D1560698

Tikunei haZohar

by
Rav Shimon bar Yochai

with
Ma'alot haSulam Commentary
by
Rav Yehuda Tzvi Brandwein

The First Unabridged English
Translation with Commentary

Published by
**Kabbalah Centre International, Inc.
Dean HaRav Berg**

Edited and Compiled by
Rabbi Michael Berg

Kabbalah Centre Publishing is a registered DBA of The Kabbalah
Centre International, Inc.

For further information:
The Kabbalah Centre
155 E. 48th St., New York, NY 10017
1062 S. Robertson Blvd., Los Angeles, CA 90035

1.800.Kabbalah   www.kabbalah.com

Printed in Canada, August 2019

ISBN: 978-1-57189-957-6

Cover Design: HL Design (Hyun Min Lee) www.hldesignco.com
Graphic Layout: Shlomit Heymann

"For a bird of the air may carry your voice."

Ecclesiastes 10:20

If my Boundary stops here

I have daughters to draw new maps of the world.

They will draw the lines of my face.

They will draw with my gestures my voice.

They will speak my words thinking they have invented them.

They will invent them.

They will invent me I will be planted again and again.

I will wake in the eyes of their children's children.

They will speak my words.

Ruth Whitman

I dedicate this volume to all

mothers, daughters, sisters, aunts, nieces,

grandmothers, granddaughters...

Women of the world, whatever race religion or creed,

we are the strength of the world, dropping

Binah upon Malchut, just as the dew

waters and brings nourishment to the

Rose and the Lily,

always with love...

Sandra Gering

TABLE OF CONTENTS

תפילה קודם הלימוד מהאר"י זיע"א

רִבּוֹן הָעוֹלָמִים וַאֲדוֹנֵי הָאֲדוֹנִים, אַב הָרַחֲמִים וְהַסְּלִיחוֹת, מוֹדִים אֲנַחְנוּ לְפָנֶיךָ ה' אֱלֹהֵינוּ וֵאלֹהֵי אֲבוֹתֵינוּ, בְּקִידָה וּבְהִשְׁתַּחֲוָיָה, שֶׁקֵּרַבְתָּנוּ לְתוֹרָתְךָ וְלַעֲבוֹדָתֶךָ, עֲבוֹדַת הַקּוֹדֶשׁ, וְנָתַתָּ לָנוּ חֵלֶק בְּסוֹדוֹת תּוֹרָתְךָ הַקְּדוֹשָׁה. מָה אֲנַחְנוּ, מֶה חַיֵּינוּ, אֲשֶׁר עָשִׂיתָ עִמָּנוּ חֶסֶד גָּדוֹל כָּזֶה. עַל כֵּן אֲנַחְנוּ מַפִּילִים תַּחֲנוּנֵינוּ לְפָנֶיךָ, שֶׁתִּמְחוֹל וְתִסְלַח לְכָל חַטֹּאתֵינוּ וַעֲווֹנוֹתֵינוּ, וְאַל יִהְיוּ עֲווֹנוֹתֵינוּ מַבְדִּילִים בֵּינֵינוּ לְבֵינֶךָ. וּבְכֵן יְהִי רָצוֹן מִלְּפָנֶיךָ ה' אֱלֹהֵינוּ וֵאלֹהֵי אֲבוֹתֵינוּ, שֶׁתְּכוֹנֵן לְבָבֵנוּ לְיִרְאָתְךָ וְאַהֲבָתֶךָ, וְתַקְשִׁיב אָזְנְךָ לִדְבָרֵינוּ אֵלֶּה, וְתִפְתַּח לְבָבֵנוּ הֶעָרֵל בְּסוֹדוֹת תּוֹרָתֶךָ, וְיִהְיֶה לִימוּדֵנוּ זֶה נַחַת רוּחַ לִפְנֵי כִסֵּא כְבוֹדְךָ כְּרֵיחַ נִיחוֹחַ. וְתַאֲצִיל עָלֵינוּ אוֹר מְקוֹר נִשְׁמָתֵנוּ בְּכָל בְּחִינוֹתֵינוּ. וְשֶׁיִּתְנוֹצְצוּ נִיצוֹצוֹת עֲבָדֶיךָ הַקְּדוֹשִׁים, אֲשֶׁר עַל יָדָם גִּלִּיתָ דְּבָרֶיךָ אֵלֶּה בָּעוֹלָם. וּזְכוּתָם וּזְכוּת אֲבוֹתָם וּזְכוּת תּוֹרָתָם וּתְמִימוּתָם וּקְדוּשָּׁתָם, יַעֲמֹד לָנוּ לְבַל נִכָּשֵׁל בַּדְּבָרִים אֵלּוּ. וּבִזְכוּתָם תָּאִיר עֵינֵינוּ בְּמַה שֶׁאֲנַחְנוּ לוֹמְדִים, כְּמַאֲמַר נְעִים זְמִירוֹת יִשְׂרָאֵל: "גַּל עֵינַי וְאַבִּיטָה נִפְלָאוֹת מִתּוֹרָתֶךָ", כִּי ה' יִתֵּן חָכְמָה מִפִּיו דַּעַת וּתְבוּנָה. יִהְיוּ לְרָצוֹן אִמְרֵי פִי וְהֶגְיוֹן לִבִּי לְפָנֶיךָ, ה' צוּרִי וְגוֹאֲלִי. רִבּוֹן עָלְמִין דְּאַנְתְּ הוּא מְגַלֶּה עֲמִיקָתָא וּמְסַתְּרָתָא וְגָלֵי רָזַיָּא. יְהֵא רַעֲוָא מִן קֳדָמָךְ לְאַסְבְּרָא מִלִּין בְּפוּמָנָא. וּלְקַיְּימָא בָּנָא מִקְרָא שֶׁכָּתוּב "וְאָנֹכִי אֶהְיֶה עִם פִּיךָ וְהוֹרֵיתִיךָ אֲשֶׁר תְּדַבֵּר". וְלֹא נִיעוּל בְּכִיסּוּפָא קֳדָמָךְ. וְנִזְכֶּה לִשְׁמוֹעַ רָזִין עִלָּאִין דְּאוֹרַיְיתָא, מִפּוּמָא דְּרֵישָׁא דִּמְתִיבְתָּא עִילָּאָה אָמֵן כֵּן יְהִי רָצוֹן אָמֵן סֶלָה.

A Prayer from the Ari (Rav Isaac Luria)
to be recited before the study of the Zohar

Ruler of the universe, and Master of all masters. The Father of mercy and forgiveness, we thank You, our God and the God of our fathers, by bowing down and kneeling, that You brought us closer to your Torah and Your Holy Work, and you enable us to take part in the secrets of your Holy Torah. How worthy are we that You grant us with such big favor, which is the reason we plead before You that You will forgive and acquit all our sins, and that they should not bring separation between You and us. And may it be Your will before You, our God and the God of our fathers, that You will awaken and prepare our hearts to love and revere You, and may You listen to our utterances and open our closed hearts to the hidden studies of Your Torah, and may our study be pleasant before Your Place of Honor, as the aroma of sweet incense, and may You emanate to us Light from the source of our soul to all of our being. And may the sparks of Your Holy servants, through which You revealed Your wisdom to the world, shine. May their merit and the merit of their fathers and the merit of their Torah and holiness support us so we shall not stumble through our study. And by their merit enlighten our eyes in our learning as it is stated by King David, the Sweet Singer of Israel: "Open my eyes so that I will see wonders from Your Torah." (Psalms 119:18)"For the Lord gives wisdom; from his mouth come knowledge and understanding." (Proverbs 2:6) "May the utterances of my mouth and the thoughts of my heart find favor before You, God my Strength and my Redeemer." (Psalms 19:15)

Introduction by Rav Berg

Blessed is He who has kept us alive and maintained us until this day, to behold the accomplishment of the sacred work of publishing the holy book, *Ha'oleh baSulam* ("Ascending the Ladder") on the Tikunei haZohar by my beloved son Rav Michael Berg, who worked and toiled with great devotion to bring merit to many.

Blessed be the Creator and praised be the Maker who gave us the merit to publish the commentary on the Tikunei haZohar for those whose hearts care and yearn to taste of the Tree of Life of the Holy Luminary, Rav Shimon bar Yochai.

As we know, the Tikunei haZohar will help to hasten the coming of the Messiah—may it happen soon in our days—and is related to, and was put aside, until the Messianic era. Do not say, "Who could know the depth of these subjects and would stand before the Ari [Rav Isaac Luria, 1534–1572] of blessed memory, understanding the depth of his mysteries, for the merciful Lord has sent us from the Eternal Heaven a watcher and a holy one from Him, out of Him a stake, and out of Him shall come forth the cornerstone." He has illuminated our eyes with a great Light, the Light of presence, "In the light of the King's countenance is life," (Proverbs 16:15), a shining and welcoming countenance, our teacher and rabbi, the holy Kabbalist Rav Yehuda haLevi Ashlag, and his distinguished disciple, Rav Yehuda Tzvi Brandwein, may their merit protect us and all of Israel. In this, our generation, we have attained the merit of their great compositions, which explain this technology in a clear, practical way so that every reader can understand, study, and be enriched by it.

Therefore "... be glad, you righteous, and shout for joy, all you who are upright in heart," (Psalms 32:11) for the mysteries of the Torah that have been concealed and hidden from the eyes of our ancestors and previous generations are published and discovered in these times. By virtue of our Torah study may we merit to attain the consolation of Zion and be redeemed by an everlasting redemption.

My teacher, my friend, and the beloved of my soul, Rav Yehuda Tzvi Brandwein, continued to write the commentary on the Zohar after the death of his teacher the holy Kabbalist Rav Yehuda haLevi Ashlag. During his lifetime, my righteous teacher also began to write a commentary on the Tikunei haZohar entitled *Ma'alot haSulam* ("Ascents of the Ladder").

My teacher, Rav Brandwein, told me that everything he understood and wrote was according to what he had learned and received from his teacher. Unfortunately for us, Rav Brandwein did not succeed in finishing his commentary on the Tikunei haZohar during his lifetime. Yet I knew that the time would come when my teacher would merit to see his plan carried out according to his understanding and sanctity.

All those years since my teacher disappeared from human eyes, I have been anxious about when his commentary would be published. Yet during those years, Rav Brandwein still came to me while I was writing all the other books that were later published, and I knew that my teacher would also come and help us publish the incomplete portion of the commentary on the Tikunei haZohar. I knew that the matter was very important and that the commentary on the Tikunei haZohar must be published to bring the Redemption closer to us.

I have seen how the words of my righteous teacher, concerning young people, have been fulfilled. Even though many movements have been founded to bring the estranged back to spirituality, my teacher wrote that without the study of Kabbalah there is no hope of bringing back young people who have already fled their roots. He said, "For every young person who returns, thousands upon thousands leave. Only the wisdom of Kabbalah can draw them near."

I knew that very few souls would come to study the Tikunei haZohar if the study was not easy. And I saw this as a favorable time to draw those estranged with classes, lectures, and books about Kabbalah and the mysteries of the Torah. I knew that I had to devote most of my time to awaken them around the world and that I could not complete my righteous teacher's plan to publish the complete commentary on the Tikunei haZohar.

I, therefore, left the sacred undertaking of the Tikunei haZohar and put all my energy into taking all that I had learned from my righteous teacher and disseminating this wisdom of Kabbalah to the layman.

During the past thirty years, together with my wife Karen ("Blessed is she more than women in the tent." (Judges 5:24), whose devotion and care brought us to this day, we have succeeded in bringing back hundreds of thousands of souls. Thousands upon thousands of women now immerse themselves in the spiritual cleansing waters of the *mikveh* today because they know the real goal of the precepts of the Torah, which are to do good to every person and not because it is so written.

When I observed the outcome of spreading the study of Kabbalah to the layman, I invested less and less time in writing books in general, to complete the sacred work of the Tikunei haZohar in particular.

Clearly, I have been feeling uncomfortable because of the delay in publishing such an important book as the Tikunei haZohar, but I learned from my righteous teacher that it is more important to save lives in this time when we see so many leaving their spiritual roots at such a fast pace. It was clear to me that had my righteous teacher not decided to participate in the Histadrut (Israeli Labor Federation), he would certainly have had time to complete his commentary on all the Tikunei haZohar, and who knows what else.

I remember once arriving in the middle of the night for our regular study and seeing my righteous teacher's face illuminated with unimaginable joy. I inquired as to what had transpired for the countenance of my righteous teacher to acquire such unusual Light. My righteous teacher answered me that he had been working on a very challenging passage of the Tikunei haZohar. Although my righteous teacher used the commentary of the Gaon of Vilna (Rav Eliyahu ben Solomon, 1720–1797) that truly explained this difficult passage, what bothered Rav Brandwein was that the Gaon of Vilna's commentary did not completely match the words.

In that article of the Tikkunnei haZohar my righteous teacher found the precise explanation for the words and because of that Rav Brandwein was so happy.

I knew that my righteous teacher's heart ached for not having enough time to complete the entire commentary on the Tikunei haZohar. "Alas," wept my teacher, "what will be of the souls who remained orphaned with no father to care for them? According to my calculation, the number who will remain vigilant will gradually diminish. Therefore, in such troubled times as this, I can in no way give up the opportunity the Creator has bestowed upon me to draw these souls back to the path of Torah with my job in the Histadrut. What will be the use of my commentary on the Tikunei haZohar if there will be no one to read the book?"

After my righteous teacher left this physical plane, I understood that the entire conversation between my teacher and myself was to teach me about priorities. Yet this did not mean that my concern for the commentary on the Tikunei haZohar was over. It pained me that my righteous teacher died before his time and did not achieve completing his commentary.

Not a day has passed without me asking my righteous teacher to help me with his desire concerning the Tikunei haZohar. Many times I have wished to discontinue my work with estranged souls and go in the direction of uncovering the commentary of my righteous teacher. I was certain that this commentary would come to me directly from my righteous teacher as it did with all the books I have written and every interpretation I have given on the weekly portions.

The fact that the commentary on the Tikunei haZohar has not yet been published is an additional reason why our redemption and the coming of the Messiah are delayed. Yet what could I do? My righteous teacher gave me all the signs that I must not stop the sacred work of distributing the study of the mysteries of Kabbalah throughout the world.

It is clear to me and my wife Karen that we have begun opening the iron wall that had previously sealed off the study of Kabbalah and the distribution of the teachings to every person whose heart desires to know the mysteries of the wisdom of Kabbalah. We never thought where this would lead. It did not occur to us that there would be Kabbalah Centre branches around the world or that we would reach a state, as we have today, where new branches open nearly every three months. And although it is clear to me that my righteous teacher stands behind every decision concerning where and when to open a new branch, the concern about publishing the commentary on the Tikunei haZohar by my righteous teacher has not ceased, even for a moment.

Therefore, when my son, Rav Michael, told me a few years ago that he felt a desire to complete the commentary of my righteous teacher, I began to weep. Although I was pained because the commentary had not yet been published, I knew that I must not cease my work for even a single day and must instead continue disseminating the wisdom of Kabbalah. And here my son, Rav Michael, turned to me and asked to begin the commentary on the Tikunei haZohar. There are no words to describe the joy I felt that day.

It is more than ten years now that my sons Rav Yehuda and Rav Michael have been studying the Study of the Ten Luminous Emanations [*Talmud*

Eser Sefirot] by the holy Kabbalist, Rav Yehuda haLevi Ashlag, the author of the *Sulam*, as well as the book of Zohar and the Writings of the Ari [*Kitvei haAri*].

On that day, it was clear to me above any doubt that both could write the commentary on the *Tikkunim*. From the time of their birth, and until the coming of the Messiah, my sons knew they had to be connected with my righteous teacher Rav Yehuda Tzvi Brandwein and his righteous teacher, Rav Yehuda haLevi Ashlag. While we lived in Israel, we would visit them on the eve of every New Moon. And whenever we visit Israel, we go to visit them—Rav Ashlag and Rav Brandwein. My sons' connection with my righteous teacher and our righteous master and teacher, Rav Ashlag, is very strong.

I remember when my sons were three and four years old and were asked by their friends where they had been, and they answered simply and without calculating: "We went to visit the righteous men in their homes." They never called that place a cemetery. I, therefore, knew that with their help there would be no problem in writing the commentary on the Tikunei haZohar. The pen would record the commentary, and the words would be those of my righteous teacher and his righteous teacher. It is a great merit to the entire world that my son, Rav Michael, will be the messenger to pass on the commentary that my righteous teacher had not personally completed while he was alive.

I felt as if the burden I had carried all those years in not publishing the commentary of my righteous teacher had disappeared because the time had come for the world to benefit from the depth of the mysteries of the Tikunei haZohar. In our time especially, before the coming of the Messiah, as we witness chaos multiply, harming the entire world in general and humanity in particular, it is no coincidence that the Prologue of the Tikunei haZohar (Volume 22 of the Hebrew Aramaic Zohar) begins with the following words:

Rav Shimon left and escaped to the desert of Lod and hid, together with his son Elazar, in a certain cave. A miracle occurred to them. One carob tree and one water fountain appeared. They ate from that carob and drank from that water, and Elijah the Prophet visited them twice each day and studied with them, and nobody had cognizance of them. This is mentioned in Zohar Chadash, Ki Tavo (Par. 1).

And this is called the Tikunei haZohar, which are seventy ways in which Rav Shimon bar Yochai interpreted the word *beresheet* from the mysteries of the Torah. Arise Rav Shimon; commence discourses in the presence of the Shechinah. He began and said, "And the wise shall shine like the brightness of the Firmament." (Daniel 12:3)

And the Cause of all Causes, MEANING THE ENDLESS LIGHT granted permission to all the Holy Names, IN GENERAL, to all the VARIOUS NAME COMPOSITIONS OF Yud-Hei-Vav-Hei and all the VARIOUS NAMES OF designated Divine attributes, to reveal to them hidden secrets— each Name, in its grade. And permitted the Ten Sefirot to reveal hidden secrets to them, as there was no permission granted to reveal those SECRETS until the arrival of the generation of the King Messiah.
~ Tikunei haZohar, 1:1-2, 4

While I was reading this prologue, several questions arose within me. First, why was this article inserted into both the Tikunei haZohar and also the Zohar Chadash, portion of Ki Tavo, when it seems that all the wisdom revealed to Rav Shimon in the cave of Peki'in is contained in the Tikunei haZohar? Which came first? And also, why does the article stress that **one** carob tree grew and **one** spring appeared, rather than just say **a** carob and **a** spring?

When we examine the first paragraph in the Tikunei haZohar, we see that Rav Shimon received teachings from Prophet Elijah. This is immediately followed, in the second paragraph, by: "It is called the Tikunei haZohar, which are seventy ways in which Rav Shimon bar Yochai interpreted the word *beresheet* from the mysteries of the Torah." Truly this is a wonder.

From the second paragraph it seems that the Tikunei haZohar was revealed to Rav Shimon before the book of the Zohar and before the Zohar Chadash. Also, it seems that all Rav Shimon learned in the cave was the Tikunei haZohar, although we know that this part in particular was not yet published in the world. From this we can understand why there are no conversations among the disciples in the Tikunei haZohar like there are in the book of Zohar and in Zohar Chadash. The entire Tikunei haZohar reached only Rav Shimon and his son Rav Elazar in the cave, there were no other disciples except for the two.

It seems that the many articles of the conversations among the disciples that are scattered throughout the books of the Zohar and Zohar Chadash have appeared after Rav Shimon came out of the cave. From Zohar, Prologue 185, concerning Rav Shimon's exit from the cave, we can understand that the Tikunei haZohar is indeed on a much more elevated level than the books of the Zohar and Zohar Chadash.

Rav Pinchas ben Yair, whose daughter was Rav Shimon's wife, was about to embark on a ship in search of Rav Shimon and his son Rav Elazar. The Zohar, Prologue 187 says:

> And he saw two birds flying over the sea towards him. He raised his voice and said: "Birds, birds, who fly over the sea, have you seen the place where the son of Yochai is?" He waited a while and then said: "Birds, birds, go and bring me back an answer." They flew away.

Rav Shimon fled the government who had issued the edict to kill him. And he and his son hid in a certain cave (Babylonian Talmud, Shabbat 33B), and they did not know where he was. For this reason Rav Pinchas sailed away to seek him among the islands. The Zohar, Prologue 188-189 continues:

> Before he embarked on the ship, the two birds came back. One was carrying a letter in its mouth informing him that Rav Shimon bar Yochai had existed in the cave, together with his son, Rav Elazar.

> Rav Pinchas went to meet him and found him completely changed. His body was full of sores and wounds from staying so long in the cave. He wept with him, and said, "Woe that I have seen you thus." Rav Shimon said to him, "Blessed is my portion that you have seen me thus for had you not seen me so, I would not have been this way."

For the many years that he lived in the cave, Rav Shimon had to immerse himself in the sand to cover his nakedness and engage in the Torah, thus his flesh was covered with earth. Rav Shimon explained to Rav Pinchas that were it not for those conditions, he would not have merited the revelation of the secrets of the Torah. All the height of his great wisdom was earned during those thirteen years when he hid in the cave.

What we understand from the article is that for Rav Shimon to be able to attain the mysteries of the Torah he had to undergo a process of annulling the body's essence. Here we learn the importance and value of the Tikunei haZohar and their elevated level of wisdom. The entire teaching of the Zohar that Rav Shimon later revealed to the disciples is incorporated in the Tikunei haZohar, and to tolerate and understand all the depths of the mysteries of the Tikunei haZohar it was necessary to annul the body. Without being divested of his body, the teaching of the Tikunei haZohar could not have reached Rav Shimon.

Rav Shimon, therefore, called the teaching he received from Prophet Elijah in the cave the Tikunei haZohar. This teaches us that whoever studies the wisdom of Kabbalah must also consider annulling their body's essence. For the student of Kabbalah there is no room for remaining with the ego because then the study of life turns into deadly poison.

The reason the above article from the Tikunei haZohar is brought again in Zohar Chadash, portion of Ki Tavo, is to indicate to us the difference between the Tikunei haZohar and the other sections of the Zohar. Only Rav Shimon and his son Rav Elazar participated in the revelation of the Tikunei haZohar. The other disciples, included in many sections of the Zohar, did not undergo the torments Rav Shimon suffered. Therefore, Rav Pinchas' story about the cave is recorded in the Prologue of the Zohar and the friends' account of Rav Shimon in the cave appears in Zohar Chadash, in the portion of Ki Tavo.

Zohar Chadash repeats the matter of Rav Shimon and his son's stay in the cave to both mark and reinforce the difference between the Tikunei haZohar and the books of the Zohar and Zohar Chadash. Thus the Tikunei haZohar is the source of all that Rav Shimon received in the cave. The book of the Zohar itself interprets the Tikunei haZohar since the revelation of the Tikunei haZohar could reach only a sage of the most elevated level such as Rav Shimon and his son.

The Tikunei haZohar was the first teaching after the giving of the Torah but the world was incapable of receiving this wisdom. The Israelites present at the giving of the Torah— the Generation of Knowledge—were of an elevated level of consciousness and thus could receive the Torah from Moses. With the revelation of the Tikunei haZohar, only Rav Shimon and his son were of this elevated level of the Generation of Knowledge and thus capable of receiving the Tikunei haZohar from Moses and Prophet Elijah.

Since the Tikunei haZohar is at a much higher level, comprehending it is very difficult, which is why the Tikunei haZohar is meant for the Messianic era and no other time. Another reason the study of the Tikunei haZohar will not be prevalent among communities prior to the coming of the Messiah is that the souls present during the Messianic era will be an incarnation of the Generation of the Wilderness—the Generation of Knowledge—and will thus comprehend the Tikunei haZohar.

We now understand why Rav Shimon bar Yochai wrote in the Zohar that after his passing from our world, the study of the Zohar will be hidden and concealed from those knowledgeable in it until the Messianic era. Even Rav Moshe Cordovero (also known as the Ramak, 1522 – 1527) stated in his commentary on the Tikunei haZohar in his book *Ohr Yakar* ("Precious Light") that the book of Zohar was composed specifically for the generation of the Messianic era and this is the reason the Zohar has disappeared for such a long time:

> "The Book of Zohar will disappear and be hidden from the eyes of the knowledgeable, and no author mentions it but the sages of later generations. For even though it was written in its time, it was concealed and hidden until this time, when it was discovered. And even after it had been discovered, it was hidden by the sages and they did not publish it until now when it was published. This is an indication that it was essentially required for the end of the exile."

To understand why the sages did not publish it until what is known as the end of the exile, this is what Rav Aba promises in the book of Zohar, Yitro 23:

> Rav Aba raised his hands to his head and wept, saying: "The Light of Torah now reaches the highest throne in Heaven. After my master leaves this world, who will shine the Light of the

Torah? Woe to the world that will remain orphaned from you. Yet my master's words will shine in the world until the coming of King Messiah. Then, it is written, 'for the earth shall be full of the knowledge of the Lord, as the waters cover the sea.'" (Isaiah 11:9)

Our master, and righteous teacher Rav Yehuda haLevi Ashlag wrote the following in his Introduction to the Zohar, paragraph 57:

"From this you will understand the dryness and darkness that we find in this generation, something unheard of in previous generations; for even the servants of the Lord have withdrawn their hands from engaging in the mysteries of the Torah."

And Maimonides (Rav Moses ben Maimon, also known as the Rambam, 1135–1204) gives an allegory to explain this. He said that if a line of a thousand blind people walk on the way and have at least one seeing person at their head, they can be certain of following the right path and not fall into holes and nets as they follow the seeing man at their head. But without that one person, they will undoubtedly stumble on anything lying in the way and will all fall into the lowest pit.

Rav Ashlag, continues:

Thus is the subject before us. If the servants of the blessed Lord were at least engaged in the inner meaning of the Torah and drawing complete Light from the blessed Endless Light, the whole generation would have followed them, and they would all be certain in their path and they would not stumble. Yet if even the servants of the blessed Lord removed themselves from this wisdom, it is no wonder that the entire generation fails because of them. I cannot speak at length of this out of the greatness of my sorrow.

Indeed I know the reason. It is because faith has diminished both in general and in the celestial holy ones, the sages of the generations, in particular. Yet the books of Kabbalah and the Zohar are filled with substantial allegories. Therefore, everyone has fear that their loss will exceed their profit, as, Heaven forbid, they might sin with regard to carved idols and images. It is this that awoke me to create a sufficient commentary on the Writings of the Ari and now for the holy Zohar, and thus I have removed this fear entirely.

I have explained and clearly proven that the spiritual allegory of anything, devoid of any material likeness, is above space and beyond time. As the readers shall see, it is to enable the multitude of the house of Israel to study the book of Zohar and warm by its sacred Light.

And I have called the commentary the *Sulam* (Ladder) to indicate that the function of my commentary is as the function of any ladder. If you have an attic filled with many good things, you merely need a ladder to reach it; then every good in the world is in your hand.

Yet the ladder is not a goal in itself. If you rest on the steps of the ladder without entering the attic you will not carry out your intent. So it is with my commentary on the Zohar; the expression that will completely explain their deepest subjects has not yet been created. Instead, with my commentary I have created a path and entrance through which everyone can rise and delve into and behold the Book of Zohar itself. Only then will my intent in my commentary be carried out.

With all the words of our righteous master and teacher Rav Ashlag, I raise the questions: Why should we wait until the Days of the Messiah, and why was the Zohar not revealed beforehand? Moreover, it is written specifically in Zohar, Naso 90:

"...and since the Israelites will taste of the Tree of Life, which is this book of Zohar, they will go out of exile with mercy."

It is also written in Zohar Chadash 114A:

"When this treatise is revealed in the world, the great gather before it."

And if the book of the Tikunei haZohar can save the entire world—especially now that the commentary of the *Sulam* has appeared, which enables us to read the words of the Zohar themselves and understand the true meaning of the stories of the Torah—why did the commentary of the *Sulam* not appear many years ago?

Not only were our people in darkness in previous generations, today we have rabbis, leaders of the nation, who seek for the flock to walk in darkness, even though the book of Zohar sharply turns our attention to not consider the context of the written words but rather to the inner meaning of the Torah, as written in Zohar, Beha'alotcha 58-64:

Rabbi Shimon says: Woe to the man who says that the Torah came to relate stories, simply and plainly, and simpleton tales. If it was so, even at the present day we could produce a Torah from simplistic matters, and perhaps even nicer ones than those. It must be that all items in the Torah are of a superior nature and are uppermost secrets. Therefore, this story of the Torah is the mantle of the Torah. He who thinks that this mantle is the actual essence of the Torah and that nothing else is in there, let him breathe his last and let him have no portion in the World to Come.

Come and behold: the world above and the world below are measured with one scale. Israel below CORRESPOND TO the lofty angels above. It is written about the lofty angels: "Who makes the winds His messengers" (Psalm 104:4). When they go down, they don with the vestments of this world. If they had not acquired the dress for this world, they would not be able to exist in this world, and the world would not be able to stand them. And if this is so for the angels, how much more so is it for the Torah that created these MESSENGERS and all the worlds that exist due to it. Once it came down to this world, if it had not donned all these garments of this world, WHICH ARE THE STORIES AND SIMPLISTIC TALES, the world would not have been able to tolerate it.

Therefore, this story of the Torah is the mantle of the Torah. He who thinks that this mantle is the actual essence of the Torah and that nothing else is in there, let him breathe his last and let him have no portion in the World to Come. Therefore, David said, "Open my eyes, that I may behold wondrous things out of Your Torah" (Psalm 119:18); that is, look what lies under that garment of the Torah.

Come and behold: There is a dress that is visible to everyone. The fools, when they see a person dressed beautifully, who appears to them distinguished by his clothing, do not observe any further. They judge him according to his distinguished apparel and consider the dress as the body of man, and the body of the person like his soul.

Similar to this is the Torah. It has a body, which is composed of the precepts of the Torah that are called the "body of the Torah." This body is clothed with garments, which are stories of this world. The ignorant look only at that dress, which is the story in the Torah, and are not aware of anything more. They do not look at what lies beneath that dress. Those who know more do not look at the dress but rather at the body beneath that dress. The wise, the sages, the servants of the Loftiest King, those that stood at Mount Sinai, look only at the soul OF THE TORAH, which is the essence of everything, the real Torah. In the time to come, they will look at the soul, the soul of the Torah.

Woe to the wicked who say that the Torah is merely a story and nothing more, for they look at the dress and no further. Praised are the righteous, who look properly at the Torah. Wine lasts only if it is in a jug. Similarly, the Torah does not endure, except in this mantle. Therefore, there is no need to look except at what is beneath the mantle. That is why all these matters and all these stories are garments.

And if everything is so clear to the point that the Zohar calls these rabbis "foolish and wicked," why is the remedy for the world only capable of being revealed at the Days of the Messiah? Another question that we must raise is: I understand the word "foolish," as they have eyes yet they do not see and they have ears but do not listen but why does the Zohar call these people "wicked," using such strong language.

The answer I received from my righteous master was so simple that I could not understand why it took years until I understood the depth of the subject. **There is order in the world, even though most of the time it seems as if things do not take place according to order.** After the sin of Primordial Adam, the world has existed in the form of the Tree of Knowledge of Good and Evil. There are times when good rules and times when evil rules. There must be that there will be a time of the influence of good, for were it not for times such as these, there would be no possibility for the world to emerge from darkness into Light. Therefore there were times, such as with the

Generation of the Wilderness, incarnations of the Generation of the Flood, and the Generation of the Tower of Babel.

When the Creator saw there was no hope for the world, he sent Moses our teacher to save the world through the giving of the Torah. But Moses alone was unable to save the world. Rather, his role was to be a teacher, to guide—just as the *Sulam*—to bring the Israelites to the well to drink of the springs of the Torah. But even Moses could not have forced the children of Israel to drink of the water.

And since the Generation of the Wilderness (Knowledge) decided not to enter the attic filled with everything good, they all died in the wilderness. At the time of the Generation of Knowledge, the Israelites were capable of choosing the right path and reaching the point of bringing the Messiah during their own time. And these same souls of the Generation of the Wilderness incarnated again during the time of the revelation of the Tikunei haZohar by Rav Shimon bar Yochai, and again they had the chance to save the world by receiving all the tools to wage war with Satan and control him, just as Rav Shimon himself had power over Satan. So why does the Zohar call them "wicked"? It is because instead of thinking of the entire world and including themselves, they decided to care for themselves alone, as is said in the Zohar concerning Rav Shimon's leaving the cave the first time.

In the Talmud, Tractate Shabbat 33B-34A, it says:

> They went and hid in a cave. A miracle happened to them and a carob tree and a spring of water were created for their sakes. They used to take off their clothes and sit up to their necks in sand. They studied the whole day and during prayer they put on their clothes and prayed. And again they took off their clothes so they would not wear out.

They lived twelve years in the cave. Elijah came and stood at the entrance to the cave and said: "Who shall inform Bar Yochai that the Caesar has died and his edict is annulled?" They heard that and came out. As they left, they saw people plowing and sewing the earth. [Rav Shimon bar Yochai] said: "They set down everlasting life and engage in transient life!"

Every place they turned their eyes, immediately burned! A Divine echo came out and said to them: "Have you come out to destroy My world? Return to your cave!" They again went and lived there twelve months. A Divine echo then resounded and said: "Leave your cave!" They came out. And wherever Rav Elazar struck [burned with his holiness] Rav Shimon healed.

In truth, it is a little difficult to understand why people were burned when Rav Shimon bar Yochai and Rav Elazar looked at them. Rashi has already remarked that people need to eat and therefore some must grow wheat to have bread to eat. How could such a thing happen?

Yet we learn from the story about the power of the Zohar. Even Rav Shimon understood that the body requires food, yet after he received the teaching from the Tikunei haZohar, Rav Shimon knew that there will no longer be any need to till the earth all day to grow wheat. If a person can conjure it with a spiritual thought anyone could grow wheat and there will be no need to work all day for food.

Rav Shimon rose to such an elevated spiritual level that he no longer recognized the limitations the material world shackles us with. Rav Shimon's consciousness was of such an elevation that he could have created any material object. He, therefore, was unable to comprehend how the multitude could be engaged in material pursuits.

Such is the power of the Tikunei haZohar to change the entire world. Yet people who wish to receive the teaching of the Tikunei haZohar must first reach the consciousness of those of the Generation of the Wilderness, who received the Torah on Mount Sinai in its entirety, together with the study of Kabbalah.

Rav Shimon bar Yochai, by virtue of the strength of his greatness and holiness, which the mind cannot grasp, and by virtue of the holiness of his generation, merited that the mysteries of the Torah and the wisdom of Kabbalah be revealed in full. Even though the wisdom of the Torah was known to individuals beforehand, such as the first published book—the *Sefer Yetzirah* ("Book of Formation"), whose authorship is attributed to the Patriarch Abraham and the Angel Raziel, books that were revealed and written even before the giving of the Torah, this book [Tikunei haZohar] contains the loftiest ideas and concepts.

For a long time, the technology of the wisdom of Kabbalah was beyond the comprehension of the layperson. Engaging in its study was kept for the few and for those of merit, since only people at the level of the Generation of Knowledge were able to understand its depths. Therefore, the Zohar wrote that during the Messianic era, the mysteries of Kabbalah shall be revealed. And the holy Ari (Rav Isaac Luria) wrote in his book, *Gate of Reincarnations*, that during the Messianic era, the souls of the Generation of the Wilderness (Knowledge) will incarnate and return to this era.

In one of my blessed righteous teacher's letters to me, dated Friday, the holy Shabbat eve, 15th of Av 5728, he wrote about the subject of unity:

> "And the publisher has already started to set part two of the Tikunei haZohar with the commentary of the *Ma'alot haSulam* ("Ascents of the Sulam"), and I have started writing part three. And I pray that the blessed Lord will let me finish all the

tikkunim because the revelations are full of awe, and silence befits them."

Unfortunately, my righteous teacher did not have the time to finish his commentary on the Tikunei haZohar. And since we have the merit that my son, Rav Michael, has completed the commentary on the Tikunei haZohar, I know that my righteous teacher is very glad to see his desire fulfilled.

With help from the blessed Creator may we merit to behold the presence of the Shechinah with the coming of the Messiah "and he will destroy death forever." Isaiah 25:8 The desire of my righteous teacher, as he wrote in his manifesto in his Prologue to the Tikunei haZohar, has already begun to be fulfilled in our own days:

> "Peace in the world, and the blotting out of envy and hatred from humanity are interconnected; and the state of 'the earth shall be full of the knowledge of the Lord as the waters cover the sea' (Isaiah 11:9) is a prerequisite for the consciousness of, "The wolf also shall dwell with the lamb." (Isaiah 11:6)

To reach the most important goal of the coming of the Messiah and peace is connected to, and depends on, the behavior among people. And what I have seen of my righteous teacher is simply the concept of love for another— something I have not seen prior or since then. Before I met my righteous teacher I had almost never heard this expression. My righteous teacher of blessed memory spoke and wrote much on the subject and stressed the importance of studying the Tikunei haZohar, which may help us in the time before the coming of the Messiah, to transform selfish love into love for others.

Human consciousness, which has not changed for 4,000 years, is still very far from understanding the concept "love for another." We see this throughout the history of the people of Israel. On the one hand, hatred increases and becomes stronger in daily life, including hatred for no reason; on the other hand, every Israelite already knows the reason for the destruction of the Temple. You may ask how we do not pay attention to the subject of hatred for no reason, which brought about the destruction, and have not learnt introspection from all the problems and pogroms that have harmed us.

In our Centers we emphasize the need and the importance of transforming the Desire to Receive for Oneself Alone into the Desire to Receive for the Sake of Sharing. What amazes everyone is how evident it is that whoever studies with us truly transforms their nature and behaves differently.

And the only cause that facilitates the change in human nature that we can speak of is connected to reading the Zohar, something that is routine throughout all the Kabbalah Centres and our students. Especially now that the commentary on the entire Tikunei haZohar has been published, certainly reading this will be very helpful in the time before the coming of the Messiah.

The Zohar also emphasizes the matter of *bila hamavet lanetzach* (death will be swallowed up forever) for our times as well as the Resurrection of the Dead, which will be awakened during the Messianic era. Even though there are those who believe in the Resurrection of the Dead and in *bila hamavet lanetzach*, the only place where they contemplate these concepts is during prayer. Apart from these times, they do not think that they can do something to hasten this at all. As far as they are concerned, one day the Creator will simply have mercy on us and the Messiah will come.

The reason these concepts are truly so far removed from their consciousness is that most people do not think it possible that a simple individual like themselves can affect the coming of the Messiah before its time, since righteous people such as Rav Shimon bar Yochai, Rabbi Akiva and others were unable to draw the Redemption nearer during their own time.

Thus, even though they believe the Messiah will come, their consciousness is very far from it, and they do not contemplate the subject at all. It is hard to believe that the Messiah could come, especially considering the fact that during our generation we see so much fragmentation, divisiveness, and hatred for no reason. The hatred existing today among individuals is truly appalling, so how can we hope and think that the Messiah will come and arrange peace in the world?

Also, what do we do with the precept: "And you shall know the Lord."? (Hosea 2:22) According to the explanation of the Zohar, complete certainty means that we raise the last letter Hei of the Name of the Lord [Yud-Hei-Vav-Hei] to the letter Vav to create and bring about a connection and uniting of Malchut, our world, with Zeir Anpin, with the Desire to Receive for the Sake of Sharing. What we absolutely need to receive, without any question or doubt, is the substance of personal providence, which is to know that there truly is a Creator Who manages the whole world.

Not being allowed to ask questions was never an issue, no command "not to ask" was ever given. Sometimes Moses asked questions, and the Creator answered "Do not ask about this." But in general the Torah requires us to ask. This is the issue of casuistry in the Gemara and the Talmud. When the holy Ari came to a teaching that was not understood, he worked wholeheartedly to remove questions and doubts, which are related to Satan who causes all doubts and every misunderstanding in the world.

With "And you shall know the Lord"—no doubts will remain. As I learned from my righteous teacher, we do not **believe** in the Lord," but we **know** the Lord, we **know** that there is a Creator who oversees every single detail. Thus when some problem appears in our life, we must not forget that everything comes from Heaven. This means that if we behave in a positive way, the Creator weighs the cause and carries out the effect, which must be positive. If our work is negative, especially between ourselves and others, then undoubtedly the effects in our life will be full of problems and disruptions.

The matter that demands the most work on our part is related to interpersonal relationships. We must also know that all prayers and petitions that are related to *bila hamavet lanetzach* and the coming of the Messiah depend on our intention during prayer. And we need to know that we do have an influence on the time and the coming of the Messiah.

It must be clear that if everything is dependent on the blessed Creator, the Creator would arrange it so that the Messiah would come immediately. The biggest problem arises from the mistake we make when we ask the Creator to send the Messiah; as if it depends on the Creator's approval or disapproval of our request. Although it seems at times that the Creator does not heed our cry, it is not worthwhile to think so, even for a moment. The Creator is ready to fulfill all requests at any given moment but there is a small problem according to the teaching and technology of Kabbalah, called Bread of Shame.

We are beholden to perform the work for the Messiah to come because the revelation of the Messiah depends on us alone, and not on the sentiments of the Creator. Therefore there are two demands in our natural laws that we require. The first is that every person must study the Tikunei haZohar and the second is to reach the level of love for another for no reason. The souls of the Generation of the Wilderness return to the world in our time, the time of the Messianic era, and it is only because they previously understood all the mysteries of our world that we now start to understand our fate.

Today, we comprehend that we must work on ourselves to transform our Desire to Receive into the Desire to Share. Our souls understand that without the study of the wisdom of Kabbalah and the Zohar in general, and in particular the study of the Tikunei haZohar, we do not stand a chance of receiving anything other than what we have for the past 3,400 years—troubles, chaos, and other terrible outcomes.

Today, we can fulfill our desire of preventing murder and persecution, which were an inseparable part of daily life. We live in the time Rav Shimon bar Yochai wrote about 2,000 years ago—the Messianic era—when all the secrets of the wisdom of Kabbalah will be revealed, as the Prophet Jeremiah prophesied concerning this time:

> "…and they shall teach no more every man, his neighbor, and every man his brother, saying, Know the Lord; for they shall all know Me, from the least of them to the greatest of them, says the Lord; for I will forgive their iniquity, and I will remember their sin no more." (Jeremiah 31:33)

Indeed, when examining this verse of Jeremiah, many questions arise and it is difficult to understand its words. What does the prophet not wish to convey by the words, "for they shall all know the Lord"? Why specifically during the Messianic era and not beforehand? What is the problem in teaching every man and his brother to know the Lord? Also it seems from the words of the prophet that the youngest (the least) would reach the knowledge of the Lord only during the Messianic era and not beforehand?

More difficult still is the promise of the Creator. Why will the Creator "forgive their iniquity, and remember their sin no more" specifically during the Messianic era but not beforehand? It seems as if the Creator is willing to forgive for the reason that everyone "already knows." What is the connection between the two subjects?

As will be explained, we shall arrive at answers for all these questions. It is written in the Zohar that after the passing of Rav Shimon bar Yochai, the world will be in darkness until the Messianic era. And everyone asks why, during these 2,000 years, the world must suffer and wait until the time of the Messianic era and have no pleasure especially as it is written in the Zohar that only the book of Zohar can bring the world to tasting of the Tree of Life—there is no other way?

The answer is that the Generation of the Wilderness (Knowledge), will bring the commentary of the Zohar into fruition. They will be incarnated during the Messianic era. They are the scientists that bring about all the technological advancements. And with the technological understanding of today, we can understand the concepts that appear in the Zohar. Without the understanding of this scientific technology it is impossible to understand the Zohar.

Although our generation is like the generation of those who came out of Egypt, there is a great difference between us and them. Unfortunately, the people of the Generation of the Wilderness found no reason to better themselves. They understood everything concerning the purpose of this world, yet they were still governed by their Desire to Receive for the Oneself Alone. Thus we find so many complaints in the Torah leveled at Moses and the Holy One, blessed be He.

They knew how to control the physical reality; they recognized the superiority of spirit over matter, yet it had not occurred to them to be happy in their own lot and to think, even a little, of sharing and giving to others. They judged what was wrong with others but did not look within to see what was wrong with themselves. Love for no reason was a foreign concept to them. They only understood hatred for no reason, accepted it, and consumed it like air for breathing.

As was discussed previously, the Generation of the Wilderness is an incarnation of the Generation of the Flood and the Generation of the Tower of Babel. The Creator thought that through slavery and hard labor in Egypt these souls would attain purification and bring the Messiah and the state of *bila hamavet lanetzach*.

Yet again, they did not take advantage of the opportunity that was granted them at the giving of the Torah, and built the golden calf. Since that time until the generation of Rav Shimon bar Yochai, no other opportunity has occurred. While the Israelites experienced no problems while living in the Holy Land, they did not think that they should work to purify their Desire to Receive. This is the reason the destructions of the First and Second Temples took place.

Rav Shimon saw that the 2,000 years of exile would cause these souls to change their nature. Even though these souls felt their ego, whenever they were expelled from one country to another amidst persecutions and death, part of their essence of being selfish was nullified.

There is no comparison between the hatred of one individual toward another and the hatred that has existed in previous generations. We truly saw in latter times how these souls [us] suddenly became simple lambs to the other nations, and this caused us to transform ourselves a little.

Rav Shimon saw in advance that when the era before the coming of the Messiah would arrive, the book of the Zohar will be discovered because these souls will have undergone numerous humiliations and purifications as a result of their experiences of exile. He knew that these souls would then be ready to receive the last purification, which is the study of the Zohar. This is what will assist us in this final stage to transform the Desire to Receive for Oneself Alone to the Desire to Receive for the Sake of Sharing.

During this time, even without the effect of the days before the coming of the Messiah, the era itself will cause every person to be more in the consciousness of "sharing." Unlike during previous generations, we truly see that the awareness of humanity is to begin caring for others.

Today, wealthy people throughout the world give away large sums to the poor; people care about our air quality and the proper hygiene of food. Governments collect taxes to care for those who have nothing. The problem of another has already started to grab the community's attention. This is why, during our time, the dissemination of the wisdom of Kabbalah has begun. At no other time in history was there such a popular interest in Kabbalah as there is today.

There is one more noteworthy fact regarding the verse from Jeremiah, "And you shall know the Lord." It seems that there was once a need to say to one another, "And you shall know the Lord," because if no one said it, people would not know the Lord. Why is that? The answer is that those who accepted and believed in the Lord, accepted it without knowing the Lord but rather accepted the precept, "and you shall know the Lord...," like the other precepts of the Torah that must be accepted, believed in, and performed. This is why the prophet emphasized the point of "and you shall know the Lord," so there would be no need to say, "know the Lord," because each will arrive at the knowledge of the Lord on his own.

Hence the Zohar, which elucidates the entire Torah, teaches us that we, as the generation of the exodus from Egypt, will know that the Torah does not speak of the Holy One, blessed be He as a man of flesh and blood, Heaven forbid, but engages in the Light of the Creator. Understanding the Light of the Creator does not need to come to a person by force or by means of a policeman as is the case with other religions, which demand performance without questioning or knowing. Kabbalah teaches us that there is no coercion in spirituality.

And in truth, Jeremiah's words become real today, when many souls have forsaken their religion because they did not wish to accept "knowing the Lord" as a precept. Individuals do not wish to be religious, nor do they wish to accept "the yoke of the Heavenly Kingdom" without understanding it. In general the religious way has involved coercion for thousands of years but with the arrival of the age preceding the Messiah everything has changed.

Our time bears witness that the words of the prophet Jeremiah are beginning to manifest. The spreading of Kabbalah is being carried out in an unusual way, and has resulted in millions of people engaging in the study of Kabbalah and the Zohar, as well as coming to know the Lord and truly transforming their nature. This has never occurred before throughout history.

Moreover, through the mission of the Kabbalah Center, which is the way of the Zohar, we can bring thousands upon thousands of souls back to spirituality without convincing them it is good. We simply disseminate the knowledge of Kabbalah, and people are beginning to realize that there is no other way to reach a joyful life.

However, every person must start by working on themselves, transforming their own nature, and then the Zohar will aid us in reaching this goal, even though there will be more difficulties along the way. The world loves this knowledge, which must eventually bear fruit, which is more difficult.

This is why I wish to add a section of the Introduction by my righteous teacher to the Tikunei haZohar:

> The whole of evil, of which it is said, "for the impulse of man's heart is evil from his youth" (Genesis 8:21) is selfish love (that is called egoism) that is imprinted on man's heart so that all his movements revolve around his own axis without any sparks of giving to another.
>
> Our sages of blessed memory have said of this (Tractate Kidushin 30b) that the Holy One, blessed be He, said: "I created the evil inclination and created the Torah to subdue it." By engaging in the Torah and the precepts for its own sake, a person is slowly educated until he is able to destroy all sparks of ego-love in himself, and to sanctify all his actions to be only for giving to another. Even the necessary things that he receives are so that he would be capable of sharing.

In his book, *Yesod Mora* ("Foundation of Awe"), page 8, the great and righteous sage Rav Abraham Ibn Ezra (1089–1167), writes: "And now pay attention and know that although all the precepts written in the Torah, or most of those accepted as composed by our ancestors, involve actions or speech, they are all to perfect the heart; 'for the Lord searches all hearts, and understands all the imaginations of the thoughts' (I Chronicles 28:9) and it is written, 'those who are upright in their hearts' (Psalms 125:4) and its opposite is 'a heart that devices wicked thoughts....'. (Proverbs 6:18) I have also found one verse that includes all precepts, which is, 'You shall fear the Lord your God and serve him.' (Deuteronomy 6:13, Ibid. 10:20) The word fear comprises all the negative precepts in speech, heart, and deed. This is the first step from which to ascend to the worship of the exalted Lord. It includes all the positive precepts, and these will train the heart and guide it until it will cleave to the upright blessed Lord, for this is what man was created for. He was not created to acquire a fortune and build structures, etc. Therefore he must seek everything that will bring him to love God, to study wisdom, and seek faith."

So we clearly see that the Torah is only the means to reach self-purification. Just as the Light of the Creator gives and shares, so too our goal is to transform the Desire to Receive for Oneself Alone into the Desire to Receive for the Sake of Sharing. This is why the prophet Isaiah prepared the removal of envy and hatred from humanity by the filling of the earth with knowledge, a condition for world peace. "...for the earth shall be full of the knowledge of the Lord" (Isaiah 11:9) is a prerequisite for, "The wolf also shall dwell with the lamb..." (Isaiah 11:6)

Unfortunately, misinterpretation has endured for two thousand years until this great Light was revealed in our generation. Both our righteous master and teacher, Rav Yehuda HaLevi Ashlag, in his great writings and especially in the *Sulam* commentary on the Zohar and Zohar Chadash; and his distinguished pupil, my righteous teacher, his right hand, who continued in his path, Rav Yehuda Tzvi Brandwein, have opened for us the gates of wisdom, and it is through them that the Heavenly book has been revealed to whomever seeks and asks for it. "Wisdom cries aloud in the street; she utters her voice in the squares," (Proverbs 10:20) thus we shall go from slavery to freedom, from enslavement to redemption, and from darkness to great Light, until "for the earth shall be full of the knowledge of the Lord," will be fulfilled soon in our own days.

I wish to add one more point that I have forgotten to put in the book Beloved of My Soul, of the letters from my righteous teacher to me, which was published by my son, Rav Michael. When I met my righteous teacher for the first time, I asked myself how I would know that my righteous teacher, Rav Ashlag's distinguished pupil, truly replaced our master and teacher Rav Yehuda haLevi Ashlag. You must remember that because I grew up at the great Yeshivas of the great men of Lithuania, the concept of Kabbalah was far from me. I had never met kabbalists until I met my righteous teacher. Yet I have learned two important things to observe from my righteous teacher:

First is to see whether the kabbalist has written any books from which one can study the wisdom of Kabbalah. Unfortunately today, since laypeople have no measuring stick to employ, they cling to many who call themselves kabbalists and after a short time leave those so-called kabbalists.

What I have witnessed is that except for my righteous teacher, the holy Rav Ashlag had no student quite like Rav Brandwein, even though there were thousands upon thousands of students who wrote about the Zohar and Kabbalah.

The second, which is more important to me, is that I have seen no other individual having love for others quite like my righteous teacher.

Rav Brandwein lived with the knowledge, the understanding, and the manifestation of the love for others. I remember a story my righteous teacher told about a famous rabbi who arrived in Israel from Europe and asked whether his disciples could show him something of the destruction of the Temple. They were all puzzled and did not understand the rabbi's question. Surely the rabbi knew of the Western Wall that has remained since the time of the destruction? When they wanted to take him to the Western Wall, the rabbi answered that he knew about the Western Wall and that his question was not of a material nature but rather something spiritual. His disciples did not know what to do.

After six months, the rabbi gathered his disciples and announced that he had truly found the spiritual object that remained from the destruction, and that it was hatred for no reason. For six months, the rabbi continued, he observed and followed the behavior of individuals, and to his grief he saw that even after 2,000 years individuals remained in their place, hating others even though others had done nothing against them.

The rabbi saw that despite the exile and all the troubles these souls had experienced, still no transformation had taken place. He therefore did not see how these souls could bring the Messiah, and that the Holy One, blessed be He, needed to take them from slavery to freedom Himself.

I know the extent of the pain of my righteous teacher when he saw individuals hating each other. And my righteous teacher told me that since the arrival of the holy master [Rav Yehuda Ashlag] in our world and the revelation of the book of Zohar, this process has changed. The time of which Rav Shimon bar Yochai had written has arrived—the book of Zohar will be rediscovered.

During the lifetimes of Rav Ashlag and Rav Brandwein, they did not sell or distribute many sets of the Zohar. Then, suddenly in 1985, the Kabbalah Center managed to distribute approximately the same amount of sets of the

Zohar in one year—a feat that had previously taken close to thirty years to achieve. Since then and until the year 1997, more and more people have become interested in the study of the Zohar.

I personally have witnessed how as the book of Zohar entered into more homes, an unreasonable resistance began to increase. Suddenly religious people, who had never opened the book of the Zohar in their lives, began to "guard" its holiness, wanting irreligious people and those who are religious but not Torah scholars to return the book of the Zohar that they had bought, claiming that they are not worthy of it, even though it is not written anywhere that it is forbidden to look at the book of Zohar.

And some tell people that they must burn the book of the Zohar that they have bought. It happened in France that one such individual, a man of about thirty years old, asked all the Jews of Paris to bring their books of the Zohar to him because he wanted to bury them. I began to understand that this nature was evil from its youth. However, that there were people saying that the Zohar must be buried or burnt, for me is a sign that we are very close to Redemption.

It is clear to me that the publication of the commentary of *Ha'oleh baSulam* ("Ascending the Ladder") on the Tikunei haZohar by my son, Rav Michael, is another step in the revelation of the wisdom of truth in the world, and through which we shall merit complete Redemption soon. It is also clear that the commentary on the Tikunei haZohar will spread throughout the Diaspora faster than we ever dreamed possible.

With the compassion of the Lord upon us, He has sent us from the Eternal Heaven a watcher and a holy one from him, out of him a stake and he has illuminated our eyes with a great Light, the Light of presence, the holy master, Rav Yehuda haLevi Ashlag, author of the *Sulam*, and we have merited in our generation to understand this discipline, study it, and be improved by it.

And in addition to all his books that shine throughout the Firmaments, Rav Ashlag has left us his student, his right hand, my righteous teacher, Rav Yehuda Tzvi Brandwein, who continued in his path, and has expanded and written a commentary, *Ma'alot haSulam*, and spread the wisdom of the author of the *Sulam*.

And now I have had the merit to see my sons, Rav Yehuda and Rav Michael, who continue in our path to bring the revelation and the spreading of the Light of the wisdom of Kabbalah to the layman. May we merit to continue the ways of our righteous teachers until we merit, through their hands, the revelation of the wisdom of Kabbalah and the study of the Zohar, and especially the study of the Tikunei haZohar with the *Ha'oleh baSulam* commentary by my son, Rav Michael, to witness the coming of the Messiah soon in our days, Amen.

~ Rav Berg, 1997

PROLOGUE

PROLOGUE

1. "And the wise shall shine like the brightness (*zohar*) of the Firmament."

1. רַבִּי שִׁמְעוֹן אָזַל לֵיהּ וְעָרַק לְמַדְבְּרָא דְלוֹד וְאִתְגַּנִּיז בְּחַד מְעַרְתָּא, הוּא
וְרַבִּי אֶלְעָזָר בְּרֵיהּ אִתְרַחֲזִיע נִיסָא, נָפַק לְהוֹן חַד חֲרוּב, וְחַד מַעֲיָינָא דְמַיָּא,
אָכְלֵי מֵהַהוּא חֲרוּב, וְשָׁתָן מֵהַהוּא מַיָּא, הֲוָה אֵלִיָּהוּ זָכוּר לַטּוֹב אָתֵי לְהוֹן
בְּכָל יוֹמָא תְּרֵי זִמְנֵי, וְאוֹלִיף לוֹן וְלָא יָדַע אִינִישׁ בְּהוֹ כו'. בְּזוֹהַר חָדָשׁ פָּרָשַׁת
תָּבוֹא (נ"ט ג) כָּתוּב שָׁם.

1. Rav Shimon left and escaped to the desert of Lod and hid, together with his son Rav Elazar in a certain cave. A miracle occurred to them. A carob tree and a spring of water emerged. They ate from that carob tree and drank from that water, and Elijah, of blessed memory, visited them twice each day and studied with them, and nobody knew of them. This is written in Zohar Chadash, [Ki] Tavo 1.

2. וְדָא אִתְקְרֵי: תִּקּוּנֵי הַזֹּהַר, דְּאִינּוּן שַׁבְעִין אַנְפִּין לְאוֹרַיְיתָא, דְּפָרִישׁ רַבִּי
שִׁמְעוֹן בַּר יוֹחָאי, בְּמִלַּת בְּרֵאשִׁית, מִסִּתְרֵי אוֹרַיְיתָא. קוּם רַבִּי שִׁמְעוֹן אַפְתַּח
מִילִין קַמֵּי שְׁכִינְתָּא. פָּתַח וְאָמַר וְהַמַּשְׂכִּילִים יַזְהִירוּ כְּזוֹהַר הָרָקִיעַ וגו'.

2. And this is called Corrections of the Zohar (Tikunei haZohar), which are seventy ways in which Rav Shimon bar Yochai interpreted the word Beresheet "In the beginning..." (Genesis 1:1), from the secrets of the Torah. Rise Rav Shimon, commence discourses in the presence of the Shechinah. He began and said, "And the wise shall shine like the brightness (*zohar*) of the Firmament...." (Daniel 12:3)

3. וְהַמַּשְׂכִּילִים אִלֵּין רַבִּי שִׁמְעוֹן וְחַבְרַיָּיא. יַזְהִירוּ, כַּד אִתְכַּנָּשׁוּ לְמֶעֱבַד הַאי
חִבּוּרָא, רְשׁוּתָא אִתְיָהִיב לְהוֹן וּלְאֵלִיָּהוּ עִמְּהוֹן, וּלְכָל נִשְׁמָתִין דִּמְתִיבְתָּאן
לְנַחֲתָא בֵּינַיְיהוּ, וּלְכָל מַלְאָכַיָּא בְּאִתְכַּסְיָא, וּבְאֹרַח שֵׂכֶל.

3. "And the wise" are Rav Shimon and the friends. "Shall shine," means when they gathered together to produce this collective composition,

permission was granted to them, and with them authority was given to Elijah and to all the souls of the Academy [Yeshiva] to descend to them, and to all the Angels in a concealed manner, and in a manner of intelligence.

4. וְעִלַּת עַל כֹּלָּא יָהִיב רְשׁוּ לְכָל שְׁמָהָן קַדִּישִׁין, וּלְכָל הֲוַיָּין וּלְכָל כִּנּוּיִין, לְגַלָּאָה לוֹן רָזִין טְמִירִין, כָּל שֵׁם בְּדַרְגָּא דִילֵיהּ. וּרְשׁוּתָא יָהִיב לַעֲשַׂר סְפִירָן לְגַלָּאָה לוֹן רָזִין טְמִירִין, דְּלָא אִתְיְהִיב רְשׁוּ לְגַלָּאָה לוֹן עַד דְּיֵיתֵי דָּרָא דְּמַלְכָּא מְשִׁיחָא.

4. And the Cause of everything, meaning the *Ein Sof* (Endless) granted permission to all the Holy Names, in general, to all the Names of the Tetragrammaton [Explicit Name—Yud-Hei-Vav-Hei] and to all the various Names of designated Divine attributes, to reveal hidden secrets to them, each Name in its grade. And permission was given to the Ten Sefirot to reveal hidden secrets to them; secrets that permission was not granted to be revealed until the arrival of the generation of King Messiah.

5. כְּזֹהַר הָרָקִיעַ, דְּאִיהוּ כְּלִיל כָּל גַּוֶון. זֹהַר טָמִיר וְגָנִיז זֹהַר בָּהִיר בַּשְׁוָקִים. זֹהַר זָרִיק נְצוֹצִין וּמַבְהִיק כְּבָרָק לְעַיְנִין. זֹהַר זָהִיר וְחִוֵּור כְּסִיהֲרָא. זֹהַר זָהִיר סוּמָקָא כְּמַאֲדִים. זֹהַר מַבְהִיק כְּלִיל יְרוֹקָא כְּחַמָּה. זֹהַר יָרוֹק כְּכֹכָב. זֹהַר כְּלִיל חִוֵּור וְסוּמָק. זֹהַר זָהִיר לְכָל עֵיבַר, כְּמָאן דְּמָחָא בַּפַּטִּישׁ וְזָרִיק עִיבִיבִין לְכָל סִטְרָא.

5. "Shall shine like the brightness (*zohar*) of the Firmament," which is comprised of all the colors, a brightness (*zohar*) that is concealed and hidden, a brilliant brightness (*zohar*) in the Heavens, a brightness (*zohar*) that emits sparks and shines like lightning to the eyes, a brightness (*zohar*) that shines white like the moon, a brightness (*zohar*) that shines red like Mars. A brightness (*zohar*) that shines with a combined illumination that is green like the Sun, a bright (*zohar*) green like a star, a brightness (*zohar*) combined of white and red, a brightness (*zohar*) that

shines to every direction, as one striking a hammer, emitting sparks of light in every direction.

6. הָכִי מֵהַאי זֹהַר זַהֲרִין כַּמָּה נִשְׁמָתִין, דְּאִינּוּן זַהֲרִין כֻּלְּהוּ בְּרָקִיעַ. וְאַלֵּין אִינּוּן נִשְׁמָתִין מֵאַלֵּין מַשְׂכִּילִים דְּאִית בְּהוֹן שֵׂכֶל לְאִשְׁתְּמוֹדְעָא בְּרָזִין דְּמָארֵיהוֹן. כֻּלְּהוּ רְשִׁימִין וּמְצוּיָּירִין בְּמַלְכוּתָא דִּרְקִיעָא, כְּכוֹכְבַיָּא דְּנָהֲרִין בִּרְקִיעָא וְהַיְינוּ יַזְהִירוּ כְּזֹהַר הָרָקִיעַ. מַאי הָרָקִיעַ. דְּנָהֲרִין בֵּיהּ נִשְׁמָתִין דְּמַשְׂכִּילִים כְּכֹכְבַיָּא בְּרָקִיעַ הָכִי נָהֲרִין בְּכָרְסְיָא.

6. So too, some souls illuminate from this brightness (*zohar*), and they all illuminate in the correction of the Firmament. These souls are from those wise ones who possess intelligence to know the secrets of their Master. All these souls are marked and shaped in the Malchut (Kingdom) of the Firmament like stars that shine in the Firmament, and this is the meaning of: "…they shall shine like the brightness (*zohar*) of the Firmament." What is this Firmament? He asks, "What is this correction called Firmament (*Rakia*)?" And answers, "It is that by which the souls of the wise illuminate like the stars in the Firmament, and similarly they illuminate in the Throne."

7. וְכֻלְּהוּ פָּרְחִין מִן רָקִיעַ וְדָא צַדִּיק חַי עוֹלָמִים, דְּמִנֵּיהּ פָּרְחִין נִשְׁמָתִין דְּצַדִּיקַיָּא. וְנָהֲרִין בְּסִיהֲרָא. וַעֲלַיְיהוּ כְּתִיב וַיִּתֵּן אֹתָם אֱלֹקִי"ם בִּרְקִיעַ הַשָּׁמָיִם לְהָאִיר עַל הָאָרֶץ.

7. And all the souls fly up from the Firmament, and it is the ever living righteous (*tzadik*), from which the souls of the righteous people fly up and illuminate in the light of the moon, Malchut, from which the Returning Light comes, and about them is written: "and God placed them in the Firmament of the Heavens to illuminate over the Earth." (Genesis 1:17)

8. וְאִיהוּ רָקִיעַ, דְּאִיהוּ לְעֵיל מֵחֵיוָון הָדָא הוּא דִכְתִיב וּמִמַּעַל לָרָקִיעַ אֲשֶׁר עַל רֹאשָׁם וַהֲפוֹךְ רָקִי"עַ וְתִשְׁכַּח לֵיהּ עִיקָ"ר וִיסוֹדָא דְּמֶרְכַּבְתָּא עִלָּאָה דַּעֲלֵיהּ קַיְימִין חֵיוָון וְכָרְסַיָּא דְּמֶרְכַּבְתָּא עִלָּאָה.

8. And that Firmament, which is higher than the living creatures, about which is written: "...and above the Firmament that was over their heads..." (Ezekiel 1:26) **Rearrange the letters of** *Rakia* **(Firmament) and you will find** [the word] *ikar* (principal) **and the foundation of the Supernal Chariot upon whom exist the living creatures and the Throne of the Supernal Chariot.**

9. וַעֲלֵיהּ אִתְּמַר וְצַדִּיק יְסוֹד עוֹלָם עַל צַדִּיק דִּלְעֵילָא קַיְּימָא עָלְמָא דְּאִתְכַּסְיָיא. וְעַל צַדִּיק דִּלְתַתָּא קַיְּימָא עָלְמָא דְּאִתְגַּלְיָיא. וְהַיְינוּ מַצְדִּיקֵי הָרַבִּים מֵהַהוּא צַדִּיקָא דְּעָלְמָא תַּלְיָין, מַאי הָרַבִּים. אִלֵּין דְּאִתְּמַר עֲלַיְיהוּ הֲלָכָה כְּרַבִּים. דְּאִינּוּן מִסִּטְרָא דַּאֲבָהָן, דְּלֵית רַבִּים פָּחוֹת מִתְּלַת.

9. And about the Firmament at the mouth of Arich Anpin is said, "... and the righteous is the foundation of the world." (Proverbs 10:25) **The concealed world exists due to the Supernal Righteous, and the revealed world exists due to the righteous below, that is: "And those that turn many to righteousness."** (Daniel 12:3) **From that righteous everlasting foundation** (Yesod) **depend** the many. He asks, **"Who are the many?"** And replies, **"Those about whom is said: 'the ruling is set by the majority'** (Tractate Shabbat 15a) **which are the aspect of the** [three] **Patriarchs, since there is no majority with less than three."**

10. הֲלָכָה כְּרַבִּים, דָּא שְׁכִינְתָּא. וּמִתַּמָּן וְעַמֵּךְ כֻּלָּם צַדִּיקִים לְעוֹלָם יִירְשׁוּ אָרֶץ הַהִיא דְּאִתְּמַר בָּהּ וְהָאָרֶץ הֲדֹם רַגְלָי. דָּא שְׁכִינְתָּא דְּאִיהִי כְּלִילָא מֵעֲשַׂר סְפִירָן, וּמִתַּמָּן אִתְקְרִיאוּ יִשְׂרָאֵל: מְלָכִים. צַדִּיקִים. חוֹזִים, נְבִיאִים, מָארֵי תוֹרָה. גִּבּוֹרִים. חֲסִידִים. נְבוֹנִים. חֲכָמִים. רָאשֵׁי אַלְפֵי יִשְׂרָאֵל.

10. **"The ruling is set by the majority,"** this is the Shechinah. **And from there: "And your people are all righteous, they will inherit the Earth forever,"** (Isaiah 60:21) **about which it is said, "And the Earth is My footstool,"** (Isaiah 66:1) **which is the Shechinah that is composed of ten Sefirot, and from whence Israel are called: kings, righteous, seers,**

prophets, masters of Torah, mighty, pious, understanding, wise, heads of the thousands of Israel.

2. "As a bird strays from her nest, so does a man stray from his place."

11. וּרְשׁוּתָא אִתְיְהִיב לְאִלֵּין נִשְׁמָתִין דְּאִתְתָּרְכוּ מֵאַתְרַיְיהוּ בָּתַר קוּדְשָׁא בְּרִיךְ הוּא וּשְׁכִינְתֵּיהּ לְקַנְּנָא בְּהַאי חִבּוּרָה דְּאִתְּמַר בָּהּ כְּצִפּוֹר נוֹדֶדֶת מִן קִנָּהּ כֵּן אִישׁ נוֹדֵד מִמְּקוֹמוֹ וְלֵית צִפּוֹר אֶלָּא שְׁכִינְתָּא דְּאִיהִי מִתְתַּרְכָא מֵאַתְרָהָא הָדָא הוּא דִּכְתִיב שַׁלֵּחַ תְּשַׁלַּח אֶת הָאֵם וְאֶת הַבָּנִים תִּקַּח לָךְ אֶת לְרַבּוֹת שְׁכִינְתָּא תַּתָּאָה, הָאֵם, שְׁכִינְתָּא עִלָּאָה, הָדָא הוּא דִּכְתִיב וּבְפִשְׁעֵיכֶם שֻׁלְּחָה אִמְּכֶם דְּתַרְוַיְיהוּ אִתְתָּרְכוּ מֵאַתְרַיְיהוּ וּבְגִין דָּא שַׁלֵּחַ תְּשַׁלַּח תְּרֵין שִׁלּוּחִין חַד מִבַּיִת רִאשׁוֹן וְחַד מִבַּיִת שֵׁנִי לְקַיְימָא בֵּיהּ אֲנִי י"י הוּא שְׁמִי וּכְבוֹדִי לְאַחֵר לֹא אֶתֵּן שְׁכִינְתָּא עִלָּאָה וּתְהִלָּתִי לַפְּסִילִים שְׁכִינְתָּא תַּתָּאָה כֵּן אִישׁ נוֹדֵד מִמְּקוֹמוֹ דָּא קוּדְשָׁא בְּרִיךְ הוּא דְּאִתְּמַר בֵּיהּ י"י אִישׁ מִלְחָמָה דְּאִתְתָּרַךְ אַבַּתְרַיְיהוּ.

11. And permission was given to those souls who were banished from their place to follow after the Holy One blessed be He, and His Shechinah, to nest in this compilation. About her, the Shechinah, it is said: "As a bird strays from her nest, so does a man stray from his place." (Proverbs 27:8) This bird is none other than the Shechinah who was banished from her place, as is written: "Send, you shall send away the (*et*) mother, and the (*et*) children take for yourself." (Deuteronomy 22:7) The word *et* comes to include the lower Shechinah, Malchut, and "the mother" is the Supernal Shechinah, Binah. This is why it is written: "And because of your transgression your Mother was banished," (Isaiah 50:1) as both, Binah and Malchut, stray from their places. Therefore, it is written: "Send, you shall send," two banishments, corresponding to Binah and Malchut, one from the first Temple, Binah, and one from the second Temple, Malchut, to fulfill the verse: "I am the Lord, that is My Name, and My glory I will not grant to others" (Isaiah 42:8) refers to the Supernal Shechinah, Binah, "nor My praise to graven idols" (Ibid.) which refers to the lower Shechinah, Malchut, "So does a man (*ish*) stray from his place," which refers to the Holy One blessed be He, of whom it

is said: "The Lord is a man (*ish*) of war," (Exodus 15:3) **who was banished following them.**

וְעוֹד כֵּן אִישׁ נוֹדֵד מִמְּקוֹמוֹ דָּא מֹשֶׁה דִּכְתִיב וְהָאִישׁ מֹשֶׁה עָנָו מְאֹד .12
דְּאִתְתָּרַךְ רוּחֵיהּ אֲבַתְרַיְיהוּ.

12. Another explanation [is]: **"So does a man (*ish*) stray from his place," concerning Moses, as it is written: "And the man (*ish*) Moses is most humble" (Numbers 12:3) because his soul wandered after** the Holy One blessed be He, and His Shechinah.

וְעוֹד כֵּן אִישׁ נוֹדֵד מִמְּקוֹמוֹ מָאן דְּאִיהוּ אִישׁ צַדִּיק דְּאָזַל נָע וָנָד מֵאֲתָרֵיהּ .13
כִּשְׁכִינְתָּא דְּאִתְּמַר בָּהּ וְלֹא מָצְאָה הַיּוֹנָה מָנוֹחַ דְּהָכִי אוּקְמוּהוּ רַבָּנָן בְּזִמְנָא
דְּאִתְחֲרַב בֵּי מַקְדְּשָׁא גְּזַר עַל בָּתֵּי הַצַּדִּיקִים דְּיִוְזְרבוּ דְּאָזְלִין כָּל חַד נוֹדֵד
מִמְּקוֹמוֹ דְּדַיּוֹ לְעֶבֶד לְמֶהֱוֵי כְּרַבֵּיהּ.

13. Another explanation, **more so** [is]: **"So does a man (*ish*) stray from his place," meaning whoever is a righteous man (*ish*) who goes and wanders from his place, like the Shechinah about whom it is written: "And the dove found no rest." (Genesis 8:9) For so have the masters explained** the verse: "In My ears said the Lord of Hosts, if not, many houses will become desolate," (Isaiah 5:9) **that at the time of the destruction of the Temple, He decreed upon the houses of the righteous to be demolished,** meaning that each individual shall continue to wander away from his home, for it suffices for the servant to be like his master.

וְרָזָא דְּמִלָּה נוֹדֵד הוּא לַלֶּחֶם אַיֵּה א"ה דִּמְרַחֵם עֲלֵיהּ אוּף הָכִי אֵין מְנַהֵל .14
לָהּ וְגוֹ' וּבְגִין דָּא דַּיּוֹ לְעֶבֶד לְמֶהֱוֵי כְּרַבֵּיהּ וְלֵית לֶחֶם אֶלָּא אוֹרַיְתָא הַאי גְּרַם
לְמָארֵי תוֹרָה דְּאָזְלִין מִתְתַּרְכִין.

14. The secret of the matter is: "He wanders for bread, where is he." (Job, 15:23) Where is anyone who would have mercy for him? Here as well, Malchut, **"she has no one to guide her, etc." (Isaiah 51:18). Therefore, it**

suffices for the servant to be like his master. And "bread" refers only to Torah; this causes the masters of Torah to go and wander.

15. זַכָּאָה אִיהוּ מָארֵי מְתִיבְתָּא מָארֵי מֶדְרָשׁ מָארֵי תוֹרָה דְּגַם צִפּוֹר מָצְאָה בַיִת בַּיִת דְּנִשְׁמָעִין בֵּיהּ פִּתְגָּמֵי אוֹרַיְיתָא דְּבַאֲתַר דְּאִית תַּמָּן תוֹרָה דְּאִיהוּ עַמּוּדָא דְּאֶמְצָעִיתָא גַּם צִפּוֹר מָצְאָה בַיִת תַּמָּן וּבְגִין דָּא אוּקְמוּהָ רַבָּנָן כָּל בַּיִת שֶׁאֵין נִשְׁמָעִין בּוֹ דִּבְרֵי תוֹרָה לְסוֹף תֶּחֱרַב.

15. Fortunate are the masters of the Yeshivah, masters of the Midrash, masters of Torah, "since the bird has also found a home," (Psalms 84:3) meaning a home in which words of Torah are heard, since in a place where Torah is found, which is the Central Column, there too "the bird has also found a home." (Ibid.) As a result of this, the masters have explained that the verse: "All darkness shall be hid in his secret places..." (Job 20:26) means that every house where there are no words of Torah heard is bound to be destroyed.

16. וְאִלֵּין דְּנִשְׁמָעִין דִּבְרֵי תוֹרָה בְּהוֹן אִתְקְרִיאוּ: בֵּיצִים. אֶפְרוֹחִים. בָּנִים. בֵּיצִים, מָארֵי מִקְרָא. אֶפְרוֹחִים, מָארֵי מִשְׁנָה. בָּנִים מָארֵי קַבָּלָה.

16. And those houses where words of Torah are heard are called "eggs, young chicks, and children." He explains, "'Eggs' are the masters of the Scriptures, 'young chicks' are the masters of the Mishnah, and 'children' are the masters of Kabbalah."

3. "Do not take the mother with the young;
but be sure to let the mother go."

17. וַעֲלַיְהוּ אִתְּמַר וְהָאֵם רוֹבֶצֶת עַל הָאֶפְרוֹחִים אוֹ עַל הַבֵּיצִים שַׁלֵּחַ תְּשַׁלַּח מִנַּיְהוּ אֲבָל עַל מָארֵי קַבָּלָה אִתְּמַר לֹא תִקַּח הָאֵם עַל הַבָּנִים.

17. Regarding them is said: "…and the mother is sitting on the young or on the eggs, you may take the young, but be sure to let the mother go." (Deuteronomy 22:6-7) from them. However, regarding the masters of Kabbalah it is said: "Do not take the mother with the young." (Deuteronomy 22:6)

18. דְּלֵית סָכְלָתְנוּ לְאִשְׁתְּמוֹדַע בִּשְׁכִינְתָּא, כְּאִלֵּין מָארֵי קַבָּלָה. וְאִלֵּין עָבְדִין לָהּ דִּירָה וְלִקוּדְשָׁא בְּרִיךְ הוּא. וּפָרְחִין עִמָּה בְּכָל אֲתַר דְּאִיהִי פָּרְחַת כֻּלְהוּ מְנַדְדִּין עִמָּה בִּעֲלִיוֹתָא דִּילָהּ אֲבָל אֶפְרוֹחֵי, לֵית גַּדְפִין דִּלְהוֹן שְׁלֵמִין דְּפָרְחִין בְּהוֹן דְּאִינוּן פִּקּוּדֵי דַּעֲשֵׂה כָּל שֶׁכֵּן בֵּצִים וּבְגִין דָּא אִתְּמַר עֲלַיְהוּ לְגַבֵּי אִימָא שַׁלֵּחַ תְּשַׁלַּח אֶת הָאֵם.

18. Since there are none who have understanding to know the ways of the Shechinah as the masters of Kabbalah do because they make a dwelling place for the Holy One blessed be He, and His Shechinah, so too, do they fly with Her; wherever She flies they all wander with her, and go on Her missions. However, the wings of young chicks with which they could properly fly, which are the positive precepts, are not complete, and all the more so their eggs. Consequently, it is said about them, in relation to the Lights of Ima in the Mochin of "sitting:" "…but be sure to let the mother go."

19. עַד דְּאָמַר מִלִּין אִלֵּין, הָא סָבָא אִזְדַּמַּן לֵיהּ וְאָמַר. וְהָא כְּתִיב וְאֶת הַבָּנִים תִּקַּח לָךְ, אָמַר לֵיהּ סָבָא, כָּל אֶתִין לְרַבּוֹיֵי, וּבְגִין דָּא לֹא אָמַר וְהַבָּנִים תִּקַּח לָךְ, אֶלָּא וְאֶת לְרַבּוֹת אֶפְרוֹחִים, אֲבָל לֹא אָמַר הַבָּנִים תִּקַּח לָךְ.

19. **While** Rav Shimon **was speaking these words, an old man came by.**
He inquired **and said,"Behold, it is written: '...you may take the young,'**
that would seem to indicate that 'but be sure to let... go' refers to the
young." Rav Shimon **replied to him, "Old man, all [instances of the word]**
'et' **comes to include the young chicks, and therefore it does not say, 'The
children take for yourself' but rather, 'And (*et*) the young' to include also
the young chicks. But it does not say, '...the children you shall take for
yourself.' That is to say that 'And (*et*) the young you may take' refers to
those children who are in the aspect of eggs, and includes those in the
aspect of young chicks, but not the masters of Kabbalah, who are with
the Mochin of Gadlut of Supernal Aba and Ima, for about them there is
nothing to add or increase. Since it is written 'and the' (*ve'et*) this means
that it refers to children who are in the aspect of eggs, and also includes
young chicks."**

20. אָמַר לֵיהּ בְּרִיךְ אַנְתְּ בּוּצִינָא קַדִּישָׁא דְּהָכִי הוּא וַדַּאי וּבָנִים אִינּוּן וַדַּאי
תְּחוֹת אִימָּא עִלָּאָה. וַחֲסִידִים. גִּבּוֹרִים. מָארֵי תוֹרָה. חוֹזִים. נְבִיאִים. צַדִּיקִים.

20. The old man **said to** Rav Shimon, **"Blessed are you, Holy Luminary,**
meaning Rav Shimon, **that is certainly so. And the children are certainly
under the Supernal Mother,** in the Mochin of Supernal Aba and Ima, and
they receive from their Six Lower Sefirot, therefore they are **pious, mighty,
masters of Torah, seers, prophets, and righteous."**

21. וַחֲסִידִים מִסִּטְרָא דְּחֶסֶד דַּרְגָּא דְּאַבְרָהָם, וְאוּקְמוּהָ עֲלֵיהּ, אֵין וְסָיד
אֶלָּא הַמִּתְחַוַּסֵּד עִם קוֹנוֹ דְּעָבִיד לֵיהּ קַן דְּאִיהוּ אַכְסַנְיָא דִּילֵיהּ וְדָא שְׁכִינְתָּא
דְּאִיהִי קַן דִּילֵיהּ בַּיִת דִּילֵיהּ. הֵיכָל דִּילֵיהּ. מָלוֹן דִּילֵיהּ. וּבְאַרְעָא קַדִּישָׁא
אִיהִי יְחוּדֵיהּ וּבֵיתֵיהּ. וְלָאו מָלוֹן וְאַכְסַנְיָא אֶלָּא כְּפוּם הַהוּא בַּר נָשׁ דְּתַקִּין
לֵיהּ וּבְגִין דָּא יָהִיב מִדַּת חֶסֶד לְאַבְרָהָם.

21. He explains, **"Pious (*Chasidim*) are from the side of** the Sefira of
Chesed, the level of Abraham. **The** masters **have explained about this
that a person is not considered pious unless he does kindness with his**

Master (*kono*), by preparing for Him, the Holy One blessed be He, **a nest (*ken*) that will be His residence, and that is the Shechinah, that is His nest, His home, His chamber, His lodging place.** The Holy Land is His only one, and His home, and the Shechinah is made into a **lodging place or residence** only in as much as that particular person has corrected it, and therefore the attribute of Chesed was given to Abraham.

22. גְּבוֹרִים מִסְּטָרָא דִגְבוּרָה, דְּיָהֲבִין תּוּקְפָּא לְמָארֵיהוֹן לְכַבּוֹשׁ עֶבֶד תַּחַת
רַבּוֹ. וְשִׁפְחָה תְּחוֹת גְּבִרְתָּהּ, בִּקְשׁוּרָא דִּתְפִּלִין. דְּמַאן דְּלֵית לֵיהּ תְּפִילִין
בְּשַׁעֲתָא קְרִיאַת שְׁמַע, מִסְּטָרָא דִּילֵיהּ שַׁלִּיט עֶבֶד וְשִׁפְחָה עַל עָלְמָא, וּבְהַהִיא
שַׁעֲתָא רַגְזָא שְׁכִינְתָּא, הָדָא הוּא דִכְתִיב עֶבֶד כִּי יִמְלוֹךְ וְשִׁפְחָה כִּי
תִירַשׁ גְּבִרְתָּהּ.

22. The mighty are from the side of the Sefira of **Gevurah, who give power to their Master to subdue the slave beneath his Master, and the handmaid under her mistress, with the bond (knot) of the Tefilin.** For whoever has no Tefilin, during the Shema reading, from his side, the slave and the handmaid control the world, and during that time the Shechinah is angered. This is the meaning of the verse: "...For a slave when he rules ... and a handmaid who inherits her mistress." (Proverbs 30: 23)

23. וְאוּף הָכִי רַגְזָא יַתִּיר, עַל נָבָל כִּי יִשְׂבַּע כִּי יִשְׂבַּע לָחֶם דְּאִתְּמַר בֵּיהּ לְכוּ
לַחֲמוּ בְלַחְמִי. דְּאִיהוּ קַמְצָן נָבָל בְּמָמוֹנֵיהּ, נָבָל שְׁמֵיהּ, דְּלָאו אִיהוּ נָדִיב,
וְלָאו אִיהוּ מִזַּרְעָא דַּאֲבָהָן, דְּאִתְּמַר עֲלַיְהוּ נְדִיבֵי עַמִּים נֶאֱסָפוּ, דְּהָא קַמְצָן
אִיהוּ עָנִי הַדַּעַת, בָּתַר דְּלָא עָבִיד טִיבוּ לְמָארֵי תּוֹרָה, לְמֶהֱוֵי מַחֲזִיק בִּידַיְיהוּ.
וְאוֹרַיְתָא בְּלָא פָקוּדַיָּא לָאו אִיהִי תּוֹרַת ה'.

23. And also, she is even more angered: "When a villain (*naval*) satiates himself with bread" (Proverbs 30:22) about which it is said: "Go eat of my bread" (Proverbs 9:5). He is considered **a villain (*naval*), because he is a miser with his money,** and he is called a villain (*naval*) since **he is not generous, nor is he from the seed of the patriarchs,** about whom it is said: "the generous of the nations gathered," (Psalms 47:10) because a miser is poor in knowledge, as he does not do good to masters of the Torah to support them [lit. hold their hands]. And Torah without precepts is not considered the Lord's Torah.

24. מָארֵי תוֹרָה, מִסִּטְרָא דְּעַמּוּדָא דְּאֶמְצָעִיתָא, דְּבֵיהּ וְצַוֹת לַיְלָה הֲוָה קָם דָּוִד, לְחַבְּרָא לֵיהּ בִּשְׁכִינְתָּא דְּאִתְקְרִיאַת לַיְלָה. וְאִיהוּ שׁוֹמֵר מַה מִּלַּיְלָה לֵיל ה', לֵיל שִׁמּוּרִים הוּא לַי"י, וּבְגִינָהּ אִתְּמַר כָּל הָעוֹסֵק בַּתּוֹרָה בַּלַּיְלָה, הַקָּדוֹשׁ בָּרוּךְ הוּא מוֹשֵׁךְ עָלָיו וְחוּט שֶׁל וֶחֶסֶד בַּיּוֹם, שֶׁנֶּאֱמַר יוֹמָם יְצַוֶּה י"י וַחַסְדּוֹ וּבַלַּיְלָה שִׁירֹה עִמִּי.

24. The masters of Torah are from the side of the Central Column, meaning the Sefira of Tiferet, which is the Central Column, that through it, with the illumination of the Central Column, which is the Torah, David would rise at midnight to connect the Sefira of Tiferet with the Shechinah which is Malchut, which is called night (lailah). This is the secret of the verse: "Watchman, what of the night (lailah)," (Isaiah 21:11), Leil-Hei, which is the secret of the verse: "a night (leil) of watchfulness for God," (Exodus 12:42) and about this is said: "Whoever studies the Torah at night, the Holy One blessed be He, draws to him a string of mercy (chesed) during the day," (Tractate Chagiga 12b) as is said: "By the day, the Lord commands his grace (chesed), and at night His song is with me." (Psalms 42.8)

25. וְחוֹזִים נְבִיאִים מִסִּטְרָא דְּנֶצַח וָהוֹד. דִּבְהוֹן כְּלִילָן תְּרֵין שְׁמָהָן דְּאִינּוּן יָאקדונה"י. דִּבְהוֹן תַּמְנְיָא אַתְוָון, לָקֳבֵל תַּמְנְיָא סִפְרֵי נְבִיאִים, וּנְבִיאִים תְּרֵין, הָא עֶשֶׂר לָקֳבֵל עֶשֶׂר סְפִירָן. לִקְבְלֵיהּ חָזָא יְחֶזְקֵאל עֶשֶׂר מַרְאוֹת. צַדִּיקִים מִסִּטְרָא דְּצַדִּיק, עַל כָּל אִלֵּין אִתְּמַר לֹא תִקַּח הָאֵם עַל הַבָּנִים.

25. Seers and prophets are from the aspect of the two Sefirot Netzach and Hod. Within them are included the two Names Yud-Hei-Vav-Hei and Alef-Dalet-Nun-Yud, and they are intertwined in Yesod that unites them. Yud-Alef-Hei-Dalet-Vav-Nun-Hei-Yud, containing eight letters

corres-ponding to the eight books of the Prophets, since the twelve
Minor Prophets are considered one book. And prophets (*nevi'im*) are two,
Netzach and Hod, so altogether they are ten, corresponding to the Ten
Sefirot. And corresponding to the Ten Sefirot, Ezekiel saw ten visions.
Righteous (*tzadikim*) are from the side of the Sefira of Yesod, which is
called Tzadik, and about all these was said, "Do not take the mother
with the young."

26. וְעוֹד, אִלֵּין דְּעָסְקִין בְּאוֹרַיְתָא לִשְׁמָהּ, וְנָטְרִין פִּקּוּדָהָא דְּאִינּוּן תַּרְיַ"ג
מִצְוֹת דְּתַלְיָין מִשֵּׁם יְקוָ"ק, כְּעִנְבִּין בְּאִתְכָּלָא, כְּדֵי לְיַחֲדָא בְּהוֹן לְשֵׁם יְ"יָ
בִּשְׁכִינָה, כְּבַר נַשׁ דְּמִתְיַחֵד עִם בַּת זוּגֵיהּ בְּכָל אֵבְרִין דִּילֵיהּ, לְאַפָּקָא זַרְעָא
מַעֲלְיָא. אִתְּמַר בְּהוֹן לֹא תִקַּח הָאֵם עַל הַבָּנִים. וְאִלֵּין דְּלָא מִשְׁתַּדְּלֵי בְּאוֹרַיְתָא
לִשְׁמָהּ, אִתְּמַר בְּהוֹן שַׁלֵּחַ תְּשַׁלַּח אֶת הָאֵם. אֶת לְרַבּוֹת שֵׁם יְ"יָ דְּאִסְתַּלַּק
עִמָּהּ מֵהַהוּא בַּר נָשׁ.

26. Furthermore, those who deal with the Torah for its own sake, and
uphold its 613 precepts, that hang on to the Name Yud-Hei-Vav-Hei, as
grapes in a cluster. And his intention is to unify the Name Yud-Hei-Vav-
Hei, which is Zeir Anpin with the Shechinah, which is Malchut, through
them, as a person who unifies himself with his soul mate, with all his
limbs, and his intention is to beget good offspring. Regarding them is
said: "Do not take the mother with the young." (Deuteronomy 22:6) And
those who do not exert effort in the Torah for its own sake, regarding
them it is said: "...but be sure to let the (*et*) mother go." (Deuteronomy
22:7) *Et* indicates the Name Yud-Hei-Vav-Hei, Zeir Anpin, who
distances Himself from that person with the mother.

27. וְעוֹד, אִלֵּין דְּאוֹכְרוּן שַׁבָּתוֹת וְיָמִים טוֹבִים, אִתְּמַר עֲלַיְיהוּ, לֹא תִקַּח
הָאֵם עַל הַבָּנִים, דְּעָבְדִין עוֹבָדָא דִּבְנִין עִם שַׁבָּת מַלְכְּתָא, וְעִם קוּדְשָׁא
בְּרִיךְ הוּא, דְּאִיהוּ יוֹם הַשַּׁבָּת. מָאן דְּקַיֵּים בֵּיהּ וְכִבַּדְתּוֹ מֵעֲשׂוֹת דְּרָכֶיךָ.
הַאי אִיהוּ כַּבֵּד אֶת אָבִיךָ וְאֶת אִמֶּךָ וְגוֹ'.

27. Furthermore, those who respect the Shabbats and the Holidays, it says about them: "Do not take the mother with the young." For they do the actions of children with the Shabbat Queen, meaning Malchut, and with the Holy One blessed be He, Zeir Anpin, which is the Sabbath day. Meaning whoever fulfills "And you shall honor it by abstaining from your own ways." (Isaiah 58:13) This is: "Honor your father and your mother...." (Exodus 20:12)

28. דְּתִכְלַת עָלְמִין נִינְהוּ. תְּרֵין יָרִית בְּכִבּוּד אָב וָאֵם. וּתְלִיתָאָה יָרִית בְּאוֹרַיְתָא דְּכָלִיל לוֹן בֵּ"ן י"ה. הֲדָא הוּא דִכְתִיב כִּי הוּא חַיֶּיךָ וְאֹרֶךְ יָמֶיךָ. כִּי הִיא חַיֶּיךָ, בְּעוֹלָם הַזֶּה, דָּא גַּן דִּלְתַתָּא. וְאֹרֶךְ יָמֶיךָ דָּא עָלְמָא דְּאָתֵי, עָלְמָא אֲרִיכָא. עַל הָאֲדָמָה אֲשֶׁר י"יָ אֱלֹהֶי"ךָ נֹתֵן לָךְ. עָלְמָא שִׁפְלָה.

28. There are three worlds. He inherits two with the precept of honoring one's father and mother, and the third he inherits in the merit of the Torah, Zeir Anpin, which also includes the first two worlds, in the secret of "son of Yud-Hei." This is what is written: "For He is your life and length of days." (Deuteronomy 30:20) "Your life" in this world, meaning the lower garden, "and length of days" is the World to Come, that is everlasting, "...in the land that the Lord your God is giving you." (Exodus 20:12) meaning the lowly world.

29. וְעוֹד, אִלֵּין דְּקָשְׁרִין לִשְׁכִינְתָּא עִם קוּדְשָׁא בְּרִיךְ הוּא בִּקְשׁוּרָא דִּתְפִלִּין, אִתְּמַר עֲלַיְיהוּ, לֹא תִקַּח הָאֵם עַל הַבָּנִים. וְאִינוּן דְּלָא קָשְׁרִין לוֹן כַּחֲדָא אִתְּמַר בְּהוֹן שַׁלֵּחַ תְּשַׁלַּח אֶת הָאֵם.

29. Furthermore, those who bind the Shechinah, which is Malchut, with the Holy One blessed be He, Zeir Anpin, through the binding of the Tefilin, it says about them: "Do not take the mother with the young." Those who do not bind them together as one, it is said about them: "...but be sure to let the mother go."

30. וְעוֹד, אִלֵּין דִּמְיַחֲדִין לוֹן כַּחֲדָא לְעַמּוּדָא דְּאֶמְצָעִיתָא, וּשְׁכִינְתָּא תַּתָּאָה, בִּקְרִיאַת שְׁמַע, אִתְּמַר עֲלַיְיהוּ לֹא תִקַּח הָאֵם עַל הַבָּנִים. וְאִלֵּין דְּלָא מְיַיחֲדִין לוֹן בְּיִחוּדָא דִּקְרִיאַת שְׁמַע, כְּתִיב בְּהוֹן שַׁלֵּחַ תְּשַׁלַּח אֶת הָאֵם.

30. Also, those who unify the Central Column, Tiferet, **and the lower Shechinah,** Malchut, **through the Shema reading, it says about them: "Do not take the mother with the young." Those who do not unify them through the unifications of the Shema reading, it says about them: "… but be sure to let the mother go."**

31. בְּכָל אֲתַר אֶת לְרַבּוֹת וְהָכָא, לְרַבּוֹת וְחָכְמָה עִלָּאָה, אֵם הָאֱמוּנָה דְּאִיהִי בִּינָה, וַעֲלָהּ אִתְּמַר בְּכָל אֲתַר הָכָא לֹא תִקַּח הָאֵם שַׁלֵּחַ תְּשַׁלַּח אֶת הָאֵם הָדָא הוּא דִכְתִיב כִּי אִם לַבִּינָה תִקְרָא. וְאִיהִי אוֹרַיְתָא דִּלְעֵילָּא דְּאִתְּמַר בָּהּ וְאַל תִּטּשׁ תּוֹרַת אִמֶּךָ.

31. Every place where "et" is written it means "to include," and here it is to include the Supernal Chochmah. He explains, **"The mother of Faith (Emunah) is Binah,** and Emunah is Malchut. Since Binah has elevated Malchut to Herself to correct Her, the Names of Chochmah and Binah changed to father and mother. **About Her,** Binah, **it says here, in every place: 'Do not take the mother.' Also: '…but be sure to let the mother go,' this is as it says: 'If** [*im*, which can be read as *em*, meaning "mother"] **you call to understanding (***binah***)….'** (Proverbs 2:3) **This applies to the Supernal Torah, about which it says: 'And do not forsake your mother's (***imecha***) teaching [Torah].'** (Proverbs 1:8)"

32. וְעוֹד, אִלֵּין דְּנַטְרִין אוֹת בְּרִית בְּתוֹחוֹמֵיהּ, דְּאִיהוּ שְׁמוֹנָה יָמִים, וְנָטְרֵי אוֹת שַׁבָּת בְּתוֹחוֹמֵיהּ דְּאִינּוּן י"י בַּן יֹ אקדרונק"י. דִּבְגִינַיְיהוּ אוּקְמוּהָ מָארֵי מַתְנִיתִין דְּלָא אִשְׁתַּכַּח בַּר נָשׁ פָּגוּם מִתַּרְוַויְיהוּ, כְּתִיב לֹא תִקַּח הָאֵם עַל הַבָּנִים. וְאִינּוּן דְּלָא אִשְׁתַּכָּחוּ בְּכָל יוֹמָא בְּשַׁעְתֵּי אוֹתוֹת אֵלּוּ, דְּאִינּוּן אוֹת תְּפִלִּין וְאוֹת בְּרִית. מִילָה וּבְשַׁבָּת אוֹת בְּרִית וְאוֹת שַׁבָּת, כְּתִיב בְּהוֹן שַׁלֵּחַ תְּשַׁלַּח אֶת הָאֵם.

32. **Also those who guard the sign of the Covenant (*Brit*) according to its parameters (*t'chum*), which is eight days,** as it says: "And on the eighth day..." **and upkeep the Shabbat in its parameters (*t'chum*),** which are two thousand cubits to each direction, and with four sides, it is eight thousand cubits; as the two signs—the Covenant (*Brit*) and the Shabbat—**are the two Yud's from the two** Names **Yud-Hei-Vav-Hei and Alef-Dalet-Nun-Yud** intertwined, **Yud-Alef-Hei-Dalet-Vav-Nun-Hei-Yud. Due to these** two signs, **the masters of the Mishnah explained, that each and every person is found with at least these two** signs daily, and regarding this person **it is written: "Do not take the mother with the young." And there are those who are not found with these two signs daily, which are** in the weekdays, **the sign of Tefilin and the sign of the Covenant, and on Shabbat with the sign of the Covenant and the sign of the Shabbat. About them it is written: "...but be sure to let the mother go."**

33. וְאִי תֵּימְרוּן אַמַאי צְרִיכִין לְמֶהֱוֵי תַּרְוַויְיהוּ בְּכָל בַּר נָשׁ בְּכָל יוֹמָא. בְּגִין דְּלָא תִשְׁתַּכַּח שְׁכִינְתָּא דְּאִיהוּ יוֹ"ד מִן אֲדֹנָ"י יְחִידָה, בְּלָא קוּדְשָׁא בְּרִיךְ הוּא דְּאִיהוּ יוֹ"ד מִן יְקֹוָ"ק. וְצָרִיךְ בַּר נָשׁ דְּלָא יִשְׁתַּכַּח בְּכָל יוֹמָא פָּחוֹת מִתַּרְוַויְיהוּ. וְאִי לָא, עֲלֵיהּ אִתְּמַר וְנִרְגָּן מַפְרִיד אַלּוּף, דְּאַפְרִיד אַלּוּפֵיהּ דְּעָלְמָא מִשְּׁכִינְתָּא.

33. He asks, **"If you say why is there a need for each man to have the two signs every day?"** He answers, **"Because you will not find the Shechinah that is Yud from Alef-Dalet-Nun-Yud alone without the Holy One blessed be He, which is Yud from Yud-Hei-Vav-Hei. And a person must** be careful **not to be found, any day, with less than two signs. If not, it** says about him: '...and a whisperer alienates his friend,' (Proverbs 16:28) meaning he separated the Chief of the World from the Shechinah."

34. נוּקְבָא אִתְּמַר בָּהּ אוֹת הִיא לְעוֹלָם. דְּכוּרָא, בְּרִית מֶלַח עוֹלָם הוּא וּבְגִין דָּא, אוֹת תְּפִלִּין נוּקְבָא. אוֹת בְּרִית דְּכוּרָא. וְרָזָא דְּמִילָה, מִ"י יַעֲלֶ"ה לָנ"וּ הַשָּׁמַיְמָ"ה, בְּרֵישֵׁי תֵּיבִין מִיכָ"ל ה, וּבְסוֹפֵי תֵּיבִין יהו"ה. בִּתְפִלִּין נוּקְבָא, הָדָא הוּא דִּכְתִיב וְהָיָה לְאוֹת עַל יָדְכָה, יַד כֵּהָה.

34. He explains the two signs, whereby the sign of the Shabbat is **Nukva,** Malchut, **about which it is said: "She is a sign forever."** (Exodus 31:17) The Circumcision is **the male,** as it says: **"It is an everlasting covenant of salt."** (Numbers 18:19) **As a result of this,** in the weekdays, **the sign of the Tefilin** is Nukva namely Malchut. **And the sign of the Covenant is male** namely Zeir Anpin. **And the secret of it is "Who will ascend for us to the Heaven (***Mi Yaaleh Lanu Hashamaymah***)."** (Deuteronomy 30:12) **Whereby the acronyms of first letters of the words spell** *Milah* **(Circumcision), and the end letters of the words are the letters of Yud-Hei-Vav-Hei.** And the hint that **the Tefilin is** the aspect of **Nukva, is when it says: "and it shall be a sign on your hand (***yad'cha***)."** (Exodous 13:16) Our masters said, **"Weaker hand (***yad-keha***)."**

35. וְעַל קַן דְּצִפּוֹרָא דָא, אִתְּמַר וְסֻכָּה תִּהְיֶה לְצֵל יוֹמָם וגו'. וְאִיהוּ לָשׁוֹן סְכָך, שֶׁמְּסַכֶּכֶת בָּה אִימָא עַל בָּנֶיהָ, אֶפְרוֹחִים דִּילָהּ, תְּלַת הֲדַסִּים, וּתְרֵי בַדֵּי עֲרָבוֹת, וְלוּלָב. אוֹ בֵיצִים, דָּא אִינּוּן אֶתְרוֹגֵּי דְכָל חַד שִׁיעוּרֵיהּ בְּכַבֵּיצָה. וְאִלֵּין דִּרְשִׁימִין בְּהוֹן, כְּתִיב עֲלַיְיהוּ לֹא תִקַּח הָאֵם עַל הַבָּנִים. סכך

35. And about this bird's nest, regarding which it says: "If you come across a bird's nest...," it says, "...there will be a booth (*sukkah*) for shade by day...." (Isaiah 4:6) The word *sukkah* is a derivative of *s'chach* (cover), whereby the mother covers and shelters her young. **"...the young..."** are **the three myrtle branches (***hadas'im***), and the two willow branches (***aravot***), and the date palm branch (***lulav***). "...or the eggs..."** are those citron fruits (*etrog*) whose minimum size is the measurement of an egg. **And those who are imprinted by them,** by the four species, **about them is written: "Do not take the mother with the young."**

36. דִּתְלַת הֲדַסִּים רְמִיזִין לִתְלַת אֲבָהָן. תְּרֵי בַדֵּי עֲרָבוֹת לִתְרֵי נְבִיאֵי קְשׁוֹט לוּלָב, צַדִּיק כַּתָּמָר יִפְרָח אֶתְרוֹג, רָמִיז לִשְׁכִינְתָּא סוּכָּה רְמִיזָא לְאִימָּא, דִּמְסַכֶּכֶת עֲלַיְיהוּ. הָא אִינּוּן תְּמַנְיָא לְקָבֵל יאקדונק"י, דְּאִיהוּ חוּשְׁבַּן סוּכָ"ה, כ"ו ה"ס.

36. He explains: **the three myrtle branches (***hadas'im***) represent the three Patriarchs,** Chesed, Gevurah, and Tiferet. **The two willow branches (***aravot***) allude to the two true prophets,** Netzach and Hod. **The lulav (date palm branch) alludes to the "righteous shall flourish like a date palm,"** (Psalms 92:12) namely Yesod. **The citron fruit (***etrog***) alludes to the Shechinah,** which is Malchut. *Sukkah* (booth) alludes to the **mother,** namely Binah that **covers them. We have a total of eight** Sefirot **corresponding to** the eight letters in the two interwoven Names: **Yud-Alef-Hei-Dalet-Vav-Nun-Hei-Yud, which equal the numerical value of the word** *sukkah,* **the letters Samech-Vav-Kaf-Hei, of which Kaf-Vav** (26) is the numerical value of **Yud-Hei-Vav-Hei,** and **Hei-Samech** (65) is the numerical value of Adonai.

‏37. וְאִלֵּין דְּלָא נָטְלִין אִלֵּין סִימָנִין בִּידַיְיהוֹן כְּתִיב בְּהוֹן שַׁלֵּחַ תְּשַׁלַּח, כֶּתֶ"ר וְחָכְמָ"ה. דְּלָא שַׁרְיָין אִלֵּין, בְּאִלֵּין תְּמַנְיָא. לְמֶהֱוֵי כֻּלְּהוּ עֲשַׂר סְפִירָן בְּכָל נְעֲנוּעַ וְנַעֲנוּעַ דִּנְעֲנוּעֵי דְּלוּלָב וּמִינָיו בְּכָל פִּקּוּדָא וּפִקּוּדָא.

37. **Those who do not take these signs in their hands, it says about them. "…but be sure to let the mother go,"** Keter and Chochmah, **for these** two, meaning Keter and Chochmah, **do not dwell with these eight,** namely Binah and Zeir Anpin [which includes Chesed, Gevurah, Tiferet, Netzach, Hod, Yesod] and Malchut, **to have all Ten Sefirot in each and every shaking of the shakings of the lulav and its species, in each and every precept.**

4. The bird whose ankles the sea reaches

‏38. וְעַל הַאי צִפּוֹר קָא רְמִיּוּ רַבָּנָן בָּהַגָּדָה דְבַתְרָא דְרַבָּה בַּר בַּר חָנָה,‏
‏דַּהֲוָה אָזֵיל בִּסְפִינְתָּא, וְחָזָא לְהַהִיא צִפָּרָא דְיַמָּא מָטֵי עַד קַרְסוּלֵוי, וּמָאן‏
‏צִפּוֹר הָכָא. חַד מֵאִלֵּין אֶפְרוֹחֵי אוֹ מֵאִינּוּן בֵּיצִים, אֶפְרוֹחִים, כְּגוֹן פְּרָחִים,‏
‏דְּלָאו אִינּוּן גְּמַר פְּרִי, מִתַּתָּא לְעֵילָּא, אוֹ מִבֵּיצִים שִׁיּת דְּאִינּוּן מֵעֵילָּא לְתַתָּא‏
‏תְּחוֹת אִימָּא עִלָּאָה, דְּהָא בֵּיצִים מִסִּטְרָא דְאִימָּא תַּתָּאָה אִינּוּן, דְּאִיהִי בֵּיצָה.‏
‏אֶפְרוֹחִים מִסִּטְרָא דְּצַדִּיק מִתַּתָּא לְעֵילָּא.‏

38. The masters alluded to this bird in the homiletics of Raba bar bar Chanah, in the Tractate Baba-Batra, that he journeyed on a ship and saw a bird, where the sea reached up to its ankles. He asks, "Which bird is hinted to here? Is it one of those 'young chicks,' which are the Lower Six of Zeir Anpin? Or, 'of those eggs,' that are the Lower Six of Malchut?" And explains, "'Young chicks (efrochim),' are like flowers (p'rachim), which are not as yet complete fruits, and their illumination spreads from below upward, since the primary illuminations of Zeir Anpin are Chasadim that ascend from below upwards. Or from the six eggs that are the Lower Six of Malchut whose illuminations are from above downward because their illumination is Chochmah, and they are beneath Supernal Ima, which is Binah, and the nature of Chochmah is to illuminate from above downward. As the eggs themselves are from the aspect of the lower mother, meaning Malchut, who is called egg (beitzah). And 'young chicks' are from the aspect of righteous (tzadik), which is Yesod, whose nature of illumination is from below upward, in the manner that Chasadim rise from below upward."

‏39. אֶלָּא לָא הֲוָה אֶלָּא מֵאִלֵּין מֵאִלֵּין אֶפְרוֹחֵי, וְצַדִּיק שְׁמֵיהּ, עַמּוּדָא חֲדָא מֵאַרְעָא‏
‏עַד רְקִיעָא, וְיַמָּא מָטֵי עַד קַרְסוּלֵוי, אִלֵּין נֶצַח וָהוֹד. דְּאִימָּא עִלָּאָה אִיהִי‏
‏יַמָּא, דְּאִתְפַּשְּׁטַת לְחַמְשִׁין תַּרְעִין, עַד קַרְסוּלֵוי דְּהַהוּא עוֹפָא, כְּגַוְונָא דָא, י׳‏
‏אִיהוּ עֶשֶׂר, ה׳ חָמֵשׁ, עֶשֶׂר וּמִנְיָן ה׳ אִינּוּן חַמְשִׁין, עֶשֶׂר בְּכָל סְפִירָה מֵאִלֵּין‏
‏חָמֵשׁ מֵחֶסֶד עַד הוֹד. יְסוֹד נָטִיל לוֹן כֻּלְּהוּ, וְאִיקְרֵי כ״ל כְּלִיל מֵאִלֵּין חַמְשִׁין.‏

39. He replies, "**There is not but** one **of those fledglings** from the aspect of Malchut, which are the Lower Six of Zeir Anpin, **whose name is righteous,** namely Yesod, which is **one pillar from the Earth to the Firmament,** which is Tiferet. '**...where the sea reached up to its ankles,' which are Netzach and Hod because the Supernal Ima,** namely Binah, is called **sea** (*yam*; 50) (sea), **that spreads to the Fifty Gates** of Binah, **to the ankles of that bird, like this: Yud is ten, Hei is five,** and through the illumination of Yud in Hei it multiplies **to ten times five, totaling 50—ten in each Sefira of these five** Sefirot **from Chesed to Hod. Yesod takes them all and is called, 'all'** (*kol*; 50) because it is comprised **of all these Fifty Gates.**"

5. "For a bird of the Heavens will carry the voice and the winged one will make the matter known."

40. וְכָרְסַיָּא דִלְתַתָּא יָם הַמֶּלַח, כִּסֵּא דִין. עוֹף דְּאִיהוּ צִפּוֹר דִּילֵיהּ אִיהוּ מטטרו"ן. עֲלֵיהּ אִתְּמַר כִּי עוֹף הַשָּׁמַיִם יוֹלִיךְ אֶת הַקּוֹל.

40. The lower throne, meaning Malchut, is **the Dead Sea** [lit. Salt Sea], and Malchut is **a throne of judgment. The bird,** meaning the bird of this sea **is Metatron,** about whom is said: **"For the bird of the Heavens will carry the voice...."** (Ecclesiastes 10:20)

41. קוֹל דִּקְרִיאַת שְׁמַע. דְּאִיהוּ כְּלִיל שִׁית יוֹמִין דְּחוֹל, וְשַׁלִּיט עֲלַיְיהוּ. וְנָטִיל הַהוּא קוֹל, וּפָרַח בֵּיהּ עַד עַמּוּדָא דְּאֶמְצָעִיתָא, דְּאִיהוּ קוֹל י"י עַל הַמַּיִם. וְלֵית מַיִם אֶלָּא תּוֹרָה. וְאִיהוּ קוֹל י"י בֶּהָדָר. עַד שִׁית קָלִין. וְאִיהוּ שְׁבִיעָאָה לוֹן. בְּאִימָא.

41. He explains which voice: **"The voice of the Shema reading because he,** Metatron, **includes the six weekdays, and rules over them. He takes that voice** of the Shema reciting, **and flies up through it until the Central Column,** namely Zeir Anpin that regulates between Chochmah and Binah and receives his Mochin, **which are "The voice of the Lord is upon the waters..."** (Psalms 29:3) **and water only means Torah. And it is the** aspect of Tiferet that is **"The voice of the Lord is majestic."** (Ibid. 29:4) **until** all **the six voices** of Zeir Anpin. **And he** also includes **the seventh** voice **among them,** meaning: "The voice of the Lord breaks the cedars ... of Lebanon," (Ibid. 29:5) which pertains **to Ima** that is Malchut.

42. וּבַעַל כְּנָפַיִם יַגֵּיד דָּבָר, דָּא צְלוֹתָא. דְּמָטֵי לָהּ עַד צַדִּיק חַי עָלְמִין. כְּלִיל חַ"י בִּרְכָאן, דְּאִתְּמַר בְּהוֹן, וּבְרָכוֹת לְרֹאשׁ צַדִּיק חַי הָעוֹלָמִים.

42. "And the winged one will make the matter (*davar*) known." (Ecclesiastes 10:20) *Davar* is **the prayer** that Metatron raises until **ever living (*chai* [18]) righteous (*tzadik*),** namely Yesod, **which includes the**

eighteen blessings about which it is said: "Blessings are upon the head of the righteous (*tzadik*)…," (Proverbs 10:6) the righteous life of the world.

43. וּצְלוֹתָא אִיהוּ דִבּוּר, דִּרְכִיבַת עֲלֵיה, וְאִיהוּ מֶרְכָּבָה לְגַבָּה בְּיוֹמִין דְחוֹל. וְדָא שְׁכִינְתָּא. וְדָא אדנ"י. קוֹל רָכִיב בְּפוּמוֹי דָא יקו"ק. וְרָזָא דִּדְבּוּר אדנ"י עֲפָתַי תִּפְתָּח וגו'. וְאִיהוּ מֶרְכָּבָה לְתַרְוַיְיהוּ, כְּגַוְונָא דָא יאקדונק"י. וְהָכִי סָלִיק מַלְאָ"ךְ כְּחוּשְׁבַּן תְּרֵין שְׁמָהָן כַּחֲדָא.

43. **Prayer is that speech that rides on him,** namely on Metatron, **and he is the chariot for it during the weekdays. This is the Shechinah, and this is the Name Adonai. The voice that rides in his mouth** internally, **that is Yud-Kei-Vav-Kei, and the secret of that speech is, "Lord open You my lips…."** (Psalms 51:17) The angel Metatron **is the chariot for both** Yud-Hei-Vav-Hei and Adonai, interwoven **like this: Yud-Alef-Kei-Dalet-Vav-Nun-Kei-Yud. And** the numerical value of **the word angel (***malach***) adds up to the total of the two Names** Yud-Hei-Vav-Hei (26) and Adonai (54) **together** equal 91.

44. וּבְגִין דָא אִתְקְרֵי מַלְאָךְ שַׂר הַפָּנִים דְּעַל יַד שְׁלִיחָא דָא מִתְיַחֲדִין בְּשִׁית יוֹמֵי דְחוֹל. אֲבָל בְּיוֹמָא דְשַׁבַּתָּא לָא סַלְקִין תְּרֵין שְׁמָהָן אִלֵין, דְּאִינּוּן: עַמּוּדָא דְאֶמְצָעִיתָא. וּשְׁכִינְתֵּיה, וְלָא מִתְיַחֲדִין עַל יְדֵי שְׁלִיחַ, אֶלָּא בְּצַדִּיק חַי עָלְמִין, וַעֲלֵיה אִתְּמַר כִּי עוֹף הַשָּׁמַיִם יוֹלִיךְ אֶת הַקוֹל, קוֹל דִּקְרִיאַת שְׁמַע. וּבַעַל כְּנָפַיִם יַגֵּיד דָבָר, דִּבּוּר דִּצְלוֹתָא, וְלָא עַל יְדֵי שְׁלִיחַ. וּבְגִין דָא וְצַדִּיק יְסוֹד עוֹלָם, הוּא כְּלִיל כֹּלָּא. וּבֵיה מִתְיַיחֲדִין תְּרֵין שְׁמָהָן אִלֵין.

44. **He,** Metatron, **is therefore called the interior ministering angel, because through this messenger,** namely Metatron, **the two Names are unified in the weekdays. But on Shabbat these two Names, which are the Central Column** Yud-Hei-Vav-Hei **and the Shechinah** Adonai, **do not ascend and are not united by the messenger, but only by the righteous (***tzadik***) life (***chai***) of worlds (***olamim***),** meaning Yesod of Zeir Anpin. **About him it is said: "For the bird of the Heavens will carry the voice…," (Ecclesiastes 10:20) the sound of the Shema reciting: "and**

the winged one will make the matter (*davar*) known," (Ibid.) this is the speech (*dibur*) of the prayer, and not through the messenger, which is Metatron. Therefore it says: "And the Righteous is an everlasting foundation," (Proverbs 10:25) which is Yesod that contains all, and by which these two Names are unified.

6. The unique unification of the two Names of
Yud Hei Vav Hei and Alef-Dalet-Nun-Yud

45. וְעַל תְּרֵין שְׁמָהָן אִלֵּין אִתְּמַר אָז יְרַנְּנוּ עֲצֵי הַיָּעַר. וְנָעֲנָה מַלְאָךְ מִגּוֹ אֶשָּׁא מִשְׁמַיָּא וְאָמַר הֵן הֵן מַעֲשֵׂה מֶרְכָּבָה, וַהֲווֹ מִתְכַּבְּצִין מַלְאֲכֵי הַשָּׁרֵת כִּבְמַזְמוּטֵי וְחָתָן וְכַלָּה.

45. **About these two Names,** meaning Yud-Hei-Vav-Hei and Alef-Dalet-Nun-Yud, **is said: "Then (***Az***) shall the trees of the wood rejoice."** (**Psalms 96:12)** *Az* [Alef-Zayin, 8] is numerically eight, like the number of the letters in the two Names. **And an angel out of fire of the Heavens responded, and said, "These are the design of the chariots,"** as the chariot is the secret of the unification of Yud-Hei-Vav-Hei and Alef-Dalet-Nun-Yud. **And the servicing angels gathered as in the bliss of the groom and bride,** which are Yud-Hei-Vav-Hei and Alef-Dalet-Nun-Yud.

46. אָמַר רַעְיָא מְהֵימְנָא, בְּרִיךְ יְהֵא בּוֹצִינָא קַדִּישָׁא, דְּאָמַר מִלִּין אִלֵּין, לְיַחֲדָא בְּהוֹן קוּדְשָׁא בְּרִיךְ הוּא וּשְׁכִינְתֵּיהּ. קוּם אֵלִיָּהוּ נְבִיאָה, לִיקָרָא דְּקוּדְשָׁא בְּרִיךְ הוּא וּשְׁכִינְתֵּיהּ, וְיִתְעָרוּן עִמָּךְ שְׁאָר נְבִיאֵי. וַעֲבִיד לֵיהּ קִנָּא בְּהַאי וְחִבּוּרָא, וּלְכָל מַשִׁרְיָין דְּאַזְלִין מִתְחַרְכֵי בָּתַר קוּדְשָׁא בְּרִיךְ הוּא וּשְׁכִינְתֵּיהּ. לְחַבְּרָא לוֹן בְּהַאי וְחִבּוּרָא.

46. **The Faithful Shepherd,** Moses, **said, "Blessed be the Holy Luminary,** namely Rav Shimon, **who said these words to unify the Holy One blessed be He, with His Shechinah through them. 'Rise Elijah the Prophet, in respect of the Holy One blessed be He and His Shechinah, and let the rest of the prophets be awakened with you, and prepare for the** Holy One blessed be He, **a nest through this compilation, and to all of the camps that go about and wander after the Holy One blessed be He, and His Shechinah to connect them to this compilation.'"

47. לְאִשְׁתַּכְּחָא בֵּיהּ נְיָיחָא, לְאִלֵּין מַשִׁרְיָין דְּנִשְׁמָתִין, דְּאַזְלִין מִתְחַרְכִין, מִשְׁכִינְתָּא דְּאִיהִי יְחִידָאָה, אֵיכָה יָשְׁבָה בָדָד. וּלְאִשְׁתַּכְּחָא בֵּיהּ נְיָיחָא

לְמִשְׁרְיָין דְּקוּדְשָׁא בְּרִיךְ הוּא, דְּאִתְּמַר בְּהוֹן הֵן אֶרְאֶלָּם צָעֲקוּ חוּצָה מַלְאֲכֵי
שָׁלוֹם מַר יִבְכָּיוּן. וְלֵית שָׁלוֹם, אֶלָּא קוּדְשָׁא בְּרִיךְ הוּא.

47. To find through it, through this compilation, **a tranquil rest to those camps of souls that go and wander away from the Shechinah that is isolated, as it says: "How deserted she lies."** (Lamentations 1:1) **And to find through it rest for the camps** of Angels **of the Holy One blessed be He, about whom it is said: "Behold, their valiant ones cry out, the ambassadors of peace weep bitterly,"** (Isaiah 33:7) **and peace can only be the Holy One blessed be He.**

7. "And he dreamed, behold, a ladder is set up on the ground."

48. קוּם לְחַבְּרָא לוֹן בְּהַאי חִבּוּרָא. דְּהָא כַּד אִית בְּיִשְׂרָאֵל מַשְׂכִּילִים,
מֵאִלֵּין דְּאִתְּמַר בְּהוֹן וְהַמַּשְׂכִּילִים יַזְהִירוּ כְּזֹהַר הָרָקִיעַ, דָּא דְּאִתְקְרֵי סֵפֶר
הַזֹּהַר. דְּיַדְעִין לְמִפְלַח לְמָארֵיהוֹן, וּלְאַפָּקָא אַזְכָּרוֹת דִּשְׁמָהָן דְּקוּדְשָׁא בְּרִיךְ
הוּא וּשְׁכִינְתֵּיה בְּכַוָּנָה. וּלְחַבְּרָא לוֹן בְּקוֹל דִּקְרִיאַת שְׁמַע. וּבְדִבּוּר דִּצְלוֹתָא,
דְּאִינוּן תְּרֵין שְׁמָהָן יאקדונק"י, דִּבְהוֹן כְּלִילָן כָּל הֲוָיָי"ן, וְכִנּוּיֵי"ן, וַעֲשַׂר
סְפִירָן.

48. Rise up to join them in this compilation because when there are
wise people among Israel, from those of whom it says: "And the wise
shall shine like the brightness (*zohar*) of the Firmament," (Daniel 12:3)
meaning this book called the Zohar, who know how to serve their master
and to recite the mentionings of the Divine Names of the Holy One
blessed be He, and His Shechinah with intention, and to unify those
Divine Names with the voice of the Shema reciting and with the speech
of the prayer, which are the two Names, Yud-Alef-Hei-Dalet-Vav-Nun-
Hei-Yud, in which are included all the Name combinations of Yud-Hei-
Vav-Hei, and all the Divine Names of the designated attributes and of
the Ten Sefirot.

49. כַּמָּה מַלְאָכִין דְּאִינוּן חֵיוָן דִּמְרַכַּבְתָּא, וּשְׂרָפִים וְאוֹפַנִּים, וְכָל עֲשַׂר כִּתּוֹת
דִּכְלִילָן בְּהוֹן, דִּמְשַׁמְּשִׁין לַעֲשַׂר סְפִירוֹת, כֻּלְּהוּ, וּפְנֵיהֶם וְכַנְפֵיהֶם פְּרוּדוֹת,
לְפִימוֹי, לְקַבֵּל אִלֵּין אַזְכָּרוֹת דְּאִינוּן יאקדונק"י, בֵּין בִּקְרִיאַת שְׁמַע, בֵּין
בִּצְלוֹתָא, בֵּין בְּשִׁירוֹת וְתִשְׁבָּחוֹת וְהוֹדָאוֹת.

49. Behold, how many angels who are the living creatures of the Chariot,
meaning the Chariot of Metatron, which are: Michael, Gabriel, Uriel, and
Raphael, and Serafim and Ofanim, and all ten groups of angels that are
included in them, that are in service to the Ten Sefirot, and about all
of them it is said: "Such were their faces and their wings were spread
upward," (Ezekiel 1:11) to the mouth of the one who prays with proper
intention, to receive those Divine mentionings, which are the Names

Yud-Alef-Hei-Dalet-Vav-Nun-Hei-Yud; either by the Shema reading or at the prayer, or at the hymns of praises and thanks.

8. The unification of Yud-Hei-Vav-Hei and Alef-Dalet-Nun-Yud

50. דְּבְכָל אַדְכָּרָה דְּיִפּוֹק מִפּוּמוֹי, בְּכָל אֲתַר, וּבְכָל מַמְלָל, צָרִיךְ לְכַוְּנָא דִּיבּוּר בְּאדנ"י, קוֹל בִּיקוּ"ק, וּלְיַחֲדָא לוֹן כַּחֲדָא, בְּיִחוּדָא דְּאִיהוּ יָחִיד נֶעְלָם, דִּמְחַבֵּר לוֹן, וּמְיַחֵד לוֹן כַּחֲדָא. וּבֵיה צָרִיךְ הַכַּוָּנָה, דְּלָא תַלְיָא לְמֵימַר בֵּיה קוֹל וְדִבּוּר, אֶלָּא מַחֲשַׁבְתָּא.

50. For any Divine Name that he utters from his mouth, at any point and in any speech, the intention must be that the speech is in the Name Adonai, and the voice is in the Name of Yud-Hei-Vav-Hei, and to unify them as one, in the oneness of the One who is Singular and Hidden, that joins those two Names and unites them as one. And for this, proper intention must be directed since it is not applicable to say voice or speech, only thought, concerning it.

51. כַּד נָחִית קוּדְשָׁא בְּרִיךְ הוּא בִּקְרִיאַת שְׁמַע, אִתְּמַר בְּחֵיוָן וָאֶשְׁמַע אֶת קוֹל כַּנְפֵיהֶם בַּעֲשָׂר מִינֵי הִלּוּלִים: בְּשִׁיר פָּשׁוּט, דְּאִיהוּ י', כֶּתֶ"ר. כָּפוּל, דְּאִיהוּ י"ה, וְחָכְמָ"ה וּבִינָ"ה. מְשׁוּלָשׁ, בִּיק"ו דְּאִיהוּ חֶסֶ"ד גְּבוּרָ"ה תִּפְאֶרֶ"ת. מְרוּבָּע בִּיקוּ"ק, דְּאִיהוּ נֶצַ"ח הוֹ"ד יְסוֹ"ד מַלְכוּ"ת.

51. At the Shema reciting, when the Holy One blessed be He, descends, it says regarding the living creatures: "And I heard the sound of their wings" (Ezekiel 1:24) with ten types of praises; with simple song, which is the letter Yud, Keter. Doubled, which are the letters Yud-Hei, Chochmah and Binah. Tripled are the letters Yud-Hei-Vav, which are Chesed, Gevurah and Tiferet. Quadrupled, are the letters Yud-Hei-Vav-Hei, which are Netzach, Hod, Yesod, and Malchut. These are ten letters that allude to the Ten Sefirot. King David said ten types of Psalm praises corresponding to them, like *Ashrei, Maskil, Mizmor, Michtam.*

52. דְּנָטְרִין צַפְרָא קַדִּישָׁא יִשְׂרָאֵל בֵּינַיְהוּ, וְקָרָאן בָּה לְיִשְׂרָאֵל דְּאִיהוּ עַמּוּדָא דְּאֶמְצָעִיתָא, וְהַיְינוּ שְׁמַע יִשְׂרָאֵל. הָא נָחִית לְגַבָּהּ, צָרִיךְ לְקַשְּׁרָא

לֵיהּ בַּחֲדָה, וּלְיַחֲדָא לוֹן בְּיִחוּדָא חֲדָא בְּלָא פֵּירוּדָא כְּלָל. וּבְגִין דָּא, מָאן דְּשָׂח בְּנְתַיִים, עֲבֵירָה הִיא בִּידוֹ הַהִיא שִׂיחָה.

52. The children of **Israel guard among them the holy bird,** meaning Malchut with the Light of Chochmah, **with which they call** and invite **Israel,** meaning Zeir Anpin, **which is the Central Column,** that shines through the control of the Light of Chasadim **and it is "Hear Israel…." He descends to Her and He must be connected with Her, and unite them in one union without any separation at all. Therefore, when someone talks during** the Shema reciting, **that conversation is the person's transgression.**

53. וְאַמַּאי קָשְׁרִין לֵיהּ בַּחֲדָה לֵא"ח עִם ד', כְּלִילָא מֵאַרְבַּע פָּרְשִׁיָּין. בְּגִין דְּלָא יְהֵא פָּרַח מִינָהּ, וְאִשְׁתְּאָרַת יְחִידָה אֵיכָה יָשְׁבָה בָדָד. וּבְגִין דָּא קָשְׁרִין לֵיהּ בַּחֲדָה בְּכַמָּה קְשׁוּרִין דִּתְפִלִּין, בְּכַמָּה קְשׁוּרֵי דְּצִיצִית, דְּלָא יָזוּז מִינָהּ.

53. He asks, **"Why when we bind Him,** meaning Zeir Anpin, **with Her,** with Malchut, Rachel, we first unify **the Alef-Chet,** which is Zeir Anpin, **with Dalet,** meaning Leah that is **composed of four portions?"** He answers, **"So that He should not fly away from Her, and She would remain alone,** as is written: **'How deserted she lies.'** (Lamentations 1:1) **Due to this, they tie Him to Her with several knots of Tefilin, and with several knots of Tzitzit so that He will not move away from Her.**

54. וְכָל קֶשֶׁר אִיהוּ מִסִּטְרָא דְּאָת י', וּתְרֵין קָשְׁרִין אִנּוּן. דְּאִנּוּן קֶשֶׁר דְּרֵישָׁא קֶשֶׁר דִּדְרוֹעָא שְׂמָאלָא. וְאִנּוּן י' בֵן יאקדונק"י.

54. And each knot is of the aspect of the letter Yud, and they are two knots: the knot of the head and the knot of the left hand. They are Yud-Yud from the two intertwined Names **Yud-Alef-Hei-Dalet-Vav-Nun-Hei-Yud.**

55. יְהוָ"ה אַרְבַּע פָּרָשִׁיָּין דִּתְפִילֵי, וְרָאוּ כָּל עַמֵּי הָאָרֶץ כִּי שֵׁם יְ"יָ וכו'.
אֲדֹנָ"י אַרְבַּע בָּתֵּי דִּתְפִלֵּי. אֶקְיֵ"ק אֲשֶׁר אֶקְיֵ"ק, מִכְלְנָּאוּ דִּתְפִלֵּי. בְּכַ"א
אֲדֻכְרוּת דִּתְפִלִּין דְּרֵישָׁא, וּבְכַ"א אֲדֻכְרוּת דִּתְפִלִּין דְּיָד. וְדָא אִימָא עִלָּאָה,
תְּפִלֵּי דְּמָארֵי עָלְמָא קָרִינַן לֵיהּ.

55. The four letters **of Yud-Hei-Vav-Hei is the secret of the four passages
of the Tefilin.** Yud, which is Chochmah, is the passage of *Kadesh* (Exodus
13:1). The first Hei, Binah, is *Vehayah Ki Yeviacha* (Exodus 13:11), Vav,
Zeir Anpin, is *Shema* (Deuteronomy 6:4). The lower Hei—Malchut, is
Vehaya Im Shamo'a (Deuteronomy 11:13), in the secret of the verse: **"And
all the nations of the land shall see that the Name of the Lord [Yud-
Hei-Vav-Hei]...."** (Deuteronomy 28:10) The four letters of the Name
Alef-Dalet-Nun-Yud are one house that includes **the four houses of the
Tefilin:** *Eheyeh Asher Eheyeh* (I will be what I will be). (Exodus 3:14) The
first *Eheyeh,* which equals 21, is the secret of Supernal Aba and Ima—
Chochmah. *Asher,* is the secret of Israel-Saba and Tevunah, Binah, in the
secret of the head (*rosh*) that goes out from the word Beresheet. The second
Eheyeh is the secret of Da'at, which reconciles Chochmah and Binah. They
are **on the inner part of the Tefilin.** They are alluded to by the **21 Divine
mentioned Names that are within the Tefilin of the head, and in the 21
Divine mentioned Names in the Tefilin of the arm. This is the Supernal
Ima,** Binah, **and they are called the Tefilin of the Master of the World,**
which is Zeir Anpin.

56. תְּפִלִּין עַל רֵישָׁא דְּעַמּוּדָא דְּאֶמְצָעִיתָא, כָּסֵי לֵיהּ אִימָא בְּגַדְפָהָא, דְּאִינּוּן
רְצוּעִין דִּתְפִלֵּי. וְקָשְׁרִין לֵיהּ יִשְׂרָאֵל בִּשְׁכִינְתָּא תַּתָּאָה, בִּתְפִלִּין דְּיָד.

56. The Tefilin on the head is of the Central Column, namely Zeir
Anpin, **and Ima covers it with her wings, which are the straps of the
Tefilin.** Because over the head two straps extend surrounding the head,
from Right and Left, which are Chesed and Gevurah. Whereby the Dalet
that is the knot on the Tefilin, which is Malchut, is held by Leah, and from
her two straps extend in the secret of Netzach and Hod, up until adjacent

to the chest, where the head of Malchut, namely Rachel, begins. **Israel bind him,** meaning Zeir Anpin, **to the lower Shechinah,** which is Rachel, **by the Tefilin of the arm.**

57. וְלֵיהּ אָמְרִין שְׁמַע יִשְׂרָאֵל, בְּרָא דְּסָבָא דְּסָבִין, וְדָא חָכְמָה עִלָּאָה. וְעַל שְׁמֵיהּ אִתְקְרֵי עַמּוּדָא דְּאֶמְצָעִיתָא, יִשְׂרָאֵל, שִׂיר א"ל. שִׂיר מִשְׂמָאלָא, שִׂיר דִּלְוִיִּם. אֵל מִימִינָא דְּכַהֲנָא. עַמּוּדָא דְּאֶמְצָעִיתָא יִשְׂרָאֵל כָּלִיל תַּרְוַיְיהוּ. וְחָכְמָה נָחִית בְּבִרְכַּה דְּכַהֲנָא, בִּימִינָא, וּבֵיהּ הָרוֹצֶה לְהַחֲכִּים יַדְרִים. אִימָא נָחִית בִּקְדוּשָׁה דְּלֵיוָאֵי מִשְׂמָאלָא. וּבֵיהּ הָרוֹצֶה לְהַעֲשִׁיר יַצְפִּין.

57. **And to him,** namely to Zeir Anpin when he ascends and regulates between Chochmah and Binah, **is said: "Hear Israel…"** For he is **the son of the elder of elders,** namely Arich Anpin, for an elder is only the one who has attained wisdom, and the aspect of revelation of Chochmah of Arich Anpin is to Aba and Ima, who are called elders, consequently, the Arich Anpin is called the elder of elders. **And this is the Supernal Wisdom,** the sealed Chochmah of Arich Anpin, **and by His Name,** meaning the Name of Chochmah of Arich Anpin, **the Central Column,** namely Zeir Anpin who goes up to regulate between Aba and Ima, **is called Israel-**Saba (as explained in Zohar, Va'etchanan). And he explains: "The name Israel is a combination of *Shir El* (a song of God). *Shir* (song) is the name of Chochmah **of the Left, the song of the Levites.** *El,* Chochmah **of the Right, of the Priests (Kohanim). The Central Column, Israel, includes both. Chochmah descends at the blessing of the Kohanim, from the Right, and by it, whoever wishes to become wise shall turn south. Ima,** in the secret of the Thirty-Two Paths of Wisdom (Chochmah), **descends in the sanctification of the Levites from the Left, and by it, whoever desires to become wealthy should turn north."**

58. עַמּוּדָא דְּאֶמְצָעִיתָא קְשׁוּרָא דְּתַרְוַיְיהוּ יְחוּדָא דְּתַרְוַיְיהוּ אוּף הָכִי יְסוֹד חַי עָלְמִין קְשׁוּרָא דְּעַמּוּדָא דְּאֶמְצָעִיתָא וּשְׁכִינְתָּא תַּתָּאָה. בְּאָן אֲתָר. בִּצְלוֹתָא דְּבֵיהּ כְּלִילָן חַ"י בִּרְכָאן, וּבֵיהּ מִתְיַיחֲדִין תְּרֵין שְׁמָהָן כַּחֲדָא, אִינּוּן יאהדונק"י.

58. The Central Column, namely Tiferet that ascends and becomes Da'at, **is a binding connection to both** Chochmah and Binah, **is the unification of both,** similarly is the righteous life of the world, the binding knot of the Central Column and the Lower Shechinah. He asks, "At which area is this unification of the Central Column, namely Zeir Anpin **with the Shechinah below,** namely Malchut of Rachel?" And replies, **"At the prayer of Amidah, which contains 18 blessings, and** by the prayer of *Shmone Esre* (Amidah) [lit. 18], **the two Names are unified, Yud-Alef-Hei-Dalet-Vav-Nun-Hei-Yud."**

59. וְחִבּוּרָא דִּתְרֵין שְׁמָהָן צְרִיכִין בַּחֲשַׁאי, וְרָזָא דְמִלָּה, בְּעָמְדָם תְּרַפֶּינָה כַנְפֵיהֶן, בְּעָמְדָם יִשְׂרָאֵל בִּצְלוֹתָא דַּעֲמִידָה, חֵיוָון תְּרַפֶּינָה כַנְפֵיהֶן, דְּלָא לְמִשְׁמַע בְּהוֹן קָלָא.

59. The joining of the two Names Yud-Hei-Vav-Hei and Alef-Dalet-Nun-Yud need to be in stillness, and the secret of the matter is: "When they stood still, they lowered their wings." (Ezekiel 1:25) He explains, **"'When they stood,' when Israel stand in the Amidah prayer,** meaning *Shmone Esre,* **'the living creatures lowered their wing' to not raise any sound."**

60. דְּתַמָּן קוֹל דְּמָמָה דַקָּה, בְּגִין דְּתַמָּן קָאָתָא מַלְכָּא. דְּהָא בְּרוּחַ גְּדוֹלָה וּבָרַעַשׁ וּבָאֵשׁ, דְּאִשְׁתַּמְעוּן בְּהוֹן גַּדְפֵי חֵיוָון, לָא אָתָא מַלְכָּא, אֶלָּא בְּקוֹל דְּמָמָה דַקָּה, דְּאִיהִי בָּתַר רוּחַ רַעַשׁ אֵשׁ. וְאִיהִי רְבִיעָאָה לוֹן.

60. Because there, in the Amidah prayer, **is "the still small voice,"** (Kings I 19:12) meaning the voice of Malchut is silence and stillness. **Because there,** in the Amidah, **comes the king,** Zeir Anpin. **Since in the great wind, the quake, and the fire, where the** sound of the wings of the living creatures is heard, the king will not come for unification **unless it is in the sound of the stillness that comes after the wind, quake, and fire. And she,** Malchut, **is fourth to them.**

61. וַעֲלַיְהוּ אָמַר יְחֶזְקָאל, וָאֵרֶא וְהִנֵּה רוּחַ סְעָרָה בָּאָה מִן הַצָּפוֹן. עָנָן גָּדוֹל
וְאֵשׁ מִתְלַקַּחַת, הָא אִינּוּן תְּלַת, דִּרְכִיבִין בְּהוֹן תְּלַת אַתְוָון קו״ק. קוֹל דְּמָמָה
דַקָּה, דָּא י' מִן הוי״ה, וְאִיהִי י' מִן אדנ״י, תַּמָּן קָא אָתָא מַלְכָּא דְּאִיהוּ
יהו״ה. דְּכָל הֲוַיָּ״ה דְּשַׁלִּיט ה' עַל ו' ה' עַל י', נוּקְבָּא אִיהִי הַהֲוַיָּ״ה. כְּגוֹן טִפָּה
דְּנוּקְבָּא, כַּד שַׁלְּיט עַל טִפָּה דִּדְכוּרָא, בַּת אִיהִי.

61. **About them,** regarding the wind, quake, and fire, **Ezekiel said, "...and I saw a storm wind coming from the north,"** (Ezekiel 1:4) corresponding to wind; **"a great cloud,"** corresponding to quake; **"and a flaring fire,"** corresponding to fire. **There are three, whereby three letters Hei-Vav-Hei ride in them, 'the still small voice' is Yud of Yud-Hei-Vav-Hei, and is Yud from Alef-Dalet-Nun-Yud there,** in Malchut of Atzilut, **comes the king, which is Yud-Hei-Vav-Hei.** He defines **every** sequence of **Yud-Hei-Vav-Hei where the Hei is dominant over,** meaning comes before, **the Vav, and the Hei over the Yud, that** sequence of **Yud-Hei-Vav-Hei is** an aspect **of Nukva,** meaning judgment, **as when the drop of the female has dominance over the drop of the male** the infant born **is female.**

62. אָתָא אֵלִיָּהוּ וְכָל מָארֵי מְתִיבְתָּא, וְאִשְׁתַּטְחוּ קַמֵּיהּ וְאָמְרוּ סִינַי סִינַי. מָאן
יָכִיל לְמֵימַר מִלִּין קַמָּךְ. אֶלָּא בְּקוֹל דְּמָמָה דַקָּה, דִּבְפוּמָךְ קָא אָתֵי מַלְכָּא.

62. **Elijah and all the Yeshiva members came and bowed before** the Faithful Shepherd **and said, "Sinai, Sinai, who could say anything in your presence. Rather the king comes through the silent voice of your mouth** and the union of the Holy One blessed be He, and His Shechinah is performed."

9. Four white garments and four gold garments

63. קוּם אֵלִיָּהוּ תַּקֵּן לְבוּשֵׁי מַלְכָּא וּמַטְרוֹנִיתָא, דְּאַנְתְּ כַּהֲנָא, תְּקֵן לֵיה לְקוּדְשָׁא בְּרִיךְ הוּא אַרְבַּע בִּגְדֵי לָבָן, וְאַרְבַּע בִּגְדֵי זָהָב לְמַטְרוֹנִיתָא, דְּאִתְּמַר בָּה, כָּל כְּבוּדָה בַת מֶלֶךְ פְּנִימָה מִמִּשְׁבְּצוֹת זָהָב לְבוּשָׁהּ.

63. The Faithful Shepherd said to **Elijah, "Rise, prepare the clothes of the King and Queen,** meaning for Zeir Anpin and Nukva. **Since you are a Kohen, prepare for Him, for the Holy One blessed be He,** Zeir Anpin, **four white garments, and four gold garments for the Queen, about whom it says: 'The king's daughter is all glorious within, Her clothing is interwoven with gold.'"** (Psalms 45:13)

64. אַרְבַּע בִּגְדֵי לָבָן כֻּלְּהוּ רַחֲמֵי בִּשְׁמָא דַיְהֹ"ה. וְלֵית מָאן דְּמָחֵיל בְּהוֹן עֲרָיִין אֶלָּא אִיהוּ, אַרְבַּע בִּגְדֵי זָהָב, כֻּלְּהוּ דִּינָא, מִסִּטְרָא דְּאדנ"י. וְלֵית מָאן דְּמָחֵיל עַל עֲבוֹדָה זָרָה, אֶלָּא אִיהִי. דְּשַׁלְטָאן שִׁפְחָה בַּאֲתַר דִּגְבִירְתָּהּ.

64. **All four white garments** illuminate **with Mercy with the Name Yud-Hei-Vav-Hei,** namely Zeir Anpin, **and no one but He pardons** the sin **of incest. All four of the gold garments** hint to **Judgment from the aspect** of the Name **Alef-Dalet-Nun-Yud,** namely Malchut, **and there is no one but She who could pardon** the sin **of idolatry** because the idol worshippers empower the rule of the handmaiden in place of the mistress.

65. כִּשְׁמֵיהּ, כֵּן כָּרְסְיֵיהּ. כֵּן לְבוּשֵׁיהּ, וּבְאִלֵּין לְבוּשִׁין לָא אִתְלַבַּשׁ עַד כְּעַן, מִיּוֹמָא דְּאִתְחֲרַב בֵּי מַקְדְּשָׁא. דְּהָא כְּתִיב, אַלְבִּישׁ שָׁמַיִם קַדְרוּת. וּשְׁכִינְתָּא אִתְּמַר בָּהּ, אַל תִּרְאוּנִי שֶׁאֲנִי שְׁחַרְחֹרֶת, בְּגִין דְּאִיהִי בְּגָלוּתָא, וְכָרְסַיָּא דִּילָהּ פְּנִימָה בְּחוֹבִין דְּיִשְׂרָאֵל. דְּתַּפָּן נִשְׁמָתִין דְּיִשְׂרָאֵל.

65. Meaning to say, **as the** union of the Holy One and His Shechinah illuminates in Atzilut that is called **Name, likewise** He illuminates in the World of Briyah that is called **the Throne,** and the Throne of Mercy unifies with the Throne of Judgment. **So too** this union illuminates **in the**

garments, in the secret of the four white garments and four gold garments of the High Priest (Kohen haGadol) in the Temple. **And he did not dress in those clothes until now, from the time of the destruction of the Temple, since it says: "I shall dress the Heavens** (meaning Zeir Anpin) **in darkness." (Isaiah 50:3)** It says about **the Shechinah,** meaning Malchut: **"Do not look at me when I am blackened," (Song of Songs 1:6) because She is in exile. Her Throne, from where the souls of Israel are, is flawed due to the sins of Israel.**

66. וּבְגִין דָּא, זַכָּאָה אִיהוּ מָאן דְּתַתְקִין לָהּ כֻּרְסַיָּא, בִּצְלוֹתָא דִּילֵיהּ, בְּפִקּוּדִין דִּילֵיהּ, בָּתַר דְּאִיהוּ כֻּרְסַיָּא פָּגִים בְּגִינַיְהוּ. וְאִסְתַּלַּק שֵׁם יְהֹוָ"ה מִתַּמָּן דְּאִיהוּ לָא שָׁרְיָא בַּאֲתַר פָּגִים. הֲדָא הוּא דִכְתִיב כָּל אֲשֶׁר בּוֹ מוּם לֹא יִקְרָב, אוּף הָכִי בְּנִשְׁמָתָא פְּגִימָא לָא שָׁרְיָא. זַכָּאָה אִיהוּ מָאן דְּאַשְׁלִים נִשְׁמָתֵיהּ, לְשָׁרְיָא בֵּיהּ שֵׁם יְקֹוָ"ק, וְעָבִיד לֵיהּ כֻּרְסַיָּא לְגַבֵּיהּ.

66. **Consequently, happy is he who fixes for Her,** for the Shechinah, **a throne through his prayer and his good deeds, since the Throne is flawed due to them,** as it is written: "since a hand is on the throne of the Lord (YaH, Yud-Hei)" (Exodus 17:16) **and the Name of Yud-Hei-Vav-Hei is moved away from there, because He does not reside in a flawed place. This is as it says: "Any person who has a defect should not approach." (Leviticus 21:18) Similarly, he does not reside in a blemished soul.** Thus, **fortunate is he who has perfected his soul to allow the Name Yud-Hei-Vav-Hei to reside in it, and prepared it as a throne for Him.**

67. וְזַכָּאָה פּוּמָא דְּמִתְחַבֵּר בָּהּ קוּדְשָׁא בְּרִיךְ הוּא עִם שְׁכִינְתֵּיהּ, דְּאִיהִי תּוֹרַת ה'. וְזַכָּאָה אִיהוּ מָאן דְּלָבֵישׁ מַלְכָּא וּמַטְרוֹנִיתָא בַּעֲשַׂר סְפִירָן דִּבְרִיאָה, דְּכָלִילָן בְּשֵׁם יאקדונק"י. כִּשְׁמֵיהּ כֵּן לְבוּשׁוֹהִי. וּמָאן דְּתַתְקִין לֵיהּ סוּסְיָא, דְּאִתְּמַר בָּהּ לְסוּסָתִי בְּרִכְבֵי פַרְעֹה דִּמִּיתִיךְ רַעְיָתִי, דְּאִיהִי מֶרְכָּבָה דִּילֵיהּ.

67. **Praiseworthy is the mouth in which the Holy One blessed be He, and His Shechinah connect, for this is the Torah of the Lord, and praiseworthy is he who dresses the King and Queen,** which are Zeir

and Nukva in Atzilut, **in the Ten Sefirot that are in Briyah that are included in the Name Yud-Alef-Hei-Dalet-Vav-Nun-Hei-Yud. As His Name, so are His clothes.** And praised is he **who prepared himself** to be **a horse** in the chariot of the Shechinah, **as she,** the Shechinah, is **His chariot,** meaning Zeir Anpin's, **about whom it says: "To the steeds among Pharaoh's chariots have I compared you my beloved."** (Song of Songs 1:9)

68. דְּבְיוֹמֵי דְּשַׁבְּתוֹת וְיָמִים טוֹבִים אִיהוּ לָבוּשׁ לְבוּשֵׁי מַלְכוּתָא, דְּאִינּוֹן עֶשֶׂר סְפִירוֹת דִּבְרִיאָה. וּבְיוֹמֵי דְּחוֹל לָבִישׁ עֶשֶׂר כִּתּוֹת דְּמַלְאָכַיָּא, דִּמְשַׁמְּשֵׁי לוֹן לַעֲשַׂר סְפִירָן דִּבְרִיאָה.

68. Since on Shabbats and Holidays He dresses in royal garments, which are the Ten Sefirot of Briyah, and in the weekdays He dresses in a garment of ten classes of angels from the World of Yetzirah **who service the Ten Sefirot of Briyah.**

69. דְּעֶשֶׂר סְפִירוֹת דַּאֲצִילוּת מַלְכָּא בְּהוֹן. אִיהוּ וְגַרְמֵיהּ חַד בְּהוֹן. אִיהוּ וְחַיָּיוֹ חַד בְּהוֹן. מַה דְּלָאו הָכִי בְּעֶשֶׂר סְפִירוֹת דִּבְרִיאָה, דְּלָאו אִינּוּן וְחַיַּיְהוֹן חַד. לָאו אִינּוּן וְגַרְמֵיהוֹן חַד. וְעִלַּת עַל כֹּלָּא הוּא נָהִיר בְּעֶשֶׂר סְפִירוֹת דַּאֲצִילוּת, וּבְעֶשֶׂר סְפִירוֹת דִּבְרִיאָה. וְנָהִיר בְּעֶשֶׂר כִּתּוֹת דְּמַלְאָכַיָּא, וּבְעֶשֶׂר גַּלְגַּלֵּי דִרְקִיעָא, וְלָא אִשְׁתְּנֵי בְּכָל אֲתַר.

69. Since in the Ten Sefirot of Atzilut, the King, the Endless Light, blessed be He, **is dressed in them. He,** meaning His essence, **and the causes,** meaning the vessels, **are one. He and the living creatures,** meaning the Lights, **are all one. It is not the case in the Ten Sefirot of Briyah; neither they**—namely their essence—**nor the living creatures,** namely the Lights, **that are in them are one. Neither they nor their causes,** namely the vessels, **are one. And the Supernal of All,** namely the Endless Light, blessed be He, **illuminates in the Ten Sefirot of Atzilut, and in the Ten Sefirot of Briyah, and He illuminates in the ten classes of angels,** namely in the World of Yetzirah, **and in the ten wheels of the Firmament,**

namely the World of Asiyah. **And in each place there is no change to Him** whatsoever, in the secret of: "I am God, I did not change" (Malachi 3:6)

10. The Chariot of Ezekiel

70. קוּם יְחֶזְקֵאל נְבִיאָה, לְגַלָּאָה אִלֵּין מַרְאוֹת קַמֵּי שְׁכִינְתָּא, דְּאִתְּמַר בְּהוֹן,
וּדְמוּת הַחַיּוֹת מַרְאֵיהֶם כְּגַחֲלֵי אֵשׁ. בְּנִקּוּדֵי אוֹרַיְתָא, וְטַעֲמֵי דְאוֹרַיְיתָא,
דַּעֲלַיְיהוּ דְאַתְוָון אִתְּמַר, וּדְמוּת הַחַיּוֹת. מַרְאֵיהֶם כְּגַחֲלֵי אֵשׁ, אִלֵּין אִינּוּן
נְקוּדִין. בּוֹעֲרוֹת כְּמַרְאֵה הַלַּפִּידִים אִלֵּין טַעֲמֵי.

70. Rise Ezekiel, the prophet, to reveal those visions in the presence of the Shechinah, of which it says: "And the image of the beasts, their looks are as fiery coals," (Ezekiel 1:13) by the vowels of the Torah, and the cantillation marks of the Torah. Because about the letters of the Torah it says: "They form image of the beasts," "their looks are like fiery coals" are the vowels, "burning as the visions of the torches" are the cantillation marks.

71. וּבְהוֹן, וְהַמַּשְׂכִּילִים יַזְהִירוּ כְּזֹהַר הָרָקִיעַ. וְהַמַּשְׂכִּילִים: אִלֵּין אַתְוָון.
יַזְהִירוּ: אִלֵּין נְקוּדִין, דְּנָהֲרִין בְּהוֹן. כְּזֹהַר: אִלֵּין טַעֲמֵי.

71. And through them, meaning by the cantillation, vowels, and letters, is written: "And the wise shall shine like the brightness (zohar) of the Firmament." (Daniel 12:3) "And the wise" refers to the letters, "shall shine" are their illuminating vowels in them, in the letters, "Like the brightness (zohar) of the Firmament" refers to the cantillation marks.

72. וּשְׁכִינְתָּא כְּלִילָא מִכֻּלְּהוּ. עֲלָהּ אִתְּמַר, הִיא מִתְהַלֶּכֶת בֵּין הַחַיּוֹת, דְּאִינּוּן
חֵיוָן עִלָּאִין דְּנִקּוּדֵי דְטַעֲמֵי. וְחֵיוָן תַּתָּאִין, דְּנִקּוּדֵי דְאַתְוָון.

72. The Shechinah, namely Malchut, includes all of the visions. Since all the illumination of Chochmah is to illuminate as needed to influence the Shechinah, as it is written: "Praised is the influencing educator to the poor." (Psalms 41:2) About Her it is said: "It walks among all the living creatures." (Ezekiel 1:13) These are the Supernal Beasts that illuminate

in the dots of the cantillation marks and Lower Beasts that illuminate in the vowels of the letters.

73. כְּגַוְונָא דָא ׃ ה ה וְאִנּוּן סְגוֹלְתָּא לְעֵילָא תְּלַת זִיוְין עִילָּאֵי דְּרְמִיזִין י"י"י בְּרֵאשֵׁי תֵּיבוֹת יהו"ה יהו"ה יהו"ה. וְאִנּוּן יהו"ה מֶלֶךְ יהו"ה מָלָךְ יהו"ה יִמְלֹךְ, אַנְפֵּי תְּלַת זִיוְין עִילָּאִין דְּאִנּוּן חֶס"ד גְּבוּר"ה תִּפְאֶר"ת.

73. The same is with (the letter) Hei, and the three Supernal Beasts are hinted by the three Yud's of the Segol (••) above the Hei at the beginning of the words Yud-Hei-Vav-Hei, Yud-Hei-Vav-Hei, Yud-Hei-Vav-Hei (Yud, Yud, Yud), pertaining to: The Lord (Yud-Hei-Vav-Hei) is reigning King, the Lord (Yud, Hei, Vav, Hei) reigned, the Lord (Yud-Hei-Vav-Hei) will reign." And they are the faces of the three Supernal Beasts: Chesed, Gevurah, and Tiferet.

74. וּלְתַתָּא סְגוֹ"ל דְּאִנּוּן זִיוְין תַּתָּאִין, אַנְפֵּי נֶצַ"ח הו"ד יְסוֹ"ד. דְּרְמִיזִין בִּיבָרֶכְ"ךָ יָאֵ"ר יִשָּׂ"א. נְקוּדָה דְּאֶמְצָעִיתָא וַיָּה שְׁמָהּ אָדָם. כְּגַוְונָא דָא ה. הִיא מִתְהַלֶּכֶת בֵּין הַחַיּוֹת, דְּאִנּוּן תְּלַת לְעֵילָא, וּתְלַת לְתַתָּא, כְּגַוְונָא דָא ה. אִיהִי רְבִיעָאָה לְכָל תְּלַת, וּשְׁבִיעָאָה לְשִׁית.

74. Below under the Hei, three Yud's Segol, which are the lower beasts, hinted by the three Yud's of Yevarechecha (May He bless you), Ya'er (May He illuminate), Yisa (May He elevate). These are the faces of Netzach, Hod, and Yesod. The Central Point is a living creature whose name is Adam, namely Malchut. Similar to this, Hei—she walks about between the living creatures that are three above, Chesed, Gevurah, and Tiferet, and the three below, Netzach, Hod, and Yesod. Similar to this—Hei is the fourth to each three, completing Chesed, Gevurah, and Tiferet and completing Netzach, Hod, and Yesod, and seventh to six, for Chesed, Gevurah, Tiferet, Netzach, Hod, and Yesod together.

75. וְרָזָא דִּתְלַת זִיוְין תַּתָּאִין, עֲלַיְיהוּ קָא רְמִיזָ, וַיְהִי בִּשְׁלִשִׁים שָׁנָה. וְעַל נְקוּדָא דְּאֶמְצָעִיתָא, קָא רְמִיזָ בָּרְבִיעִי, דְּאִיהוּ אַרְבַּע אַנְפֵּי אָדָם, וְזָכְמָה

עִלָּאָה, כְּ"וַו בַּ"ה, דְּאִתְּמַר בֵּיהּ דְּמוּת כְּמַרְאֵה אָדָם עָלָיו מִלְמַעְלָה, וְכֹלָּא בְּרָזָא דִּנְקוּדֵי דְּאָת הֵ.

75. The secret of the three living creatures below, the verse alludes about them: "And it was on the thirtieth year...," (Ezekiel 1:1) because each Sefira is composed of ten. **And about the middle point, which is Malchut, he hints: "On the fourth" meaning the four faces of man,** as is written: "And the image of their faces was the face of man." (Ezekiel 1:10) Meaning the **Supernal Chochmah,** first two letters **Kaf-Chet** means "power," and **Mem-Hei,** which numerically equals 45. **Of whom it says: "And above the throne was an image like that of a man."** (Ezekiel 1:26) **All is in the secret of the dots of the letter Hei.**

76. וּבַחֲמִשָּׁה לַחֹדֶשׁ: דָּא אָת הֵ', דְּאִיהִי אֱלֹקִי"ם, כִּנּוּ"י לְשֵׁם יְקוּ"ק. וְאִיהִי כָּרְסַיָּא, דְּהָכִי סְלִיק הַכִּסֵּ"א כְּחוּשְׁבַּן אֱלֹקִי"ם. וְאִיהִי כֶּתֶר עֶלְיוֹן, וַחֲמִישָׁאָה לְאַרְבַּע חֵיוָון עִלָּאִין, וַחֲמִישָׁאָה לְאַרְבַּע תַּתָּאִין. וְאִיהִי כָּרְסַיָּא לְמָארֵי כֹלָּא. אָדוֹן עַל כֹּלָּא דְּאִיהוּ טָמִיר וְגָנִיז.

76. "On the fifth of the month," (Ezekiel 1:1) as mentioned in the verse, **refers to the letter Hei,** and not the punctuation, **alluding to the five letters of the Name Elokim, a byname for the Name Yud-Kei-Vav-Kei,** that is a throne to Zeir Anpin. Because the numerical value of *hakise* (the Throne) is the same as Elokim (86). And it is the Supernal Keter to Briyah, Yetzirah and Asiyah, **the fifth to the four Supernal Animals, and the fifth to the four lower animals. And it is a throne to the Ruler of all. The Master of all, which is hidden and sealed.** Meaning Endless Light, blessed be He that reaches to the end of Atzilut.

77. וְאִי תֵּימָא דְּרָזָא דָּא חָזָא יְחֶזְקֵאל, לָא הֲוָה אֶלָּא דְּמוּת דְּאִלֵּין חֵיוָון, וְלָא רָזָא חֵיוָון. אֶלָּא כְּמַלְכָּא דְּשַׁלְחוּ שְׁטָר בַּחֲוֹתָמֵיהּ, וְדִיּוֹקְנָא דְּמַלְכָּא רְשִׁימָא עַל שַׁעֲוָה בַּחֲוֹתָמֵיהּ.

77. He asks, "**Did Ezekiel see this secret** of the Supernal Chariot?" He answers, "**No. It was merely the image of those animals. But he did not see** actual **animals. It is a parable to a king who sent a certificate with his stamp, and the form of the king was marked in the wax from** the king's **stamp.**"

78. דְּבִסְפִירָן דַּאֲצִילוּת אִיהוּ דִּיוֹקְנָא דְמַלְכָּא מַמָּשׁ. וּבִסְפִירָן דִּבְרִיאָה, וְחוֹתָמָא דְמַלְכָּא. וּבִסְפִירָן דִּיצִירָה, וּבְמַלְאָכִין דְּאִינּוּן חֵיוָן, צִיּוּרָא דְחוֹתָמָא בְּשַׁעֲוָה. וּבְגִין דָּא אִתְּמַר בְּמַרְאוֹת יְחֶזְקֵאל, דְּמוּת כְּמַרְאֵה אָדָם. וּדְמוּת הַחַיּוֹת, וְלָא הַחַיּוֹת מַמָּשׁ. לְמַאן דְּכָל יוֹמוֹי לָא חָזָא מַלְכָּא וְהוּא בֶּן כְּפַר, וְשָׁאִיל בְּגִינֵיהּ, וְרָשִׁימִין לֵיהּ עַל טַבְלָא, אוֹ עַל נְיָיר, דִּיוּקְנֵיהּ.

78. He explains, "**Because in the Sefirot of Atzilut is the actual form of the King, and in the Sefirot of Briyah is the stamp of the King, and in the Sefirot of Yetzirah and in the angels, the animals** of Yetzirah, **it is a depiction of the wax stamp. Therefore, it says in the visions of Ezekiel: 'A face in the likeness of man.'** (Ezekiel 1:5) **The image of the animals, but not the animals themselves.** Comparable to **someone who never saw the king in his life, he is a village dweller, and asks about** the king, to recognize him **and they mark down for him the image** of the king **on a tablet or on a paper.**"

79. וַאֲנִי בְּתוֹךְ הַגּוֹלָה עַל נְהַר כְּבָר, דָּא נְהַר דִּינוּר נָגֵיד וְנָפֵיק מִן קֳדָמוֹהִי וְגוֹ'. וְרִבּוֹא רִבְבָן דְּמַלְאֲכַיָּא קֳדָמוֹהִי יְקוּמוּן. דִּינָא יְתִיב וְסִפְרִין פְּתִיחוּ, דְּאִינּוּן תְּלַת סִפְרִין דְּנִפְתָּחִין בְּרֹאשׁ הַשָּׁנָה, וּבֵיהּ, טָבְלִין נִשְׁמָתִין בְּהַאי נְהַר דִּינוּר, מִוּהֲבָמְתָן דִּמִוּוהֲבָמִין בְּעָלְמָא שָׁפֵלָה.

79. "And I am within the exiled, on the river Kvar" (Ezekiel. 1:1)**: this refers to the "the Dinur [lit. fire] River that issued and came forth ... and tens of thousands of these ministering angels stood before him, set to judge, and the books were open,"** (Daniel 7:10) **referring to the three books opened on Rosh Hashanah. In this very same Dinur River, the**

souls immerse to cleanse themselves **from their filth that contaminates them in the lowly world.**

80. וְדָא מטטרו"ן בְּדִיוּקְנָא דְצַדִּיק יְסוֹד עָלְמָא, דְּאִיהוּ נָהָר דִּינוּר מִסִּטְרָא דִּגְבוּרָה. נָהָר פְּלָגָיו, מִסִּטְרָא דְחֶסֶד, פַּלְגֵי מַיִם. וְהַאי אִיהוּ עַל נְהָר כְּבָר. מַאי כְּבָ"ר. דָּא מטטרו"ן, רֶכָ"ב לְעַמּוּדָא דְאֶמְצָעִיתָא. וַיִּרְכַּב עַל כְּרוּב וַיָּעֹף, וְאִיהוּ רֶכֶב אֵשׁ וְסוּסֵי אֵשׁ, כְּלִיל שִׁתִּין רִבּוֹא מֶרְכָּבוֹת.

80. **This** angel **Metatron in the image of the righteous** (*tzadik*) **foundation of the world,** meaning Yesod, called *Kol* (All), for Yesod is not a Sefira on its own but only a composition of all the five Sefirot, **which is the Dinur River** from the aspect of Gevurah, **and it is the river of small streams from the aspect of the Chesed,** the secret of "small streams," and **this is "on the River Kvar."** He asks, **"What is** the definition of **Kvar?"** And replies, **"This is Metatron."** Kvar is the letter combination of *rechev* **(the chariot) to the Central Column,** meaning Tiferet. In the secret of the verse: **"He rode on a Cherub and flew"** (Psalms 18:10) **and this is "the chariot of fire and horses of fire,"** (Kings II 2:11) **inclusive of 600,000 of chariots.**

81. וּמִסִּטְרָא דְצַדִּיק חַי עָלְמִין, הוּא כְּלִיל י"ח רִבּוֹא מֶרְכָּבוֹת, וְהַיְינוּ רֶכֶב אֱלֹקִי"ם רִבּוֹתַיִם אַלְפֵי שִׁנְאָן. וְאוּקְמוּהָ מָארֵי מַתְנִיתִין, תְּרֵי אַלְפֵי שֶׁאֵינָן מִתְּרֵין רִבּוֹא, דְּאִנּוּן כָּל רִבּוֹא עֲשֶׂרֶת אֲלָפִים. רִבּוֹתַיִם: עֶשְׂרִים אֲלָפִים. תְּרֵי שֶׁאֵינָן. אִשְׁתָּאֲרוּ תַּמְנֵי סְרֵי אַלְפֵי, דְּנָחֲתִין עִם מטטרו"ן לְקַבְּלָא י"ח בִּרְכָאן דִּצְלוֹתִין דְּיִשְׂרָאֵל, לְסַלְקָא לוֹן קַמֵּי קוּדְשָׁא בְּרִיךְ הוּא בַּוַ" י עָלְמִין, צַדִּיק יְסוֹד עוֹלָם, וּבְרָכוֹת לְרֹאשׁ צַדִּיק.

81. **From the aspect of the righteous life of the world,** namely Yesod, **it includes 180,000 chariots, and this is** the secret of the verse: **"God's chariot are twice ten thousand, and thousands of thousands of angels."** (Psalms 68:17) **The masters of the Mishnah established** the meaning of **"twice ten thousand, and thousands of thousands (shin'an)" to mean two that are not included in the twice ten thousands (shtyaim she'einam),**

leaving only eighteen thousand that descend with Metatron, to receive the eighteen blessings from the prayers of Israel and to uplift them to the presence of the Holy One blessed be He, in eighteen worlds, meaning: "the righteous (tzadik) foundation of the world" (Proverbs 10:25) "and blessings to the head of the righteous (tzadik)." (Proverbs 10:6)

82. וַאֲנִי בְּתוֹךְ הַגּוֹלָה, דָּא שְׁכִינְתָּא נְפָתְחוּ הַשָּׁמַיִם, ה' רְקִיעֵי דְּיוֹמָא קַדְמָאָה, ה' דְּהַשָּׁמַיִם, דִּבָהּ רְשִׁימִין חֵיזוּ דְּמִקּוֹרֵיהוֹן יו"ד ק"י וא"ו ה"י. יהו"ה.

82: "And I am (ani) within the exile," (Ezekiel 1:1), refers to the Shechinah, that is called "I" (ani), in the meaning of Ve'Ani tefilah (And I, the prayer), "The Heavens opened" (Ibid.) the Hei (5) five Firmaments mentioned on the first day. The letter Hei of the word haShamayim (the Heavens) meaning Binah, in which are marked the visions of the source of the Firmaments, which is Yud-Vav-Dalet Hei-Yud Vav-Alef-Vav Hei-Yud; Yud-Kei-Vav-Kei.

83. וָאֶרְאֶה מַרְאוֹת אֱלֹקִי"ם, וָחֲמֵשׁ אוֹר דְּיוֹמָא קַדְמָאָה. לָקֳבֵל ה' קַדְמָאָה. כְּלִילָא מֵחֲמֵשׁ אוֹר. דְּאִיהוּ אָאאאא פְּתוּחֵי וְזֹתָם קֹדֶשׁ לַי"י. וְכָל א' אַחֲזֵי אקי"ק.

83: "I saw visions of God (Elokim)." (Ezekiel 1:1) Five Lights (or) of the first day, corresponding to the first Hei of the Name Yud-Hei-Vav-Hei that is comprised of five lights: Chesed, Gevurah, Tiferet, Netzach, and Hod. Since in the Hei exist five Alef's punctuated with the vowels Kametz, Tzere, Cholem, Chirek and Shuruk, such as the verse: "Engraved as on the signet ring, Holy to the Lord." (Exodus 28:36) And each letter Alef indicates the Name Alef-Kei-Yud-Kei (Eheyeh), because Light (or) begins with Alef, and Alef-Kei-Yud-Kei begins with Alef.

84. וּנְקוּדִין אִלֵּין סָלְקָן אֱלֹקִי"ם, דִּבְהוֹן שֶׁבַע נְקוּדִין, תְּלַת לְעֵיל, תְּלַת לְתַתָּא, וֹחַ"ל"ם בְּאֶמְצָעִיתָא. וְחַד רְקִיעָא תְּמִינָאָה לוֹן, דְּאִתְּמַר בֵּיהּ וַיִּתֵּן אֹתָם אֱלֹקִי"ם בִּרְקִיעַ הַשָּׁמָיִם.

84. These vowels amount to Elokim, and contain seven vowels, three on top, three on the bottom, Cholem in the middle and one Firmament— this is eighth for them, as it is said: "And God (Elokim) placed them in the Firmament of the Heaven." (Genesis 1:17)

‎85. וְשֶׁבַע נְצוֹצֵי דִנְקוּדֵי אָאאאא לָקֳבֵל שֶׁבַע כֹּכְבֵי לֶכֶת. תְּלַת מִכָּאן, וּתְלַת מִכָּאן וַחַמָּ"ה בְּאֶמְצָעִיתֵיה, רְבִיעָאָה לְכָל תְּלַת, וּשְׁבִיעָאָה לְשִׁית, וְאִיהִי בְּצוּרַת חֹלֶ"ם.

85. The seven sparks of dots of the vowels of the five Alef's correspond to the seven planets: Saturn, Jupiter, Mars, the Sun, Venus, Mercury, and the Moon, three from here, and the three from there, the sun in the middle, the fourth to each group of three, and the seventh to the group of six, and this is in the form of Cholem.

‎86. בְּאִלֵּין חָמֵשׁ וְקָמַץ הַכֹּהֵן מִשָּׁם מְלֹא קֻמְצוֹ קָמֵץ אִיהוּ י', כַּד אִתְפַּתַּח בַּה' נְקוּדִין אִיהוּ ה', חָמֵשׁ אֶצְבְּעָאן דִּבְהוֹן אִתְפַּתַּח קוֹמֵץ דְּאִיהוּ י', לַחֲמִשִׁין תַּרְעִין דְּחֵירוּ.

86. Regarding these five vowels it is said: "And the priest (Kohen) should take from it his handful (*vaKametz kumtzo*)." (Leviticus 2:2) The origin of the punctuation dots in the **Kametz is Yud,** and this is alluded when he closes the palm of his hand, **and when he opens (*pote'ach*) with the five dots, it is a Hei,** which hints **to the five fingers by which** the palm of the hand is opened from its scooped position, which is Yud, to Fifty Gates of Freedom.

‎87. וְאַתְוָון י"ק כְּחֶשְׁבַּן חֹלֶ"ם, דְּאִיהוּ אֶמְצָעִי. וְחֹרֶ"ק, כְּחֶשְׁבַּן ו"ק. ו' דְּרוֹעָא, ה' כָּתֵף, קָמֵ"ץ י"ד פִּרְקִין דְּאֶצְבְּעָן.

87. The letters Yud-Hei (15) equal the numerical value of Cholem (78), which in small numerical value is 15 (78; 7+8=15), **which is in the middle,** namely Tiferet. **Chirek (308; 3+0+8=11) equals the numerical value of**

Vav-Hei (11). Vav (6) is the arm and Hei is the shoulder. Kametz (194) in small numerology is 14 (1+9+4=14) alluding to the fourteen joints in the fingers of the hand.

88. וְהַאי אִיהוּ וַיֹּאמֶר כִּי יָד עַל כֵּס יָ"קָ, וְאִינּוּן רְמִיזִין יְקֹנָ"ק אֱלֹהֵי"נוּ יְקֹנָ"ק. וּבְחָמֵשׁ אֶצְבְּעָאן דְּיַד שְׂמָאלָא י"ד פִּרְקִין, רְמִיזִין כוז"ו, במוכס"ז כוז"ו, וְאִינּוּן כ"ח. דְּאִתְּמַר עֲלַיְיהוּ וְעַתָּה יִגְדַּל נָא כֹּ"חַ יְ"יָ.

88. This is the explanation of the verse: "He said, the hand (*yad*, Yud-Dalet) is on the throne of the Lord (Yud-Hei)." (Exodus 17:16) Those fourteen joints alluded in the Names of "...the Lord, our God, the Lord..." (Deuteronomy 6:4) Yud-Kei-Vav-Kei, Elokenu, Yud-Kei-Vav-Kei are the secret of the right hand. In the five fingers of the left hand, are alluded fourteen joints, in the Names Kaf-Vav-Zayin-Vav; Bet-Mem-Vav-Kaf-Samech-Zayin; Kaf-Vav-Zayin-Vav, totaling in small number 28, about which it is said: "And now let the strength (*ko'ach*, 28) of God be increased." (Numbers 14:17)

89. וְהָכִי סָלִיק אי"ה או"ה, כ"ח. דִּרְמִיזִין בְּכִסֵּא כָבוֹד מָרוֹם מֵרִאשׁוֹן. מִיָּד דְּאִסְתַּלְקוּ, וַיֵּלְכוּ בְלֹא כֹחַ לִפְנֵי רוֹדֵף. וּבְגִין דָּא אוֹקְמוּהָ מָארֵי מַתְנִיתִין, כָּל הָאוֹמֵר אָמֵן יְהֵא שְׁמֵיהּ רַבָּא בְּכָל כּוֹחוֹ קוֹרְעִין לוֹ גְּזַר דִּינוֹ שֶׁל שִׁבְעִים שָׁנָה.

89. Similarly, Alef-Yud-Hei and Alef-Vav-Hei also equal 28, which are hinted in "The Throne of Honor exalted from the beginning," (Jeremiah 17:12) as soon as these 28 were removed, it says: "And they went without strength (*ko'ach*, 28) before the pursuer." (Lamentations 1:6) Consequently, the masters of the Mishnah have defined: "Whoever utters the *Amen yehei shemei rabah* (Amen, may the great Name...) with all his strength (*ko'ach*) tears up his decreed sentence of seventy years."

90. דְּאִינּוּן שַׁבְעִין שְׁנִין, בָּתַר אֶלֶף וּמָאתָן שְׁנִין דְּאִתְחֲרַב בֵּי מַקְדְּשָׁא. וְאִית דְּחָזִיב לוֹן מִשְּׁבוּטַל הַתָּמִיד. בְּגִין דְּבַדְרְגָּא דְיַעֲקֹב קֵן דְּפוּרְקָנָא,

דְּדַרְגֵּיהּ אֱמֶת. הָדָא הוּא דִכְתִיב, תִּתֵּן אֱמֶ"ת לְיַעֲקֹב, דְּאִיהוּ סִימָן אֶלֶף מָאתַיִם וְתִשְׁעִים.

90. As they are seventy years after the twelve hundred years from the time of the destruction of the Temple. Some figure the time from when they ceased the Tamid Sacrifice, since the final end for the redemption depends upon Jacob's level, namely Zeir Anpin, **whose level is truth (*emet*),** Tiferet, **as it says: "You granted truth to Jacob."** (Micah 7:20) **Because it,** truth (*EMeT*, Alef-Mem-Tav), **is the acronym of 1,290** (*Elef*, 1000; *Matayim*, 200; *Tishim*, 90).

91. וְאִית דְּאוֹסִיף בֵּיהּ ב' קָרוֹב יְ"יָ לְכָל קוֹרְאָיו לְכֹל אֲשֶׁר יִקְרָאֻהוּ בֶאֱמֶת. לָדַעַת בָּאָרֶץ דַּרְכֶּךָ. אוּף הָכִי אֶרֶץ אַלֶף ר"ץ מָאתַיִם וְתִשְׁעִים. לְקַיְּימָא בְהוֹן אֱמֶ"ת מֵאֶרֶ"ץ תִּצְמָח. כַּד יְהוֹן לְבָר כְּחוּשְׁבַּן אֶרֶ"ץ. אֲבָל גְּזַר דִּינָם שִׁבְעִים שָׁנִים.

91. **There are those who add** the letter **Bet (2)** to hint the word *be'EMeT* (in truth), like the verse: **"The Lord is close to all those who call on Him, to all who call Him in truth (*be'EMeT*)."** (Psalms 145:18) **Similarly: "That Your ways may be know on earth (*baAReTZ*),"** (Psalms 67:2) **because also** in the word *AReTZ*, the first letter **Alef** means **one thousand, Resh (200)** and **Tzadik (90) equal 290, to maintain in them,** in Zeir and Nukva: **"Truth (*EMeT*) will sprout from the land (*me'AReTZ*)"** (Psalms 85:11), **after they will be** exiled **outside as the numerical value of *AReTZ* (1290). But their decreed sentence is seventy years.**

11. The Torah of Briyah and the Torah of Atzilut

‫92. דָּבָר אַחֵר, וְהַמַּשְׂכִּילִים: אִינוּן נְקוּדֵי. יַזְהִירוּ: דְּנָהֲרִין בְּאַתְוָון. דְּאִנּוּן‬
‫נְקוּדִין עֲגוּלִין, אַתְוָון מְרוּבָּעִין. דְּבְאַתְוָון אִתְבְּרִיאוּ אַרְבַּע חֵיוָון דְּכָרְסְיָא,‬
‫דְּאִתְּמַר עֲלַיְיהוּ בְּעִנְיָנָא דִּיחֶזְקֵאל, וּדְמוּת הַחַיּוֹת. מַרְאֵיהֶם כְּגַחֲלֵי אֵשׁ,‬
‫אִלֵּין אִינוּן נְקוּדֵי דְּאוֹרַיְתָא, דְּאִינוּן תִּשְׁעָה. דְּבְהוֹן אִתְבְּרִיאוּ תִּשְׁעָה גַּלְגַּלֵּי‬
‫דְּכָרְסְיָא. כָּרְסְיָא אִיהִי עֲשִׂירָאָה לְתִשְׁעָה גַּלְגַּלִּים. דְּנָהֲרִין בְּהוֹן עֶשֶׂר אַתְוָון,‬
‫דְּאִנּוּן יֹו"ד קֵ"א וָ"ו קֵ"א. וּבְהוֹן אִתְבְּרִיאוּ וְאַרְבַּע אַתְוָון דְּאִינוּן יְקֹוָ"ק,‬
‫נָהֲרִין בְּאַרְבַּע חֵיוָון וּבְהוֹן אִתְבְּרִיאוּ.‬

92. Another matter: "The wise" (Daniel 12:3) **pertains to the vowel punctuation** [yet above in verse 71: the Zohar says that "the wise" are the letters]; **"shall shine"** (Ibid.) because **they shine to the letters. The dots are circular** meaning they illuminate from below upward, **and the letters are squared** meaning they illuminate from above downward. **The letters created the four animals of the Throne, as was mentioned in the story of Ezekiel: "And the image of the animals;"** (Ezekiel 1:1) **"Their appearance like coals of fire"** (Ezekiel 1:13). **This pertains to the punctuation vowels in the Torah, amounting to nine:** Kametz, Patach, Tzere, Segol, Sh'va, Cholem, Chirek, Shuruk and Melopum **by which the nine wheels of the throne were created, and the Throne** itself **is tenth to the nine wheels, and by them the ten letters illuminate, which are** Yud-Vav-Dalet, Hei-Alef, Vav-Alef-Vav, Hei-Alef, **and by them were they created. The four letters, Yud-Kei-Vav-Kei, illuminate in the four animals, and by them were they created.**

‫93. וְשֵׁם הוִי"ה אִיהוּ עַמּוּדָא דְּאֶמְצָעִיתָא, אֱמֶת. וּשְׁכִינְתֵּיהּ, תּוֹרַת אֱמֶת. בָּהּ‬
‫אִתְבְּרִיאַת כָּרְסְיָא, דְּאִיהִי אֱלֹקִי"ם. וְהַיְינוּ בְּרֵאשִׁית בָּרָא אֱלֹקִי"ם: בְּאוֹרַיְתָא‬
‫דְּאִיהִי רֵאשִׁית, בָּרָא כָּרְסְיָא, דְּאִיהִי אֱלֹקִי"ם. דְּהָכִי סָלִיק הַכֵּ"א לְחוּשְׁבַּן‬
‫אֱלֹקִי"ם.‬

93. The Name Yud-Kei-Vav-Kei is the Central Column, Tiferet, whose attribute is **truth, and its Shechinah,** namely Malchut, is called **Torah**

of truth. **With Her, the Throne, which is Elokim,** the World of Briyah, **was created. The meaning** of the verse: **"In the beginning God (Elokim) created…"** (Genesis 1:1) is that **with the Torah, which is "beginning"** (*resheet*)**, he created** the World of **the Throne, which is Elokim. The** numerical value **of "the throne"** (*hakise*) **amounts to the numerical value of Elokim (86).**

94. וְאִית אוֹרַיְתָא דִּבְרִיאָה, וְאוֹרַיְתָא דַּאֲצִילוּת. אוֹרַיְתָא דִּבְרִיאָה יְ"יָ קָנָנִי רֵאשִׁית דַּרְכּוֹ. וְאוֹרַיְתָא דַּאֲצִילוּת, תּוֹרַת יְ"יָ תְּמִימָה. וּבָהּ תָּמִים תִּהְיֶה עָם יְ"יָ אֱלֹהֶי"ךָ. וּמִסִּטְרָא דִּילָהּ אִתְּמַר עַל יִשְׂרָאֵל בָּנִים אַתֶּם לַי"יָ.

94. And there is the Torah about Briyah (Creation), and Torah about Atzilut (Emanation). Concerning the Torah of Briyah, it says: **"God brought me back as the first of His works,"** (Proverbs 8:22) **and about the Torah of Atzilut** it says: **"The Torah of God is complete."** (Psalms 19:8) **Regarding** the Torah of Atzilut: **"Be complete with the Lord your God."** (Deuteronomy 18:13) **And from that aspect it is said about Israel: "You are children to the Lord** your God." (Deuteronomy 14:1)

95. וּמְנָא לָן דְּאוֹרַיְתָא דַּאֲצִילוּת אִיהִי תּוֹרַת יְ"יָ דְּתַלְיָא בִּשְׁמֵיהּ. אֶלָּא הָכִי אוּקְמוּהָ, זֶה שְׁמִי לְעֹלָם, שְׁמִי עָם י"ק שס"ה. זִכְרִ"י עָם ו"ק רמ"ח. תּוֹרָה בְּחָשְׁבָּן אַתְווֹי תרי"א, וְעָם אָנֹכִי וְלֹא יִהְיֶה לְךָ, אִיהִי תרי"ג. וְהַיְינוּ ב' דְּאִתּוֹסְפַת בַּתּוֹרָה. זֹאת הַתּוֹרָה אָדָם, דָּא יו"ד ק"א וא"ו ק"א.

95. And he asks, "Where do we have a hint in the scriptural verse **that the Torah of Atzilut is the Torah of the Lord, which is dependent on His Name Yud-Hei-Vav-Hei?"** He replies, **"So the masters explained: 'This is My Name forever** and this is My memorial unto all generations' (Exodus 3:15): 'My Name' (*Shmi*; 350) with Yud-Hei (15) amounts to 365, and 'My Memorial' (*Zichri*; 237) with Vav-Hei (11) amounts to 248, which all together amounts to 613. The numerical value of the word 'Torah' is 611, and together with the two utterances of 'I am (the Lord your God)' and 'you shall not have…' (Exodus 20:2) it is also **613. The two**

extra utterances amount to **the Bet (2)** of Beresheet, **which is an addition to the Torah,** as is said: '**This is the Torah, man (45)…**' (Numbers 19:14) **meaning** Yud-Hey-Vav-Hei spelled out with Alef: Yud-Vav-Dalet, Hei-Alef, Vav-Alef-Vav, Hei-Alef, which equals 45."

96. וּבְגִין דָּא כָּבוֹד חֲכָמִים יִנְחָלוּ, וְאוּקְמוּהוּ רַבָּנָן דְּמַתְנִיתִין, אֵין כָּבוֹד אֶלָּא תּוֹרָה. וְאִית כָּבוֹד נִבְרָא. וְאִית כָּבוֹד נֶאֱצָל. מִסְטְרָא דְּאוֹרַיְתָא דִּבְרִיאָה, אִתְּמַר בְּיִשְׂרָאֵל כִּי לִי בְנֵי יִשְׂרָאֵל עֲבָדִים. וּמִסְטְרָא דַּאֲצִילוּת בָּנִים אַתֶּם לַיְיָ וְגוֹ' וּלְעֵילָא עַל כֹּלָּא, עֵלַּת עַל כֹּלָּא, דְּלֵית אֱלֹקִי עֲלֵיהּ, וְלָאו תְּוֹחֹתֵיהּ, וְלָאו לְאַרְבַּע סְטְרֵי עָלְמָא. וְאִיהוּ מְמַלֵּא כָּל עָלְמִין.

96. And about this is said: **"The wise will inherit honor,"** (Proverbs 3:35) **and the masters of the Mishnah established that there is no** other meaning for **honor but the Torah. And there is a created honor** of Briyah (Creation) **and there is an emanated honor** of Atzilut (Emanation). **From the aspect of the Torah of Briyah it is said about Israel: "Because the children of Israel are servants to Me,"** (Leviticus 25:55) **and from the aspect** of the Torah **of Atzilut it says: "You are children of the Lord…."** (Deuteronomy 14:1) **And above everything is He, the Highest of all, that there is no God above Him or below Him, and neither in the four directions of the world, and He fills all the worlds.**

97. וְאִיהִי אַסְחַר, וּמְקַבֵּל בָּהּ יִסּוּרִין וּמַרְעִין וּמַכְאוֹבִין, בְּדִוְזִילוּ דְּמָארֵיהּ אַהֲבָה בְּסוֹפָהּ. כְּגַוְונָא דְּאוּקְמוּהָ מָארֵי מַתְנִיתִין, עַל אִלֵּין מָארֵי קוּשְׁיָין וּמַוְזָלוֹקוֹת, אֶת וָהֵב בְּסוֹפָהּ, וְאוּקְמוּהָ אַהֲבָה בְּסוֹפָהּ. דְּמַה דַּהֲוַת לוֹן שְׁכִינְתָּא סוֹף דְּכָל דַּרְגִּין קוּשְׁיָא וְדִין מִסְטְרָא דִּגְבוּרָה. אִתְוַזְּוֶרֶת לוֹן אַהֲבָה מִסְטְרָא דִּימִינָא אַהֲבַת חֶסֶד.

97. The first four levels in the awe of the Lord are missing here and this is the ending of the fourth level: and he revolves and receives through it awe of his master, sufferings, afflictions and pains, and at the end he merits and attains **love. As the masters of the Mishnah have established about those who constantly engage in difficult discussions and disputes, this**

verse: "What he gave at the Sea of Reeds (*et vahev besufa*)" (Numbers 21:14) They explained: "love at the end (*ahava besufa*)," because at first, the Shechinah was at the end of all levels for them, and therefore an aspect of a difficulty and judgment from the Left side that is Gevurah, went back to being for them love from the Right side, the love of Chesed (Kindness).

98. וּבְגִין דָּא כָּל הַמְקַיֵּים אֶת הַתּוֹרָה מֵעוֹנִי. סוֹפוֹ לְקַיְּימָה מֵעוֹשֶׁר. וְהַאי אִיהוּ אַהֲבָה בְּסוֹפָה. וְכָל מָאן דְּלָא מְקַיֵּים לָהּ מֵעוֹשֶׁר, יְקַיְּימָהּ מֵעוֹנִי.

98. Subsequently, everyone who observes to upkeep the Torah in poverty is bound at the end to upkeep it in a state of wealth. And whoever does not seek to upkeep it in wealth, will uphold it in a state of poverty, and then will he merit to uphold it in wealth.

12. The fifth level in the awe of Heaven

99. דַּרְגָּא וַחֲמִישָׁאָה בְּיִרְאַת יְ"יָ, אוּקְמוּהוּ מָארֵי מַתְנִיתִין, כָּל הַקּוֹדֵם יִרְאָתוֹ לְחָכְמָתוֹ, וְחָכְמָתוֹ מִתְקַיֶּמֶת. וְכָל הַקּוֹדֵם חָכְמָתוֹ לְיִרְאַת וְחֶטְאוֹ, אֵין וְחָכְמָתוֹ מִתְקַיֶּמֶת. דְּכָל הַקּוֹדֵם חָכְמָתוֹ לְיִרְאָתוֹ, לְמָה הוּא דוֹמֶה, לְמִי שֶׁמָּסְרוּ לוֹ מַפְתְּחוֹת הַפְּנִימִיִּים, וְלֹא מָסְרוּ לוֹ מַפְתְּחוֹת הַחִיצוֹנִיִּים, בַּמֶּה יִכָּנֵס.

99. The masters of the Mishnah have set the fifth level in awe of Heaven as: Anyone who sets up his awe as a priority to his wisdom, his wisdom will last; and whoever sets his wisdom as a priority to his fear of sinning, his wisdom will not last. Because whoever sets his wisdom as a priority to his awe is comparable to someone who was given the inner keys but not the external keys. How can he enter?

100. וּבְאָרַח רָזָא: אדנ"י, תַּמָּן י' יִרְאַת יְ"יָ. וְאִלֵּין אַרְבַּע אַתְוָון, אִינּוּן מַפְתְּחוֹת הַחִיצוֹנִיִּים דִּילָהּ. י' מִן יְקוֹ"ק, אִיהִי וְחָכְמָה. וְאַרְבַּע אַתְוָון דְּהַאי שְׁמָא, אִינּוּן מַפְתְּחוֹת הַפְּנִימִיִּים.

100. Understanding it **in a manner of secrecy;** in the Name **Adonai** there are four letters: Alef-Dalet-Nun-Yud, **the Yud** at the end hints to **the awe of the Lord, and the four letters therein,** in the Name **Alef-Dalet-Nun-Yud, are its external keys. The Yud from** the Name **Yud-Kei-Vav-Kei is Chochmah, and the four letters of this Name,** Yud-Kei-Vav-Kei **are the inner keys.**

101. וּבְגִין דָּא אַקְדִּימוּ בִּצְלוֹתָא, אדנ"י שְׂפָתַי תִּפְתָּח, וּלְבָתַר וְחָתְמִין לָהּ בְּשֵׁם יְקוֹ"ק, בָּרוּךְ אַתָּה יְ"יָ מָגֵן אַבְרָהָם. וְאוּף הָכִי אַקְדִּים שְׁבָ"א דְּאִיהִי יִרְאָה, בְּשֵׁם יְהֹוָה, לְאַהֲבָה דְּאִיהָי קָמֵ"ץ רַחֲמֵי שְׁבָ"א מִסִּטְרָא דִּגְבוּרָה, כִּי בָאֵשׁ יְ"יָ נִשְׁפָּט. קָמֵ"ץ, מִיָּמִינָא, וְקָמַ"ץ הַכֹּהֵן, מִשּׁוּם בְּגִין דְּמַעֲלִין בַּקֹּדֶשׁ, וְלֹא מוֹרִידִין. וּבְגִין דָּא, אַקְדִּימוּ שָׁסַ"ה לֹא תַעֲשֶׂה, דְּאִינּוּן דְּחִזִילוּ, לְרַמַ"ח פִּקּוּדִין, דְּאִינּוּן רְחִימוּ. הָדָא הוּא דִּכְתִיב זֶה שְׁמִי לְעוֹלָם וכו'. שְׁמִי עִם י"ק שָׂסַ"ה, זִכְרִי עִם ו"ה רַמַ"ח.

101. **Therefore,** in the Amidah prayer **they precede** to say **"God (Adonai), may You open my lips," and after** that they seal **by** the Name Yud-Kei-Vav-Kei: **"Blessed are You Lord (Yud-Kei-Vav-Kei) the shield of Abraham."** Similarly, he **precedes** the vowel Sh'va, **which hints to awe, in the Name of Yud-Kei-Vav-Kei that is punctuated by the vowels, Sh'va, Cholem and Kametz,** and he precedes the Sh'va, which alludes to awe, **to love, which is** indicated **by the Kametz,** which is **Mercy.** He explains that the vowel **Sh'va is from the aspect of Judgment,** in the secret of the verse: **"For with fire (va'esh) will the Lord judge...."** (Isaiah 66:16) *Va'esh* באש are the letters of the word Sh'va שבא. **The vowel Kametz is on the right,** in the meaning of the verse: **"And the priest (Kohen) shall scoop (*veKametz*)"** (Leviticus 5:12) **because you upgrade in sanctity, and do not downgrade. Therefore, they preceded the 365 negative precepts, which allude to awe, to the 248 positive precepts,** which allude **to love. This is as it was said: "My Name"** (*Shmi;* 350) **with Yud-Hei (15) amounts to 365, and "My Memorial"** (*Zichri;* 237) **with Vav-Hei (11) amounts to 248.** (Exodus 3:15)

13. The sixth level in the awe of Heaven

102. דַּרְגָּא שְׁתִיתָאָה בְּיִרְאַת יְ"יָ, וְהָיָה אֱמוּנַת עִתֶּיךָ כו'. אֱמוּנַת: סֵדֶר
זְרָעִים. עִתֶּיךָ: סֵדֶר מוֹעֵד. וֹחֹסֶן: סֵדֶר נָשִׁים. יְשׁוּעוֹת: סֵדֶר נְזִיקִין. וְחָכְמַת:
סֵדֶר קָדָשִׁים. וָדָעַת: סֵדֶר טָהָרוֹת. אִי אִיכָּא יִרְאַת ה' אִין, וְאִי לָא לָא. וְסִימָן
זְמַ"ן גָּק"ט.

102. The sixth level in awe of Heaven. It is written: "**Wisdom and
knowledge shall be the stability** [lit. faith] **of your time** and strength of
salvation, wisdom, and knowledge; **awe of Heaven, that is his treasure.**"
(Isaiah 33:6) "**Stability (faith)**" is the Order of Zera'im (seeds) because
by man's faith he trusts to set apart his tithes appropriately; "**Of your
time**" is the Order of Mo'ed (Festivals); "**strength**" is the Order of
Nashim (Women), from the same root word as inheritors (*yorshin*),
and through women are born inheritors; "**salvation**" is the Order of
Nezikin (Damages). Their redeemer cautions to separate apart from
harm, and from being obligated for monetary damages; "**wisdom**" is the
Order of Kodashim (Holy Things) since any sanctity is by wisdom; **and
"knowledge" is the Order of Taharot (Purifications).** Da'at is more
preferred than Chochmah. Nonetheless, the awe of the Lord is his treasury,
which means, **if there is awe of the Lord, there is, and if not, no. And
its signature sign is Zayin-Mem-Nun-Kof-Tav** (Zera'im, Moed, Nashim,
Nezikin, Kodashim, Taharot). The Mishnah is divided into Six Orders,
each order containing multiple Tractates.

103. וְאִלֵּין שִׁית סִדְרֵי מִשְׁנָה, בְּאֹרַח רָזָא אִינּוּן מֵעַמּוּדָא דְאֶמְצָעִיתָא דְכָלִיל
שִׁית סִדְרֵי מַתְנִיתִין. וּמַאן דְּבָעֵי לְנַטְלָא לֵיה בְּלָא שְׁכִינְתֵּיה, דְּאִיהִי יִרְאַת
יְ"יָ, עֲלֵיה אִתְּמַר, וְנִרְגָּן מַפְרִיד אַלּוּף. כְּאִלּוּ עָבִיד קִצּוּץ וּפְרוּד בֵּין קוּדְשָׁא
בְּרִיךְ הוּא וּשְׁכִינְתֵּיה.

103. And these Six Orders of the Mishnah, in a manner of secret, are
from the Central Column, meaning Tiferet, containing all Lower Six
Sefirot, **which includes the Six Orders of the Mishnah. Whoever wishes**

to acquire it, Tiferet, **without his Shechinah,** namely Malchut, **which is his awe of the Lord,** it says: "And the complainer separates chief friends," (Proverbs 16:28) **as if he undercut and separates the Holy One blessed be He and His Shechinah.**

104. וּבְגִין דְּלָא יַעַבְדוּן פֵּרוּדָא, אַף עַל גַּב דְּאוֹלִיף אָדָם שִׁית סִדְרֵי מִשְׁנָה, וְלָא אַקְדִּים לֵיהּ יִרְאַת יְ"יָ דְּאִיהוּ שְׁכִינְתֵּיהּ, קוּדְשָׁא בְּרִיךְ הוּא לָא שָׁרְיָא לְגַבֵּיהּ. וּבְגִין דָּא, אִי אִיכָּא יִרְאַת יְ"יָ אִין. וְאִי לָא לָא. כְּאִלוּ לָא הֲוָה כְּלוּם בִּידֵיהּ.

104. And so as not to make a separation between the Holy One blessed be He, and the Shechinah, therefore, **although a person studied the entire Six Orders of the Mishnah without having first prioritized for himself the awe of the Lord, which is the Shechinah, the Holy One blessed be He, does not reside with him. It is therefore** said: "Awe of the Lord is his treasure," (Isaiah 33:6) **if there exists awe of the Lord,** it is **good,** and he merits the Light of the Torah, which is the revelation of the Holy One blessed be He. **If not,** he does not make a study with the awe of the Lord as his priority, it is **as though he has nothing in his hands.**

105. אֱמוּנַת: אִיהִי אִימָא עִלָּאָה, מִסִּטְרָא דְּחֶסֶד. דְּבָה קְרִיאַת שְׁמַע דְּאִיהִי אֱמוּנָה. וְאִיהִי עִתֶּיךָ מִסִּטְרָא דִּגְבוּרָה, דְּבֵיהּ אִתְּמַר וְאַל יָבֹא בְכָל עֵת אֶל הַקֹּדֶשׁ וְגו'. וֹסֶן: אִיהִי מִסִּטְרָא דְּעַמוּדָא דְּאֶמְצָעִיתָא.

105. He now explains how Chesed, Gevurah, Tiferet, Netzach, Hod, and Yesod in Zeir Anpin are the Six Orders of the Mishnah, and they are hinted in the above verse, starting from above downward, from Chesed to Yesod, and says: **"Stability (faith),"** which is the Order of Zera'im (Seeds) **is the Supernal Ima,** meaning **from the aspect of Chesed, which contains the Shema reading,** which is accepting the yoke of the Heavenly Kingdom, **that is the faith.** And this is in the Sefira of Chesed, as it says: "And to unify You, with love." And the ruling laws pertaining to the Shema reading are in the Order of Zera'im (Seeds). **"Your time"** is from the aspect of

Gevurah, the Left Column, **about which it says: "…that he shall not approach, at any time, to the Holy…,"** (Leviticus 16:2) meaning that he should not draw the Upper Three Sefirot of the left, but "only with this (*zot*) shall Aaron come to the Holy," meaning from below upward, which are the Lower Six Sefirot of the Left, and not the entire complete cycle; and this is the Order of Mo'ed (Festivals). **"Strength" is from the aspect of the Central Column,** Tiferet, since from Tiferet begins the correction of the separated Nukva, (as mentioned in Idra Raba, 306): "This Tiferet spreads from the center of the heart, permeates, and crosses to the other side and restores the face of the Nukva (female)" and this is the Order of Nashim (Women).

106. יְשׁוּעֹ֫ת: אִתְקְרִיַּ֫ת, מִסִּטְרָא דְּנֶ֫צַח, וְגַם נֵצַח יִשְׂרָאֵל לֹא יְשַׁקֵּר וְלֹא יִנָּחֵם. וְחָכְמַת: אִיהִי סֵ֫דֶר קָדָשִׁים, דְּאִיהוּ הוֹד. וְדַעַת: אִיהוּ יְסוֹד, דְּאִיהוּ סֵ֫דֶר טָהֳרוֹת.

106. "Salvations" is named after the aspect of Netzach because the Nukva contains five Gevurot (Judgments), in the secret of five strong leaves, which are the forces of judgment in the curtain that prevents the higher Light from getting clothed below the curtain, since the drawing of Chochmah below the divider caused the damages and the shattering of the vessels. In the time of Gadlut, when there is a mating upon them, and the five Chasadim of Direct Light are clothed within the five Gevurot, then they are called salvations (*yeshuot*). And Malchut is called a cup of salvation (*kos yeshuot*), or a cup of blessing. They extend from above downward, in the aspect of Netzach, which is the Right Column that illuminates from above downward. Then is said: **"And also the eternal (*netzach*) strength of Israel will not lie nor repent."** (Samuel I 15:29) This is the Order of Nezikin (Damages). **Wisdom is the Order of Kodashim (Holy Things), which is Hod,** meaning the Chochmah of the left that illuminates with holiness from down upwards, as is the nature of Hod. **Knowledge (Da'at) is Yesod** the Central Column that regulates between Netzach and Hod, **which is the Order of Taharot (Purifications),** which cleanses the Left

Column to illuminate from the down upward, and not to go lower than
the divide, and for this, Da'at is better and preferred than Chochmah, as
mentioned before.

107. וְאִית דְּיֵימָא בְּהִפּוּכָא. מִסִּטְרָא דִשְׁכִינְתָּא תַּתָּאָה אִיהִי אֱמוּנָה. וּמִסִּטְרָא
דְּצַדִּיק, דְּבֵיהּ כְּלִילָן תְּרֵין שְׁמָהָן, אָמֵן. דְּאִנּוּן יאקדונק"י. וּבְצַדִּיק, עֵץ פְּרִי
עֹשֶׂה פְּרִי לְמִינוֹ אֲשֶׁר זַרְעוֹ בוֹ עַל הָאָרֶץ. וּבְגִין דָּא אִתְקְרֵי סֵדֶר זְרָעִים.

107. It could be said the other way, to define the six words in the verse:
"...stability, in your time, strength, salvations, wisdom, and knowledge,"
starting from below upward, from Yesod to Chesed that the Shechinah
below, which is Malchut, is stability (faith), from the aspect of the
righteous (tzadik), which is Yesod, in which Malchut is included, since in it,
in Yesod, are included two Names, whose letters' numerical value amount
to Amen (91), and they are Yud-Alef-Hei-Dalet-Vav-Nun-Hei-Yud [Yud-
Hei-Vav-Hei is 26; Alef-Dalet-Nun-Yud is 65]. Regarding righteous,
meaning Yesod, it says: "fruit trees on the earth bearing fruit according
to their kind with seed in them...," (Genesis 1:11) meaning Malchut.
Therefore, stability (faith) is called the Order of Zera'im (Seeds).

108. עִתֶּיךָ: אִיהִי מִסִּטְרָא דְּהוֹד, דְּאִיהִי סֵדֶר מוֹעֵד, דְּבֵיהּ אוֹכְלִין כָּל
אַרְבַּע, וְתוֹלִין כָּל חָמֵשׁ, וְשׂוֹרְפִין בִּתְחוֹלַת שֵׁשׁ.

108. "Your time" is from the aspect of Hod, which is the Order of Mo'ed
(Festivals), in which they eat every four [hours] and hang on every fifth
[hour] and burn at the beginning of every sixth [hour].

109. וֹחֹסֶן: אִיהוּ מִסִּטְרָא דְּעַמּוּדָא דְּאֶמְצָעִיתָא, דְּבֵיהּ סֵדֶר נָשִׁים. יְשׁוּעוֹת:
אִיהִי סֵדֶר נְזִיקִין, מִסִּטְרָא דִּגְבוּרָה. דְּתַמָּן כָּל דִּינִין נָפְקִין, לְמַאן דְּעָבִיד נֶזֶק
לְחַבְרֵיהּ.

109. "Strength" is from the aspect of the Central Column, Tiferet,
within which is the Order of Nashim (Women). "Salvations" is the

Order of Nezikin (Damages), from the aspect of Gevurah, meaning the Left Column, because **from there come all the laws for whoever does damage to his friend.** And when the five aspects that are in the curtain (*masach*), whose source is the Left Column, get restored to clothe the five Chasadim, then they are called five Gevurot and called salvations.

110. וְחָכְמַת: אִתְקְרִיאַת מִסִּטְרָא דְחֶסֶד, דְּבָה הָרוֹצֶה לְהַחְכִּים יַדְרִים, דְּאִיהוּ סֵדֶר קְדְשִׁים. וְעִמֵּיה נֶצַח. הָדָא הוּא דִכְתִיב, נְעִימוֹת בִּימִינָךְ נֶצַח. דַּעַת דְּאִיהוּ סֵדֶר טְהָרוֹת.

110. **"Wisdom" is named after the aspect of Chesed,** meaning the Chochmah of the right that shines with Chasadim, **about which** they said: **"Whoever wishes to get wise, let him face south." This is the Order of Kodashim (Holy Things). And with it is Netzach, as it is written: "Sweet pleasures in your right, power of victory (*netzach*)."** (Psalms 1:11) and namely **Da'at,** Zeir Anpin in Chasadim, because Chesed, Gevurah, and Tiferet are Keter, Chochmah, and Binah, and Netzach is Da'at that includes the Lower Six Sefirot, **and that is the Order of Taharot (Purifications).**

111. וְאִינּוּן שִׁית סִדְרֵי מַתְנִיתִין, בְּרָזָא דְלַהַט הַחֶרֶב, הַמִּתְהַפֶּכֶת מֵרַחֲמֵי לְדִינָא, וּמִדִּינָא לְרַחֲמֵי.

111. **These are the Six Orders of the Mishnah in the secret of "the fiery sword that turns"** (Genesis 3:24) **from Mercy to Judgment and from Judgment to Mercy.**

14. The seventh level in the awe of Heaven

112. דַּרְגָּא שְׁבִיעָאָה בְּיִרְאַת יְ"יָ, כָּל מָאן דְּאִית בֵּיהּ יִרְאַת יְ"יָ אוּקְמוּהוּ
מָארֵי מַתְנִיתִין דְּלֵית לֵיהּ חוּסֵר. הָדָא הוּא דִכְתִיב יְראוּ אֶת יְ"יָ קְדוֹשָׁיו
כִּי אֵין מַחְסוֹר לִירֵאָיו. לַאו יְהֵא מֵאִינוּן דְּאִתְּמַר בְּהוֹן, וְחוֹשֵׂךְ מִיּוֹשֶׁר אַךְ
לְמַחְסוֹר. וְלָא יְהֵא לֵיהּ חוּסֵר בְּאוֹרַיְתָא, אִם הוּא מָארֵי תּוֹרָה.

112. The seventh level in the awe of Heaven: according to the masters
of the Mishnah anyone who has awe of Heaven lacks nothing, as it says:
"Fear [have awe for] the Lord, you, His holy people, because those who
fear [have awe for] Him have no shortage." (Psalms 34:10) And he will
not be of those about whom it is written: "one withholds what is right,
only to become poor," (Proverbs 11:24) and he should not have shortage
in the Torah if he is a master of Torah.

113. דִּבְלָאו אוֹרַיְתָא לֵית דְּוֹחִילוּ, כְּמָא דְאַתְּ אָמָר אֵין בּוּר יֵרֵא חֵטְא. וּכְגַוְונָא
דְּלֵית אוֹרַיְתָא בְּלָא דְּוֹחִילוּ, אוּף הָכִי לֵית דְּוֹחִילוּ בְּלָא אוֹרַיְתָא, וְלָא יְהֵא
חוּסְרוֹן בְּבֵיתֵיהּ. וְלָא יְהֵא חוּסְרוֹן בְּנִשְׁמָתֵיהּ וְלָא יְהֵא חוּסְרוֹן בְּעוֹבָדוֹי טָבִין,
דְּלֵית חוּסֵר וַעֲנִיּוּת כְּחוּסֵר דְּאוֹרַיְתָא וּפִקּוּדַיָּיא טָבִין, כְּמָה דְּאוּקְמוּהוּ מָארֵי
מַתְנִיתִין, אֵין עָנִי אֶלָּא מִתּוֹרָה וּמִן הַמִּצְוֹת.

113. Since without Torah there is no awe, as said, "An ignoramus has
no fear of sin," (Tractate Avot 2:5) and as there is no Torah without fear,
so too there is no fear without Torah. There should be no lack in his
house, and neither a lack in his soul. And he should not lack in good
deeds, since no shortage and poverty can be compared to the deficiency
of Torah, precepts, and good deeds. As the masters of the Mishnah
established that there is no poverty other than (poverty) in Torah and
precepts.

114. דְּגוּפָא אִיהוּ עוֹבָדֵי יְדוֹי דְּבַר נָשׁ, לֵית חוּסֵר סַגִּי מִנֵּיהּ, בָּתַר דְּלַאו אִיהוּ
עוֹבָדוֹי דְּקוּדְשָׁא בְּרִיךְ הוּא. הָדָא הוּא דִכְתִיב אִם יְ"יָ לֹא יִבְנֶה בַיִת שָׁוְא
עָמְלוּ בוֹנָיו בּוֹ. וְדָא גָּרַם דְּיִתְחֲרַב בֵּי מַקְדְּשָׁא, דְּלָא הֲוָה עוֹבָדֵי יְ"יָ.

114. Meaning **if a person's handiwork are intended merely for the body, you have no bigger deficiency than this, since his activities do not relate to the Holy One blessed be He. This is what is written: "Unless the Lord builds the house, the builders labor in vain."** (Psalms 127:1) As was said to the High Priest (Kohen Gadol), "Be careful in your service, it should be for the sake of Heaven and desired because if it is not desirable your effort will amount to nothing." (Tractate Yoma 19b) **This caused the destruction of the Temple because they were not in the Lord's service.**

15. The eighth level in the awe of Heaven

115. דַּרְגָּא תְּמִינָאָה בִּירְאַת יְ"י. לְמֶהֱוֵי לֵיהּ בֹּשֶׁת אַנְפִּין, מָאן דְּאִית לֵיהּ בֹּשֶׁת אַנְפִּין, דְּלָא לְמֶעֱבַד עֲבֵירָה דְּאָתֵי לִידוֹי, בְּגִין דְּוֹחֵילוּ דְּקוּדְשָׁא בְּרִיךְ הוּא, כְּאִלּוּ בֵּיהּ אִתְבְּרִי עָלְמָא, וּבְגִין דָּא בְּרֵאשִׁי"ת: יָרֵ"א בֹּשֶׁ"ת. הֲרֵי יִרְאָה עִם בֹּשֶׁת כֹּלָּא חַד. וּמָאן דְּלֵית בֵּיהּ בֹּשֶׁת אַנְפִּין אוֹקְמוּהוּ מָארֵי מַתְנִיתִין בְּוַדַּאי שֶׁלֹּא עָמְדוּ רַגְלֵי אֲבוֹתָיו עַל הַר סִינַי.

115. The eighth level in the awe of Heaven is that one should feel shame. Whoever is shamefaced and does not commit a sin because of his awe of Heaven, it is considered as if the world was created for him. Therefore, the letters in Beresheet could be reorganized as *yare boshet* (fear of shame). So we see that fear together with shame are all one. And whoever is not shamefaced, the masters of the Mishnah established (Tractate Nedarim 20a) that certainly his ancestor's feet were not standing at Mount Sinai.

116. וַהֲפוֹךְ בֹּשֶׁ"ת, וְתִשְׁכַּח עֹֽבַ"ת. וְהַיְינוּ בְּרֵאשִׁית: יָרֵ"א שַׁבָּ"ת, דְּלָא תְּחַלֵּל לֵיהּ בְּפַרְהֶסְיָא, כְּבַר נַשׁ דְּלָאו בֵּיהּ בֹּשֶׁת אַנְפִּין. וַוי לֵיהּ מָאן דִּמְחַלֵּל שַׁבָּת מַלְכְּתָא, דְּאִיהִי קֹדֶשׁ, לְמֶעֱבַד לֵיהּ וֹוֹל. דְּאוּקְמוּהוּ מָארֵי מַתְנִיתִין, כָּל הַמִּשְׁתַּמֵּשׁ בְּתַגָּא וְחָלַף, זֶה הַמִּשְׁתַּמֵּשׁ בְּמִי שֶׁשּׁוֹנֶה הֲלָכוֹת. כָּל שֶׁכֵּן בְּשַׁבָּת מַלְכְּתָא.

116. Rearrange the letters of the word *boshet* בֹּשֶׁת (shame), and you will find the word *shabbat*. Rearrange the letters of Beresheet and you get *yare Shabbat* (fear of Shabbat) to not publicly profane it, as a person who has no shame. Woe to him who profanes Shabbat, the Queen, that is holy, and makes Her secular. He is even more so than the category of what was set by the masters of the Mishnah: "He who uses the crown [of Torah], passes away," (Tractate Megilah 28b) which relates to one who uses the service of one who studies Laws (*Halachot*). All the more so with relation to Shabbat, the Queen.

117. וְעוֹד, בּוֹשׁ פָּנִים לְגַן עֵדֶן. עַז פָּנִים לְגֵיהִנֹם. אִנּוּן דְּעָבְרִין עֲבֵירָה בְּיַד רָמָה, וְלֵית לוֹן בֹּשֶׁת אַנְפִּין מִקּוּדְשָׁא בְּרִיךְ הוּא, דְּאִתְּמַר בֵּיהּ מִשָּׁמַיִם הִבִּיט יְ"יָ רָאָה אֶת כָּל בְּנֵי הָאָדָם. וְאִתְּמַר בֵּיהּ, מְלֹא כָל הָאָרֶץ כְּבוֹדוֹ, וְאִתְּמַר בֵּיהּ וּחֹפֵשׂ כָּל חַדְרֵי בָטֶן רוֹאֶה כְּלָיוֹת וָלֵב.

117. In addition, said the masters: **"A shamed face to the Garden of Eden, and an impudent face to Hell (Gehenom)."** (Tractate Avot 5:20) Meaning those who sinfully transgress high handedly, and have no shame for the Holy One blessed be He, about them it says: **"From Heaven the Lord gazed and saw all mankind."** (Psalms 33:13) **And it says about Him: "The earth is full of His glory."** (Isaiah 6:3) **And it says about Him: "… searches out all the inward parts of the bell;"** (Proverbs 20:27) **"Sees the heart and the mind."** (Jeremiah 20:12)

118. וַעֲנָוָה קְטִירָא בִּדְחִילוּ, הֲדָא הוּא דִכְתִיב עֵקֶב עֲנָוָה יִרְאַת יְ"יָ. מָאן דְּאִית בֵּיהּ יִרְאַת יְ"יָ אַיְיתֵי לֵיהּ לִידֵי עֲנָוָה, דְּאִיהִי שְׁכִינְתָּא עִלָּאָה, דְּיִרְאַת יְ"יָ עֵקֶב לְגַבָּהּ. וְדָא דַרְגָּא דְמשֶׁה, דְּאִתְּמַר בֵּיהּ וְהָאִישׁ משֶׁה עָנָיו מְאֹד. וּבְגִין דְּאִיהִי יִרְאָה עֵקֶב לְגַבָּהּ. אוּקְמוּהָ מָארֵי מַתְנִיתִין יִרְאָה מִלָּה זוּטַרְתִּי הִיא לְגַבֵּי משֶׁה.

118. Humility is tied to awe, as is written: **"following humility is the fear (awe) of the Lord."** (Proverbs 22:4) **"Whoever has fear (awe) of the Lord will become humbled"** refers to the upper Shechinah, Leah, Malchut of Binah, **whose awe of the Lord,** namely Rachel, **is on her heels. This is the level of Moses, about whom is said: "And the man Moses was very humble,"** (Numbers 12:3) and because humility is at the heels of awe the masters of the Mishnah established that awe was a small matter to Moses.

16. The ninth level in the awe of Heaven

119. דַּרְגָּא תְּשִׁיעָאָה בְּיִרְאַת ה' כָּל מָאן דְּאִית בֵּיה יִרְאַת יְ"יָ יִתְהַלָּל. וְכִי אִית לְבַר נַשׁ לְשַׁבָּחָא גַּרְמֵיה. אֶלָּא אִיהוּ מְשֻׁבָּח קֳדָם יְ"י. הָדָא הוּא דִכְתִיב, שֶׁקֶר הַחֵן וְהֶבֶל הַיֹּפִי וגו' דָּא דָּרָא דְּחִזְקִיָּהוּ. דְּבְיִרְאַת יְ"י קָא אָתֵי בַּר נַשׁ לְקַיְימָא תַּרְיַ"ג מִצְוֹת, כְּחֻשְׁבַּן בְּיִרְאַ"ת.

119. The ninth level in the awe of Heaven is: Whoever has awe of Heaven should be praised. He asks, "Should then a person praise himself?" And answers, "Rather, he is praiseworthy before the Lord, as is written, 'Charm is deceptive, and beauty is fleeting....' (Proverbs 31:30) This refers to the generation of Hezekiah [Tractate Sanhedrin; page 20]. Since with the awe of Heaven a person comes to uphold all the 613 precepts. Also, the numerical value of 'with fear [lit. awe] (beyirat)' is 613."

17. The tenth level in the awe of Heaven

120. דַּרְגָּא עֲשִׂירָאָה בְּיִרְאַת י"י. אִית יִרְאָה וְאִית יִרְאָה. לָאו כָּל אַפַּיָּא שָׁוְיָן. אִית יִרְאָה דְּדָחִיל בַּר נַשׁ לְקוּדְשָׁא בְּרִיךְ הוּא, בְּגִין דְּלָא יִלְקֵה לֵיהּ בִּרְצוּעָה, דְּאִתְּמַר בָּהּ וְהָאָרֶץ הָיְתָה תֹהוּ וָבֹהוּ, מִסִּטְרָא דְּאִילָנָא דְּטוֹב וָרַע, דְּאִיהִי אַרְעָא רֵקַנְיָא שִׁפְחָה בִישָׁא. כְּגַוְונָא דְּחַד מֵאַרְבַּע אֲבוֹת נְזִיקִין, דְּאִיהוּ הַבּוֹר. וּכְגַוְונָא דְּבוֹר דְּיוֹסֵף, דְּאוֹקִמוּהוּ עֲלֵיהּ הַבֹּרָה, וְהַבּוֹר רֵק וכו'. הַבֹּרָה: נָקְבָא בִישָׁא. בּוֹר: דְּכוּרָא. וּבוֹר בְּגִין דְּאִיהוּ מִתַּמָּן, אוֹקִמוּהוּ עֲלֵיהּ, אֵין בּוֹר יְרֵא חֵטְא. בָּתַר דְּלֵית בֵּיהּ יִרְאַת י"י.

120. **The tenth level in the awe of Heaven. There is awe and there is awe,** and **not all aspects are equal. There is such awe when a person is scared that the Holy One blessed be He, might lash him with a strap, regarding which it is said:** "And the earth was without form and void…," (Genesis 1:2) **from the aspect of the Tree of Good and Evil. This type of awe is a land that is desolate and empty. An evil handmaiden** that is as evil as **a pit (bor), which is one of the four sources of harmful damage. Similar to the pit of Joseph, as they defined it** "And they sent him into **the pit (haborah), and the pit (bor) was empty…."** (Genesis 37:24) **"Into the pit (haborah)" is the wicked female** of the Klipah, **and "the pit (bor)" the male** of the Klipah: "And it was empty, it did not contain any water" (Ibid.), [water means] the Torah, **and because the bor is from there,** from the Klipah, **they established about it:** "No ignoramus (bur) fears sin," since he does not have that awe of the Lord. *Bor,* which means "pit," and *bur,* which means "ignoramous," are spelled the same.

121. מַאן דְּאִיהוּ דָּחִיל מִגּוֹ אוֹרַיְיתָא, דְּאִיהִי תִּפְאֶרֶת, דְּמִנֵּיהּ נָפְקַת. כְּגוֹן דָּא, אִיהִי עֲקוּלָא לְגַבֵּיהּ, וּבְגִין דָּא אֵין כָּל יִרְאָה שָׁוָה: דְּהָא יִרְאַת ה' הִיא מַלְכוּת דִּילֵיהּ, כְּלִילָא מִכָּל פִּקּוּדֵי אוֹרַיְיתָא בְּגִין דְּאִיהִי יִרְאָה דְּנָפְקַת מִגּוֹ תּוֹרָה, דְּאִיהוּ עַמּוּדָא דְּאֶמְצָעִיתָא, דְּאִיהוּ יהו"ה.

121. **One who has awe of Heaven as a result of Torah, which is Tiferet, from where it emanates,** as mentioned later, **to that degree is its value.**

Consequently, not every fear (awe) is equal, since the awe of the Lord is his Malchut, which encompasses all the precepts of the Torah. Thus, it was called the awe of Heaven **because it is an awe that results from Torah, which is the Central Column, which is Yud-Hei-Vav-Hei.** And because this awe results from the Torah, **which is** called Yud-Hei-Vav-Hei, therefore it is considered awe of Heaven.

122. דִּבְגִינֵיהּ אוּקְמוּהוּ מָארֵי מַתְנִיתִין, גְּדוֹלָה תּוֹרָה שֶׁמְּבִיאָה לְאָדָם לִידֵי מַעֲשֶׂה. דְּאִי בַּר נָשׁ לָא יָדַע אוֹרַיְיתָא, וְאַגְרָא דְּפִקּוּדַיָּיא דִּילָהּ, וְעוֹנְשִׁין דִּילָהּ לְמַאן דְּעָבַר עַל פִּקּוּדַיָא. וּמַאן הוּא דְּבָרָא לֵיהּ וּבָרָא אוֹרַיְתָא, וּמַאן הוּא דִּיהֵיב לָהּ לְיִשְׂרָאֵל, אֵיךְ דָּחִיל לֵיהּ, וְנָטַר פִּקּוּדוֹי.

122. Since about it, the masters of the Mishnah established: "Great is the Torah since it leads the person to take an action." If a person does not know the teachings of the Torah and the benefits attributed to its precepts, as well as the punishments for whomever transgresses the precepts, and if a person does not know who it is that created the Torah and who it is that gives it to Israel, how could he possibly fear Him and keep His precepts?

123. וּבְגִין דָּא, אָמַר דָּוִד לִשְׁלֹמֹה בְּנוֹ, דַּע אֶת אֱלֹקֵ"י אָבִיךָ וְעָבְדֵהוּ. דְּאִי בַּר נָשׁ לָא אִשְׁתְּמוֹדַע הַהוּא דִּיהֵיב לֵיהּ אוֹרַיְתָא, וּמַנֵּי לֵיהּ לְנַטְרָא לָהּ, אֵיךְ דָּחִיל מִנֵּיהּ, וְעָבִיד פִּקּוּדוֹי.

123. Therefore King David said to his son Solomon, "…know the God of your father and serve Him…." (I Chronicles 28:9) since if a person does not know He who gave him the Torah and instructed him to keep it, how could he fear Him and fulfill His precepts?

124. וּבְגִין דָּא אוּקְמוּהוּ רַבָּנָן, וְלֹא עַם הָאָרֶץ חָסִיד וְאֵין בּוּר יְרֵא חֵטְא. בְּגִין דְּאוֹרַיְתָא דְּאִיהִי תְרֵ"א, מִתְּרֵין דַּרְגִּין אִתְיְהִיבַת, מֵחֶסֶד וּגְבוּרָה, דְּמִתְחַפְּנָן תְּרֵין פִּקּוּדִין, אַהֲבַת חֶסֶד וּדְחִילוּ דִּגְבוּרָה, דְּאִיהִי יִרְאָה. דִּבְהוֹן אִשְׁתְּלִימוּ

תַּרְיַ"ג פִּקוּדַיָא. וּבְגִין דְּכָל אוֹרַיְתָא וּפִקוּדַיָא מִתְּרֵין סִטְרִין אִתְיְהִיבַת, אוּקְמוּהוּ רַבָּנָן, וְלֹא עַם הָאָרֶץ חָסִיד וְאֵין בּוּר יְרֵא חֵטְא.

124. Therefore our masters established: "And no common simpleton is pious, nor could an ignoramus fear sin." Because Torah, which numerically is 611 was given from two levels, from Chesed and Gevurah. Two precepts were given from there—the love of kindness (Chesed) and fear of the judgment (Gevurah), which is awe. By these, the two precepts of love and fear, which are the secret of the first two precepts: "I am" and "You shall not have," **were 613 commandments completed. And because the entire Torah and its precepts were given from both ends, our masters have established: "No common simpleton could be pious, nor could an ignoramus fear sin."**

125. וְאִי תֵּימָא, הָא חֶסֶד גְּבוּרָה, דְּמִתַּמָּן מַלְכוּת אִיהִי אַהֲבָה וְיִרְאָה, אֵיךְ אוּקְמוּהוּ רַבָּנָן גְּדוֹלָה תּוֹרָה שֶׁמְּבִיאָה אָדָם לִידֵי מַעֲשֶׂה. דְּמֵהָכָא מַשְׁמַע דְּכָל הַקּוֹדֵם יִרְאָתוֹ לְחָכְמָתוֹ וְחָכְמָתוֹ מִתְקַיֶּימֶת.

125. If you ask, "We have here Chesed and Gevurah, from where Malchut illuminates with love and awe, so how did our masters state: 'great is the Torah since it leads the person to take an action,' since from here we learn, that a person who gives precedence to his awe before his wisdom, his wisdom endures?" (Avot, 3:9)

126. אֶלָּא כֹּלָּא קְשׁוֹט תִּפְאֶרֶת אִתְקְרֵי אָדָם, כְּגַוְונָא דִּילֵיהּ הֲוָה אָדָם ה"א דִּלְתַתָּא, דְּאוּקְמוּהוּ עֲלֵיהּ, דַּהֲוָה רִאשׁוֹן לְמַחֲשָׁבָה וְאַחֲרוֹן לְמַעֲשֶׂה. וּבְגִין דָּא אוּקְמוּהוּ רַבָּנָן יִשְׂרָאֵל עָלָה בְּמַחֲשָׁבָה לְבְּרָאוֹת, דְּאִתְּמַר עֲלַיְיהוּ אָדָם אַתֶּם.

126. He answers, "But all is true; Tiferet is called Adam. Similarly he, the lower Hei, namely Malchut, **is called Adam,** as the masters **explained that he was preconceived first in his thought, and was last in creation. As a result of this our masters have established: Israelites came as a**

thought to be created, about them it is said: "You My Sheep... are man [lit. *adam*]...." (Ezekiel 34:31)

127. אוּף הָכִי תִּפְאֶרֶת דְּאִיהוּ יְהֹו"ה, אִיהוּ רִאשׁוֹן לְמַחֲשָׁבָה דְּאִיהִי וְחָכְמָה עִלָּאָה. וְאַחֲרוֹן לְמַעֲשֶׂה דְּאִיהוּ י' מִן אדנ"י חָכְמָה תַּתָּאָה. יִרְאַת ה' מַלְכוּת דִּילֵיהּ.

127. Likewise, Tiferet, Zeir Anpin, which is Yud-Hei-Vav-Hei, is first in a thought that starts with the letter Yud in Supernal Wisdom, and last in actual action, which is the Yud of Alef-Dalet-Nun-Yud, the lower wisdom. Awe of Heaven is His (Malchut) Kingdom.

128. וּבְגִין דָּא אִתְּמַר בָּה אִשָּׁה כִּי תַזְרִיעַ אִתְּתָא אִית לָהּ לְאַקְדָּמָא בְּכָל פִּקּוּדַיָּא, דְּאִתְּמַר בָּה אִשָּׁה יִרְאַת יְ"י הִיא תִתְהַלָּל. וּבְגִין דָּא, מָצָא אִשָּׁה בְּקַדְמֵיתָא, מָצָא טוֹב. דְּאִתְּמַר בֵּיהּ טוֹב יְ"י לַכֹּל. וְאִי אַקְדִּים לָהּ בִּצְלוֹתָא, כְּמָה דְּאוּקְמוּהוּ אדנ"י שְׂפָתַי תִּפְתָּח, מִיָּד וַיָּפֶק רָצוֹן מֵיְ"י.

128. This is why it says: "If a woman has conceived..." (Leviticus 12:2) Meaning that the aspect of the woman must be given priority in all the precepts. As it says about her: "A woman who fears (is in awe of) the Lord, she is to be praised." (Proverbs 31:30) Therefore, it first says: "whoever finds a wife..." and only then it says "...finds good." (Proverbs 18:22) About him it says: "The Lord is good to all" (Psalms 145:9) and if he puts her ahead in his prayer, as they established: "Lord (Adonai), open You my lips...," (Psalms 51:17) immediately "he obtains favor from the Lord." (Proverbs 18:22)

129. וּבְגִין דָּא, כַּוָּנָה דְּאִיהִי מַחֲשָׁבָה, צָרִיךְ לְאַקְדָּמָא לְמִצְוָה וּבְגִין דָּא עַוִּיאוּ רַבָּנָן, כַּוֵּין מַחֲשָׁבְתָּא דִּצְלוֹתָא בְּבִרְכָה קַדְמָאָה. דְּהָכִי אוּקְמוּהוּ, אִם לָא כַּוֵּין בְּבִרְכָה רִאשׁוֹנָה חוֹזֵר לָרֹאשׁ.

129. Consequently, intention (*kavanah*), which is thought, needs to be before the precept. Therefore our masters have organized to direct the

intention at the first blessing of the prayer because they have established that if he did not direct his intention at the first blessing he must return to the beginning.

בְּגִין דָּא, צָרִיךְ לְאַקְדְמָא יִרְאָה מִסִּטְרָא דִּשְׁכִינְתָּא בֵּין בְּאוֹרַיְתָא בֵּין .130
בְּפִקּוּדַיָּא. אֲבָל מִסִּטְרָא דְקוּדְשָׁא בְּרִיךְ הוּא, צָרִיךְ לְאַקְדְמָא אוֹרַיְתָא
לְיִרְאָה בְּכָל פִּקּוּדַיָּא. דְּיִרְאָה דְּאוֹרַיְתָא אִית, דְּאִתְקְרֵי נוּקְבָּא תּוֹרָה שֶׁבְּעַל
פֶּה דִּבְגִינָהּ אִתְּמַר תַּמָּן, אָז יְרַנְּנוּ עֲצֵי הַיָּעַר. עָנָה מַלְאָךְ מִן הַשָּׁמַיִם, וְאָמַר,
הֵן הֵן מַעֲשֵׂה מֶרְכָּבָה.

130. Therefore, from the aspect of the Shechinah, namely Malchut, **awe must be placed first, both in Torah and in precepts. But from the aspect of the Holy One blessed be He,** namely Zeir Anpin, **Torah needs to be placed before awe in all of the precepts because when there is** awe **resulting from Torah, the Nukva is called Oral Torah, and pertaining to Her it was said there: "Then (az) all the trees of the forest will sing...."** (I Chronicles 16:33) **An angel from Heaven responded: "These, these, are the Workings of the Chariot."**

מֵהַאי אָ"ז תַּלְיָין ע"ב שְׁמָהָן דְּהַיְינוּ חֶסֶד. דְּבֵיהּ צָרִיךְ לְאַתְקָנָא כָּרְסַיָּא .131
לְמָארֵיהּ בְּכַנְפֵי מִצְוָה, וְיָשַׁב עָלָיו בֶּאֱמֶת, עָשׂוֹר אֱמֶת. מ"ה יו"ד ק"א, וא"ו
ק"א מוֹרִיד הַטַּל, לְאַנְהָרָא לְגַבֵּי ה"א. דְּאִיהוּ כְּלִיל תְּלַת בִּרְכָאָן קַדְמָאִין
דִּצְלוֹתָא, וּתְלַת בַּתְרָאִין.

131. From that az, meaning from the unification of the two Names Yud-Hei-Vav-Hei and Alef-Dalet-Nun-Yud, **72 Names hang,** the 72 Lights from the Name of 72, **is Chesed, which is** numerically 72 that hints to Chochmah that is clothed in Chasadim, **by which,** by the attribute of Chesed that is 72, **the throne** Malchut, **needs to be prepared for its Master,** Zeir Anpin, **by the wings of a precept (mitzvah).** (As explained in Zohar, Pinchas paragraph 256): **"A person will be distinguished by the 72 knots and bindings of Tzitzit, to attain the 72 bridges of the throne, which are 18 knots and bindings to each direction..."** Meaning five knots and thirteen bindings equals eighteen, and four times for the four directions, altogether is 72: "...and He sat thereon in truth (*emet*)...," (Isaiah 16:5) which is Zeir Anpin, in the secret of the verse "You will give truth (*emet*) to Jacob." A tenth of *emet* (450) is 45, **Mem-Hei, which equals** the Yud-Hei-Vav-Hei spelled out with Alef: **Yud-Vav-Dalet, Hei-Alef, Vav-Alef-Vav, Hei-Alef, "Who brings down the dew (*tal*; 39)"** as the first nine Sefirot Yud-Vav-Dalet, Hei-Alef, Vav-Alef-Vav whose numerical value equals 39. Dew (*tal*) **to illuminate towards** the last **Hei-Alef,** meaning Malchut [and see Zohar, Pinchas 287]; "And about her we learned: like the image of Adam, is upon him from above...and is called in the Name Yud-Vav-Dalet, Hei-Alef, Vav-Alef-Vav, Hei-Alef, since Malchut is called by the Name Mem-Hei (45). And Hei–Alef is numerically six, hinting to the illumination of Zeir Anpin, **which includes the first three blessings in the prayer** of the Amidah (*Shmone Esre*), which are Chesed, Gevurah, and Tiferet, **and the last three,** which are Netzach, Hod, and Yesod.

18. "One golden pan of ten [sanctuary] shekels..."

132. וְדָא עֶשֶׂר סְפִירוֹת בְּלִי מָה. דְּאִינּוּן לְקָבְבְלַיְיהוּ תְּרֵין שְׁמָהָן יְקֹו"ק אדנ"י. וּתמַנְיָא אַתְוָון. דְּאִינּוּן עֲשָׂרָה עֲשָׂרָה הַכַּף עֲשָׂרָה בְּשֶׁקֶל הַקֹּדֶשׁ, וְדָא כ' מִן כֶּתֶר עֲשָׂרָה מִן שְׁכִינְתָּא תַּתָּאָה אדנ"י מִתַּתָּא לְעֵילָא מִן אֲנִ"י עַד אַיִ"ן עֲשָׂרָה מֵעֵילָא לְתַתָּא מֵעַמּוּדָא דְאֶמְצָעִיתָא דְּאִיהוּ יהו"ה. וּבְגִין דָא כ' כְּלִיל לוֹן.

132. This, meaning the ten letters of the Name Mem-Hei, **are Ten Sefirot without substance, which correspond to the two Names Yud-Kei-Vav-Kei and Alef-Dalet-Nun-Yud, and the eight letters** of the two Names, **totaling ten.** And since each Name is composed of the Ten Sefirot, **which are "...one golden pan (kaf) of ten shekels."** (Numbers 7:80) **This is the kaf of Keter** that includes **Ten Sefirot from the lower Shechinah,** meaning Malchut, **which is Alef-Dalet-Nun-Yud, from below upward,** meaning the Ten Sefirot of the Returning Light **from ani (me; Alef-Nun-Yud),** which is Malchut, **to ayin (nothingness; Alef-Yud-Nun),** which is Keter. **The Ten** Sefirot of Direct Light **from above downward, from the Central Column, Tiferet, which is Yud-Hei-Vav-Hei, and therefore kaf,** which alludes to Keter, which is the root-source, **includes them.**

133. וּבְקֵץ דְּפוּרְקָנָא, מְ'דַלֵּג עַל הֶ'הָרִים, דָּא מ"ה, וְלֵית הָרִים, אֶלָּא אֲבָהָן, דְּאִינּוּן מֶרְכַּבְתֵּיהּ. אוּף הָכִי מְ'קַפֵּץ עַל הַ'גְּבָעוֹת אִנּוּן אִמָּהָן, אקְי"ק אדנ"י. בְּהַהוּא זִמְנָא, אָ"וֹ יָשִׁיר מֹשֶׁה וכו', וְכֹלָּא אִתְקְשַׁר וְאִתְכְּלִיל בּוֹ"י בְּרְכָאן דִּצְלוֹתָא, דְּכְלִיקָן בּוֹ"י עָלְמִין. הָדָא הוּא דִכְתִיב בְּרָכוֹת לְרֹאשׁ צַדִּיק.

133. At the final redemption: "...leaping (m'daleg) over the mountains (heharim)," (Song of Songs 2:8) and Rashi explains: "for the sake of the mountains." (Tractate Rosh Hashanah 11) **This** acronym **is Mem-Hei (45), and "mountains" refer only to the Patriarchs, who are His chariot,** as mentioned that the Patriarchs are the chariot, Chesed, Gevurah and Tiferet. **Similarly: "jumping (mekapetz) over the hills (hag'va'ot),"** (Ibid), is also Mem-Hei (45). **Hills (hag'va'ot) are the Matriarchs: Alef-Kei-Yud-Kei,** meaning Binah, and **Alef-Dalet-Nun-Yud, meaning Malchut. At that**

period of time: "Then (*Az*) Moses will sing...." (Exodus 15:1) Similarly the Zohar (Beresheet A, 248) says, "About that time we learn about Moses and the Israelites: 'then (*az*) you will take pleasure in the Lord.'" "Pleasure" (*oneg*) contains the letters Ayin עָ, Nun גָ, Gimel גָ, which are the acronym of Eden עֵדֶן, River נָהֵר, Garden גַּן. Upholding that scriptural verse starting with: "Then (*Az*) Moses will sing...." (Exodus 15:1) "Eden" is the secret of Alef-Hei-Yud-Hei, which is Binah. "River" is Zeir Anpin–Mem-Hei (45). "Gan" is Malchut, Alef-Dalet-Nun-Yud. **And everything, all these specific unifications and Names, connect and are comprised in the eighteen blessings of the Amidah (18)** *Shmone Esre* **prayer service, which are included in the [righteous] life of the world,** (*chai*, meaning "life," is numerically 18) **which is why it says: "Blessings to the head of the Righteous,"** (Proverbs 10:6) referring to the Yesod that unites them, one with the other. [See Zohar, Pinchas 308] **Alef-Dalet-Nun-Yud in action, Yud-Kei-Vav-Kei, in speech, Alef-Kei-Yud-Kei in thought.**

134. וְאִית כָּבוֹד נִבְרָא, כִּגְוְונָא דְכָבוֹד נֶאֱצָל. מִסִּטְרָא דְכָבוֹד נִבְרָא, אָמְרִין יִשְׂרָאֵל לְגַבֵּי אָדוֹן עַל כֹּלָּא, אִם כַּעֲבָדִים. וּמִסִּטְרָא דְכָבוֹד נֶאֱצָל אִתְּמַר בְּהוֹן אִם כְּבָנִים.

134. There is a created honor, as mentioned above [verse 96] that there is no other meaning for honor but Torah, and that is the Torah of Briyah (Creation), **as there is an emanated honor,** Torah of Atzilut (Emanation). **From the aspect of the created honor, Israel say to the Master of all: "if like servants," and from the aspect of the emanated honor, it is said about them,** Israel: "**if like children.**"

135. אִיהוּ עִלַּת עַל כֹּלָּא, לֵית אֱלוֹהַּ עֲלֵיהּ, וְלָא תְוֹוֹתֵיהּ, וְלָא לְאַרְבַּע סִטְרִין דְּעָלְמָא אִיהוּ מְמַלֵּא כָּל עָלְמִין וְאִיהוּ אַסְחַר לְכָל סִטְרָא, דְּלָא מִתְפַּעְטִין יַתִּיר מִגְּבוּל דְּשַׁוֵּי לְכָל חַד, וּמִדָּה דְּשַׁוֵּי לְכָל חַד. וְכֻלְּהוּ בִּרְשׁוּ דִּילֵיהּ, בִּרְשׁוּת הַיָּחִיד.

135. He, meaning the Endless Light, **is above everything. There is no Godly-power over and above Him, nor below Him, and neither in any of the four directions of the world. He fills all the worlds,** with the Internal Light. **He surrounds all directions, and they do not expand beyond the boundaries that He assigned to each one, and from the measured size that He prepared for each one. All is within His domain, His private domain** of the Endless Light, blessed is He.

136. אדנ"י, מֶרְכָּבָה לַיהו"ה, וּבָהּ אִתְעַטַּף. וְאוּף הָכִי יהו"ה אִתְעַטַּף בְּאהי"ה, לְמִבְרֵי עָלְמָא. אֲבָל שֵׁם יהו"ה, אִיהוּ מֶרְכָּבָה לְמָארֵיהּ, לְכֶתֶר עִלָּאָה. וּבְגִין דָּא, אֵין קָדוֹשׁ כַּיְ"יָ.

136. The Name Alef-Dalet-Nun-Yud is the chariot to the Name Yud-Hei-Vav-Hei, meaning **it reveals its illumination,** like the rider is revealed through his chariot, **and through it He covers Himself. So too the Name Yud-Hei-Vav-Hei is covered in the Name** Alef-Hei-Yud-Hei **to create the world. But the Name Yud-Hei-Vav-Hei is a chariot to its Master, which is the Supernal Keter (Crown). Therefore,** it is written: **"There is no holy sanctity like the Lord (Yud-Hei-Vav-Hei)."** (Samuel I 2:2)

137. עִלַּת עַל כֹּלָּא טָמִיר וְגָנִיז בְּכֶתֶר, וּמִנֵּיהּ אִתְפַּשַּׁט נְהוֹרֵיהּ, עַל יקו"ק דְּאִיהוּ: י' חָכְמָה. ה', בִּינָה. ו', כְּלִיל שִׁית סְפִירָן. ה', מַלְכוּת. וְהַאי אִיהוּ אִתְפַּשְׁטוּתֵיהּ מֵעֵילָא לְתַתָּא.

137. The Cause of All, meaning the Endless Light, blessed be He, **is concealed and hidden in Keter,** and this is the secret of tip of the Yud of Yud-Hei-Vav-Hei, **and from it,** from Keter, **the Light** of the Endless Light, blessed be He, **expanded over the** four letters of the Name **Yud-Kei-Vav-Kei, which are: Yud–Chochmah, the first Hei–Binah, Vav–that comprises the six Sefirot:** Chesed, Gevurah, Tiferet, Netzach, Hod, and Yesod. **The last Hei–Malchut. This is the expansion** of the Direct Light **from above downward.**

138. וְאוֹף הָכִי אִתְפַּשַּׁט נְהוֹרֵיהּ, עַל י' מִן אדנ"י, מִתַּתָּא לְעֵילָא, עַד אֵין סוֹף, דְּאִתְרַבִּיוּ בְּאדנ"י אַיִ"ן. ב וּבְגִין דָּא י' י' מִן יאקדונה"י, עֲשָׂרָה עֲשָׂרָה הַכַּף דָּא כ' מִן כֶּתֶר. וּמָארֵי דְּכלָּא לֵית בֵּיהּ צִיּוּר דְּאוֹת וּנְקוּדָה, הָדָא הוּא דִכְתִיב וְאֶל מִי תְדַמְיוּנִי וְאֶשְׁוֶה וְאֶל מִי תְדַמְיוּן אֵ"ל וּמַה דְּמוּת תַּעַרְכוּ לוֹ.

138. So too, His Light expands over the Yud of the Name Alef-Dalet-Nun-Yud, in the secret of the Binding by Striking from below upward, the secret of the Ten Sefirot of the Returning Light, until the Endless Light. Thus, in the Alef-Dalet-Nun-Yud is alluded the word *ayin* (nothingness), meaning the Endless Light. Consequently, Yud, Yud, from the combination Yud-Alef-Hei-Dalet-Vav-Nun-Hei-Yud, which contains twice the Ten Sefirot from the Direct Light and the Returning Light, and this is the secret of "ten [lit. ten, ten] sanctuary shekels per ladle." This is the letter Kaf of Keter. And the Master of all, meaning the Endless Light, blessed be He, contains no delineating picture of any letter or dot. This is what it says: "And to whom will you compare Me, that I will be equal." (Isaiah 40:25) "To whom then will you liken God or what likeness will you compare Him to?" (Ibid. 18)

139. אִיהוּ צַיֵּיר בִּתְרֵין אַתְוָון, תְּרֵין עָלְמִין. בְּאָת י' צַיֵּיר עָלְמָא דְּאָתֵי. וּבְאָת ה' עָלְמָא דֵין. הָדָא הוּא דִכְתִיב, כִּי בְּי"ה י"י צוּר עוֹלָמִים וּמְקוֹרִין דְּכָל שְׁמָהָן אִינּוּן: יו"ד ה"י ו"יו ה"י, יהו"ה. יו"ד ה"א וא"ו ה"א יהו"ה. כָּל יו"ד אִיהִי אַוְחֲזֵי יהו"ה. כָּל א' אַוְחֲזֵי אהי"ה לְעֵילָא. אדנ"י לְתַתָּא.

139. With the two letters, Yud-Hei, He depicted the two worlds, the World to Come and this world. With the letter Yud, He drew the World to Come, and with the letter Hei, He drew this world, as it says: "... for the Lord is God (Yud-Hei), an everlasting Rock." (Isaiah 26:4) The sources of all the Names are Yud-Vav-Dalet, Hei-Yud, Vav-Yud-Vav, Hei-Yud, which equals the numerical value of the Ayin-Bet (72) Name of Yud-Hei-Vav-Hei. Yud-Vav-Dalet, Hei-Alef, Vav-Alef-Vav, Hei-Alef, which equals the numerical value of the Mem-Hei (45) Name of Yud-Hei-Vav-Hei. Each Yud indicates, that is to say alludes to the Name Yud-Hei-

Vav-Hei. Each Alef indicates, meaning to say, alludes to the Name **Alef-Hei-Yud-Hei above,** meaning Binah, **and** the Name **Alef-Dalet-Nun-Yud below,** meaning Malchut.

140. הָכָא שֵׁם יהו"ה אִיהוּ בְּכִנּוּיֵיהּ וַד, בְּגִין דְּמִנֵּיהּ אִשְׁתְּכַח כִּנּוּיֵיהּ. אֲבָל מִסִּטְרָא דַעֲשַׂר סְפִירָן דִּבְרִיאָה, לָאו שֵׁם יהו"ה וְכִנּוּיֵיהּ וַד. הָדָא הוּא דִכְתִיב, כֹּל הַנִּקְרָא בִשְׁמִי וְלִכְבוֹדִי בְּרָאתִיו כו'. הֲרֵי דְאִית סְפִירוֹת אִתְקְרִיאוּ בְּשֵׁם יהו"ה, וּבְשֵׁם אדנ"י, וְאִנּוּן דְּאדנ"י אִתְבְּרִיאוּ.

140. Here, in the World of Atzilut, **the Name Yud-Hei-Vav-Hei is with its appellation as one, since the appellation is found from it. However, from the aspect of the Ten Sefirot of Briyah the Name Yud-Hei-Vav-Hei and its appellation are not one. As it is written: "All that is called by My Name and for My honor, I created it...."** (Isaiah 43:7) **So there** are **Sefirot that are called by the Name Yud-Hei-Vav-Hei** and there are Sefirot called by **the Name Alef-Dalet-Nun-Yud, and those** Sefirot by the Name **Alef-Dalet-Nun-Yud illuminate in Briyah.**

141. וּבְגִין דָּא, אִית שְׁמָהָן דַּמְיָין לְחוֹתָמָא דְּמַלְכָּא, דִּבְהוֹן אִשְׁתְּמוֹדַע דְּיוּקְנָא דְּמַלְכָּא וּמַטְרוֹנִיתָא, צִיּוּרָא מַמָּשׁ. וְאִית שְׁמָהָן דְּאִינּוּן כְּגַוְונָא דִרְשִׁימוּ דְּצִיּוּרָא דְּחוֹתָמָא בְּשַׁעֲוָה, וְהָכִי דְּוְחִילִין מֵהַהוּא רְשִׁימוּ, כְּאִילּוּ הֲוָה מַלְכָּא מַמָּשׁ. אֲבָל אָדוֹן עַל כֹּלָּא, לֵית לֵיהּ מִכָּל אִלֵּין צִיּוּרִין כְּלָל. הָדָא הוּא דִכְתִיב וְאֶל מִי תְּדַמְּיוּן אֵ"ל וכו'.

141. As a result, there are Names similar to the King's Seal, by which the form of the King and Queen are recognizable—a real drawing. Then, there are also Names that are like a drawing impressed on wax. And so there is awe and fear from that stamped marking in the King's Seal, **as if it was the King himself. But the Master of all,** meaning the Endless Light, blessed be He, **has none of these depictions, at all. As it is written: "And to whom will you liken Me...?"** (Isaiah 40:25)

142. וּמִסִּטְרָא דְּצִיּוּרִין דְּשַׁעֲוָה, תַּמָּא יְחֶזְקֵאל כָּל אִלֵּין מַרְאוֹת דְּוָחָמָא. וּבְגִין דָּא אִתְּמַר בְּהוֹן, וּדְמוּת כְּמַרְאֵה אָדָם, וְלָא מַרְאֶה מַמָּשׁ. כְּמַרְאֵה וַשְׁמַ"ל, וְלָא וַשְׁמַ"ל. כְּמַרְאֵה אֵשׁ בֵּית לָהּ סָבִיב הוּא מַרְאֶה דְּמוּת כְּבוֹד יְ"יָ, וְלָא כְּבוֹד יְ"יָ מַמָּשׁ, אֶלָּא מַרְאֶה צִיּוּר דִּילֵיהּ.

142. And from that aspect of the drawing in wax, which is from the World of Formation, did Ezekiel see all those visions, as it says about them: "...and a likeness like the appearance of man..." (Ezekiel 1:26) but not an actual appearance, "...as an appearance of fire (*chashmal*) [lit. electricity]" (Ezekiel 1:27) but not a vision of fire, "so was the radiance around him. This was the appearance of the likeness of the glory of the Lord." (Ibid. 28) Not actually the Lord's glory, but a vision, just His depiction.

19. The secret of the structure of Ezekiel in the secret of the dots

143. פָּתַח וְאָמַר, יְחֶזְקֵאל נְבִיאָה קוּם מִשֵּׁינָתָךְ, לְגַלְּאָה הָכָא מַרְאוֹת דְּאִתְגַּלְיָין לָךְ. דְּכֻלְּהוּ לְנַצְבָּךְ בְּאֹרַח סָתִים, וּבְאִתְגַּלְיָא. בְּאִתְגַּלְיָא, צִיּוּרִין. אֲבָל בִּסְתִימוּ דְּעַיְינִין, דְּיוֹקְנָא דְּמַלְכָּא וּמַטְרוֹנִיתָא. כָּל שֶׁכֵּן וְכָל שֶׁכֵּן הַהוּא דְּלֵית לֵיהּ דְּיוֹקְנָא, דִּבְגִינֵיהּ אִתְּמַר הַאי קְרָא, לְמָאן דְּצַיֵּיר בֵּיהּ דְּיוֹקְנָא, אָרוּר הָאִישׁ אֲשֶׁר יַעֲשֶׂה פֶסֶל וכו' וְשָׂם בַּסָּתֶר בְּסִתְרוֹ שֶׁל עוֹלָם. וַאֲפִילּוּ מִכָּל מַה דְּבַר נַשׁ יָכִיל לְאַסְתַּכָּלָא בְּעֵינָא, וַאֲפִילּוּ מִכָּל דְּיוֹקְנִין דְּאִתְחֲזֵי לִנְבִיאֵי, צוּרַת הַדְּיוֹקְנָא דְּכָלִילָא מִכַּמָּה נְהוֹרִין.

143. The Faithful Shepherd **began and said, "Ezekiel the prophet rise from your sleep, to reveal here the visions that were revealed to you. Both, those** that shine **in a sealed manner,** meaning Supernal Aba and Ima, and those that shine **openly,** meaning Yisrael-Saba and Tevunah." He then explains, "Those that shine **openly are the images,** Lights revealed in Chochmah **but those that shine by closed eyes,** meaning by Lights covered from Chochmah, since eyes are Chochmah, is **the form of the King and Queen,** meaning a form stripped of any matter, **most definitely and certainly so, that which has no form at all,** meaning the Endless Light, blessed be He, that illuminates in a concealed manner. **Regarding someone who tries to draw a picture form of Him,** the Endless Light, blessed be He, **the verse says: 'Cursed is the person that will produce an engraved image… and places it in a concealed place,'** (Deuteronomy 27:15) **in the Concealed One of the world** [meaning to draw an image of the Concealed One of the world, namely, the Creator], **and even what a person could contemplate with his** logical **eye,** not necessarily an actual engraved image. **Even if it is from the forms that appeared in the visions of the prophets,** as is written: '…and in the hands of the prophets I shall be likened,' **that is, the likeness of the form that is composed from the many Lights,** meaning Malchut. As the masters said, 'All the prophets prophesied with *Ko* (so [said]);' all this is not applicable in the Light of the Endless, blessed be He because thought has no grasp in the Endless."

144. וַזֹד וּמִמַּעַל לָרָקִיעַ אֲשֶׁר עַל רֹאשָׁם, א כְּמַרְאֵה אֶבֶן סַפִּיר דְּמוּת כִּסֵּא, דָּא אֶבֶן סַפִּיר דְּמִתְכַּסֵּא וְאִיהוּ לְעֵילָּא, כְּגַוְונָא דָא א וְתַחַת רַגְלָיו כְּמַעֲשֵׂה לִבְנַת הַסַּפִּיר, כְּגַוְונָא דָא א וְכֹלָּא א'.

144. One vision: "And above the Firmament that is over their heads, was the likeness of a throne as the appearance of a sapphire stone…," (Ezekiel 1:26) which is the precious stone that gets covered, and it is higher above. Similar to this א; "and underneath His feet, was something like the paved working of the sapphire stone…" (Exodus 24:10). Similar to this א, and all is Alef.

145. נְקוּדָה דָא הוּא כְּגוֹן וֹלֶ"ם לְעֵילָּא, כֶּתֶר עֶלְיוֹן דְּרָכִיב עַל יָ"ה דְּאִינּוּן חָכְמָה וּבִינָה כְּחֻשְׁבַּן וֹלֶם וְתַחַת רַגְלָיו כְּמַעֲשֵׂה לִבְנַת הַסַּפִּיר וְזָרֵק וְדָא מַלְכוּת וְהָאָרֶץ הֲדוֹם רַגְלָי, אִיהִי תְּחוֹת ו"ה דְּאִיהוּ חֶשְׁבּוֹן חִרֵ"ק וְהָכִי סְלִיק יהו"ה יו"י.

145. This dot, called the sapphire stone, is like the vowel Cholem that is above the letters, and alludes to the Supernal Keter that rides upon Yud-Hei (15), which are Chochmah and Binah, as the numerical value of the word Cholem (78), which in small numerical value amounts to 15 like Yud-Hei (7+8=15), "…and under His feet is the paved work of the sapphire stone…" (Exodus 24:10) that refers to the Chirek that sits beneath the letters, which is Malchut, as it says: "…and the earth is My footstool" (Isaiah 66:1) that is under the letters Vav-Hei, amounting numerically to 11, the numerical value of Chirek (308) in small numerical value (3+0+8=11). This is how the letter Alef amounts to Yud-Hei-Vav-Hei (26), since the shape of Alef is a Vav with two Yud's, which in total equals 26 (Vav=6, Yud=10, Yud=10).

146. וְעוֹד רָקִיעַ דָא עַמּוּדָא דְּאֶמְצָעִיתָא דְּכָלִיל שֵׁם יהו"ה, וְאִיהוּ כְּלִיל שִׁית סְפִירָן בְּאֶמְצָעִיתָא דַּעֲלֵיהּ אִתְּמַר נָטוּי עַל רָאשֵׁיהֶם מִלְמַעְלָה דַּעֲלֵיהּ אִתְּמַר נוֹטֶה שָׁמַיִם כַּיְרִיעָה, כְּגַוְונָא דָא א בְּאֶמְצַע א נוֹטֶה שָׁמַיִם לְבַדִּי. מָאן נָטָה לֵיהּ. עָלַת עַל כֹּלָּא. לְבַדּוֹ: יְחִידָא בְּלָא תִנְיָינָא לְמֶעֱבַד לֵיהּ.

146. Also, it could be defined that **this Firmament is the Central Column,** namely Zeir Anpin **that includes the Name Yud-Hei-Vav-Hei, and it includes Six Sefirot,** Chesed, Gevurah, Tiferet, Netzach, Hod, and Yesod, **in the middle.** Since it rises and regulates between the Right and Left of Yisrael-Saba and Tevunah, in the secret of "three emanate from one," **about which it is said: "...stretched over their heads from above,"** (Ezekiel 1:22) **and about which it is said: "...Who stretches out the Heavens like a curtain." (Psalms 104:2) It is like this line in the middle of the letter Alef: "...that stretched forth the Heavens alone...." (Isaiah 44:24) Who stretched it out? The Cause of all Causes, Himself, alone, independently, without another to help Him.**

147. תִּנְיָינָא וְעַל דְּמוּת הַכִּסֵּא דְּמוּת כְּמַרְאֵה אָדָם עָלָיו מִלְמָעְלָה. דָּא אִיהוּ יֹו"ד הֵ"א וָא"ו הֵ"א כְּלִיל תֵּשַׁע נְקוּדִין וַעֲשִׂירָאָה שְׁכִינְתָּא כְּלִילָא מִכֹּלְהוּ.

147. The second vision is: "And above the Firmament that was over their heads was the likeness of a throne...." (Ezekiel 1:26) **This is Yud-Hei-Vav-Hei of Mem-Hei (45), which includes the nine vowels, and the tenth is the Shechinah,** Malchut, inclusive of all.

148. וְכֹלָּא א דְּלֵית אָדָם בְּלָא א'. וְכֹלָּא אִיהוּ עַמּוּדָא דְּאֶמְצָעִיתָא אִיהוּ יְהֹו"ה דְּכָלִיל וְאִיהוּ שְׁמָא מְפָרַשׁ דְּכָלִיל א. לְאַחֲזָאָה דְּאִם רָץ לִבְּךָ שׁוּב לְאָחוֹר.

148. This entire correction is hinted at in the letter **Alef since there is no man,** the secret of the Light of the face, in the secret of "The wisdom of man illuminates his face," **that exists without Alef,** which is the secret of clothing Chochmah in Chasadim. **All is the Central Column, which is the Yud-Hei-Vav-Hei, inclusive of the** letter **Alef, and it is the Explicit Name that includes the Alef,** meaning Yud-Hei-Vav-Hei of Mem-Hei (45) when spelled out with the full Alef letters, **to indicate "should your heart run forward"** to draw the Chochmah from above downward **"draw back"** (Book of Formation, Chapter 1), and you will arouse the curtain of the Chirek with both actions, by which the Left Column diminishes, and it returns to be Mochin [Light] of the face.

149. תְּלִיתָאָה כְּמַרְאֵה אֵשׁ בֵּית לָהּ סָבִיב וְדָא שְׁכִינְתָּא. דְּהָכִי אוּקְמוּהוּ רַבָּנָן דְּנִשְׁמָתִין דּוֹמִין קֳדָם שְׁכִינְתָּא כִּנֵּרוֹת לִפְנֵי הָאֲבוּקָה. וּבְגִין דָּא כְּמַרְאֵה אֵשׁ בֵּית לָהּ, וְאִיהִי בֵּית כְּנִישְׁתָּא דִלְעֵילָא, אָ"שׁ נֹגַ"הּ, כִּי בֵיתִי בֵּית תְּפִלָּה יִקָּרֵא לְכָל הָעַמִּים.

149. The third vision is: **"as the appearance of fire round about enclosing it [her],** (Ezekiel 1:27) **and that is the Shechinah. Since so have the masters established: the souls** of the righteous **are similar before the Shechinah, like candles before a torch.** (Tractate Psachim 8a) **Therefore** it says regarding the Shechinah: **"as the appearance of fire round about enclosing it [her]," and this refers to the Supernal House of Congregation,** meaning Binah, since the souls of the righteous receive from the aspect corresponding to them, which is Binah. **And it is called the fire of radiance** (*nogah*), in the secret of: **"Since my house is to be called a house of prayer for all the nations."** (Isaiah 56:7)

150. וְאִיהִי אֵשׁ בֵּית לָהּ מִסִּטְרָא דִגְבוּרָה, דְּאִיהִי ב', יוֹמָא תִנְיָינָא, דְּאִתְבְּרֵי בֵּיהּ גֵּיהִנָּם. א', יוֹמָא קַדְמָאָה דְּאִתְבְּרֵי בֵּיהּ גַּן עֵדֶן, וְדָא חֶסֶד. עַמּוּדָא דְּאֶמְצָעִיתָא, כְּמַרְאֵה אָדָם כְּלִיל תַּרְוַיְהוּ. וָא"וּ לִימִינָא. ל"ב יוֹ"ד ה"א ה"א.

150. He explains, how Binah includes Chesed, Gevurah, Tiferet, Netzach, and Hod and spreads into them, and says: **It is "fire round about enclosing it"** (Ibid.), **from the aspect of Gevurah,** in the secret of: "I am Binah, for mine is the Gevurah," **which is the Bet, the second day, in which Gehenom (Hell) was created,** which is the Left Column. **Alef is the first day, in which the Garden of Eden was created, and this is Chesed,** the Right Column. **The Central Column is Tiferet: "...as the appearance of a man..."** (Ezekiel 1:26) **including both Right and Left. Vav to the Right,** meaning Chasadim, **Lamed-Bet (32),** as also the combination of the letters **Yud-Hei-Hei** spelled out as Yud-Vav-Dalet; Hei-Alef; Hei-Alef (which together equals 32) to the Left, the illumination of Chochmah in the Left, Thirty-Two Paths of Wisdom (Chochmah) that are clothed in the Chasadim of the Right, and both shine in the secret of the Name Mem-Hei (45), which is the numerical value of Vav-Alef-Vav (13) plus Lamed-Bet (32).

151. מִבַּוְרְאֵה מָתְנָיו וּלְמַעְלָה, וּמִבַּוְרְאֵה מָתְנָיו וּלְמַטָּה, אִינּוּן תְּרֵין שׁוֹקִין. תְּרֵין נְבִיאֵי קְשׁוֹט. וְאִינּוּן רְבִיעָאָה וַחֲמִשָּׁאָה לְחֶסֶד. דְּמִתַּמָּן בִּנְיָנָא דְּעָלְמָא. הָדָא הוּא דִּכְתִיב עוֹלָם חֶסֶד יִבָּנֶה ה'. עִלָּאָה אִתְפַּשְּׁטַת עַד הוֹד, וַחֲמִשִׁין תַּרְעִין. וּבְגִין דָּא קָא רָמִיז עָלָה, רָאִיתִי כְּמַרְאֵה אֵשׁ בֵּית לָהּ, וּבָהּ שֵׁשׁ מַרְאוֹת.

151. "From the appearance of his loins and upward...and from the appearance of his loins and downward," (Ezekiel 1:27) these are the two thighs, which are Netzach and Hod, two true prophets, and they are fourth and fifth to Chesed, from whence is the construction of the world. As is written: "Forever is mercy (Chesed) built...." (Psalms 89:3) The upper Hei, Binah, spreads to Hod, and comprises Chesed, Gevurah, Tiferet, Netzach, and Hod, each comprised of ten, thus totaling Fifty Gates. As a result of this, it is alluded about Binah: "...I saw as it were the appearance of fire...." (Ezekiel 1:27) And within Binah there are six visions.

152. שְׁבִיעָאָה כְּמַרְאֵה הַקֶּשֶׁת. הַקֶּשֶׁת: דָּא צַדִּיק יְסוֹד עָלְמָא. כְּמַרְאֵה דִּילָהּ לְתַתָּא מטטרו"ן, דָּא חֶזְוָא יְחֶזְקֵאל, דְּאִיהוּ כְּלִיל כָּל מַרְאוֹת. וְחֵזוּ תְּמִינָאָה כֵּן, מַרְאֵה הַנֹּגַהּ סָבִיב, דָּא שְׁכִינְתָּא תַּתָּאָה, דְּאִתְּמַר בָּהּ נְקֵבָה תְּסוֹבֵב גָּבֶר. וּבְגִין דָּא כֵּן מַרְאֵה הַנֹּגַהּ סָבִיב אֵשׁ נֹגַהּ.

152. The seventh vision is: "Like the appearance of the bow...." (Ezekiel 1:28) This bow is the righteous, the foundation of the world, meaning the crown of Yesod [see Zohar, Noach 267] like her appearance below, which is Metatron. Ezekiel saw him, meaning Metatron, who includes all the visions. The eighth vision: "...as the appearance of fire round about

enclosing" (Ibid.), **which** refers to **the lower Shechinah,** which is called by
the Name Elohim or Adonai. **Regarding which it says: "…a woman shall
court a man."** (Jeremiah 31:21) **As a result of this: "…there was radiance
(*nogah*) round about him,"** and it is called: **"The fire of radiance,"** meaning
house of prayer.

153. תְּשִׁיעָאָה הוּא מַרְאֶה דְּמוּת כְּבוֹד יְ"יָ, וְחָכְמָה עִלָּאָה, דְּמוּת דִּילָהּ וַזָּא
יְחֶזְקֵאל לְתַתָּא וְלָא וָחָכְמָה. וְכַד מָטָא לִדְמוּת כֶּתֶר דְּאִיהוּ דַרְגָּא עֲשִׂירָאָה,
וַחֲזֵי מַה כְּתִיב בֵּיהּ, וָאֶרְאֶה וָאֶפּוֹל עַל פָּנַי, דְּלָא יָכוֹל לְמִסְבַּל, וְאִם מַרְאוֹת
דִּלְתַתָּא הָכִי, כָּל שֶׁכֵּן וְכָל שֶׁכֵּן מַרְאוֹת עִלָּאִין דִּסְפִירוֹת דִּבְרִיאָה כָּל שֶׁכֵּן
וְכָל שֶׁכֵּן מַרְאוֹת דַּאֲצִילוּת.

153. The ninth vision **is: "The appearing image of the glory of the Lord,"**
(Ezekiel 1:28) which is the **Supernal Chochmah. Ezekiel had a vision of
Her lower image but not Chochmah,** meaning the Chochmah revealed in
Malchut. **When he reached the image of Keter, which is the tenth level,**
which is revealed in Malchut of Malchut, **see what is written about that:
"and when I saw it, I fell upon my face"** (Ezekiel 1:28) **because he was
unable to bear it. If the lower visions,** in Yetzirah, **are such, how much
more so are the Supernal visions of the Sefirot of Briyah (Creation),**
which only contain one curtain over them, **and even more so the visions of
Atzilut (Emanation),** which are completely without any curtain.

154. וּבְרָזָא דְאָת א, תִּשְׁכַּח וֹל"ם וְזֵיר"ק שׁוּרֶק, כְּגַוְונָא דָא וֹ, וְאִיהוּ גַּלְגַּל
דְּאִתְהַפַּךְ לְשִׁית סִטְרִין לְעֵילָא וּלְתַתָּא וּלְאַרְבַּע סִטְרִין, אִתְהַפַּךְ לִימִינָא וְסָהִיד
עַל עֲלַת עַל כֹּלָּא, דְּלֵית אֱלָךְ אָחֱרָא לִימִינָא דְעָלְמָא. אִתְהַפַּךְ לִשְׂמָאלָא,
וְסָהִיד עֲלֵיהּ. וְהָכִי לְכָל סִטְרָא סָהִיד עַל יִחוּדֵיהּ, דְּלֵית אֱלָךְ אָחֱרָא עֵילָא
וְתַתָּא וּלְאַרְבַּע סִטְרִין. הַאי אִיהוּ דְאוּקְמוּהוּ מָארֵי מַתְנִיתִין, כְּדֵי שֶׁתַּמְלִיכֵהוּ
עַל הַשָּׁמַיִם וְעַל הָאָרֶץ וְעַל אַרְבַּע רוּחוֹת הָעוֹלָם.

154. In the secret of the letter Alef **you will find** the vowels **Cholem,
Chirek, Shuruk, like this Vav** וֹ namely Melopum, which is a Vav with a
dot within, called Shuruk, and also a dot above and a dot below. **And it is a**

turning wheel to six ends, which are Chesed, Gevurah, Tiferet, Netzach, Hod, and Yesod. Above–Netzach, below–Hod, and to the four sides, which are Chesed–South; Gevurah–North; Tiferet–East; Yesod–West. It turns around to the right and testifies about the Cause of All, that there is no other God to the right side of the world. Turns around to the left and testifies about it, and so to each side, testifying about its singularity, that there is no other God above, below, and on all four sides. This is why it was set by the masters of the Mishnah to prolong the reciting of echad (one), to extend His reign over the Heavens and over the Earth and on all four directions of the world.

155. וְ' כְּלִיל תְּלַת נְקוּדִין, עֵילָּא וְתַתָּא וְאֶמְצָעִיתָא דְּסַהֲדִין. וּתְלַת סַהֲדִין תְּווֹתַיְיהוּ לְתַתָּא, עַל עִלַּת עַל כּלָּא, דְּאִיהוּ רִאשׁוֹן וְאַחֲרוֹן וּמִבַּלְעָדָיו אֵין אֱלֹקִי"ם, דְּאִיהוּ כְּלִיל שִׁית נְקוּדִין כְּחוּשְׁבַּן ו'. דְּסַהֲדִין עַל עִלַּת עַל כּלָּא, דְּלֵית אֱלֹוֹהַּ אָחֳרָא לְשִׁית סִטְרִין אֶלָּא הוּא. הָא תֵּשַׁע נְקוּדִין דְּכְלִילָן בְּאָת ו' מִן א. וְאָת א' בֵּיהּ אִשְׁתַּלִּימוּ לְעֶשֶׂר. וּבֵיהּ כֻּלְּהוּ אָזְלִין לַאֲתַר וְזָד. הָא הָכָא רָזָא דְּבִנְיָנָא דִּיחֶזְקֵאל, בְּרָזָא דִּנְקוּדִין.

155. The letter Vav includes three dots: above, below and in the middle, that testify, and three witnesses down below, that testify about the Cause of All, Who is first and last, and without or beside Him there is no Godly power (Elokim). Since it contains six dots like the numerical value of the letter Vav (6), and it testifies about the Cause of All that there is no other Godly power (Elokim) in the six ends, but Him. Together there are nine dots, contained in the letter Vav, from the Alef, and together with the letter Alef, where the Vav is, it completes them to ten dots. And all follow to one place by it. Here, therefore, is the secret of the structure of Ezekiel in the secret of the dots.

20. The secret of the vowels

156. וְעוֹד רָזָא נְקוּדֵי צָרִיךְ לְאַוְזָרָא עֲלַיְיהוּ. פָּתַח, בְּחוֹשְׁבַּן אוֹתִיוֹתָיו, אִיהוּ
יו"ד וּכְתִיב, פּוֹתֵחַ אֶת יָדֶךָ וּמַשְׂבִּיעַ לְכָל חַי רָצוֹן. וְאוּקְמוּהוּ, אַל תִּקְרֵי
יָדֶךָ, אֶלָּא יוּדֵ"ךָ, וְאִינּוּן י' י' מִן יאקדונה"י. וּבְאָן אֲתַר מִתְפַּתְּחִין. בִּרְקִיעָא,
דְּאִיהוּ פָּתַח, וְאִיהוּ מַפְתְּחָא, כְּלִיל אקדונ"ה, שִׁית אַתְוָון בְּאֶמְצַע י"י'. וּתְרֵין
יוּדִין עִם רָקִיעַ דְּאִיהוּ ו', סְלִיק לְחוּשְׁבַּן יְהֹוָ"ה.

156. **Furthermore, we need to repeat** and explain **the secret of the
vowels. The sum value of the letters** of the vowel **Patach** פָּתַח **(Pei-Tav-
Chet, 488) is 20,** in small numerical value **(4+8+8=20), which is the value
of Yud-Vav-Dalet (20).** The Rav Isaac Luria (the Ari) wrote that the
reason Rav Shimon uses the small numerical value is because his intention
is to correct the World of Asiyah (Action) within which small numerical
values exist. **And it is written: "Open (pote'ach) your hands (yadecha) and
satisfy the desire of each living thing,"** (Psalms 145:16) **and** the masters
**established: do not read yadecha (your hands) rather yud-echa (your
Yud's), referring to the two Yud's of** the interlinked Names Alef-Dalet-
Nun-Yud and Yud-Hei-Vav-Hei, which are Zeir Anpin and Nukva, **Yud-
Alef-Hei-Dalet-Vav-Nun-Hei-Yud. In which area are they opened?** The
answer is: **in the Firmament,** Yesod, **which is Patach (opening) and is a
key (maphte'ach)** that includes Alef-Hei-Dalet-Vav-Nun-Hei, **six letters in
between the two Yud's, and the two Yud's,** which equal twenty, **plus the
Firmament, which is six, amounts to the sum of Yud-Hei-Vav-Hei (26).**

157. קָמֵ"ץ, רָקִיעַ וְנִיצוֹץ, אִינּוּן י"ו, אִיהוּ קוֹמֶץ כָּל נְקוּדִין, דְּאִינּוּן שִׁית סָרֵי
כְּחוּשְׁבַּן שִׁית סָרֵי אַנְפִּין דְּחֵוְיָן, וּבְגִין דָּא, אִיהוּ קוֹמֶץ כָּל נְקוּדִין.

157. **In the vowel Kametz** קָמֵ"ץ **there is a Firmament and a spark,** which
is a line over a dot, **and they are like a Yud,** the spark, **and a Vav,** the line.
**The secret of the Kametz is the kometz (handful compression) of all the
vowels,** in the secret of resistance to enclothing, (see paragraph 87). **And
they,** the Firmament and the spark, **amount to sixteen, like the number**

in the sixteen faces of the Holy **Beasts** of the chariot, whereas the face of man is also composed of four, which amount to sixteen faces. **And as a result of this,** that each is inclusive of four faces, even the face of man, **it compresses (kometz) all the vowels,** so they will not illuminate to the bodies of the levels.

158. צֵרֵ"י אִיהוּ ווּשְׁבַן ו'"ו, וּתְחוֹת צַדִּיק תְּרֵין נִיצוֹצִין, דְּאִינוּן י"י אֶת שְׁנֵי הַמְּאוֹרוֹת הַגְּדוֹלִים, וְאִינּוּן ו'"ו י"י סַלְקִין ל"ב. וְאִינּוּן ל"ב נְתִיבוֹת פָּלִיאוֹת וָחָכְמָה. וּנְקוּדָה תְּחוֹת, מִן צֵרֵ"י דְּאִיהִי י', עֶשֶׂר סְפִירוֹת הֲרֵי מ'"ב. וּבְגִין דָּא צֵרֵ"י בֵּיהּ צָיֵיר עָלְמִין, וַיִּצֶר תַּפָּן צֵר"י, בֵּיהּ צָיֵיר אָדָם. הֲרֵי רָזָא דְּנָקִיד צֵרֵי מ'"ב, וּתְלַת אַתְוָון, הֲרֵי מ'"ה כְּווּשְׁבַן אָדָ"ם.

158. The vowel **Tzere** צֵרֵ"י (Tzadik=90, Resh=200, Yud=10) in the small numerical value is 12 (9+0, 2+0+0, 1+0=12), just like **the amount of two letter Vav's (6+6 = 12). Under** the letter **Tzadik** of Tzere are **two sparks** צ **the two Yud's (20),** and they allude to the scriptural verse: **"The two great lights,"** (Genesis 1:16) which are Zeir Anpin and Nukva. **Those two Vav's plus two Yud's amount to 32, and they are the Thirty-Two Paths of wonders of Wisdom (Chochmah). The dot under the Resh** of Tzere רֵ **is ten, and alludes to the Ten Sefirot; thus we have altogether 42 (32+10). Consequently, the Tzere contains the impression of** the two **worlds. Therefore: "He formed (vayitzer)," (Genesis 2:7) the Tzere** is alluded there; with the Tzere **He delineated and formed the man** [lit. *Adam*]. **We have here the secret of the vowel Tzere, which is 42, and the three letters** of the word **Tzere,** Tzadik, Resh, Yud, **together amount to** the value **of 45, like the sum value of Adam (Alef=1, Dalet=4, Mem=40).**

159. שְׁבָא אוּף הָכִי, אֶת הַמְּאוֹר הַגָּדוֹל לְמֶמְשֶׁלֶת הַיּוֹם וְאֶת הַמְּאוֹר הַקָּטֹן וְגוֹ', וּבֵיהּ רָזָא מ'"ב, וּבֵיהּ רָזָא דְּאָדָם, כְּגַוְונָא דָא, וְשַׁעְבַן שְׁבָא ו', וּתְלַת נִיצוֹצוֹת וְרָקִיעַ יי"ו, דְּווּשְׁבַנְהוֹן ל'"ו הֲרֵי מ'"ב. וּתְלַת אַתְוָון שָׁבָ"א, הֲרֵי מ'"ה. וְרָזָא דְּמִלָּה וְאָמְרוּ כְּ'י מַ'ה שְׁמֹ'ו מַ'ה אוֹמֵר אֲלֵיהֶם. וְנָקוּד שָׁבָ"א נָקִיד בְּשֵׁם יְהוֹ"ה בְּאוֹרַיְתָא.

159. The vowel Sh'va שְׁבָא is also the secret of: **"The greater light to rule the day, and the lesser light..."** (Genesis 1:16) **in it is the secret of 42, and in it is the secret of Adam (45), as follows: the value of Sh'va** (Shin=300, Bet=2, Alef=1) **is six** (3+0+0+2+1=6), **the three dots and the Firmament** of the punctuation of Sh'va (as Sh'va is two dots, and the Kametz is a dot and a line, thus three dots and a line) **are three Yud's and a Vav, which amount to 36.** The small numerical value of the letters in Sh'va (Shin=300, Bet=2, Alef=1) is six (3+0+0+2+1=6), **thus 42, and the actual three letters, Shin-Bet-Alef, with 42 equals 45. The secret of the matter is: "Ve'amru li mah Shmo Mah omar aleihem (and they will say to me 'what is His Name,' what shall I tell them?")** (Exodus 3:13) hinting at the end of the words *"...Li mah shmo mah..."* to the Name Yud-Hei-Vav-Hei, **and the vowel Sh'va is marked under the Yud of the Name Yud-Hei-Vav-Hei in the Torah.**

‏160. סֶגּוֹל וַ"י וְשֶׁבָנֵיה, וְאִיהוּ וו"ו מִן וַיִּסַּע וַיָּבֹא וַיֵּ"ט. וּתְלַת נְקוּדִין יי"י אִיהוּ ‏וֹ"ם. וְאַרְבַּע אַתְוָון מִן סֶגּוֹ"ל אִיהוּ וֹם"ד. וְתֵיבָה, הָא אִינוּן וַֽמֵּ"ה. פְּנֵי מֹשֶׁה ‏כִּפְנֵי וַֹמָּה.

160. The sum value of the letters **of Segol** סֶגּוֹל (Samech=60, Gimel=3, Vav=6, Lamed=30) **equals eighteen** (6+0+3+6+3+0=18), which is the value **of three Vav's (3x6) from** the scriptural verses: **"Vayisa, vayavo, vayet"** (Exodus 14:19-21), the secret of the 72 Names. **The three dots** of Segol **are like three Yud's (30), and together with** the three Vav's (18) together amounts to 48, which is: *cham* **(hot). And** together with **the four actual letters of Segol, it is 52, plus the word** itself **together, it is 53, which is** *chamah* **(sun), and this is the secret of: "The face of Moses is like the face of the sun."** (Bava Batra 75a)

‏161. וֹלֶם חָסֵר ו', וֹושֶׁבָנֵיה י"ק וּתְלַת נִיצוֹצוֹת יי"י, הָא אִינוּן מ"ה. שְׁמָא ‏מְפָרֵשׁ יו"ד ה"א ה"א וא"ו ה"א. וְעִם תְּלַת אַתְוָון וְתֵיבָה הָא אִיהוּ מ"ט, כְּחוּשְׁבָּן ‏מ"ט אַתְוָון שְׁמַע יִשְׂרָאֵל וכו' בָּרוּךְ שֵׁם כְּבוֹד וכו'.

161. The vowel **Cholem** וֹלֶם (Chet=8, Lamed=30, Mem=40), **without the Vav, amounts** in small numerical value to fifteen (8+3+0+4+0=15), which is **Yud-Hei, and the three sparks,** one dot on the Chet of Cholem, and the Tzere (two dots) under the Lamed, like this: וֹלֵם, create **Yud, Yud, Yud (30) that altogether equals 45, which is the Explicit Name** Yud-Hei-Vav-Hei spelled out with Alef: <u>Yud-Vav-Dalet; Hei-Alef; Vav-Alef-Vav; Hei-Alef.</u> **And with the three letters** Chet, Lamed, and Mem, **plus the word,** altogether **they are 49, like the number of letters in the verses of** *"Shema* **(Hear) Israel...,"** (Deuteronomy 6:4) which is 25, and together with the 24 letters of *"Baruch Shem Kevod..."* amounts to 49 letters.

162. וְאוּקְמוּהוּ רַבָּנָן דְּמַתְנִיתִין וַחֲמִישִׁים שַׁעֲרֵי בִּינָה נִבְרְאוּ בְּעוֹלָם, וְנִתְּנוּ לְמֹשֶׁה, חוּץ מֵאֶחָד, שֶׁנֶּאֱמַר וַתְּחַסְּרֵהוּ מְעַט מֵאֱלֹהִי"ם. וּלְתַתָּא בְּמַלְאָכִים, אִינּוּן מ"ט פָּנִים טָהוֹרַת מִן מטטרו"ן, דְּאִיהוּ וֹלֶ"ם בְּמַלְאָכִים.

162. The masters of the Mishnah explained (Tractate Rosh Hashanah 21b) **that Fifty Gates of Binah were created in the world, and were given to Moses, except one, as said: "You have made him but a little lower than the angles..."** (Psalms 8:6) meaning in worlds of Creation (Briyah), Formation (Yetzirah) and Action (Asiyah), **are the forty-nine faces of purity of Metatron, which is the** vowel **of Cholem among the angels.**

163. וֹר"ק עִם וֹושְׁבַן אַתְוָון, אִיהוּ א"ם וֹחֶרֶק וֹושְׁבַּנֵיהּ ו"ה, וּתְלַת נִיצוֹצוֹת י'י'י' תְּלָתִין הָא אִיהוּ א"ם.

163. The vowel Chirek וֹרֶק (Chet=8, Resh=200, Kuf=100) **with the** small **numerical value of the letters** of the word Chirek **is Alef-Mem (41).** He explains how the letter **value of Chirek is eleven, and the three sparks,** the dots under the letters וֹרֶק, **are Yud, Yud, Yud, which is thirty,** and with the number eleven are **altogether 41.**

164. שָׁרֶק אִיהוּ וֹושְׁבַן אַתְווֹי ו', וְוֹמֵשׁ נִיצוֹצוֹת וַחֲמִשִׁין, הָא נ"ו. תְּלַת אַתְוָון וְתֵיבָה, הָא אִנּוּן ס', סוֹד י"י לִירֵאָיו. וּבֵיהּ רָזוּ לְיַעֲקֹב שְׂמוֹחָה. דְּכַד נְקוּדֵי,

מֵחָכְמָה עִלָּאָה מִתְפַּשְׁטָאן, תִּשְׁעָה עַד מַלְכוּת. וְטַעֲמֵי, מִכֶּתֶר עַד מַלְכוּת.
וְשׁוּרֶ"ק צַדִּיק יְסוֹד עָלְמָא, בֵּיהּ סוֹד שׁוּרֶק תִּנְיָינָא, בְּתוֹסֶפֶת ו' מ"ב.

164. The numerical value of Shurek שׁוּרֶק (Shin=300, Resh=200,
Kof=100) in small numerical value **is six** (6+0+0) **and the five sparks** of
the vowel שׁוּרֶק, which are **fifty, and with the** numerical value **six** of the
letters, **together are 56.** The actual number of **the letters themselves is
three, with the word** it is four, **which is** 60, which is the value of the letter
Samech, and Samech hints to *sod* (secret), like the verse: **"The secret (*sod*)
of the Lord is with those who fear Him."** (Psalms 25:14) **Regarding this:
"...sing praise to Jacob joyfully"** (Jeremiah 31:6) **because** all the **dots,
from the level of the Supernal Wisdom spread up, nine to Malchut.
And the cantillation marks** are from the level **of Keter to Malchut,
and the Shurek, the Righteous, foundation of the world,** meaning
Melopum, which is the Sefira of Yesod, **in it** is the secret of **the second
Shurek,** meaning Melopum, **with the additional Vav,** on top of the value
of Shuruk, and **the** three dots, resulting to 36, and with the addition of the
Vav amounts to **42.**

165. וְעוֹד קָמֵ"ץ אוּקְמוּהוּ מָארֵי דְּקְדּוּק, דְּאִיהוּ תְּנוּעָה גְּדוֹלָה, בְּגִין דְּאִיהוּ
קַדְמָאָה דְּכֻלְּהוּ נְקוּדִין דִּסְפִירָאן. אַף עַל גַּב דְּכֻלְּהוּ שְׁמָהָן קַדִּישִׁין, אִתְעֲבִידוּ
דָּא כִּסֵּא לְדָא, כְּגוֹן בְּרָא דְּצָרִיךְ לְמִפָּלַח לַאֲבוֹי וּלְאָמֵּיהּ, וּלְמֶעֱבַד לְגַרְמֵיהּ
לְגַבַּיְיהוּ כְּעֶבֶד וְשַׁמָּשׁ וְכָרְסַיָּא וּמַצָּב תְּחוֹתַיְיהוּ, הָכִי אִינּוּן סְפִירָן דָּא לְדָא.
וּבְגִין דָּא, אִית נְקוּדָה מַלְכָּא, וְאִית נְקוּדָה עַבְדָּא לְגַבֵּיהּ. כְּגוֹן שְׁבָ"א, דְּאִיהוּ
עֶבֶד לְקָמֵ"ץ, וְרָץ בִּשְׁלִיחוּתֵיהּ, וּמְזַגֵּב אַחֲרָיו אֲבָל בְּאַתְרֵיהּ מַלְכָּא אִיהוּ.

165. It could **further** be explained that the vowel of **Kametz was set by the
masters of grammar to be a long vowel, because it is the first of all the
vowels in the Sefirot,** since Kametz is considered Keter. **And although
all the Sefirot are Holy Names,** nonetheless, **they become benchmarks
one to the other, just as a son required to assist his father and mother,
allowing himself to be for them a servant, assistant, a chair and a stool
under them, so are the Sefirot** one to each other. **Consequently, there**

exists a vowel that is **a king and there is a vowel** that is **a servant to it, similar to the** vowel **Sh'va that is subservient to the Kametz, and runs for** [the Kametz's] **mission, and also trails after it. However, in its** [the Sh'va's] **own place it is a king.**

166. וְרָזָא דְקָמֵ"ץ, וְוּשְׁבָּן קָמֵץ י"ד, וּתְלַת נִיצוֹצֵי וְרָקִיעַ, נ'. מ' דְאִיהוּ
מֶלֶךָ, אִנּוּן רְמִיזִין, אַרְבַּע יוּדִי"ן, מִן יו"ד ה"י וא"ו ה"י. יו"ד ה"א וא"ו ה"א
וְלַאו לְמַגָּנָא אִתְּמַר בֵּיהּ מֶלֶךָ. דְאִיהוּ מֶלֶךָ גָּדוֹל עַל כָּל מַלְכִין.

166. The secret of the Kametz קָמֵץ (Kuf=100, Mem=40, Tzadik=90), **the** small **numerical value of the Kametz is 14** (1+0+0+4+0+9+0). **The three sparks,** (three dots, which are three Yud's; see verse 163) equal 30, and plus 14 equals 44. **The Firmament** of the Kametz (see verse 157), which looks like the letter Vav (6), plus the 44, equals **50.** This [50] is a complete level with five elevations, since there are ten Sefirot in each of them, and all together it is fifty. This is because Kametz is Keter, and there is a principle that Keter, which is the highest in the Partzuf, contains all that exists in the lower Sefirot and levels. **The Mem** (40) of the Nun (50) indicates **that it is king (***melech***), and they are hinted in the four Yud's of** Yud-Vav-Dalet, Hei-**Yud**, Vav-**Yud**-Vav, Hei-**Yud,** meaning the level of 72 (Ayin-Bet or AV) of Adam Kadmon, which is the second expansion of Adam Kadmon, and the level of Chochmah and the dots that are hinted by the Yud's, since each Yud is hinted in the shape of a dot. Also, the Yud (10) from the Nun (50), hints to Yud-Vav-Dalet, Hei-Alef, Vav-Alef-Vav, Hei-Alef, which is the Name of 45 (Mem-Hei, MaH), because the name 72, which is the elevation of Chochmah, is the source root of the Name 45. **And not in vain does it say regarding Him "king" (***melech***), since He is the greatest king over all kings.** Since all the Lights that exist in the worlds are derived from the second expansion of Adam Kadmon by the mating of 72 (AV) 63 (Samech-Gimel, SaG) of Adam Kadmon, whose illumination brings down the lower Hei to its place, and the Upper Three Sefirot illuminate in the Partzuf.

167. פָּתָ"ח אִיהוּ מ"ב, וחוּשְׁבַּן פַּתָחוֹ אִיהוּ כ', וְנִיצוֹץ וּתְרֵין רְקִיעֵי וו"י, הָא
מ"ב. כ"י ב"י וְחָשַׁק וַאֲפַלְטֵהוּ, פִּתְחוּ לִי שַׁעֲרֵי צֶדֶק אַבָּא בָּם וכו', בָּ"ם
אַרְבָּעִים וּתְרֵין, כִּי בִי וְחָשַׁק וַאֲפַלְטֵהוּ, וְחָשַׁק וְזֵירַק שְׂבָא קָמֵץ מִן אֲבָגִיתָץ.

167. The numerical value of the vowel **Patach** פַּתָחוֹ with its vowels **is 42.**
And explains, **the numerical value of Patach** (Pei-Tav-Chet, 488) in small
numerical value **is 20** (4+8+8). And the spark, which is the dot below the
Kametz under the Tav of the Patach תָ, **and the two Firmaments** (which
are the horizontal lines of the vowels), are **two Vav's (12), plus the Yud (10),
totaling 42.** This is in the secret of verse: **"Because He has set his love
upon me (*ki vi*; 42) therefore I will deliver him,"** (Psalms 91:14) and in
the secret of the verse: **"Open (*pitchu*) for me the gates of righteousness; I
will enter them (*bam*; 42)...."** (Psalms 118:19) **"For He desired (*chashak*)
me."** *Chashak* (Chet-Shin-Kof) **is** the acronym of the vowels **Chirek** (Chet),
which is Netzach, **Sh'va** (Shin), which is Gevurah, **and** *Kametz* (Kof),
which is Keter of the vowels under the letters **Alef-Bet-Gimel-Yud-Tav-
Tzadik** (אֲבָגִיתָץ).

168. קָמֵ"ץ קוֹמֵץ סָתִים בְּאָת יוּ"ד. פַּתָ"ח אִתְפַּתּחוֹ בֵּיהּ בְּחָמֵשׁ אֶצְבְּעָאן,
דְּאִינּוּן ה', וְכַמָּה רָזִין בְּנִקּוּדֵי, וְהַאי אִיהוּ אַבָּא בָּם אוֹדֶה יָ"ה. וּפַתָ"ח עֲלֵיהּ
אִתְּמַר, פִּתְחוּ לִי כו', זֶה הַשַּׁעַר לַי"י.

168. The vowel **Kametz** קָמֵץ is from the word *kometz* (**shut tightly**), since
its Light **is sealed within the** letter Yud, in contrast to the extension from
above to below. **Patach, within which** Chochmah **opens and develops
with the five fingers,** meaning in an entire level of Ten Sefirot **that are
alluded to in the letter Hei, and similarly, many secrets in the vowels,**
which are Chochmah, **are developed and opened** in secret of the Patach.
This is the meaning of: "I will enter into them (*bam*=42)..." (Psalms
118:19) referring to the Name 42; **"...I will give thanks to the Lord."**
(Ibid.) referring to the Mochin of Keter, Chochmah, and Binah. **About the
Patach it was said: "Open (*pitchu*) for me..."** (Ibid.) **"This is the gate of
the Lord...."** (Ibid. 20)

169. מַלְאָכִין אִית דִּמְשַׁמְּשִׁין לְאַלֵּין נְקוּדִין. וְאִינּוּן אַתְוָון. דְּאִינּוּן כְּסוּסְוָון לִנְקוּדֵי. וְטַעֲמֵי מַנְהִיגֵי לוֹן, וְאִינּוּן תְּנוּעוֹת לְגַבַּיְיהוּ, כְּגוֹן עַל פִּי יְ"יָ יַחֲנוּ וְעַל פִּי יְ"יָ יִסָּעוּ.

169. There are messengers that service these vowels, and they are the letters, which are like horses upon which **the vowels** ride on. **And the cantillation marks lead** the letters and the vowels **and they cause their movements, as it says: "At the Lord's command they rest and at the commandment of the Lord they journeyed…."** (Numbers 9:23)

170. וְאִינּוּן נְקוּדִין לְגַבֵּי טַעֲמֵי, כְּעָאנָא בָּתַר רַעְיָין, דְּאַנְהִיגִין לוֹן לְכָל סִטְרָא, לְסַלְקָא וּלְנַחְתָּא עֵילָא וְתַתָּא, וּלְאַנְהָגָא לוֹן לְכָל סִטְרָא, לִימִינָא וּשְׂמָאלָא, לְקַמָּא וְלַאֲחוֹרָא.

170. In relation to the cantillation marks, these vowels are like sheep that follow **their shepherd who leads them in every direction. To rise and descend, up and down, and to lead them in each direction, to right and left,** which is related to the Light of Chasadim, for example, to increase or diminish Chasadim, **to conduct forward and backward** that occurs in the Light of Chochmah.

171. וְטַעֲמֵי אִינּוּן נִשְׁמָתִין, וּנְקוּדִין רוּחִין, וְאַתְוָון נַפְשִׁין, אִלֵּין מִתְנַהֲגִין בָּתַר אִלֵּין, וְאִלֵּין בָּתַר אִלֵּין. אַתְוָון מִתְנַהֲגֵי בָּתַר נְקוּדֵי, וּנְקוּדֵי בָּתַר טַעֲמֵי. כִּי גָּבֹהַּ מֵעַל גָּבֹהַּ שׁוֹמֵר.

171. The cantillation marks are the Neshamas, the vowels are the Ruachs, and the letters are the Nefeshs. These behave according to those, and these according to the others. He explains: **the letters behave according to the vowels, the vowels behave according to the cantillation marks,** as is written: **"For he that is higher than the highest is protected by a higher one."** (Ecclesiastes 5:7)

172. וְעוֹד אַתְוָון אִנּוּן אֶשׁ, נְקוּדֵי רוּחַ, אֶל אֲשֶׁר יִהְיֶה שָׁמָּה הָרוּחַ לָלֶכֶת יֵלֵכוּ. וְאִנּוּן כְּמַבּוּעֵי מַיָּא, דְּאִתְּמַר עֲלַיְיהוּ הַמְשַׁלֵּחַ מַעְיָנִים בַּנְּחָלִים. יַשְׁקוּ כָּל חַיְתוֹ שָׂדָי וְגוֹ', אִלֵּין אַתְוָון. וְאִית דְּשַׁוּוּ לוֹן לְאַתְוָון מַיִם אֵשׁ רוּחַ וְעָפָר, אַרְבַּע רַגְלִין דְּכָרְסַיָּא. נְקוּדֵי אָדָם לָשֶׁבֶת עַל הַכִּסֵּא.

172. It can be explained **further: the letters are the fire, the vowels are the wind,** and the fire follows the wind, as written: "...wherever the spirit was to go they went..." (Ezekiel 1:12) and the cantillation marks **are like the water springs,** about which was said: "He who sends forth springs into the valleys... they give drink to every beast of the fields..." (Psalms 104:10-11) **which are the letters. And there are those who equate the letters to water, fire, wind, dust,** which are **four legs to the throne, and the vowels** are the aspect **of man to sit on the throne.**

21. Seventy-two combinations of Yud-Hei-Vav-Hei,
like the numerical value of Chesed

173. מִסְטְרָא דְּאִימָּא הֵהֵי"ן לְעֵילָא, מִסִיטְרָא דִּבְרַתָּא הֵהֵי"ן לְתַתָּא. מִסְטְרָא
דְּאַבָּא יוּדִי"ן לְעֵילָא, מִסְטְרָא דִּבְרַתָּא יוּדִי"ן לְתַתָּא. מִסְטְרָא דְּבֵן וָוִי"ן
לְעֵילָא, כְּגַוְונָא דָא וו"י. מִסְטְרָא דְּאַבָּא וָוִי"ן לְתַתָּא, כְּגַוְונָא דָא יו"ו. הֵהֵי"ן
דְּאִימָּא כְּגַוְונָא דָא: הה"ו הה"י. הֵהֵי"ן דִּבְרַתָּא כְּגַוְונָא דָא: יה"ה וה"ה.
וְהָכִי בְּכָל הֲוַיֵ"ה וַהֲוַיֵ"ה.

173. **From the side of Ima,** namely Binah, **the** letters **Hei** in the Name Yud-Hei-Vav-Hei **are above,** meaning are the cause. **From the aspect of the daughter,** namely Malchut, **the letters Hei** in the Name Yud-Hei-Vav-Hei **are below,** meaning are the effect. **From the aspect of Aba,** namely Chochmah, **the Yud's** in the Name **are above. From the aspect of the daughter,** namely Malchut, **the Yud's** in the Name are **below. From the aspect of the son,** Zeir Anpin, the letters **Vav** in the Name are **above, like this: Vav-Vav-Yud. From the aspect of Aba,** namely Chochmah, **the** letters **Vav** in the Name are **below, like this: Yud-Vav-Vav. The** letters **Hei** in the Name **from the aspect of Ima,** namely Binah, are **like this: Hei-Hei-Vav; Hei-Hei-Yud. The** letters **Hei** in the Name from the aspect of **the daughter,** namely Malchut, are **like this, Yud-Hei-Hei, Vav-Hei-Hei. And so it is in each and every Yud-Hei-Vav-Hei.**

174. וְעוֹד מַאן דְּאוֹלִיף אִלֵּין הֲוַיֵי"ן, צָרִיךְ לְאוֹלְפָא לוֹן, לְמִבְנֵי בְּהוֹן בִּנְיָנָא
לְקוּדְשָׁא בְּרִיךְ הוּא דְּאִתְּמַר בֵּיהּ וַיְרַפֵּא אֶת מִזְבַּח י"י הֶהָרוּס. וְרָזָא דְמִלָּה,
דְּיָכְלִין לְמֶהֱרַס בְּאַתְוֵוי דִּשְׁמֵיהּ. הֲדָא הוּא דִכְתִיב, פֶּן יֶהֶרְסוּ אֶל י"י. וּבְגִין
דָּא דְיֶהֶרְסוּ לוֹן בְּחוֹבַיְיהוּ, צָרִיךְ לְמִבְנֵי לוֹן בִּצְלוֹתְהוֹן.

174. **In addition, whoever studies these** different sequences of Names of **Yud-Hei-Vav-Hei, must learn them to build the structure for the Holy One blessed be He through them. Regarding it is said: "And he fixed up the demolished Altar** (*mizbe'ach*) **of the Lord...."** (I Kings 18:30) Malchut is called the Altar of the Lord, and when it is in unification with the first

nine Sefirot, which are Yud-Hei-Vav, then all is healed and the structure is whole. **The secret of the matter is that it is possible** through sins **to cause destruction in the letters of Yud-Hei-Vav-Hei,** since through this flaw they destroy the structure of Malchut, and her nine lower Sefirot are destroyed as well and fall to the Klipot. **This is what is written: "Lest they break through to the Lord…."** (Exodus 19:21) **And since they destroy by their sins, they must** repent **and be built up by their prayers.** Through prayer, the Sefirot and the letters will return and ascend to Atzilut and [the Israelites] can complete the structure of Malchut.

175. דְּאָת י' אִיהִי אֶבֶן, יְסוֹדָא דְּבִנְיָנָא. י"י בֶּן יי"ה בֶּן יי"ו בֶּן וי"י, בְּהוֹן אֲבָנִים שְׁלֵמוֹת תִּבְנֶה אֶת מִזְבַּח י"י אֱלֹקֶ"יךָ. דָּא ה'. ו' דָּא קוֹרָה וְעַמּוּדָא לִסְמוֹךְ עֲלָהּ בַּיִת. וּבְגִין דָּא וְזָבוּרָא דִתְכַלַּת אַתְוָון. ב' בִּנְיָנָא. י' יְסוֹד בִּנְיָנָא. ת' תִּפְאֶרֶת. וְאִנּוּן בְּמַלְכוּת.

175. The letter **Yud is the stone,** namely Malchut with the Mochin of the face, **the foundation of the structure.** The letters **Yud-Yud, from** the combinations of **Yud-Yud-Hei, from Yud-Yud-Vav, from Vav-Yud-Yud,** which are combinations from the Name of 72 (Ayin-Bet), as further explained. **Regarding these** combinations it is written: **"You shall build the Altar of theLord your God of unhewn stones."** (Deuteronomy 27:6) **This is the Hei,** namely Malchut that is called the "Altar," as mentioned by Elijah: "And Elijah took twelve stones, according to the number of the tribes of the sons of Jacob…." (I Kings 18:31) **This Vav is a column and pillared beam upon which to support the house,** meaning when Malchut, which is considered the house, is with Mochin of the back and there is a need to support Her. **Thus, the connection of the three letters: Bet—**_binyan_ **(structure), Yud—Yesod (foundation) of the structure, Tav—Tiferet;** (Bet-Yud-Tav) spells _bayit_ (house). **They,** Yesod and Tiferet, illuminate in **Malchut.**

176. י' יְסוֹד, סְפִירָה תְּשִׁיעָאָה, דְּאִיהוּ סוֹמֵךְ גְּאוּלָה לִתְפִלָּה, וּבֵיהּ סוֹמֵךְ י"י לְכָל הַנּוֹפְלִים. ת' תִּפְאֶרֶת, דְּאִתְּמַר בֵּיהּ כְּתִפְאֶרֶת אָדָם לָשֶׁבֶת בָּיִת. וּבֵיהּ

כָּל הַזּוֹקֵף זוֹקֵף בְּשֵׁם. אֲבָל לְגַבֵּי יְסוֹד, כָּל הַכּוֹרֵעַ כּוֹרֵעַ בְּבָרוּךְ. הָדָא הוּא דִכְתִיב, בְּרָכוֹת לְרֹאשׁ צַדִּיק.

176. Yud is Yesod, the ninth Sefira from top to bottom, from Keter to Yesod, **which combines the Ge'ulah (Redemption) prayer,** as Yesod is called "redeemer" [see Zohar Chadash, Ruth 617] **with the** Amidah **prayer,** meaning Malchut called "prayer" (*tefilah*). **And through it: "The Lord upholds all who fall…"** (Psalms 145:14) since it shines to Malchut with the Chasadim of the Mochin of the face. The letter **Tav, Tiferet,** Zeir Anpin, **about which is said: "Like the beauty of man to dwell in the house."** (Isaiah 44:13) **Regarding it,** Tiferet, they said: **"Whoever straightens up, straightens up by the Name"** (Tractate Berachot 12a) meaning by the Mochin of the back, as the level of Zeir Anpin and Nukva are equal and both suckle from Ima. **However, by Yesod,** meaning the Mochin of the face, they said (Ibid.): **"whoever kneels, kneels at *Baruch*,"** as it is written: **'Blessings upon the head of the righteous.'"** (Proverbs 10:6)

177. וְאִיהוּ עֵרוּב דְּיַשְׁפִּיל בֵּיהּ הַקּוֹרָה, אִם הִיא לְמַעְלָה מֵעֶשְׂרִים, דְּאִיהִי יוּ"ד דִּלְעֵילָא מִכ', דְּאִיהוּ כ' כֶּתֶר, אִיהוּ עִלַּת הָעִלּוֹת עַל כֹּלָּא, דְּלֵית עֵינָא שַׁלִּיט עֲלֵיהּ.

177. And He, Yesod **is** indicated in the precept of **Eruv** pertaining to Shabbat, when the Lights [Mochin] of the face illuminate, **that he should lower down the beam if it is higher than twenty, which is Yud-Vav-Dalet,** which equals the numerical value of Kaf (20) hinting to Keter. **Since above twenty, which is Kaf, Keter, is the Cause of All, as the eye has no access [lit. control] to see,** and has no grasp at all, and what cannot be grasped cannot be defined by a Name.

178. וּבְגִין דָּא מָבוֹי דְּאִיהִי שְׁכִינְתָּא תַּתָּאָה, דְּאִיהִי י' וְעֵירָא, עֲשָׂרָה טְפָחִים שִׁעוּרָהּ. בֵּיהּ צָרִיךְ לְהַשְׁפִּיל הַקּוֹרָה דְּאִיהוּ ו'. אֲבָל לְגַבֵּי סָכָּה דְּאִיהִי אִימָּא, דְּשִׁעוּר דִּילָהּ יו"ד, דְּאִיהוּ כ' כֶּתֶר, לְעֵילָא מִכֶּתֶר לֵית אָדָם דְּמֶרְכָּבָה דָּר בֵּיהּ, גוֹ סָכָּה, דְּלֵית עֵינָא שַׁלִּיט עֲלֵיהּ.

178. Thus, an alleyway, which hints to **the lower Shechinah**, namely Malchut, **which is a small Yud, its measurement is ten palm widths,** which allude to the Ten Sefirot of Malchut. **In it,** in the alleyway, **the requirement is to lower the beam, which is Vav,** and to illuminate it with the Mochin of the face. **However, as concerning a Sukkah, which is Ima,** Binah, **whose measurement is Yud-Vav-Dalet,** numerically **twenty,** which hints **to Kaf (20), Keter,** meaning the Mochin of the back, where both Zeir Anpin and Nukva draw from Binah equally, **higher than Keter, no man of the chariot dwells in it,** within the Sukkah, **since the eye has no access** [lit. control] **to see it.**

179. וּמָקוֹר דְּאִלֵּין הֲוַיָי"ן כְּחֶשְׁבַּן חֶסֶד, דִּבְהוֹן צָרִיךְ לְמִבְנֵי בִּנְיָנָא דָא, דְּאִנּוּן מֵחֶסֶד, דְּמָקוֹר הַוַויָיתֵי"ה אִיהוּ יוֹד הֵי וִיו הֵי, דְּסָלְקֵי לְע"ב הֲוַיָי"ן, כְּחוּשְׁבַּן חֶסֶ"ד. כֻּלְּהוּ, אֶבֶן. וְקוֹרָה. וּבִנְיָנָא דְּאִתְבְּנֵי בְּתַרְוַויְיהוּ.

179. **The source** of these combinations **of the Names of Yud-Hei-Vav-Hei,** which are **like the numerical value of Chesed (72), by which it is necessary to build this structure,** namely Malchut, **and they are derived from Chesed,** meaning by the clothing of Chochmah in Chasadim, **and the sources of these** Names of **Yud-Hei-Vav-Hei is <u>Yud</u>-Vav-Dalet, <u>Hei</u>-Yud, <u>Vav</u>-Yud-Vav, <u>Hei</u>-Yud,** ten letters **that amount to 72 Yud-Hei-Vav-Hei's,** meaning 72 combinations, **like the numerical value of Chesed,** which is 72. **All of them,** meaning all the various combinations, are **a stone,** (*even*, Alef-Bet-Nun) which is Yud, **a structural beam,** which is Vav, **and a structure,** meaning Malchut, which is Hei **that is built by both** the Yud and the Vav.

180. וְאִלֵּין אִינּוּן ע"ב הֲוַיָי"ן, דְּנָפְקִין מִן יוֹ"ד הֵ"י וִי"ו הֵ"י. יַהֲוְ הֲיֵ הֲיֵ הֲהֵוּ הַוֵהּ יְהַהּ יַוֵהּ וָיַהּ הֲיֵוּ הֲהֵוּ הַהֵוּ הַהֵוֹ יַהֲיֵ יְהֵהּ וְהֵהּ וַיַהּ וִיהּ וְהֵוֹ וְוַיֵ וַיַן הֲוֵי הַוֵי הַוֵהּ יֵוֵהּ וֵיֵהּ וִיו וְוֵהּ וְהָו יְהֵן יַהֵוּ יְהֵן יַהֵוּ יַוֵהּ יֵוֵהּ וְיֵהּ יַהֵיהּ יָהֵי וַיֵ וְהֵי וַהֵי וְהֵי יֵהּ יֵהּ יַוֵ יֵוֵ הֲיֵ הֲוֵי הֲוֵי הֲהֵי הֲהֵי הֲהֵי הֲהֵי יְהֵהּ יַהֵהּ יֵהֵ יִיהּ הֲוָה וְהֵהּ וַהֵ וְוַהּ וְהָו הַהֵוּ הַהֵוֹ וַהּ יִוּן יַהּ יִיוּ יִיוּ יֵיוֹ וֵיֵ וְוַיֵ וְוַיֵ.

180. These are the 72 combinations of Yud-Hei-Vav-Hei that come out of the Name <u>Yud</u>-Vav-Dalet, <u>Hei</u>-Yud, <u>Vav</u>-Yud-Vav, <u>Hei</u>-Yud.

22. "Whoever reads the Shema reading, it is as though he holds a double-edged sword in his hand."

181. שֵׁם יְהֹוָ"ה, י' דִילֵיהּ בְּרֵישָׁא דְּחַרְבָּא, דְּלֵית מָאן דְּנָצַח וַדַּאי לְמָארֵי חַרְבָּא דָא, וּבָהּ נָצַח לְכָל סִטְרִין אָחֳרָנִין, וְלֵית חַד קַיְּימָא קַמֵּיהּ. גּוּפָא דְּהַאי חַרְבָּא ו'. זַכָּאָה אִיהוּ מָאן דְּיָדַע לְאַנְּפָּה לֵיהּ בִּידֵיהּ, לְכָל סִטְרָא, עֵילָא וְתַתָּא וְאַרְבַּע סִטְרִין, בְּשִׁית סְפִירָן. תְּרֵין פִּיפִיּוֹת דְּחַרְתָּיהּ בְּהוֹן עֵילָא וְתַתָּא מִתְּרֵין סִטְרִין, אִינּוּן ה"ה. וּנְקוּדָא אֱלֹקִי"ם וְהַיְינוּ נַרְתֵּק דִּילֵיהּ, וּבְגִין דָּא בִּינָה נְקוּדָה אֱלֹקִי"ם כְּגַוְונָא דָא יֱהֹוִ"ה כְּמָה דְּאִתְּמַר.

181. Concerning the four letters of **the Name Yud-Hei-Vav-Hei,** its Yud **is at the top of the sword. Since certainly, there is no-one who could be victorious against the master of this sword. By this** sword he wins **all other sides, and none can last in front of it. The body of that sword is Vav** of the Name Yud-Hei-Vav-Hei. **Fortunate is he who knows how to wield that up with his hands to all sides, up and down and to four directions in the six Sefirot.** As Netzach and Hod are up and down, and Chesed, Gevurah, Tiferet, and Yesod are to the four winds. **The two sharp edges of the sword by which he cuts up and down from both sides are** the letters **Hei, Hei,** of the Name Yud-Hei-Vav-Hei. **The vowels** of the Name are the vowels of the Name **Elokim,** meaning Chataf–Segol, Cholem and Chirek. **This is the sheath of** the sword, **and therefore, this Binah has the Name Yud-Hei-Vav-Hei with the vowels of Elokim: like this:** יֱהֹוִ"ה Yud with Chataf Segol, **Hei** with Cholem, and **Vav** with Chirek, as we learned.

182. וְהַאי אִיהוּ דְּאוּקְמוּהוּ מָארֵי מַתְנִיתִין, כָּל הַקּוֹרֵא קְרִיאַת שְׁמַע, כְּאִלּוּ אוֹחֵז חֶרֶב פִּיפִיּוֹת בְּיָדוֹ. וְהָא אוּקְמוּהוּ עַל מִטָּתוֹ לְהַגֵּן מִן הַמַּזִּיקִין, אֲבָל בִּקְרִיאַת שְׁמַע דִּצְלוֹתָא, אֲדוֹן הַמַּזִּיקִין קָשׁוּר, לֵית לֵיהּ רְשׁוּ לְמִבְרַח. וְזַכָּאָה אִיהוּ מָאן דְּשָׁוֵוית לֵיהּ בְּהַהוּא זִמְנָא, לְקַיֵּים הַשְׁכֵּם לְהָרְגוֹ בִּצְלוֹתָא, דְּאִתְּמַר בָּהּ וַיַּשְׁכֵּם אַבְרָהָם בַּבֹּקֶר.

182. This is what the masters of the Mishnah established: "Whoever recites the Shema, it is as if he holds a double-edged sword in his hand."

(Berachot 5a) **They established that** the evening Shema reading **on his bed is to protect from the damaging [entities]. However, with the Shema reading during** Shacharit **(Morning) Prayer, the master of damaging [entities] is bound, and has no authority to escape. Praised is he who can slaughter him during that period to fulfill** the verse: "He who comes to kill you, **rise up earlier and kill him."** (Sanhedrin 72) **This is the rising up earlier** in the morning **to pray,** as mentioned: **"And Abraham rose up early in the morning...."** (Genesis 22:3)

183. כָּל שֶׁכֵּן מָאן דְּלָא חָשַׁשׁ לִיקָרֵיהּ, לְשַׁחֲטָא יִצְרֵיהּ וְשַׂנְאֵיהּ, דְּלֵית שַׂנְאֵיהּ לְחוֹד אֶלָּא שַׂנְאֵיהּ דְּקוּדְשָׁא בְּרִיךְ הוּא. דִּבְכָל יוֹמָא תָּבַע חוֹבִין דִּבְנוֹי לְשַׁחֲטָא לוֹן.

183. Certainly, whoever does not worry about his own **respect, to slaughter his inclination and his own foe** by himself, **since that** Evil Inclination **is not only his adversary but also of the Holy One blessed be He, since he demands daily for the sins of His children** in order **to slaughter them.** And whoever hates the children, proves that he also hates their father.

184. וְאוּף הָכִי צָרִיךְ לְאַעֲבָרָא לֵיהּ מִשְּׁמַיָּא וְאַרְעָא, כְּגַוְונָא דְּאַעֲבָרֵיהּ מִשִּׁמְשָׁא וְסִיהֲרָא. וְאוּף הָכִי צָרִיךְ לְאַעֲבָרָא לֵיהּ וּלְבַת זוּגֵיהּ מִתְּרֵין כָּרְסַיָּין. הָדָא הוּא דִכְתִיב, כִּסֵּא כָבוֹד מָרוֹם מֵרִאשׁוֹן, דְּתַמָּן קוּדְשָׁא בְּרִיךְ הוּא וּשְׁכִינְתֵּיהּ בִּתְרֵין כָּרְסַיָּין, וְתַמָּן קוּדְשָׁא בְּרִיךְ הוּא וּשְׁכִינְתֵּיהּ בְּשִׁמְשָׁא וְסִיהֲרָא, וְעַל שְׁמַיְיהוּ אִתְקְרֵי, כִּי שֶׁמֶשׁ וּמָגֵן יְ"יָ אֱלֹקִי"ם. וּבְהַהוּא זִמְנָא יִתְקַיֵּים בֵּיהּ, לֹא יָבֹא עוֹד שִׁמְשֵׁךְ וִירֵחֵךְ לֹא יֵאָסֵף.

184. In the same way it is necessary to remove him, so that he will not have a grasp in Heaven and Earth, which is up and down, Netzach and Hod, **just like he removed him** so that he will have no attachment **in the sun and the moon,** Tiferet, Yesod, and Malchut. **Similarly, it is required to remove** the Samech-Mem [Sama"el] **and his mate from the two chairs,** Chesed and Gevurah, **as written: "Your Throne of Glory, exalted from**

the beginning...," (Jeremiah 17:12) **where the Holy One blessed be He, and His Shechinah are** united **with the two chairs.** The chair of mercy and grace, and the chair of judgment and might. **And there the Holy One blessed be He, and His Shechinah are** united **in the sun,** Tiferet, **and moon,** Malchut, **and** the Sun and Moon **are named after** the Holy One blessed be He, and His Shechinah, **"For the Lord God is a sun and shield...."** (Psalms 84:12) **During that period of time,** in the future to come, **will** the following verse **come true: "Your sun will no more go down, neither your moon withdraw itself...."** (Isaiah 60:20)

185. וְהָכִי צָרִיךְ לְאַעֲבָרָא לֵיהּ מִשְּׂמָאלָא דְּקוּדְשָׁא בְּרִיךְ הוּא, דְּאִיהִי גְּבוּרָה, דְּמִתַּמָּן מִצָּפוֹן תִּפָּתַח הָרָעָה, וְתַמָּן יֵיתֵי לְמִתְבַּע חוֹבִין, מֵאִלֵּין דְּאִתְּמַר בְּהוֹן בָּנִים אַתֶּם לַי"יְ אֱלֹקֵי"ם.

185. **Similarly it is required to remove him from the Left of the Holy One blessed be He, which is Gevurah,** the Left Column, and correct him so that he will illuminate only from below upward. **Since from there,** from the Left Column, **it is said: "Out of the north, the evil shall break forth...."** (Jeremiah 1:14) **There** the Evil Inclination **comes** to corrupt and spoil the restorations of the Central Column, which diminishes the Left Column and clothes it in Chasadim of the Right, **to seek the sins from those regarding whom is mentioned: "You are children of the Lord your God...,"** (Deuteronomy 14:1) referring to the righteous that attained the Neshama of Zeir Anpin and Nukva of Atzilut, and they are considered children.

186. מִתַּמָּן וְאֵילֵךְ אִנּוּן עָרִים וַעֲבָדִים, מִסִּטְרָא דְחֵיוָון דְּכָרְסַיָּא עָרִים וּמִמַּנָּן, מִסִּטְרָא דְכֹכְבַיָּא דְנָהֲרִין בִּשְׁמַיָּא וְאַרְעָא, עֲבָדִין. וְהַאי אִיהוּ אִם כְּבָנִים אִם כַּעֲבָדִים. וְהַאי אִיהוּ דְּצָרִיךְ לְאַנָּפָא לֵיהּ וַרְבָּא לְשִׁית סִטְרִין, דְּאִנּוּן שְׁמַיָּא וְאַרְעָא שִׁמְשָׁא וְסִיהֲרָא, כִּסֵּא דִין וְכִסֵּא רַחֲמִים. לְאַעֲבָרָא סמא"ל וְנָחָ"שׁ מִנֵּיהוּ, דְּמִסִּטְרָא דִּלְהוֹן שַׁלִּיט סמא"ל וּבַת זוּגוֹ.

186. From there, from Atzilut and below, in the worlds of Briyah, Yetzirah, and Asiyah, are **ministers and servants from the aspects of the living creatures of the throne,** meaning Briyah, are **ministers and appointees,** who have the Light of Neshama that illuminate in Briyah, **and from the aspects of the stars,** which are tiny drops of Light **that illuminate in the Heavens,** which is Yetzirah in the secret of Zeir Anpin that nests in Yetzirah, **and earth,** which is Asiyah in the secret of Malchut that nests in the *Ofan,* **they are slaves. This is** what we say in the prayer service of Rosh Hashanah: **"Either like sons or like slaves,"** and that means, **that there is a need to wield up that sword to the six sides, which are Heaven and Earth,** up and down—Netzach and Hod, **Sun and Moon**—Tiferet and Malchut, **the chair of justice and the chair of mercy,** meaning Chesed and Gevurah that are Zeir Anpin and Nukva in all the realms, and it is necessary **to remove Sama"el and the serpent from them, since Sama"el and his mate dominate from their aspect,** from the aspect of the lower Briyah, Yetzirah, and Asiyah.

187. וְצָרִיךְ לְקַשְׁרָא לֵיהּ בִּרְצוּעִין דִּתְפִלִּין, תְּרֵין בִּתְרֵין קַרְנוֹי, וְחַד בִּדְרוֹעָא. וּלְבָתַר יִשְׁחוֹט לֵיהּ בִּקְרִיאַת שְׁמַע. בְּגִין דְּלָא יִתְקָרִיב לְסִטְרָא דִּגְבוּרָה. אֲבָל מִסְּטְרָא דִּסְפִירָן וַהֲוַויּ"ת דִּלְהוֹן, אִתְּמַר לֹא יְגוּרְךָ רָע, וְהֹדָר הַקָּרֵב יוּמָת.

187. It is required to bind him with the binding straps of the Tefilin of the head that draw the illuminations of Mochin from the head to the body. **Two** binding straps **in his two horns, and one** binding strap **on the arm,** since by the drawing down of the Mochin of the Tefilin, which are called strength (*oz*), we manifest the verse regarding: "And all the nations of the Earth will see that the Name of the Lord is called upon you and they will fear you." (Deuteronomy 28:10) **He then must slaughter him,** Sama"el (Samech-Mem), **by the Shema reading,** where Zeir Anpin receives the Lower Six of Gadlut of Ima, by which he diminishes the Left Column, which is considered the slaughtering of the Samech-Mem, who suckles from the Upper Three Sefirot, **so that he should not approach closely to the side of Gevurah,** the Left Column, to draw down the illumination of

Chochmah from above downward. **However, about the aspects of their Sefirot and various** combinations of **Yud-Hei-Vav-Hei, it is said: "No evil shall sojourn with You"** (Psalms 5:5) **"...and the common man who comes near shall be put to death."** (Numbers 1:51) as is written in Etz Chayim: "Every Sefira that we mentioned are all Godliness and complete unity, from the beginning of the Ten Sefirot of Atzilut until the end of the Ten Sefirot of Asiyah, and only the Nefesh and Ruach of Briyah, Yetzirah, and Asiyah it is said about them "...and from there it will separate." (Genesis 2:10) However, the Neshama is Godliness and the outsider has no portion in it."

188. וְעוֹד ה' דְּיַד כֵּהָה, דְּאִיהִי יוֹנָה קַדִּישָׁא, מְצַפְצְפָאן לָהּ בְּנָהָא בְּכַמָּה צִפְצוּפִין דִּזְמִירוֹת שִׁירוֹת וְתוּשְׁבְּחוֹת וְהוֹדָאוֹת, עַד דְּנַחְתִּין לָהּ לְגַבַּיְיהוּ, הָא נַחֲתִין לָהּ לְגַבַּיְיהוּ, קָשִׁרִין לָהּ בִּרְצוּעָה, דְּאִיהִי ו', שִׁית תֵּיבִין דְּיִחוּדָא.

188. Furthermore, it is necessary to meditate when putting on Tefilin on the **Hei of the the weaker hand** (*yad keh'ah*) that alludes to Malchut being built from Gevurah, which is the left hand, **which is the holy dove,** the Shechinah, **and her children,** Israel, **chirp to her with various chirps of hymns, songs, praises and thanks, until they bring her down to them, and when they have brought her down to them,** they then **bind her with the strap** of Tefilin, **which is the Vav (6),** alluding **to the six words of unification** in *Shema* (Hear) *Yisrael.*

189. וְהַיְינוּ רָזָא וְהָיָה לְאוֹת עַל יָדְכָה. קְשׁוּרָא דְּתַרְוַיְיהוּ, דָּא י', וְדָא יְחוּד. וּבְגִין דָּא בְּקִשּׁוּרָא דְּתַרְוַיְיהוּ, מַאן דְּשָׁוֵי עֵיזָקָא בֵּינַיְיהוּ, דְּאִיהִי שִׁיוַּת חוּלְקִין, עֲבִירָה הִיא בְּיָדוֹ, דְּעָבַד בָּהּ פְּרוּדָא בֵּין ו"ה דְּאִיהוּ עַמּוּדָא דְּאֶמְצָעִיתָא וּמַלְכוּתֵיהּ.

189. This is the meaning of the verse: **"And it shall be a sign on your hand** (*yadchah*)...." (Exodus 13:16) *Yad keh'ah* (the weaker hand), **the binding of the two,** meaning Zeir Anpin and Nukva, **this is Yud,** Chochmah, **and is is the unification. Consequently, at the binding of the two** Tefilin straps, **whoever utters speech between them, which is mundane speech, commits a transgression because he makes a separation between the Vav and Hei, which is the Central Column,** Vav–Zeir Anpin, **and His Malchut**–the Hei.

23. The Yud-Hei-Vav-Hei in the middle

190. תְּפִלִּין דְּרֵישֵׁיהּ דְּקוּדְשָׁא בְּרִיךְ הוּא, דְּאִיהוּ ו' אִיהִי ה' עִלָּאָה אִימָא עִלָּאָה, עֲטֶרֶת תִּפְאֶרֶת. עֲלָהּ אִתְּמַר, פְּאֵרְךָ חֲבוֹשׁ עָלֶיךָ, אִלּוּ תְּפִלִּין שֶׁבָּרֹאשׁ. וְהַאי אִיהוּ רָזָא דַּהֲוָי"ה, דְּאִתְּמַר בֵּיהּ הִנֵּה יַד יְ"יָ הֹוָי"ה וכו'.

190. The head Tefilin of the Holy One blessed be He, which is Vav, Zeir Anpin, **are the upper** letter **Hei, Supernal Ima,** Binah, **a crown of Tiferet,** because Binah is Keter, the crown of Zeir Anpin, which is Tiferet. **About** Zeir Anpin, **it is said: "Bind on your turban...."** (Ezekiel 24:17) **These are the Tefilin of the head. This is the secret** of the combination **of Yud-Hei-Vav-Hei, regarding which** the meaning of this combination **is mentioned, "Behold, the hand of the Lord** יְהֹוָה **shall be upon** (hoya) **הֹוָיָה your livestock...."** (Exodus 9:3) The word "shall be" in Hebrew is hoya, which is also the combination Hei-Vav-Yud-Hei of the Yud-Hei-Vav-Hei. So, the first letter, Hei is the Tefilin, Binah. The second letter, Vav is the person who puts on the Tefilin, Zeir Anpin. The third letter, Yud is the knot of the hand Tefilin, and the last letter Hei is the Tefilin of the hand, Malchut. Together it is the combination of Hei-Vav-Yud-Hei.

191. וּבְגִין דָּא אוּקְמוּהָ מָארֵי דְּתַלְמוּדָא יְרוּשַׁלְמִי, הֲוָיֹ"ת בְּאֶמְצַע, יַד יְהֹוָ"ה מִימִינָא דְּאִתְּמַר בָּהּ וַיַּרְא יִשְׂרָאֵל אֶת הַיָּד הַגְּדוֹלָה, מִסִּטְרָא דְּחֶסֶד. יַד רָמָה, מִסִּטְרָא דְּתִפְאֶרֶת, דְּאִתְּמַר בָּהּ וּבְנֵי יִשְׂרָאֵל יוֹצְאִים בְּיָד רָמָה. יַד חֲזָקָה בְּאֶמְצָעִיתָא דְּאִיהִי יַד יְהֹוָ"ה הֹוָיֹ"ה לְמֶהֱוֵי רַחֲמֵי מִכָּל סִטְרָא, דְּיָנָּא כָּבוּשׁ בְּאֶמְצָעִיתָא.

191. Therefore the masters in the Jerusalem Talmud have set up Yud-Hei-Vav-Hei combinations **in the middle,** meaning to prepare the combination of Yud-Hei-Vav-Hei, which is the secret of the Left Column in the secret of Isaac, in the middle, between the right, the secret of Abraham, and between the Central Column, the secret of Jacob, [See Zohar, Emor 197]: "So are both united in Isaac, this from this side...." He explains: **"The hand of the Lord" is from the right,** meaning the right hand that binds the Tefilin, **about which is mentioned: "Israel saw the great hand…"** (Exodus 14:31) and that was **from the aspect of Chesed. "…high hand"** (Exodus 14:8) **is from the aspect of Tiferet,** Zeir Anpin that puts on the Tefilin, **about which it is said: "And the children of Israel went out with a high hand." (Ibid.) "Strong hand" is in the middle, which is "…the hand of the Lord shall be** (*hoya*) הוֹיָה…" (Exodus 9:3) **to place mercy on each side, and the judgment is subdued in the middle.**

192. יָד רָמָה עֲלָהּ אִתְּמַר וְהָיָ"ה יְ"יָ לְמֶלֶךְ עַל כָּל הָאָרֶץ. וּתְלַת זִמְנִין יָ"ד, אִנּוּן מ"ב אַזְכָּרוֹת דִּתְּפִלִּין דְיָד, וּתְפִלִּין דְרֵישָׁא. יָ"ד שְׁכִינְתָּא תַּתָּאָה אִיהִי.

192. **About the "high hand,"** meaning Zeir Anpin, Tiferet, **is said: "And the Lord will be King over all the Earth…."** (Zachariah 14:9) **Three times "hand"** [*yad*=14] **is 42,** which alludes to the 42 **times the** Yud-Hei-Vav-Hei **is mentioned in the Tefilin of the hand and Tefilin of the head.** Tefilin of **the hand are the lower Shechinah,** Malchut.

193. הַיָּד הַגְּדוֹלָה, מִימִינָא דְחֶסֶד, דְתַמָּן וְחָכְמָה. יָד הַחֲזָקָה, מִסִּטְרָא דִגְבוּרָה, דְתַמָּן בִּינָה. יָד רָמָה, מִסִּטְרָא דְעַמּוּדָא דְאֶמְצָעִיתָא, מְעוּטָּר בְּכֶתֶר עַל רֵישֵׁיהּ תְּפִלֵּי דְמָארֵי עָלְמָא.

193. **The great hand is** from the aspect of **the Right of Chesed, where Chochmah is,** since Chesed ascends to Chochmah during Gadlut. **The strong hand is from the aspect of Gevurah, the Left Column, where Binah is,** since in Gadlut, Gevurah rises to Binah. **A "high hand" is from the aspect of the Central Column, Tiferet, decorated by a crown on his head, the Tefilin of the Master of the World.**

194. שִׁין שֶׁל תְּפִלִּין, הֲלָכָה לְמֹשֶׁה מִסִּינַי. שׁ דְתִתְלַת רָאשִׁין, שׁ דְאַרְבַּע רָאשִׁין, לְקָבֵּל שֶׁבַע הַנַּעֲרוֹת הָרְאוּיוֹת לָתֶת לָהּ מִבֵּית הַמֶּלֶךְ. וְאִנּוּן בְּשַׁוַּחַר שְׁתַּיִם לְפָנֶיהָ, וְאַחַת לְאַחֲרֶיהָ, וּבָעֶרֶב שְׁתַּיִם לְפָנֶיהָ וּשְׁתַּיִם לְאַחֲרֶיהָ. וּלְקַבֵּל אֵלֶּין שִׁבְעָה, אִית שִׁבְעָה רוֹאֵי פְּנֵי הַמֶּלֶךְ, הַיּוֹשְׁבִים רִאשׁוֹנָה בַּמַּלְכוּת.

194. The letter **Shin on the Tefilin** box **is a law** given **to Moses on Mount Sinai.** There are two types of Shin, the right **Shin has three heads** שׁ, the left **Shin has four heads** שׂ, **corresponding to "….the seven maids appropriate for her assignment, given from the king's house."** (Esther 2:9) **Also, they** correspond to the seven blessings in the Shema reading, **whereby, in Shacharit,** the Morning Prayer, **he recites two** blessings **before and one after. In Arvit,** the Evening prayer, **two before and two after, and corresponding to these** seven, there are seven **"…who see the king's face, and sat first in the kingdom."** (Esther, 1:14)

195. וְתִפְאֶרֶת אִיהוּ כָּבוּשׁ בְּאָת יוּ"ד עִם ה' תַּתָּאָה, וְנַפְשׁוֹ קְשׁוּרָה בְּנַפְשׁוֹ. וְאִיהוּ וְלָבוּשׁ עִם אָת י' מִסִּטְרָא דְה' עִלָּאָה. וּבְגִין דָּא אֵין וְלָבוּשׁ מַתִּיר עַצְמוֹ מִבֵּית הָאֲסוּרִין, דְּאִיהוּ בְּגָלוּת עִם יִשְׂרָאֵל. הָדָא הוּא דִכְתִיב בְּכָל צָרָתָם לוֹ צָר בּוֹ'. לֹא צָר בְּא' בְּהַהוּא זִמְנָא דְּאִיהוּ עִם יִשְׂרָאֵל, לֹא צָר וַדַּאי, וְלֵית צָר אֶלָּא יֵצֶר הָרָע, דְּהַדָּר הַקָּרֵב יוּמָת. וְרָזָא דְמִלָּה, כִּי בִי וָשָׁק וַאֲפַלְּטֵהוּ, כִּי בִי בְּגִימַטְרִיָּא מ"ב אַזְכָּרוֹת דִּתְפִלֵּי. אֲשַׂגְּבֵהוּ כִּי יָדַע שְׁמִי.

195. Tiferet, namely Zeir Anpin, **is subjected in the letter Yud,** the knot on the Tefilin of the hand, **with the lower Hei,** Malchut, in the secret of **"…that his soul is bound up with the lad's soul."** (Genesis 44:30) **And it is bound with the letter Yud,** namely with the Mochin of the illumination of Chochmah that appear in Malchut, in the secret of: "bind on your turban," **from the aspect of the upper Hei,** Binah, as all the Lights, both of Chochmah and Chasadim, he receives from Binah. **Consequently, "A bound prisoner cannot extricate himself from the jailhouse,"** (Tractate Berachot 5:2) during the period **when he is in exile with Israel,** as it is said: "As a bird wanders from her nest, so does man wander from his area." And the Shechinah is his jailhouse, **as written: "In all their afflication was He (Lo) afflicated…,"** (Isaiah 63:9) Lo (not), **with an Alef, was not distressed, during the time when he was with Israel,** and they were performing precepts, and elevating Mayin Nukvin (Feminine Waters), **certainly not afflicted (tzar). Tzar is but the Evil Inclination of "…the common man who approaches close shall be put to death."** (Numbers

3:10) **And the secret of the matter is: "Because he has set his love upon Me (ki vi), therefore I will deliver him..."** (Psalms 91:14) *Ki vi* **numerically is 42 mentions of** Yud-Hei-Vav-Hei **in the Tefilin,** in the secret of the three times *yad* (hand, 14), which is the Name of 42, called the Name that elevates, since by the descent of the higher to the lower realm, in the secret of *"Lo tzar"* (*lo* with a Vav כֹל, which means "He is" afflicted), then through the ascent of Mayin Nukvin he brings up to him the lower, and the Mochin of the Name of 42 illuminates in him, which is the regular Yud-Hei-Vav-Hei, with the full spelling out, and the full spelling out of that spelling out. It then becomes *Lo tzar* with an Alef (*Lo* with an Alef לֹא means "He is not" afflicted). **"...I will elevate him for he has known My Name"** (Psalms 91:14) in the secret of the verse: "And all the nations of the world will see that the Name of the Lord is called upon you and they shall fear you." (Deuteronomy 28:10)

196. יִקְרָאֵנִי בִּקְרִיאַת שְׁמַע וְאֶעֱנֵהוּ, הָדָא הוּא דִּכְתִיב, אָז תִּקְרָא וַי"יְ יַעֲנֶה. יְהֹ"ה, בְּאַרְבַּע בָּתֵּי דִּתְפִלֵּי דְּרֵישָׁא, דְּאִינּוּן אַרְבַּע אַתְוָון אהי"ה. וַי"יְ יַעֲנֶה, יְהֹ"ה. בְּאַרְבַּע בָּתֵּי דִּתְפִלִּין דְּיָד, דְּאִינּוּן אדנ"י.

196. What is written in the verse: **"He shall call on Me..."** (Psalms 91:15) **refers to the Shema reading, "...and I will answer him,"** (Ibid.) **as it says: "Then (Az) you will call, and the Lord will answer..."** (Isaiah 58:9) and explains "Then (Az) you will call," meaning the Name **Yud-Hei-Vav-Hei** in the four paragraphs, **in the four housings of the Tefilin of the head, which are four letters** of the Name **Alef-Hei-Yud-Hei אהי"ה.** The four letters Yud-Hei-Vav-Hei plus the four letters Alef-Hei-Yud-Hei add up to *Az* (8), **"...and the Lord will answer..."** meaning the four letters **Yud-Hei-Vav-Hei** that are in the four passages **in the four housings in the Tefilin of the hand, which are** the four letters of **Alef-Dalet-Nun-Yud,** since "... and the Lord means He and His court house.

197. וְאִי תֵימָא לַאו אִינּוּן בְּיָד אֶלָּא בֵּית א' וַחֲמִשָׁאָה, יַד כֵּהָה. הָכִי הוּא וַדַּאי, דְּאִיהִי וַחֲמִשָׁאָה, וְאִיהִי רְבִיעָאָה רְבִיעָאָה לְיה"ו, יַד כֵּהָה. יה"ו אִיהוּ

אֲהִי"ה, וְסָלִיק לְחוּשְׁבַּן כ"א, וְאַרְבַּע אַתְוָון בִּכְלָל, כ"ה. ה' מִן יְהֹו"ה,
רְבִיעָאָה לֵיהּ. וְחַמְשָׁאָה לְאֲהִי"ה, דְּאִיהוּ אַרְבַּע בָּתֵּי. וְאִיהוּ בַּיִת וַחֲמִשָׁאָה.
וְעוֹד אֲהִי"ה אֲדֹנָ"י, סָלְקֵי לְחוּשְׁבַּן אֱלֹהִי"ם, דְּאִיהוּ כְּלָלָא דַחֲמִשָּׁה בָּתֵּי
תְּפִלֵּי.

197. **If you say that the hand** Tefilin **is only but a fifth housing,** called **the weak hand** (*yad keh'ah*)**,** how could you say that there are four housings in the Tefilin of the hand? And answers, **so, certainly it is,** that it is only one housing, **refers to the fifth,** Malchut, **and this one is the fourth** that completes the first nine, which are three times Yud-Hei-Vav, and therefore this fourth one includes all. He explains further, **the fourth to Yud-Hei-Vav is *yad kehah*,** whereas in general the Tefilin of the head and hand are considered one all encompassing Yud-Hei-Vav-Hei, and the Tefilin of the head with four housings are **Yud-Hei-Vav** of Yud-Hei-Vav-Hei, this and the the weak hand (*yad keh'ah*) meaning the hand Tefilin, complete this Yud-Hei-Vav to Yud-Hei-Vav-Hei. And they, too, are composed of four housings. Yud-Hei-Vav, namely the Mochin that are Chochmah, Binah, and Da'at, **is** Alef-Hei-Yud-Hei, since the Mochin of Da'at is composed of Chasadim and Gevurot, and therefore they are four Mochin and are clothed in four vessels, that are four leters Alef-Hei-Yud-**Hei, amounting numerically to twenty one,** exactly as the value of Yud-Hei-Vav, which are the Mochin, **and with the inclusion of the four letters**—Alef-Hei-Yud-Hei—amounts to **25. Hei from Yud-Hei-Vav-Hei is the fourth to Yud-Hei-Vav and the fifth to Alef-Hei-Yud-Hei,** which is the four housings of Tefilin of the head and the Tefilin of the hand, **and it is the fifth housing, then,** it could **also** be explained that Alef-Hei-Yud-**Hei and Alef-Dalet-Nun-Yud are 86, which amounts to the value of Elohim (86). This is the total composition of the five housings of the Tefilin.**

198. יְקוּ"ק אַרְבַּע, פָּרָשִׁיִּין: י', קַדֶּשׁ לִי, וְדָא חָכְמָה ה', וְהָיָה כִּי יְבִיאֲךָ,
וְדָא בִינָה. וְאִינּוּן לִימִינָא וּשְׂמָאלָא, דְּאִינּוּן חֶסֶד גְּבוּרָה. ו', שְׁמַע יִשְׂרָאֵל,
תִּפְאֶרֶת, כְּלִיל שִׁית תֵּיבִין דְּיִחוּדָא. ה', וְהָיָה אִם שָׁמֹעַ, מַלְכוּת שְׁכִינְתָּא
תַּתָּאָה.

198. The four letters of the Name **Yud-Hei-Vav-Hei** is the secret of the four Mochin, the secret of **the four portions. Yud** of Yud-Hei-Vav-Hei is the secret of the first portion **"Sanctify unto Me…"** (Exodus 13:2)**, and that is Chochmah.** The first **Hei,** of Yud-Hei-Vav-Hei, is the secret of the second portion: **"And it will be when the Lord will bring you"** (Ibid. 13:11)**, which is Binah, and they are to the Right and Left, which are Chesed and Gevurah.** That is to say, that Chochmah and Binah of Zeir Anpin are not set consistent, except during the prayers and on Shabbats and Holidays, and they are therefore not considered to be actual Chochmah and Binah, but only Chesed and Gevurah that ascend during Gadult to Chochmah and Binah, in the secrect of "The head of the king is established in Chesed and Gevurah." [See Zohar, Mishpatim 520] **Vav** of Yud-Hei-Vav-Hei is the third passage: **"Hear (*Shema*) Israel…,"** (Deuteronomy 6:4) **Tiferet, which is composed of the six words of the unification:** *"Shema Yisrael Adokai Elokenu Adokai Echad"* (Hear Israel the Lord is our God, the Lord is One) (Ibid.) that allude to the Lower Six Sefirot of Zeir Anpin of the Mochin. **The** bottom **Hei,** is the fourth passage: "If you will be dilligent to listen…" (Deuteronomy 11:13), **Malchut** of Mochin**, and this is the lower Shechinah.**

199. תְּלַת רְצוּעִין: נֶצַח, וְהוֹד, וִיסוֹד. יְסוֹד, רְצוּעָה דְקָשִׁיר וָא"ו עִם ה'. כִּי כֹל בַּשָּׁמַיִם וּבָאָרֶץ, דַּאֲחִיד בִּשְׁמַיָּא וּבְאַרְעָא. תְּרֵין רְצוּעִין נֶצַח וְהוֹד, דַּאֲחִידָן בֵּהּ' עִלָּאָה. וְהַקָּרְנַיִם גְּבוֹהִים וְהָאַחַת גָּבוֹהַ מִן הַשֵּׁנִית. אוּף הָכִי תְּרֵין רְצוּעִין, חַד אֲרוּכָה, וְחַד קְצָרָה, קְצָרָה עַד חֲזֶה. אֲרוּכָה עַד טַבּוּרָא.

199. Three binding straps are Netzach, Hod and Yesod. **Yesod is the strap that connects the Vav,** namely Zeir Anpin, **with Hei,** namely Malchut. About Yesod is mentioned: **"…all (*kol*) that is in the Heaven and on the Earth…."** (1 Chronicles 29:11) Targum Pseudo-Jonathan translates: **"That all is unified in Heaven and Earth,"** because *Kol* (All) is the name of Yesod, and is attached to Zeir Anpin called *Shamayim* (Heavens), and to Malchut, called *Aretz* (Earth). [See Zohar, Mishpatim 405] **The two binding straps are Netzach and Hod, which are attached**

to the upper Hei, the Tefilin of the head, about which is mentioned: "And the two horns were high, but one was higher than the other...." (Daniel 8:3) So too, the two binding straps, one is longer, which shines the illumination of Chochmah called "long," and one is shorter, which shines with Chasadim, shortened to the chest because up to there the Lights are covered, and the long one is to the navel because from there the revealed Chasadim shine the illumination of Chochmah.

200. וְאִתְפַּשְׁטוּתָא דְה' עִלָּאָה עַד הוֹד, בָּאת י' אִיהוּ. דְּאִיהוּ קֶשֶׁר שֶׁל תְּפִלִּין דְּרֵישָׁא. דְּאִיהִי ה' עִלָּאָה, סְלִיקַת לְחַמְשִׁין, חָמֵשׁ זִמְנִין עֲשָׂר בָּאת י'. וְהַיְינוּ ה"י מִן אֱלֹקִי"ם, חָמֵשׁ זִמְנִין ה' בָּאת י', חַמְשִׁין בְּחָמֵשׁ סְפִירָן. יְסוֹד, כָּ"ל, נָטִיל לוֹן כֻּלְּהוּ. וְיָרִית לוֹן לְכַלָּה. וְהַיְינוּ כָּ"ל, כַּלָּ"ה.

200. The extension of the upper Hei until Hod is with the letter Yud, meaning by Chochmah, called Yud, since the upper Hei that is the knot of the Tefilin of the head, in the secret of Leah, which is Binah, amounting to fifty, five times ten in the letter Yud, namely the letters Hei-Yud (Hei=5, Yud=10) in the Name Elokim, five times the letter Hei by the letter Yud, fifty, in five Sefirot: Chesed, Gevurah, Tiferet, Netzach and Hod, as each one is composed of ten, and ten times five is fifty, and they are the Fifty Gates of Binah. Yesod, which is called *Kol* (All; Kaf-Lamed), the numerical value fifty encompasses all of them, and bequeaths them to Malchut called *Kalah* (bride; Kaf-Lamed-Hei) namely *Kol–Kalah*, Yesod and Malchut.

201. בָּאת ה' תַּתָּאָה קֶרֶן אַחַת, וְרָזָא דְּמִלָּה אוּקְמוּהוּ רַבָּנָן שׁוֹר שֶׁהִקְרִיב אָדָם הָרִאשׁוֹן קֶרֶן אַחַת הָיְתָה לוֹ בְּמִצְחוֹ, שֶׁנֶּאֱמַר מִשּׁוֹר פָּר מַקְרִן מַפְרִיס, מַקְרִן חָסֵר יו"ד. וְדָא רְצוּעָה דְּיָד, דְּתִתְפְּלֵי דְּמָארֵי עָלְמָא.

201. In the lower letter Hei, namely Malchut, there is one horn, meaning one strap. And the meaning of the matter the masters have explained is "The ox that Adam sacrificed had only one horn on its brow," (Tractate Shabbat 28b) as mentioned: "more than an ox or bullock that produced

horn and hoof." (Psalms 69:32) *Makreen* (produced horn) is missing a letter **Yud, and that is the** one **binding strap of the Tefilin on the arm of the Master of the world.**

202. כ', כֶּתֶר דְּמָארֵי עָלְמָא. אִיהוּ שְׁמֵיהּ תְּפִלִּין דְּרֵישָׁא, אֲבָל כֶּתֶר תְּפִלִּין עֲלֵיהּ, וְרָזָא דְּמִלָּה, אֵין קָדוֹשׁ כַּיְיָ' כִּי אֵין בִּלְתֶּךָ. לֵית פִּקּוּדָא דְּלָא אִתְכְּלִילָן בֵּיהּ עֲשַׂר סְפִירָן.

202. The letter **Kaf** indicates **the Keter (Crown) of the Master of the world, the Name** of the Keter is **Tefilin of the head. However, it** also **contains on it** in the rear **the Keter** binding-knot **of Tefilin. And the secret of it is: "There is none as Holy as (*ke*; Kaf) the Lord, as there is none but You...."** (I Samuel 2:2) As the secret of this Kaf is the two Yud's in the combination of the two Names Yud-Alef-Hei-Dalet-Vav-Nun-Hei-Yud, the meaning of "ten, ten to the *kaf* (spoon) in the sanctuary Shekel," meaning the Kaf of Keter, since **there is no precept in which the Ten Sefirot are not included,** from the Ten Sefirot of Direct Light cloaked in the Ten Sefirot of the Returning Light.

203. וְעִיקָּר דִּתְפִלִּין מִשְּׂמָאלָא, וּבְגִין כַּךְ נִשְׁבַּע יְ"יָ בִּימִינוֹ, זוֹ תּוֹרָה. וּבִזְרוֹעַ עֻזּוֹ אֵלּוּ תְּפִלִּין וּמִסִּטְרָא דִּשְׂמָאלָא, ה' תְּפִלִּין עַל ו'. אִימָא עַל בְּרָה. בְּגִין דְּבָהּ אִתְבְּנֵי, הֲדָא הוּא דִּכְתִיב כּוֹנֵן שָׁמַיִם בִּתְבוּנָה. י' אַבָּא, תְּפִלִּין עַל בְּרַתָּא, ה' דְּבֵיהּ אִתְבְּנִיאַת. הֲדָא הוּא דִּכְתִיב, יְ"יָ בְּחָכְמָה יָסַד אָרֶץ. וְדָא הוּא הֲוָיָ"ה. וְדָא הוּא רָזָא אַרְבַּע מִשְׁמָרוֹת הוּ"י לַיְלָה.

203. Although there is no precept that is not composed of all Ten Sefirot, nonetheless, **the main part of the Tefilin** precept stems **from the Left aspect,** meaning the illumination of Chochmah as revealed through Binah that ascends to Chochmah. **Consequently,** they said: **"The Lord has made an oath by His right hand..."** (Isaiah 62:8) Right **is the Torah,** whose base is Chasadim, which are Right. **"...and with the arm of His strength..."** (Ibid.) **refers to the Tefilin,** whose root is the illumination of Chochmah **and from the Left side. The first Hei** of Yud-Hei-Vav-Hei, is

Tefilin on Vav, meaning Tiferet, Zeir Anpin, **Ima,** which is Binah, **on her son,** Zeir Anpin **because through her is all his,** Zeir Anpin's, **structure,** whose root is from the Light of Chasadim and is now being built by the illumination of Chochmah that he receives from Binah, as **it is written: "By understanding (*tevunah*) He establish the Heavens (Zeir Anpin)."** (Proverbs 3:19) **Yud** of Yud-Hei-Vav-Hei, **Aba**–Chochmah, **Tefilin on the daughter**–Malchut, called the lower **Hei** of Yud-Hei-Vav-Hei **by which,** by the Lights of Aba, Malchut **is built up. Thus, it is written: "The Lord by wisdom (*chochmah*) established the Earth…"** (Proverbs 3:19) meaning Malchut, called *Aretz* (Earth), since Malchut from its source is Chochmah of the Left lacks Chasadim, now it receives Chasadim from Supernal Aba, the Chochmah of the Right, which is Chesed. **And this is the** order of combinations of **Yud-Hei-Vav-Hei, and this is the secret of** what the masters said: **"Four posts is the night (*Lailah*; Hei-Vav-Yud)."** (Tractate Berachot 3b) And *lailah* (night) is the secret of the illumation of the Left.

204. וְאִית דְּאָמַר הֲוַיּ"ת בְּאֶמְצָע, כְּגַוְונָא דָא יהה"ו: י', קַדֶּשׁ לִי. ה', ה', וְהָיָה כִּי יְבִיאֲךָ, וְהָיָה אִם שָׁמֹעַ. ו' שְׁמַע יִשְׂרָאֵל. הוי"ה ו"י בְּאֶמְצָעִיתָא. יהה"ו ה"ה בְּאֶמְצָעִיתָא.

204. Some say that the Yud-Hei-Vav-Hei combination **in the middle** refers to the order of the four paragraph from the Torah where the two middle paragraphs begin with a combination of Yud-Hei-Vav-Hei. These are: "It shall be (*Vehayah*) when the Lord will bring you…," (Exodus 13:11) and "It shall come to pass (*Vehayah*) if you listen…" (Deuteronomy 11:13) are in the middle, like this **Yud-Hei-Hei-Vav: Yud,** the first passage: **"Sanctify (*kadesh*) for Me…."** (Exodus 13:2) Meaning Chochmah, **Hei, Hei,** the second and third are the two paragraphs of **"When (*vehayah*) He will bring you"** (Ibid.): **"If (*vehayah*) you listen…,"** (Deuteronomy 11:13) which are Binah and Malchut. **Vav: "Hear (*Shema*) Israel"** (Ibid.) Zeir Anpin, as the order of the Tefilin of Rabenu Tam. And in the order of Tefilin according to Rashi, the Mochin are organized thus: **Hei-Vav-Yud-Hei,** and the letters **Vav-Yud** are in the middle. **Thus he summarizes the**

difference between the two versions in the explanation of what is meant by the Yud-Hei-Vav-Hei are in the middle.

24. The twelve combinations of Yud-Hei-Vav-Hei

‫205. וּבְצֵרוּף מִי"ב הֲוָיָי"ן אִשְׁתְּמוֹדְעוּ כֻּלְּהוּ. וְאִלֵּין אִינּוּן: יהו"ה יהה"ו יוה"ה‬
‫דְּרָמִיזֵי בְּשֵׁם יו"ד ה"י ו"י ה"י. הַאי שְׁמָא מְקוֹרָא דְּאַתְוָון וּמְקוֹרָא דִּלְהוֹן‬
‫בִּקְרָאֵי בְּנִקּוּדֵי יְהוּ"הָ יִשְׂמְחוּ הַשָּׁמַיִם וְתָגֵל הָאָרֶץ מְקוֹרָא דִּנְקוּדֵי מַן יִתְהַלֵּל‬
‫יִתְהַלֵּל הַמִּתְהַלֵּל הַשְׂכֵּל וְיָדוֹעַ. יוה"ה יְדוֹתָיו וּלְצֶלַע הַמִּשְׁכָּן הַשֵּׁנִית, תְּלַת‬
‫וָוִי"ן בְּהַאי שְׁמָא יו"ד ה"י ו"י ה"י. והי"ה והה"י ויה"ה. וּנְקוּדִין דִּלְהוֹן,‬
‫וַיִּרְאוּ אוֹתָהּ שָׂרֵי פַרְעֹה והי"ה. והה"י הי"ו היה"ה. ויה"ה,‬
‫וַיֵּרַע יוֹשֵׁב הָאָרֶץ הַכְּנַעֲנִי. הוה"ה הי"ו ההי"ו, מְקוֹרָא דִּלְהוֹן הוה"י וְכָל זֶה‬
‫אֵינֶנּוּ שֹׁוֶה לִי. היו"ה הָמֵר יַמְרוּנוּ וְהָיָה הוּא. ההי"ו עִירֹה וְלַשֹּׂרֵקָה בְּנִי אֲתֹנוֹ.‬
‫היה"ו היו"ה ההו"י. היה"ו לַיהו"ה אִתִּי וּנְרוֹמְמָה שְׁמוֹ. הוי"ה: הִנֵּה יַד יְ"יָ‬
‫הוֹיָה. ההו"י: וּצְדָקָה תִּהְיֶה לָּנוּ כִּי.‬

205. In the combination of the twelve possible combinations of Yud-Hei-Vav-Hei, all these following combinations **are recognized.** They are: **Yud-Hei-Vav-Hei; Yud-Hei-Hei-Vav; Yud-Vav-Hei-Hei,** meaning these are the three combinations starting with Yud **that are hinted in the Name Yud-Vav-Dalet, Hei-Yud, Vav-Yud-Vav, Hei-Yud,** which is the Name of 72, the Yud-Hei-Vav-Hei spelled with Yud. **This Name is the source of the letters,** since each letter begins to be written by a point, which is Yud, **and the sources** of the combinations are **in the verses and** their **vowels.** He explains: the first combination, **Yud-Hei-Vav-Hei,** comes from the verse: *Yismechu Hashamaim Vetagel Ha'aretz* "The Heavens will rejoice and the Earth will be glad." (Psalms 96:11) **The source and vowels of** the combination **Yud-Hei-Hei-Vav is** *Yit'hallel Hamit'halel Haskel Veyodoa* "Let he that glories, glory in this, that he understands and knows Me...." (Jeremiah 9:23) The source and combination of **Yud-Vav-Hei-Hei** is: "*Yedotav Uletzela Hamishkan Hashenit* "for its two pegs, and for the second side of the Tabernacle...." (Exodus 26:19-20) There are **three Vav's in the Name** Yud-Vav-Dalet Hei-Yud Vav-Yud-Vav, Hei-Yud, and they hint to the three combinations: **Vav-Hei-Yud-Hei; Vav-Hei-Hei-Yud; Vav-Yud-Hei-Hei, which all begin with the letter Vav,** and **their** source and **vowels are from** the verse: *Vayiru Otah Sarey Pharaoh* "And the ministers of Pharaoh saw her…," (Genesis 12:15) since the last letters of each word make up **Vav-Hei-Yud-Hei.** The second combination: **Vav-Hei-Hei-Yud** comes from: *…Udvash Hayom Hazeh Yud-Hei-Vav-Hei* "…and honey. This day the Lord…." (Deuteronomy 26:15-16) The third combination: **Vav-Yud-Hei-Hei** comes from: *Vayar Yoshev Ha'aretz Hakna'ani* "And when the inhabitants of the land, the Canaanites saw…." (Genesis 50:11) There are also six combinations that start with Hei, three combinations with each Hei from the two Hei's in the Name, and they are: Hei-Vav-Hei-Yud; Hei-Yud-Vav-Hei; Hei-Hei-Yud-Vav. These are three combinations starting with the first Hei, and three combinations that start with the last Hei: Hei-Yud-Hei-Vav; Hei-Vav-Yud-Hei; Hei-Hei-Vav-Yud. And there are three combinations from Binah, which are: **Hei-Vav-Hei-Yud; Hei-Yud-Vav-Hei; Hei-Hei-Yud-Vav. Their sources are Hei-Vav-Hei-Yud** that comes from the last letters of the words: *Vekol Zeh Einenu Shoveh Liy* "Yet all this is not worthwhile for me…." (Esther 5:13) **Hei-Yud-Hei-Vav** comes from: *Hamer Yemirenu Vehayah Hu* "…and if he shall exchange it, then it and its substitute shall both be…." (Leviticus 27:33) **Hei-Hei-Yud-Vav** comes from the last letters of the words: *"Iroh Velasorekah Beniy Atono* "Tying his donkey to a vine, his young donkey to a vine branch…." (Genesis 49:11) **Hei-Yud-Hei-Vav; Hei-Vav-Yud-Hei; Hei-Hei-Vav-Yud.** The combination of **Hei-Yud-Hei-Vav** comes from *LaYud-Hei-Vav-Hei Itiy Unromemah Shemo* "Give greatness to the Lord with me, and let us exalt His Name together." (Psalms 34:4) The combination of **Hei-Vav-Yud-Hei** is *"Hine Yad* (יהו״ה, Yud-Hei-Vav-Hei) *Hoyah* (הֹוְיָה, Hei-Vav-Yud-Hei)" "Behold the hand of the Lord is…." (Exodus 9:3) The combination **Hei-Hei-Vav-Yud** is from the last letters of the words: *Utzdakah Tihiyeh Lanu Kiy* "and it will be a merit [lit. charity] for us when we…." (Deuteronomy 6:25)

206. וְכָל קְרָאִין דְּקָא אַתְיָין הֲוַיָ״ן אִלֵּין בְּרֵאשֵׁי אַתְוָון, אוֹ בְּסוֹפֵי אַתְוָון, בֵּין מִן הַתּוֹרָה, בֵּין מִן הַנְּבִיאִים, בֵּין מִן הַכְּתוּבִים. יָכוֹל לְנַחֲדָא לוֹן בְּנִקּוּדַיְיהוּ. אוּף הָכִי כָּל הֲוַיָ״ן דְּקָא אַתְיָין מִתַּלַת אַתְוָון, נְקוּדָה דִּלְהוֹן בְּקְרָאִין. כְּגוֹן יְהֹה מִקְוֹרָא דִּילֵיהּ כִּי יְהֹו״ה יְהֹיָ״ה בְּכִסְלֵהּ. וְאִית דְּנָקִיד לוֹן מֵרֵאשֵׁי תֵּבִין, לַהֲוַיָ״ה דְּבְסוֹפֵי תֵּבִין. וְאִם הֲוַיָ״ה בְּרֵאשֵׁי תֵּבוֹת נְקוּדָא דִּילֵיהּ בְּסוֹפֵי תֵּבִין.

206. All these Yud-Hei-Vav-Hei sequences **that come from these scriptures are either from the first letters of the words** like: *Yismechu Hashamaim Vetagel Ha'aretz* "Let the Heavens be glad, and let the Earth rejoice…" (Psalms 96:11) **or from the last letters of the words** like: *Iroh Velasorekah Beniy Atono* "Tying his donkey to a vine, his young donkey to a vine branch…" (Genesis 49:11) **either from** verses in **the Torah or from the Prophets or from the writings. These Yud-Hei-Vav-Hei** sequences **could be punctuated by the vowel** of the letters from which they are derived. **So too, all** the Names of **Yud-Hei-Vav-Hei that come from** the combination of **three letters, like Yud-Hei-Hei, whose source is** from the verse: *Kiy Yud-Hei-Vav-Hei Yehiyeh Bekislecha* "For the Lord will be your confidence…." (Proverbs 3:26) **And there are those that punctuate the** Names of **Yud-Hei-Vav-Hei that come from the last letters of the words** with the vowels **of the beginning letters of the words, and if the Yud-Hei-Vav-Hei comes from the beginning of the words, the vowels will be from the last letters of the words.**

‏207. וְאִית נְקוּדָה בְּרָזָא אָחֳרָא. כְּגַוְונָא דָא. יְהֹו"ה מֶלֶךְ. יְהֹו"ה מַלַךְ יְהֹו"ה יִמְלֹךְ. שְׁמָהָן לְעֵילָּא, נְקוּדָאן דִּלְהוֹן כְּתִיבִין דִּתְחוֹתַיְיהוּ.

207. There is **another** way and **secret to punctuate, for example:** "The **Lord is sovereign King, the Lord was sovereign King and the Lord will be sovereign King." Whereby the Names** of the Yud-Hei-Vav-Hei **mentioned first above are punctuated with the vowels of the words that follow** the Names.

‏208. אַרְבַּע שְׁמָהָן תַּלְיָין מִכָּל שְׁמָא וּשְׁמָא, וַעֲלַיְיהוּ אִתְּמַר וְקָרָא זֶה, לְקָבֵל י"ב אַנְפִּין דִּתְכֵלֶת חֵיוָון, אֶל זֶה י"ב גַּדְפִין דִּתְכֵלֶת חֵיוָון. וְעַל כֻּלְּהוּ פְּנֵי אָדָם, וּתְפִלִּין הוּא פְּנֵי אָדָם, צִיצִית פְּנֵי חֵיוָון.

208. Four Names come from each Name of these three Names: "the Lord is King, the Lord was sovereign King, and the Lord will be sovereign King," since one Name comes from each letter of the Yud-Hei-Vav-Hei, and thus twelve Names. **Regarding them is mentioned: "And they called unto another this (zeh;12)," (Isaiah 6:3) corresponding to the twelve faces of the three creatures** of the chariot: lion, ox, and eagle, each of which has four faces, **"to this (zeh;12)," (Ibid.) these are the twelve wings of the three creatures:** lion, ox, and eagle, **and above them is the face of man,** which is the secret of the verse: "...and upon the likeness of the throne, was a likeness appearing as a man upon it above." (Ezekiel 1:26) **And Tefilin is the face of man,** namely the Mochin of Chochmah, and **Tzitzit are the faces of the living creatures and the wings of the living creatures,** meaning the illumination of Chochmah with Chasadim, which is the white in the Tzitzit.

209. וְאוּקְמוּהוּ רַבָּנָן, שֵׁם בֶּן י"ב, כָּל הַיוֹדְעוֹ וְהַזָּהִיר בּוֹ, כָּל תְּפִלוֹתָיו מִתְקַבְּלוֹת. וּמְקוֹרוֹ יוֹד הֵי וָאו הֵי. כָּל י' אִיהוּ אַנְפּוֹי א' וּדְמוּת פְּנֵיהֶם פְּנֵי אָדָם הָכָא בְּהַאי שְׁמָא, רָזָא דִתְפִלִּין. וְצִיצִית.

209. Our masters of blessed memory have established the Name of twelve, meaning the three Names related to *melech* [is sovereign King], *malach* [was sovereign King], and *yimloch* [will be sovereign King], **anyone who knows it and is careful with it, all his prayers are accepted. Its source is Yud-Vav-Dalet, Hei-Yud, Vav-Alef-Vav, Hei-Yud,** the Name of 63 that has three Yud's and an Alef. **Each face of a Yud is an Alef,** in the secret of the verse **"...they had a face of a man...." (Ezekiel 1:10) Here in this Name** that equals 63 **is the secret of the Tefilin and Tzitzit.**

210. תָּא חֲזֵי, כָּל הֲוָי"ה דְאִיהִי ה' עַל י' ה' עַל ו', נוּקְבָּא. כָּל הֲוָי"ה דְתַרֵין הֵהִי"ן כַּחֲדָא בְּאֶמְצַע, אִינוּן אַחְוָיוֹת, כְּגַוְונָא דָא יהה"ו. כָּל הֲוָי"ה י"ו כַּחֲדָא בְּאֶמְצַע, הֵיו"ה, אִינוּן אַחִים. כִּי יֵשְׁבוּ אַחִים יַחְדָו.

210. Come and see, any Yud-Hei-Vav-Hei whose combination is Hei over Yud, Hei over Vav, for example: *LaYud-Hei-Vav-Hei Itiy Unromemah Shemo* (Psalms 34:4) **is in the feminine** aspect that illuminates from below upward. **Any Hei-Vav-Yud-Hei whose two Hei's are together in the**

middle are sisters, Binah and Malchut, **like this: Yud-Hei-Hei-Vav,** from the secret of the verse *Yit'halel Hamit'halel Haskel Veyado'a,* (Jeremiah 9:23) which shine with Chochmah, in the secret of the verse: "Say to wisdom (*chochmah*) 'you are my sister'" (Proverbs 7:4) **Any Yud-Hei-Vav-Hei** whose combination is **Yud-Vav in the middle together,** such as **Hei-Yud-Vav-Hei** that comes from the verse: *Hamer Yemirenu Vehayah Hu* (Leviticus 27:33) **are brothers,** Chochmah and Zeir Anpin, in the secret of the verse: **"When brothers dwell together...."** (Deuteronomy 25:5)

211. תְּרֵין הֵהִי"ן כַּחֲדָא, וַתֵּלַכְנָה שְׁתֵּיהֶן. י"ו רְחוֹקִים דָּא מִן דָּא, אוֹ קְרוֹבִים דָּא מִן דָּא, עֲלַיְיהוּ אִתְּמַר, שָׁלוֹם שָׁלוֹם לָרָחוֹק וְלַקָּרוֹב וְגוֹ'. דְּהַיְינוּ קָרְבָּן עוֹלָה וְיוֹרֵד, יהה"ו, ה' דְּאִיהִי אִימָא עוֹלָה, סְלִיקָא לְגַבֵּי י', הִיא הָעוֹלָה. ה' דְּאִיהִי בְּרַתָּא, נְחִיתַת לְגַבֵּי ו', וַיֵּרֶד מֵעֲשׂוֹת הַחַטָּאת, עַל כֵּן יַעֲזָב אִישׁ אֶת אָבִיו וְאֶת אִמּוֹ וְגוֹ', וְהַאי אִיהוּ קָרְבָּן עוֹלָה וְיוֹרֵד, חָמֵשׁ אֲשׁוֹת סָלְקִין, וְחָמֵשׁ נְחִיתִין.

211. Two Hei's of the Name **as one,** is the secret of the verse: **"So they went...,"** (Ruth 1:19) which are Binah and Malchut. **Yud-Vav** of the Name **when they are far apart from each other,** meaning with the illumination of Chochmah that is called "far," in the secret of the verse: "...I said 'I will get wisdom but it is far from me.'" (Ecclesiastes 7:23) **or they are close to each other,** meaning with the Light of Chasadim, on which there is no contraction (*tzimtzum*), and therefore it is called close. **About them,** about these two Lights, **is said: "Peace, peace, to him that is far off and to him that is near...,"** (Isaiah 57:19) **which is like a sacrifice that ascends and descends. This is hinted to in the combination of Yud-Hei-Hei-Vav** that comes from the verse: *"Yit'halel Hamit'halel Haskel Veyado'a."* (Jeremiah 9:23) **Hei, which is Ima,** Binah, **ascends,** meaning it **elevates to Yud,** which is Chochmah, in the meaning of the verse: **"It is the law of the burnt offering [lit. elevates]...."** (Leviticus 6:2) **Hei, which is the daughter,** Malchut, **descends to the Vav,** namely Zeir Anpin, in the secret of the verse: **"And he came down from offering the sin offering...,"** (Leviticus 9:22) and then it is said: **"Therefore shall a man leave his father and**

mother...," (Genesis 2:24) and then this combination is made: _Yismechu Hashamayim Vetagel Ha'aretz._ (Psalms 96:11) **This is a sacrifice [whose price] rises and falls. Five fires rise and five fires descend.**

212. לֵית הֲוָיֵ"ה דְּלָא אַחֲזֵי עַל רָזָא עִלָּאָה. הוה"י, כַּד נוּקְבִין שָׁלְטִין עַל דְּכוּרִין, דִּינָא אַחֲזֵי בְּעָלְמָא, וּמִיתָה וְעוֹנִי. וְדָא אִיהוּ רָזָא דְּהָפַךְ מֹשֶׁה שְׁמֵיה, וְקָטַל לְמִצְרִי, דְּאִתְּמַר בֵּיה וְאָמְרוּ לִי מַה שְּׁמוֹ מָה, וּמֹשֶׁה הָפַךְ לֵיהּ כְּגַוְונָא דָא, מַה שְּׁמוֹ מָה לִי הוה"י וּנְקוּדָה הָוְהָי, מִצְרִי דְּמְזַלְזֵל בִּשְׁמֵיה, וְאָמַר מַה שְּׁמוֹ מַה מַה יָכִיל לְמֶעְבַּד לִי לִקְטֵיל לֵיה בֵּיה. וְאִם אַתְוָון בְּסוֹפֵי תֵּיבוֹת, נְקוּדִין אִנּוּן מֵרֵאשֵׁי תֵּיבִין.

212. There exists no combination of the Name **Yud-Hei-Vav-Hei** that does not indicate a Supernal secret. **Hei-Vav-Hei-Yud** is a reverse combination **when** the aspects of **femininity,** meaning the Hei's in the Name **dominate over** the aspects of **masculinity,** which are **Yud-Vav** of the Name, **judgment, death, and poverty** is seen in the world. **This is the secret that Moses turned around the Name** of Yud-Hei-Vav-Hei **and killed the Egyptian,** as it says concerning it: "**...and they say to me 'what is His name, what....'**" (_ve'amru Liy Mah Shmo Mah_ [Yud-Hei-Vav-Hei]) (Exodus 3:13) in a straight order that indicates mercy, **and Moses turned it around** in reverse, **thus:** _Mah Shmo Mah Liy_ and the combination is **Hei-Vav-Hei-Yud. Its vowel is Hei with Kametz, Vav with Sh'va, Hei with Kametz, Yud with Chirek,** since **the Egyptian disparaged His Name and said: "What is His Name, what could He do to me?"** he said **"kill him with the Name."** See Zohar, Emor 318: "...as they established, as it is written: '...do you intend to kill me [by your uttering]...' (Exodus 2:14) that Moses killed him by uttering the Holy Name." **If the letters** of the Name **are at the end of the words, then the vowels are from the beginning of the words.**

25. Beresheet: *Bat Rashei* (Daughter of the Heads)

213. תִּקוּנָא ה', בְּרֵאשִׁית: בַּ"ת רָאשֵׁ"י, אֵלֶּה רָאשֵׁי בֵית אֲבוֹתָם, בַּת, עֵלָּה
אוּקְמוּהוּ מָארֵי מַתְנִיתִין, בַּת בְּתְחוֹלָה, סִימָן יָפֶה לְבָנִים. וְאִיהִי י' מִן אדנ"י,
מַרְגָּלִית יְקָרָא, כְּלִילָא מִכָּל גַּוְונִין.

213. The fifth correction, Beresheet: meaning the word *beresheet* contains
bat rashei (daughter of the heads), in the meaning of the verse: "These
are the heads (*rashei*) of houses of their fathers...." (Exodus 6:14)
About *bat* (daughter), which is Malchut, the masters of the Mishnah
have established: "A daughter in the beginning is a good sign for sons,"
(Tractate Bava Batra 141a) meaning the Lower Six Sefirot of Zeir Anpin.
And she, Malchut, is the letter **Yud of Adonai (Alef-Dalet-Nun-Yud), a
precious pearl composed of all colors,** meaning Ten Sefirot of Zeir Anpin.

214. דְּאָת י' מִן יהו"ה, לָא תָּפִיס בֵּיה גַּוְון כְּלָל, הֲדָא הוּא דִכְתִיב אֲנִי י"י
לֹא שָׁנִיתִי. לָא יִשְׁתַּנֵּי בְּשׁוּם גַּוֶון כְּלָל, אֶלָּא נָהִיר מִלְּגָאו דְּגַוְונִין. דְּשֵׁם יהו"ה,
כְּנִשְׁמָתָא בְּגוּפָא דְּאֵינִישׁ. אוֹ כִּשְׁרָגָּא בְּהֵיכְלָא. וְאָת י' מִן אדנ"י, אִיהוּ
סַפִּיר. נָטִיל גַּוְון תְּכֵלֶת וְאוּכָם מִסִּטְרָא דְּדִינָא, וְנָהִיר בֵּיה נְהוֹרָא וְחִוְורָא,
מִסִּטְרָא דְּרַחֲמֵי.

214. Since the letter Yud of the Name Yud-Hei-Vav-Hei has no color
whatsoever associated with it, as it says: "For I the Lord, do not
change...." (Malachi 3:6) I do not change by any color of the Sefirot at all,
but rather illuminate within the colors, in the secret of the Ten Sefirot of
Direct Light, as the Name Yud-Hei-Vav-Hei is like the soul within the
human body or like a candle within the chamber. And the letter Yud
from the Name Alef-Dalet-Nun-Yud is a sapphire stone, which takes
the blue and black colors from the side of judgment, which is the Left
Column that is Judgment, and the white Light illuminates through it
from the side of Mercy, the Right Column, which is Mercy and Chasadim.

215. וְאִיהוּ אָת י' מִן אדנ"י, אוֹדֶם מִסִטְרָא דִגְבוּרָה, פִּטְדָה מִסִטְרָא דִימִינָא, בָּרֶקֶת מִסִטְרָא דְעַמּוּדָא דְאֶמְצָעִיתָא. אִיהִי אל"ף דל"ת נו"ן יו"ד, כְּלִילָן מי"ב גַּוְונִין. וְכֻלְהוּ מְשׁוּלָשִׁין בַּאֲבָהָן, מְשׁוּלָשִׁין בְּכֹהֲנִים לְוִים וְיִשְׂרָאֵלִים. קְדוּשָׁה לְךָ יְשַׁלֵשׁוּ.

215. And this letter Yud from the Name **Alef-Dalet-Nun-Yud** is called *Odem* (Carnelian), from the aspect of Gevurah, and is called *Piteda* (Topaz) from the Right aspect, which is Chesed. It is called *Bareket* (Agate) from the aspect of the Central Column, which is Tiferet. **Malchut is Alef-Lamed-Pei, Dalet-Lamed-Tav, Nun-Vav-Nun, Yud-Vav-Dalet, composed of twelve colors,** which are Chochmah, Binah, Tiferet and Malchut, each one includes three Columns, and 4 x 3=12. **All are in threes by the Patriarchs,** Chesed, Gevurah, and Tiferet, **in threes: Cohens, Levites, and Israel,** which is Netzach, Hod, and Yesod, that are composed from Chesed, Gevurah, and Tiferet, **and "sanctification is tripled for you,"** meaning the Upper Three: Chochmah, Binah, and Da'at.

216. כָּל אֶבֶן דְּגַוְון דִּילָהּ וְזִיוּוֹר, נְטִילַת מֵחֶסֶד. וְאִיהִי סְגוּלָה דִילֵיהּ רְחִימוּ. וְרָזָא דְמִלָּה, וְאַהֲבַת עוֹלָם אֲהַבְתִּיךְ עַל כֵּן מְשַׁכְתִּיךְ חָסֶד. אַבְנָא סוּמְקָא, נְטִילַת מִן גְּבוּרָה. וּסְגוּלָה דִילָהּ לְמֶהֱוֵי אֵימָתוּ מוּטֶלֶת עַל בִּרְיָין דְעָלְמָא. אַבְנָא כְּלִילָא מִתְּרֵין גַּוְונִין חִיוּוֹר וְסוּמָק, אִיהִי מֵעַמּוּדָא דְאֶמְצָעִיתָא. יָרוֹק כְּדַהֲב, מִסִטְרָא דְאִימָא עִלָּאָה דְאִיהִי תְּשׁוּבָה, קַו יָרוֹק דְּאַסְחַר כָּל עָלְמָא.

216. **Every stone whose color is white takes from Chesed, and its unique quality is love,** and the secret of the matter is: **"…I have loved you with an everlasting love, therefore with mercy (*chesed*) I have drawn you."** (Jeremiah 31:2) **A stone** whose color is **red takes from Gevurah, and its unique quality is to cast His fear on the creatures of the world. A stone comprised from the two colors, white and red, takes from the Central Column,** meaning Tiferet, composed of Chesed and Gevurah. **Green as gold takes from the aspect of Supernal Ima,** Binah, **which is repentance (*teshuvah*), a green line that encircles the entire world.**

217. וְאִית גַּוֶן פָּשׁוּט, כָּפוּל, מְשׁוּלָשׁ, מְרוּבָּע, עַד דְּסָלִיק לַעֲשָׂרָה גַּוְונִין, דִּנְהִירִין בְּהוֹן עֲשַׂר אַתְוָון, דְּאִינּוּן י' י"ה יה"ו יהו"ה. וְסַלְקוּ אִלֵּין עֲשַׂר, לְע"ב נְהוֹרִין דְּנָהֲרִין בְּע"ב גַּוְונִין.

217. **And there is a simple color,** namely Keter, **doubled,** Chochmah and Binah, **tripled,** Chesed, Gevurah, and Tiferet, **quadrupled,** Netzach, Hod, Yesod, and Malchut, **until it gets to ten colors,** the Ten Sefirot, **by which ten letters illuminate,** which are: **Yud, Yud-Hei, Yud-Hei-Vav, Yud-Hei-Vav-Hei,** which is Yud-Hei-Vav-Hei in Ribua. **These ten** letters **amount to 72 Lights that shine in 72 colors.**

218. חָשַׁ"ק: וֹלֶ"ם, שְׁבָ"א, קָמֵ"ץ. אִינּוּן נִקּוּד צְבָאוֹת. נֵצַח וְהוֹד יְסוֹד, וְכֻלְּהוּ נָהֲרִין בְּאַבְנָא יַקִּירָא מַלְכוּת, כְּלִילָא מִכָּל סְגוּלוֹת. שְׁבָ"א גַּוֶן סוּמָק דִּגְבוּרָה, דְּנָטִיל מִנֵּיהּ הוֹד. קָמֵ"ץ גַּוֶן חִוָּור. וְלָא צָרִיךְ לַאֲרָכָא בְּהוֹן, דְּהָא אִתְּמָרוּ לְעֵילָּא.

218. *Chashak,* an abbreviation of the vowels: **Cholem, Sh'va, and Kametz, under the word** *tzva'ot,* under the Tzadik there is Sh'va, under the Bet there is Kametz, and there is Cholem above the Vav. **Netzach, Hod, and Yesod** are called *tzva'ot,* and **all illuminate in the precious stone** that is Malchut, **which is composed of all unique qualities. And Sh'va, its color is red from Gevurah and Hod,** which is in the Left Column, **takes from it. Kametz, its color is white,** meaning it shines in Chasadim, and Netzach takes from it. **There is no further need to expound** about the vowels **as we studied** their meaning **earlier.**

26. Beresheet: That is love

219. וְעוֹד תִּקּוּנָא ו', וְהַמַּשְׂכִּילִים יַזְהִירוּ, אִלֵּין אִינּוּן דְּיָדְעִין רָזָא בְּפִקּוּדָא תִּנְיָנָא, בְּמִלַּת בְּרֵאשִׁי"ת דְּאִיהִי אַהֲבָ"ה, דְּאִיהִי לְחֶשְׁבַּן זְעֵיר בְּרֵאשִׁי"ת. בְּמַתְקְלָא חֲדָא סָלְקִין. דָּא בְּדָא, דָּא תְּלֵיסַר וְדָא תְּלֵיסַר.

219. Also, the sixth correction, it is written: **"And the wise shall shine…"** (Daniel 12:3) **these are those who know the meaning of the second precept in the word Beresheet** because the first precept is awe, in the secret of: "The fear [lit. awe] of the Lord is the beginning of wisdom…" (Psalms 111:10) and similarly: "The fear [lit. awe] of the Lord is the beginning of knowledge." (Proverbs 1:7) And the second precept **is *ahavah* (love), which equals the same as *beresheet* in small numerical value,** since *beresheet* and *ahava* **equal the same value, one with the other** because **one,** *beresheet,* **equals 13** and **the other,** *ahavah,* also **equals 13.**

220. וְדָא אַהֲבַת חֶסֶד, דְּאִיהִי ע"ב בְּחוּשְׁבָּן, לָקֳבֵל שְׁמָא מְפָרֵשׁ וַיִּסַּע וַיָּבֹא וַיֵּט. דְּבֵיהּ וָא"ו, כְּחוּשְׁבָּן אֶחָ"ד. דְּהַיְינוּ מַאֲמַר וָד, דְּאִיהוּ בְּרֵאשִׁית. דְּאוּקְמוּהוּ עֲלֵיהּ, וַהֲלֹא בְּמַאֲמַר אֶחָד יָכוֹל לְהִבָּרְאוֹת.

220. And this is *ahavat chesed* (loving kindness), which Chesed **equals 72, corresponding to the Explicit Name** that results from the verses: **"And he went…and came…and he stretched…"** (*Vayisa, vayavo, vayet*), (Exodus 14:19-21) which are the 72 Names [see Zohar, Beshalach 173]; **in it exists Vav-Alef-Vav,** which equals 13, **like the numerical value of *echad* (one),** referring to the Thirteen Attributes of Mercy that are hinted at in the three words: Vav-Hei-Vav, Alef-Nun-Yud, and Vav-Hei-Vav, which comprise the 72 Names, at the beginning Vav-Hei-Vav, in the middle Alef-Nun-Yud, and towards the end Vav-Hei-Vav, which are the initials of Vav-Alef-Vav. **This is one utterance,** which is Beresheet, **about which the masters said: "The world could have been created in one (*echad*) utterance."** (Tractate Rosh Hashanah 31a; Avot 5:1)

221. וְהַאי אִיהוּ רְחִימוֹי דְּמָארֵיהּ, מָאן דְּמָסַר נַפְשֵׁיהּ בְּאֶחָד, בִּרְחִימוּ דְּמָארֵיהּ. וּבְגִין דָּא, וְאָהַבְתָּ אֵת יְיָ אֱלֹהֶיךָ, אֲפִילוּ נוֹטֵל אֵת נַפְשֶׁךָ, דְּאִם חֲבִיב עֲלֵיהּ נַפְשֵׁיהּ מִגּוּפָא, לְכַךְ נֶאֱמַר וּבְכָל נַפְשְׁךָ. וְאִם חֲבִיב עֲלֵיהּ גּוּפֵיהּ מִמְּמוֹנֵיהּ, לְכַךְ נֶאֱמַר בְּכָל לְבָבְךָ. וְאִם חֲבִיב עֲלֵיהּ מָמוֹנָא מִגּוּפָא, לְכַךְ נֶאֱמַר בְּכָל מְאֹדֶךָ. בַּמֶּה דְחָבִיב עֲלָךְ, מְסוֹר לֵיהּ בִּרְחִימוּ דְּמָארָךְ בְּעֵת צָרָה.

221. This is the love of one's master; anyone who is ready to sacrifice himself at the word *echad* with love for his master. It is subsequently said after *Shema Yisrael Adonai Elokeinu Adonai Echad*: "Love the Lord your God, with all your heart and soul," (Deuteronomy 6:5) even when he takes away your soul. In case his soul is dear to him more than his body, meaning sufferings, it also says: "…and with all your soul…." (Ibid.) If his body is dearer to him than his wealth, it says: "…with all your heart…," (Ibid.) and if his wealth is dearer to him than his body, it says: "…and with all your might." Whatever is dear to you, pass it on with love for your master, in time of trouble and distress because then is the test, and true love is recognized.

222. וְדָא אִיהוּ נִסָּיוֹן דַּעֲתִידִין יִשְׂרָאֵל לְאִתְנַסָּאָה, בְּשַׁבְעִין שְׁנִין דְּגָלוּתָא בַּתְרָאָה. דְּעָנִי וְחָשׁוּב כַּמֵּת, וּכְאִלּוּ נָטְלִין נַפְשֵׁיהּ. גּוּפָא וְנַפְשָׁא וּמָמוֹנָא, כֻּלְּהוּ שְׁקוּלִין. בַּמֶּה דְחָבִיב עֲלֵיהּ, מְסוֹר לֵיהּ בִּרְחִימוּ דְּמָארֵיהּ. וּבְהַהוּא זִמְנָא, אִתְקַשַּׁר בְּמִלַּת אַהֲבָ"ה, דְּאִיהִי בְּרֵאשִׁי"ת, וּכְאִלּוּ בֵּיהּ בָּרָא עָלְמָא.

222. And this will be the test for Israel during the seventy years of the last exile. Since a poor person is considered as dead, and if money is taken from him it is as if they took his soul. Body, soul, and wealth are equal; whatever is dear to him he should pass it on with love for his master. And during that period, when he gives over everything in time of trouble, he connects to the word love (*ahavah*), which is Beresheet, and it is as if the world was created for him, as it says: "In the beginning God created…," meaning that for the sake of love, which is "In the beginning," God made the Creation.

223. וּמָאן דְּלָא מָסַר נַפְשֵׁיהּ אוֹ גּוּפֵיהּ אוֹ מָמוֹנֵיהּ בִּרְחִימוּ דְּמָארֵיהּ בְּשַׁעֲתָא דִּשְׁמַד, כְּאִלּוּ אַחֲזַר עָלְמָא לְתֹהוּ וָבֹהוּ. וּבְגִין דָּא, קְרָא סָמִיךְ לֵיהּ, וְהָאָרֶץ הָיְתָה תֹהוּ וָבֹהוּ.

223. And he who is not ready to give up his soul, body or wealth with love for his master, during times of persecution, it is as if he brought the world to a state of formlessness and emptiness. And thus it is written, next to the verse of Genesis 1:1, the verse: "And the earth was without form and void...." (Genesis 1:2)

224. וְאָהַבְתָּ יְ"יָ אִיהִי מַלְכוּת, כְּלִילָא מִכָּל סְפִירָן, וְאִיהִי פִּקּוּדָא דְּקוּדְשָׁא בְּרִיךְ הוּא בְּכָל תַּרְיַ"ג פִּקּוּדִין. וּבְגִינָהּ אִתְּמַר, מַדּוּעַ אַתָּה עוֹבֵר אֶת מִצְוַת הַמֶּלֶךְ, וְאִיהִי בִּנְיַן עָלְמָא. שִׁפְחָה בִּישָׁא אִיהִי וְחָרְבַּן עָלְמָא, וּבְגִין דָּא אִתְּמַר בָּהּ, וְהָאָרֶץ הָיְתָה תֹהוּ וָבֹהוּ, וְאִיהִי רְצוּעָה בִּידָא דְּקוּדְשָׁא בְּרִיךְ הוּא, לְאַלְקָאָה בֵּיהּ חַיָּיבַיָּא.

224. Malchut is the love of the Lord, comprised of all the Sefirot, and it is the precept (*mitzvah*) of the Holy One blessed be He, concerning all the 613 precepts. For her sake is mentioned: "...'Why are you transgressing the command of the king?'" (Esther 3:3) and she is the building structure of the world. The wicked maid is the destruction of the world, and therefore about her is said: "...and the earth was without form and void...." (Genesis 1:2) And she is a strap by which the Holy One blessed be He, punishes the wicked.

225. וּבְגִין דָּא, מָאן דְּרָחִים לְקוּדְשָׁא בְּרִיךְ הוּא מִגּוֹ נַפְשֵׁיהּ אוֹ גּוּפֵיהּ אוֹ מָמוֹנֵיהּ, דְּיִנְטַר לֵיהּ קוּדְשָׁא בְּרִיךְ הוּא. הָא רְחִימוּ דִּילֵיהּ תְּלוּיָּה, בְּהַהִיא דְּיָהִיב לֵיהּ, וְלָאו עִקָּר רְחִימוּ דִּילֵיהּ דְּלָאו אִיהוּ. הַאי רְחִימוּ, דְּאִם נָטַל מָמוֹנֵיהּ אוֹ גּוּפֵיהּ, כָּפַר בֵּיהּ.

225. That is, if someone loves the Holy One blessed be He, out of his soul, body or wealth in order that the Holy One blessed be He, should protect him, then that love is dependent on something that he hopes to

get, **and that is not a primal love,** rather, that thing is primary and the love is dependent on it. **For this love, if money, body or soul are taken from him, he is in denial,** since the root of his love is based on some material thing, if that material thing is denied and voided, then so is his love.

226. לָאו אִיהוּ עִקָּר רְחִימוּ, עַד דְּיִמְסַר נַפְשֵׁיהּ בִּרְחִימוּ דְּמָארֵיהּ. וְאִם כָּל תְּלַת שְׁקוּלִין לְגַבֵּיהּ, יִמְסוֹר לוֹן כֻּלְּהוּ עַל קְדוּשַׁת שְׁמֵיהּ, בִּרְחִימוּ. וְהַאי אִיהוּ עִקָּרָא דִּרְחִימוּ, דְּאִיהִי אַהֲבַת י"י מַלְכוּת, דְּאִיהִי אַהֲבַת חֶסֶד. דְּיִרְאָה מִסִּטְרָא דִּגְבוּרָה אִיהִי. וּמֵחֶסֶד אִיהִי מַלְכוּת אַהֲבַת י"י, כְּמָה דְּאִתְּמַר. מִגְּבוּרָה אִיהִי יִרְאַת י"י. וְאוֹרַיְיתָא דְּאִיהִי תרי"א, מִתַּרְוַיְיהוּ אִתְיַהִיב לְיִשְׂרָאֵל, וְדָא עַמּוּדָא דְּאֶמְצָעִיתָא. מִסִּטְרֵיהּ אִתְקְרִיאַת מַלְכוּת תּוֹרַת י"י תְּמִימָה. וְאִיהִי מִצְוָה דִּילֵיהּ, בְּכָל תרי"ג פִּקּוּדֵי דְּתַלְיָין בִּשְׁמֵיהּ, דְּאִינּוּן שְׁמִ"י עִם י"ק שס"ה. זִכְרִ"י עִם ו"ה רמ"ח, הוּא בְּצַלְמוֹ כִּדְמוּתוֹ.

226. Love is a primary matter and root cause, only **when one gives his soul out of love for his master. And if all three are of equal balance to him,** his soul, body, and health, **then he should give them all for the sanctity of His Name lovingly. And this is the essential root of this love, the love of Malchut,** which is called **loving kindness (**ahavat chesed**),** when Chesed illuminates in it, **and it is called "awe" from the aspect of Gevurah,** when Gevurah illuminates in it. **And from Chesed,** when Malchut illuminates in the aspect of Chesed, **Malchut is** the aspect of **love of the Lord, as we have learned. And from Gevurah is the awe (fear) of the Lord. And Torah,** which is numerical value **611 was given to Israel from between the two,** Chesed and Gevurah, **and this** Torah **is the Central Column,** Tiferet, **from the aspect** of the Central Column, **Malchut is called: "The statutes of the Lord are perfect…."** (Psalms 19:8) **She is His precept (**mitzvah**),** as Zeir Anpin is Torah, and Malchut is mitzvah, **inclusive in all 613 commandments that depend on the Name** Yud-Hei-Vav-Hei, **which are: "My Name" (**Shmi; 350**) with Yud-Hei (15) is 365 negative precepts, "My Memorial" (**Zichri, 237**) with Vav-Hei (11) is 248 positive precepts, and 365+248=613. It is in his image and form,** inclusive of all the precepts of the Torah, which is Zeir Anpin.

27. Beresheet: *Brit Esh* (Covenant of Fire)

‫227. וְעוֹד תִּקּוּנָא ז', וְהַמַּשְׂכִּילִים יַזְהִירוּ, אִלֵּין דְּיָדְעִין בְּמִלַּת בְּרֵאשִׁית,‬
‫פְּקוּדָא תְּלִיתָאָה, דְּאִיהִי בְּרִית מִילָה. וְהַיְינוּ בְּרֵאשִׁי"ת, דְּאִיהוּ בְּרִי"ת אֵ"שׁ.‬
‫וּבְרִית אִיהִי י', וְעִם אֵ"שׁ, אִתְעֲבִיד אִי"שׁ וְאוֹף הָכִי עִם ה', עִם אֵשׁ, אִיהִי‬
‫נוּקְבָא, וְעַל תְּרֵין אֶשּׁוֹת, אִתְּמַר בְּקַדְמֵיתָא כָּתְנוֹת אוֹר. דִּבְהוֹן עֲקָבוֹ מַכְהֶה‬
‫גַּלְגַּל חַמָּה.‬

227. Furthermore, [concerning] the seventh correction, it is written:
"The wise shall shine…" (Daniel 12:3) **referring to those who recognize
the third precept in the word Beresheet,** which is **the Covenant of
Circumcision (*Brit Milah*). The letters in the word Beresheet** spell *Brit
Esh* [lit. Covenant of Fire], **the *Brit* is Yud, and with *Esh* (Alef, Shin)
it becomes *ish* (man, Alef, Yud, Shin). Similarly, also, the letter Hei
with *esh* becomes *isha* (woman, Alef, Shin, Hei), female. About** these **two
types of fire we learned that at first,** before the sin, Primordial Adam
wore **garments of Light, by which** Primordial Adam **was able to dim the
circuit of the sun** by the bulge on his **ankle.**

‫228. וְהַיְינוּ בּוֹרֵא מְאוֹרֵי הָאֵשׁ, דְּאִינוּן בְּהַבְדָּלָה, י"ה מִן אִישׁ וְאִשָּׁה, בָּתַר‬
‫דְּחָאבוּ, וַיַּעַשׂ יְ"יָ אֱלֹקִי"ם לְאָדָם וּלְאִשְׁתּוֹ כָּתְנוֹת עוֹר וַיַּלְבִּישֵׁם, וְדָא עוֹר‬
‫שֶׁל נָחָשׁ לְאִתְדַּכָּאָה בַּמֶּה דְּחָאב.‬

228. The reason that at the end of Shabbat we recite **the blessing over the
lights of fire is because** the lights of fire shine **on the separation of Yud-
Hei,** which are illuminations of Light, **from *ish* (man) and *isha* (woman),
after they sinned,** and then is mentioned: **"And the Lord God made for
Adam and his wife garments of skin and clothed them"** (Genesis 3:21)
**and this is the skin of the serpent, in order to get purified from what
he sinned.**

‫229. וּבְגִין דָּא, צַדִּיקִים דְּנָטְרֵי בְּרִית, שׁוּב אֵינָם חוֹזְרִים לְעַפְרָן, דְּאִיהוּ עוֹר,‬
‫מִשְׁכָא דְּחִוְיָא, דְּאִתְבְּרֵי מֵעַפְרָא, דְּאִתְּמַר בֵּיהּ וְנָחָשׁ עָפָר לַחְמוֹ.‬

229. As a consequence, the righteous who safeguard the Covenant (*Brit*), and continue the great Mochin of the Light of Chaya, **do not return again to their dust, which is the skin**, Malchut of the attribute of Judgment, which is the greatness of the Desire to Receive, in the aspect **of the serpent that was created from dust, as mentioned about it: "…and dust shall be the serpent's food."** (Isaiah 65:25)

230. וּבְגִין דָּא, מָאן דְּלָא נָטִיר בְּרִית, אִתְדָּן בְּחִבּוּט הַקֶּבֶר בְּהַהוּא עַפְרָא. וְאִלֵּין אִינּוּן, דְּגוּפָא דִּלְהוֹן אִינּוּן כוֹן קֶבֶר בְּחַיֵּיהוֹן, דְּדוֹחֲקִין לוֹ שַׁעְתָּא בְּכָל יוֹמָא. וּבְמִלְאָכָא דִּלְהוֹן, דְּאִתְבַּקַּע דְּמָא בְּצִפָּרְנֵיהוֹן.

230. Consequently, whoever does not guard the Covenant, to receive in order to give pleasure to his Creator, **is sentenced to the shaking of the grave (*chibut hakever*), in that dust, and these bodies are to them** an aspect **of a grave in their own lifetime**, as the masters said: "The wicked are called dead while they are alive" (Berachot 18b) **because they are daily in a state of distress,** and constantly scream "give, give" as the masters said: "Whoever has a hundred wants two hundred." **And during their occupation,** meaning when they do the work to improve themselves, **blood** flows out **from their split fingernails.**

231. וּבְגִין דָּא, תַּקִּינוּ לְאַחֲזָאָה צִפָּרְנַיִם בְּהַבְדָּלָה, דַּהֲוָה אָדָם מִלְבָּשׁ בִּכְתְנוֹת צִפָּרְנַיִם, דַּהֲווֹ נָהֲרִין כַּעֲנָנֵי כָבוֹד. וְאִיהוּ בְּהַבְדָּלָה מִנַּיְיהוּ, וַיֵּדְעוּ כִּי עֲרוּמִּים הֵם מִנַּיְיהוּ, בְּגוּפָא וְנִשְׁמָתָא וְרוּחָא וְנַפְשָׁא, עֲרוּמִּים מִכִּתְנוֹת אוֹר, דְּאִינּוּן מְאוֹרֵי הָאֵשׁ.

231. Consequently, they set the custom to look at the fingernails during the Havdalah ceremony, at the end of Shabbat, **because Primordial Adam was dressed up in garments of fingernails, which shone like the Cloud of Glory, and** due to the sin of the Tree of Knowledge Good and Evil **it was separated from them,** and then it is mentioned **"and they knew they were naked…"** (Genesis 3:7) **from these, in Body, Neshama, Ruach,**

and Nefesh, and naked from the garments of Light, which are the Lights of Fire.

232. וּבְגִין דִּבְשַׁבָּת אִתְוַזָּא לוֹן בְּאַדְלָקַת שְׁרָגָּא דְשַׁבָּת, בִּתְרֵין פְּתִילוֹת דְּאֵשׁ, וּבְמוֹצָאֵי שַׁבָּת יִתְעַבְרוּן מִנַּיְיהוּ. תַּקִּינוּ לְמֵימַר בְּמוֹצָאֵי שַׁבָּת הַבְדָּלָה בְּאֵשׁ.

232. Because on Shabbat, these Lights of Fire **can be seen when lighting the Shabbat candles with two wicks of fire, and at the end of Shabbat they are removed from them,** therefore **they set the custom to recite the Havdalah ceremony with fire at the end of Shabbat.**

233. וּבְגִין דִּבְשַׁבָּת וְיוֹמִין טָבִין מִתְלַבְּשִׁין נִשְׁמָתִין בִּכְתָנוֹת אוֹר, אָמַר הַנָּבִיא עַל כֵּן בָּאוּרִים כַּבְּדוּ יְ"יָ, וְאוּקְמוּהוּ רַבָּנָן, כַּבְּדוּהוּ בִּכְסוּת נְקִיָּה. מִיָּד דְּאָמַר מִלִּין אִלֵּין, אִשְׁתַּטְחוּ קַמֵּיהּ כֻּלְּהוּ בְּנֵי מְתִיבְתָּא. דְּלֵית חֶדְוָה בֵּינַיְיהוּ, כְּחֶדְוָה כַּד אִתְחֲדֵשׁ בֵּינַיְיהוּ רָזָא דְאוֹרַיְיתָא.

233. And since in Shabbat and Holidays the souls are dressed up in garments of Light, therefore the prophet said: "Therefore, glorify you the Lord in the regions of light...." (Isaiah 24:15) And the masters defined it to honor Him with clean clothes. As soon as the Faithful Shepherd **said these things, all the members of the Academy (Yeshivah) prostrated themselves before him because no joy is as great among them as the joy when new secrets in the Torah is revealed anew among them.**

234. וּבְגִין דָּא, מָאן דְּנָטִיר בְּרִית אֵשׁ, קָרֵי אִישׁ צַדִּיק תָּמִים. וְאוֹת י' דְּשַׁדַּ"י, אִיהִי וְוֹלְיָא עַל צַוָּאר דְּשַׁ"ד, יֵצֶר הָרָע, וְוֹלְיָא דְשַׁלְשְׁלָאָה. וּבְגִין דָּא רְשִׁים עַד"י בִּבְרִית, וְרַשִׁים בַּמְּוֹוָה, דְּמִזְדַעְזְעִין כֻּלְּהוֹן מֵהַאי שַׁלְשְׁלָאָה, דְּאִיהִי אוֹת שַׁבָּת, אוֹת בְּרִית, אוֹת יָמִין טָבִין, אוֹת תְּפִלִּין.

234. That is why he who guards this Covenant of Fire, and does not draw the Mochin without the correction of the Central Column that diminishes the Upper Three of the Left, **is called "A completely righteous man," and the Yud of** the Name **Shadai (Shin-Dalet-Yud) is a ring on the neck of the demon (shed, Shin-Dalet) of the Evil Inclination, a ring that chains him,** the secret of the curtain in the Central Column. **Therefore,** the Name **Shadai is marked on the Covenant (Brit),** meaning that it is marked with the Mochin that are revealed through the precept of Circumcision, **and it is marked in the Mezuzah because they all tremble from this chain, which is the sign of Shabbat, the sign of the Covenant, the sign of Holidays,** and **the sign of Tefilin.**

235. וּמִיָּד דְּאִיהוּ תָּפִיס בָּהּ יֵצֶר הָרָע דְּאִיהוּ שֵׁ"ד. נָטִיל בַּר נָשׁ חַרְבָּא, דְּאִתְּמַר בָּהּ רוֹמְמוֹת אֵ"ל בִּגְרוֹנָם, דְּאִיהוּ י' רֵישָׁא דְּחַרְבָּא, ו' גּוּפָא דְּחַרְבָּא, ה"ה תְּרֵי פִּפְיוֹת דִּילָהּ. וְשָׁחִיט לֵיהּ. וּבְגִינֵיהּ אִתְּמַר, הַבָּא לְהָרְגָךְ הַשְׁכֵּם לְהָרְגוֹ בִּצְלוֹתָא, דְּאִתְּמַר בָּהּ וַיַּשְׁכֵּם אַבְרָהָם בַּבֹּקֶר.

235. **Immediately when he grasps the Evil Inclination, which is** *shed* **(Shin-Dalet), with this** Yud of Shadai, **the person takes the sword, about which is mentioned: "Let the high praises of God be in their mouth…,"** (Psalms 149:6), meaning he draws the aspect of Chasadim on the curtain that is called Yud Hei Vav Hei **because the Yud** of Yud-Hei-Vav-Hei **is the top point of the sword, the Vav of** Yud-Hei-Vav-Hei is **the body of the sword, the Hei-Hei of** Yud-Hei-Vav-Hei are **the two sharp edges of the sword, and he slaughters him. About him was mentioned: "Whoever comes to kill you, get up earlier and kill him" by prayer, regarding which is said: "And Abraham rose early in the morning…."** (Genesis 22:3)

236. וְעוֹד קְרִיאַת שְׁמַע אִיהִי רוֹמַ"ח, כְּלִילָא מִשִּׁית תֵּיבִין דְּיִחוּדָא, וּמֵרְמַ"ח תֵּיבִין, עִם י"ָ אֱלֹקֵ"יכֶם אֱמֶת. וְהוּא קִירְטָא, וְהָא אִתְּמַר, וְחָמֵשׁ אַבְנִין, ה' דְּאִתְעֲבִידוּ חַד אַבְנָא בְּאָת י', וְקָטִיל בָּהּ לְיֵצֶר הָרָע.

236. Also, the Shema reading is a *romach* (spear; 254), that is, he adds the idea of the spear to what he said before regarding the sword, **composed from the six words of the unification,** meaning *Shema Yisrael Adonai Elokeinu Adonai Echad* [Hear Israel, the Lord our God, the Lord is one], **and from the 248 words** of the entire Shema reading **with: "Your God is truth"** that together equals *romach* (254). **It is a slingshot, and it was said** (in Zohar, Ekev, verse 27): "The Shema reading is like a slingshot" that slings **five stones,** which are *Shema Yisrael Adonai Elokeinu Adonai,* the **Hei** of the Name, **which become one stone** in the word *Echad* (one) **by the letter Yud** of the Name, **and with it kills the Evil Inclination.**

237. וּבְאָן אֲתַר אִיהִי קִירְטָא בִּתְפִלִּין. חוּט דְּקִלְעָא כָּרִיךְ בְּיָד, דָּא רְצוּעָה דְּיָד, דְּאִיהוּ כְּוֹוּט דְּוַרְקָא. וְאִיהוּ קְרִיאַת שְׁמַע קֶשֶׁת, דְּזָרִיק וְיִצִּים, מִסְטְרָא דְּבָרוּךְ שֵׁם כְּבוֹד מַלְכוּתוֹ, וּבְרָכוֹת לְרֹאשׁ צַדִּיק, דְּאִיהוּ קֶשֶׁת הַבְּרִית. רוֹמְחָא דָּא עַמּוּדָא דְּאֶמְצָעִיתָא, בְּחָמֵשׁ אֶצְבְּעָאן דְּיָד, דְּאִיהוּ ה' תַּתָּאָה, וְאִיהִי לִימִינָא דְּחֶסֶד, דַּרְגָּא דְּאַבְרָהָם, דְּחוּשְׁבְּנֵיהּ רמַ"ח, וְעִם ו' דְּעַמּוּדָא דְּאֶמְצָעִיתָא אִתְעֲבִיד רוֹמַ"ח. קֶלַע, ה' עִלָּאָה, לִשְׂמָאלָא. י' אַבְנָא דְקִלְעָ. י"ק דִּתְפִלִּין וְכֹלָּא י"ק עִם שְׁמִ"י שְׁסָ"ה, זְכְר"י עִם ו"ק רמַ"ח.

237. He asks, **"At which place is this slingshot** indicated also **in the Tefilin?"** And answers, **"The string of the slingshot is wound around the hand; this refers to the binding strap from the Tefilin on the arm, as a sling string that throws** (*zarka*), and furthermore, **the Shema reading is the bow that shoots off the arrows,** from the aspect of the lower Hei, Malchut, **from** *Baruch Shem Kevod Malchuto...* **'And blessings to the head of the righteous...'** (Proverbs 10:6) **refers to the stringed bow of the Covenant. The** *romach* (spear) **of the Tefilin is the Central Column,** Tiferet, Vav of the Name, **with the five fingers of the right hand** that ties the Tefilin, **which is the lower Hei of the Name, and it is to the right,** which is Chesed, **the level of Abraham** (Alef, Bet, Resh, Hei, Mem) **whose numerical value is 248, and with the Vav of the Central Column, it becomes** *romach* (spear; 254). **The sling is the upper Hei** of the Name, **to the left. Yud** of the Name **is the stone of the sling,** and they are the

Yud-Hei from the Name Yud-Hei-Vav-Hei in the Tefilin. All Names of Yud-Hei-Vav-Hei share Yud-Hei (15) with Sh'mi (250) equals 365, which represent the 365 negative precepts, in the secret of *zeh Shmi le'olam...* (... this is My Name forever (*Zichri*)...) (Exodus 3:15), *Zichri* (237) with Vav-Hei (11) equals 248 positive precepts, in the secret of ...*zeh Zichri ledor dor dor* '...this is My Memorial unto the all generations.'" (Ibid.)

238. וּמַאן דְּאִיהוּ נָטִיר י' בִּתְמַנְיָא יוֹמִין דְּמִילָה, בִּתְמַנְיָא אַלְפֵי תְחוּם שַׁבָּת, בִּתְמַנְיָא פָּרְשִׁיָן דִּתְפִלֵּי. אִיהוּ נָטִיר מִכָּל מַזִּיקֵי דִּתְחוֹת יְדָא דְּיֵצֶר הָרָע, דְּאִיהוּ מְמַנָּא עַל שִׁתִּין רִבּוֹא. כָּל שֶׁכֵּן מָאן דְּקָשִׁיר לֵיה בְּשַׁלְשְׁלָאין וְקָטִיל לֵיהּ.

238. He who keeps the Covenant, which is the letter Yud, by the eighth day of Circumcision (*Milah*), and guards the sign of the Shabbat, by eight thousand cubits of the domain of Shabbat, and keeps the sign of the Tefilin, by the eight passages inside the Tefilin, four on the head and four on the arm, is guarded from all the destroyers that are under the authority of the Evil Inclination, who is appointed over 600,000 agents of destruction. All the more so about he who binds him in chains and kills him.

239. וְעוֹד, בְּרִית דְּתַקִּינוּ בֵיה מָנָא בְּעַפְרָא, לְשַׁדְּיָיא לָה בְּעַפְרָא, וְדָם דְּאַטִּיפִין מִנֵּיה אִתְחֲשִׁיב לֵיה כְּאִלּוּ עָבִיד לֵיה עוֹלָה, וְהַהוּא עַפְרָא לְתַקָּנָא בֵּיה מִזְבַּח אֲדָמָה, וְדָם דִּבְרִית, כְּאִלּוּ דָבַח עֲלָה עֲלָוָון. הָדָא הוּא דִכְתִיב מִזְבַּח אֲדָמָה תַּעֲשֶׂה לִי וְגוֹ'. וְשָׁזִיב לֵיה בְּהַהוּא עַפְרָא מֵחִבּוּט הַקֶּבֶר, וּבְדַם מִילָה, שָׁזִיב לֵיה, מִשְׁחִיטַת מַלְאַךְ הַמָּוֶת.

239. Furthermore, at the precept of Circumcision, which is *Brit*, they established the requirement to prepare a vessel with soil to throw the foreskin membrane, into the soil. The blood that drips from the child is considered as if he made him a burnt sacrifice offering, and from the soil is amended the earthen altar, and the blood of the Circumcision is as if he slaughtered on the altar sacrifices and burnt offerings, as it says:

"...prepare me an altar out of stone...." (Exodus 20:21) That soil will save him from the agitating punishment of the grave (*chibut hakever*), and the blood of the Circumcision will save him from the slaughter by the Angel of Death.

240. וְאִם הַהוּא דְקַבִּיל בְּרִית אִיהוּ מַמְזֵר, הַהוּא עַפְרָא תַּקִּין לֵיהּ לְחִוְיָא, דְאִתְּמַר בֵּיהּ וְנָחָשׁ עָפָר לַחְמוֹ. וְאִיהוּ מִן הָאֲדָמָה אֲשֶׁר אֲרֲרָהּ יְ"יָ דְאִתְּמַר בָּהּ אֲרוּרָה הָאֲדָמָה. וְאִיהִי עַפְרָא מֵהַאי דְאִתְּמַר בָּהּ, וְהָאָרֶץ הָיְתָה תֹהוּ וָבֹהוּ, דְאִתְּמַר בָּהּ וְהָאָרֶץ כַּבֶּגֶד תִּבְלֶה, עֲמֵיהּ יְהֵא וְחוּלְקֵיהּ. כְּאִלּוּ קָשִׁיר לֵיהּ לְמֶיעֱבַד עוֹלָה לַעֲבוֹדָה זָרָה.

240. Meaning **if the circumcised child is a bastard** (*mamzer*), **that soil prepared him for the serpent,** about whom is mentioned: "...and dust is the serpent's food...." (Isaiah 65:25) **And this** altar is "...from the ground (soil) that the Lord has cursed." (Genesis 5:29), about which was said: "...the ground will be cursed...." (Genesis 3:17) **And this soil is from the** one about which is said: "And the earth was without form and void..." (Genesis 1:2), **and regarding it was also said:** "...and the earth will wax old like a garment..." (Isaiah 51:6) **the one who makes an altar for him will share in his destiny, and it is as if he binds him to prepare him for a burnt sacrifice to idol worship.**

241. דְּהַהוּא בֵּן אוֹ בַּת אִינוּן פֶּסֶל וּמַסֵּכָה, וְעַל דָּא אִתְּמַר, אֲשֶׁר יַעֲשֶׂה פֶסֶל וּמַסֵּכָה, וְאִתְּמַר וְשָׂם בַּסָּתֶר בְּסִתְרוֹ שֶׁל עוֹלָם, וְאָמַר כָּל הָעָם אָמֵן. דְּהַהוּא בַּר מִנָּחָשׁ הַקַּדְמוֹנִי אִיהוּ. דִּגְרִים מָוֶת לְאָדָם וּלְאִתְּתֵיהּ, דְאִתְּמַר בֵּיהּ אָרוּר אַתָּה מִכָּל הַבְּהֵמָה וכו'.

241. **Because that son or daughter,** which are bastards, **are like the carved and molten images, and about this one,** meaning their father, **was said:** "...the man that makes a graven or molten image..." (Deuteronomy 27:15), **and is mentioned further:** "...and places it in a hidden place" (Ibid.) **that is, what the world keeps hidden and secret:** "And all the people say, Amen." (Ibid.) **because that child's source is** rooted **from the**

primordial serpent, who brought on death to Adam and his wife, as is said about him, the primordial serpent: "...cursed are you from all the beasts...." (Genesis 3:14)

242. קְלִיפָה דְּעָרְלָה דְּכַסֵּי עַל י', אִית לָהּ תְּלַת קְלִיפֵי כְּגִלְדֵי בְּצָלִים דָּא עַל דָּא. וְאִינוּן כִּקְלִיפִין דֶּאֱגוֹזָא, דְּאִתְּמַר עֲלַיְיהוּ וְהָאָרֶץ הָיְתָה תֹהוּ, דָּא קַו יָרוֹק, קְלִיפָה קַדְמָאָה דֶּאֱגוֹזָא. וָבֹהוּ, אֲבָנִים מְפוּלָמוֹת דָּא קְלִיפָה תִּנְיָנָא דֶּאֱגוֹזָא, קָשֶׁה כְּאֶבֶן. וְחֹשֶׁךְ, קְלִיפָה תְּלִיתָאָה. וּבְהוֹן אוּקְמוּהוּ רַבָּנָן, אֵין דּוֹרְשִׁין בַּעֲרָיוֹת בִּשְׁלֹשָׁה. שָׁלֹשׁ שָׁנִים יִהְיֶה לָכֶם עֲרֵלִים. וּלְקָבֵל מוֹחָא אִיהוּ וּבַשָּׁנָה הָרְבִיעִית יִהְיֶה כָּל פִּרְיוֹ קֹדֶשׁ הִלּוּלִים לַי"יָ.

242. The Klipa (negative shell) of foreskin that sheaths the Mochin, the secret of Yud, has three shells, like the layers of onions, one over the other, and they are like the shells (membrane) of an nut (egoz), about which was said: "And the earth was without form...," (Genesis 1:2) which is the green line, the first shell of the nut. "...and void...," (Ibid.) meaning smooth stones, is the second shell as hard as stone, and "...darkness..." (Ibid.) is the third shell. Concerning them the masters have established: "One may not expound the laws of forbidden sexual relations before three people," (Mishnah Chagigah 2:1) "...three years its growth shall be forbidden...." (Leviticus 19:23) and corresponding to the brain is said: "And on the fourth year all the fruit thereof shall be holy, for giving praise unto the Lord." (Leviticus 19:24)

243. וּבְהוֹן מִסִּטְרָא דָּא, אַרְבָּעָה נִכְנְסוּ לְפַרְדֵּס, שְׁלֹשָׁה אָכְלוּ מֵאִלֵּין קְלִיפֵי וּמֵתוּ, רְבִיעָאָה אָכַל אִיבָּא, וְזָרַק קְלִיפִין וְחַי. כְּגַוְונָא דָּא אִתְּמַר, רַבִּי מֵאִיר רִמּוֹן מָצָא, תּוֹכוֹ אָכַל קְלִיפָתוֹ זָרָק.

243. And from this aspect, of these Klipot, we learned: "four entered the orchard (pardes) the acronym for P'shat (simple meaning), Remez (hint, allusion), Derash (interpretation) and Sod (secret). Three ate from these outer shells and died, and they were Ben Zoma, Ben Azai and Acher, and the fourth, Rav Akiva, ate the fruit and threw away the Klipot,

and survived because he entered and existed in peace." (Chagigah 14b) **Similarly, we learned that Rav Meir:** "Found a pomegranate, ate the inner fruit and disposed of the outer shell."

244. וּכְגַוְונָא דְּאִלֵּין קְלִיפִין, אִינוּן קוּשְׁיָין דְּחַפְיָין עַל הֲלָכָה. דְּאִיהִי מוֹחָא מִלְּגָּאו. וְלֵית בַּר נָשׁ יָכִיל לְמֵיכַל בְּנַהֲמָא דְאוֹרַיְיתָא, דְּאִתְּמַר בָּהּ עֵץ חַיִּים הִיא, עַד דְּזָרִיק קוּשְׁיָין מֵהֲלָכוֹת. וְאִית הֲלָכָה, דְּכָל קוּשְׁיָין דִּילָהּ אִינוּן, כְּאִילָנָא דִּקְלִיפָה דִּילֵיהּ וְקַנֶּה דִּילֵיהּ, וְעֵצָיו, וְעַלִּין, וְאִיבָּא, כֻּלְּהוֹן שָׁוִין לְמֵיכַל, וַעֲלֵיהּ אִתְּמַר, נֵרְדְ וְכַרְכּוֹם וְגוֹ'. וּבְגִין דָּא לָאו כָּל קָשְׁיָין שָׁוִין.

244. And similar to these shells are the difficult questions that surround the Halachah (law), which is like the inner brain (the fruit of the nut), and a person cannot digest the bread of Torah, about which it is said: "She a Tree of Life...," (Proverbs 3:18) **until he disposes and answers the difficult questions arising from these laws. And there is such accepted law, whereby all the difficulties about it are like a tree whose shells, bark, sprigs, woody parts, leaves, and fruits are all equally edible and digestible. And about such a tree is said:** "Spikenard and saffron...," (Song of Songs 4:14) which are not fruits at all, but types of woody parts and shell bark from the trees. **Thus, not all questionable difficulties are equal.**

28. Beresheet: Is the Torah

245. פִּקוּדָא רְבִיעָאָה בְּמִלַּת בְּרֵאשִׁית, דָּא אוֹרַיְתָא, דְּאִתְּמַר בָּהּ יְ"יָ קָנָנִי רֵאשִׁית דַּרְכּוֹ. וְדָא שְׁכִינְתָּא תַּתָּאָה, דְּאִיהִי רֵאשִׁית לְנִבְרָאִים. וְאִיהִי אַחֲרִית לְחָכְמָה עִלָּאָה. וּבְגִינָהּ אִתְּמַר, מַגִּיד מֵרֵאשִׁית אַחֲרִית.

245. The fourth precept indicated by the word Beresheet is Torah, called *resheet*, as said about it: "The Lord made me as the beginning of His way…." (Proverbs 8:22) And this refers to the lower Shechinah, Malchut, which is the first to all creations and last to the Supernal Wisdom (Chochmah), and for her sake was said: "Declaring the end from the beginning…." (Isaiah 46:10)

246. כַּד אִתְנְטִילַת מִכֶּתֶר, אִתְקְרִיאַת עֲטֶרֶת תִּפְאֶרֶת, עֲטָרָה בְּרֹאשׁ כָּל צַדִּיק, תַּגָּא דְּסֵפֶר תּוֹרָה וּבְגִינָהּ אִתְּמַר כָּל הַמִּשְׁתַּמֵּשׁ בְּתַגָּא וְחָלַף. כַּד אִתְנְטִילַת מֵהַאי חָכְמָה עִלָּאָה דְּהִיא רֵאשִׁית, אִתְקְרִיאַת עַל שְׁמָהּ.

246. When She is taken from Keter it is called a "decoration of splendor," as it is a crowning decoration to Zeir Anpin, called Tiferet, a crown to the head of every righteous, a crown to the Torah scroll. For its sake we were taught: "He who uses the crown [of Torah], passes away," (Tractate Megilah 28b; see verse 116 above) As this is the end goal of the growth of Nukva, and this stature is only reached in the back or outer (*achorayim*) state, and there is a need to be cautious not to detain Zeir [Anpin] and Nukva in an outer state and continue immediately the Mochin of the face. And when She is taken from this Supernal Wisdom, which is called *resheet*, She is named after it, Chochmah.

247. וְכַד אִתְנְטִילַת מִבִּינָה, אִתְקְרִיאַת עַל שְׁמָהּ תְּבוּנָה וְכַד אִתְנְטִילַת מֵחֶסֶד, אִתְקְרִיאַת תּוֹרָה שֶׁבִּכְתָב, דְּאִתְיְהִיבַת מִימִינָא, דִּכְתִיב מִימִינוֹ אֵשׁ דָּת לָמוֹ. וְכַד אִתְנְטִילַת מִגְּבוּרָה, אִתְקְרִיאַת תּוֹרָה שֶׁבְּעַל פֶּה. דְּהָכִי אוּקְמוּהוּ מָארֵי מַתְנִיתִין, תּוֹרָה שֶׁבְּעַל פֶּה מִפִּי הַגְּבוּרָה נִתְּנָה, וּמִתַּמָּן גְּבוּרִים

עוֹמְדִים בַּפֶּרֶץ, וְלָא יָכִיל לְמֵיקַם בָּהּ, אֶלָּא גִּבּוֹר בְּמִלְחַמְתָּהּ שֶׁל תּוֹרָה, גִּבּוֹר בְּיִצְרוֹ.

247. And when She is taken from Binah, She is named Tevunah after it. And when She is taken from Chesed, She is called the Written Torah, which was given from the Right, as it says: "...at His right hand was a fiery law unto them." (Deuteronomy 33:2) And when She is taken from Gevurah, She is called the Oral Torah, as the scholars of the Mishnah established: "...the Oral Torah was given from the mouth of the Almighty [lit. Gevurah]." And there, in Oral Torah, the mighty stand in the breach, and only the mighty could endure the battle [lit. war] of the Torah, mighty against his inclination.

248. וּבְיוֹמָא תְּלִיתָאָה, נָחִיתַת לְעַמּוּדָא דְּאֶמְצָעִיתָא עַל יְדֵי דְמֹשֶׁה, הָדָא הוּא דִּכְתִיב וַיְהִי בַיּוֹם הַשְּׁלִישִׁי בִּהְיוֹת הַבֹּקֶר, בָּתְרֵי לוּחֵי אַבְנִין נֵצַח וְהוֹד. הָדָא הוּא דִּכְתִיב, כְּתוּבִים מִשְּׁנֵי עֶבְרֵיהֶם, וְאִינּוּן תְּרֵין נְבִיאֵי קְשׁוֹט. וּמִסִּטְרָא דְּעַמּוּדָא דְּאֶמְצָעִיתָא אִתְקְרִיאוּ נְבִיאֵי הָאֱמֶת. וּשְׁכִינְתָּא תּוֹרַת אֱמֶת, הָדָא הוּא דִּכְתִיב תּוֹרַת אֱמֶת הָיְתָה בְּפִיהוּ. וְאִתְקְרִיאַת מַרְאֵה דִּנְבוּאָה, וְרוּחַ הַקֹּדֶשׁ, מִסִּטְרָא דְּתַרְוַויְיהוּ.

248. And on the third day, Tiferet, She descended to be Nukva to the Central Column, through Moses, in the secret of Moses's bride (kalat Moshe), as it says "...Moses finished (kalot) setting up the Tabernacle...," (Numbers 7:1) as it says: "And it came to pass on the third day when it was morning...." (Exodus 19:16) This was the unification of face-to-face, with the two stone tablets, which are Netzach and Hod of Arich Anpin, as He is in Netzach and She is in Hod, as it says: "...written on both their sides..." (Exodus 32:15) meaning Right and Left, front and back, and they are two true prophets, since they are from the Central Column aspect, which is the secret of: "...grant truth to Jacob." (Micah 7:20), they are called prophets of truth. And the Shechinah is the Torah of Truth, as it says: "The law [Torah] of truth was in his mouth...," (Malachi 2:6)

and it is called the mirror of prophecy (*nevua*) and Spirit of Holiness (*Ruach haKodesh*), from both aspects, Netzach and Hod.

249. וּבְיוֹם הַזֶ' נִתְּנָה, דָּא צַדִּיק יְסוֹד עוֹלָם, וּבְדַרְגָּא דִילֵיה מַלְכוּת מַלִּיל עִמְּהוֹן, וְהָא אוּקְמוּהוּ לִי' מַלְכִין, שֶׁמָּא לָא יוּכְלוּ לְדַבֵּר עַל פֶּה אֶחָד, נָגַע בְּבַת, וְכָלַל בָּהּ כָּל הַי'.

249. The Torah was given on the Shabbat day, as the masters said, "... everyone agrees that the Torah was given on Shabbat." (Shabbat 86b) **This is the "...righteous is an everlasting foundation."** (Proverbs 10:25) meaning that on Shabbat Yesod is found complete, **and in its level,** meaning in the unification of Yesod and Malchut, **Malchut spoke with them. Thus they established it to ten Malchuts,** meaning that Malchut includes all Ten Sefirot. **In case they all will not be able to speak as one mouth,** rather **he touched the daughter,** since the Supernal Light spread from each Sefira until Malchut, **and included in her all Ten,** since by Returning Light She completes each Sefira and is inclusive of each Sefira, and they all get revealed through Malchut.

250. וְדָא י', בַּ"ת אַחַת, תְּחוֹת, הַי' מִן אֱלֹקִי"ם, י' מִן אדנ"י, י' מִן שד"י. כְּלִילָא מִכָּל כִּנּוּיִי"ן, וּמִכָּל הֲוַיִי"ן, כְּגוֹן קוק"י אוֹ כְּוָותֵיהּ דִיהֵא י' תְּחוֹת ה', בְּכָל שֵׁם דְּכִינּוּ"י וַהֲוַיִ"ה, אִיהִי נוּקְבָא.

250. And this, meaning Malchut, **is Yud, one daughter,** which is **beneath,** meaning the last of the Sefirot, and is **the Yud of** the Name **Elokim** אֱלֹקִי"ם, hinting to Malchut, and also **Yud from** the Name **Adonai** אדנ"י, **and Yud from Shadai** שד"י. She is included in all the Names and Yud-Hei-Vav-Hei's, as Hei-Vav-Hei-Yud. **And similar to it, in all Names and Yud-Hei-Vav-Hei's that Yud is under the Hei, she is** an aspect of **Nukva.**

251. וּבְגִין דְּאוֹרַיְתָא מִינָּהּ אִתְיְהִיבַת, אָמַר לְמֹשֶׁה וְרָאִיתָ אֶת אֲחוֹרָי כו'. דְּלֵית נָבִיא וְחָכָם יָכִיל לְעַאֲלָא לְעֵילָא פָּחוֹת מִן דָּא.

251. And because the Torah was given from Her, since all the Lights of Chochmah are revealed only in Her, the Holy One blessed be He **said to Moses: "…and you shall see My back…"** (Exodus 33:23) **since there is no prophet or sage that is able to ascend above** in the Supernal levels **besides Her.**

252. וּבְגִין דָּא אִתְקְרִיאַת מַפְתְּחוֹת הַחִיצוֹנִיִּים, אַנְפִּין דִּילָהּ. וְאַנְפִּין דִּלְגָאו, מַפְתְּחוֹת הַפְּנִימִיִּים. וְהָא אִתְּמַר לְעֵיל, דְּאִם בַּר נָשׁ לֵית בִּידוֹי מַפְתְּחוֹת הַחִיצוֹנִיִּים, בְּמַאי יֵיעוּל. וּבְגִין דָּא אִתְּמַר בָּהּ, זֶה הַשַּׁעַר לַיְיָ.

252. And due to this, that Her illumination is the illumination of Chochmah, which shines in the external vessels, **Her face is called the outer keys, and Her inner face,** when she shines with Chasadim by clothing the Lights of Chochmah in Chasadim, **is called the inner keys. And we already learned earlier** (verse 99) **that if a person does not possess the outer keys, with what would he enter? And therefore, it says regarding Her: "This is the gate of the Lord…."** (Psalms 118:20)

253. וּבְגִין דְּלֵית הַשָּׁעָה לְנָבִיא וְחוֹזֶה וְחָכָם פָּחוֹת מִינָהּ, אָמַר הַנָּבִיא כֹּה אָמַר יְ"י אַל יִתְהַלֵּל חָכָם בְּחָכְמָתוֹ גו', כִּי אִם בְּזֹאת יִתְהַלֵּל גו', וְיָדוֹעַ אוֹתִי. וּבְגִין דָּא יַעֲקֹב אוֹלִיף לָהּ לִבְנוֹי, וְיָהִיב לוֹן קַבָּלָה מִינָהּ, הֲדָא הוּא דִכְתִיב וְזֹאת אֲשֶׁר דִּבֶּר לָהֶם אֲבִיהֶם. וְדָוִד דַּהֲוָה לֵיהּ קַבָּלָה מִינָהּ, אָמַר לְגַבָּהּ, אִם תַּחֲנֶה עָלַי מַחֲנֶה כו', רָמִיז לָהּ בְּהַאי תַּגָּא, וְסָלִיק מַחֲשַׁבְתֵּיהּ לְגַבָּהּ, וְאָמַר לֹא יִירָא לִבִּי וכו'.

253. And since the prophet, seer, and sage have no grasp except through Her, the prophet declares: "So said the Lord, 'Let not the wise be praised by his wisdom…but let him that glorifies praise, in this (*zot***)… and knows Me….'"** (Jeremiah 9:22-23) **And therefore, Jacob taught about Her to his children and passed on to them the accepted traditional accounts of Her,** meaning they merited the complete clothing of Malchut, which shines in all the Lights of the first nine Sefirot, **and David that had the accepted traditional accounts of Her,** meaning he became a chariot to Her, **said to**

Her, "Though a host should encamp against me...." (Psalms 27:3) He
hinted to Her with this Keter (Crown), meaning Keter of Malchut, and
raised his thoughts towards Her and said: "...my heart shall not fear...."
(Ibid.)

254. וְאַהֲרֹן דַּהֲוָה לֵיהּ קַבָּלָה מִינָהּ, לָא הֲוָה עָאל לְפַנִּי לִפְנִים, פְּווֹת מִינָהּ.
הֲדָא הוּא דִכְתִיב, בְּזֹאת יָבֹא אַהֲרֹן אֶל הַקֹּדֶשׁ, דַּהֲוָה יָדַע דְּאִיהִי עִקָּרָא
דְכֹלָּא, דְּאִיהִי קָרְבָּן לַי"יָ, עוֹלָה לַי"יָ, אִשֶּׁה לַי"יָ.

254. And Aaron that had the accepted traditional accounts from Her,
did not enter into the inner sanctuary except through Her, as it says:
"With this (zot) shall Aaron come into the holy place..." (Leviticus 16:3)
because he was aware that Malchut is the essence of everything, that
She is a sacrificial offering (korban) for the Lord, a burnt offering (olah)
for the Lord, a fire offering (isheh) for the Lord. Korban is Right Column,
isheh is Left Column, and olah is Central Column.

255. וְיִשְׂרָאֵל דַּהֲוָה לוֹן קַבָּלָה מִינָהּ, לָא בָעוּ מִקּוּדְשָׁא בְּרִיךְ הוּא מַשְׁכּוֹנָא
אָחֳרָא, דִּיפְרְדוֹן לוֹן בְּגִינָהּ מִן גָּלוּתָא אֶלָּא זֹאת. הֲדָא הוּא דִכְתִיב וְאַף גַּם זֹאת
בִּהְיוֹתָם בְּאֶרֶץ אוֹיְבֵיהֶם וכו', וְנָבִיא אָמַר בְּגִינָהּ, כַּד חָזָא בִּנְבוּאָתָא דוֹחֲקָא
דְיִשְׂרָאֵל תַּקִּיפָא אָמַר זֹאת אָשִׁיב אֶל לִבִּי כו' וְזֹאת לִיהוּדָה וַיֹּאמַר.

255. And Israel who had the accepted traditional accounts from Her did
not want another collateral from the Holy One blessed be He to assure
them that he will redeem them from their exile for His own sake, except
for this (zot), which is the Shechinah, as it written: "And for all this (zot)
when they are in the land of their enemies...." (Leviticus 26:44) When the
prophet saw in prophecy how great Israel's oppression will be, he said
about Her: "This (zot), I will bring back to my heart..." (Lamentations
3:21) "And this (zot) for Yehuda, and he said...." (Deuteronomy 33:7)

256. אִיהִי מַרְגָּלִית כְּלִילָא מִכָּל גַּוְונִין נְהִירִין דְּאִינּוּן נְהִירִין בְּגַוְּרְמַיהּ וּסְגוּלָה דִּילֵיהּ בְּכָל נְקוּדִין דְּאַתְוָון וְטַעֲמֵי בְּכָל שֵׁם וָשֵׁם. מִסִּטְרָא דְּחוֹלֶ"ם אִיהִי סְגוֹלְתָּא.

256. Malchut **is a pearl that is composed of all colors,** meaning from all Sefirot **that illuminate** in Her. **They illuminate in Her by the essence** of Zeir Anpin, since she has nothing of her own, **and She is His** *segula* (unique and special quality), meaning that through her he is corrected with the Central Column, which is the secret of Segol, **in all the vowel points of the letters, and also by the cantillation marks,** such as Segolta, **in each and every Name, from the aspect of Cholem She is the Segolta** of the cantillation marks.

257. וְחוֹלֶם מָלֵא בְּוָא"ו סָלִיק בְּאַתְוֹוֹי אהי"ה. וּתְלַת נִיצוֹצִין יי"י כְּחוּשְׁבַּן יהו"ה, דְּאִיהוּ כ"ו, וְאַרְבַּע אַתְוָון. סָלִיק לְחָשְׁבָּן יהו"ה אהי"ה נ"א. בְּרָזָא יהו"ה דְּיי"י. וּסְגוּלָה דִּילֵיהּ אֵ"ל נָא רְפָא נָ"א לָהּ. אָנָּא יְ"י הוֹשִׁיעָה נָּ"א.

257. The vowel **Cholem** וֹחוֹלֶם **spelled with Vav** (Chet=8, Vav=6, Lamed=30, Mem=40)**, amounts to** 21 in small numerical value (8+6+3+0+4+0)**, like the amount of the Name Alef-Hei-Yud-Hei (21), and with the three sparks,** meaning with the vowel over the Vav and the two dots of the Tzere under the Lamed, together they are **three Yud's** since each dot is considered a Yud, thus amounting to 30, **like the numerical value** of the four letters of **Yud-Hei-Vav-Hei, which is 26 plus the four letters** themselves, which is thirty. **Thus, Cholem amounts to the numerical value of Yud-Hei-Vav-Hei (26) and Alef-Hei-Yud-Hei (21), which is 51 (Nun-Alef), in the secret of the three Yud's,** meaning 26 and the four letters of the Name, **and its** *segula* **(unique quality),** meaning Segol, which is the Central Column, is *El Na Refa Na* **(Nun-Alef, 51)** *Lah* "Heal her now God, I beseech You." (Numbers 12:13) *"Ana haShem hoshiah Na* **(Nun-Alef, 51)** "We beseech you Lord, save now...." (Psalms 118:25)**.**

258. אֲהִי"ה כ"א: כ' כֶּתֶר. א' אֵין סוֹף. אֵין קָדוֹשׁ כַּי"ָ וגו' וְחוֹלֵם סְגוּלָתֵיה לְעָלְמָא, דְּבֵיה אִתְּמַר וַיַּחֲלם וְהִנֵּה סֻלָּם מֻצָּב אַרְצָה כו'. וְעוֹד חוֹלֵם מוֹחֵל עֲוֹנוֹת יִשְׂרָאֵל.

258. The numerical value of the Name **Alef-Hei-Yud-Hei** is **21** (which is also Kaf-Alef; 21); **Kaf** hints **to Keter, Alef** hints to the **Endless** Light, in the secret of the verse: **"There is no holy as the Lord...."** (I Samuel 2:2) **And the Cholem is good for dreams** (*chalom*), about which it is said: **"And he dreamed** (*vayachalom*), and behold there was a ladder set up on the earth...."** (Genesis 28:12) **In addition, the letters in the word** *cholem* can be rearranged to the word *mochel* (forgives) the sins of Israel.

259. וֹלֵם וָחָסֵר. אִיהוּ ה'"י מִן אֱלֹקִי"ם, תְּלַת נִיצוֹצוֹת כ' מִן אֱלֹקִי"ם. אִשְׁתָּאַר א"ם דְּאִתְּמַר בָּהּ כִּי אִם לַבִּינָה תִקְרָא וְלָאו צָרִיךְ לְאַרְכָא בְּנִקּוּדֵי דְהָא אִתְאַמְרוּ.

259. Cholem וֹלֵם **without** the Vav is the same as **Hei-Yud** (15) in small numerical value (since Cholem is 78, and 7+8=15) **of the Name Elokim** (Alef-Lamed-Hei-Yud-Mem) **and the three sparks,** one dot over the Chet, and two [dots] of the Tzere under the Lamed from Cholem equal **Lamed (30) from the Name Elokim. There remains the Alef-Mem of Elokim, regarding which it says: "If** (*im*; Alef-Mem) **only you will call out for understanding...."** (Proverbs 2:3) **There is no need to further explain** at length the subject of **the punctuation vowels, as we already studied them** above in the article Secrets of the Vowels.

29. Beresheet: *Yere Shabbat* (Awe of Shabbat)

260. דָּבָר אַחֵר וְהַמַּשְׂכִּלִים אִלֵּין דְּיַדְעֵי בְּפִקּוּדָא וַחֲמִישָׁאָה בְּמִלַת בְּרֵאשִׁי"ת יְרֵ"א שַׁבָּ"ת אַזְהָרָה דִּילֵיהּ דְּלָא לְחַלְלָא בְּרַתָּא דְּמַלְכָּא בְּטַ"ל מְלָאכוֹת דְּאִינּוּן אַרְבָּעִים מְלָאכוֹת חָסֵר אַחַת לָקֳבֵל אַרְבָּעִים מַלְקִיּוֹת חָסֵר חָד.

260. Another definition of "And the wise..." (Daniel 12:3); these are those who are aware of the fifth precept (*mitzvah*) **that is indicated in the word Beresheet and that is:** *Yere Shabbat* (Awe of Shabbat), **His cautious warning that one should not desecrate the daughter of the king,** meaning Malchut, **with the thirty-nine prohibited actions, which are forty actions minus one,** which are applied in the secular weekdays, corresponding to the forty lashes minus one.

261. רְצוּעָה לְאַלְקָאָה אִיהִי שִׁפְחָה בִּישָׁא. שַׁעַטְנֵ"ז כְּלִילָא מִשּׁוֹר וַחֲמוֹר דְּאָמַר יַעֲקֹב וַיְהִי לִי שׁוֹר וַחֲמוֹר עַל כָּל דְּבַר פֶּשַׁע עַל שׁוֹר עַל חֲמוֹר דְּאֵין מַלְקִין בְּשַׁבָּת דְּלָא שַׁלְטָא שִׁפְחָה בִּישָׁא עַל עָלְמָא וַוי לֵיהּ לְמַאן דְּאַשְׁלִיט לָהּ עַל עָלְמָא.

261. The wicked maiden is the lashing strap. *Shatznez* (incompatible mixture; Shin, Ayin, Tet, Nun, Zayin) stands for *Satan oz* (Satan strength; Shin, Tet, Nun; Ayin, Zayin), **comprised of an ox and a donkey,** the two damagers, **about which Jacob mentioned: "And I have** [under my control] **oxen and donkeys..."** (Genesis 32:6) and similarly it is mentioned: **"In every matter of guilty negligence whether it be for ox, for donkey...."** (Exodus 22:8) **But on Shabbat there is no lashings, since this wicked maiden has no power to dominate over the world on Shabbat. Woe to him that allows her to dominate over the world.**

262. וּבְגִין דָּא אֶת שַׁבְּתוֹתַי תִּשְׁמֹרוּ דָּא בַּת יְחִידָה דְּאִיהִי שְׁמִירָה אַחַת לְשַׁבָּתוֹת הַרְבֵּה, בָּהּ תַּלְיָין כָּל שְׁמִירָתָן דְּעֶשֶׂר סְפִירוֹת דְּאִתְקְרִיאוּ שַׁבָּתוֹת הַרְבֵּה, וְשָׁמְרוּ בְנֵי יִשְׂרָאֵל אֶת הַשַּׁבָּת דָּא בַּת יְחִידָה דְּאִיהִי שְׁמִירָה לְיִשְׂרָאֵל בְּכָל שַׁבָּת וְשַׁבָּת.

262. Therefore it says: *Et* (redundant singular) *Sabtotai Tishmoru* "My Shabbats you shall keep..." (Leviticus 26:2) referring also to **the singular daughter,** Malchut, **which is one guard to many Shabbats,** meaning **on her are dependent all the safeguards of the Ten Sefirot, which are called "many Shabbats,"** since each Sefira is composed of ten Sefirot, and includes the Upper Three and the Lower Seven, which are called "the six days of activity and Shabbat." **"Thus, Israel should keep** (also, protect; guard) **the Shabbat...."** (Exodus 31:16) **This is the only daughter,** Malchut, **that is the guard to Israel each and every Shabbat.**

263. וּמָאן דִּמְחַלֵּל לָהּ לַאו אִיהוּ נָטִיר מִקּוּדְשָׁא בְּרִיךְ הוּא. וְלֹא עוֹד אֶלָּא דְּאִתְּמַר בָּהּ מְחַלְלֶיהָ מוֹת יוּמָת. מָאן דְּאָעִיל בִּרְשׁוּת דִּילָהּ שִׁפְחָה וַחֲלָלָה וְזוֹנָה. דִּרְשׁוּת דִּילָהּ אִיהוּ תְּחוּם שַׁבָּת כְּגַוְונָא דִּתְחוּם וּגְבוּל דְּיַמָּא דְּאִתְּמַר עַד פֹּה תָבוֹא וְזֹל גְּבוּל לַיָּם.

263. **One who desecrates the Shabbat, the Holy One blessed be He, does not guard him. Furthermore, it says about it: "...every one that profanes it shall surely be put to death..."** (Exodus 31:14) **meaning anyone who places a profaned immoral maiden in her domain. As her domain is the border limits of Shabbat, similar to the limits and borders of the sea, as it says: "...Who have placed sand for border limit to the sea..."** (Jeremiah 5:22) **which is the correction of the dividing curtain (masach) so no Light will pass from the masach of Malchut and below.**

264. וּמַאי נִיהוּ. וְהָיָה מִסְפַּר בְּנֵי יִשְׂרָאֵל כְּחוֹל הַיָּם וְלֵית יָם אֶלָּא אוֹרַיְתָא. מָאן דְּאַעֲבַר עֲלָהּ, כְּאִלּוּ חָזַר עָלְמָא לְתֹהוּ וָבֹהוּ. וּבְגִין דָּא קְרָא סָמִיךְ לֵיהּ וְהָאָרֶץ הָיְתָה תֹהוּ וָבֹהוּ.

264. **He asks, "Who is this** border of the sea?" He answers, "his is what is written: **'And the number of the children of Israel shall be as the sand (chol) of the sea (yam)...'"** (Hosea 2:1) meaning to say that the children of Israel watch themselves not to draw down the Mochin of Shabbat from above downward, **and "sea" means the Torah,** meaning the Mochin that

are called Torah. **Whoever transgresses this** and wishes to draw Light from the *masach* and below, **it is as if he returns the world to a shapeless and empty state. Therefore, next to** Beresheet, which is *Yere Shabbat*, **it is written: "The earth was without form and void…."** (Genesis 1:2)

265. דְּאִיהוּ חוֹל לְיָם, כְּחוֹּלָא דְּשַׁלְשְׁלָאָה לְכַלְבָּא, מָאן דְּאַפִּיק לֵיהּ מִשַּׁלְשְׁלָאֵיהּ גְּרִים כַּמָּה נְשׁוּכִין דִּיסוּרִין דְּנָשִׁיךְ לֵיהּ. וּבְגִינֵיהּ אָמַר דָּוִד הַצִּילָה מֵחֶרֶב נַפְשִׁי מִיַּד כֶּלֶב יְחִידָתִי וְדָא סמא"ל דְּאִיהוּ תָּפִיס בְּקוֹלָר מִסִּטְרָא דְּאִלֵּין דְּקָשְׁרִין לֵיהּ בְּאוֹת דִּתְפִלִּין וּרְצוּעָה בְּקֶשֶׁר עַל דְּרוֹעֵיהּ. וְקָשׁוּר בִּתְרֵין רְצוּעִין עַל קַרְנוֹי. דְּאִיהוּ שׁוֹר מוּעָד.

265. This correction, **which is like sand to the sea,** meaning not to extend the Mochin from the *masach* and below, **is like the collar that links the dog to the chain. Whoever removes him from the chain causes many painful bites** by the dog that will bite him. **About him, David said: "Deliver my soul from the sword, mine only one from the power of a dog."** (Psalms 22:21) **And this** dog **is** Sama"el, **who is seized in the collar chain, from the aspect of those who tie him up by the sign of the Tefilin** that is called *ot* (sign) **and a strap on his arm, and is bound by two straps over his horns, since** Sama"el **is a forwarned ox** (*shor mu'ad*), about whom it says: "… the ox shall be stoned…." (Exodus 21:29)

266. וּשְׁכִינְתָּא שַׁבָּת יְחִידָה אִיהִי, רְשׁוּת הַיָּחוּדָא דְּעָלְמָא. דְּאִיהוּ גָּבְהוֹ עֶשֶׂר אַתְוָון דְּשְׁמָא מְפָרַשׁ יו"ד ה"א וא"ו ה"א, וְרָחְבּוֹ אַרְבְּעָה יהו"ה.

266. And the Shechinah, Malchut, **on Shabbat is singular,** [and is] **the private domain of the singularity of the world,** Zeir Anpin, **whose height is ten letters of the Explicit Name, Yud-Vav-Dalet, Hei-Alef, Vav-Hei-Vav, Hei-Alef, and whose width is four** letters **Yud-Hei-Vav-Hei** without the full spelling.

267. עָנ"ג שַׁבָּת בְּהִפּוּכָא נֶג"ע מָאן דְּאִית לֵיהּ וְלָא מְקַיֵּים לֵיהּ אִתְהַפַּךְ לֵיהּ לְנֶג"ע צָרַעַת. שִׂפְתָּה דַּחֲרִיבַת בֵּיתֵיהּ וְנָתַץ אֶת הַבַּיִת אֶת אֲבָנָיו וְאֶת עֵצָיו

וְדָא הוּא עֲנִיּוּתָא, דְּאִיהוּ בַּאֲתַר דְּנֶגַע צָרַעַת. וְחָזַר בִּתְיוּבְתָּא, וְטִהֲרוּ הַכֹּהֵן דָּא מִיכָאֵ"ל כֹּהֵן גָּדוֹל מְמַנָּא תְּחוֹת יַד וְחֶסֶד.

267. The "delight or pleasure" (*oneg*, Ayin-Nun-Gimel) **of Shabbat rearranged is "affliction"** (*nega*, Nun-Gimel-Ayin), meaning **whoever has** the means and capability to delight the Shabbat **and does not fulfill it, it turns around for him to be an afflicting plague, a maid who will destroy his home, as is written** regarding the *tzara'at* (leprosy) affliction: "...**the house should be demolished, the stones of it, and the wood beams thereof...,**" (Leviticus 14:45) **and this is poverty that takes the place of** this *tzara'at* (leprosy) affliction. And if **he repents,** then it says regarding him: "...**then the priest shall declare it clean...,**" (Ibid. 14:48) **this is Michael, the High Priest,** who is **appointed under the hand of the Sefira of Chesed.**

268. עֲנָ"ג אִיהוּ נָהָ"ר יוֹצֵא מֵעֵ"דֶן לְהַשְׁקוֹת אֶת הַגָּ"ן דְּאִיהוּ עֵדֶן נְהַר גָּן דְּאִיהוּ נְשָׁמָתִין. ו' נָהָר דְּנָפִיק מֵעֵדֶן מִבֵּין י"ה. וְלֵית עֵדֶן אֶלָּא כֶּתֶר עֶלְיוֹן דְּאִיהוּ מוּפְלָא וּמְכוּסֶה. וּבְגִין דָּא אִתְּמַר בְּעֵדֶן, עַיִן לֹא רָאָתָה אֱלֹהִי"ם זוּלָתְךָ. לְהַשְׁקוֹת אֶת הַגָּן דָּא ה' תַּתָּאָה.

268. *Oneg* (delight or pleasure) is "...**a river emanating from Eden to water the Garden...**" (Genesis 2:10) which is to say, *oneg* עֲנג is an acronym of *eden* ע (Eden), *nahar* נ (river), and *gan* ג (garden), **which is the pleasure of the souls. Vav is the river that emanates from Eden from between Yud-Hei,** which is the secret of Chochmah. **This Eden is strictly the Supernal Keter,** the Upper Eden, **which is marvelously covered,** meaning the sealed *mocha* (brain), **and therefore it says about Eden: "...neither has the eye seen a God, besides You...."** (Isaiah 64:3) "...**to water the garden...**" (Genesis 2:10) **this lower Hei,** Malchut.

269. אַרְבְּעִים מַלְקִיּוֹת חָסֵר חַד כְּחֶשְׁבַּן טַ"ל, מַאן דְּנָטִיר לָהּ מִנַּיְיהוּ נָחִית טַ"ל עֲלֵיהּ, דְּאִיהוּ יו"ד ק"א וא"ו. טַ"ל לְהַחֲיוֹת הַמֵּתִים. הָדָא הוּא דִּכְתִיב, כִּי טַל אוֹרוֹת טַלֶּיךָ וּמִיָּד וְאֶרֶץ רְפָאִים תַּפִּיל וַעֲלֵיהּ אוּקְמוּהוּ רַבָּנָן דְּמַתְנִיתִין

כָּל הָעוֹסֵק בְּטַל תּוֹרָה טַל תּוֹרָה מְחַיֵּיהוּ וְכָל מִי שֶׁאֵינוֹ עוֹסֵק בְּתוֹרָה אֵין טַל תּוֹרָה מְחַיֵּיהוּ.

269. Forty lashes minus one is the value of *tal* (dew; 39). **Whoever guards the Shabbat from them,** meaning he does not perform forbidden work, **dew descends on him,** which is <u>Yud</u>-Vav-Dalet, <u>Hei</u>-Alef, <u>Vav</u>-Alef-Vav, which equals 39. [It is the] **dew to revive the dead, as it is written: "...for Your dew is like the dew of light..."** (Isaiah 26:19) **and right afterward it says: "...and the earth shall bring to life the shades."** (Ibid.) **About this the masters of the Mishnah have explained that: "whoever deals with the dew of Torah, the dew of Torah revives him. Whoever does not deal with the Torah, the dew of Torah does not revive him."**

30. Beresheet contains the word *bayit* (house)

270. וְעוֹד וְהַמַּשְׂכִּלִים יַזְהִירוּ, אִלֵּין דְּיַדְעִין בְּפִקּוּדָא שְׁתִיתָאָה דְּאִתְרְמִיזַת בְּמִלַּת בְּרֵאשִׁית: בַּי"ת תַּמָּן, דְּאִתְּמַר בָּה, גַּם צִפּוֹר מָצְאָה בַיִת וּדְרוֹר קֵן לָהּ. וְהָא יְנוֹקִין יַדְעִין דִּדְרוֹר קֵן לָהּ, וּמַאי אָתֵי דָוִד לְמֵימַר בְּרוּחַ קוּדְשָׁא. אֶלָּא דָא מִצְוַת קַן צִפּוֹר דְּאִית בֵּיהּ כַּמָּה רָזִין. וַעֲלֵיהּ אִתְּמַר גַּם צִפּוֹר מָצְאָה בַיִת, דִּכְתִיב בְּגִינָהּ כִּי בֵיתִי בֵּית תְּפִלָּה דָּא בֵּי בֵּי כְּנִישְׁתָּא. וּדְרוֹר קֵן לָהּ דָּא בֵּי בֵּי מִדְרָשָׁא, אֲשֶׁר שָׁתָה אֶפְרוֹחֶיהָ אִלֵּין מָארֵי תוֹרָה מָארֵי מִשְׁנָה מָארֵי קַבָּלָה דְּבִגִינְהוֹן לָא זָזֶה שְׁכִינְתָּא מִיִּשְׂרָאֵל.

270. Furthermore: "And the wise shall shine" refers to those who are aware of the sixth precept (*mitzvah*) alluded to in the word Beresheet, since it contains the word *bayit* (house), meaning [the word Beresheet is the letters of] *rosh* (head) *bayit* (house), about which is written: "Also a bird has found a house, and a sparrow a nest for herself...." (Psalms 84:4) He asks, "Is David coming to tell us through Divine Inspiration (*Ruach Hakodesh*), something everyone knows? Even little children know that the sparrow has a nest." He answers, "Rather, he is referring to the precept of sending away the nesting mother bird (*shiluach hakan*), which contains many secrets." About this he mentions: "Also a bird has found a house...," about whom it is written: "...My home shall be called a house of prayer..." (Isaiah 56:7) which is the House of Prayer: "...and a sparrow a nest for herself" (Psalms 84:4) which is the House of Study, "...where she may place her young" (Ibid.) who are the masters of the Torah, the masters of the Mishnah, [and] the masters of Kabbalah, who in their merit, the Shechinah did not move out from Israel.

31. "And the wise" are the letters; "shall shine" are the vowels; "like the brightness (zohar)" are the cantillation marks

271. בְּרֵאשִׁית בָּרָא אֱלֹקִי"ם פָּתַח רַבִּי שִׁמְעוֹן וְאָמַר וְהַמַּשְׂכִּילִים יַזְהִירוּ כְּזֹהַר הָרָקִיעַ וְהַמַּשְׂכִּילִים אִלֵּין אַתְוָון. דְּאִינּוּן לְבוּשִׁין דְּאוֹרַיְיתָא מְרַקְמָן מִכָּל גַּוְונָא דְּנוּרָא. חִוָּור וְסוּמָק וְיָרוֹק וְאוּכָם. וּמִנְּהוֹן אִתְפָּרְשָׁן לְכַמָּה גַּוְונִין. וְכֻלְּהוּ גַּוְונִין אִינּוּן מְרַקְמָן בְּמַשְׁכָא דְּגוּפָא דְּבַר נָשׁ דְּאִיהוּ בְּגִנְתָּא דְּעֵדֶן. וּרְקִיעָא בְּאִלֵּין אַתְוָון אִיהוּ מְצוּיָיר וּמְרוּקָם בְּגִין דִּבְהוֹן אִתְבְּרֵי.

271. Rav Shimon opened and said: "And the wise shall shine like the brightness of the Firmament..." (Daniel 12:3) "The wise" refers to the letters, which are the garments of the Torah, Zeir Anpin, embroidered from all types of colors of fire, and they are four inclusive colors: white, red, green, and black. And from them divide and expand other types of colors. And all the colors are embroidered in the skin of the body of Adam that is in the Garden of Eden and the Firmament that is above the Garden of Eden is decorated and embroidered by these letters of Zeir Anpin because it was created by them, by these letters was he created.

272. יַזְהִירוּ אִלֵּין נְקוּדִין דְּנַהֲרִין בְּאַתְוָון. וּבְהוֹן נְהִירִין כֹּכְבַיָא בִּרְקִיעָא בְּגִנְתָּא דְּעֵדֶן. וְכֻלְּהוּ נְהִירִין בְּעַיְינִין דְּגוּפָא בְּגִנְתָּא דְּעֵדֶן.

272. "...shall shine..." are the vowels that shine within the letters, and by them, the vowels, the stars in the Firmament of the Garden of Eden shine. And all the vowels and the stars shine in the eyes of the body in the Garden of Eden.

273. כְּזֹהַר אִלֵּין טַעֲמֵי אוֹרַיְיתָא דִּבְהוֹן מִתְנַהֲגִין אַתְוָון וּנְקוּדֵי. וּבְהַהוּא גוּפָא דְּגִנְתָּא. כְּזֹהַר דָּא נִשְׁמָתָא דְּאִיהִי תְּנוּעָה דְּאַתְוָון. וּנְקוּדֵי. דְּנַהֲרִין בְּאַנְפִּין וּבְעַיְינִין. וְנַפְשָׁא אִיהִי כְּלָלָא דְּאַתְוָון. וְאִיהִי שִׁתּוּפָא דְּגוּפָא. רוּוְחָא אִיהִי כְּלָלָא דִּנְקוּדֵי דְּנַהֲרִין בְּעַיְינִין.

273. "...like the brightness..." are the cantillation marks (*Ta'amei Torah*, [lit. Tastes of the Torah]) by which the letters and vowels are conducted. And the meaning of "...like the brightness..." in that body of the garden is the Neshama that moves the letters and the vowels that illuminate in the face and eyes of that body in the Garden of Eden. And the Nefesh is the collective of the letters and is the partner of the body, and Ruach is the collective of the vowels that illunimate in the eyes.

274. קָם סָבָא חַד פָּתַח וְאָמַר בּוֹצִינָא קַדִּישָׁא כַּמָּה וְחֵילִין נַטְרִין לָךְ בְּגִנְתָּא דְעֵדֶן. כַּמָּה מַשִׁרְיָן דְּמַלְאָכִין מִסְתַּכְּלִין מִבְּשׁוּקוֹפֵי רְקִיעָא בְּגִנְתָּא בְּזִמְנָא דְתֵעוֹל תַּמָּן. וְכֻלְּהוּ מִסְתַּכְּלִין בָּךְ וְגַוְונִין דִּרְקִיעָא בָּךְ יַזְהִירוּ. בְּגִין דִּבָךְ נַהֲרָא שְׁכִינְתָּא דְּאִיהוּ זֹהַר הָרָקִיעַ. וְגַן אִיהוּ סָתִים וְחָתִים עַד דְּתֵיעוֹל בֵּיה שְׁכִינְתָּא הָדָא הוּא דִּכְתִיב גַּן נָעוּל אֲחוֹתִי כַלָּה.

274. One elder rose up, opened and said: "Holy Luminary, meaning Rav Shimon, how many hosts of angels wait for you in the Garden of Eden. How many camps of angels gaze through the windows of the Firmament in the Garden when you enter there, and they all look at you and the colors of the Firmament of the Garden of Eden will illuminate through you because the Shechinah, which is the brightness of the Firmament, shines through you? And the Garden is covered and sealed until the Shechinah enters, which is the Malchut of Atzilut, as it written: 'A locked garden is my sister, my bride...' (Song of Songs 4:12)"

275. וְגַוְונִין לָא נָהֲרִין בִּרְקִיעָא עַד דְּיֵעוֹל תַּמָּן קוּדְשָׁא בְּרִיךְ הוּא. וּמִיָּד דְּיֵעוֹל תַּמָּן אִתְּמַר בְּהוֹן, נִפְתְּחוּ הַשָּׁמַיִם וָאֶרְאֶה מַרְאוֹת אֱלֹקִי"ם. מַאי מַרְאוֹת, אֶלָּא מַ"ר אוֹ"ת מַר דְּאִתְּמַר בֵּיה מַלְאֲכֵי שָׁלוֹם מַר יִבְכָּיוּן וְאִיהוּ אוֹת בַּצָּבָא דִּילֵיהּ לֵיהּ מִתְפַּתְּחִין רְקִיעִין. וּבֵיה נָהֲרִין כָּל גַּוְונִין דִּלְהוֹן.

275. And the colors of the Firmament do not illuminate until the Holy One blessed be He, enters there. And as soon as He enters there, it is mentioned regarding them: "The Heavens opened and I saw visions (*marot*) of God." (Ezekiel 1:1) He asks, "What are visions?" and answers,

"**Rather** read it as *mar ot*," and he explains, "*mar* (bitter) **as regarding it is written: '…angels of peace weep bitterly.'** (Isaiah 33:7 **He is a sign** (*ot*) **in His army. For Him the Heavens open, and all their colors illuminate by Him.**"

276. וּכְעַן בּוֹצִינָא קַדִּישָׁא קוּם נְהִיר גַּוְונִין דִּרְקִיעָא בְּאַתְוָון דְּאוֹרַיְתָא. וְנָהִיר כֹּכְבַיָּא בְּהוֹן בְּנִקוּדֵי. כְּזֹהַר: דָּא כֻּרְסַיָּא יְקָרָא, דְּכָל נִשְׁמָתִין קַדִּישִׁין מִתַּמָּן אִתְגְּזָרוּ.

276. **"And now, Holy Luminary, rise to illuminate the colors of the Firmament by the letters of the Torah, and to illuminate the stars** in the Firmament **by the vowels" "…like the brightness…"** this is the Throne of Glory, from whence all the holy souls were hewn.

277. קָם בּוֹצִינָא קַדִּישָׁא פָּתַח כְּמִלְקַדְמִין, וְאָמַר וְהַמַּשְׂכִּילִים יַזְהִירוּ. אִלֵּין אַתְוָון. דְּכֻלְּהוּ כְּלִילָן בְּאָת ב' מִן בְּרֵאשִׁית. ב' אִיהִי בַּיִת בֵּי מַקְדְּשָׁא דְּתַמָּן בָּה נָהֲרִין כָּל אַתְוָון. רֵאשִׁית, נְקוּדָה בְּהֵיכְלֵיהּ. כְּגַוְונָא דָא ב עֲלָהּ אִתְמַר כָּל כְּבוּדָּה בַת מֶלֶךְ פְּנִימָה.

277. Rav Shimon, who is called **the Holy Luminary, rose up and opened as before and said: "'…and the wise shall shine…,' refers to the letters, as all are included in the letter Bet of Beresheet. Bet also hints to** *bayit* **(house), meaning the Holy Temple** (*Bet haMikdash*), **where all the letters illuminate.** *Resheet* [of Beresheet], meaning Arich Anpin, **a dot,** meaning Malchut, **in his chamber,** is Malchut in Binah because he elevated his Malchut into Binah **similar to this Bet ב, about which is said: "All glorious is the king's daughter within…."** (Psalms 45:14)

278. תֵּשַׁע נְקוּדִין תַּלְיָין מִינָהּ וְאִלֵּין אִינּוּן דְּאִתְגַּלְיָין וְאִינּוּן סְפִירָן דְּתַלְיָין מִנֵּהּ וְאִיהִי סַפִּיר גִּזְרָתָם עֲשִׂירִית כֹּון וְאִלֵּין אִינּוּן דְּנָהֲרִין בְּאָת ב' דְּאִיהִי בֵּי מַקְדְּשָׁא דִּלְעֵילָּא.

278. Nine dots, which are the Supernal Aba and Ima, Yisrael-Saba and Tevunah, and Zeir Anpin **hang** and extend **from Her,** from Binah of Arich Anpin, which is Bet and a vowel. **And they are the ones that are revealed, and they are the Sefirot that hang from Her. And She,** Malchut that extends with them, **is carved from sapphire,** as She illuminates from them all, **and is tenth to them,** as She completes them all, **and they are the ones that illuminates in the letter Bet, which is the Supernal Temple,** Binah.

279. וְסַפִּירִים אִתְקְרִיאוּ, עַל שֵׁם הַשָּׁמַיִם מְסַפְּרִים כְּבוֹד אֵ"ל. וּלְבָתַר דְּאִינוּן מְסַפְּרִים כְּבוֹד אֵ"ל, אִתְקְרִיאוּ עֶשֶׂר סְפִירוֹת בְּלִי מָה, וְנָוֵית בְּהוּ יֹו"ד ה"א וא"ו ה"א לְאַנְהָרָא בְּהוֹן. דְּעַל שְׁמֵיהּ אִתְקְרִיאוּ. וְכֻלְּהוּ נְהִירִין בְּאַתְוָון אִלֵּין.

279. The vowels **are called Sefirot, according to** the verse: **"The Heavens declare the glory of God [El]…"** (Psalms 19:2) as Heavens are Zeir Anpin with the Mochin of Chochmah and Binah, and 'the glory of God [El] is Malchut. **And after they relate (***mesaprim***),** meaning "mate," from the expression "A woman relates and discusses (*mesaperet*) with her husband" (Tractate Berachot 3a), and illuminates **to the glory of God,** which is Malchut, **they are called Ten Sefirot without anything else (***bli mah***),** meaning Ten Sefirot of Direct Light clothed in Ten Sefirot of Returning Light, without any additions to the number ten. **And in them descends Yud-Vav-Dalet, Hei-Alef, Vav-Alef-Vav, Hei-Alef,** meaning Zeir Anpin in Gadlut, **to illuminate in them, since they are named after it,** by the Name MaH (Mem-Hei; 45), as Yud-Hei-Vav-Hei spelled with the Alef's equals 45. **And all illuminate by these letters** of the Name Mem-Hei.

280. סְפִירָן וְאַתְוָון דִּי בְּהוֹן אִתְבְּנִיאַת. דְּאִיהִי ב' כְּגַוְונָא דָא. וְדָא אִיהוּ רָזָא דְּמִלָּה בְּחָכְמָה יִבָּנֶה בָּיִת וּבֵיתָא דָא אִית לֵיהּ תְּלַת מִכָּל גַּוְונִין. וְאִינוּן תְּלַת עַמּוּדִין דְּסַמְכִין לָהּ, וְאִינוּן וו"ו. עֲלַיְיהוּ אִתְּמַר וְוֵי הָעַמּוּדִים וַחֲשׁוּקֵיהֶם כֶּסֶף תְּלַת עַמּוּדִים, אִלֵּין תְּלַת אֲבָהָן דְּסַמְכִין לְבֵיתָא, דְּאִיהִי שְׁכִינְתָּא. וַחֲשׁוּקֵיהֶם, אִלֵּין תְּרֵין סַמְכֵי קְשׁוֹט, דְּאִתְּמַר בְּהוֹן יָכִין וּבוֹעַז, וַעֲלַיְיהוּ בֵּיתָא קַיְּימָא.

280. By the illumination **of the Sefirot to the letters** Malchut **is built up, which is like a Bet, from** the expression of *bayit* (house), **and this is the secret of the matter** about what it is written: **"Through wisdom (*chochmah*) is a house built…."** (Proverbs 24:3) As Binah is a house to the Supernal Chochmah, similarly Malchut is a house to the lower Chochmah, and **this house,** that is Malchut, **has three colors,** which are Chesed, Gevurah, and Tiferet, and Chesed includes the Upper Three Sefirot, **and they are the three Columns that support her, and they are three hooks (*vavin*; Vav's** וו"ו**),** as each includes the Lower Six, **and about them is said: "…their hooks are silver and their sockets are silver…."** (Exodus 27:17) **The three Columns are the three Patriarchs,** Chesed, Gevurah, and Tiferet **that support the house, which is the Shechinah,** Malchut, **and their sockets are the two pillars of truth,** about which it is said: **"…Yachin and … Boaz."** (I Kings 7:21) meaning Netzach and Hod, **and upon them stands the house,** Malchut, since Malchut is structured from Netzach and Hod of Zeir Anpin.

281. וְהַבְּרִיחַ הַתִּיכוֹן דָּא נְקוּדָה מִלְּגָּאו דְּסָתִים מִלְּגָּאו. מַבְרִיחַ דָּא ו' אִתְפַּשְּׁטוּתָא דְּהַהִיא נְקוּדָה דְּאִיהִי י' מַבְרִיחַ מִן הַקָּצֶה וַדַּאי מִן קָצֶה דָּא ה' עִלָּאָה. אֶל הַקָּצֶה, דָּא ה' תַּתָּאָה.

281. "And the middle bar [in the midst of the boards shall pass through from end to end.]**"** (Exodus 26:28) **is this inner dot** within the Bet **that is sealed inside. "…shall pass through…" is Vav,** which is **the extension of this dot, which is Yud** that hints to Chochmah since the ascent of the dot, which is Malchut to the chamber, which is the Binah of Arich Anpin, is the root of the extension of Chochmah into all the levels and Partzufim of the four Worlds of Atzilut, Briyah, Yetzirah, and Asiyah, **shall certainly extend and pass through "…from end…," which is the upper Hei,** Binah **"…to end." which is the lower Hei,** Malchut. **Meaning before he explained the shape of the Bet, which is the structure of Malchut, in the secret of the letters, and now he is explaining the extension of the dot inside the Bet, in the secret of illuminating the vowels within the letters.**

282. קְשׁוּרָא דִּתְכַת עַמּוּדִים, דְּאִינּוּן וָוֵי הָעַמּוּדִים, דָּא וַ"י עָלְמִין. דְּכַךְ
אִינּוּן סָלְקִין תְּכַת ו'ו'ו' כְחוּשְׁבַּן חַ"י, דְּאִיהוּ צַדִּיק יְסוֹד עוֹלָם.

282. The connection of the Three Columns that ties them to Malchut, **which are the hooks of the Columns,** Chesed, Gevurah, and Tiferet **is this** *chai* [18] *ha'olamim* (life of the worlds), which is Yesod, **since the three Vav's [3 x 6] equal 18, which is "the Righteous, the foundation of the world."**

283. ה"ה, כַּד נָטְלִין מֵעַמּוּדָא דְּאֶמְצָעִיתָא, דְּאִתְקְרֵי הַבְּרִיחַ הַתִּיכוֹן,
אִתְקְרִיאוּ אִינּוּן בְּרִיחִים עַל שְׁמֵיהּ. הָדָא הוּא דִכְתִיב, וַחֲמִשָּׁה בְרִיחִים
לְקַרְשֵׁי צֶלַע הַמִּשְׁכָּן כו'.

283. Hei, Hei, which are Leah and Rachel, in the secret of Binah and Malchut, **when they receive from the Central Column,** which is Zeir Anpin, since they clothe the entire stature of Zeir Anpin; Leah from the chest and above, and Rachel from the chest and below, **which is called the middle bar,** as it regulates between the Right and Left of Binah, in the secret of "three come out of one, one is sustained by three," **are also named after it, called "bars," as it is written: "And five bars to the beams on the side of the Tabernacle...."** (Exodus 26:27) The secret of the Explicit Name sequence Yud-Vav-Hei-Hei shines here, which comes from: *Yedotav Uletzela Hamishkan Hashenit* "...its two pegs; and for the second side of the Tabernacle..." (Exodus 26:19-20; see verse 205 above), which means that Zeir Anpin ascends towards Aba, Vav joins with Yud, and Binah is Left above Malchut.

284. וְתִקּוּנָא דְּמַשְׁכְּנָא, הֲוָה צִיּוּרָא דְּעוֹבָדָא דִּבְרֵאשִׁית, וְגִנְּתָא דְּעֵדֶן.
וּבְאִלֵּין צִיּוּרִין דִּנְקוּדִין, וּרְקִימוּ דְּגַוְונִין דְּתַמָּן, הַמַּשְׂכִּילִים יַזְהִירוּ וְכו'.

284. And the preparation of the Tabernacle (*Mishkan*) was already illustrated in the image of the acts of Creation and in the image of the Garden of Eden. And by these images of the vowels and the colorful embroidery that is there in the Tabernacle, acts of Creation and the Garden of Eden: "...the wise shall shine...." (Daniel 12:3)

285. בְּרֵאשִׁית: ב' רֵאשִׁית, בָּהּ וְהַמַּשְׂכִּילִים יַזְהִירוּ. כְּזֹהַר: דָּא אֱלֹקִ"ם, וְהוּא הַכִּסֵ"א לְוֹשְׁבָּנָא. אַדְהָכִי, הָא סָבָא אִתְחֲזַר כְּמִלְּקַדְמִין, וְאָמַר, בּוֹצִינָא קַדִּישָׁא וַזֹּיר בָּךְ, עָאלַת לְגִנְתָּא וְאִתְבְּהֵילַת לְנַפְקָא מִתַּמָּן, וּמִתַּמָּן עָאלַת לְמַשְׁכְּנָא, דְּאִיהוּ צִיּוּר דְּעוֹבָדָא דִּבְרֵאשִׁית, וְנָפְקַת מִתַּמָּן.

285. Beresheet is the letters of Bet resheet; Bet that is second in number and is Chochmah, is first in the count of the Sefirot, and not Keter, since Keter is not included in the count. In it, in Chochmah: "the wise shall shine..." "...like the brightness" is God (Elokim), which is Binah that is a throne for Chochmah, and it is the root of the World of Briyah, and it equals the numerical value of the throne (hakiseh). In the meantime, the elder returned, as before, and the Holy Luminary said: "Withdraw yourself! You entered the Garden of Eden and you hurried to get out of there, and from there you entered the Tabernacle, which is in the image of the acts of Creation, and you left from there."

286. אִית לָךְ לְאַוְזָרָא תַּמָּן, דְּהָא כַּמָּה וַיְילִין נָטְרִין לָךְ מֵעַמָּא קַדִּישָׁא, לְמִשְׁמַע מָאן צִיּוּרִין דְּתַמָּן, דְּאִינוּן כְּגַוְונָא דְּדִיּוּרִין דִּשְׁכִינְתָּא, דְּאִתְּמַר בְּהוֹן, וְעָשׂוּ לִי מִקְדָּשׁ וְשָׁכַנְתִּי בְּתוֹכָם. דְּוַדַּאי מַשְׁכְּנָא וּמְנַרְתָּא וּמַקְדְּשָׁא וּמַדְבְּחָא וּפָתוֹרָא, כֹּלָּא אִיהוּ דִּיוּקְנָא דְּדִיּוּרִין דִּשְׁכִינְתָּא לְעֵילָא וְתַתָּא.

286. It is imperative that you return there, as there are many soldiers from the Holy Nation that are waiting to hear from you concerning what these illustrations are there, which are like abodes of the Shechinah, about which it is said: "And let them prepare Me a sanctuary so I shall dwell among them." (Exodus 25:8) because, certainly, the Tabernacle, the Menorah (Candelabra), the sanctuary, the altar and the table are all in the image of the abodes of the Shechinah, above and below.

32. Wise at heart: Thirty-Two Paths of Wisdom

287. מִיָּד פָּתַח רַבִּי שִׁמְעוֹן וְאָמַר, וַיַּעֲשׂוּ כָל חֲכַם לֵב בְּעוֹשֵׂי הַמְּלָאכָה
וְגוֹ'. מַאי כָל חֲכַם לֵב. הַהוּא דְּאִיהוּ חָכָם בְּחָכְמָה, וּבְל"ב נְתִיבוֹת דִּילָהּ,
דְּאִינּוּן כְּלִילָן בְּשִׁית יוֹמֵי דִּבְרֵאשִׁית, וְהַיְינוּ שֵׁשׁ מָשְׁזָר, דְּאִינּוּן שִׁית יוֹמֵי
דִּבְרֵאשִׁית, כְּלִילָן בַּעֲשָׂר מֵעֲשַׂר אֲמִירָן, וְל"ב שְׁבִילִין, דְּאִינּוּן ל"ב זִמְנִין אֱלֹקִי"ם
בְּעוֹבָדָא דִּבְרֵאשִׁית. וְהַמַּשְׂכִּילִים בְּהוֹן, אִשְׁתְּמוֹדְעִין אַתְוָון, דְּאִתְּמַר בְּהוֹן,
יוֹדֵעַ הָיָה בְּצַלְאֵל לְצָרֵף אוֹתִיּוֹת שֶׁבָּהֶם נִבְרְאוּ שָׁמַיִם וָאָרֶץ.

287. **Immediately, Rav Shimon opened and said,** it is written: **"And the
wise hearted man among them that wrought the work...."** (Exodus 36:8)
He asks, **"Why** does it say **'wise hearted** (*chacham lev*)? Surely intellectual
wisdom resides in the head,'" and answers, "this is the wise at heart, **he who
is wise in Wisdom (Chochmah) and its Thirty-Two (Lamed-Vav) Paths
that are included in the six days of Creation. This is the meaning of: '...
twined linen per six...'** (Ibid.) meaning **that those six days of Creation
are comprised of the ten utterances,** which are Ten Sefirot, since Chesed
includes the First Three Sefirot, and Yesod includes Malchut, **and the
Thirty-Two Paths, which are the 32 times Elokim** is mentioned **in the
acts of Creation. And those who are wise and knowledgeable in them,**
in the Ten Sefirot and Thirty-Two Paths of Wisdom of the six days of
Creation, **know how** to combine **the letters, about which we learned:
'Betzalel was familiar and knowledgeable on how to combine the letters
by which the Heavens and Earth were created.'** (Tractate Berachot 55a)"

288. וְאִינּוּן כ"ח אַתְוָון, וְאַרְבַּע סְרֵי אָחֳרָנִין גְּנִיזִין בְּהוֹן. וְאִלֵּין אִינּוּן כ"ח
אַתְוָון בְּרֵאשִׁית בָּרָא אֱלֹקִי"ם אֵת הַשָּׁמַיִם וְאֵת הָאָרֶץ. וַעֲלֵיהוּ אִתְּמַר, כֹּחַ
מַעֲשָׂיו הִגִּיד לְעַמּוֹ.

288. **And they are the 28 letters** of Binah, **and the 14 other** letters of
Keter and Chochmah **are stored and hidden in them,** that they are
wrapped within the vessel of Binah. **And these are the 28 letters** in the
first verse in the Torah: **"In the beginning, God created the Heavens and**

Earth." (Genesis 1:1) **About them was said: "He declared to His people the strength of His works…."** (Psalms 111:6) [See explanation of Rashi on the first verse Beresheet]

289. וּבְגָלוּתָא אִסְתַּלַּק הַאי כֹּ"חַ מִנַּיְיהוּ, וְאִתְּמַר בְּהוֹן, וַיֵּלְכוּ בְּלֹא כֹחַ לִפְנֵי רוֹדֵף. וּבְגִין דָּא אָמְרִין בְּקַדִּיש וְעַתָּה יִגְדַּל נָא כֹחַ יְ"יָ, לְקֵבֵל כֹּ"חַ אַתְוָון אָחֳרָנִין, דְּאִית בְּאִלֵּין שֶׁבַע תֵּיבִין, דְּאִינּוּן: יְהֵא שְׁמֵיהּ רַבָּא מְבָרַךְ לְעָלַם וּלְעָלְמֵי עָלְמַיָּא. וְדָא אִיהוּ הָעוֹנֶה אָמֵן יְהֵא שְׁמֵיהּ רַבָּא בְּכָל כֹּחוֹ.

289. In exile this strength (ko'ach; 28) disappeared from them, from Zeir Anpin and Nukva, **and we learned about them,** about Israel: **"…and they go without strength (ko'ach) before the pursuer."** (Lamentations 1:6) **For this reason they say in Kaddish: "And now, I pray You, let the power (ko'ach) of the Lord be great…,"** (Numbers 14:17) **corresponding to the other 28 letters that are in the seven words, which are:** *Yehe Shmei Raba Mevorach Le'olam Ule'almei Almaya* **"May His great Name be blessed forever and ever." And this is** what the masters of blessed memory said, **"One who responds with, 'Amen, let His Name be great' with all his strength (ko'ach), tears up his decreed judgment sentence.** (Tractate Shabbat 119b)

290. י"ד אָחֳרָנִין אִינּוּן יְהֹוָ"ה אֱלֹהֵי"נוּ יְהֹוָ"ה. וְסִימָן, אוֹר לְאַרְבָּעָה עָשָׂר בּוֹדְקִין אֶת הֶחָמֵץ לְאוֹר הַנֵּר. וּבְאִלֵּין י"ד אַתְוָון אוּמָאָה, הָדָא הוּא דִכְתִיב כִּי יָ"ד עַל כֵּס יָ"ה. קָם סָבָא וְאָמַר, בּוֹצִינָא קַדִּישָׁא, בְּוַדַּאי אִלֵּין אַרְבַּע סְרֵי דְפוּרִים, אִינּוּן בְּאַרְבָּעָה עָשָׂר בּוֹ, וּבַחֲמִשָּׁה עָשָׂר בּוֹ, דָּא י"ד י"ה. אֲבָל סִימָנִין דְּכֹ"חַ אִינּוּן אוֹר אַרְבָּעָה עָשָׂר י"ד קַדְמָאִין דְּכֹ"חַ, י"ד תִּנְיָינִין, אִינּוּן בְּרֵאשׁוֹן בְּאַרְבָּעָה עָשָׂר יוֹם כו'.

290. The other fourteen letters are: "…the Lord, our God, the Lord (Yud-Hei-Vav-Hei Eloheinu Yud-Hei-Vav-Hei)…" (Deuteronomy 6:4) **and their sign is: "On the night of the fourteenth we check for the Chametz to the light of the candle," and by these fourteen letters is the oath, as it is written: "The hand (yad; 14) upon the throne of the Lord**

(Yud-Hei)…." (Exodus 17:16) **The elder rose up and said to** Rav Shimon, **"Holy Luminary, these are certainly the fourteen of Purim,** which refer to the wiping out of the memory of Amalek, hinted in the Mishnah (Tractate Megillah 1:1) **on the fourteenth and fifteenth of the month, which is Yud-Dalet (14) and Yud-Hei (15). But the signs of strength** (*ko'ach*; 28) **are the Light of the fourteenth, the first fourteen of the 28, and the second fourteen are** indicated in what the Torah says: **"…on the first [month] on the fourteenth day…"** (Numbers 9:5)

291. וְאִינּוּן: י"ד פִּרְקִין דְּי"ד יְמִינָא, וְי"ד שְׂמָאלָא, וְי"ד פִּרְקִין דְּגוּפָא. וְאִינּוּן: תְּלַת פִּרְקִין דִּדְרוֹעָא יְמִינָא, וּתְלַת דִּדְרוֹעָא שְׂמָאלָא, וּתְלַת דְּשׁוֹקָא יְמִינָא, וּתְלַת דְּשׁוֹקָא שְׂמָאלָא, וּתְרֵין דְּגוּפָא. וְרָזָא דְּמִלָּה, וּשְׁלֹשָׁה פֹּנִים יָמָּה וּשְׁלֹשָׁה פֹּנִים נֶגְבָּה וכו'.

291. And they are the fourteen sectional parts of the fingers **of the right hand** (*yad*; 14), **Chesed, and fourteen** sectional parts **of the left** hand, Gevurah, **and the fourteen sectional parts of the body,** Tiferet, which is comprised of Right and Left. **And they, the [joints of the body] are: three sections of the right arm,** meaning the upper arm connected to the shoulder, the forearm, and the palm of the fingers, **three section of the left arm, and three** sections **of the right thigh,** meaning the bone of the upper thigh, the lower leg and the foot, **and the three** sections **of the left thigh, and two** sections **of the body,** namely the body and the sexual organ (*brit*). **The secret of the matter is: "…three looking toward the west** (*yama*) [lit. sea], **and three looking toward the south…"** (I Kings 7:25) and the body, which is the sea, includes two sections that stand above them.

292. וְכֹלָּא דָּא כְּגַוְונָא דְּדָא, תִּקּוּנָא דְּגוּפָא, כְּתִקּוּנָא דְּמַשְׁכְּנָא. הָא תְּלַת זִמְנִין אַרְבַּע סְרֵי: פּוּרִים בְּאַרְבָּעָה עָשָׂר בּוֹ, פֶּסַח לְאַרְבָּעָה עָשָׂר, תְּלִיתָאָה, בָּרִאשׁוֹן בְּאַרְבָּעָה עָשָׂר יוֹם, וְסַלְקִין לְאַרְבָּעִין וּתְרֵין יוֹמִין, וְדָא אִיהוּ וַיַּעֲשׂוּ כָל חֲכַם לֵב וכו'.

292. All are corrected **similar to each other.** He explains: "**The correction of the body,** which is Zeir Anpin that includes the Lower Six, **is like the correction of the Tabernacle,** which is Malchut that is comprised of all the corrections of Zeir Anpin. **Thus, there are three times 14: on Purim in the fourteenth day** [of Adar]; **Pesach, in the morning of the fourteenth; and the third is: "...in the first [month], on the fourteenth [day]."** (Numbers 9:5) **And they** ascend in number from below upward, in the secret of: "Lift up your hands to the sanctuary..." (Psalms 134:2) until they **equal 42 days,** and they attain the illumination of the Upper Three Sefirot from the Supernal Forty-Two, and they are made into the secret of the 32 times the word Elohim is mentioned [in the acts of Creation] plus the ten utterances [of Creation], **and this is the meaning of: "And every wise hearted man among them that wrought the work...."** (Exodus 36:8)

293. וְעָשׂוּ אָרוֹן, דָּא שַׁבָּת. דְּמַשְׁכְּנָא אִיהוּ שֵׁשׁ מָשְׁזָר, כְּלִיל שִׁית יוֹמִין דִּבְרֵאשִׁית, דְּאִינוּן תְּרֵין דְּרוֹעִין, חֶסֶד וּגְבוּרָה. וְגוּף, עַמּוּדָא דְאֶמְצָעִיתָא. וּתְרֵין שׁוֹקִין, תְּרֵין נְבִיאֵי קְשׁוֹט, וְצַדִּיק אוֹת בְּרִית בֵּינַיְיהוּ. מַשְׁכְּנָא, שְׁכִינְתָּא תַּתָּאָה, כְּלִילָא מִכָּלְּהוּ תִּקּוּנִין דְּגוּפָא.

293. "And they shall make an Ark..." (Exodus 25:10) **this is** hinting to **Shabbat** day, meaning Malchut when it shines with the illumination of the Upper Three Sefirot, **because the Tabernacle is twined-linen by six, comprising the six days of Creation, which are: two arms,** Chesed and Gevurah, **the body, the Central Column,** Tiferet, **the two thighs,** which are **the two true prophets,** Netzach and Hod, **and Tzadik, the sign of the Covenant** (*Brit*), Yesod, **in between them.** These are the Lower Six Sefirot of Zeir Anpin, **and the Tabernacle,** meaning **the lower Shechinah,** Malchut, **is comprised of all the corrections of the body,** meaning the structure of Malchut in the Mochin of the Lower Six Sefirot.

294. צֶלַע הַמִּשְׁכָּן דָּא מטטרו"ן, שִׁפְחָה דְּמַטְרוֹנִיתָא, עֲלָהּ אִתְּמַר עֶצֶם מֵעֲצָמַי. עֶצֶם הַשָּׁמַיִם לָטֹהַר.

294. The side of the Tabernacle is Metatron in the aspect of **the maid of the Queen.** Study in the Zohar, beginning of Mishpatim: "From the body of the queen's daughter," is Metatron, and "this body," is Ima of the Shechinah," **about which is said: "This is now bones (etzem) of My bones…"** (Genesis 2:23) **"…and the like [essence] (etzem) of the Heavens for purity."** (Exodus 24:10) meaning it is always found with the Light of Chasadim, which is white and is called essence (etzem).

295. אָרוֹן, וַדַּאי דָּא לֵ"ב, נוּר דָּלִיק, כָּלִיל לֵ"ב נְתִיבוֹת, וְאִיהוּ שַׁבָּת. וּבֵיהּ שְׁכִינְתָּא עִלָּאָה, דְּאִיהִי תּוֹרַת וְכָם. וּבָהּ לֵב מֵבִין, וְאִיהוּ נְשָׁמָה יְתֵירָה דְּשַׁבָּת, וְאִיהוּ חֵירוּ דְשַׁבָּת, דִּבְגִינָהּ לָא שָׁלְטִין מָארֵי דְגֵיהִנָּם עַל עָלְמָא.

295. The Ark is certainly the heart (lev; 32), a burning fire comprised of **Thirty-Two Paths** of Wisdom (Chochmah). **And it is Shabbat,** Malchut, **and in it,** in Malchut, is included **the Supernal Shechinah,** Binah, **which** is called **the Teachings of the Wise (Torat Chacham),** since Binah is the Nukva (female) to Aba that is Chochmah, and therefore it is called the Teachings of the Wise. **With it,** meaning with the inclusion of Binah, **is an understanding heart, and the heart is the additional soul of Shabbat, and it is the freedom of Shabbat, for whose sake the masters of Hell (Gehenom) have no control on the world.**

296. וּמַאי נִיהוּ גֵּיהִנָּם בְּגוּפָא. דָּא כָּבֵד. וְאִיהִי מִזְבַּח הַנְּחוֹשֶׁת, לְאַעֲבָרָא לֵיהּ מֵעָלְמָא. וְכָבֵד בֵּיהּ מָרָה גֵּיהִנָּם דְּאוֹקִיד בֵּיהּ. כַּפֹּרֶת הַלֵּב, דָּא פָּרִישׂוּ דְסֻכַּת שָׁלוֹם, דְּאִתְּמַר בָּהּ הַפּוֹרֵשׂ סֻכַּת שָׁלוֹם.

296. He asks, **"And what is the subject of Hell (Gehenom) in the body?"** And answers, **"This is the liver, and it,** meaning the heart, **is the copper altar** in the Tabernacle. And the fire on the altar is **to remove it,** Hell, **from the world. And in the liver, which is Hell (Gehenom), is the bile, which is the fire that consumes in it. The cover [lit. atonement] (kaporet) of the heart is the covering of the Sukkah of peace,** which is Malchut illuminated with the Chasadim of Binah, **about which it is said: "He who spreads over Sukkah (booth) of peace."**

297. מְנַרְתָּא דָא רֵישָׁא. וְשִׁבְעָה נֵרוֹתֶיהָ עֲלֵיהּ, אִינּוּן: תְּרֵין אוּדְנִין, וּתְרֵין עַיְינִין, וּתְרֵין נוּקְבֵי וְחוֹטְמָא, וּפוּמָא. וּמְנַרְתָּא לִימִינָא, וְאִתְּמַר בָּהּ הָרוֹצֶה לְהַחְכִּים יַדְרִים. בְּגִין דְּתַמָּן מוֹחָא בְּרֵישָׁא. וְחָכְמָה בְּמוֹחָא שַׁרְיָא, וּבֵיהּ נָהִיר מְנַרְתָּא, בְּגִין דְּאִיהוּ מִשְׁחָא, דְּאִתְּמַר בֵּיהּ כַּשֶּׁמֶן הַטּוֹב עַל הָרֹאשׁ.

297. This Menorah (Candelabra) is the head, meaning Zeir Anpin, **and the seven-arm candles over it are: two ears, two eyes, two nostrils of the nose and the mouth,** which are Chesed, Gevurah, Tiferet, Netzach, Hod, Yesod, and Malchut of the skull of Zeir Anpin, and in Gadlut they are Chochmah, Binah, Tiferet, and Malchut: sight, hearing, sense of smell, and speech. **And the Menorah is to the right,** that is to say, it shines by the illumination of Chochmah of the Right, **and about it was mentioned: "He who wants to be wise should turn south"** (Tractate Bava Batra 25b) **because the brain is in the head there, and Chochmah resides in the brain. The Menorah illuminates by it,** by the brain of Chochmah, **because it is oil, as concerning it is said: "…like the precious oil upon the head…"** (Psalms 133:2)

298. כַּנְפֵי רֵיאָה, עֲלַיְיהוּ אִתְּמַר וְהָיוּ הַכְּרֻבִים פּוֹרְשֵׂי כְנָפַיִם לְמַעְלָה סוֹכְכִים בְּכַנְפֵיהֶם עַל הַכַּפֹּרֶת, דָא כַּפֹּרֶת הַלֵּב. פָּתוֹרָא דָא לִבָּא, וְאִתְּמַר בֵּיהּ שֻׁלְחָן בַּצָּפוֹן.

298. About the wings of the lungs, which blow over the heart, **is said: "And the Cherubs shall spread their wings upward, shielding the ark cover (kaporet) with their wings…,"** (Exodus 25:20) **this is the cover** [lit. atonement] of the heart (kaporet halev). **The table,** Malchut, **is the heart, about which it is said: "The table is to the north."**

299. וְדָא שְׁכִינְתָּא תַּתָּאָה, אִיהִי מְנַרְתָּא כַּד נָטְלָא מִימִינָא, וְשַׁרְיָא עֲלָהּ וְחָכְמָה, וְאִתְּמַר בָּהּ הָרוֹצֶה לְהַחְכִּים יַדְרִים. וְכַד נָטְלָא מִשְׂמָאלָא דְּאִיהִי

גְּבוּרָה, אִתְקְרִיאַת פָּתוֹרָא, וְאִתְּמַר בָּהּ הָרוֹצֶה לְהַעֲשִׁיר יַצְפִּין, וְשַׁרְיָא עֲלָהּ בִּינָה, דְּאִתְּמַר בָּהּ בִּרְכַּת יְ"יָ הִיא תַעֲשִׁיר. וְכַד נָטְלָא מִגּוּפָא, דְּאִיהוּ עַמּוּדָא דְּאִמְצָעִיתָא אִתְקְרִיאַת מַשְׁכְּנָא כְּלִיל מִתַּרְוַיְיהוּ. כִּיּוֹר וְכַנּוֹ, אִינּוּן תְּרֵין כֻּלְיָין, וּבְהוֹן שַׁרְיָין תְּרֵין סַמְכֵי קְשׁוֹט.

299. And this lower Shechinah, Malchut, when it receives from the Right it is called Menorah, and Chochmah of the Right dwells upon her, and concerning it is mentioned: "He who wants to be wise should turn south." (Tractate Bava Batra 25b) And when it receives from the Left, which is the Chochmah of the heart, Thirty-Two Paths, which is Gevurah that ascends to Binah, it is called *shulchan* (a table), and concerning it is mentioned: "He who wishes to get rich should face north," (Ibid.) since the Chochmah of the Left is called "wealth," in the secret of the verse: "... out of the north comes golden splendor...." (Job 37:22) And Binah dwells upon it, as concerning it is mentioned: "It is the blessing of the Lord that enriches...." (Proverbs 10:22) And when it receives from the body, Tiferet, which is the Central Column that is comprised of Right and Left, it is considered a Tabernacle composed of both. The copper laver and its base are the two kidneys, in which dwell the two supports of truth, Netzach and Hod.

300. מוֹחָא, עֲלֵיהּ אִתְּמַר, וּפְנֵי אַרְיֵה אֶל הַיָּמִין, וְתַמָּן מְנַרְתָּא דָּלִיק. לִבָּא, וּפְנֵי שׁוֹר מֵהַשְּׂמֹאל, וְתַמָּן פָּתוֹרָא מִתַּתְקְנָא, בְּגִין דְּלִבָּא אִיהוּ לִשְׂמָאלָא. גּוּפָא עֲלֵיהּ אִתְּמַר, וּפְנֵי נֶשֶׁר, וְתַמָּן מַשְׁכְּנָא מִתַּתְקְנָא.

300. About the brain is said: "...the face of a lion on the right" (Ezekiel 1:10) and there the Menorah illuminates, in the Chochmah of the Right. About the heart is said: "...the face of an ox on the left" (Ibid.) and there is set the table, to illuminate with the Thirty-Two Paths of Wisdom (Chochmah), because the heart (*lev;* 32) is to the left and illuminates in the Chochmah of the Left. About the body is said: "...and the face of an eagle" (Ibid.), meaning Tiferet, which is Compassion, inclusive of Right and Left, **and that is where the setting of the Tabernacle is,** meaning the contruction of Malchut with the illumination of the Lower Six Sefirot.

301. וּשְׁכִינְתָּא אִיהִי דְּמוּת אֶחָד לְאַרְבַּעְתָּם. וְאִיהִי ד' דְּאֶחָד. וְאִיהִי אַרְבַּע אַנְפִּין דְּכָל חַיָּה. בְּגִין דְּבָה אַרְבַּע אַתְוָון נְהִירִין. דְּאִינּוּן יהו"ה, וְאִיהִי דְּמוּת אָדָם, דְּאִיהוּ יו"ד ה"א וא"ו ה"א.

301. And the Shechinah, which is Malchut, **is the image of Adam (man) [lit. one].** Since lion, ox, and eagle are Chesed, Gevurah, and Tiferet, and Malchut is the face of Adam (man) **to all four.** Since She receives from all of them, and all are included in Her, and She completes them. **And She,** Malchut, is the **Dalet of** *echad* (one; Alef-Chet-Dalet), since the Alef and Chet of *echad* is Chesed, Gevurah, and Tiferet, and the Dalet of *echad* is Malchut. **And** Malchut **is the four faces each living creature, since through Her the four letters shine, which are: Yud-Hei-Vav-Hei,** which hint to the four living creatures, **and She is the image of man (*adam*; 45),** which is Yud-Vav-Dalet, Hei-Alef, Vav-Alef-Vav, Hei-Alef, which is the same numerical value as Adam, the Name of (MaH; Mem-Hei; 45).

302. וְעֶשֶׂר אַתְוָון אִלֵּין, אִנּוּן שִׁעוּר קוֹמָא דְּגוּפָא דָא, דְּאִיהוּ מַשְׁכְּנָא, וַעֲלֵיהּ, אִתְּמַר עֶשֶׂר אַמּוֹת אֹרֶךְ הַקֶּרֶשׁ. וָאֲמַלֵּא אֹתוֹ רוּחַ אֱלֹקִים בְּחָכְמָה בִּתְבוּנָה וּבְדַעַת וּבְכָל מְלָאכָה. בְּחָכְמָה: דָּא י' בִּתְבוּנָה דָּא ה'. וּבְדַעַת: דָּא ו'. וּבְכָל מְלָאכָה: דָּא ה'.

302. And these ten letters of the Name of 45 **are the stature of this body called the Tabernacle, and about it is said: "Ten cubits shall be the length of each beam..."** (Exodus 26:16) **"I have filled him with the spirit of God, in wisdom and in understanding, and in knowledge, and all manner of workmanship."** (Exodus 31:3) **"...with wisdom" is Yud; "...understanding" is Hei; "...knowledge" is Vav; "...all workmanship" is Hei.**

33. "And the wise" is the body; "shall shine" are the four living creatures; "like the brightness (*zohar*)" is Neshama

303. וְהַבָּר אַוֹר, וְהַמַּשְׂכִּילִים: אִלֵּין אַרְבַּע יְסוֹדִין דְּגוּפָא. יַזְהִירוּ: בְּהוֹן אַרְבַּע
חֵיוָון, דְּאִינוּן מַזָּל אַרְיֵה, מַזָּל שׁוֹר, מַזָּל נֶשֶׁר, מַזָּל אָדָם. דִּפַרְצוּפָא דְּבַר
נַשׁ אִשְׁתְּמוֹדַעַת בְּהוֹן בְּאַנְפּוֹי דְּבַר נַשׁ, וְדָא אִיהוּ הַכָּרַת פְּנֵיהֶם עָנְתָה בָּם.
כְּזֹהַר: דָּא נִשְׁמָתָא. וּמַצְדִּיקֵי הָרַבִּים: בְּאֵבָרִין דְּגוּפָא. יְהוֹן נַהֲרִין בְּמַזָּלַיְיהוּ
כַּכּוֹכָבִים לְעוֹלָם וָעֶד.

303. Another explanation: "And the wise…" are the four elements [lit. foundations] of the body, which are: fire, air, water and earth, which come from the internal of Chesed, Gevurah, Tiferet, and Malchut. "…shall shine" in them, in the faces of the four creatures of the chariot, which are: the sign of Lion, the sign of Ox, the sign of Eagle and the sign of Man, since by the face of Man one recognized the face that resides on man. And this is what is meant by: "The show of their facial countenance bears witness against them…." (Isaiah 3:9) "…like the brightness" is the Neshama. "…and those who teach righteousness to the multitudes" (Daniel 12:3) the Light of the *mazalot* (signs, merits) will illuminate "…like the stars, for ever and ever," in the limbs of the body, which are many.

34. "And the wise" are the world; "shall shine" are the four Angels; "like the brightness (zohar)" is the Throne

304. דָּבָר אַחֵר וְהַמַּשְׂכִּילִים: אִלֵּין אַרְבַּע סִטְרֵי עָלְמָא. יַזְהִירוּ: אִלֵּין אַרְבַּע מַלְאֲכַיָּא, דְּאִינּוּן מִיכָאֵ"ל גַּבְרִיאֵ"ל רְפָאֵ"ל נוּרִיאֵ"ל כְּזוֹהַר: דָּא כָּרְסַיָּא יְקָרָא.

304. Another interpretation: "And the wise" are the four directions of the world, which are south, north, east and west, drawn from the external aspect of Chesed, Gevurah, Tiferet, and Malchut. "...shall shine" are the four Angels: Michael, Gabriel, Raphael and Nuriel. "...like the brightness (zohar)" is the Throne of Glory, which is Malchut. [See Zohar, Vaera 33]

35. "And the wise" are the lips; "shall shine" are the eyes;
"like the brightness (zohar)" are the faces

‫305. דָּבָר אַחֵר, וְהַמַּשְׂכִּילִים: אִלֵּין שִׂפְוָון, דְּאִתְּמַר בְּהוֹן וְשִׂפְתוֹתֵינוּ שֶׁבַח.‬
‫וּבְהוֹן, אוח"ה"ע בומ"ף גיכ"ק דטלנ"ת זסשר"ץ, דִּמְשַׁמְּשִׁין בְּפוּמָא, בְּכ"ב‬
‫אַתְוָון. וּבְהוֹן חַתּוּךְ הַדִּבּוּרָא הַצְּלוֹתָא, לְשַׁבְּחָא לְמַלְכָּא.‬

305. Another interpretation: "And the wise" are the lips, about which it
is said in the prayer book, "And our lips are full of praise." In them are
five expressions, which are: **Alef, Chet, Hei, and Ayin** from the throat.
Bet, Vav, Mem, and Pei from the lips. **Gimel, Yud, Kaf, and Kof** from
the palate. **Dalet, Tet, Lamed, Nun, and Tav** from the tongue. **Zayin,
Samech, Shin, Resh, and Tzadik** from the teeth. These correspond to
Chochmah, Binah Tiferet, and Malchut, and Keter that is their source.
They serve the mouth with the 22 letters, and by them we articulate the
prayer to give praise to the King.

‫306. יַזְהִירוּ: אִלֵּין עַיְנִין, דְּאִתְּמַר בְּהוֹן וְעֵינֵינוּ מְאִירוֹת כַּשֶּׁמֶשׁ וְכַיָּרֵחַ. שִׁבְעָה‬
‫גְלְדֵּי עֵינָא אִינוּן, דְּנַהֲרִין בְּהוֹן שִׁבְעָה כֹּכְבֵי לֶכֶת, וְשִׁמְשָׁא וְסִיהֲרָא דְּאִתְּמַר‬
‫בְּהוֹן, וְעֵינֵינוּ מְאִירוֹת כַּשֶּׁמֶשׁ וְכַיָּרֵחַ, הָא תִּשְׁעָה. כְּגַוְונָא דְּתֵשַׁע נְקוּדִין‬
‫דְּאוֹרַיְיתָא.‬

306. "...shall shine" are the eyes about which it is said in the prayer
book, "And our eyes shine like the sun and the moon." There are seven
membranes in the eye, and the seven celestial bodies (planets) illuminate
in them, which are: Saturn, Jupiter, Mars, the Sun, Venus, Mercury, and
the Moon. And with the Sun and Moon, about which it is said: "...and
our eyes shine like the Sun and Moon," (ibid) all together they are nine,
like the nine punctuation marks in the Torah.

‫307. וְהָא חַמָּה וּלְבָנָה בִּכְלָל שִׁבְעָה כֹּכְבַיָּא אִינוּן אֵיךְ וְשִׁיב לוֹן תּוֹסֶפֶת עַל‬
‫שֶׁבַע. אֶלָּא חַמָּה אִיהִי נוּקְבָא, לְגַבֵּי שִׁמְשָׁא. לְבָנָה, נוּקְבָא לְגַבֵּי יָרֵחַ. וְשִׁמְשָׁא‬

וְיָרֵחַ, אִינוּן נַהֲרִין לְשִׁבְעָה כֹּכְבֵי לֶכֶת, דְּאִינוּן כְּשִׁבְעָה גִּלְדֵי עֵינָא. וְשִׁמְשָׁא
וְסִיהֲרָא, הָא תִּשְׁעָה. בַּת עֵין, עֲשִׂירִית לוֹן, כַּלָּה דְּכָלִילָא מִכָּלְהוּ.

307. The Zohar asks, "**Are the Sun and Moon not already included in
the seven planets, so how could he consider them again as an addition
to the seven** celestial bodies (planets)?" He answers, "**Rather,** *Chamah*
(Sun) **is the female aspect of** *Shemesh* (Sun), which is male, **and** *Levanah*
(Moon) **is the female aspect of** *Yare'ach* (Moon), which is male. **The Sun
and the Moon shine to the seven celestial bodies (planets), which are
like the seven membranes in the eye, and together with the Sun and the
Moon they are nine. The pupil of the eye is the tenth one, and is called**
kalah **(bride), because it includes** (*kolel*) **all of them.**

308. כְּזֹהַר הָרָקִיעַ, דָּא אַסְפַּקְלַרְיָאה דְּנַהֲרָא בְּאַנְפּוֹי דְּאָדָם, דְּמִינָהּ תַּלְיָין
אוּדְנִין וְעַיְינִין וְחוֹטָמָא וּפוּמָא, דְּאִינוּן מַנְהִיגֵי גוּפָא וְאֶבְרִין דִּילֵיהּ. כְּגַוְונָא
דְטַעֲמֵי דְּאִינוּן מַנְהִיגֵי אַתְוָון וּנְקוּדֵי דְּאוֹרַיְיתָא.

308. "**...like the brightness** (*zohar*) **of the Firmament**" **is the reflective
mirror that illuminates the face of man, from which hang the ears, the
eyes, the nose, and the mouth, which conduct the body and its limbs like
the cantillation marks** (*te'amim*) **that conduct the letters and the vowels
in the Torah.**

309. כְּמָה דְּשִׂפְוָון וְשִׁינַיִן וְחֵיךְ וְלָשׁוֹן וְגָרוֹן אִנּוּן מְשַׁמְּשִׁין לְאַתְוָון, הָכִי כְּגַוְונָא
דָא, כַּנְפֵי עֵינָא, וְעַסְעַפֵּי עֵינָא, וּתְלַת גַּוְונֵי דְּעֵינָא אִינוּן מְשַׁמְּשִׁין לְעֵינָא.

**309. Just like the lips, teeth, palate, tongue, and throat serve the
letters,** by which the five expressions of the mouth are produced, **in a
similar manner, the eye lashes [lit. wings] and eye lids,** which are Keter,
Chochmah, Binah, Zeir Anpin, and Malchut, on the cover over the eyes,
and the three colors in the eyes, serve the eyes, which are the vowels.

310. וְכֹלָּא אִתְקַשַׁר בְּחָמֵשׁ נְקוּדִין, כְּגַוְונָא דָא אַאֶאֶאֶ אַתְוָון וּנְקוּדֵי וָחָמֵשׁ
בְּגוֹ וָחָמֵשׁ. וַעֲלַייהוּ אִתְּמַר רָאשֵׁיכֶם שִׁבְטֵיכֶם זִקְנֵיכֶם וְשֹׁטְרֵיכֶם כֹּל אִישׁ
יִשְׂרָאֵל, הָא וָחָמְשָׁה. טַפְּכֶם נְשֵׁיכֶם וְגֵרְךָ אֲשֶׁר בְּקֶרֶב מַחֲנֶיךָ מֵחֹטֵב עֵצֶיךָ
עַד שֹׁאֵב מֵימֶיךָ. הָא וָחָמֵשׁ אָחֳרָנִין, וָחָמֵשׁ לְגוֹ וָחָמֵשׁ, אִלֵּין ה"ה, וּמִנַּייהוּ
אִתְיְיהִיבוּ עֲשַׂר דִּבְּרָן, דָּא י'. וְכָל הָעָם רוֹאִים אֶת הַקּוֹלוֹת מִסִּטְרָא דְו'.

310. **And all,** meaning all five expressions of the mouth, which are the 22 letters in Malchut, **connect with the five vowels** of Yisrael-Saba and Tevunah **in this manner: אַאֶאֶאֶ Alef with Chirek, Alef with Shuruk, Alef with Tzere, Alef with Cholem, and Alef with Kametz. The letters and vowels are five,** which are Keter, Chochmah, Binah, Tiferet, and Malchut of Yisrael-Saba and Tevunah, **within five,** which are Keter, Chochmah, Binah, Tiferet and Malchut of Malchut. **About them it is said: "…your heads, your tribal chiefs, your elders, your officers, even all the men in Israel"** (Deuteronomy 29:9) **which are five** levels of Yisrael-Saba and Tevunah: **"Your children, your wives, and the stranger in your camp, even your wood cutters and water drawers"** (ibid. 29:10) **thus another five** levels of Malchut. **Five** illuminate **into five, and they are the** two letters **Hei-Hei,** of the Yud-Hei-Vav-Hei, **and from them** that is, through the joining of the two Hei's, **the Ten Utterances were given, which are the Yud (10)** of the Name Yud-Hei-Vav-Hei: **"…and all the nation saw the voices [lit. thunderings]…"** (Exodus 20:14) **from the aspect of the Vav** of Yud-Hei-Vav-Hei, since voice and speech are the secret of Vav-Hei.

36. "And the wise" are the masters of Scripture; "shall shine" are the masters of Mishnah; "like the brightness of the Firmament" is the Halachah

‏311. דָּבָר אַחֵר וְהַמַּשְׂכִּילִים: אִלֵּין מָארֵי מִקְרָא. יַזְהִירוּ: אִלֵּין מָארֵי מִשְׁנָה. דְּאִינּוּן מָארֵי מַתְנִיתִין, מ"ט אַנְפִּין טָהוֹר, וּמ"ט אַנְפִּין טָמֵא. מ"ט אַנְפִּין טָהוֹר, אִנּוּן מ"ט אַתְוָון דְּפַרְשָׁה דְיִחוּדָא עִלָּאָה, דְּאִיהוּ שְׁמַע יִשְׂרָאֵל, כ"ה אַתְוָון. וְכ"ד אַתְוָון דְּפַרְשָׁה תִּנְיָינָא דְיִחוּדָא דְּאִיהִי בָּרוּךְ שֵׁם כְּבוֹד מַלְכוּתוֹ לְעוֹלָם וָעֶד.

311. Another explanation: "And the wise" are the masters of Scripture, "…shall shine" are the masters of Mishnah, since these masters of the Mishnah can clearly distinguish and select **the 49 faces** or aspects **of purity** in the oral Torah, **and the 49 faces of impurity. The 49 faces of purity are the 49 letters in the portion of the Supernal Unification, which is the** *Shema Yisrael* "Hear Israel…" that has **25 letters, plus 24 letters in the second passage: "Blessed be the Name of His Kingdom for ever,"** which together equal 49.

‏312. כ"ה אַתְוָון, עֲלַיְיהוּ אִתְּמַר, כֹּה תֹאמַר לְבֵית יַעֲקֹב. וּבְכ"ד אַתְוָון, דְּכְלִילָן בְּהוֹן כ"ד סְפָרִים, דְּאִינּוּן כ"ד דְּשָׁאִיב מִן יַמָּא דְאוֹרַיְתָא, אִתְּמַר בְּהוֹן וְתַגֵּיד לִבְנֵי יִשְׂרָאֵל.

312. Concerning **the 25 letters** of the above mentioned Supernal unification there is another verse **that says: "So (*KoH*, Kaf=20, Hei=5) shall you say to the house of Jacob…."** (Exodus 19:3) **Concerning the 24 letters** of the lower unification **that include the 24 books** of the written Torah, (24 in letters is Kaf=20 and Dalet=4; *KaD*) **which is a pitcher (*kad*) that draws water from the sea of Torah of which** the verse continues: "…and tell the children of Israel." (Ibid.)

313. וּמַאי נִיהוּ דְּשָׁאֲבִין מִנֵּיה הַאי כ"ד דְּאִיהִי שְׁכִינְתָּא, כְּלִילָא מִכ"ד סִפְרֵי
דְּאוֹרַיְתָא. דָא צַדִּיק, דְּאִיהוּ נָהָר דְּנָפִיק מֵעֵדֶן עִלָּאָה. בְּגִין דְּנָחִית בֵּיה ו',
דְּאִיהוּ בֵּן י"ה.

313. He asks, "And who is this river from which they draw the 24, which
is the Shechinah that is comprised of the 24 books of the Torah?" He
answers, "This is the righteous (*tzadik*), meaning Yesod, that is the river
that emanates from Supernal Eden, because the Light of Vav, Zeir
Anpin, descends and clothes it with Mochin of Aba and Ima; [the Vav] is
the son of Yud-Hei, since Yud is Aba, and Hei is Ima."

314. וּבְגָלוּתָא אִסְתַּלַּק מִנֵּיה, וְאִתְּמַר בֵּיה וְנָהָר יֶחֱרַב וְיָבֵשׁ. יֶחֱרַב בְּבַיִת
רִאשׁוֹן. וְיָבֵשׁ בְּבַיִת שֵׁנִי. וְאִיהוּ דָךְ, בְּכ"ד סְפָרִים, וְעִם כָּל דָא דְּאִיהוּ חָרֵב
וְיָבֵשׁ. אִתְּמַר בֵּיה, אַל יָשׁוֹב דַּ"ךְ נִכְלָם. אַל יָשׁוֹב דַּךְ, דְּאִיהוּ צַדִּיק בָּרוּךְ
שֵׁם כְּבוֹד מַלְכוּתוֹ לְעוֹלָם וָעֶד, דַּ"ךְ בִּשְׁכִינְתָּא, דְּאִיהִי כ"ד אַתְוָון דְּיִחוּדָא.
עֲלֵיה אִתְּמַר, וְהַמֶּלֶךְ שְׁלֹמֹה בָּרוּךְ. וְעַל אִלֵּין כ"ד אַתְוָון אִתְּמַר וְשַׂמְתִּי כ"ד
כ'ד שִׁמְשֹׁתַיִךְ כו'.

314. During the time **of exile,** the Light of Zeir Anpin **disappears** from
Yesod, **and it is said about it: "The river bed will be desolate and dry."**
**(Isaiah 19:5) "...desolate" in the first Temple; "...and dry" in the second
Temple. He is depressed** (*DaK*, Dalet-Kaf, the reverse of *KaD* that is Kaf-
Dalet) **in the 24 books of the Torah, and in spite of all this,** meaning
desolate and dry, **it is said about it: "Let not the oppressed turn back
[his prayers to] to You ashamed." (Psalms 74:21) "Let not the oppressed
(*DaK*),"** which is the righteous that **says: "Blessed is the glorious Name
of His Kingdom for ever..."** and unites the *DaK* in the Shechinah, [let
him not] **return** ashamed, rather let him **merit to transform the *DaK*
(oppressed) to the *KaD* (pitcher; 24) letters of the unification,** and then
it will be said about him: **"But King, Solomon shall be blessed...." (I
Kings 2:45) About these 24 letters,** which are the secret of Malchut, **it
is said: "And I will set your glass windows with rubies" (Isaiah 54:12)**
KaDKaD; Kaf-Dalet-Kaf-Dalet; equals twice 24, as mentioned in Zohar,

Prologue 206: "What was devoid and dry will become a land producing fruits and vegetation growths, and suitable for tree plantings."

315. הַאי עָנִי אִיהוּ דַ"ךְ, וּבַת זוּגֵיהּ דַכָ"ה. וְאִיהִי כַדָ"ה עַל שִׁכְמָהּ, כ"ד ה', דְּאִיהִי חֲמִשָּׁה חוּמְשֵׁי תוֹרָה. וְאִינּוּן ה' אֶצְבְּעָאן, דִּבְהוֹן אִתְּמַר, וַתְּמַלֵּא כַדָ"הּ וַתָּעַל.

315. This pauper, Yesod, **is *DaK*, and his paired mate,** Malchut, **is *DaKah*, and she** transforms *DaKah into KaDah* **in the meaning of: "Her pitcher (*KaDah*) on her shoulder." (Genesis 24:15) The word *KaDah* has the acronym *Kad* plus Hei (5), which is the five books of Torah, and the five fingers,** [as mentioned in Zohar, Beresheet 129]: "The fingers of man represent the most hidden of all levels and secrets of the Supernal World" **about which is mentioned "…she filled her pitcher and came up again"** (Genesis 24:16) in Returning Light that ascends from below upward.

316. וּמֵאַיִן שׁוֹאֲבִין. מִכ"ה אַתְוָון. וְרָזָא דְמִלָּה, כ"ה תְּבָרְכוּ אֶת בְּנֵי יִשְׂרָאֵל אֶת וַדַּאי. בְּמַאי אִתְבָּרְכַת וְאִתְמַלְיָאַת. בְּאָת ו'. דְּאִיהוּ כָּלִיל שִׁית תֵּיבִין דְּיִחוּדָא, דְּאִינּוּן שְׁמַע יִשְׂרָאֵל יְ"יָ אֱלֹקֵי"נוּ יְ"יָ אֶחָ"ד. וּבֵיהּ אִתְעֲבִידַת אוֹת. כ"ה, אִיהִי אִימָא עִלָּאָה, יַמָּא דְאוֹרַיְיתָא. ו', נָהָר דְּנָפִיק מֵעֵדֶן, וּמִנֵּיהּ אִתְמַלְיָאַת כ"ד דְּאִיהִי שְׁכִינְתָּא תַּתָּאָה.

316. He asks, "From which level **do** the small Zeir Anpin and Nukva, which are the lower unification of Yesod and Malchut, **draw?"** He answers, **"From the 25 letters of** *Shema Yisrael,* meaning from the higher unification **and it is the secret meaning of: '…so (*KoH*) shall you bless the children of Israel…,' (**Numbers 6:23)" He asks, **"By what is she blessed and fulfilled?"** He answers, **"By the letter Vav,** which is Zeir Anpin **that includes the six words of the Supernal Unification that are** *Shema Yisrael Adonai, Elokeinu Adonai Echad,* **and by this** [letter Vav] **a sign** (*ot*) [lit. letter] **is produced.** He explains, *KoH* (25) **is the Supernal Ima,** Binah, **which is the sea (*yam*) of Torah,** since twice 25 of Shacharit and Arvit are *yam* (50) that are the Fifty Gates of Binah. **Vav,** Zeir Anpin, is a river that emanates from there, from Binah, and from it the Pitcher (*KaD*; 24), which is the lower Shechinah, Malchut, is filled as it is said: "...to water the garden...." (Genesis 2:10)

317. וּמִנָּהּ אִתְשַׁקְיָא בְּגָלוּתָא, מַה דַּהֲוָה בְּקַדְמֵיתָא, הִיא אִתְשַׁקְיָא מִנֵּיהּ, הֲוָה מִנֵּיהּ. וְרָזָא דְמִלָּה, וַתְּמַהֵר וַתּוֹרֶד כַּדָּהּ עַל יָדָהּ וַתַּשְׁקֵהוּ. וַעֲלָהּ אִתְּמַר, וַתּאֹמֶר שְׁתֵה אֲדֹנִי דְּאִיהוּ אָדוֹן דִּילָהּ.

317. During the exile, He, Zeir Anpin, is watered from Her, Binah, unlike before where She, Malchut, was watered from Him. Here, in the time of exile, He is watered from Her, and this is the secret of the words: "And she quickly lowered her pitcher (*KaDah*) over her hand and gave him to drink..." (Genesis 24:18) As is mentioned about it: "She said, 'Drink my lord (*adoni*)'..." (Ibid.), meaning that He is Her master.

318. וַתְּכַל לְהַשְׁקוֹתוֹ וַתּאֹמֶר גַּם לִגְמַלֶּי"ךָ אֶשְׁאָב, אִלֵּין רְמַ"ח תֵּיבִין דִּקְרִיאַת שְׁמַע, דְּאִינּוּן שְׁקִילִין לִרְמַ"ח פִּקּוּדִין דְּאוֹרַיְיתָא, דִּבְהוֹן גְּמוּלֵ"י וָלָב יָנְקִין. וְעַתִּיקֵי מִשָּׁדַיִם, דְּאִתְּמַר בְּהוֹן, שְׁנֵי שָׁדַיִךְ כִּשְׁנֵי עֲפָרִים תְּאוֹמֵי צְבִיָּה, וְאִינּוּן תְּרֵי לוּחֵי אוֹרַיְיתָא.

318. "And when she done giving him drink, she said, 'I will also draw water for your camels'...." (Genesis 24:19) "...your camels (*gemalecha*)" numerically is 248 corresponding to the 248 words in the Shema reading, which correspond to the 248 positive precepts in the Torah, by which those weaned (*gemulei*) of suckling milk and draw. And [they are also called] "those removed from the breasts," about which it is mentioned: "Your two breasts are like two fawns that are twins of a gazelle" (Song of Songs 7:4) and they are the two Tablets of the Torah.

319. כ"ה, אִיהִי שְׁכִינְתָּא עִלָּאָה דְּבָהּ נָפְקֵי יִשְׂרָאֵל מִמִּצְרַיִם. כְּמָה דְאַתְּ אָמַר, כֹּה אָמַר יְ"יָ כַּחֲצוֹת הַלַּיְלָה וְכוּ', אִיהִי כ"ה אַתְוָון דְּיִחוּדָא דְּשַׁחֲרִית, וְכ"ה אַתְוָון דְּיִחוּדָא דְּעַרְבִית.

319. *KoH* (So; 25) **is the Supernal Shechinah,** Binah enclothed in the Mochin of Zeir Anpin, **by which Israel got out of Egypt, as you say:** *"KoH (So) said the Lord, around midnight..."* (Exodus 11:4) **meaning the 25 letters of the** *Shema Yisrael* **unification in Shacharit, and the 25 letters of the** *Shema Yisrael* **unification in Arvit,** hinting to the Fifty Gates of Binah.

320. וְשַׂמְתִּי כ"ד כ"ד שִׁמְשׁוֹתַיִךְ, דָּא שְׁכִינְתָּא תַּתָּאָה דְּאִיהִי כ"ד אַתְוָון דְּיִחוּדָא קַדְמָאָה דְּשַׁחֲרִית, וְכ"ד אַתְוָון דְּיִחוּדָא דְּעַרְבִית. כ"ה כ"ד דְּשַׁחֲרִית אִינוּן מ"ט אַנְפִּין.

320. *"And I will set your glass windows with rubies (KaD KoD; 24, 24)..."* (Isaiah 54:12) **which is the lower Shechinah,** Malchut, **that** comprises **24 letters of the first unification in Shacharit, and 24 letters of the Arvit unification,** meaning the 24 letters in *Baruch Shem Kevod Malchuto Le'olam Va'ed.* **The 25 and 24 of** the prayer of **Shacharit are the 49 faces.**

321. וְאִית מ"ט אַנְפִּין לְתַתָּא, מִסִּטְרָא דְּיִשְׂרָאֵל זוּטָא, דְּאִיהוּ מטטרו"ן, וְאִיהוּ מ"ט אַנְפִּין, וּבְהוֹן יַזְהִירוּ מָארֵי מִשְׁנָה, דְּאִיהִי תִּנְיָינָא לַהֲלָכָה, שִׁפְחָה דִּילֵיהּ, בְּגִין כִּי מָרְדְּכַי הַיְּהוּדִי מִשְׁנֶה לַמֶּלֶךְ, כְּגַוְונָא דָּא מִשְׁנָה, מִשְׁנֶה לַמֶּלֶךְ. וּבֵיהּ יַזְהִירוּ מָארֵי מַתְנִיתָא.

321. Below, in Briyah, Yetzirah, and Asiyah, **there are 49 faces from the aspect of the small Israel, which is the Angel Metatron, and he includes 49 faces. And by them the masters of the Mishnah will illuminate, since** the Mishnah **is secondary to Law (***Halachah***),** which is Malchut, **and is her maidservant, therefore** it is said: *"Mordechai, the Judean is second (mishneh) to King Achasverus...."* (Esther 10:3) **Similarly, the Mishnah** from the word *mishneh* is **second to the King, and through her the masters of the Mishnah will illuminate.**

322. כְּזֹהַר הָרָקִיעַ, דָּא הֲלָכָה, דְּאִיהִי קַבָּלָה לְמֹשֶׁה מִסִּינַי. וְכַמָּה עוֹלִימָתָאן אִית לָהּ, דְּאִינוּן הֲלָכוֹת פְּסוּקוֹת, דְּאִתְּמַר בְּהוֹן, וַעֲלָמוֹת אֵין מִסְפָּר.

322. "...like the brightness (*zohar*) of the Firmament..." this refers to Halachah, meaning the Malchut of Atzilut, which is a teaching received by Moses on Sinai, since Moses is the aspect of Zeir Anpin. She has many maidens that are undisputed laws, as it says about them: "... and innumerable maidens" (Song of Songs 6:8) meaning they illuminate with Chasadim, as "numerable" means the Mochin of the illumination of Chochmah, and "innumerable" indicates the Mochin of Chasadim.

323. וְאִיהִי סָלְקָא עַל כֻּלְּהוּ, הֲדָא הוּא דִּכְתִיב וְאַתְּ עָלִית עַל כָּלָּנָה. וְאִיהִי עִם כֻּלְּהוּ, כְּמָה דְּאוּקְמוּהוּ הֲלָכָה כְּרַבִּים. וּמַצְדִּיקֵי הָרַבִּים, בָּהּ יְהוֹן כַּכּוֹכָבִים לְעוֹלָם וָעֶד. כַּכּוֹכָבִים וַדַּאי, דְּלֵית לוֹן חוּשְׁבָּנָא.

323. And she surpasses all of them, as it is written: "And you excelled them all." (Proverbs 31:29) She, Malchut, goes with all, meaning She is included within them, as the masters have established that the law follows the majority opinion. "And those who teach righteousness to the majority..." in Malchut "shall shine ... as stars for ever as ever." (Daniel 12:3) Because they shine with the Mochin of the Upper Three Sefirot, certainly like the stars that are innumerable to count.

324. דְּכָל כּוֹכָבָא וְכוֹכָבָא אִתְקְרֵי עָלְמָא יְחִידָא, וְדָא הוּא וַעֲלָמוֹת אֵין מִסְפָּר, וְאִלֵּין עֲלָמוֹת, אַל תִּקְרֵי עֲלָמוֹת, אֶלָּא עוֹלָמוֹת וּבְגִין דְּצַדִּיקַיָּיא אִינּוּן כַּכּוֹכָבִים, וְכָל חַד אִית לֵיהּ כּוֹכָב. בְּגִין דָּא אוּקְמוּהוּ קַדְמָאִין, כָּל צַדִּיק וְצַדִּיק אִית לֵיהּ עוֹלָם בִּפְנֵי עַצְמוֹ.

324. Each and every star is considered as a world of its own, and this is the meaning of: "...and innumerable maidens (*alamot*)" (Song of Songs 6:8) do not read as *alamot*, but *olamot* (worlds). And because the righteous are like stars, and each has his own star, therefore the earlier masters have said: "Each and every righteous has a world on its own."

325. וְכָל מָאן דְּזָכָה לַהֲלָכָה חַד, יָרִית עָלְמָא וְדָא, כָּל שֶׁכֵּן מָאן דְּזָכֵי לְמַסֶּכְתָּא חֲדָא, אוֹ לִתְרֵין, אוֹ לִשְׁתִּין, דְּאִתְּמַר בְּהוֹן שִׁשִּׁים הֵמָּה מְלָכוֹת,

דְכָל מַסֶּכְתָּא מַטְרוֹנִיתָא אִיהִי בְּגַרְמָהּ, זַכָּאָה אִיהוּ מָאן דְיָרִית לָהּ בְּהַאי עָלְמָא.

325. Whoever had the merit to attain one Halachah inherits one world, [and] most certainly he who merits a complete tractate or two, or even sixty tractates, about whom is said: "There are sixty queens…" (Song of Songs 6:8) because each tractate is a queen on her own. Fortunate is he who inherits her in this world.

326. הֲלָכָה עוּלֵימָא דְמַטְרוֹנִיתָא דְאִיהִי קַבָּלָה, זַכָּאִין אִינוּן דְמִשְׁתַּדְּלִין בִּשְׁכִינְתָּא, דְאִיהִי עַל כֻּלְהוּ בַּהֲלָכָה. לְאַפָּקָא לָהּ מִן גָּלוּתָא, דְאִתְּמַר בָּהּ וּבְפִשְׁעֵיכֶם שֻׁלְחָה אִמְּכֶם. וּלְמֵיזַל לָהּ לְגַבֵּי בַּעְלָהּ, לְמֶהֱוֵי לָהּ קַבָּלָה בִּדְרוֹעוֹי, לְקַיֵּים בָּהּ שְׂמֹאלוֹ תַּחַת לְרֹאשִׁי וכו'.

326. Halachah is the attending maid, the exterior aspect of Malchut, of the queen who is Kabbalah, the inner aspect. Happy are those who make efforts for the Shechinah, as She dwells over all who occupy themselves with Halachah for its own sake to bring Her, the Shechinah, out of exile, as said about Her: "…and for your transgressions, your mother was banished" (Isaiah 50:1) and lead Her to Her husband, so that She will be received (*kabbalah*) in the arms of Her husband, to fulfill the verse: "…his left hand is under my head…." (Song of Songs 2:6)

327. דִּבְגָלוּתָא, מִשְׁנָ"ה דְּאִיהִי מטטרו"ן שָׁלְטָא, וְאִיהוּ מִשְׁנֶה לַמֶּלֶךְ. בַּאֲתַר דְּמַטְרוֹנִיתָא, יָתְבָא מִשְׁנֶה, וְדָא אִיהוּ וְשִׁפְחָה כִּי תִירַשׁ גְּבִירְתָּהּ. וּבְיוֹמוֹי דְמֹשֶׁה לָא שָׁלְטָא שִׁפְחָה אֶלָּא מַטְרוֹנִיתָא, לְבָתַר דְּמִית מֹשֶׁה וְיָרִית יְהוֹשֻׁעַ דְּאִיהוּ נַעַר, בַּאֲתַר מַלְכוּתָא שָׁלְטָא שִׁפְחָה. כְּמָה דְאַתְּ אָמַר, אֲנִי שַׂר צְבָא י"י עַתָּה בָאתִי.

327. Since during the time of exile the Mishnah, which is the aspect of Metatron, rules, and he is second (*mishneh*) to the King, instead of the queen, a viceroy (*mishneh*) takes her place, and this is the meaning of: "And a maidenservant that is heir to her mistress." (Proverbs 30:23)

During Moses' time the maidenservant did not rule, only the queen. After Moses died, and Joshua, who is called *na'ar* (young lad), took over, as is written: "And his servant Joshua ben Nun, was a young lad" (Exodus 33:11) then **instead of the queen the maidenservant ruled, as it says: "I am the captain of the host of the Lord, now I have come…."** (Joshua 5:14)

328. וְהָא אוּקִימְנָא, מְטַטְרוֹ"ן אִיהוּ מַעֲשֵׂה מֶרְכָּבָה, וַעֲלֵיהּ אִתְּמַר אֵין דּוֹרְשִׁין בְּמֶרְכָּבָה בְּיָחִיד, מַאי בְּיָחִיד. בְּיִחוּדָא דְעָלְמָא. אֶלָּא אִם כֵּן הָיָה חָכָם וּמֵבִין מִדַּעְתּוֹ, וְחָכָם בְּחָכְמָה, וּמֵבִין בְּבִינָה, וְיוֹדֵעַ בְּדַעַת. דְּאִתְּמַר בְּהוֹן, וָאֲמַלֵּא אוֹתוֹ רוּחַ אֱלֹקִי"ם בְּחָכְמָה בִתְבוּנָה וּבְדַעַת. בְּגִין דְּאִיהוּ מַשְׁכְּנָא, דְּאִתְמַלֵּי בִּתְלַת דַּרְגִּין אִלֵּין.

328. **And we have already established Metatron is of the secret of the Workings of the Chariot (*Ma'ase Merkavah*)** as Metatron comprises all four creatures of the Chariot, [see Zohar, Pinchas, 259] **about which it was said, "No teaching or expounding is permitted regarding the Workings of the Chariot before a single individual."** (Tractate Chagigah 11b) He asks, **"What is the meaning of 'before a single individual'?"** and answers, **"by the singular force of the world (the Creator): '… except if the individual is wise and understands from his knowledge'** meaning he attained Chochmah (wisdom), Binah (understanding) and Da'at (knowledge) **because a wise man is one who merits and attained Chochmah and understands Binah, and has knowledge in Da'at. As is said about them: 'And I filled him with the Divine Spirit of God, in wisdom (*chochmah*), in understanding (*tevunah*), and in knowledge (*da'at*)…'** (Exodus 31:3) **because he,** Metatron, **includes the Tabernacle,** meaning the structure of Malchut with Mochin of the Lower Six Sefirot, **that gets filled up by these three levels,** Chochmah, Binah, and Da'at."

329. וּבְכָל מְלָאכָה: דָּא מַעֲשֵׂה בְרֵאשִׁית, שְׁכִינְתָּא תַּתָּאָה. דְּאֵין דּוֹרְשִׁין לָהּ בְּעוֹבָדָא דִּבְרֵאשִׁית בִּשְׁנַיִם, אֶלָּא בְּיִחוּדָא דְעָלְמָא. מֶ"רְכָּבָ"ה דִּילָהּ אִיהוּ מְטַטְרוֹ"ן, גּוּף שְׁכִינְתָּא.

329. "And in all types of craftsmanship" (Ibid.), this refers to the **Workings of Creation (*Ma'aseh Beresheet*), meaning the lower Shechinah,** the Malchut of Atzilut, that **"you may not expound the Workings of Creation in front of two but only with the singular force of the world,"** since in Atzilut, He, His living creatures, and causes are all one. [See Prologue to Tikunei Zohar, 69] **Her chariot is Metatron, the body of the Shechinah,** meaning her extension from above downward, to Briyah, Yetzirah, and Asiyah.

וּשְׁכִינְתָּא אִיהִי מ"ה: יו"ד ה"א וא"ו ה"א אִתְקְרִיאַת בְּגִין דְּאִיהִי כְּלָלָא .330
דַּעֲשַׂר סְפִירָן. רֶכֶב דִּילָהּ מטטרו"ן, עֲלֵיהּ אִתְּמַר, רֶכֶב אֱלֹקִי"ם רִבּוֹתַיִם
אַלְפֵּי שִׁנְאָן. מַאי שִׁנְאָ"ן. שׁוֹר, נֶשֶׁר, אַרְיֵה, אָדָם. וְדָא אִיהוּ סוֹד מֶרְכָּבָ"ה:
רֶכֶ"ב מ"ה וַדַּאי.

330. And the Shechinah is Mem-Hei (45), called Yud-Vav-Dalet, Hei-Alef, Vav-Alef-Vav, Hei-Alef, which is Yud-Hei-Vav-Hei spelled out with Alef's that adds up to 45 because she includes all Ten Sefirot of the Name Mem-Hei, and all calculations and summations are in Malchut, as is known. Her riding chariot is Metatron, about whom is said: "The Chariots of God myriads, even thousands upon thousands (*alfei shinan*)...." (Psalms 68:18) What is *shinan* (Shin-Nun-Alef-Nun)? It is an acronym of *Shor, Nesher, Aryeh,* Adam (ox, eagle, lion, and man), and see Zohar, Beresheet A, 83, which says: "and Nun is man." This is the secret of chariot (*merkavah*; מרכבה); Mem-Resh-Kaf-Bet-Hei, which is *rechev* Mem-Hei רכב מה; Resh-Kaf-Bet, Mem-Hei (45), specifically, since Metatron is a *rechev* (chariot) to Malchut of Atzilut, called Mem-Hei.

וּמטטרו"ן אִיהוּ אָרוֹן, גּוּפָא לְאוֹרַיְתָא דְּבִכְתַב, דְּאִיהוּ עַמּוּדָא .331
דְּאֶמְצָעִיתָא. וְאִיהוּ שְׁלֹמֹן, פָּתוֹרָא דִשְׁכִינְתָּא, דְּאִיהִי כ"ב, דְּאִתְּמַר בֵּיהּ
כ"ב בְּנִין, וְאִיהוּ לִשְׂמָאלָא. וּבְגִין דָּא אָמְרוּ מָארֵי מַתְנִיתִין, שְׁלֹמֹן בַּצָּפוֹן.

331. And Metatron is the Ark, the body to the written Torah, which is the Central Column, meaning Zeir Anpin of Atzilut that is clothed in him.

He is in the aspect of the table (*shulchan*) of the Tabernacle, the table of the Shechinah, meaning Malchut of Atzilut that is called heart (*lev*, 32), which is named after the Thirty-Two Paths of Wisdom (Chochmah) that are revealed in her, about which the masters said: "A heart that understands" (Tractate Berachot 61b) in the secret of the verse, "...unto all that are wise hearted, whom I have filled with the spirit of wisdom (*chochmah*) ...." (Exodus 28:3) It is to the Left, meaning Chochmah of the Left, and therefore, the masters of the Mishnah said "The table is to the north" (Tractate Yoma 21b) meaning on the left side.

332. וְאִיהוּ מְנוֹרָה, נוּר דָּלִיק, מִסְטְרָא דִשְׁכִינְתָּא, דְּאִתְּמַר בָּהּ נֵר יְ"יָ. וְצָרִיךְ לְמֶהֱוֵי לִימִינָא, לְקַבְּלָא מִשְׁחָא. וּבְגִין דָּא מְנוֹרָה בְּדָרוֹם, דָּא אִיהוּ מָאנָא, לְקַבְּלָא פְּתִילָה וּמִשְׁחָא וּנְהוֹרָא. פְּתִילָה, שְׁכִינָה. מִשְׁחָא דִילָהּ צַדִּיק שֶׁמֶן כָּתִית. נְהוֹרָא דִּילָהּ, עַמּוּדָא דְּאֶמְצָעִיתָא. כְּגַוְונָא דָּא נַפְשָׁא, דְּאִיהִי שֻׁתּוּפָא דְגוּפָא, אִיהִי פְּתִילָה. רוּחַ, דָּא מִשְׁחָא. נְהוֹרָא, דָּא נִשְׁמָתָא. מָאנָא דָּא גוּפָא אִיהוּ עֶבֶד, וְאִיהוּ רֵכֶב לִתְלַת סְטְרִין אִלֵּין, דְּאִינוּן קִיטּוֹרָא דִּיְחוּדָא וַחֲדָא, דְּאִינוּן נֶ"ר יְ"יָ נִשְׁמַת אָדָם.

332. And He, Metatron, is called Menorah (candelabra), from the aspect of the Right a lit candle from the aspect of the Shechinah, Malchut, about which it is said: "...a lamp of the Lord...." (Proverbs 20:27) The Menorah needs to be in the Right to receive the oil, which is Chochmah of the Right that illuminates with Chasadim, and because of this, the Menorah needs to be on the south, which is the Right. This is a vessel, meaning the Menorah, to receive in her a wick, oil, and Light, which are Nefesh, Ruach, and Neshama. The wick is the Shechinah, which is Nefesh. Her oil is righteous (*tzadik*) meaning Yesod Ruach pressed oil. Her Light, the Central Column, which is Zeir Anpin with Mochin of the Upper Three Sefirot of Binah, and it is Neshama. He explains, in this way the Nefesh that is a partner to the body is this wick, Ruach is the oil and the Light is Neshama. The vessel, the body, meaning Metatron, is the servant and is chariot to these three aspects, Nefesh, Ruach, Neshama, which are a

tie of one unification, which are "…the spirit of man is the lamp of the Lord…." (Ibid.)

37. No speculative interpretation may be made,
neither in the Divine Chariot nor individually

333. וְהַאי עֶבֶד, אִיהוּ כְּנוּיָא לְכָל שְׁמָהָן, עִנּוּי לְכָל שְׁמָהָן. וּבֵיהּ מַרְכִּיבִין
כָּל אִלָנִין עִלָּאִין, מִסִּטְרָא דְטוֹב. מֶרְכָּבוֹת דְּסִטְרָא דְרַע, עֲלַיְיהוּ אִתְּמַר,
וְלֹא בָּעֲרָיוֹת בִּשְׁלֹשָׁה. מַאי עֲרָיוֹת. סמא"ל וְנָחָשׁ. לָא צָרִיךְ לְמֶהֱוֵי בִּשְׁלֹשָׁה,
דְּאִינּוּן: מַשְׁחִי"ת, אַ"ף, וְחֵימָ"ה, לְמֶהֱוֵי. תְּלִיתָאָה בֵּינַיְיהוּ, דְּלָא מִתְקַשְׁרִין
בְּהוֹן. אֶלָּא דִּיהוֹן תַּרְוַיְיהוּ בִּפְרוּדָא. וּבְגִין דָּא אֵין דּוֹרְשִׁין בַּעֲרָיוֹת בִּתְלָתָא.

333. **And this servant,** Metatron, **includes all the appellations of all
the Names,** such as, Merciful (*Rachum*), Gracious (*Chanun*), Good (*Tov*),
Upright (*Yashar*) **and the changes to all the Names,** like Mem-Tzadik-Pei-
Tzadik, Kaf-Vav-Zayin-Vav, Bet-Mem-Vav-Kaf-Samech-Zayin, and Kaf-
Vav-Zayin-Vav, **and through him they graft all Supernal trees,** which are
the Sefirot **from the good side,** since he becomes a chariot for them to
ride on. **About the chariots from the evil side is said** in the Mishnah in
Chagigah: **"And neither in incest (sexual immorality) by three." What
incest (sexual immoralities;** *arayot*)? **They are Sama"el and the Serpent.
They must not be in three, which are destroyer (***mashchit***), anger (***af***)
and heated fury (***cheima***),** in the way of Right, Left, and Central that **the
third one is in the middle** like in holiness, **so that there is no bonding
connection with them,** meaning not to give them a stirring cause to bond,
rather, that both Sama"el and the Serpent **shall be separated, thus:
"regarding incest (sexual immoralities) do not study with three."**

334. וְעוֹבָדָא דִּבְרֵאשִׁית בְּהִפּוּכָא, אֵין דּוֹרְשִׁין בְּמַעֲשֵׂה בְרֵאשִׁית בִּשְׁנַיִם,
דְּלָא יַעַבְדוּן פְּרוּדָא, אֶלָּא בְּיָחִיד, דְּאִיהוּ יְחוּדָא וָחָד. וּבְגִין דָּא לֹא יֹאכַל
אָדָם תְּרֵי, וְלֹא יִשְׁתֶּה תְּרֵי.

334. **And regarding the Workings of Creation, it is the opposite:
"two may not expound the Workings of Creation"** so as not to cause
a separation: **"rather, only a single individual,"** which is the Singular

One. Thus a person should not eat two and neither drink two, meaning in pairs.

335. וְלֹא בְּמֶרְכָּבָה בְּיָחִיד, בְּגִין דְּיָחִיד לֵית לֵיהּ שׁוּתּוּף דְּאִיהוּ מטטרו"ן, כְּגַוְונָא דְּנִשְׁמָתָא דְּלֵית לָהּ שׁוּתּוּף בְּגוּפָא. וְאַמַּאי אָמַר אֶלָּא אִם כֵּן הָיָה וְחָכָם וּמֵבִין מִדַּעְתּוֹ, הָכָא מַשְׁמַע דְּאִית לֵיהּ מֶרְכָּבָה לְעֵילָא לְקוּדְשָׁא בְּרִיךְ הוּא, דְּאִיהוּ מְלָאכָה דִּילֵיהּ, וּמַאי אִיהוּ, הַהִיא דְּאִיהִי כְּלִילָא מֵחָכְמָה וּבִינָה וָדַעַת, דְּאִינּוּן יה"ו.

335. And it is not permitted to expound **on the Divine Chariot individually, since individual** connotes that it **has no partner, which is Metatron,** about whom it is mentioned: "...for My Name is within him." (Exodus 23:21) **similar to the Neshama** when **it has no partnership with the body.** He asks, **"Why does it say: 'Except if he was wise and understands from his knowledge' which means that he has a chariot above to the Holy One blessed be He, and this is his work? What is the work that is comprised of Chochmah, Binah, and Da'at, which are** the letters **Yud**–Chochmah, **Hei**–Binah and **Vav**–Da'at?"

336. מְלָאכָה דִּתְלַת אַתְוָון אִיהִי ה', שְׁכִינְתָּא תַּתָּאָה, שָׁלִימוּ דִּתְלַת אַתְוָון, עֲלָהּ אִתְּמַר וַתֵּכֶל כָּל עֲבוֹדַת מִשְׁכַּן וְגוֹ'. וְאִיהִי ה' דְּיוֹם הַשִּׁשִׁי, וּבְגִין דָּא, אַף עַל גַּב דְּאַמְרִינָן אֵין דּוֹרְשִׁין בַּמֶרְכָּבָה בְּיָחִיד, חָזַר וְאָמַר אֶלָּא אִם כֵּן הָיָה וְחָכָם וּמֵבִין מִדַּעְתּוֹ. דְּוַדַּאי בְּאִלֵּין תְּלַת, דּוֹרְשִׁין בַּמֶרְכָּבָה בְּיָחִיד. וּבְלָא אִלֵּין תְּלַת לָאו אִיהוּ יְחוּדָא דִּילֵיהּ. וְדָא אִיהוּ רָזָא דְּאִיהוּ קוּדְשָׁא בְּרִיךְ הוּא לְעֵילָא וַדַּד בִּשְׁכִינְתֵּיהּ.

336. The answer, **"This work of the three letters,** Yud-Hei-Vav, **is Hei, the lower Shechinah,** Malchut, **that completes,** with her Returning Light, **the three letters Yud-Hei-Vav,** which are the first nine Sefirot of Direct Light, because the thorn of the tip of the Yud is Keter. Yud itself is Chochmah, Hei is Binah, and Vav is the Six Sefirot: Chesed, Gevurah, Tiferet, Netzach, Hod and Yesod. **About** Malchut **it says, 'Thus was finished all the work of the Tabernacle...,'** (Exodus 39:32) which connotes end-goal and completion, **and it is the** letter **Hei of *yom hashishi*** (the sixth day; Genesis 1:31), since it should have said *yom shishi* (day six). **Consequently, though we say 'you cannot expound on the Chariot individually,' he repeats and says, 'except if he was a sage and understands from his knowledge.' Definitely so, since with these three,** Chochmah, Binah, and Da'at, **expounding on the Chariot is permitted individually. If these three are lacking, this select individuality is not His unification and this is the secret meaning behind the idea that the Holy One blessed be He, is One above in His Shechinah."**

337. וְכַד אִיהוּ לְתַתָּא בִּמְטַטְרוֹ"ן בְּלָא שְׁכִינְתֵּיה, אִשְׁתַּנִּי בֵּיה, וּבְגִין דָּא אֲמַר אֱלִישָׁע אַחֵר, שֶׁמָּא חַס וְשָׁלוֹם שְׁתֵּי רְשׁוּיוֹת יֵשׁ. וּבְגִין דָּא אֲמַר, אַל תַּמֵּר בּוֹ כִּי שְׁמִי בְּקִרְבּוֹ, בְּגִין דִּמְטַטְרוֹ"ן אִיהִי שֵׁנִי לַמֶּלֶךְ.

337. **When** the Holy One blessed be He**, is below,** clothed up in Briyah, Yetzirah, and Asiyah **in Metatron, without the Shechinah,** that is to say, the the Right Column rules alone, **changing in him,** and only shines with the illumination of the Lower Six Sefirot, **and because of this, Elisha "the other" said: "Perhaps, God forbid, there are two authorities." For this reason** the verse said: "...be not rebellious against him...for My Name is in him..." (Exodus 23:21) **since Metatron is secondary to the King.**

338. וְכַד אִיהִי שְׁכִינְתָּא בְּלָא בַּעֲלָהּ, אִתְקְרֵי הַאי מַלְאָךְ, מְשַׁנֶּה לָהּ, וְאִשְׁתַּנִּיאַת דְּלָא אִשְׁתְּמוֹדְעִין בָּהּ חֵילִין, וּמַה דְּאִיהִי מַטְרוֹנִיתָא. וּבַמַּאי הִיא מִתְכַּסְיָא. בְּהַהוּא דְּאִתְקְרִיאַת אָמָה. וְדָא הוּא דְּאֲמַר קְרָא, וְכִי יִמְכֹּר אִישׁ אֶת בִּתּוֹ לְאָמָה, אִישׁ: דָּא קוּדְשָׁא בְּרִיךְ הוּא. בִּתּוֹ: דָּא שְׁכִינְתָּא. לְאָמָה: בַּת זוּגֵיה דִּמְטַטְרוֹ"ן, דְּאִיהִי מִיטַטְרוֹ"ן, בְּתוֹסֶפֶת יוּ"ד.

338. **When She, the Shechinah,** Malchut that is clothed below in Briyah, Yetzirah, and Asiyah, **is without Her husband,** meaning with the external illumination of Chochmah that also shines in Briyah, Yetzirah, and Asiyah, **this angel,** Metatron, **is considered a viceroy and secondary to Her, and She changes so that Her hosts** of Briyah, Yetzirah, and Asiyah **do not**

recognize Her as a Queen. He asks, "By what is She covered, to say, what is the form of her clothing," and answers, "by that which is called a maid-servant." As the verse says: "And if a man shall sell his daughter as a maid-servant…" (Exodus 21:7); "man" is the Holy One blessed be He, "his daughter" is the Shechinah, this "maid-servant" is the mate of Metatron, who is Mitatron, with an additional Yud.

339. דְּשִׁפְחָה בִּישָׁא, הִיא אָמָה דְּעֵרֶב רַב, וּבְגִין דְּהַהִיא שִׁפְחָה בִּישָׁא וּבְנָהָא לָא אִשְׁתְּמוֹדְעִין בָּה, אִיהִי מִתְכַּסְיָא בְּעַבְדָא דִּילָה, כְּנִשְׁמָתָא בְּגוּפָא.

339. Since the negative maid-servant, meaning the Other Side, is the mother of the mixed multitudes, and so that this maid and her children do not recognize Her, She covers and is clothed within Her servant, Metatron, as the soul clothes itself within the body.

340. וּבְגָלוּתָא קַדְמָאָה דְּלָא וָזְרַת לְמַלְכוּתָהָא בְּרַתָּא דְּמַלְכָּא, וְלָא נָפְקַת מֵהַהוּא גוּפָא, לָא נָפְקַת וְזָפָשִׁית, וּבְגִינָהָא אִתְּמַר בְּהוֹן, עֲבָדִים הָיִינוּ לְפַרְעֹה בְּמִצְרַיִם, בְּגִין דַּהֲווֹ תְּחוֹת רְשׁוּ דְּהַהוּא עֶבֶד. וּבְגִין דָּא אָמַר פַּרְעֹה בְּהַאי אֲתַר, לֹא יָדַעְתִּי אֶת יְ"יָ וְגַם אֶת יִשְׂרָאֵל לֹא אֲשַׁלֵּחַ. וּבְגִין דָּא נָפְקוּ בִּמְנוּסָה, כְּעַבְדָּא דְּלֵית לֵיהּ כְּתַב חֵירוּ, וּבְרַח מֵרִבּוֹנֵיהּ.

340. In the first exile, namely the exile in Egypt, where the daughter of the king did not return to her royal kingdom, and did not leave this body meaning Metatron, she was not liberated. And for her sake it was said about them, Israel: "we were slaves," in the first exile "to Pharaoh in Egypt" because Pharaoh had the power in Egypt to enslave the children of Israel because they were under the dominant authority of that slave-servant Metatron, and therefore Pharaoh said about this place: "Who is this Lord… that I should let Israel go?" (Exodus 5:2) It is for this reason that during the exodus of Egypt the Shechinah escaped in a hurried flight, like a slave that has not received his liberating document, and escapes from his Master.

341. אֲבָל בְּפוּרְקָנָא בַּתְרָאָה, לָא נָפְקַת בְּרַתָּא בְּהַאי עַבְדָּא, כִּשְׁפָחָה. אֶלָּא בְּקוּדְשָׁא בְּרִיךְ הוּא. בְּגִין דְּאוֹרַיְתָא דְּאִיהִי חֵירוּ אִיהִי עִמָּה בְּגָלוּתָא בַּתְרָאָה, דְּאִיהִי חֵירוּ דִּילָהּ. מַה דְּלָא הֲוָה הָכִי בְּגָלוּתָא קַדְמָאָה, דְּלָא הֲוָה לָהּ וְלִבְנָהָא אוֹרַיְתָא, דְּאִיהוּ חֵירוּ, דְּאוֹרַיְתָא וַדַּאי אִיהִי חֵירוּ, בְּמַלְכוּתָא דִּילָהּ, בִּיקָרָא דִּילָהּ, הָדָא הוּא דִכְתִיב יְקָרָה הִיא מִפְּנִינִים.

341. However, in the Final Redemption, this Daughter of the King will not leave like a maid-servant but rather through the Holy One blessed be He because the Torah, which is Zeir Anpin with the Mochin of Binah that is freedom (*cherut*), as the masters said: "Do not read engraved (*charut*) but rather freedom (*cheirut*)." (Tractate Eruvin 54a) **She** the Torah **is with Her in the last exile and it is Her freedom.** This was not the case in the first exile, in Egypt, where this Malchut and Her children Israel did not have the Torah, which is freedom, **since the Torah** that is Zeir Anpin **is definitely freedom,** when the Torah illuminates **in her own Malchut, in her own honor and glory, as it says: "She is more precious than rubies...."** (Proverbs 3:15)

342. וּבְגִין דָּא, לֹא תֵצֵא כְּצֵאת הָעֲבָדִים. וְדָא הוּא דְּאָמַר, כִּי לֹא בְחִפָּזוֹן תֵּצֵאוּ וּבִמְנוּסָה לֹא תֵלֵכוּן כִּי הֹלֵךְ לִפְנֵיכֶם יְ"יָ. יהו"ה וַדַּאי, אִיהוּ יוֹקִים לוֹן מֵעַפְרָא, וְאִיהוּ נָהִיר עַל אַנְפּוֹי דְּיִשְׂרָאֵל. וּבֵיהּ אִשְׁתְּמוֹדְעִין כָּל עָלְמִין, דְּאִינוּן זֶרַע בֵּרַךְ יְ"יָ.

342. Thus it says: "...she will not go out as the men-servants do" (Exodus 21:7), and it says: "For you will not go out in haste, neither shall you go in flight, for the Lord will go before you...." (Isaiah 52:12) **Yud-Hei-Vav-Hei definitely, He will raise them up from the dust, and He will illuminate the faces of Israel, and through Him it will be recognized in all worlds, that they are "...the seed the Lord has blessed."** (Isaiah 61:9)

343. וְאִתְפָּשַׁט קוּדְשָׁא בְּרִיךְ הוּא בְּכָל כִּנּוּיִין וּמֶרְכָּבוֹת דְּמֶטַטְרוֹ"ן, דְּאִינוּן כוז"ו בְּמוּכְס"ז כוז"ו, מצפ"ז. וְאִתְּמַר בֵּיהּ, וְלֹא יִכָּנֵף עוֹד מוֹרֶיךָ וְהָיוּ עֵינֶיךָ רוֹאוֹת אֶת מוֹרֶיךָ. בְּהַהוּא זִמְנָא, כִּי עַיִן בְּעַיִן יִרְאוּ בְּשׁוּב יְ"יָ צִיּוֹן.

343. **The Holy One blessed be He, will unfold** Himself **from all the apellations and chariots of Metatron, which are Kaf-Vav-Zayin-Vav, Bet-Mem-Vav-Kaf-Samech-Zayin, Kaf-Vav-Zayin-Vav,** meaning the letters immediately following the Names Yud-Hei-Vav-Hei, Eloheinu, Yud-Hei-Vav-Hei, **and Mem-Tzadik-Pei-Tzadik,** the letters of the Name Yud-Hei-Vav-Hei with the *at-bash* cipher (where Alef becomes Tav and Bet becomes Shin, etc.). **It was said about Him: "…yet shall not your Teacher hid Himself any more, but your eyes shall see your Teacher."** (Isaiah 30:20) **About that time** it was said, **"…for they shall see eye to eye, the Lord returning to Zion."** (Isaiah 52:8)

38. Six-sided Yud-Hei-Vav

344. וְאִתְפָּשַׁט מִמֶּרְכָּבוֹת דִּלְתַתָּא, וְאִתְלַבַּשׁ בְּמֶרְכָּבָה דִּילֵיהּ, דְּאִיהִי
אֲדֹנָ"י, שֵׁם הַמֶּרְכָּבָה דָא יהו"ה. כִּנּוּ"י דָא אֱלֹקִי"ם דְּסָלִיק לְחֶזְבָּן אהי"ה
אֲדֹנָ"י, וְאִיהוּ כִּנּוּ"י דִּתְרֵין שְׁמָהָן אִלֵּין וּבֵיהּ אִתְכַּסְיָין.

344. **He will unfold from the chariots below** of Briyah, Yetzirah, and
Asiyah, because the screen separating Atzilut from Briyah, Yetzirah, and
Asiyah will be abolished, **and He will be donned in His own chariot,
which is Alef-Dalet-Nun-Yud,** meaning the Malchut of Atzilut, which
will descend to the place where the feet of Adam Kadmon (Primordial
Adam) end, equating the ending feet of Atzilut to the ending feet of Adam
Kadmon. **The Name of this chariot** of the final correction is **Yud-Hei-
Vav-Hei. The appellation** of this chariot is **Elokim (86), which equals
the numerical value of Alef-Hei-Yud-Hei (21) plus Alef-Dalet-Nun-Yud
(65),** which includes Binah and Malchut to illuminate equally, **and this**
Name Elokim **is a designation (***kinui,* **86) of these two Names, Alef-Hei-
Yud-Hei (21) and Alef-Dalet-Nun-Yud (65), and they are clothed in it,**
in the secret of the verse: "know this day, and take to heart that the Lord,
He is God…." (Deuteronomy 4:39)

345. אקי"ק אִיהוּ יה"ו. ו' דְּאִיהוּ כְּלִילָא דְּשִׁית סְטְרִין, דִּבְהוֹן וְאָתִים שִׁית
סְטְרִין. וְאִינּוּן: יה"ו הו"י וה"י וי"ה הי"ו יו"ה.

345. The Name **Alef-Hei-Yud-Hei,** which is Binah, **is Yud-Hei-Vav,** which
are the Chesed, Gevurah, and Tiferet of Zeir Anpin that ascend to Binah
and become the aspect of Alef-Hei-Yud-Hei because the lower that ascends
to the upper becomes like it. **Vav, which includes the Lower Six Sefirot,**
of Zeir Anpin, ascends and regulates between Chochmah and Binah of
Yisrael-Saba and Tevunah **by which** meaning the Upper Three Sefirot, **he
seals the Lower Six Sefirot** because Zeir Anpin receives these Chochmah,
Binah, and Da'at from Yisrael-Saba and Tevunah by his ascension and
regulation of the Chochmah and Binah of Yisrael-Saba and Tevunah in

the secret of, "three come out of one," because any measure of Light that the lower causes in the upper, the lower also gains it, in the secret of, "one is sustained by three." Each one of the Lower Six Sefirot has Mochin, which are Chochmah, Binah, and Da'at, and this is considered as if they were stamped by the Upper Three Sefirot, and they illuminate according to the dominance of each end, according to the dominance of that Column. Similarly, the combination changes in each one of the ends, **and they are: Yud-Hei-Vav,** Chesed in the Right, **Hei-Vav-Yud,** Gevurah in the Left, **Vav-Hei-Yud,** Tiferet, the Central Column, **Vav-Yud-Hei,** Netzach, **Hei-Yud-Vav,** Hod, and **Yud-Vav-Hei,** Yesod.

346. יה"ו נָטִיל לֵיהּ יְמִינָא דְּאִיהוּ חֶסֶ"ד, וְחָתִים בֵּיהּ לְחָכְמְתָא. וּבֵיהּ הָרוֹצֶה לְהַחְכִּים יַדְרִים. הו"י נָטִיל לִשְׂמָאלָא, דְּאִיהוּ גְּבוּרָה וְחָתִים בֵּיהּ לְעוּתְרָא, וּבֵיהּ הָרוֹצֶה לְהַעֲשִׁיר יַצְפִּין. וה"י פָּנָה לְמִזְרָחוּ, וְנָטִיל לֵיהּ עַמּוּדָא דְאֶמְצָעִיתָא, וְחָתִים בֵּיהּ בְּנֵי.

346. The combination of **Yud-Hei-Vav is taken by the Right Column, which is Chesed, and stamps in it for wisdom** because each lower grade receives from the higher [grade] in the way of a stamp and a stamped impression, **and about it,** the Right Column, the masters **said: "He who wants to get wiser, let him turn to the south." Hei-Vav-Yud is taken by the Left Column that is Gevurah, and stamps in it for wealth, and about it,** the masters said: **"He who wants to be wealthier should turn to the north." Vav-Hei-Yud turns to the east and is taken by the Central Column,** Tiferet, **and stamps in it for children,** meaning the abundant flow of souls.

347. וי"ה נָטִיל לֵיהּ יַרְכָא יְמִינָא, וְאִסְתַּכַּל בֵּיהּ לְעֵילָא, וְחָתִים בֵּיהּ וַזֵּי הִי"ו נָטִיל לֵיהּ יַרְכָא שְׂמָאלָא, וְאִסְתַּכַּל לְתַתָּא, וְחָתִים בֵּיהּ מְזוֹנֵי.

347. The combination of **Vav-Yud-Hei is taken by that right thigh,** Netzach, **and looks at it above,** as the nature of the Right, whose manner is to illuminate from below upward, **and stamps in it life** to the lower beings. The combination, **Hei-Yud-Vav is taken by that left thigh,** Hod, **and looks down,** as is the nature of the Left that illuminates from above downward, **and stamps in it sustenance** to the lower beings.

348. אִסְתַּכֵּל לְעֵילָא לְגַבֵּי חָכְמָה, וְאִתְקַשַּׁר בְּיַרְכָא יְמִינָא, וְרָשִׁים בֵּיהּ חַיִּים, בְּגִין דְּחָכְמָה עֲלֵיהּ אִתְּמַר, הַחָכְמָה תְּחַיֶּה בְּעָלֶיהָ. אִסְתַּכֵּל לְעֵילָא לְגַבֵּי אִימָא עִלָּאָה, וְאִתְקַשַּׁר בְּיַרְכָא שְׂמָאלָא, וְרָשִׁים בֵּיהּ מְזוֹנֵי.

348. Zeir Anpin **looks up to Chochmah** and receives the illumination of Chochmah and it **gets tied in the right thigh,** Netzach, **and stamps life in the** Light of Chochmah, **since it was said about the wisdom (*chochmah*): "…for wisdom (*chochmah*) preserves the life of him that has it."** (Ecclesiastes 7:12) Zeir Anpin **looks up to the Supernal Ima,** Binah, and receives her illumination, and she **gets connected to the left thigh,** Hod, and the Light of Binah **stamps in it sustenance.**

349. יו"ה פָּנָה לְמַעֲרָב, בְּצַדִּיק דְּאִיהוּ עֵרוּב, דְּתַמָּן מִתְעָרְבִין כָּל חֲיָילִין, וְאִתְכְּלִיל בְּחַ"י אַתְוָון, דְּאִינּוּן יה"ו הו"י וי"ה הי"ו יו"ה וה"י. אִלֵּין אִינּוּן י"ח אַתְוָון, דִּבְהוֹן חַ"י עָלְמִין אִתְקְרִיאוּ וְצַדִּיק בְּהוֹן אִתְקְרִי חַ"י עָלְמִין.

349. The combination **Yud-Vav-Hei turned to the west (*ma'arav*), in that Righteous,** Yesod, **that is a blending (*eruv*) because there,** in Yesod, **are blended** and included **all the hosts, and it includes the eighteen letters** of all the six combinations, **which are Yud-Hei-Vav, Hei-Vav-Yud, Vav-Yud-Hei, Hei-Yud-Vav, Yud-Vav-Hei, Vav-Hei-Yud. These are the eighteen letters by which the eighteen (*chai*; 18) worlds are called, and the Righteous,** Yesod that includes them, **is named "the life of the worlds" (*chai ha'olamim*) after them.**

350. כָּל הֲווָיֵ"ת אִלֵּין מֵאִימָּא עִלָּאָה תַּלְיָין, דְּאִיהִי חַיִּים, וְצַדִּיק עַל שְׁמֵיהּ אִתְקְרִי חַ"י. חֲיוֹת הַמֶּרְכָּבָה עַל שְׁמָהּ אִתְקְרִיאוּ בְּגִין דְּאִיהִי אִימָּא עִלָּאָה חַיִּים, כְּמָה דְּאַתְּ אָמַר עֵץ חַיִּים הִיא לַמַּחֲזִיקִים בָּהּ, וְאִיהִי מֶרְכָּבָה לְחָכְמָה.

350. **All these** Names of **Yud-Hei-Vav-Hei depend** and shine **from the Supernal Ima, Binah, which is life** that shines with the Mochin of Chaya, **and Righteous,** Yesod, **which is named "life"** (*chai*) **after it. The chariot's creatures** that receive Her illumination **are named after Her** living creatures (*chayot*) **because Supernal Ima is "life,"** as you say: **"She is a Tree of Life to those who hold onto Her...."** (Proverbs 3:18) Binah is **a chariot to Chochmah** because due to Chochmah She is called "Life" (*Chaim*), in the secret of the verse: "...for wisdom (*chochmah*) preserves the life of him that has it." (Ecclesiastes 7:12)

351. מַלְכוּת תַּמָּן ה', וּבָה אִתְקְרֵי יהו"ה בִּשְׁלִימוּ. שִׁבְעָה זִמְנִין אִתְקְרִיאַת בָּה יהו"ה יהו"ה יהו"ה יהו"ה יהו"ה יהו"ה יהו"ה. וְאִית בְּהוֹן כ"ח אַתְוָן, דְּאִתְּמַר בְּהוֹן, וְעַתָּה יִגְדַּל נָא כ"ח יְ"יָ, וּבְאִלֵּין שֶׁבַע שְׁמָהָן אִתְקְרִיאַת הִיא בַּת שֶׁבַע, וַעֲלַיְיהוּ אִתְּמַר, שֶׁבַע בַּיּוֹם הִלַּלְתִּיךָ.

351. In Malchut, Nukva of Zeir Anpin, **is** the lower letter **Hei** of the Name Yud-Hei-Vav-Hei, **and with** Malchut, Zeir Anpin **is called a complete** Name of **Yud-Hei-Vav-Hei.** Since Malchut, which is Hei, completes Yud-Hei-Vav and becomes Yud-Hei-Vav-Hei. **Seven times** Malchut **is called Yud-Hei-Vav-Hei.** Six times from the Names that Zeir Anpin illuminates in her, and one of her own. **Together they contain 28 letters** [7 x 4] **about which it is said: "Now, I pray you, let the power** (*ko'ach;* 28) **of the Lord (Yud-Hei-Vav-Hei) be great...."** (Numbers 14:17) **She is named Bat-sheva (daughter of seven) after these seven Names** that illuminate in her, **about which was said: "Seven times a day, do I praise You...."** (Psalms 119:164)

352. י"ה תְּלָתִין וּתְרֵין זִמְנִין, בִּתְלָתִין וּתְרֵין אֱלֹקִי"ם, אִינוּן ל"ב נְתִיבוֹת חָכְמָה. א' עִם י"ה אֱלֵ"ה מְקוֹם כְּבוֹדוֹ.

352. There are thirty-two times Yud-Hei in the 32 Names of Elokim that are mentioned is the Acts of Creation in Genesis, since in every Name of Elokim there is Hei-Yud. **They are the Thirty-Two Paths of Wisdom**

(Chochmah), as Yud is Chochmah, and Hei that is Binah is a chariot to Chochmah, since the rider is revealed through his chariot. **Alef** of Elokim, which alludes to Keter, **together with** the letters **Yud and Hei** that are Chochmah and Binah **is the secret meaning of** the word **"where"** (*Ayeh*) as in the verse: **"Where (Alef-Hei-Yud-Hei,** *Ayeh***) is the place of His glory."** (From the *Kedusha* of the Musaf prayer)

39. "And the wise" are the chambers

353. וְהַמַּשְׂכִּילִים אִינּוּן הֵיכָלִין וְצִיּוּרִין דְּגִנְתָּא דְעֵדֶן, כֻּלְּהוּ מְצֻיָּירִין וּמְרוּקָמִין בְּאַתְוָון. א' צִיּוּרָא דְּהֵיכָלָא גְּנִיזָא, דְּאִיהִי אָנֹכִ"י, דְּסָלִיק לְחוּשְׁבַּן כִּסֵּ"א, וְאִיהוּ מְצֻיָּיר בְּנִקּוּדִין. דְּאִינּוּן כְּכַכְבַיָּא, דְּנַהֲרִין בִּרְקִיעָא, וּבְהוֹן מְצֻיָּירִין נִשְׁמָתִין וְרוּחִין וְנַפְשִׁין דְּצַדִּיקַיָּא.

353. "And the wise" are the chambers and images of the Garden of Eden, all illustrated and embroidered with letters. Alef is the illustration of a hidden chamber, and it alludes to "I am" (anochi; 81), which equals the numerical value of Throne (Kise; 81). It is illustrated by vowels, which are shining stars in the Firmament, and the Neshamot, Ruchot, and Nefashot of the righteous are shaped by these vowels.

354. וְצִיּוּרָא דִּילֵיהּ כְּגַוְונָא דָא א דָא אִיהוּ דְּיוֹקְנָא דְקָמֵץ ▼, דְּאִיהוּ נִיצוֹץ וְרְקִיעַ. נִיצוֹץ אִיהוּ כֹּכָב, וַעֲלֵיהּ אִתְּמַר, דָּרַךְ כֹּכָב מִיַּעֲקֹב. רְקִיעַ, וְקָם שֵׁבֶט מִיִּשְׂרָאֵל. נִיצוֹץ אִיהוּ כֹּכָב, וַמָּה דְּנַהֲרָא בִּרְקִיעָא, עֲטָרָה עַל רֵישֵׁיהּ. לְתַתָּא אִתְפַּלַּג א כְּגַוְונָא דָא א, סִיהֲרָא דִּתְחוֹת רָקִיעַ וְתַרְוַויְיהוּ בְּצִיּוּרָא דָא.

354. Its shape is similar to this א, which is the shape of an inverted vowel Kametz ▼, which is a spark and a Firmament. The spark is a star, about which was said: "...there shall step forth a star out of Jacob..."(Numbers 24:17) and Firmament is a tribe about which was said: "...and a tribe will rise from among Israel..." (Ibid.) This spark is a star, which is the Sun that shines in the Firmament, and is a crown above its head. At the lower side, the Alef is divided like this א, the Moon below the Firmament, and both the Sun and the Moon are included in this illustration of Alef.

355.)) ‎ـ‎ כַּד יֵיתֵי סמא"ל לְאִסְתַּכְּלָא בָהּ לְתַתָּא, אִסְתַּכְּלַת לְעֵילָא, וְאִתְכְּסִיאַת אַנְפָּהָא מִנֵּיהּ, וְהָדְרַת אַנְפָּהָא מִנֵּיהּ לְתַתָּא, וְאִיהִי אִתְרַחֲקָא מִנֵּיהּ, בְּהַהוּא זִמְנָא תִּקְעוּ בַחֹדֶשׁ שׁוֹפָר בַּכֶּסֶא לְיוֹם חַגֵּנוּ.

355. This illustration of the Moon that faces upward, **when Sama"el comes to gaze at the** moon, meaning to draw her abundance **downward, she looks up and covers her face from him, and turns her face away from him,** not to look **down, and she distances herself from him. About this time is said: "Blow the Shofar on the new month, on the covered moon for our feast day."** (Psalms 81:4)

356. בְּאָן יַרְחָא, בְּיַרְחָא דְּאִתְכַּסְיָא בֵּיהּ סִיהֲרָא. וּמָאן הוּא דִּמְכַסֵּי עֲלָהּ, יְהֹוָ"ה דְּכֵן סָלִיק א' בְּחוּשְׁבָּן: י' לְעֵילָא. ו' בְּאֶמְצָעִיתָא. וְאִיהוּ נָטִיר לָהּ, הֲדָא הוּא דִּכְתִיב אֲנִי יְהֹוָ"ה הוּא שְׁמִי וכו'.

356. He asks, **"Which month?"** He answers, **"In the month that the Moon covers itself."** He asks, **"Who is the cover over it?"** He answers, **"Yud-Hei-Vav-Hei, since Alef has the same numerical value,** 26, which is the value of Yud-Hei-Vav-Vei. Alef **with Yud above, Yud below, and Vav in the middle. And he guards her,** as it says 'I am the Lord; that is My **Name** and My glory will I not give to another...' (Isaiah 42:8) 'My Name' and 'glory' are associated Names to Malchut, in the secret of: 'Blessed is the Name of the glory of His Kingdom (*Malchuto*) for ever.'"

357. ב' הֵיכְלָא לִנְקוּדָה, גַּג דִּילָהּ אִיהוּ רָקִיעַ, וְאִיהוּ פָּתַח, עֲלֵיהּ אִתְּמַר, נוֹטֶה שָׁמַיִם כַּיְרִיעָה. וְאִיהוּ ו' דִּמְכַסֵּי עַל נְקוּדָה עִלָּאָה וְתַתָּאָה וְאֶמְצָעִיתָא, כְּגַוְונָא דָא ב.

357. Bet is the chamber for the dot ב. Since up to here he explained the secret of the Kametz in the letter Alef, which includes two Kametz's; one regular Kametz and one inverted, in the secret of Atik and Arich Anpin, two halves of Keter of BaN (Bet-Nun; 52), and the Light of Chochmah in the vessel of Keter. He now returns to explain the secret of the vowel Patach in the aspect of Binah's Light in the vessel of Chochmah, which is the Supernal Aba and Ima that became a chamber to that dot that is Chochmah. Because they are the Upper Three of Binah, which is entirely Chasadim, it is therefore illustrated by two Vav's, which are the secret of

Chasadim. **Its roof is a Firmament, and it is Patach,** meaning Chochmah of the Right, **about it is said: "...Who stretches out the Heavens like a curtain." (Psalms 104:2) And it is the Vav that covers over the dot, above, below and in the middle. Meaning to say, it is a composite of three Vav's, like this: נ.**

358. צ' תְּרֵין נְצוֹצוֹת דְּאָת צ', אִינּוּן צֵר"י, תְּרֵי רֵאשִׁין דְצ', אִינּוּן תְּרֵין דְע'. ע' אִית לָהּ תְּלַת רֵאשִׁין, וְאִינּוּן סֶגּוֹ"ל, וְאִינּוּן תְּלַת נְקוּדִין שׁוּרֵ"ק.

358. Tzadik צ, **the two sparks of the letter Tzadik are** the vowel **Tzere,** which is the secret of Yisrael-Saba and Tevunah, the Lower Seven of Binah, which are the sources of Zeir Anpin and Nukva, which are hinted in Tevunah, son (*ben*) and daughter (*bat*). Two dots that appear in Tzadik, in the secret of Yud and an inverted Nun, in the secret of back to back. **The two heads of the Tzadik are two** heads **of Ayin** when they unify face-to-face, and Ayin is the secret of Chochmah, in the meaning of: "A man's wisdom illuminates his face." **The letter Shin** ש **has three heads, and they are** the vowel **Segol,** the Chesed of the vowels **and they are three dots of** the vowel **Shuruk,** the Hod of the vowels and the root of Malchut, and when they illuminate in Malchut, the dots are positioned one on top of the other, without Right, Left and Central like in Segol, in the secret of "the Da'at of Nukva is Light," and the dots are apportioned to top, middle, and end.

359. ו' רֵישָׁא דִילָהּ חוֹלָ"ם וְחִירֵ"ק שׁוּרֵ"ק בּוּ', קוּצָא מִלְּגָאו וְחִירֵ"ק. קוּצָא דְאָת ג'. וְכֹלָּא אִתְרְמִיּוֹ בְּאָת א, נְקוּדָה לְעֵילָא חוֹלָ"ם. נְקוּדָה לְתַתָּא וְחִירֵ"ק. בְּאֶמְצָעִיתָא שׁוּרֵ"ק כְּגַוְונָא דָא ו.

359. Vav ו, which is the secret of Tiferet, **its top are** the vowels **Cholem, Chirek, and Shuruk in Vav,** meaning Melapum because Vav is the secret of Zeir Anpin that ascends and regulates between the Right and Left of Yisrael-Saba and Tevunah in the meaning of the two vowels, Cholem and Shuruk, since Cholem is the secret of the Keter and Chochmah that remained in the level and were never affected ever, and it is the secret of the Right Column. Shuruk is the secret of Binah, [Tiferet and Malchut], which left to a lower level and later returned to their level, and are considered to be Left Column. It is known that when the two Columns, Right and Left, come forth, a conflict develops between them and they are unable to shine until Zeir Anpin ascends with Feminine Waters and unites the two Columns together, and then they can shine, and this is the secret of the Central Column and Chirek. It is a general principle that any Light that is caused above by the lower, the lower also merits it, and therefore the Vav has all three vowels, Cholem, Shuruk, and Chirek. **The tip [lit. thorn] from the inner** side of the Vav **is the tip of the letter Gimel** גּ in the secret of Chesed that comes from the Chirek**,** which is the prime cause to diminish the Left Column and unite it with the Right (mercy) in the secret of: "Who recompenses (*gomel*) good Chasadim." **All** these vowels, Cholem, Chirek, and Shuruk, **are hinted in the letter Alef,** which is in the Partzuf of Yisrael-Saba and Tevunah from which the vowels are derived as is known that the Supernal Aba and Ima are cantillation marks, and Yisrael-Saba and Tevunah are vowels. **The upper point** of the Alef **is the** vowel **Cholem, the lower point** of the Alef **is the** vowel **Chirek, and in the middle is** the vowel **Shuruk, like this Vav** ו within the Alef, meaning Melopum, Vav and a dot.

360. וְעוֹד, תְּרֵין נְקוּדִין דְּאָת א, אִינּוּן צֵרֵ"י, וְאִינּוּן שָׁבָ"א. וְאִינּוּן בְּדְיוֹקְנָא אָחֳרָא א', כְּגוֹן י' לְעֵילָא, ו' בְּאֶמְצָעִיתָא, ד' לְתַתָּא. אִיהוּ קוֹצָא לְעֵילָא קוֹצָא לְתַתָּא, קוֹצָא בְּאֶמְצָעִיתָא, וְאִיהוּ סְגוֹ"ל, וְאִיהוּ שׁוּרֵ"ק תְּלַת נְקוּדִין, כֻּלָּא אִיהוּ א.

360. Also, besides the vowels Cholem, Shuruk and Chirek, **the two vowels of the letter Alef are Tzere and Sh'va,** thus there are also Tzere and Sh'va in the letter Alef, **and are hinted in another form** of the **Alef,** as is known that Alef hints to Yud-Vav-Yud and also to Yud-Vav-Dalet, **like this: Yud above, Vav in the middle, Dalet at the bottom,** the letter Alef has a thorn at its origin, **that is the tip above the Yud, a tip at the bottom** of the Dalet, a tip in the middle of the Vav, and it is a Segol and Shuruk consisting of three dots. Thus, all nine dots are alluded in the Alef. (See verse 353, where it says: "Alef is the illustration of a hidden chamber, and it alludes to "I am" [anochi; 81], which equals the numerical value of Throne [Kise; 81]. It is illustrated by vowels...")

361. אַתְוָון אָחֲרָנִין, הֵיכָלִין וְכִסּוּיִין לְאִלֵּין אַתְוָון. וְכֹלָּא אִיהוּ מְרוּקָם וּמְצוּיָיר בְּכָרְסַיָּא. ו', שִׁית דַּרְגִּין לְכָרְסַיָּא. ס', שִׁתִּין גַּלְגַּלּוֹי דְּכָרְסַיָּא דְּאַתְוָון דְּאוֹרַיְתָא אִתְּמַר בְּהוֹן, אֵין מוּקְדָם וּמְאוּחָר בַּתּוֹרָה, אֲבָל בְּכָרְסַיָּא, כֻּלְּהוּ מִתְתַּקְּנָן כִּדְקָא יָאוּת. וְרָזָא דָּא לְחַכִּימֵי לִבָּא אִתְמַסַּר.

361. Other letters that illuminate in the Garden of Eden are chambers and covers for these letters, of Alef, which is the inner chamber, and all is embroidered and illustrated in the throne, which is Briyah. And even though we are discussing the letters in Atzilut, it is only mentioned as root source, but the essence of the letters themselves were not able to come out until the World of Briyah, meaning below the dividing curtain (masach) of Atzilut, where the curtains have control. However, in Atzilut itself there is no controlling power of a curtain at all, and without the power of the dividing curtain the letters do not take on their latent shape. And what we determine and distinguish dividing curtains and letters in Atzilut are merely for the source roots that activate such in the lower worlds. Vav is six levels to the throne, which are the Lower Six Sefirot of Zeir Anpin. Samech is the sixty wheels of the throne, which are the Lower Six Sefirot of Malchut, in the secret of the verse, "Behold, it is the bed of Solomon; sixty mighty men are surrounding it...." (Song of Songs 3:7) Regarding the letters of the Torah, we studied: "there is no earlier and later in the Torah," but in the throne all are properly organized, and this secret was given to the wise at heart.

40. The 22 letters

362. דָּבָר אַחֵר וְהַמַּשְׂכִּילִים יַזְהִירוּ, אֵלֵּין אִינוּן אַתְוָון, דַּהֲוָה לוֹן שֵׂכֶל לְאַעֲלָא קֳדָם מַלְכָּא, כָּל חַד עַל תִּקּוּנוֹי. מִסִּטְרָא דִּגְבוּרָה עָאלוּ כֻּלְּהוּ לְמַפְרֵעַ, בְּגִין דְּאִיהִי דְרוֹעָא שְׂמָאלָא, תִּשְׁרֵ"י. וְדָא אִיהוּ בְּרֵאשִׁי"ת, ב"א תִּשְׁרֵ"י. בְּגִין דִּבְמִדַּת הַדִּין אִתְבְּרֵי עָלְמָא, וּבְגִין דָּא עָאלוּ לְמַפְרֵעַ.

362. Another explanation: "And the wise shall shine" are the letters, since the 22 letters are the particulars of all the top levels existing in the four Worlds of Atzilut, Briyah, Yetzirah, and Asiyah, **that had the intellectual sense to enter the King's presence, each one in its proper order,** because each letter has a specific instruction about its level in holiness, and figured out its level by which the people of the world will be able to reach to the Final Correction, and therefore claimed that it is worthy to create the world by its attributes. **From the side of Gevurah, all entered retroactively,** in the order of Tav, Shin, Resh, Kuf, **because** Gevurah **is the left arm,** which is the secret of the month of **Tishrei [Tav-Shin-Resh-Yud],** since the month of Nissan is Right, Chesed, and Tishrei in Left, Gevurah. **This is Beresheet,** anagram of **Bet-Alef Tishrei (came in the order of Tav-Shin-Resh), because the world was created with the attribute of judgment,** as it says that at first the thought was to create the world with the attribute of judgment. **Therefore, the** letters entered in the backward order, in the secret of Mayin Nukvin (Feminine Water).

363. וְהָא אוּקְמוּהוּ דְּבִּימִינָא אִתְבְּרֵי עָלְמָא, וּבֵיהּ עָאלוּ אַתְוָון כְּסִדְרָן. וְרָזָא דְּמִלָּה, אָמַרְתִּי עוֹלָם חֶסֶד יִבָּנֶה. וּבְגִין דָּא, כַּד עָאלוּ אַתְוָון לְמַפְרֵעַ, וּמְנַיְיהוּ כְּסִדְרָן, לָא בָּעָא קוּדְשָׁא בְּרִיךְ הוּא לְמִבְרֵי בְּהוֹן עָלְמָא, עַד דְּשִׁתֵּף לוֹן בִּימִינָא וּשְׂמָאלָא, וּבָרָא בְּהוֹן עָלְמָא.

363. **Thus, it was established** by the masters **that the world was created by the Right,** Chesed, since He foresaw that the world will not endure, He brought forward the attribute of mercy binding it with the attribute of judgment, as will be explained later, **and by it,** the Right Column, **the**

letters entered in their correct order, in the straight forward manner, Alef, Bet etc. This is the secret of: "I said 'forever is mercy (*chesed*) built….'" (Psalms 89:3) Therefore, when the letters began to enter backwards, and some of them in order, the Holy One blessed be He, did not wish to create by them the world until He united them with right and left together, and then He created the world with them.

‏364. נָטַל א"ב מִכְּסִדְרָן, וְנָטַל תש"ר מִלְמַפְרֵעַ, וְשִׁתֵּף בְּהוֹן אֶת י' מִן שְׁמֵיהּ, וּבָרָא בְּהוֹן עָלְמָא, בְּגִין דְּיִתְקַיַּים בִּנְיָינָא, בְּגִינֵיהּ וְאִינוּן אב"י תש"ר: אב"י אֲ"שֶׁר בְּ"יָדוֹ נֶ"פֶשׁ כָּל חָ"י. ת': תּוֹרַת י"י תְּמִימָה. ש': שַׁבָּת. ר': רֵאשִׁית וְחָכְמָה יִרְאַת י"י.

364. He took the letters **Alef and Bet from their direct order,** which is the secret of the Right Column, **and He took the letters Tav, Shin, and Resh from the backwards order,** which is the secret of the Left Column, **and combined the Yud of His Name with them,** which is the secret of the Masach (curtain; dividing line) of Chirek from the Central Column, **and created the world with them,** with the above mentioned six letters, which are also the six letters of the word Beresheet, **so that the structure of the world will endure. They are** the anagram of **Alef-Bet-Yud, Tav-Shin-Resh. Alef-Bet-Yud** which is the secret of: **"In Whose hand is the soul of all living…"** (Job 12:10) that hints to Malchut, the bundle of life. **Tav** ת is for **"The law of the Lord is perfect [lit. complete]…"** (Psalms 19:8) Zeir Anpin, Tiferet. **Shin** ש is for: *Shabbat,* Binah. **Resh is for** *Resheet* (the beginning) **"The fear [lit. awe] of the Lord is the beginning of wisdom…,"** (Psalms 111:10) and together they are one level with a full stature of Chochmah, Binah, Tiferet, and Malchut.

‏365. וּבְכֻלְּהוּ לָא בָעָא לְמִתְחַל אֶלָּא בְּאָת ב', בְּגִין דְּאִיהוּ בִּנְיַן אָב, בִּנְיָינָא דְעָלְמָא, וּבָהּ שָׁארֵי לְמִתְחַל. בְּגִין דְּבָהּ עָתִיד לְמִבְנֵי יְרוּשָׁלַיִם, כְּמָה דְאַתְּ אָמַר בּוֹנֵה יְרוּשָׁלַיִם י"י, דְּאִם י"י לֹא יִבְנֶה בַיִת שָׁוְא עָמְלוּ בוֹנָיו בּוֹ. וּבִנְיָינָא דְאוֹרַיְיתָא וְדְעָלְמָא, בְּאָת ב' עֲתִידָה לְמִבְנֵי, וַעֲלָהּ קַיְימָא עָלְמָא. וּבְהַהוּא

זִמְנָא דְּאִתְבְּנִיאַת, כְּאִלּוּ בְּהַהוּא זִמְנָא יִתְבְּרֵי עָלְמָא וְיִתְבְּנֵי, וְדָא בְּרֵאשִׁית בָּרָא אֱלֹקִי"ם.

365. Of all the letters, the Holy One blessed be He, **only wished to start with the letter Bet ב, because it is a** *binyan av* (DNA) [lit. father structure], meaning a structure for the Light of Chochmah, called "father," which is **the structure of the world. He wanted to begin with it because with it He is destined to build Jerusalem, as you say: "The Lord built up Jerusalem…"** (Psalms 147:2) and with it He will build the Holy Temple, as it says: **"If the Lord will not build a house, in vain did its builders labor…."** (Psalms 127:1) **The structure of the Torah and the** structure of the **world are destined to be built by the letter Bet, and the world is sustained through** this letter. **That time when** the Temple **was built, was as if at that very time the world was created and built up, and this is the meaning of:** *Beresheet* **"In the beginning God created…."** (Genesis 1:1)

366. אֲבָל כַּד וְחָרַב בַּיִת רִאשׁוֹן, כְּאִלּוּ הֲוָה עָלְמָא תֹהוּ וָבֹהוּ, וְדָא אִיהוּ וְהָאָרֶץ הָיְתָה תֹהוּ. מִיָּד דְּאִתְבְּנִיאַת, וַיֹּאמֶר אֱלֹקִי"ם יְהִי אוֹר. בְּגִין דְּכָל אַתְוָון נְהִירִין בָּהּ.

366. But at the actual time **when the first Temple was destroyed,** meaning during the actual time of the destruction, and see in Etz Chayim (Gate of the Diminishment of the Moon, Chapter 2), and this is what it says, "had it not been for this great diminishment, the Klipot and the nations of the world would not have been able to destroy the Holy Temple, **it was as if the world was formless and desolate, and this is** what is says: **"and the earth was without form and void…."** (Genesis 1:2) **As soon as** the Holy Temple **was built,** it says: **"And God said, 'let there be light…'"** (Genesis 1:3) since all the letters illuminate in the Holy Temple.

367. וְאַף עַל גַּב דְּאוֹר הוּא א', אוֹר דִּילֵהּ דְּנַהֲרָא בָּהּ, ב'. בְּחָמֵשׁ נְהוֹרִין, דְּאִינוּן ה' עִלָּאָה דִּשְׁמָא קַדִּישָׁא.

367. And even though Light (*or*), which is Chochmah, **is Alef א,** in the meaning of the verse: "...I will teach you wisdom" (Job 33:33) **it is Light by which it illuminates Bet ב,** meaning Chochmah does not illuminate in its Upper Three Sefirot, except through Yisrael-Saba and Tevunah, which are the secret of Binah and the Lower Six of Chochmah, **that illuminates in the five Lights,** which are Keter, Chochmah, Binah, Zeir Anpin and Malchut, **which are the upper Hei (5) ה of the Holy Name,** Yud-Hei-Vav-Hei, as Supernal Aba and Ima are the secret of the Yud of Yud-Hei-Vav-Hei, and Yisrael-Saba and Tevunah are the first Hei.

368. ג' עַמּוּדָא דְסָמִיךְ בֵּיתָא, דְאִיהוּ גְמִילוּת וַחֲסָדִים טוֹבִים. אִיהוּ סָמִיךְ לְד', דְאִיהוּ דַּלַּ"ת. וּבְאָן אֲתַר סָמִיךְ לָהּ, בִּגְלוּתָא. א' סָמִיךְ וְנָהִיר לְבּ'. ג' גָמִיל וְחֶסֶד עִם ד'.

368. The letter **Gimel ג is the pillar that supports the house,** which is Malchut that is called "house," and this pillar is: **"Beneficial acts of kindness"** (Avot 1:2) **it is a support for the** letter **Dalet ד,** which **literally means "poor or deprived"** (*dalat*). He asks, **"And in which area does [Gimel] support [Dalet]?"** and answers, **"In exile. Alef supports and illuminates Bet, and Gimel acts kindly with Dalet."**

369. וּבְמַאי. ג' אִיהוּ גַלְגַּל, וּבָהּ כָּל אַתְוָון מִתְגַּלְגְּלִין בְּכַמָּה גְלִילֵי דְדַהֲבָא. הֲדָא הוּא דִכְתִיב, יָדָיו גְּלִילֵי זָהָב מְמֻלָּאִים בַּתַּרְשִׁיש.

369. He asks, **"And by what** does Gimel support and help the Dalet?" He explains, **"Gimel is like a wheel, and all the letters turn in many rolls of gold by it, as is said: 'His hands are rods of gold set with beryl (*batarshish*)....'** (Song of Songs 5:14)"

370. מַאי בַּתַּרְשִׁיש. אֶלָּא בְּתָרֵי שֵׁת. וְאִינוּן תְּרֵין דְרוֹעִין, גְּדוֹלָה גְבוּרָה דִּבְהוֹן שָׁרֵי אוֹרַיְיתָא בְּב'. וּבְהוֹן שִׁית פִּרְקִין, דְאִינוּן ו' אַתְוָון בְּרֵאשִׁית, דִּכְלִילָן בְּעַמּוּדָא דְאֶמְצָעִיתָא, דְאִיהוּ ו'. וַעֲלֵיהּ אִתְּמַר, וַיְרַא רֵאשִׁית לוֹ, לוֹ: לְאָת ו'. כִּי שָׁם חֶלְקַת מְחוֹקֵק סָפוּן.

370. He asks, "What is *"batarshish* (בַּתַּרְשִׁישׁ)"? And explains, "Rearrange the letters, *bitrei shesh* (2x6; בְּתְרֵי שֵׁשׁ), and they are for the two arms: 'the great'—Chesed, right arm, 'the mighty'—the left arm, **which by both of them,** Chesed and Gevurah, **the Torah begins with the Bet (2)** of Beresheet, **and there are six parts in** the two arms, since each has three joints **that are** hinted **in the six letters of the word Beresheet. All** six parts of the two arms, right and left **are included in the Central Column,** Tiferet, **which is Vav** ו, and they are 2x6, one of the two arms and one of Tiferet. **About it,** Tiferet that is the Central Column, **is said: 'And he chose a first part for himself (resheet lo)....'** (Deuteronomy 33:21) *Lo* (Lamed-Vav), means 'for himself' and also means 'to the **letter Vav;'** that by the ascension of the Mayin Nukvin (Feminine Waters) from the Central Column that rises and regulates between the Columns, Right and Left of Binah, and causes a revelation of Mochin of Chochmah, Binah, and Da'at in Binah, in the secret of 'three emanate from one.' Thus he also attains them, since each measure of Light that the lower causes in the upper, the lower also merits. Therefore, 'He saw the beginning of the Vav,' meaning it also merits the top, Chochmah, Binah, and Da'at in the secret 'one is sustained by three' **'...for the portion of a revered chieftain is there...'** (Ibid.), referring to the Masach of Chirek that includes the two points: lock *(man'ula)*, and key *(maftecha)*, and all the Mochin get revealed in *maftecha,* and the point of *man'ula* is concealed. And it is the secret of the Hei of Moshe (Mem-Shin-Hei) that was a collateral to Abraham. **And since Moses was not given the chance to correct it it, even though on his own right he was able to reveal its completeness, therefore no one knew his burial place, since the burial represents the flaw, and since he had no flaw, no person could know his burial until the Final Correction, when Moses completeness will be revealed. Therefore, 'there' in the Central Column, 'a portion of a ruler (burial plot)' which is Moses, 'is hidden [lit. reserved].'"**

371. ד' דַּלֶת דְּבֵיתָא דִירוּשְׁלַיִם. ו' עַמּוּדָא דְּסָמִיךְ לְדַלֶת וְאִיהִי דַלֶת דִּתְרֵין תַּרְעִין, דְּאִתְּמַר בְּהוֹן פִּתְחוּ לִי שַׁעֲרֵי צֶדֶק.

371. Dalet ד is the door (delet) of the house, which is Malchut that **is called Jerusalem,** since by the acts of kindness of the Gimel, it goes from *dalat,* an idiom of "poverty and emptiness," to *delet,* a "doorway and opening" where all the Lights can enter inside. **Vav,** Zeir Anpin that illuminates with acts of kindness, **is the supporting pillar to this door (delet), and it** becomes a **doorway of two gates,** the Gate to the Light of Chochmah and the Gate to the Light of Chasadim, **as said about them: "Open to me the Gates of Righteousness…."** (Psalms 118:19)

372. וּבְגִין דָּא אִית לְדָלֶ"ת תְּרֵין גַּגִּין, וְאִינּוּן תְּרֵין דְּרוֹעִין וְכָל אֶחָד ו' דְּאִינּוּן שִׁית פִּרְקִין. אִיהִי דֶלֶת, וְדָא אִיהוּ דַּלוֹתִי וְכִי יְהוֹשִׁיעַ וְאָת ד' הִיא דְּרוֹעָא דְּאִית בֵּיהּ תְּרֵין אַמִּין.

372. This Dalet, therefore, has two rooflines, which are two Columns, **and they are two arms, each one is also a Vav (6) ו, which are six joints,** which are the Lower Six Sefirot of Chochmah and the Lower Six Sefirot of Chasadim. The Lower Six of Chochmah are hinted in the long vertical line, and the Lower Six of Chasadim are hinted in the shorter horizontal line, lying on its width from right to left, as is known that length hints to Chochmah and width to Chasadim, and both together form the Dalet. **This is** the meaning of: **"I am destitute (daloti)…"** (Psalms 116:6) meaning poverty and destitute: **"…and He saved me"** (Ibid.), as this poverty became the gateway and doorway to the chamber of Chochmah. **The letter Dalet ד is an arm that has two cubits (amot)** to measure the height of the levels.

373. ה' שְׁלִימוּ דִּתְרֵין דְּרוֹעִין וְגוּפָא. דְּאִיהִי כְּלָלָא דִּתְלַת אַבָהָן. ו' יְהוּדָא, שְׁלִימוּ דְּאָת ד', דְּאִיהִי סִיהֲרָא. כַּד נָהִיר בָּהּ, אִתְּמַר בָּהּ, וְהָיָה אוֹר הַלְּבָנָה כְּאוֹר הַחַמָּה וְאוֹר הַחַמָּה יִהְיֶה שִׁבְעָתַיִם כְּאוֹר שִׁבְעַת הַיָּמִים. וְדָא שְׁלִימוּ דְּחַמָּה וְסִיהֲרָא, דְּאִינּוּן ה"ה. בְּגִין דְּאִיהִי ז' כְּלִיל י"ו. וּבְגִין דָּא אִיהוּ זָכוֹר וְשָׁמוֹר, זָכוֹר מִסִּטְרָא דְּה' עִלָּאָה, שָׁמוֹר מִסִּטְרָא דְּה' תַּתָּאָה.

373. Hei ה has 3 lines and **is the completion of the two arms and the body,** Chesed, Gevurah, and Tiferet, **as this Hei is a composite of the**

three Patriarchs, in the secret of the three legs of the throne, and it is the fourth leg that completes them in the secret of the Kingdom of David. This is because Dalet is the secret of drawing down of Chochmah, and before Malchut cleaved to the Central Column it was under the control of Chochmah of the Left Column that was not yet joined with the Right Column, and therefore she was lacking (*dalah*) and poor because she was unable to shine without Chasadim. After cleaving to Zeir Anpin, which is the secret of the Central Column, then Chochmah is clothed with the many Chasadim of Zeir Anpin and completes Zeir Anpin, and then she is also composed of three Columns and becomes a Hei. **Vav ו is the unity that completes the letter Dalet ד,** which is **the Moon, and when it illuminates in her it is said: "Moreover the light of the Moon will be like the light of the Sun, and the light of the Sun will be sevenfold as the light of the seven days...."** (Isaiah 30:26) **This is the completion of the Sun and the Moon, which are the two Hei's of the Name Yud-Hei-Vav-Hei, because this** Malchut that **is Zayin (7) ז is comprised of Yud-Vav. Therefore, it is "remember (*zachor*)" and "guard (*shamor*),"** which is said regarding the Shabbat, **"remember" from the aspect of the upper Hei,** Binah, **"guard" from the aspect of the lower Hei,** Malchut.

374. וֹ' אִית לָהּ תְּכַת גַּגִּין, וְאִינוּן ו'ו'ו', דְּכָלִיקָן בְּחַ"י עָלְמִין. וֹ' אִיהִי מִפְּשַׁר וְלְכְמִין טָבִין בְּט'. וְהָא אוּקְמוּהוּ, וְלְכְמָא טָבָא מִסִּטְרָא דְּאַת ט', דְּאִיהוּ סָחוֹר לָהּ. כַּמָה דְּאוּקְמוּהוּ, וְלְכְמָא טָבָא וְחֵיזַת, וַדַּאי מִתַּמָּן קָא אַתְיָא. בְּגִין דְּאַת ט' אִיהִי סְפִירָה תְּשִׁיעָאָה מֵעֵילָּא לְתַתָּא. וֹ' סְפִירָה תְּמִינָאָה, מִתַּתָּא לְעֵילָּא. וֹ' מִסִּטְרָא דְּאַת א'.

374. The letter Chet ח has in its shape **three roof lines, and they are Vav-Vav-Vav that are included in life of the worlds (*chai olamim*),** which is Yesod, and three times Vav (6) [3x6=18; the numerical value of *chai* (life)]. **Chet is** he who merited to be a Chariot to the attribute of Yesod, the attribute of Joseph the Righteous; **he who knows how to interpret the dreams for good (*tovah*), with a Tet ט,** which is also an attribute of Yesod, as Chet (8) and Tet (9) equal *Tov* (good; 17). **They have established that**

a good dream is of the aspect of the letter Tet that surrounds the letter
Chet, as was established about interpreting dreams that you need to say,
chelma tava chazeita "You have seen a good dream." **Definitely it comes
from** that letter Tet **since this letter Tet is the ninth Sefira,** Yesod, when
you count **from top to bottom** in Direct Light. **Chet (8) is the eighth
Sefira, Yesod, from bottom to top** when the Lights leave, when the Light
of Keter came out first and the Light of Yesod entered the vessel of Hod,
and thus the Light of Yesod is in the vessel of Hod and circles about it from
the outside. **Chet** is Yesod **from the aspect of the letter Alef א,** which
alludes to the Light of Chochmah in the vessel of Keter, in the secret of
the verse: "...I will teach you wisdom (*chochmah*)..." (Job 33:33), and Chet
is the eighth Sefira from Chochmah. The second expansion is the secret of
Ayin-Bet of Primordial Adam (Adam Kadmon), and it is the root of all the
Lights of Chochmah in all the worlds.

375. י' סְפִירָה עֲשִׂירָאָה, עֲשִׂירִית הָאֵיפָה. כַּד נָחֵית ו' לְגַבָּהּ, אִתְעֲבִידַת
וַ"י. וְאָת י' כַּד סַלְקָא בְּכ', אִתְקְרִיאַת כֶּתֶר. וַעֲלֵיהּ אִתְּמַר כֶּתֶר יִתְּנוּ לְךָ
יְהֹו"ָה אֱלֹהֵ"נוּ. אַבָּא וְאִימָא, מַלְאָכִים הֲמוֹנֵי מַעְלָה, אֵלֶּין נִשְׁמָתִין, דְּאִינּוּן
מַלְאָכִים מִסִּטְרָא דְּמַלְכוּת.

375. Yudn (10) י **is the tenth Sefira,** Malchut, in the secret of: **"and the
tenth of an ephah...."** (Numbers 28:5) **When Chetn (8)** ח Yesod, **descends
to Yudn (10)** י Malchut, **it becomes** *chai* וַ"י, **(life; 18),** since the Yesod is
only alive during its unification with Malchut, in the 18 Sefirot, nine of
Direct Light and nine of Returning Light. **The letter Yud,** Malchut, **when
it ascends to Kafn (20)** כ, meaning that the Returning Light of Malchut
ascends with Ten Sefirot up to Keter, and clothes the Ten Sefirot of Direct
Light, which together are Twenty Sefirot, then Malchut **is called Keter.
About** Zeir Anpin **is said** then: **"A crown will they give to you Lord our
God,"** meaning to You Lord, our God (Elokim), Zeir Anpin, the Elokim
of the lower ones, **will Aba and Ima** that are called **angels, multitudes of
above, give an aspect of their Keter, which are the Neshamot,** since the
Keter of Aba and Ima is Binah of Arich Anpin, and Binah is the Neshama,

they are angels of the aspect of **Malchut** that ascended to the head of Arich Anpin. They rearranged the verse to say: "to You, Lord our God, will the angels, multitudes of above, give a crown." It says in the Gate of Meditations of our teacher, the Ari of blessed memory, in the section of the Musaf of Shabbat: "It was already explained in the Tikunei HaZohar that Aba and Ima are called the angels of Arich Anpin, the Keter of Atzilut." That which they call Zeir Anpin and Nukva "Lord our God" is because of the rule that a lower [Sefira] that elevates to a higher [Sefira] becomes like [the upper Sefira], and in the Musaf of Shabbat Zeir Anpin and Nukva stand in the place of Aba and Ima, and they are named after Aba and Ima.

376. יַחַד כֻּלָּם קְדוּשָׁה לְךָ יְשַׁלֵּשׁוּ, קְדוּשָׁה וַדַּאי אִיהִי שְׁכִינְתָּא. לְךָ יְשַׁלֵּשׁוּ, אִינּוּן תְּלַת אֲבָהָן, דְּאִינּוּן קָדוֹשׁ קָדוֹשׁ קָדוֹשׁ יְ"יָ צְבָאוֹ"ת, מַאי צְבָאוֹ"ת. אֶלָּא תְּרֵין נְבִיאֵי קְשׁוֹט. מְלֹא כָל: דָּא צַדִּיק. הָאָרֶץ כְּבוֹדוֹ: דָּא שְׁכִינְתָּא, דְּאִיהוּ קְדוּשָׁה, דַּעֲלָהּ אִתְּמַר, אֵין קְדוּשָׁה פָּחוּת מֵעֲשָׂרָה, וְדָא אִיהוּ כ'.

376. "Together they will all recite the *Kedusha* (Holiness) three times." The Holiness definitely refers to the Shechinah, since Zeir Anpin is called holy (*kadosh*) and Malchut is called holiness (*kedusha*). The meaning is that from the elevations the Nukva has **"they will recite three times."** Three times "Holy" **are the three Patriarchs:** Chesed, Gevurah, and Tiferet. **Holy,** in Chesed, **Holy** in Gevurah and **Holy** in Tiferet, *Hashem Tzeva'ot* (the Lord of Hosts.) What is *Tzva'ot* (Hosts)? They are two true **prophets,** Netzach and Hod, **filling all** (*melo kol*), this is *Tzadik*, Yesod called "All" (*Kol*), **"the earth from His glory,"** which is the Shechinah, Malchut **that is** called **Holiness** (*Kedusha*) when she has the illumination of the Upper Three Sefirot, **about which we learned:** *Kedusha* is **not** recited with **less than ten** people, **and this is Kaf** that alludes to Keter.

377. ל', וַיַּחֲלוֹם וְהִנֵּה סֻלָּם מֻצָּב אַרְצָה, דָּא שְׁכִינְתָּא תַּתָּאָה. וְרֹאשׁוֹ מַגִּיעַ הַשָּׁמַיְמָה, דָּא שְׁכִינְתָּא עִלָּאָה. וְהִנֵּה מַלְאֲכֵי אֱלֹהִי"ם, דָּא מ' עוֹלִים בְּל', וְיוֹרְדִים בְּנ'. דְּאִתְּמַר בָּהּ, אֵיךְ נָפַלְתָּ מִשָּׁמַיִם הֵלֵל בֶּן שָׁחַר, אִתְּמַר בֵּיהּ

וְיוֹרְדִים בּוֹ. אֲבָל בְּסָ׳, בָּהּ סַלְקִין, בְּגִין דְּאִיהִי סָ״נֶה, אִיהִי סָ״לָם, לְסַלְקָא בָּהּ.

377. The letter **Lamed ל** is the secret of the verse: **"And he dreamed, and behold, there was a ladder set upon the earth...,"** (Genesis 28:12) **which is the lower Shechinah,** Malchut: **"...and the top of it reached toward Heaven...,"** (Ibid.) **which is the Supernal Shechinah,** Binah. Lamed is "a tower flying in the air" meaning Binah, when Malchut ascended to it and was reduced from "light" (or; Alef-Vav-Resh) to "air" (avir; Alef-Vav-Yud-Resh), that during the time of Gadlut it becomes Chochmah to the head of Arich Anpin, and it expands to Zeir Anpin, and the Yud that hints to Malchut goes out of avir. **"...and behold, there were angels of God..."** (Ibid.): **This is Mem,** and they are from the left side, and that is why it says angels of Elokim and not angels of Yud-Hei-Vav-Hei [See Zohar, Vayikra 284]. **"...ascending..." with a Lamed,** which is Binah: **"...and descending..." with Nun** that is Malchut, **about which the verse says: "How did you fall from the high Heaven, morning star, son of the morning (ben shachar)."** (Isaiah 14:12), since Malchut is so called because of her two situations. In the first situation she is dark (shechorah), and in the second situation she is praised, **and it says about this** in the ladder: **"...and descending by it."** (Ibid.) **However, in the letter Samech ס they ascend because this** Malchut is a bush סָ״נֶה (s'neh, Samech-Nun-Hei), **and that is a ladder** סָ״לָם (sulam; Samech-Lamed-Mem) **to go up in the Lamed.**

378. ע׳ בָּהּ מִסְתַּכֵּל, וּבֵיהּ מְצַפֶּה, וְרָזָא דְמִלָּה, וְכָל עַיִן לָךְ תְּצַפֶּה. פ׳ בָּהּ כָּל לָשׁוֹן לָךְ תְּשַׁבַּח, בְּזִמְנָא דְסָלִיק לְאַתְרֵיהּ. וְכִי כְעַן לָא מְשַׁבְּחִין לֵיהּ כָּל לָשׁוֹן. לָא. עַד דְּיִתְקַיֵּים קְרָא, וְהָיָה יְ״יָ לְמֶלֶךְ לְמֶלֶךְ וַדַּאי בָּאת ל׳. וּבְהַהוּא זִמְנָא יִתְקַיֵּים כָּל פֶּה וְכָל לָשׁוֹן יִתְּנוּ הָדָר לְמַלְכוּתָךְ.

378. With the letter **Ayin ע** which hints to the eyes, the secret of Chochmah, **He looks,** meaning He observes and watches, **and through it He hopes and waits,** because when the lower ones improve their deeds they merit to attain His watchfulness and care. **This is the secret of: "And every**

eye (*ayin*) will hope and wait to see you." (Nishmat prayer) The letter **Pei
פ, by it:** "Every tongue will praise you" (Ibid) since the letter Pei hints
to the mouth, **when it ascends to its place.** Since at the time of Malchut's
ascension to Binah, the mouth descended to the aspect of the navel, and
in the future the Pei will return to its place in the head. He asks, **"Now,
do not all tongues praise him?"** And answers, **"Not until the verse: 'And
the Lord shall be a King [lit. *lemelech*; to the King]...' (Zachariah 14:9)
will be fulfilled definitely with the letter Lamed,** which is Binah—the
Name of Samech-Gimel (63)." See Zohar, Pinchas, 646: "Lamed ascended
above all letters...because it equals the Name Yud-Vav-Dalet, Hei-Yud, Vav-
Alef-Vav, Hei-Yud, which has three times Yud (10) that equals Lamed (30),"
and the Name Bet-Nun (52) in the future will be Samech-Gimel (63). **In
that time will be fulfilled: "Every mouth and every tongue will give a
splendor crown of glory to Your reign."**

379. צ', בְּהַהוּא זִמְנָא אִתְּמַר בָּהּ, צְדָקָה תְּרוֹמֵם גּוֹי. וְלֵית צְדָקָה אֶלָּא
צְלוֹתָא, הָא אוּקְמוּהוּ. וְאִיהִי אִימָא עִלָּאָה דְנָחֲתָא לְגַבֵּי צֶדֶק, וְאִתְעֲבִידַת
צְדָקָה וְאִתְכַּלִּיל י"ה בְּתַרְוַיְהוּ, בְּצַדִּיק וּצְדָקָה.

379. The letter **Tzadik צ** hints to charity (*tzedakah*) **regarding that
time it says about** Malchut: **"Charity [lit. Righteousness] will elevate
a nation...."** (Proverbs 14:34) **And *tzedakah* צְדָקָה is only prayer, as
they established** in Tractate Brachot 14a, and Rashi explains that justice
(*tzedek*; צֶדֶק) is prayer because one justifies his Creator. **And it is Supernal
Ima,** Binah, **that descends** to the aspect of *tzedek*, Malchut, **and from**
tzedek **it becomes** *tzedakah* **(charity). The Yud-Hei** from Aba and Ima **are
included in both,** in Yesod and Malchut; **Yud in *Tzadik*,** which is Yesod,
and Hei in *Tzedakah*, which is Malchut. See Zohar, Bechukotai 21 and
Tractate Sotah 17a, where it says that man (*ish*) and woman (*isha*), if they
merit the Shechinah is amongst them.

380. ק' בְּהַהוּא זִמְנָא, יִסְלְקוּן לֵיהּ קָלִין דִּצְלוֹתָא, קָלִין דְּאוֹרַיְיתָא, וּבְהַאי
זִמְנָא יְהֵא הַקוֹל קוֹל יַעֲקֹב. ר' רִאשׁוֹן לְצִיּוֹן הִנֵּה הִנָּם וְלִירוּשָׁלַיִם מְבַשֵּׂר אֶתֵּן.

ע׳ בָּה שָׁלוֹם שָׁלוֹם לָרָחוֹק וְלַקָּרוֹב אָמַר יְ"י וּרְפָאתִיו. לָרָחוֹק שֶׁנִּתְקָרֵב.
דְּקָרוֹב קָרוֹב הֲוָה. ת׳ בָּה תַּם עֲוֹנֵךְ בַּת צִיּוֹן לֹא יוֹסִיף לְהַגְלוֹתֵךְ.

380. The letter **Kof** ק hints to "voice" (*kol*), and **at that time the voices of prayer and voices of Torah will ascend** to the Holy One blessed be He, **and at this time it will be: "The voice is the voice of Jacob…."** (Genesis 27:22) The letter **Resh** ר hints to **"The first (*rishon*) who shall say to Zion, 'Behold, here they are, and to Jerusalem I will give a messenger of good tidings,'"** (Isaiah 41:27) meaning he will illuminate to Malchut from the aspect of the sealed Chochmah, called "first" (*rishon*). The letter **Shin** ש hints to **peace** (*shalom*), in it: **"'Peace, Peace to him that is far and to him that is near,' said the Lord, '…and I will heal him'."** (Isaiah 57:19) and explains: **him who was far and came closer because he was already near and close.** Since *shalom* is the secret of the unification (*zivug*), and **there are two types of unifications, one to draw Chochmah and one to draw Chasadim. The unification to draw Chochmah to Zeir Anpin and Nukva is considered "far,"** in the secret of the verse "From afar the Lord appeared unto to me," (Jeremiah 31:2) and in the secret of the verse, "…I said, 'I will get wisdom,' but it is far from me." (Ecclesiastes 7:23) **Since Zeir Anpin and Nukva are not able to receive Chochmah without Chasadim, and this is meant by, "…who was far and came closer…." But in the Upper Three [Sefirot] this subject of far and close does not apply, and they receive Chochmah without clothing, and that is the secret of "as to the near he is already close and near" meaning in the Upper Three Sefirot. The letter Tav** ת hints to "finished" (*tam*), in it: **"The punishment of your iniquity is accomplished (*tam*), daughter of Zion, He will no longer carry you away into captivity."** (Lamentations 4:22)

PETICHAT ELIYAHU

PETICHAT ELIYAHU

For the first day of the month of Elul

1. בְּרֵאשִׁית בָּרָא אֱלֹקִי"ם וְגוֹ' כְּתִיב, וְהַמַּשְׂכִּילִים יַזְהִירוּ כְּזֹהַר הָרָקִיעַ וְגוֹ', אִלֵּין אִינּוּן רַבִּי שִׁמְעוֹן בֶּן יוֹחָאי, וַחֲבֵרָיו, רַבִּי אֶלְעָזָר בְּרֵיה, וְרַבִּי אַבָּא, וְרַבִּי יוֹסֵי, וְרַבִּי חִיָּיא, וְרַבִּי יִצְחָק, וּשְׁאָר חַבְרַיָּא. דְּאִזְדַּהֲרוּ וְזֹהֲרוּ לְעֵילָא, כְּזֹהַר הָרָקִיעַ.

1. **"In the beginning God created…"** (Genesis 1:1) **It is written: "…and the wise shall shine like the brightness (*zohar*) of the Firmament…."** (Daniel 12:3) **These are Rav Shimon bar Yochai and his friends, Rav Elazar his son, Rav Aba, Rav Yosi, Rav Chiya, Rav Yitzchak, and the rest of the friends who are shining brightly above,** in the upper worlds, **like the brightness (*zohar*) of the Firmament.**

2. מַאי כְּזֹהַר, אֶלָּא כַּד עָבְדוּ הַאי וִחְבּוּרָא, אִסְתַּכְּמוּ עֲלֵיה לְעֵילָא, וְקָרְאוּ לֵיהּ סֵפֶר הַזֹּהַר וּמַצְדִּיקֵי הָרַבִּים בֵּיהּ יְהוֹן נְּהִירִין, כַּכּוֹכָבִים. לְעוֹלָם וָעֶד, דְּלָא אִתְחַשִׁיךְ נְהוֹרָא דִלְהוֹן, לְעָלַם וּלְעָלְמֵי עָלְמִין.

2. **He asks, "What is the meaning of brightness (*zohar*)?"** And answers, **"When they prepared this composition, those above agreed and named it the Book of the Zohar."** The explanation of the matter is found in the Tikunei Zohar, Prologue 5. **"And those who turn many to righteousness"** (Ibid.) **by this** brightness (*zohar*) **of the Firmament, will multiply "like the stars"** (Ibid.) **so that their light will never diminish."'**

3. בְּהַהוּא זִמְנָא דְּאִתְחַבַּר הַאי וִחְבּוּרָא, רְשׁוּתָא אִתְיְהִיב לְאֵלִיָּהוּ, לְאַסְכָּמָא עִמְּהוֹן בֵּיה. וּלְכָל מָארֵי מְתִיבְתָּא דִלְעֵילָא וְתַתָּא, וְכָל חֵילִין דְּמַלְאָכִין עִלָּאִין, וְנִשְׁמָתִין עִלָּאִין, לְמֶהֱוֵי עִמְּהוֹן בְּאַסְכָּמוּתָא, וּרְעוּתָא כַּחֲדָא.

3. **At the time that this composition was written, permission was given to Elijah to endorse it** with the Tanaim, Rav Shimon bar Yochai and his friends, **along with the deans of the Academies (Yeshivot), above and**

below, and all Supernal hosts of angels, and all the Supernal souls, together as one endorsement and one desire.

Elijah opened

4. פָּתַח אֵלִיָּהוּ וְאָמַר, רִבּוֹן עָלְמִין, אַנְתְּ הוּא חַד וְלָא בְּחֻשְׁבָּן אַנְתְּ הוּא עִלָּאָה
עַל כָּל עִלָּאִין, סְתִימָא עַל כָּל סְתִימִין, לֵית מַחֲשָׁבָה תְּפִיסָא בָּךְ כְּלָל.

4. Elijah opened and said: Master of the worlds, meaning the Endless
Light, blessed be He, **You are One without enumeration,** meaning
simple Light without change, addition, or a sweetened curtain, called
"enumeration." **You are above all the Supernal beings, the most concealed
of all concealed beings,** since the Upper Three Sefirot, Keter, Chochmah,
and Binah are considered Supernal and concealed, and the Endless Light,
blessed be He, is above them. **No [human] consciousness can grasp You
at all,** since He is the essence of reality and He is the secret of reality. We
have no grasp of our own essence let alone the essence of reality.

5. אַנְתְּ הוּא דְאַפִּיקַת עֲשַׂר תִּקּוּנִין, וְקָרֵינָן לוֹן עֲשַׂר סְפִירָן, לְאַנְהָגָא בְּהוֹן
עָלְמִין סְתִימִין, דְּלָא אִתְגַּלְיָין, וְעָלְמִין דְּאִתְגַּלְיָין. וּבְהוֹן אִתְכְּסִיאַת מִבְּנֵי נָשָׁא.
וְאַנְתְּ הוּא דְקָשִׁיר לוֹן וּמְיַחֵד לוֹן. וּבְגִין דְּאַנְתְּ מִלְּגָאו, כָּל מָאן דְּאַפְרִישׁ חַד
מִן חַבְרֵיהּ מֵאִלֵּין עֲשַׂר, אִתְחֲשִׁיב לֵיהּ כְּאִלּוּ אַפְרִישׁ בָּךְ.

5. You are the one Who produced Ten Corrections, meaning in relation
to the lower beings so that they can conceive them. **And we call them Ten
Sefirot, to conduct with them obscure worlds that are not revealed** with
the illumination of Chochmah, **and revealed worlds** that shine with the
illumination of Chochmah. **Through them, You are hidden from people,**
like someone who hides himself from others but the person is not affected
by that covering but others are. **You are the One who connects them and
unites them and because You are from within** the Sefirot and illuminate
in them, **then anyone who separates these Ten Sefirot one from the
other, to give dominance to that one Sefira alone, it is considered for
him as if he separates You,** meaning it is as if he separates the unity of the
Endless, blessed be He.

6. וְאִלֵּין עֲשַׂר סְפִירָן, אִינּוּן אָזְלִין כְּסִדְרָן, חַד אֲרִיךְ, וְחַד קָצָר, וְחַד בֵּינוּנִי. וְאַנְתְּ הוּא דְּאַנְהִיג לוֹן, וְלֵית מָאן דְּאַנְהִיג לָךְ. לָא לְעֵילָא, וְלָא לְתַתָּא, וְלָא מִכָּל סִטְרָא.

6. These Ten Sefirot follow their order, through the three Columns, **one** the Right Column: Chochmah, Chesed, and Netzach **is long,** as its illumination spreads from above downward, **one,** the Left Column: Binah, Gevurah, and Hod, **is short,** as its illumination illuminates from below upward, **and one,** the Central Column: Da'at, Tiferet, Yesod, and Malchut **is average,** comprised of Right and Left. **You,** the Endless Light, blessed be He, **conducts them, and there is no other who will lead You, neither above** in the Upper Three Sefirot, **nor below** in Malchut and Briyah, Yetzirah, and Asiyah, **nor in any other side,** in the Lower Six Sefirot, as He surrounds all worlds and fills all worlds.

7. לְבוּשִׁין תְּקִינַת לוֹן, דְּמִנַּיְיהוּ פָּרְחִין נִשְׁמָתִין לִבְנֵי נָשָׁא. וְכַמָּה גוּפִין תְּקִינַת לוֹן, דְּאִתְקְרִיאוּ גוּפָא, לְגַבֵּי לְבוּשִׁין דִּמְכַסְיָין עֲלֵיהוֹן.

7. For the Ten Sefirot of Atzilut **You prepared garments,** which are the Ten Sefirot of Briyah, **from which the Neshamot (Souls) fly to humankind,** since Neshama is from Briyah, Ruach is from Yetzirah, Nefesh from Asiyah. For the Sefirot **You prepared several bodies,** as each Sefira is comprised of Ten Sefirot and is considered a body on its own, **and they are called bodies** in relation **to the clothing that covers them,** which are Briyah, Yetzirah, and Asiyah.

8. וְאִתְקְרִיאוּ בְּתִקּוּנָא דָא, חֶסֶד דְּרוֹעָא יְמִינָא, גְּבוּרָה דְּרוֹעָא שְׂמָאלָא, תִּפְאֶרֶת גּוּפָא, נֶצַח וְהוֹד תְּרֵין שׁוֹקִין, וִיסוֹד סִיּוּמָא דְּגוּפָא, אוֹת בְּרִית קֹדֶשׁ. מַלְכוּת פֶּה. תּוֹרָה שֶׁבְּעַל פֶּה קָרִינָן לֵיהּ.

8. And the Sefirot **are named after this correction,** meaning after the correction of the shape of the stature of Adam of Atzilut. **Chesed is the right arm, Gevurah is the left arm, Tiferet is the body** meaning the chest, **Netzach and Hod** are **the two thighs, Yesod is the final part of the body,** which is Tiferet, **the sign of the Holy Covenant, and Malchut is the mouth,** meaning the Malchut of the head, **and we call it the Oral Torah.**

9. וְחָכְמָה מוֹחָא, אִיהוּ מַחֲשָׁבָה מִלְּגוֹ, בִּינָה לִבָּא, וּבָה הַלֵּב מֵבִין, וְעַל אִלֵּין תְּרֵין כְּתִיב, הַנִּסְתָּרוֹת לַי"יָ אֱלֹהֵי"נוּ.

9. Chochmah is the brain, meaning **the thought within** the brain, which is Light and vessel. **Binah is the heart, and through it,** Binah, **the heart understands,** and these are Light and Vessel. **About these two,** Chochmah and Binah, **it is written: "The hidden [lit. secret] matters belong to the Lord our God...."** (Deuteronomy 29:28)

10. כֶּתֶר עֶלְיוֹן, אִיהוּ כֶּתֶר מַלְכוּת. וַעֲלֵיהּ אִתְּמַר, מַגִּיד מֵרֵאשִׁית אַחֲרִית. וְאִיהוּ קַרְקַפְתָּא דִּתְפִלֵּי.

10. The Supernal Keter is the crown Malchut, meaning it spreads in the Ten Sefirot of Direct Light to attain Binding by Striking on Malchut, and the Ten Sefirot elevated by Returning Light, from Malchut until Keter, and the stature of Keter and Malchut become equal. **About this is said: "Declaring the end from the beginning...,"** (Isaiah 46:10) meaning a complete stature, from Keter to Malchut. **And this is the skull of the Tefilin,** which is the Surrounding Light.

11. מִלְּגוֹ אִיהוּ יוֹ"ד קֵ"א וַא"ו הֵ"א, דְּאִיהוּ אֹרַח אֲצִילוּת, אִיהוּ שַׁקְיוּ דְּאִילָנָא בִּדְרוֹעוֹי וְעַנְפוֹי, כְּמַיָּא דְּאַשְׁקֵי לְאִילָנָא, וְאִתְרַבֵּי בְּהַהוּא שַׁקְיוּ.

11. Within the stature of Atzilut is **Yud-Vav-Dalet, Hei-Alef, Vav-Alef-Vav, Hei-Alef,** which is the Name of Mem-Hei (45), **which is in the path of Atzilut,** meaning the stature of Chochmah that illuminates in Atzilut, as is known that Adam Kadmon and Atzilut, Briyah, Yetzirah, and Asiyah are in this order: Adam Kadmon is Keter, Atzilut is Chochmah, Briyah is Binah, Yetzirah is the Lower Six, and Asiyah is Malchut. And the Light of

Chochmah does not extend below Atzilut. **It is the watering of the tree in its arms and branches, as waters that water that tree and** the tree **multiplies and** grows **by this watering.**

12. רִבּוֹן הָעוֹלָמִים, אַנְתְּ הוּא עִלַּת הָעִלּוֹת, וְסִבַּת הַסִּבּוֹת, דְּאַשְׁקֵי לְאִילָנָא בְּהַהוּא נְבִיעוּ, וְהַהוּא נְבִיעוּ אִיהוּ כְּנִשְׁמָתָא לְגוּפָא, דְּאִיהוּ חַיִּים לְגוּפָא וּבָךְ לֵית דִּמְיוֹן, וְלֵית דְּיוֹקְנָא, מִכָּל מַה דִּלְגָו וּלְבָר.

12. Master of the worlds, meaning the Endless Light, blessed be He, **You are the Cause of all Causes, and the Reason for all Reasons, that waters the tree** of Atzilut **by that spring,** which is the Name of Mem-Hei (45), **and that spring is like a soul to the body, that is the life of the body. And You have no likeness nor form from all that is inside or outside** of Atzilut.

13. וּבְרָאת שְׁמַיָּא וְאַרְעָא, וְאַפִּיקַת מִנְּהוֹן שִׁמְשָׁא וְסִיהֲרָא וְכֹכְבַיָּא וּמַזָּלֵי. וּבְאַרְעָא, אִלָּנִין וְדִשְׁאִין וְגִנְתָא דְעֵדֶן וְעִשְׂבִּין וְחֵיוָן וְעוֹפִין וְנוּנִין וּבְנֵי נָשָׁא. לְאִשְׁתְּמוֹדְעָא בְּהוֹן עִלָּאִין, וְאֵיךְ יִתְנַהֲגוּן בְּהוֹן עִלָּאִין וְתַתָּאִין. וְאֵיךְ אִשְׁתְּמוֹדְעָאן עִלָּאֵי מִתַּתָּאֵי. וְלֵית דְּיָדַע בָּךְ כְּלָל, וּבַר מִינָךְ לֵית יְחוּדָא בְּעִלָּאֵי וְתַתָּאֵי, וְאַנְתְּ אִשְׁתְּמוֹדַע אָדוֹן עַל כֹּלָּא.

13. You created Heaven and Earth and produced from them, from the Heavens, **Sun, Moon, stars, and constellations. In the Earth** You created **trees, grasses, the Garden of Eden, plants, animals, fowl, fish, and human beings to acknowledge the Supernal beings through them,** as is written: "Lift up your eyes on high..." (Isaiah 40:26) and similarly: "...without my flesh I shall see God," (Job 19:26) since every branch reflects its root, **and how the higher and lower ones behave,** meaning the development of the Worlds from above downward in the way of cause and effect, reason and result, **and how the lower ones recognize** and perceive to attain the Divine Light **from the higher ones. And in You,** Your blessed Essence, **there is absolutely** no one **who is knowledgeable,** since there is no conception of His Essence, at all. **Besides Your unification, there is no**

such unique unity in the upper and lower ones, and You are recognized as the overall Cause and **Master over All** because we recognize You by Your actions, just like man does not grasp his own essence but nevertheless has no doubt in his existence, so too one who cleaves to the Creator has no doubt in His existence, yet he does not understand His essence.

14. וְכָל סְפִירָן, כָּל חַד אִית לֵיהּ שֵׁם יְדִיעַ, וּבְהוֹן אִתְקְרִיאוּ מַלְאָכַיָּא. וְאַנְתְּ לֵית לָךְ שֵׁם יְדִיעַ, דְּאַנְתְּ הוּא מְמַלֵּא כָּל שְׁמָהָן, וְאַנְתְּ הוּא שְׁלִימוּ דְכֻלְּהוּ. וְכַד אַנְתְּ תִּסְתַּלֵּק מִנְּהוֹן, אִשְׁתָּאֲרוּ כֻּלְּהוּ שְׁמָהָן, כְּגוּפָא בְּלָא נִשְׁמָתָא.

14. Among all of the Sefirot, each one has a known Name, since the Ten Names in the Torah that may not be erased are the secret of the Ten Sefirot, as mentioned in the Zohar [Vayikra 168]. The Sefira of Keter is called Alef-Hei-Yud-Hei, the Sefira of Chochmah is Yud-Hei, the Sefira of Binah is Yud-Hei-Vav-Hei with the vowels of Elokim, Chesed is El, Gevurah is Elokim, Tiferet is Yud-Hei-Vav-Hei, the two Sefirot Netzach and Hod are named Tzeva'ot, Yesod is El Chai (Living God), and Malchut is Alef-Dalet-Nun-Yud, **and the angels are named by them,** by the Names of the Sefirot, for example, Elim, Elokim etc. **Yet You have no known Name,** as He cannot be perceived and whatever we cannot perceive we cannot define by Name. We recognize **that You are He who fills all the Names with Inner Light, and it is You who completes them all** with Surrounding Light, **and when You are gone from them, all the Names remain as a body without a soul.**

15. אַנְתְּ חַכִּים, וְלָאו בְּחָכְמָה יְדִיעָא. אַנְתְּ הוּא מֵבִין, וְלָא מִבִּינָה יְדִיעָא. לֵית לָךְ אֲתַר יְדִיעָא אֶלָּא לְאִשְׁתְּמוֹדְעָא תּוּקְפָךְ וְחֵילָךְ לִבְנֵי נָשָׁא, וּלְאַחֲזָאָה לוֹן, אֵיךְ אִתְנַהֲגָ עָלְמָא בְּדִינָא וּבְרַחֲמֵי, דְּאִינוּן צֶדֶק וּמִשְׁפָּט, כְּפוּם עוֹבְדֵיהוֹן דִּבְנֵי נָשָׁא.

15. You are wise but not from known wisdom. You understand but not from known understanding, since He is wise on His own and understands on His own, and wisdom is only called wisdom (*chochmah*), and understanding is only called understanding (*binah*) because He filled them with wisdom and understanding. [See Zohar, Bo 224] **You do not occupy any known place** that would limit you, since the Holy One blessed be He, is the place of the world but the world is not His place. The reason He emanated Atzilut is only **so that human beings would perceive His strength and might and to show them how the world conducts itself with judgment and mercy, which are righteousness and justice, according to the deeds** of the lower ones, human beings.

16. דִּין, אִיהוּ גְּבוּרָה. מִשְׁפָּט, עַמּוּדָא דְּאֶמְצָעִיתָא. צֶדֶק, מַלְכוּתָא קַדִּישָׁא מֹאזְנֵי צֶדֶק, תְּרִין סַמְכֵי קְשׁוֹט, הִין צֶדֶק, אוֹת בְּרִית. כֹּלָּא לְאַחֲזָאָה אֵיךְ אִתְנַהֲיג עָלְמָא, אֲבָל לַאו דְּאִית לָךְ צֶדֶק יְדִיעָא דְּאִיהוּ דִּין. וְלַאו מִשְׁפָּט יְדִיעָא דְּאִיהוּ רַחֲמֵי, וְלַאו בְּכָל אִלֵּין מִדּוֹת כְּלָל.

16. Judgment (*din*) is Gevurah, the Left Column. **Justice (*mishpat*) is the Central Column,** Tiferet. **Righteousness (*tzedek*) is the Holy Malchut. Just scales are the two supporters of truth,** Netzach and Hod, **and a truly measured *hin* is this sign of the Covenant,** Yesod. Malchut, which is named "righteousness," is the secret of the well, and the three flocks of sheep that rest upon her are Netzach, Hod, and Yesod, and therefore all are named "righteousness." [See Zohar, Vayetze 98] **Everything is to show how the the world is conducted** by righteousness and justice, **but it is not as if there is certain righteousness that is judgment, and not a certain justice that is mercy, nor of any of these attributes, at all.** Rather it is a simple unified Light, as the masters of blessed memory said about the *manna* that it was "bread from Heaven," since it did not materialize as it got clothed in this world, and whoever would taste from it would taste whatever he desired. It must be that it was a different and opposite form, since there is nothing that can give what it does not contain, so how could there be two opposites in one item? So it must be that it is simple and stripped of all taste, and it includes all of the tastes in a way that the physical receiver would be able to differentiate to himself any taste he wanted. In this way we can understand every spiritual entity that in and of itself is single and stripped of any worldly form, and when it comes to the lower receiver it turns into a certain limited form, according to its quality.

יז. קוּם רַבִּי שִׁמְעוֹן, וְיִתְחַדְּשׁוּן מִלִּין עַל יְדָךְ, דְּהָא רְשׁוּתָא אִית לָךְ לְגַלָּאָה רָזִין טְמִירִין עַל יְדָךְ מַה דְּלָא אִתְיְיהִיב רְשׁוּ לְגַלָּאָה לְשׁוּם בַּר נַשׁ עַד כְּעַן.

17. Elijah said to Rav Shimon, "**Rise, Rabbi Shimon, and let new ideas come through you, as you have permission to reveal hidden secrets, permission that was not granted to any person until now to reveal** them."

יח. קָם רַבִּי שִׁמְעוֹן, פָּתַח וְאָמַר, לְךָ יְ"יָ הַגְּדוּלָה וְהַגְּבוּרָה וכו', עִלָּאִין שְׁמָעוּ, אִינוּן דְּמִיכִין דְּחֶבְרוֹן וְרַעְיָא מְהֵימְנָא, אִתְּעָרוּ מִשֵּׁנַתְכוֹן. הָקִיצוּ וְרַנְּנוּ שׁוֹכְנֵי עָפָר, אִלֵּין אִינוּן צַדִּיקַיָּא, דְּאִינוּן מִסִּטְרָא דְּהַהוּא דְּאִתְּמַר בָּהּ, אֲנִי יְשֵׁנָה וְלִבִּי עֵר, וְלָאו אִינוּן מֵתִים, וּבְגִין דָּא אִתְּמַר בְּהוֹן הָקִיצוּ וְרַנְּנוּ וכו'.

18. Rav Shimon stood up, opened and said: "**Yours, Lord, is the greatness, and the power,** and the glory, and the victory, and the majesty; for all that is in the Heavens and on Earth is Yours." (I Chronicles 29:11) **Listen, Supreme Ones, they who rest in Chevron,** which are the Patriarchs, **and the Faithful Shepherd,** Moses our teacher, **be shaken off from your sleep. "...awake and sing, you that dwell in dust...."** (Isaiah 26:19) **It is those righteous that are from this aspect about which it is said: "I sleep, but my heart wakes..."** (Song of Songs 5:2) meaning Malchut, **and they are not dead,** just slumbering, **and therefore it says about them, "Awake and sing..."** As the terminology of "awake" is applied to the concept of sleep.

יט. רַעְיָא מְהֵימְנָא, אַנְתְּ וַאֲבָהָן, הָקִיצוּ וְרַנְּנוּ לְאִתְּעָרוּתָא דִּשְׁכִינְתָּא דְּאִיהִי יְשֵׁנָה בְּגָלוּתָא. דְּעַד כְּעַן צַדִּיקַיָּא כֻּלְּהוּ דְּמִיכִין וְשֵׁינָתָא בְּחוֹרֵיהוֹן, מִיָּד יְהִיבַת שְׁכִינְתָּא תְּלַת קָלִין לְגַבֵּי רַעְיָא מְהֵימְנָא, וְיֵימָא לֵיהּ קוּם רַעְיָא מְהֵימְנָא, דְּהָא עֲלָךְ אִתְּמַר קוֹל דּוֹדִי דוֹפֵק לְגַבַּאי, בְּאַרְבַּע אַתְוָון דִּילֵיהּ. וְיֵימָא בְּהוֹן, פִּתְחִי לִי אֲחוֹתִי רַעְיָתִי יוֹנָתִי תַמָּתִי, דְּהָא תַם עֲוֺנֵךְ בַּת צִיּוֹן לֹא יוֹסִיף לְהַגְלוֹתֵךְ.

19. Faithful Shepherd, you and the Patriarchs, awake and sing to the waking of the Shechinah that sleeps in exile, as up until now all the righteous are sleeping, and the sleep is in the caverns of their eyes. Instantly, the Shechinah emits three sounds toward the Faithful Shepherd, and says to him, "Rise, faithful Shepherd, since about you it was said, 'hark, my beloved is knocking' (Song of Songs 5:2) **by me, with His four letters,** the full Yud-Hei-Vav-Hei, as the first three letters: Yud-Hei-Vav are the secret of the Patriarchs, and the last letter Hei is Moses that will reveal himself at the conclusion of all the corrections. **And he will say about them, 'Open to me, my sister, my love, my dove, my undefiled...'** (Ibid.) corresponding to Chochmah, Binah, Tiferet, and Malchut. **Since, 'The punishment of your iniquity is accomplished, daughter of Zion, He will no more carry you away into captivity....'** (Lamentations 4:22)

20. שֶׁרֹאשִׁי נִמְלָא טָל, מַאי נִמְלָא טָל. אֶלָּא אָמַר קוּדְשָׁא בְּרִיךְ הוּא אַנְתְּ וְשֵׂיבָא דְּמִיּוֹמָא דְּאִתְחֲרַב בֵּי מַקְדְּשָׁא דְּעָאלְנָא בְּבֵיתָא דִּילִי, וְעָאלְנָא בְּיִשּׁוּבָא לַאו הָכִי. דְּלָא עָאלְנָא כָּל זִמְנָא דְּאַנְתְּ בְּגָלוּתָא, הֲרֵי לָךְ סִימָנָא שֶׁרֹאשִׁי נִמְלָא טָל. הֵ"א, שְׁכִינְתָּא בְּגָלוּתָא, שְׁלִימוּ דִילָהּ וְחַיִּים דִּילָהּ, אִיהוּ טָל. וְדָא אִיהוּ יוּ"ד הֵ"א וָא"ו. וְהֵ"א אִיהִי שְׁכִינְתָּא, דְּלָא מְוִוישְׁבַן טָ"ל. אֶלָּא יוּ"ד קַ"א וָא"ו, דְּסַלְּיקוּ אַתְוָון לְחָשְׁבַּן טָ"ל. דְּאִיהוּ בּוּלְיָא לִשְׁכִינְתָּא, מִנְּבִיעוּ דְּכָל מְקוֹרִין עִלָּאִין. מִיָּד קָם רַעְיָא מְהֵימָנָא, וַאֲבָהָן קַדִּישִׁין עִמֵּיהּ.

20. "'...for my head is filled with dew....'" (Song of Songs 5:2) He asks, "What is the meaning of 'filled with dew'?" But the Holy One blessed be He, said, "You think that from the day of the Temple's destruction, I entered My abode, and I entered the settlement of Celestial Jerusalem? Not so, as I have not entered, since there is no internal mating of Supernal Aba and Ima, called Celestial Jerusalem, as long as you are in exile." And here is your proof, "For my head" the secret of the Upper Three Sefirot, "Is filled with dew (tal)" and the Upper Three Sefirot of the Upper Three Sefirot do not extend, before the End of Correction, when the entire Malchut will be corrected, only the Lower Six of the Upper Three Sefirot. He explains what is dew (tal); the last letter Hei spelled out as **Hei-Alef**

of the Name of Mem-Hei (45) **is the Shechinah,** and She is **in exile. Her completion and Her life is** *tal* **(39), and this is** the first three letters Yud-Hei-Vav spelled out **Yud-Vav-Dalet (20), Hei-Alef (6), Vav-Alef-Vav (13),** which equals *tal* (39) from the Name of Mem-Hei. **And the** last **Hei-Alef, the Shechinah,** Malchut, **was not** included **in the counting of** *tal,* but only the **Yud-Vav-Dalet, Hei-Alef, Vav-Alef-Vav, whose letters equal** *tal* **(39).** It, the Yud-Hei-Vav spelled-out, **fills the Shechinah from the fountain of all the Supernal Sources,** which is the skull of Arich Anpin. **The Faithful Shepherd immediately rose up, and the holy Patriarchs with him,** meaning to say, that they merited the great Illuminations of the Final Correction.

21. עַד כָּאן רָזָא דְיִחוּדָא, מִכַּאן וְאֵילַךְ פַּרְשָׁתָא קַדְמָאָה דְסִתְרֵי אוֹרַיְיתָא. פָּתַח רַבִּי שִׁמְעוֹן וְאָמַר, בְּרֵאשִׁית בָּרָא אֱלֹקִ"ם, סוֹד יְ"יָ לִירֵיאָיו וּבְרִיתוֹ לְהוֹדִיעָם, סוֹ"ד: אִלֵּין אִינּוּן שַׁבְעִין דְּאִתְפָּרַשׁ מִלַּת בְּרֵאשִׁית בְּהַאי פַּרְשָׁתָא.

21. Up to here was explained **the secret of the unification** of the Name of Mem-Hei. **From here onward** he explains **the first chapter of the concealed** parts **of the Torah (***sitrei torah***). Rav Shimon opened and said, "In the beginning God created..."** (Genesis 1:1)**; "The secret of the Lord is to those who fear Him, and His covenant to make them know it."** (Psalms 25:14) **"Secret (***sod***),"** which equals 70, **these are the seventy manners** by which **the word Beresheet** of the beginning of the Torah is **explained in this passage.**

TIKKUNIM 1-17

TIKKUNIM 1-17

For the second day of the month of Elul
First Tikkun
Beresheet: *Bet Resheet*

1. בְּרֵאשִׁית: בּ' רֵאשִׁית. זֶה הַשַּׁעַר לַי"יָ צַדִּיקִים יָבֹאוּ בוֹ, דָּא אִיהוּ תַּרְעָא דְּצַדִּיקַיָּיא, דְּאִית לוֹן רְשׁוּ לְאַעֲלָא תַּמָּן וְאָחֳרָנִין דְּלַאו אִינּוּן צַדִּיקַיָּא, אִתְדַּחְיָין מִתַּמָּן.

1. The word **Beresheet** is spelled with the letter **Bet**, which is Malchut, and *resheet* (beginning) with which to enter into the Supernal levels, as it is written: "**This is the gate of the Lord; the righteous shall enter into it.**" (Psalms 118:20) **This is the gate that the righteous people have permission to enter, and others who are not righteous are rejected from there.**

2. בָּהּ רְשִׁימִין וּמְצוּיָּירִין וּמִתְחַקְּקָין, דִּיוֹקְנִין דְּעִלָּאִין וְתַתָּאִין. צִיּוּרָא דְּאָדָם רְשִׁימָא תַּמָּן, וְאִיהוּ דְּמוּת אָדָם, רְשִׁימָא דְּאַרְיֵה תַּמָּן לִימִינָא. וּרְשִׁימָא דְּשׁוֹר לִשְׂמָאלָא. וּרְשִׁימָא דְּנִשְׁרָא בְּאֶמְצָעִיתָא. וְרָזָא דְּמִלָּה, וּדְמוּת פְּנֵיהֶם פְּנֵי אָדָם וּפְנֵי אַרְיֵה אֶל הַיָּמִין לְאַרְבַּעְתָּם וכו' וְאַרְבַּע וַיֵּיתָא אַרְבַּע אַנְפִּין. אִלֵּין אַרְבַּע אַתְוָון דִּשְׁמָא קַדִּישָׁא דִּיהֹו"ה דְּנָהִיר בְּהוֹן.

2. **In Malchut are impressed, fashioned, and engraved**, meaning Nefesh, Ruach, and Neshama, **all of the shapes and forms of the higher and lower beings** because Malchut includes all of the Supernal levels, and is a Keter, meaning a root, to all those below her. **The shape of a man**, which is Zeir Anpin, **is impressed there, which is the image of a man. An impression of a lion is** impressed **there to the right**, which is Chesed; **an impression of an ox is** impressed **to the left**, which is Gevurah. **An impression of an eagle is** impressed **in the middle. The secret of the matter is: "As for the likeness of their faces, they had the face of a man, all four of them had the face of a lion on the right side...,"** (Ezekiel 1:10) **each beast has four faces,** as each one is composed of all four; **these are the four letters of the Holy Name Yud-Hei-Vav-Hei.** Yud is the secret of Chesed, the face of a

lion, Hei is the secret of Gevurah, the face of an ox, Vav is the secret of the face of an eagle. The lower Hei is the secret of Malchut, the face of man **that shines in them** in all four beasts of the Chariot.

3. מַלְכָּא דְּכֻלְּהוּ חֵיוָן, דָּא אָדָם, דְּאִיהוּ יוֹ״ד ה״א וא״ו ה״א, דְּסָלִיק בְּחֻשְׁבָּן חַד. דְּמוּת אָדָם: דָּא שְׁכִינְתָּא קַדִּישָׁא, דְּאִיהוּ דְיוֹקְנֵיהּ. אִיהִי חוֹתָם דִּילֵיהּ.

3. The King of all the beasts is man [lit. *adam*] **that rides on the Throne, which is Yud-Vav-Dalet, Hei-Alef, Vav-Alef-Vav, Hei-Alef,** the Yud-Hei-Vav-Hei of Mem-Hei (45) **that equals the same numerical value** of *adam* (man), which is 45. **The image of a man, this is the Holy Shechinah,** meaning Malchut, **that She is his shape,** that is included in him, **and She is his seal.**

4. וַעֲלָהּ אִתְּמַר, שִׂימֵנִי כַחוֹתָם עַל לִבֶּךָ, דְּהָכִי אָמְרַת שְׁכִינְתָּא, אַף עַל גַּב דְּאַנְתְּ תִּסְתַּלַּק לְעֵילָא דְיוֹקְנָךְ לָא אִתְעֲדֵי מִנָּאי לְעָלַם, כְּהַהוּא חוֹתָם, דְּבְהַהוּא אֲתַר דְּאִתְדַּבַּק בֵּיהּ, רְשִׁימוּ דְּמָארֵי וֹחוֹתְמָא, לָא אִתְעֲדֵי מִנֵּיהּ דְיוֹקְנָא דְיוֹחוֹתְמָא, לְאִשְׁתְּמוֹדְעָא בֵּיהּ, וּבְגִין כָּךְ אָמְרָה כְּנֶסֶת יִשְׂרָאֵל בְּגָלוּתָא שִׂימֵנִי כַחוֹתָם עַל לִבֶּךָ, כִּרְשִׁימוּ דִּתְפִלִּין דְּיָד, דְּאִינוּן לָקֳבֵל לִבָּא. כַחוֹתָם עַל זְרוֹעֶךָ, כִּתְפִלִּין דְּרֵישָׁא, דְּאִינוּן תַּלְיָין רְצוּעִין לְכָל סְטָרִין. עַל לִבָּא וּדְרוֹעָא.

4. About the Shechinah **it is said: "Set me as a seal upon your heart…,"** (Song of Songs 8:6) **since the Shechinah,** which is Malchut **says** to Zeir Anpin **"even though you go up and away,** meaning after the prayer, since the Mochin of Zeir Anpin leave, **your shape was never removed from me like that seal. For the shape of the seal is not erased from the place the impression of the owner of the seal cleaves to, since it is recognizable** to the owner of the seal, which is Zeir Anpin, and all of this is during the day." **Therefore, the Congregation of Israel,** Malchut, **said in exile** or at night, which is called "exile," meaning when the Mochin leave completely, when even the impression is gone, which is a time of separation between

Zeir Anpin and Malchut, she pleads and says to him, **"Set me as a seal upon your heart..."** (Ibid.) Do it in such a manner that my seal will be upon your heart, which is **like** the impression **of the hand Tefilin, which corresponds to the heart: "as a seal upon your arm"** (Ibid.) **like the head Tefilin, whose straps hang to each side on the heart and the arm**, and through my impression remaining on your heart you will be able to draw to me an illumination from there.

וּבְהוֹן אִינּוּן רְשִׁימִין, דְּאִינּוּן עַמֵּיהּ דְּקוּדְשָׁא בְּרִיךְ הוּא, וְעוֹד שִׂימֵנִי כַּחוֹתָם דָּא חוֹתָם דְּאוֹת בְּרִית קֹדֶשׁ, וְהוּא אוֹת בְּרִית שַׁבָּת קֹדֶשׁ, וְיָמִים טוֹבִים. .5

5. And by them, meaning by the Tefilin, the children of Israel **are marked, who the people of the Holy One blessed be He are, are marked** because the Tefilin are the seal of the Holy One blessed be He. **Also, "Set me as a seal"** (Ibid.) **refers to the sign [lit. seal] of the Covenant,** since circumcision is also known as a seal, as it is said, "....and He marked His offspring with the sign of the Holy Covenant" [from the blessing of the circumcision]. **It is also the sign of the Covenant of the Holy Shabbat and Holidays.** See Zohar Chadash, Song of Songs, 205-206, where it says that the Light that rests on us on the Holidays is called Tefilin and the Supernal Signet Ring of the King. And surely so on Shabbat that Shabbat Eve is called the hand Tefilin, and the day of Shabbat is called the head Tefilin.

כִּי עַזָּה כַמָּוֶת אַהֲבָה, תַּקִּיפָא אִיהִי אַפְרָשׁוּתָא דְּקוּדְשָׁא בְּרִיךְ הוּא וּשְׁכִינְתָּא מִיִּשְׂרָאֵל, כִּפְרִישָׁא דְּנִשְׁמְתָא וְרוּחָא וְנַפְשָׁא מִגּוּפָא. וְתוּ כִּי עַזָּה כַמָּוֶת אַהֲבָה, כַּד יִשְׂרָאֵל מְיַחֲדִין שְׁמָא דְּקוּדְשָׁא בְּרִיךְ הוּא בִּרְחִימוּ, וְאָמְרִין הַבּוֹחֵר בְּעַמּוֹ יִשְׂרָאֵל בְּאַהֲבָה. .6

6. "...for love is as strong as death...," (Song of Songs 8:6) **this separation of the Holy One blessed be He, and His Shechinah from Israel as strong** and hard **as the parting of the Neshama, Ruach, and Nefesh from the body. Also, "...love is as strong as death"** (Ibid.) means that **when Israel**

unify the Name of the Holy One blessed be He, with love and say: "He who chooses His nation Israel with love." [From the Morning Prayer]

7. קְשָׁה כִשְׁאוֹל קִנְאָה, דְּקוּדְשָׁא בְּרִיךְ הוּא מְקַנֵּי עֲלַיְיהוּ, בְּזִמְנָא דְּיִפְּקוּן מִן גָּלוּתָא, דְּאִיהוּ יְהֵא בְּהַהוּא זִמְנָא קַנָּא וְנוֹקֵם וּבַעַל חֵמָה. רְשָׁפֶיהָ רִשְׁפֵּי אֵשׁ, בְּהַהוּא זִמְנָא יִתְעַר שְׂמָאלָא בְּשַׁלְהוֹבִין דִּילֵיה, דְּאִנּוּן רִשְׁפֵּי אֵשׁ שַׁלְהֶבֶת יָ"הּ, וְיוֹקִיד כַּמָּה הֵיכָלִין דְּבָתֵּי עֲבוֹדָה זָרָה, וְיִטּוֹל נוּקְמִין מֵעֲמָלֵק, דְּאִיהוּ אוֹמֵי בִּתְרֵין אַתְוָן דִּשְׁמָא קַדִּישָׁא דְּאִינּוּן יָ"הּ, לְנָטְלָא נוּקְמָא מִנֵּיה. הָדָא הוּא דִּכְתִיב וַיֹּאמֶר כִּי יָד עַל כֵּס יָ"הּ. וְדָא אִיהוּ רִשְׁפֵּי אֵשׁ שַׁלְהֶבֶת יָ"הּ.

7. "Jealousy is as cruel as Sheol" (Ibid.) means the Holy One blessed be He is jealous for Israel at the time when they will leave the exile, He will be jealous and avenging and wrathful at that time. "The coals thereof are coals of fire, the flame of the Lord (Yud-Hei)" (Ibid.) means that at that time, when Israel will leave the exile, He will arouse the left side with its flames that are "fire and flames of the Lord (Yud-Hei)" meaning the Left Column of Ima, and it will burn many temples of idol worshippers and take revenge upon Amalek, as He made an oath by the two letters of the Holy Name, Yud-Hei, to get His revenge of them. This is the meaning of the verse: "...the hand upon the throne of the Lord (Yud-Hei)..." (Exodus 17:16) and this is the meaning of: "coals of fire and flames of the Lord (Yud-Hei)." (Song of Songs 8:6)

8. וְיִשְׂרָאֵל אָמְרִין, רִבּוֹן עָלְמִין, אַף עַל גַּב דַּאֲנָא בְּגָלוּתָא מְרַוֲחָקָא מִנָּךְ, שִׂימֵנִי כַחוֹתָם עַל לִבֶּךָ, וְלָא יִתְעֲדִי מִנָּן דִּיוּקְנָךְ, דְּאִיהִי וֹחוֹתָם דִּילָךְ, שְׁכִינְתָּא דִּילָךְ. דִּבְגִינָהּ אַנְתְּ הֲוֵית דָּכִיר לָן בְּגָלוּתָא, וְחוֹתָמָא דְּקוּדְשָׁא בְּרִיךְ הוּא וַדַּאי אִיהִי שְׁכִינְתָּא.

8. When they are in exile, Israel says: "Master of the universe, even though I am in exile, far away from You 'Set me as a seal upon Your Heart' (Song of Songs 8:6) and thus Your Image will not be erased from us, which is Your Seal and is Your Shechinah, for whose sake You always remember us in exile, and the Seal of the Holy One blessed be

He, is assuredly the Shechinah for two reasons: firstly, She is the last Sefira, which is likened to the seal at the end of a letter. Secondly, because all of the Mochin can only be revealed in Her and they shine only from Her and above, and in this aspect She is the signet of the king. This is similar to a king who sits in his throne and the countrymen recognize him by his signet, and when they see the signet it is as if they see the king himself."

9. בְּרֵאשִׁ֖ית בָּרָ֑א, ב' אִיהִי וַדַּאי, בָּהּ פָּתְוָוֹת אוֹרַיְיתָא בְּב', וְדָא בְּרֵאשִׁית: ב' רֵאשִׁית. ב' אִיהוּ וַדַּאי אוֹצָרָא דְּכֹלָּא, עֲלָהּ אִתְּמַר, יִרְאַת יְ"יָ הִיא אוֹצָרוֹ.

9. This is a continuation to that which it says in verse 8: "and the seal of the Holy One blessed be He, is assuredly the Shechinah." **"In the beginning (Beresheet) God created…"** (Genesis 1:1) The letter **Bet is certainly the** Shechinah, which is called *bayit* (house), **with which the Torah starts with the letter Bet, and this is Beresheet;** which is spelled **Bet** *resheet.* **Bet** that is Malchut **is assuredly the treasury of all** the levels. **About it is said, "…the awe of the Lord is His treasure."** (Isaiah 33:6)

For the second day of the month of Elul
Second Tikkun
Resheet is the Torah

‫1. בְּרֵאשִׁית, וְזִמְנִין סַגִּיאִין אִינּוּן בְּאוֹרַיְיתָא רֵאשִׁית, וְכָל חַד אִתְפָּרַשׁ‬
‫בְּאַתְרֵיהּ, כַּדְקָמָא אִיהוּ, יְ"יָ קָנָנִי רֵאשִׁית דַּרְכּוֹ, וְדָא אוֹרַיְיתָא, דְּאִית בָּהּ‬
‫טַעֲמֵי וּנְקוּדֵי וְאַתְוָון, וְכַמָּה פִּקּוּדִין דַּעֲשֵׂה וְלֹא תַעֲשֶׂה, דְּכֻלְּהוּ תַּלְיָין בְּשֵׁם‬
‫יהו"ה הָדָא הוּא דִכְתִיב, זֶה שְׁמִי לְעֹלָם וכו'. שְׁמִ"י עִם י"ה שָׂ"ה. זִכְר"י‬
‫עִם ו"ה רמ"ח. שָׂ"ה מִשְּׂמָאלָא, מִדְּחִילוּ דִּגְבוּרָה אִתְיַהִיבוּ, פַּחַד יִצְחָק.‬

1. Prior to this, he explained that the letter Bet of Beresheet is the Shechinah and here he continues to interpret *resheet* (beginning) of Beresheet as the Torah. And he says, the word *resheet* appears many times in the Torah and each one is defined in its place to mean "the first," as it is written "The Lord made me as the beginning (*resheet*) of His way…." (Proverbs 8:22) **This is the Torah,** called "beginning," **which contains cantillation marks, vowels, and letters, and many positive precepts and negative precepts, which all originate in the Name Yud-Hei-Vav-Hei,** namely, in He who commanded these precepts, which is why it says "God made me." **This is the meaning of: "this is My Name (*Shmi*) forever, and this is My memorial (*Zichri*)…."** (Exodus 3:15) ***Shmi* (350) plus Yud-Hei (15)** equals the numerical value of **365** negative precepts. ***Zichri* (237) plus Vav-Hei (11)** equals the numerical value of **248** positive precepts. **The 365** negative precepts were given **from the Left, from awe,** the aspect of **Gevurah,** which is the **fear of Isaac.** (The rest is missing)

For the third day of the month of Elul

THIRD TIKKUN

Beresheet: *Shev Beyir'at haShem* (Dwell in the Awe of Heaven)

1. בְּרֵאשִׁית, תַּמָּן יְרָא"ת. מָה דְּאִשְׁתְּאַר מֵאִינּוּן אַתְוָון, ע"ב וְרָזָא דְמִלָּה, שֵׁב בְּיִרְאַת יְ"יָ. וְאִם לֵית דְּחִילוּ, לֵית חָכְמָה, כְּמָה דְּאוּקְמוּהָ, אִם אֵין יִרְאָה אֵין חָכְמָה. בְּגִין דְּיִרְאָה הִיא אוֹצָרָא לְחָכְמָה, אִיהִי גְּנִיזָה דִילָהּ, אִיהִי טְמִירוּ דִילָהּ, אִיהִי בֵּיתָא דְמַלְכָּא.

1. The word **Beresheet** (Bet-Resh-Alef-Shin-Yud-Tav) **contains** [the word] *yir'at* (the awe of, Yud-Resh-Alef-Tav). **The remaining letters** of Beresheet **are Shin-Bet** (*shev*, dwell), **and the secret of the word is "dwell in the awe of Heaven."** As the awe of Heaven must be permanent as a house in which to dwell, in the secret of the verse, "…according to the beauty of a man, to dwell in a house" (Isaiah 44:13) **and without awe there is no wisdom, as it is said, "Without awe, there is no wisdom."** (Tractate Avot, Chapter 3) **Because awe is a treasure house for Chochmah, its treasury; it is its hidden place, and it is the King's house.**

2. וְדָא תִּקּוּנָא תְּלִיתָאָה, כְּגַוְונָא דָא בְּרֵאשִׁית: רֹא"שׁ בַּי"ת. וְרָזָא דְמִלָּה, בְּחָכְמָה יִבָּנֶה בָּיִת. וּמַאן דְּבָעֵי לְמֶחֱזֵי לְמַלְכָּא, לֵית לֵיהּ רְשׁוּ לְמֶחֱזֵייהּ, אֶלָּא בְּבֵיתֵיהּ. וְרָזָא דְמִלָּה, חָכְמָה לָא אִשְׁתְּמוֹדְעָא, אֶלָּא בְּבֵיתֵיהּ. כְּגַוְונָא דָא עַמּוּדָא דְּאֶמְצָעִיתָא, דְּאִיהוּ יְקוּ"ק, לָא אִשְׁתְּמוֹדַע לִנְבִיא וְחוֹזֶה, אֶלָּא בְּהֵיכָלֵיהּ, דְּאִיהוּ אדנ"י. וְרָזָא דְמִלָּה וַי"יָ בְּהֵיכַל קָדְשׁוֹ.

2. And this Third Tikkun (Correction) of the Seventy Corrections is thus: **Beresheet is the** [same] **letters of the words** *rosh bayit* **(head of the house). The secret of the matter is: "Through wisdom (*chochmah*) a house is built…"** (Proverbs 24:3) **and whoever wishes to see the King may only see Him in His house, and the secret of the matter is that Chochmah is known only in its house,** meaning in Malchut. Since from Chochmah to Malchut there is none among all the Sefirot that could receive the illumination of Chochmah for itself, and Malchut is only considered a house when it contains Chochmah. **Similar to this is the Central Column**, which is Zeir Anpin that illuminates within Chasadim with the illumination of Chochmah, **which is Yud-Hei-Vav-Hei. It is not known to a prophet or seer, rather only in His chamber**, namely Malchut that is sweetened with the mercy of Binah because then it is considered a sanctuary like Binah, The chamber **is the Name Alef-Dalet-Nun-Yud. The secret of the matter is "And the Lord,"** which is Zeir Anpin, **"But the Lord is in his Holy Chamber…"** (Habakkuk 2:20), which is Malchut.

‎3. וְאִיהִי כְּלִילָא מִשֶּׁבַע הֵיכָלִין, מִשֶּׁבַע אַרְעִין. וַעֲלַיְיהוּ אָמַר דָּוִד, אֶתְהַלֵּךְ לִפְנֵי יְ"יָ בְּאַרְצוֹת הַחַיִּים. וְעַמּוּדָא דְאֶמְצָעִיתָא אִיהוּ כְּלִיל שֶׁבַע רְקִיעִין, וַעֲלַיְיהוּ אָמַר דָּוִד הַשָּׁמַיִם שָׁמַיִם לַי"יָ.

3. And Malchut **is comprised of Seven Chambers** that are Ten Sefirot, as the upper chamber includes the Upper Three Sefirot, and the lower chamber includes both Yesod [six] and Malchut; **from seven lands**, whose root is the seven chambers of Malchut of Atzilut, and the highest land, called "World" (*Tevel*), includes the Upper Three Sefirot. **About them David said, "I will walk before the Lord in the lands of the living,"** (Psalms 116:9) meaning many lands. **And the Central Column**, Zeir Anpin, **comprises seven Firmaments, about which David said, "The Heavens are the Heavens of the Lord…"** (Psalms 115:16) as there are several aspects of Heaven. [See Zohar, Vayakhel 283]

‎4. וְלֵית יְדִיעָה כְּלָל בְּמַלְכָּא וּבְמַלְבּוּשׁיֵּה וּבְתִקּוּנֵיה לְבַר נָשׁ בְּעָלְמָא, עַד דְיֵעוּל מַלְכָּא לְבֵיתֵיה וּלְהֵיכָלֵיה, דְּאִיהִי ב', וַעֲלָהּ אִתְּמַר כִּי בֵיתִי בֵּית תְּפִלָּה יִקָּרֵא לְכָל הָעַמִּים.

4. And there is no conception at all to any person in the world **about the King** Himself **and the garments** of the King **and His corrections, until the King enters** to **His house** or **His chamber**, referring to the mating of Zeir Anpin and Malchut, **which is the** letter **Bet. And about her**, Malchut,

it is said, "For My house shall be called a house of prayer for all nations."
(Isaiah 56:7)

5. וּמַאן דְּאִיהוּ אָדָם בְּדִיוֹקְנָא דְּעַמּוּדָא דְּאֶמְצָעִיתָא, עֲלֵיהּ נֶאֱמַר, אֵין
תְּפִלָּתוֹ שֶׁל אָדָם נִשְׁמַעַת, אֶלָּא בְּבֵית הַכְּנֶסֶת, וְהָא אוּקְמוּהָ מָארֵי מַתְנִיתִין
וּמַאן דְּנָטִיר בְּרִית, אִתְקְרֵי אִישׁ תָּמִים. וְתַמָּן בְּרֵאשִׁית: בְּרִי"ת אֵ"שׁ דְּנָטִיר
לֵיהּ מֵאֶשָּׁא דְּגֵיהִנָּם.

5. And about he, a man who bears the form of the Central Column,
namely is a Chariot to Zeir Anpin, is said, "A person's prayer is only
listened to in the synagogue," because through him a union is made
between the Supernal Zeir Anpin and Nukva, and the masters of the
Mishnah have established this (Tractate Berachot 6a). And he who
guards the Covenant is considered a complete man and becomes a
Chariot to Yesod, and there Beresheet is spelled with the letters of *brit esh*
(a Covenant of fire) for the Holy One blessed be He saves him from the
fire of Hell (Gehenom).

6. אֲבָל מָאן דְּאִתְעַסַּק בְּאוֹרַיְתָא, וְנָטִיר לָהּ, אִתְקְרֵי אָדָם בְּדִיוֹקְנָא דְּהַהוּא
דִּלְעֵילָּא, הָדָא הוּא דִכְתִיב כְּתִפְאֶרֶת אָדָם לָשֶׁבֶת בָּיִת. תָּא חֲזֵי, כָּל
מָאן דְּנָטִיר אוֹת בְּרִית, דְּיוֹקְנֵיהּ רָשִׁים בִּשְׁכִינְתָּא וְצַדִּיק. וּמַאן דְּאִשְׁתַּדַּל
בְּאוֹרַיְתָא, דְּיוֹקְנֵיהּ רָשִׁים בְּעַמּוּדָא דְּאֶמְצָעִיתָא.

6. But he who studies Torah and guards it is considered a man who
bears the form of the Supernal Man, Zeir Anpin, as written, "...the
beauty of a man, to dwell in a house." (Isaiah 44:13) Come and see,
anyone who protects the sign of the Covenant, his form is impressed
on the Shechinah and the Righteous, Yesod and Malchut, the small Zeir
Anpin and Nukva. And he who makes an effort in Torah, his image is
imprinted in the Central Column, which is the great Zeir Anpin that is
called Israel.

For the third day of the month of Elul

Fourth Tikkun

Beresheet contains *rashei* (heads) and *bat* (daughter)

1. בְּרֵאשִׁית, כְּתִיב פִּתְחוּ לִי שַׁעֲרֵי צֶדֶק אָבֹא בָם אוֹדֶה יָ"הּ. פִּתְחוּ לִי,
דָּא אִינוּן תְּרֵין, עַפְעַפֵּי עֵינָא, דְּאִינוּן פָּתְחִין וְסָגְרִין. וַעֲלַיְיהוּ אִתְּמַר, וְהָיוּ
הַכְּרוּבִים פֹּרְשֵׂי כְנָפַיִם לְמַעְלָה. כְּרוּבִים: אֵלֵּין תְּרֵין כְּרוּבֵי עֵינָא, פֹּרְשֵׂי
כְנָפַיִם: עַפְעַפֵּי עֵינָא.

1. **Beresheet: It is written, "Open to me the gates of righteousness; I
will go into them, I will give thanks to the Lord (Yud-Hei)."** (Psalms
118:19) **"Open to me"** refers to **the two eyelids that open and close** the
eyes, **about which it is said, "And the Cherubs shall spread their wings
on high…."** (Exodus 25:20) **The Cherubs are the two Cherubs of the eye**,
meaning the flesh where the eye lashes come out; **"shall spread," refers to
the eyelids**, which are called the wings of the eye.

2. וְעוֹד פִּתְחוּ לִי שַׁעֲרֵי צֶדֶק, אֵלֵּין אִינוּן תְּרֵין עַיְינִין, בְּזִמְנָא דְּאִינוּן מִסְתַּכְּלִין
בְּאֹרַח מֵישׁוֹר, אִתְּמַר בְּהוֹן וּפְנֵיהֶם אִישׁ אֶל אָחִיו. וּבְזִמְנָא דְּלָאו אִינוּן מִסְתַּכְּלִין
בְּאֹרַח מֵישׁוֹר, הָא נָחָשׁ עֲקַלָּתוֹן תַּמָּן. עֲלֵיהּ אִתְּמַר, כִּי הַמָּוֶת יַפְרִיד וְגוֹ'.

2. **Another** interpretation of **"Open to me the gates of righteousness."
These are the two eyes when they look straight**, meaning that when Zeir
Anpin and Malchut are face-to-face, **it is said about them, "…with their
faces one to another…,"** (Ibid.) as the Shechinah also includes the two
Cherubs, which are Metatron and Sandalphon. [See Zohar, Acharei Mot
56] **And when they do not look straight**, meaning they are not mating, **the
crooked serpent is there, about which it is said, "…but death parts…."**
(Ruth 1:17)

3. תְּלַת גַּוְונֵי עֵינָא, אִנּוּן תְּלַת אֲבָהָן. דְּאִתְּמַר בְּהוֹ אֵלֶּה רָאשֵׁי בֵית אֲבוֹתָם.
בַּת עַיִן, דְּאִיהִי דְקִיקָא זְעֵירָא, דָּא שְׁכִינְתָּא, דְּאִשְׁתַּתְּפַת בַּאֲבָהָן. וַעֲלָהּ

אִתְּמַר, שֶׁמְּרֵנִי כְּאִישׁוֹן בַּת עָיִן. וְכֹלָּא בְּרָזָא דִּבְרֵאשִׁית, תַּמָּן רָאשֵׁ"י, תַּמָּן בַּ"ת.

3. The three colors in the eyes correspond to **the three Patriarchs**, Chesed, Gevurah, and Tiferet, **about whom it is said, "These are the heads of their fathers' houses…."** (Exodus 6:14) **The pupil [lit. daughter] of the eye is faint and small. This is the Shechinah,** Malchut **that joins the Patriarchs,** which are Chesed, Gevurah, and Tiferet in the secret of the Kingdom of David **and about Her it is said, "Keep me as the pupil of the eye…."** (Psalms 17:8) **It is all in the secret of** the word **Beresheet,** as beresheet **contains the heads** (rashei)**,** Chesed, Gevurah, and Tiferet, **and daughter** (bat; pupil)**,** Malchut.

4. קָם רַבִּי שִׁמְעוֹן עַל רַגְלוֹי וְאָמַר, רִבּוֹן עָלְמִין, אַפְתַּח עֵינַי לְאִסְתַּכְּלָא בְּהוֹן לְעֵילָּא, אָבָא בָּ"ם, בְּאַרְבָּעִים וּתְרֵין אַתְוָון דִּשְׁמָא מְפָרַשׁ, לְמִנְדַּע כָּל אָת וְאָת עַל תִּקּוּנֵיהּ, בְּרֵאשִׁית וכו', וְהָאָרֶץ הָיְתָה תֹהוּ וָבֹהוּ וכו', וְאִינּוּן אֲבַ"ג ית"ץ. קר"ע שט"ן. נג"ד יכ"ש. בט"ר צת"ג. חק"ב טנ"ע. יג"ל פז"ק. שק"ו צי"ת בָּרוּךְ שֵׁם כְּבוֹד מַלְכוּתוֹ לְעוֹלָם וָעֶד.

4. Rav Shimon rose up on his feet and said, "Master of the worlds, let me open my eyes to look up with them, 'I will go in to them (bam, **Bet-Mem, which equals 42)' by the 42 letters of the Explicit Name, to know each and every letter properly: 'In the beginning…and the earth was without form and void…'** (Genesis 1:1-2) Since there are 42 letters in the work of Creation from Beresheet to the Bet of bohu (void). And they comprise the Name of Mem-Bet (42) letters of **Alef-Bet-Gimel Yud-Tav-Tzadik; Kof-Resh-Ayin Sin-Tet-Nun; Nun-Gimel-Dalet Yud-Kaf-Shin; Bet-Tet-Resh Tzadik-Tav-Gimel; Chet-Kof-Bet Tet-Nun-Ayin; Yud-Gimel-Lamed Pei-Zayin-Kof; Shin-Kof-Vav Tzadik-Yud-Tav;** Baruch Shem Kevod Malchuto Le'olam Va'ed **"Blessed is the glorious Name of His Kingdom forever and ever."**

5. כָּל אָת וְאָת אִית לֵיהּ מַאֲמָר, וְאִית לֵיהּ נְתִיב. עֶשֶׂר אֲמִירָן אִינּוּן, וְל"ב שְׁבִילִין. וְכֻלְּהוּ תַּלְיָין מִן אִי"ה. וְדָא אִיהוּ אָבֹא בָם אוֹדֶה יָ"הּ, אִי"ה בְּחוּשְׁבַּן אוֹדֶ"ה יָ"הּ.

5. **Each and every letter** of the 22 letters in the Torah, which is Zeir Anpin, **has a saying** of the Ten Utterances, which is the secret of the Ten Sefirot of Supernal Aba and Ima, **and has a path** from the Ten Sefirot of Yisrael-Saba and Tevunah. **They are Ten Utterances and 32 paths,** which together are 42, **all originating from** *ayeh* (where), which is the secret of Keter. **This is the meaning of:** *Avo bam odeh Yah* "I will go into them, I will give thanks to the Lord." (Psalms 118:19) *Ayeh* **(16) equals the same numerical value as** *odeh* **(I will give thanks; 16)** which is the secret of Keter; *Yah* is the secret of Chochmah and Binah. [Study in the Prologue to Tikunei Zohar, 167.]

6. וְאִינּוּן שֶׁבַע סְפִירָן, כְּלִילָן בְּשֶׁבַע שְׁמָהָן, וְכֻלְּהוּ כְּלִילַת לוֹן בַּת שֶׁבַע. וְלֵית סְפִירָה מִכֻּלְּהוּ סְפִירָן דְּיְהֵא לָהּ רְשׁוּ לַאֲרָקָא בִּרְכָאן, וּלְאַשְׁפָּעָא לְתַתָּאִין אֶלָּא בְּבַת שֶׁבַע. בְּגִין דְּאִיהִי קְשׁוּרָא דְכֻלְּהוּ סְפִירָן. דְּאִי סְפִירָן הֲווֹ מְרִיקִין לְבַר מִינָהּ הֲוָה פְּרוּדָא. וּבְגִין דָּא לֵית רְשׁוּ לַאֲרָקָא סְפִירָה לְשׁוּם אֲתַר, בַּר מִינָהּ, לְגַבֵּי תַּתָּאִין.

6. **And those Seven Sefirot** of Zeir Anpin, that became Mem-Bet (42) **are included in the seven Names** of the Ana Bekoach and Batsheva [lit. **daughter of seven]** that is Malchut **includes all of them.** Thus after the Ana Bekoach it is written: *Baruch Shem Kevod Malchuto Le'olam Vaed* "Blessed is the glorious Name of His kingdom forever and for eternity." **And no Sefira among all the other Sefirot is allowed to pour its blessings and bestow abundance to the lower beings except to Batsheva,** which is Malchut, **for She is the connection of all the Sefirot, because if the Sefirot would pour out their abundance outside of Her there would be a separation between the Sefirot and consequently no Sefira is permitted to pour** abundance **anywhere to the lower beings except to Her,** meaning Malchut.

7. וּבְגִין דָּא אִתְּמַר בָּהּ, אַל יִתְהַלֵּל חָכָם בְּחָכְמָתוֹ וְגוֹ' כִּי אִם בְּזֹאת. בְּזֹאת
יָבֹא אַהֲרֹן אֶל הַקֹּדֶשׁ. דְּלֵית רְשׁוּ לִנְבִיא וְחַכִּימָא לְמִנְדַּע לְעֵילָא שׁוּם מַדַּע,
אֶלָּא בָּהּ.

7. Thus it is said about Her, Malchut: "Let not the wise glory in his
wisdom... but glory in this (*zot*)..." (Jeremiah 9:22-23) which is Malchut.
"Herewith (*zot*) shall Aaron come into the holy place...." (Leviticus 16:3)
As no prophet or sage is permitted to gain any higher knowledge except
through Her, Malchut.

8. וּבְגִינָהּ אִתְּמַר, וּמֹשֶׁה עָלָה אֶל הָאֱלֹהִי"ם. וְדָוִד בְּגִינָהּ אָמַר, אִם אֶתֵּן שְׁנָת
לְעֵינָי לְעַפְעַפַּי תְּנוּמָה עַד אֶמְצָא מָקוֹם לַי"י. אִיהוּ שְׁלִימוּ דְּאָדָם. שְׁלִימוּ
דְּיִחוּדָא. שְׁלִימוּ דִשְׁמָא קַדִּישָׁא. שְׁלִימוּ דְּכָל סְפִירָה וּסְפִירָה.

8. Due to Malchut **it is said, "And Moses went up to God (Elokim),"**
(Exodus 19:3) which is a Name of Malchut. **And David said about Her,**
"I will not give sleep to my eyes nor slumber to my eyelids until I find
a place for the Lord (Yud-Hei-Vav-Hei)...." (Psalms 132:4-5) And
Malchut is called "a place," in the secret of the verse: "... there is a place
with Me." (Exodus 33:21) **She is the completion of man (*adam*)** meaning
of the Name of Mem-Hei (45) that equals the numerical value of *adam*.
[See Tikunei Zohar, Elijah Opened, 20] She is **the completion of the**
union, as Malchut is the secret of the Dalet in *echad* (one). [See Zohar,
Pinchas, 846] She is **the completion of the Holy Name** Yud-Hei-Vav-Hei,
as Malchut represents the lower Hei that completes Yud-Hei-Vav, and She
is **the completion of each and every Sefira,** because by the union that is on
Malchut each Sefira is comprised of Ten Sefirot.

For the fourth day of the month of Elul
Fifth Tikkun
Beresheet: A dot in its chamber

1. בְּרֵאשִׁית: ב' רֵאשִׁית. נְקוּדָה בְּהֵיכְלֵיהּ. וְהַאי נְקוּדָה אִיהִי מַחֲשָׁבָה סְתִימָא. אֲדְהָכִי, הָא אֵלִיָּהוּ אוֹזְדַּמַּן לְגַבֵּיהּ דְּרַבִּי שִׁמְעוֹן, אָמַר לֵיהּ רַבִּי רַבִּי, וְהָא ב' פְּתִיחָא אִיהִי, אִם כֵּן בְּמַאי אִיהִי מַחֲשָׁבָה סְתִימָא בָהּ.

1. The word *beresheet* is made up of the **Bet** and the word *resheet* (beginning). **The dot,** that is the secret of Chochmah called *resheet* (beginning), **is in its chamber,** the secret of Yisrael-Saba and Tevunah, meaning Binah called "chamber." **And this dot is a sealed thought** that does not illuminate with revealed Light. **In the meantime, Elijah came to Rav Shimon.** Elijah **said to him, "Teacher, teacher, if Bet is open** and alludes to revealed Lights, **and if so, why is thought** which is Chochmah, **concealed within it?**

2. אֶלָּא בְּרֵישׁ הוּרְמָנוּתָא דְּמַלְכָּא בּוֹצִינָא דְּקַרְדִּינוּתָא, כַּד מָדִיד מְשִׁיחֲזָא, הַאי נְקוּדָה נָפִיק מִינָּהּ קַו, דְּסָתִים הַהוּא מַחֲשָׁבָה, כְּגַוְונָא דָא ם. בְּקַדְמֵיתָא אִיהִי מֵ"ם סְתִימָא, וְכַד אִתְפַּשַּׁט קַו דְּאִיהִי ו' מִן הַמּוּדָה, אִיהִי אִתְפַּתְּחַת וְאִתְעֲבִידַת ב'. וְדָא בְּרֵאשִׁית: ב' רֵאשִׁית, נְקוּדָה בְּהֵיכְלֵיהּ.

2. And he replies, **"At the beginning of the revelation of the King's wish,** meaning when the King first wished to emanate and create the worlds, **the hard spark,** which is the power of the harsh judgment that is in the vessel of Malchut, and is why the Light around the middle dot, which is Malchut, constricted and left, **measured the stature,** meaning in the World of Atzilut after the correction, **the dot** that is the middle dot, which is the aspect of the essence of the lock that got corrected in the Supernal Aba and Ima **produced from itself a line,** meaning Yisrael-Saba and Tevunah that are the Lower Seven of Binah, since the Supernal Aba and Ima are the secret of the "air that is not known," which is the secret of the middle dot that serves only in the Partzufs of Adam Kadmon and not in the World

of Atzilut. Therefore, there is no comprehension in the Supernal Aba and Ima that are the Lower Seven of Binah, and the Chochmah that is bestowed in Atzilut is only from the Lower Seven of Binah, which are Yisrael-Saba and Tevunah, **that blocked the thought,** meaning the illumination of Chochmah that is called "thought," since before the regulation of the Central Column, the Chochmah that was in Yisrael-Saba and Tevunah was blocked **like so:** ם [final letter Mem]. **At first it is a closed final Mem, but when the line, that is the** letter **Vav, expands from the measurement,** by the elevation of Zeir Anpin with the Masach of Chirek (Central Column) that regulates between the Right and Left Columns of Yisrael-Saba and Tevunah, then Yisrael-Saba and Tevunah open their blockage and three Mochin, Chochmah, Binah, and Da'at come out—which are the secret of "three come out of one," and because of this Zeir Anpin also merits all of these Mochin in the secret of "one is sustained by three." **This** closed Mem (Yisrael-Saba and Tevunah) **opens up and becomes** the letter **Bet** ב. **This is Beresheet: Bet** *resheet*, in which **the dot,** that is Chochmah called *resheet* **is in its chamber,** and illuminates with the illumination of Chochmah.

3. וְכַד אִיהִי ם סְתִימָא, דְּאִיהִי מֵ"ם רַבְּתָא מִלְּמַרְבֵּה הַמִּשְׂרָה וְאִתְעֲבִידַת עִזְקָא. וּבְגִינָה אִתְּמַר לְגַבֵּי כַּלָּה, תְּהֵא לִי מְקוּדֶּשֶׁת בְּטַבַּעַת זוֹ ם, וַעֲלָהּ אִתְּמַר, קוּטְרָא בְּגוֹלְמָא נָעוּץ בְּעִזְקָא. וְאִיהִי חִוָּור, וְלָא סוּמַק, וְלָא אוּכַם, וְלָא יָרוֹק, וְלָא גָּוֶון כְּלָל. וְכַד אִתְפַּשְׁטָא לְאַנְהָרָא, אִיהִי עֲבִידַת גַּוְונִין לְאַנְהָרָא.

3. **And when it is a closed final Mem** ם, **which is the large final Mem of the verse: "That the government may be increased (**ulemarbeh, וּלְמַרְבֵּה**)...."** (Isaiah 9:6) Even though Mem occurs in the middle of the word, the accepted way is to write it with a closed final Mem, as when occurring at the end of a word, and **it becomes a ring** like the Supernal Aba and Ima whose Lights of Chochmah are blocked. **And about this** ring, which is a closed Mem, **it is said when** marrying **a bride that "She shall be sanctified to me with this ring," [**ם, final Mem] by which she is forbidden to anyone else in the world. **And about** Binah, meaning Yisrael-Saba and Tevunah when they are blocked, **it is said to be the form in its raw shape,**

meaning it is formless and unrecognizable, **stuck in this ring** because without the Central Column there is no spreading, and the Mochin split into Chochmahs, Binahs, Chasadim, and Gevurot, each one comprised of ten, which amounts to 40. And the Chasadim and Gevurot do not join as Da'at to be a third *Mo'ach* that unites them. **And this** point of Malchut that ascended to Binah **is neither white nor red, neither black nor green, but absolutely colorless.** Because colors are the aspect of judgments that make differences between the levels, since white represents the Light of Chochmah, red is the color of Binah, green is the color of Tiferet, and black is the color of Malchut. As long as there is no extension from the Mem then they are like the Lights of the head, and by the illuminations of the head there is no revelation of any color because no lack or density can be activated above its level of existence. **And when** Binah **expanded to illuminate** from above downward, **it produced colors to illuminate** on them.

4. וְרָזָא דְמִלָּה עוֹטֶה אוֹר כַּשַּׂלְמָה וכו'. כַּד אִיהִי אוֹר מְעוּטָף, וְלָא אִתְפָּשַׁט וְאִיהוּ סָתִים, אִתְקְרֵי אֲוִיר. אוֹר סָתִים בְּאָת יוּ"ד, נְקוּדָה בְּהֵיכָלֵיהּ. כַּד אַפִּיק י' מֵאֲוִי"ר, אִתְגַּלְיָא אוֹ"ר וְדָא אִיהוּ וַיֹּאמֶר אֱלֹקִי"ם יְהִי אוֹר.

4. **And the secret of the matter [is in the verse]: "covers Himself with light as with a garment...,"** (Psalms 104:2) **that when the light is covered without expanding and is closed off,** then **it is called air** (*avir*, אֲוִיר, Alef-Vav-Yud-Resh), meaning that **the Light** (*Or*, אוֹר, Alef-Vav-Resh) **is closed by the letter Yud,** which is Malchut, **a dot in its chamber.** As the Yud went into the word *Or*, and the combination *avir* (air) was made. **And when He withdrew the Yud from air, Light was revealed. And this is the meaning of: "And God said, 'Let there be light.'"** (Genesis 1:3)

5. וְחָמֵשׁ זִמְנִין אוֹר אִינּוּן בְּעוֹבָדָא דִּבְרֵאשִׁית, וְאִינּוּן ה'. וַעֲלֵיהוֹ אִתְּמַר, מִי מָדַד בְּשָׁעֳלוֹ מַיִם, וְדָא דְרוֹעָא יְמִינָא, וְאִיהוּ גַּוָון חִוָּור. וְשָׁמַיִם בַּזֶּרֶת תִּכֵּן, דָּא דְרוֹעָא שְׂמָאלָא דְאִיהוּ גַּוָון סוּמָק. וְכָל בַּשָּׁלִישׁ עֲפַר הָאָרֶץ, דָּא גוּפָא, עַמּוּדָא דְאֶמְצָעִיתָא וְדָא גַּוָון יָרוֹק. וְשָׁקַל בַּפֶּלֶס הָרִים וּגְבָעוֹת בְּמֹאזְנָיִם, תְּרֵי

סָמְכֵי קְשׁוֹט. וְהַאי ה' אִיהִי אִתְפַּשְׁטַת לְאַנְהָרָא בְּחָמֵשׁ גַּוְונִין, דְּאִינּוּן חָמֵשׁ זִמְנִין אוֹר.

5. In the acts of Creation, "Light" (*Or*) is written five times. They are Hei (5), namely, Binah that spreads to Chesed, Gevurah, Tiferet, Netzach, and Hod. **And regarding them it is said, "Who,"** that is Binah **"has measured the waters in the hollow of His hand…."** (Isaiah 40:12) **And this is the right arm, and the white color,** namely Chesed; **"…and meted out Heaven with the span (*zeret*)…,"** (Ibid.) **this is the left arm, the red color,** meaning Gevurah, as *zeret*, which is derived from *zarut* (strangeness) hints to the Left Column; **"…and comprehended the dust of the earth in a measure…"** (Ibid.) **is the body, the Central Column, and the green color,** meaning Tiferet; **"…and weighed the mountains in scales, and the hills in a balance"** (Ibid.) **refers to the two true supports,** meaning Netzach and Hod. **And this Hei,** that is Binah, **spreads to illuminate the five colors, which are five times "Light":** "Let there be <u>light</u>; and there was <u>light</u>. And God saw the <u>light</u>…and God divided the <u>light</u>… And God called the <u>light</u>…" (Genesis 1:3-5)

ו. י', אִיהִי מִדָּה דִּילָהּ ה' עִלָּאָה, וְחָמֵשׁ אוֹר. ה' תַּתָּאָה, וְחָמֵשׁ גַּוְונִין, דְּנַהֲרִין בְּהוֹן וְחָמֵשׁ אוֹר. וְכַד אִתְפַּשְׁטַת ה' עִלָּאָה לְאַנְהָרָא בָּהּ תַּתָּאָה, בְּחָמֵשׁ גַּוְונִין דְּנַהֲרִין דִּילָהּ, מִיָּד אִתְפַּשַּׁט ו' לְגַבָּהּ, וְדָא אִיהוּ נוֹטֶה שָׁמַיִם כַּיְרִיעָה.

6. Yud, which is Chochmah—the first phase of the four phases of Desire to Receive—**is the measurement** of the dot. Meaning the entire measurement of Light that is in the desire of the Emanator, which is Keter, to bestow to the created being, is received by the first phase. **The upper Hei,** meaning Binah that is the second phase of the Desire to Receive, hints to **five Lights.** For in the first phase, the receiving is because of the Supernal desire of the Emanator to give, and the Light does not yet extend and go out of the category of Emanator into the category of "created being," until the second phase when there is a pushback (strengthening) from the created being itself, and the five Lights hint to this [phase]. **The lower Hei,**

meaning Malchut that is the fourth phase of desire, **hints to five colors,** which totally complete the establishment of the Desire to Receive, since it is revealed when there is no Light of Wisdom (Or DeChochmah) in the Partzuf, and the craving for Light of Wisdom is revealed. This craving establishes in it the Desire to Receive, thus completing the vessel. **And the five Lights illuminate** on the five colors of Malchut that spread from Binah. **And when this upper Hei,** which is Binah, **extends to shine on the lower Hei,** which is Malchut, **in her five colors,** immediately **the letter Vav,** which is Zeir Anpin **extends towards her,** as no Light is received by Malchut, except through Zeir Anpin. **And this is the meaning of "…Who stretches out the Heavens** [Zeir Anpin] **like a curtain."** (Psalms 104:2)

7. וְוַדַּאי כַּד אִיהִי נְהִירָא בְּגַוְונִין דִּילָהּ, אִתְּמַר בָּהּ, וּרְאִיתִיהָ לִזְכּוֹר בְּרִית עוֹלָם. וּרְאִיתִיהָ בְּתַכְשִׁיטָהָא, כְּכַלָּה דְּמִתְקַשְׁטָא לְגַבֵּי בַּעְלָהּ. וּמִיָּד נוֹטֶה שָׁמַיִם כַּיְרִיעָה, דְּאָתֵי בַּעְלָהּ לְגַבָּהּ.

7. **For surely when** Malchut **illuminates in her colors,** Her Ten Sefirot, it says about her: **"…and I will look upon it, that I may remember the everlasting Covenant…."** (Genesis 9:16) **"…and I will look upon it (her),"** "look" stands for Chochmah called "sight," **in her ornaments, as a bride adorns herself for her husband, and he immediately: "…stretches out the Heavens like a curtain,"** (Psalms 104:2) **as her husband comes to her.**

8. וְדָא אִיהוּ רָזָא דְּקַו הַמִּדָּה, דְּאִיהִי ו' מֵהַהִיא מִדָּה דְּאִיהִי י', וּלְבָתַר דְּאִיהִי נָטְלָא שְׁמָא קַדִּישָׁא, אִתְעֲבִידַת אִיהוּ מִדָּה מִתַּתָּא לְעֵילָא, בְּרָזָא דִּנְקוּדָה י'.

8. **And this is the secret of the "measuring line,"** which is the Vav that **extends from that measure that is Yud,** Chochmah. **And after** Malchut **takes on this Holy Name,** meaning She includes all the Ten Sefirot, which stands for Yud-Hei-Vav-Hei, where the tip of the Yud is Keter, the Yud is Chochmah, the first Hei is Binah, the Vav is Zeir Anpin, and the lower Hei is Malchut Herself, **She then becomes a measurement** to the Ten

Sefirot of Returning Light **from below upward, in the secret of a dot, Yud.** Meaning just like the Supernal Dot is the secret of Yud and the secret of Chochmah that extends from above downward in the Ten Sefirot of Direct Light, so too, Malchut is the secret of the Yud of Alef-Dalet-Nun-Yud that extends in the Ten Sefirot of Returning Light from below upward.

9. אִיהִי מִדָּה לְעֶשֶׂר יְרִיעָן, כַּךְ הִיא אַמָּה מִסִּטְרָא דְאוֹת ו', כְּלִילָא מֵעֶשֶׂר אַמּוֹת. הֲדָא הוּא דִכְתִיב עֶשֶׂר אַמּוֹת אֹרֶךְ הַקֶּרֶשׁ, וְדָא י'. וְאַמָּה ה' עִלָּאָה. וַוֵּאצֵי הָאַמָּה, ה' תַּתָּאָה. אֹרֶךְ הַיְרִיעָה הָאַחַת דָא ו'. וְאַמַּאי אִתְקְרֵי ה' תַּתָּאָה וַוֵּצֵי הָאַמָּה. בְּגִין דְאִתְקְרֵי מַצָּה פְרוּסָה, לֶחֶם עוֹנִי.

9. Malchut **is the measure for the ten curtains** that cover the Tabernacle, which stand for the Ten Sefirot of the head. **Thus, she is a cubit from the aspect of the letter Vav,** meaning the Ten Sefirot of the body that extend from Malchut of the head from above downward. **She includes the ten-cubit measure, which is referred to by "Ten cubits shall be the length of the board...."** (Exodus 26:16) **And this is the Yud** of the Name Yud-Hei-Vav-Hei that illuminates on the body, and is Chochmah, as length hints to Chochmah. **And one cubit** from the width **is the upper Hei,** which is Binah that shines with Chasadim, as each width hints to Chasadim. **And the half-cubit** is **the lower Hei,** Malchut. **"The length of each curtain"** (Exodus 26:2) **is the Vav,** meaning Zeir Anpin that shines with the illumination of Chochmah with Chasadim. He asks, **"Why is the lower Hei,** Malchut, **called a half-cubit?"** And answers, **"Because** Malchut **is called a piece of Matzah, bread of poverty."** The lower half of Malchut, from the chest below, is not complete with all the corrections of the 6,000 years until the Final Correction, in the secret of the verse: *Ve'amdu raglav beyom hahu al Har haZeytim* "And his feet shall stand in that day upon the Mount of Olives." (Zechariah 14:4)

10. וְהַאי נְקוּדָה כַּד סָלְקָא לְגַבֵּי א', דְאִיהוּ אֲוִירָא סָתִים, אִתְקְרֵי קָמֵ"ץ, קוֹמֵץ סָתִים, בְּגִין וְקָמַץ הַכֹּהֵן מִשָּׁם מְלֹא קֻמְצוֹ. וְאִיהִי בַּוֲשָׁבָה סְתִימָא, ם

סְתִימָא, בַּפְּתִיחָא דִּילָהּ מַאי נִיהוּ. פָּתַח. וְדָא ו'. וְאִיהִי נָטוּי כְּגַוְונָא דָא ﹅ כַּד
אִתְפָּרִישׁ מִנְּקוּדָה, אִיהִי רָקִיעַ פְּתוּחַ וַדַּאי.

10. And this dot, Malchut **when it ascends towards Alef,** meaning under Chochmah of Arich Anpin, as Chochmah is called Alef, as in the verse: "...and I will teach you (ve a'alfecha) wisdom" (Job 33:33) **which is concealed air (אֲוֵירָא סְתִים).** Since through the ascent of Malchut, which is the secret of Yud, to the Light (Or, Alef-Vav-Resh), that is Chochmah, Light becomes air (Alef-Vav-Yud-Resh). **It is called Kametz,** which means **contracted and sealed, because** it says: **"...and the priest shall take his handful (kametz) of it...."** (Leviticus 5:12) By the elevation of Malchut to Chochmah of Arich Anpin, Arich Anpin is left with two vessels, Keter and Chochmah, which in them are the two Lights, Nefesh and Ruach. **And it,** meaning Chochmah, is **an undisclosed thought, a closed final Mem,** because it only shines with the Lower Six Sefirot, which are the Light of Chasadim. He asks, **"Who is this key** that opens **Her to shine with the illumination of the Upper Three?"** and answers, **"Patach** vowel, **which is Vav. And this** Vav **is stretched out like this ﹅,** meaning diagonally, from front backward. **When it is extended out from the point,** meaning when Malchut descends to her place, **it is certainly an open Firmament,** which shines with the illumination of the Upper three Sefirot."

11. נָטוּי עַל רָאשֵׁי הַחַיָּה, דְּאִיהִי נִיצוֹצָא דְּקָמֵץ, הַה"ד, וּדְמוּת עַל רָאשֵׁי
הַחַיָּה רָקִיעַ. מַאן חַיָּה. דָּא מַלְכוּת. דְּאִיהִי נִיצוֹץ לְתַתָּא מִן רָקִיעַ, כְּגַוְונָא דָא
ﬡ מַאן רָקִיעַ. דָּא צַדִּיק. וְהַאי אִיהִי חַיָּה, אֲשֶׁר תַּחַת אֱלֹהֵי יִשְׂרָאֵל. רָאשֵׁי
הַחַיָּה דִּלְתַתָּא נֶצַח וְהוֹד.

11. Stretched over the heads of the living creature that is the spark, meaning the dot **of the Kametz. This is the meaning of the verse: "And over the heads of the living creatures there was the likeness of a Firmament...."** (Ezekiel 1:22) **Who is this living creature? That is Malchut, which is the spark below the Firmament, like this: ﬡ. Who is the Firmament? It is the Righteous,** meaning Yesod of Zeir Anpin, **and**

this Malchut **is the living creature that is beneath of the God (Elokim) of Israel,** meaning Binah, called the God (Elokim) of Israel, that is Zeir Anpin, called "Israel." **The heads of the living creature below are Netzach and Hod.**

12. וְאִית חַיָּה עִלָּאָה, כְּגַוְונָא דָא א וְדָא י' דְּאִיהִי עִלָּאָה דְּאִיהִי עַל הָרְקִיעַ, וְאִיהִי מַחֲשָׁבָה עִלָּאָה. וְהַאי אִיהִי אדנ"י, עֲטֶרֶת עִלָּאָה, אִיהִי כֶּתֶר בְּרֵישָׁא דְּכֹלָּא רָקִיעַ דִּילָהּ, ו' עִלָּאָה, וְהַאי אִיהִי עֲטֶרֶת תִּפְאֶרֶת. רֵאשִׁין דִּילָהּ, תְּרֵין דְּרוֹעִין.

12. There is also a Supernal living creature, which is Malchut that is above the chest in the secret of "...the face of man..." (Ezekiel 1:10) **like this: א. It is the Supernal Yud above the Firmament,** which is the curtain in the chest. **It is the Supernal thought,** above the chest, **and it is** that which is called **Adonai,** since it is **a Supernal Coronet, a crown on the head of all of them.** Meaning the head [beginning] of all the levels that are below the chest and Briyah, Yetzirah, and Asiyah. **Its Firmament is the upper** letter **Vav,** meaning Tiferet, **and it is a Crown of Glory (Tiferet). Its heads are its two arms,** Chesed and Gevurah.

13. וְאִית עֲטָרָה בְּרֹאשׁ אַבָּא וְאִימָא. וְאִיהִי כֶּתֶר עִלָּאָה וַדַּאי, וְרֵישִׁין דִּילָהּ לְעֵילָא, אִינּוּן אַבָּא וְאִימָא.

13. There is also a crown on the head of Aba and Ima, meaning Binah of Arich Anpin, which because of the elevation of Malchut to the head of Arich Anpin, Binah went out of the head of Arich Anpin and became Keter to Aba and Ima. **This is surely Supernal Keter** to all of the Partzufs of Atzilut, **and her heads above** that receive her abundance **are Aba and Ima.**

14. אִיהִי י' בְּכָל אֲתַר, קוֹצָא דִּילָהּ לְעֵילָא, וְגוּו דִּילָהּ בְּאֶמְצָעִיתָא, וְסוֹפָא דִּילָהּ לְתַתָּא. כְּכָלָּא דְּאַתְוָון דִּשְׁמָא מִפָרַשׁ.

14. Yud ' is divided **everywhere** to beginning, middle, and end; **its upper tip** is the beginning [lit. head]. **Its body in the center is the middle, and its ending is below. It includes the** four **letters of the Explict Name pronounced in full** Yud-Hei-Vav-Hei. The head stands for Chochmah, Binah, and Da'at; the middle for Chesed, Gevurah, and Tiferet; and the end stands for Netzach, Hod, and Yesod with Malchut that includes them. They are the four letters of Yud-Hei-Vav-Hei: Yud is Chochmah, Hei is Binah, Vav is Chesed, Gevurah, Tiferet, Netzach, Hod, and Yesod, and Hei is Malchut.

15. רֵישָׁא דִילָהּ לְעֵילָא בְּרָזָא דְטַעֲמֵי. וְגֵיוֹ דִילָהּ בְּאֶמְצָעִיתָא, בְּרָזָא דְאַתְוָן, גּוּפָא לְתַרְוַיְיהוּ. וְקוֹצָא דִילָהּ לְתַתָּא, בְּרָזָא דִנְקוּדֵי.

15. **The upper head** of the letter Yud **signifies the cantillation marks (te'amim); the body** of the Yud that is **in the middle signifies the letters, a body to both** the cantillation marks and vowels, **and its lower thorn is in the secret of the vowels.**

16. וּלְתַתָּא אִיהִי הַאי נְקוּדָה מַיִם נוּקְבִין, וּלְעֵילָא מַיִם דְּכוּרִין, רָקִיעַ בְּאֶמְצָעִיתָא, כְּגַוְונָא דָא א, עֲלָהּ אִתְּמַר וִיהִי מַבְדִּיל בֵּין מַיִם לָמָיִם.

16. **And the dot below** the line in the letter Alef indicates **Mayin Nukvin (Feminine Waters), the upper** dot **Mayin Duchrin (Masculine Waters),** and the middle line **is the Firmament in the middle, thus** א Alef. **About** the dividing line within the Alef it is said: **"...and let it divide the waters from the waters."** (Genesis 1:6).

17. וְהַאי אִיהִי מַחֲלוֹקֶת שֶׁהִיא לְשֵׁם שָׁמַיִם, דְּאִיהוּ סוֹפָה לְהִתְקַיֵּים, וּלְאַעֲלָא שֵׁלָם וְיִחוּדָא בְּתַרְוַיְיהוּ.

17. **And this is a dispute,** meaning a division done by the establishing of the dividing line that separates between water and water **that is for the sake of Heaven (LeShem Shamayim) to unite** Malchut that is called "Name"

(Shem), with Zeir Anpin that is called "Heaven (Shamayim)," **which will have a constructive outcome, and bring peace and unity in both.**

18. וְלָאו מַחֲלוֹקֶת דְּפֵרוּדָא, כְּגוֹן מַחֲלוֹקֶת קֹרַח וַעֲדָתוֹ בְּאַהֲרֹן, וּמַחֲלוֹקֶת הַאי דְּאִיהוּ לֵשֵׁם שָׁמַיִם, בְּגִין דְּמַיִם תַּתָּאִין אִינוּן בּוֹכִין, וְאַמְרִין אֲנַן בַּעְיָין לְמֶהֱוֵי קָדָם מַלְכָּא עִלַּת הָעִלּוֹת, וּבְעָן לְסַלְקָא לְעֵילָא. רְקִיעַ אַפְרִישׁ בֵּינַיְיהוּ, עַד דְּעִלַּת הָעִלּוֹת שַׁוֵּי לוֹן שָׁוִין. י'. מִסִּטְרָא דָּא, וְי' מִסִּטְרָא דָּא. ו' בְּאֶמְצָעִיתָא. כְּגַוְונָא דָּא יוֹ"י, דְּאִיהִי א, וְאֵלֵּין כֻּלְּהוּ קְרֵבִין לְעִלַּת הָעִלּוֹת. וְרָזָא דְּמִלָּה, וַיַּעַשׂ אֱלֹקִי"ם אֶת שְׁנֵי הַמְּאוֹרוֹת הַגְּדֹלִים, וְאִינוּן שָׁוִין. הָדָא הוּא דִכְתִיב, וְהָיָה אוֹר הַלְּבָנָה כְּאוֹר הַחַמָּה.

18. It is not a dispute of dissension, like the dispute of Korach and his congregation, (Numbers, Chapter 17-18) who was a Levite from the Left Column, **against Aaron** who was a Kohen from the Right Column. Korach wanted to give power of domination only to the Left Column, as Rashi writes: "He betook himself on one side to separate himself from out of the community to raise a protest regarding the priesthood." **But this dispute is for the sake of Heaven because the lower waters weep and say, "We want to be in the presence of the King, the Cause of all Causes, and wish to ascend high,** meaning to return to their Keter and Chochmah, so that they will not descend to the lower level. **The Firmament,** which is the secret of the dividing line, **separates between them, until the Cause of all Causes** by the unification of AV (72) with SaG (63), brings down Malchut to her original place, and Binah, Tiferet, and Malchut return to their level, **makes them equal** with Keter and Chochmah. The letter **Yud from this side** on the Right, **and Yud from that side** on the Left, **and** the letter **Vav,** that is the dividing line, **in the middle, thus: Yud-Vav-Yud that is the shape of Alef א. And they are all close to the Cause of all Causes, and the secret of the matter is: "And God (***Elokim***) made the two great luminaries...."** (Genesis 1:16) **And they are rendered as equals. This is why it is written: "...the light of the moon shall be as the light of the sun..."** (Isaiah 30:26)

"...for, behold, we were binding sheaves"

‎19. תָּא חֲזֵי, קָמֵ"ץ אִיהוּ סָתִים בְּאָת י', מִכָּל סִטְרָא, עֵילָא וְאִמְצָעִיתָא וְתַתָּא. וְדָא קוֹמֵץ סָתִים בִּתְלַת סְפִירָן. פְּתִיחוּ דִּילֵיהּ אִיהוּ בַּחֲמֵשׁ אוֹר, דְּאִינּוּן חֲמֵשׁ אֶצְבְּעָאן עִלָּאִין. וְאִינּוּן ה' עִלָּאָה, חֲמֵשׁ, אָאָאאָא דְּאִינּוּן אוֹר אוֹר אוֹר אוֹר אוֹר, חֲמֵשׁ זִמְנִין, חֲמֵשׁ נְהוֹרִין דְּעוֹבָדָא דִּבְרֵאשִׁית. וּנְקוּדָא דִּלְהוֹן אָאָאאָא חֲמֵשׁ דְּסַלְקָן לְעֶשֶׂר.

19. Come and see, the vowel **Kametz is concealed within the letter Yud** in the time of Katnut (smallness) when there are only the Keter, Chochmah, and the upper three of Binah **in all aspects** of the Yud, that are "head" (beginning), "inside" (middle) and "end," **up**, that is head, **middle**—inside, **and bottom**—end. **And it is compressed [Kometz] and sealed into three Sefirot,** which are the Upper Three of the Vessels and the Nefesh of Ruach of Lights. **It is opened** in the time of Gadlut (Greatness) **by the five Lights that are five Supernal Fingers.** Meaning a full stature of Nefesh, Ruach, Neshama, Chaya, and Yechida. **And they are the upper Hei,** meaning Yisrael-Saba and Tevunah, **the five** times the letter **Alef** with five different vowels: אָאָאאָא **of five times** the word *Or* (Light) with Alef, **five Lights** mentioned **in the Workings of Creation. And their vowels are Alef with** the vowel **Kametz, Alef with Tzere, Alef with Cholem, Alef with Chirek, and Alef with Shuruk.** Meaning five Lights are hinted by the vowels, in **five** vessels that are letters, **which equal ten,** which is an entire structure made of vessels [letters] and Lights [vowels].

‎20. וְרָזָא דְּמִלָּה, וְהִנֵּה אֲנַחְנוּ מְאַלְּמִים וְגוֹ', וְהִנֵּה קָמָה אֲלֻמָּתִי וְגַם נִצָּבָה. דָּא א' בְּחוֹלָ"ם, דְּאִיהִי לְעֵילָא מִכָּל נְקוּדִין, בְּקוֹמָה זָקוּף. וּבֵיהּ אִסְתַּלַּק יוֹסֵף בְּחֶלְמָא. וְכֵן יַעֲקֹב. הֲדָא הוּא דִכְתִיב, וַיַּחֲלֹם וְהִנֵּה סֻלָּם מֻצָּב אַרְצָה וְרֹאשׁוֹ מַגִּיעַ הַשָּׁמָיְמָה, דָּא א', דְּאִיהִי רֹאשׁ.

20. This is the meaning of: "...for, behold, we were binding sheaves... and, lo, my sheaf arose, and also stood upright...." (Genesis 37:7) **It is** the letter **Alef with** the vowel **Cholem that is above all vowels, stands**

upright. And through it Joseph ascended in the dream, and Jacob also, as it is written: "And he dreamed, and behold a ladder set up on the earth, and the top of it reached to Heaven…." (Genesis 28:12) This is Alef with Cholem, which is the head.

21. וְהִנֵּה מַלְאֲכֵי אֱלֹקִי"ם עוֹלִים וְיוֹרְדִים בֹּו, אָמְרוּ מָארֵי מַתְנִיתִין, עוֹלִים תְּרֵי וְיוֹרְדִים תְּרֵי. וְאִנּוּן אָ אָאָא.

21. "…and behold the angels of God ascending and descending on it." (Ibid.) The masters of the Mishnah said, "Two were ascending and two were descending." They are Alef with Kametz and Alef with Tzere ascending, Alef with Chirek and Alef with Shuruk descending.

22. וְהַאי אָת דְּאִיהִי אַלֶ"ף וֹלֶ"ם, דְּאִיהִי בְּאֶמְצָעִיתָא, אִיהִי כֶּתֶר עִלָּאָה דְּאַסְחַר עַל רֵישָׁא דְּעַמּוּדָא דְּאֶמְצָעִיתָא.

22. And this letter Alef with Cholem that is in the center of other Alef's, hints to Supernal Keter, meaning Tiferet of Ima, which surrounds the top of the Central Column, Zeir Anpin. Therefore, meaning to not delay Zeir Anpin and Nukva from receiving these Mochin of Chochmah from Yisrael-Saba and Tevunah, which are called "gladdening wine," which concerning Noah it says, "…and he drank from the wine and got drunk," (Genesis 9:21) therefore: "and, behold, your sheaves came round about, and bowed down to my sheaf" (Genesis 37:7) to draw the Mochin of Panim (Face) from the Supernal Aba and Ima.

"The stone which the builders rejected has become the chief corner stone."

23. כַּד שְׁכִינְתָּא אִסְתַּלְּקַת לְגַבֵּי, וּבְגִין דָּא וְהֵגֵּה תִסְבְּעָה אֲלֻמֹתֵיכֶם וַתִּשְׁתַּחֲוֶין לַאֲלֻמָּתִי. הַאי כִּתְרָא אִתְּמַר בָּהּ, אֶבֶן מָאֲסוּ הַבּוֹנִים הָיְתָה לְרֹאשׁ פִּנָּה. וְאִיהִי אַבְנָא דְּאִתְגְּזֶרֶת דְּלָא בִּידִין. הָדָא הוּא דִכְתִיב, עַד דִּי הִתְגְּזֶרֶת אֶבֶן דִּי לָא בִּידִין וְגו'.

23. **When the Shechinah,** Malchut, **ascends to** Keter, **it says about Her: "The stone which the builders rejected has become the chief corner stone"** (Psalms 118:22) since she attained the level of Keter that is considered to be the chief corner stone. **And that is a stone not hewn by human hands. This is written in: "A stone was cut out without hand"** (Daniel 2:34) since "This is the Lord's doing...." (Psalms 118: 23)

24. וּבְגִין דְּלָא אַשְׁכְּחָן לָהּ אֲתַר מֵאָן אִתְגְּזָרוּ, שָׁאֲלִין מַלְאֲכַיָּא קַדִּישַׁיָּא, אַיֵּה מְקוֹם כְּבוֹדוֹ לְהַעֲרִיצוֹ. וְלָא אַשְׁכְּחִין לָהּ אֲתַר. עַד דְּאָמְרִין בָּרוּךְ כְּבוֹד יְ"יָ מִמְּקוֹמוֹ.

24. **Since they cannot find the place from where they are hewn,** meaning they were hewn from the Mochin of face-to-face that is in the Upper Three, and it does not have a unification, and in the Lower Six Sefirot. the crown of Yesod completes the place of Malchut, **the holy angels ask, "Where is the place of His glory to adore Him,"** but they do not find their place, so they said: **"Blessed be the glory of the Lord from His place."** (Ezekiel 3:12)

25. וְהַאי אֶבֶן, אִיהִי סְגֻלַּת מְלָכִים, וְאִיהִי שִׂיחַת מַלְאֲכֵי הַשָּׁרֵת. שִׂיחַת חַיִּין וּשְׂרָפִים וְאוֹפַנִּים. שִׂיחַת כָּל עֶלָּאִין וְתַתָּאִין.

25. **This stone,** meaning Malchut, **is the treasure (segulah) of kings,** because through it all were completed with the Central Column, called Segol. It, Malchut, **is also the talk of the ministering angels, holy living**

creatures, Seraphim and Ofanim, the talk of all beings higher and lower because she pertains to speech.

26. יְדִיעַת שִׁמְשָׁא וְסִיהֲרָא בְּעָתִּים. עֵת וּזְמַן לְכֹלָּא. כָּל טַעֲמֵי וּנְקוּדֵי וְאַתְוָון כְּלִילָן בָּה. קָלָא דִּבּוּר וּמַחֲשָׁבָה, כְּלִילָן בָּה.

26. The science of calculating the cycles **of the Sun and Moon in the seasons, of every period and time** rests in Malchut, since all changes of weekdays, times, Holidays and Shabbats come in the stature of the Mochin that are in Malchut. **Cantillation marks, vowels, and letters are included in it,** since Light does not extend from the Endless, blessed be He, except by the Binding by Striking from the Supernal Light on the *masach* (curtain) that is in the vessel of Malchut, and therefore all are included in her and revealed by her. **Voice, speech, and thought are included in it** because thought that is the secret of Chochmah and voice that is the secret of Zeir Anpin are revealed by speech, which is the secret of Malchut.

27. אִיהִי כֶּתֶר תּוֹרָה, וְכֶתֶר כְּהוּנָה, וְכֶתֶר מַלְכוּת. וְאִיהִי תַּגָּא בְּרֵישׁ כָּל אַתְוָון כְּגַוְונָא דָא שׁ' וְעַל הַאי אַבְנָא אָמַר רַבִּי עֲקִיבָא לְחַבְרוֹי, כְּשֶׁתַּגִּיעוּ לְאַבְנֵי שַׁיִשׁ טָהוֹר אַל תֹּאמְרוּ מַיִם מַיִם.

27. It is the Torah Crown [Keter] in the secret of the Central Column, **the Crown [Keter] of priesthood,** in the secret of the Right Column, **and the Crown [Keter] of Kingship,** in the secret of the Left Column. **And it is hinted in the crowns at the top of the all letters, like** the letter **Shin** שׁ, **with three crowns,** that allude to the Crowns in the Three Columns. **And about this stone,** which is Malchut of Atzilut, **Rav Akiva said to his friends, "When you arrive to the pure marble stones, do not say 'water, water.'"**

28. וְאִיהִי קוֹצָא דְּכָל אַתְוָון, ב' כְּגַוְונָא דָא ד' קוֹץ דְּכָל אָת וְאָת, שִׁיעוּר קוֹמָה דִּלְהוֹן ו' מֵעֵילָא לְתַתָּא וּמִתַּתָּא לְעֵילָא. וְרָזָא דְּמִלָּה וּלְמִקְצֵה הַשָּׁמַיִם

וְעַד קְצֵה הַשָּׁמָיִם. וְרָזָא דָא לְךָ יְ"יָ הַגְּדֻלָּה וְהַגְּבוּרָה וְהַתִּפְאֶרֶת וְגוֹ'. לְךָ יְ"יָ
הַמַּמְלָכָה, דָא מַלְכוּת, דְּאִיהִי בְּכֹלָּא.

28. And it, Malchut, **is hinted in the tip in all the letters, such as Bet and
Dalet,** as without the strokes the Bet ב changes into a Kaf כ and the Dalet
ד into Resh ר. **The stroke of each letter** that alludes to the illumination
of Chochmah that is in each and every letter, **their stature is a Vav from
above downward,** Direct Light, **and from below upward,** Returning
Light. As is known that because of the correction of the Central Column
the illumination of Chochmah shines only in the Lower Six Sefirot, and
the Upper Three of Chochmah become surroundings. **The secret of
the matter is in the verse: "And from the one end of Heaven unto the
other..."** (Deuteronomy 4:32) which is the stature of Zeir Anpin Whose
secret is Vav. **This secret is** mentioned in the verse **"Yours, Lord, is the
greatness** Chesed **and the power (Gevurah), and the glory (Tiferet),
and the victory (Netzach), and the majesty (Hod), for all..."** meaning
Yesod called "all," **"...Yours is the kingdom, Lord...."** (I Chronicles 29:11)
"Kingdom" is Malchut that is included **in all.**

29. וְאִיהוּ צִפְצוּף עוֹפִין קַדִּישִׁין, דְּאִתְּמַר בְּהוֹן, כִּי עוֹף הַשָּׁמַיִם יוֹלִיךְ אֶת
הַקּוֹל. צִפְצוּפָא דְּכָל צִפֳּרִין, דְּאִינּוּן נִשְׁמָתִין קַדִּישִׁין, דִּמְצַפְצְפִין בְּכַמָּה
צְלוֹתִין. שִׂיחַת חַיּוֹן דְּאִינּוּן ת"ח.

29. It is also the chirping of holy birds, meaning souls, **about which it
says: "...for a bird of the air shall carry the voice...."** (Ecclesiastes 10:20)
**It is the chirping of all birds, which are holy souls, that chirp many
prayers, the talk of the living creatures that are wise students. And for
the Shechinah's sake it says: "And Isaac went out to meditate** (lasu'ach)
in the field..." (Genesis 24:63) **Speech** (sichah) **is but prayer,** which
is Malchut.

30. וּבְגִינָהּ אִתְּמַר, וַיֵּצֵא יִצְחָק לָשׂוּחַ בַּשָּׂדֶה וכו', וְלֵית שִׂיחָה אֶלָּא צְלוֹתָא.
וּבְגִינָהּ אִתְּמַר, תְּפִלַּת שַׁחֲרִית חוֹבָה. תְּפִלַּת עַרְבִית רְשׁוּת, דְּאִיהִי רְשׁוּת

דְּלֵילְיָא, בְּפָנֵי עַצְמָהּ, וּבְגִין דָּא לֵית לָהּ קְבִיעוּת בַּלַּיְלָה דְּרַדְמְיָא, לִצְלוֹתָא אֶלָּא
זִמְנִין אִשְׁתַּכַּחַת תַּמָּן, וְזִמְנִין לָא אִשְׁתַּכַּחַת.

30. And of her we learned that Shacharit (Morning Prayer) that is daytime of Chasadim **is obligatory.** Meaning it is an obligation to draw Chasadim to Malchut. **Arvit (Evening Prayer) is optional (*reshut*), being the domain of the night time,** a domain **on its own,** without the Chasadim of the daytime. **Thus** the Arvit prayer **during the night, which is like the exile, has no set time,** because the time to recite it is all night. **Rather, sometimes** the Shechinah **is there and sometimes She is not.** Meaning by coincidence.

31. זַכָּאָה אִיהוּ מָאן דְּפָגַע בָּהּ, כְּגוֹן יַעֲקֹב, דְּאִתְּמַר בֵּיהּ וַיִּפְגַּע בַּמָּקוֹם וַיָּלֶן
שָׁם, עִמָּהּ כִּי בָא הַשֶּׁמֶשׁ, עַד דְּאָתָא בַּעְלָהּ וְנָטִיר לָהּ, וּבָת תַּמָּן עִמָּהּ. מִתַּמָּן
וְאֵילֵךְ קָבְעוּהָ חוֹבָה.

31. Fortunate is he who happens to meet up with Her, like Jacob, about whom it says: "And he lighted upon the place, and tarried there [with her] all night because the sun was set..." (Genesis 28:11) **until Her husband came,** that is Zeir Anpin. And Jacob **guarded Her and spent the night with Her. From then on, it was instituted as obligatory.**

32. אֲבָל בְּשַׁבָּת אִיהִי רְשׁוּת הַיָּחִיד, דְּאִיהִי בִּרְשׁוּתָא דְּבַעְלָהּ וְלַאו כְּגַוְונָא
דְּלֵילְיָא דַּהֲוַת יְחִידָה בִּרְשׁוּתָא דִּילָהּ, הָדָא הוּא דִכְתִיב, אֵיכָה יָשְׁבָה בָדָד.

32. But on Shabbat, when Zeir Anpin and Nukva ascend to the Supernal Aba and Ima, **She is in private domain because She is in Her husband's domain,** meaning Zeir Anpin, **and not like at night when She was alone in Her** own **domain, as is written: "How does the city sit solitary?"** (Lamentations 1:1)

‫.33 וְיַעֲקֹב בְּגִין דְּקָרִיב לָהּ לְבַעְלָהּ בִּפְגִיעָה דִּילֵיהּ, וַדַּאי עֲבִיד לָהּ חוֹבָה. וְכַד‬
‫אָתָא שִׁמְשָׁא בְּשַׁחֲרִית, דְּאִתְּמַר בֵּיהּ, כִּי שֶׁמֶשׁ וּמָגֵן יְ"יָ אֱלֹקִי"ם, אִתְּמַר‬
‫בֵּיהּ וַיִּזְרַח לוֹ הַשֶּׁמֶשׁ.‬

33. And Jacob, because he brought Her closer to Her husband, and drew to Her the Light of Chasadim **by his meeting, definitely made** the Arvit prayer **obligatory,** to sweeten Her from Gevurot that are sweetened by the attribute of mercy of Binah. **And when the sun rises in Shacharit, regarding which is mentioned: "For the Lord God is a sun and shield..."** (Psalms 84:12) **it says concerning** Jacob: **"And the sun rose upon him..."** (Genesis 32:32) meaning he received the stature of the Light of Chasadim.

‫.34 מִתַּמָּן וְאֵילֵךְ קָשַׁר לָהּ עִמֵּיהּ, דְּאִיהִי קֶשֶׁר דִּתְפִלִּין דְּיָד. קָשִׁיר לָהּ‬
‫עִמֵּיהּ, דְּלָא תָזוּז מִינֵּיהּ לְעָלְמִין. מִסִּטְרָא דִשְׂמָאלָא קָשִׁיר לָהּ בִּתְפִלִּין דְּיָד,‬
‫דְּאִינּוּן בִּדְרוֹעָא שְׂמָאלָא. מִסִּטְרָא דִימִינָא, שַׁוִּי לָהּ כִּתְרָא עַל רֵישֵׁיהּ, תְּפִלִּין‬
‫דְּרֵישָׁא. וְהַאי בְּיוֹמָא דְּאִיהִי קְשִׁירָא עִם בַּעְלָהּ, אִתְּמַר בָּהּ יְשַׁחֲרוּנְנִי וְאָז‬
‫יִמְצָאוּנְנִי. אֲבָל בְּלֵילְיָא דְּאִיהִי גָּלוּתָא, דְּאִיהִי לְבַר מִבַּעְלָהּ, וְאִיהִי רְשׁוּת‬
‫בִּפְנֵי עַצְמָהּ, אִתְּמַר בָּהּ אַל תִּתְוַדַּע לָרָשׁוּת. וּבְגִין דָּא אָמַר דָּוִד, אִם אֶתֵּן‬
‫שְׁנָת לְעֵינָי וְגוֹ' עַד אֶמְצָא מָקוֹם לַיְ"יָ.‬

34. From there on he bound Malchut to him, **as she is in the knot of the hand Tefilin, where he binds her to him,** through the drawing of the illumination of the Mochin of the Tefilin, **so she would never move away from him. From the left side he binds her with the hand Tefilin, which is on the left arm. From the right side he places her as a crown on his head,** in the secret of the verse: "And all people of the earth shall see that the Name of the Lord is called upon you..." (Deuteronomy 28:10), referring to **the head Tefilin. During the daytime when she is bound with her husband it is said: "they shall seek Me** [*yeshacharuneni,* from the word *shachar,* meaning early morning] (Proverbs 1:28) **and then will "find Me." However at night** that alludes to **exile, when she is away from her husband,** meaning in Briyah, Yetzirah, and Asiyah, **and is in her own domain** (*reshut*), it says of her, **"Do not make yourself known**

to the authorities (*rashut*)," to draw the illumination of Chochmah that is in Malchut without clothing it in Chasadim. **Thus, David said: "I will not give sleep to my eyes...until I find a place for the Lord...."** (Psalms 132:4-5) Explanation: *makom* (place) is the secret of Malchut, in the secret of the verse "...there is a place by Me..." ("by Me" *iti*, Alef-Tav-Yud, can spell out *ot yud*, meaning the "letter Yud"); the letter Yud will connect to the Hei, meaning Chochmah of Malchut will be clothed with Chasadim called Yud-Hei-Vav-Hei.

The secret of the vowels

‏35. עַד כַּאן רָזָא דְקָמֵ"ץ, דְאִיהוּ רָזָא דְמַחֲשָׁבָה עִלָּאָה וְתַתָּאָה, דְאִיהוּ נְקוּדָה בִּרְשׁוּת בַּעְלָה דְאִיהוּ ו', רָקִיעַ. וּפַתָּ"ח בְּלָא נְקוּדָה, רְשׁוּ בִּפְנֵי עַצְמָהּ. וּנְקוּדָה בְּלָא פַתַּ"ח, רְשׁוּ בִּפְנֵי עַצְמָהּ. דִכְמָה דְאַתְוָון אִינוּן דְכַר וְנוּקְבָא, הָכִי נְקוּדִין אִינוּן דְכַר וְנוּקְבָא. אֲבָל אַתְוָון אִנּוּן לְגַבֵּי נְקוּדֵי, כְּגוֹן גּוּפָא לְגַבֵּי רוּחָא.

35. Thus far the secret meaning of the Kametz has been discussed, which stands for the upper and lower thought, meaning Binah and Malchut, which is the elevation of the desire, Malchut, to Binah that is called "thought." **It is a dot under her husband's domain, who is Vav, the Firmament.** Meaning the Firmament is the secret of the dividing line that is diagonal; Supernal Heavens that are male above the line, like this: אֲ, and lower Feminine waters below the line, like this: אַ. The secret of the Kametz vowel is not the dot that is under the line, which is the feminine domain, but it is the dot that is above the line, which is the masculine domain. **The Patach by itself without a dot is a domain of its own,** the aspect of Zeir Anpin, **and a dot without the Patach is a domain on its own,** the aspect of Malchut. **As the letters are divided into male and female,** meaning letters that bestow and letters that receive, **so too the dots have masculine and feminine aspects. However, in relation to the vowels all the letters are like the body to the soul,** and just like the soul gives life to the body, so too the vowels move and give life to the letters.

‏36. וְכֵן נְקוּדָה בִּלְבַד, כְּגוֹן חֹלֶ"ם, אוֹ חִיר"ק, אוֹ שׁוּר"ק. חֹלֶם לְעֵילָא מִן ו' אִתְעֲבִיד ז'. חִיר"ק, לְתַתָּא, אִתְעֲבִיד זָנָב גִּימַ"ל. שׁוּר"ק בְּאֶמְצָעִיתָא, קוֹצָא דְאָת ד', בְּאֶמְצָעִיתָא. כֹּלָּא חַד. אֲנִי רִאשׁוֹן וַאֲנִי אַחֲרוֹן וּמִבַּלְעָדַי אֵין אֱלֹקִי"ם.

36. Also a vowel by itself, without a letter, **like Cholem, Chirek, or Shuruk.** A vowel with a letter like **Cholem above the Vav becomes a Zayin. Chirek below turns to a stroke** before the Vav, so the Vav becomes the shape **of a Gimel. Shuruk in the middle of a Vav,** meaning Melopum, is the secret of **the thorn** behind the letter **Dalet,** which is **in the middle** between the two Vav's in the Dalet, one vertical from below upward, and one Vav horizontal from right to left. **And all** is in one perfection, and is the secret of **one,** as in the verse: "I am the first, and I am the last; and beside Me there is no God." (Isaiah 44:6)

37. שְׁבָ"א מָאן אִיהוּ. כַּאֲשֶׁר יִהְיֶה הָאוֹפָן בְּתוֹךְ הָאוֹפָן. וְאִינּוּן אֶת הַמָּאוֹר הַגָּדוֹל וְאֶת הַמָּאוֹר הַקָּטֹן. וְאִינּוּן גּוּף וּבְרִית. וּלְקֳבְלַיְיהוּ חַמָּה וּלְבָנָה, דְּאִינּוּן לְקָבֵל אִימָא עִלָּאָה וְתַתָּאָה.

37. He asks, **"What is** the meaning of the two dots of **Sh'va?"** and answers, "This is the inner meaning of the verse: '...as it were a wheel in the middle of a wheel.' (Ezekiel 1:16) Since a dot signifies Malchut, and a wheel signifies Malchut, and when Malchut ascends and is sweetened by Binah, Malchut is considered to be two wheels, and likewise to be two dots one beneath the other, like the Sh'va. **And they represent "the greater light,"** since She receives from Binah that is clothed in Zeir Anpin**, and "the lesser light"** (Genesis 1:16) meaning Malchut. **And they are the body** that is the secret of Tiferet, Zeir Anpin, **and the Covenant,** which is the secret of Yesod, which is from the chest downward, and anything from the chest downward pertains to Malchut. **And** the **corresponding** aspects **are the Sun and the Moon** that are Zeir Anpin and Malchut**, which correspond to Supernal Ima** clothed with Zeir Anpin, **and lower** Ima, meaning Malchut.

38. וְהִנֵּה אוֹפָן אֶחָד בָּאָרֶץ אֵצֶל הַחַיּוֹת, דָּא נְקוּדָה דִּתְחוֹת סְגוֹ"ל, נְקוּדָה דִּלְתַתָּא, אֵצֶל הַחַיּוֹת, דְּאִינּוּן צֵרֵ"י, אֶת שְׁנֵי הַמְּאוֹרוֹת הַגְּדוֹלִים.

38. The secret meaning of the verse: "...behold one wheel upon the earth by the living creatures..." (Ezekiel 1:15) **is the dot underneath the Segol,** that is, **the bottom dot** in Segol that hints at the Central Column. **"By the living creatures"** refers to the two dots **of the Tzere,** called the "living creatures" after the Light of Chochmah that is also called the Light of

Chaya (living creature), as is written: "...wisdom preserves the life of him who has it." (Ecclesiastes 7:12) This is also the secret meaning of the verse: "And God made **the two great lights...,**" (Genesis 1:16) which stand in equal stature, and divide into Right and Left.

39. וְכֵן אִיהוּ בְּתוֹךְ הָאוֹפַנִּים שׁוּרַ"ק, אוֹפַן חַד לְעֵילָא, וְאוֹפַן חַד לְתַתָּא, וְאִיהוּ עַמּוּדָא דְּאֶמְצָעִיתָא בֵּינַיְיהוּ. וְהִנֵּה אוֹפַן אֶחָד בָּאָרֶץ, דָּא חִירֵק, דְּאִיהוּ לְתַתָּא. כָּל נִיצוֹץ אִיהוּ י', וְכָל רָקִיעַ ו'.

39. And so the Segol **within the wheels,** which are the vowels of Malchut **Shuruk** of three dots. **One wheel,** meaning vowel, **is above,** meaning the right dot in the Segol that hints to Keter of Chochmah; **and one wheel below,** meaning the dot of the Segol that hints to Binah, Tiferet, and Malchut. **And it is the Central Column between them** that is the middle dot from Zeir Anpin that ascended as Feminine Water (Mayin Nukvin) to Binah and reconciles between the Columns. And in the Shuruk it is the bottom of the dot; and it is what is meant by: "**...and behold one wheel is in the ground...**" that is Chirek that is below. **Each spark is a Yud** that is a dot, and stands for Chochmah and for Malchut, **and each Firmament** stands for **Vav,** Chasadim, and Zeir Anpin.

40. יְהֹוָה שְׁבָ"א אִיהוּ דִּינָא. קָמֵ"ץ רַחֲמֵי. שְׂמָאלָא וִימִינָא. דְּמִתַּמָּן אוֹרַיְיתָא אִתְיְיהִיב, דְּאִיהוּ עַמּוּדָא דְּאֶמְצָעִיתָא. וּבְזִמְנָא דְּאִינּוּן שְׁבָ"א קָמֵ"ץ וֹכֵ"ם, אִיהוּ רָמוּז כִּי בִי וָשַׁ"ק וַאֲפַלְטֵהוּ רַק בַּאֲבוֹתֶיךָ וָשַׁ"ק יִ"י.

40. When the Name **Yud-Hei-Vav-Hei** is voweled with Sh'va, Cholem, and Kametz, **Sh'va is** the dot of Gevurah that is **Judgment. Kametz is Mercy,** in the secret of the verse: "...and the priest shall take his handful (*kametz*) of it..." (Leviticus 5:12) [Kohen] is Chesed, and they are two lines (columns). **Left is Sh'va, Right is Kametz,** in the secret of the verse: "...at His right hand went a fiery law unto them." (Deuteronomy 33:2) Right is Chesed, fire is Gevurah. The secret of the letters that spell Sh'va (Shin-Bet-Alef) derives from the verse: "For with fire (*ba'esh;* Bet-Alef-Shin) will the Lord execute judgment…" (Isaiah 66:16) **since the Torah was given from there, which is the Central Column,** Tiferet, the dot in the Cholem. **And when** the Three Columns shine, which are **Sh'va, Kametz, and Cholem it is an allusion to the verse: "Because he has set his love upon Me, therefore will I deliver him…"** (Psalms 91:14) which is the secret of the 42-letter Name, since "in me" (ki vi) equals 42. **"Only the Lord had a delight in your father to love them…"** (Deuteronomy 10:15) which is the secret of Ayin-Bet (72) that is revealed in Chesed, Gevurah, and Tiferet, which are called "fathers."

41. מִסִּטְרָא דְּא' דְּאִיהוּ רָזָא יו"י, דְּסָלִיק יהו"ה, הֲוָה קוּדְשָׁא בְּרִיךְ הוּא הוּא וּשְׁמֵיהּ לְחוֹד בְּכִתְרָא, קֳדָם דְּאִתְבְּרֵי עָלְמָא. עַד דְּסָלִיק בְּמַחֲשַׁבְתֵּיהּ לְמִבְרֵי אָדָם, דְּאִיהוּ י' בְּרֵישָׁא דְּא' תַּגָּא לְעֵילָא, וּלְתַתָּא נְקוּדָה.

41. From the aspect of Alef, which is the secret of Yud-Vav-Yud, whereby the bottom Yud has the same stature as the upper Yud, which is the Alef **that equals the numerical value of Yud-Hei-Vav-Hei (26), the Holy One blessed be He, and His Name alone was in Keter,** which is the Endless Light, blessed be He, **before the creation of the world. Until He entertained the thought to create man,** meaning in the world of correction. The form of **Yud on the top of Alef is the crownlet above,** meaning the cantillation mark, **and the Yud on the bottom is a dot.** That is to say, there is a difference between the upper Yud and the lower Yud.

42. וּבְנְקוּדֵי דְּאַתְוָן, אִשְׁתְּמוֹדְעָן כָּל סְפִירָן, דְּתֵשַׁע נְקוּדֵי אִינוּן וּבְהוֹן י"ד נִיצוֹצִין, וַעֲלַיְהוּ אִתְּמַר, וּבְנֵי יִשְׂרָאֵל יוֹצְאִים בְּיָ"ד רָמָה.

42. And by the vowels illuminating **on the letters, all the Sefirot are made known. There are nine vowels** as follows: Kametz, Patach, and Tzere are the Upper Three Sefirot of Keter, Chochmah, and Binah. Segol, Sh'va, and Cholem are Chesed, Gevurah, and Tiferet. Chirek, Kubutz, and Shuruk, also called Chirek, Shuruk, and Melopum are Netzach, Hod, and Yesod. Malchut that has nothing of her own has no vowel. The vowels

contain **fourteen sparks,** as Kametz, Cholem, Chirek, and Melopum, each
has one dot, which together add up to four dots. Tzere has two, Sh'va two,
and Segol three, and Shuruk three, which altogether equal fourteen. **About
them is written: "...for the children of Israel went out with a high hand
(*yad;* 14)."** (Exodus 14:8)

43. וְאִינּוּן לָקֳבֵל פִּרְקִין דְּחָמֵשׁ אֶצְבְּעָן, דְּאִינּוּן י"ד, וּתְרֵין רְקִיעִין תַּמָּן, וַד
בְּן קָמֵ"ץ, וְוָד בְּן פַּתַ"ח. לָקֳבֵל תְּרֵין קָנֵי דִדְרוֹעֵי. וְכָל נִיצוֹץ אִיהוּ פֶּרֶק,
וְאִיהוּ מִדָּה. וּרְקִיעַ אַמָּה, וְקָנֶה, וְקַו הַמִּדָּה.

43. And these fourteen **correspond to the joints of the five fingers** in the
hand **that are fourteen. And two Firmaments are there,** meaning two
lines laid horizontal in the vowels, **one line from the Kametz** vowel, **and
one** line **from the Patach** vowel **corresponding to the two arm lengths.
And each spark** of the dots **is a joint, and a measure** that limits the Light.
Movements are made by the joints, and likewise the letters move by the
vowels that animate them. **And the Firmament is a cubit, a** measuring
stick and a measuring line, namely the extent of the Light.

44. טַעֲמֵי אִינּוּן מְן כִּתְרָא. וְאִינּוּן בְּרֵישָׁא דְעַמּוּדָא דְּאֶמְצָעִיתָא. נְקוּדִין מְן
מוֹחָא, וְאִינּוּן בִּרְכָאן עַל רֵישָׁא דְצַדִּיק. כְּמָה דְאַתְּ אָמַר, בְּרָכוֹת לְרֹאשׁ
צַדִּיק. וְאִינּוּן תְּלַת טִפִּין, דְּאִתְמַשְׁכוּ מְן מוֹחָא לְגַבֵּי בְּרִית מִילָה. אַתְוָון
מִסִּטְרָא דְאִימָא עִלָּאָה, וְכֻלְּהוּ אִתְכְּלִילָן בְּמַלְכוּתָא.

44. Cantillation marks are from Keter of Zeir Anpin **and are at the
top of the Central Column,** Zeir Anpin. **Vowels come from the brain,**
which is Chochmah, **and are blessings upon the head of the righteous,**
meaning internal Mochin, **as it says: "Blessings are upon the head of the
righteous"** (Proverbs 10:6) **They are three drops** that stand for the Three
Columns **that flow from the brain to the circumcised organ,** which is
Yesod. **Letters,** which are vessels, **flow from the part of Supernal Ima,**
which is Binah. They are the Seven Lower Sefirot of Binah, dressed in Zeir

and Nukva, because the Upper Three Sefirot of Binah are crownlets. **And all** cantillation marks, vowels, and letters, **are included in Malchut.**

45. וּנְקוּדֵי לְאַתְוָון, כְּנִשְׁמָתָא לְגוּפָא. דְגוּפָא אִיהוּ כְּסוּס לְרוֹכֵב, וְאַתְוָון אִינּוּן פְּתוּחִין לִנְקוּדֵי, לְקַבְּלָא לוֹן. וַעֲלַיְיהוּ אִתְּמַר, וְכַנְפֵיהֶם פְּרוּדוֹת מִלְּמַעְלָה, לְקַבְּלָא עֲלַיְהוּ נְקוּדֵי. וּנְקוּדֵי בְּכָל אֲתַר בַּת קוֹל. טַעֲמֵי אִינּוּן מָאנֵי קְרָבָא.

45. Vowels illuminate in the **letters as the soul** illuminates **in the body because the body is like a horse, in relation to the rider. And letters open towards the vowels to receive them, and about them it is said: "And their wings stretched upwards..."** (Ezekiel 1:11), **to receive upon them the vowels. And the vowels,** meaning Malchut that illuminates with the illumination of Chochmah, **are always** called **Bat Kol (Heavenly Voice; lit. daughter of voice).** Since Zeir Anpin is called "voice" and Malchut is called "daughter of voice," as her Chochmah is clothed with Chasadim. **And cantillation marks are weapons of battle** to slaughter the Other Side, and to draw life, which is Mochin, to Zeir Anpin and Nukva and to Israel.

46. רָפֶ"ה אִיהוּ לְעֵילָּא מֵאַתְוָון, וַעֲלֵיהּ אִתְּמַר וּדְמוּת עַל רָאשֵׁי הַחַיָּה רָקִיעַ כְּעֵין הַקֶּרַח הַנּוֹרָא נָטוּי עַל רָאשֵׁיהֶם מִלְּמַעְלָה וְדָא אִיהוּ רָפֶ"ה. נָטוּי עַל רָאשֵׁי חֵיוָן, דְאִינּוּן יהו"ה, אַרְבַּע אַתְוָון וַדַּאי, דַּגֵ"שׁ אִיהוּ מִלְגָאו דְאַתְוָון, כְּגַוְונָא דָא יהו"ה. רָפֶ"ה מִלְּבָר כְּגַוְונָא דָא יהוה. וְאִינּוּן כְּמֶתֶג וְרֶסֶן לְאוֹתִיּוֹת וּבְהוֹן וְהַחַיּוֹת רָצוֹא וָשׁוֹב, רָצוֹא בְּדַגֵ"שׁ, וָשׁוֹב בְּרָפֶ"ה.

46. A sign to a weak sounding letter (*rafeh*) **is above the letters,** meaning a horizontal line, indicating Chasadim. **About it is said: "And over the heads of the living creatures there was the likeness of a Firmament, like the color of the terrible ice, stretched out over their heads above."** (Ezekiel 1:22) **This is weak (*rafeh*), stretched out over the heads of the living creatures, which assuredly are the four letters Yud-Hei-Vav-Hei.** The lion stands for Yud of the Name Yud-Hei-Vav-Hei, the ox is the first Hei, the Vav stands for the eagle, and the lower Hei stands for the face of man. **And the sign of Dagesh is inside the letters like this:**

יְהֹוּ"ה, and weak (*rafeh*) is outside like this: יְהֹוֹה. And they are like reins and bridle for the letters, so they may shine in the order of the Central Column, where Chochmah illuminates from below upward and Chasadim from above downwards. And in them lies the secret meaning of the verse: "And the living creatures ran and returned" (Ezekiel 1:14) "ran" with a Dagesh; "returned" with a weak (*rafeh*) Dagesh.

For the fourth day of the month of Elul

Sixth Tikkun
A bird's nest

1. בְּרֵאשִׁית: קָם רַבִּי שִׁמְעוֹן, וְאָמַר לְאֵלִיָּהוּ, אֵלִיָּהוּ בְּאוֹמָאָה עֲלָךְ, בְּמַלְכוּתָא קַדִּישָׁא דְּאִיהִי נְפִילָא בְּגָלוּתָא. טוֹל רְשׁוּתָא דְּלָא תָזוּז מִינָן. דְּהָא שְׁכִינְתָּא וְחֵילָהָא נָטְרִין לָךְ.

1. **Beresheet: Rav Shimon rose up and said to Elijah: "Elijah, by an oath upon you, receive permission** from the Holy One blessed be He, **not to move away from Him** to raise **the Holy Malchut that is fallen in exile. The Shechinah and Her hosts await you.**

2. מַלְאֲכֵי הַשָּׁרֵת, דְּאִתְּמַר בְּהוֹן, הֵן אֶרְאֶלָם צָעֲקוּ חוּצָה, צָוְוחִין לְבַר מֵהֵיכָלִין, לָא אִית מָאן דִּמְקַבֵּל צְלוֹתִין דְּיִשְׂרָאֵל. כַּמָּה צִפָּרִין מְצַפְצְפִין בִּצְלוֹתִין לְגַבֵּי אִמְּהוֹן, דְּאִינוּן מְקַנְנָן עַל אַרְעָא דְּנָטְרִין לָךְ.

2. **The ministering angels**—about which it is said: **"Behold, the mighty ones shall cry outside"** (Isaiah 33:7) because they are **shouting outside the temples**—wait for you. **But there is no one there to receive the prayers of Israel. How many birds,** the souls of Israel, **are nesting on the ground and cry out prayers towards their mother** that is Malchut, **waiting for you.**

3. וְכֻלְּהוּ אִתְקְרִיאוּ צִפָּרִים, עַל שֵׁם קַן צִפּוֹר, דְּאִיהִי אִימָא קַדִּישָׁא, דְּאִתְּמַר בָּהּ, כִּי יִקָּרֵא קַן צִפּוֹר לְפָנֶיךָ. וַעֲלָהּ אִתְּמַר, גַּם צִפּוֹר מָצְאָה בַיִת, וְדָא בֵּ' מִבְּרֵאשִׁית דְּאִתְּמַר בָּהּ, בְּחָכְמָה יִבָּנֶה בָיִת.

3. **All** the souls **are called birds,** after the bird's nest, which is the Holy **Ima,** meaning Malchut, **about whom it is said: "If a bird's nest chance to be before you..."** (Deuteronomy 22:6) **And regarding her is also said: "Even the sparrow has found a home** (*bayit*)..." (Psalms 84:4) **It is also Bet from Beresheet, about which it is said: "Through** (*be*) **wisdom,"** that

is called *resheet* (beginning) "...a house (*bayit*) is built," (Proverbs 24:3) which is Malchut that is called "house."

וּדְרוֹר קֵן לָהּ, דָּא אִימָא עִלָּאָה, יוֹבֵל, דְּאִתְּמַר בָּהּ וּקְרָאתֶם דְּרוֹר בָּאָרֶץ. .4
בְּזִמְנָא דְּצִפּוֹר מָצְאָה בַיִת, דְּאִיהִי בֵּי מַקְדְּשָׁא, וְאִתְבְּנִיאַת וְאִתְתַּקְנַת, מִיָּד
דְּרוֹר דְּאִיהִי שְׁכִינְתָּא עִלָּאָה, אַשְׁכְּחַת קֵן לָהּ לְעֵילָא. וּמִיָּד אֲשֶׁר שָׁתָה
אֶפְרוֹחֶיהָ, אִלֵּין שִׁית בְּנִין דִּילָהּ, שִׁית סְפִירָן, דְּאִינּוּן שֵׁשֶׁת יְמֵי הַמַּעֲשֶׂה,
כֻּלְּהוּ פָּרְחִין לְגַבָּהּ, בְּכַמָּה חַגִּין וּזְמַנִּין וְיוֹמִין טָבִין.

4. "...and the sparrow (*dror*) a nest for herself...." (Psalms 84:4) **This is Supernal Ima,** meaning Binah called **Jubilee, about which is written: "... and proclaim liberty (*dror*) throughout all the land...."** (Leviticus 25:10) **When the bird** Malchut **found a house, which is the Holy Temple,** meaning the illumination of the Upper Three Sefirot called "Holy," **and gets rebuilt and restored, then immediately *dror* that is the Supernal Shechinah** Binah **finds herself a nest above.** As Malchut ascends to the place of Binah and it becomes a nest for her. **And instantly: "...she may lay (*shatah*, which in Aramaic means "six") her young."** (Psalms 84:4) **These are her six children, the six Sefirot,** Chesed, Gevurah, Tiferet, Netzach, Hod, and Yesod, **the six working days. They all fly to her,** to Malchut, **during the many festivals, festive times, and Holidays.**

וְאֶפְרוֹחִים דְּאִינּוּן יִשְׂרָאֵל לְתַתָּא, כֻּלְּהוּ פָּרְחִין עִמָּהּ בְּגָלוּתָא. וּבְזִמְנָא .5
דְּאִינּוּן בֵּיצִים, דְּלֵית לוֹן גַּדְפִין בְּפִקּוּדִין דַּעֲשֵׂה לְפָרְחָא, אִתְּמַר בָּהּ לֹא תִקַּח
הָאֵם עַל הַבָּנִים.

5. He returns to explain the verse he began with: "A bird's nest," is Holy Ima, as is said, "If a bird's nest chance to be before you," and birds are the souls of Israel. Now he explains, her **young, who are Israel below,** those who merited the Light of Ruach, **all fly with** the Shechinah **in exile. And when they,** the children of Israel, are in the stage of **eggs,** meaning with the Light of Nefesh alone, and they **do not have wings to fly with the positive precepts, it says about her: "...you shall not take the mother bird with**

the young." (Deuteronomy 22:6) Rather, she should stay with them, to protect them until they grow.

6. אִי הָכִי מַאי כִּי יְקָרֵא קַן. אֶלָּא בְּזִמְנָא דְלֵית לָהּ לִשְׁכִינְתָּא אֲתַר לְשַׁרְיָא תַּמָּן בִּקְבִיעוּ, אִיהִי אָזְלַת בְּמִקְרֶה. וְדָא אִיהוּ כָּל הַקּוֹבֵעַ מָקוֹם לִתְפִלָּתוֹ וכו'. כְּמָה דְּנִשְׁמָתִין עָבְדִין, הָכִי שַׁרְיָא שְׁכִינְתָּא עִמְהוֹן. נִשְׁמָתָא דְּאִיהִי קְבוּעָה בִּצְלוֹתָא אוֹ בְּאוֹרַיְתָא. אִיהִי אֲתַר קָבוּעַ לְשַׁרְיָא בָּהּ שְׁכִינְתָּא. אֲבָל נִשְׁמָתָא דְּלֵית לָהּ קְבִיעוּ בִּצְלוֹתָא אוֹ בְּאוֹרַיְתָא, אֶלָּא אִי אִזְדַּמְנַת לָהּ בְּמִקְרֶה. הָכִי אִיהִי שַׁרְיָא עֲלָהּ בְּמִקְרֶה.

6. He asks, "If that is the case, why does it say: "If a bird's nest chance (*yikare*) to be…" (Deuteronomy 22:6) which is derived from incidence (*mikreh*), is it not necessary to have more permanency, so the mother can reside with the young as long as they are small?" And he answers, **"Rather, it is a time when the Shechinah has no room to remain there permanently,** which is the Katnut stage, **She goes** and comes **by chance."** **This is the meaning of** what the masters of blessed memory said, **"He that designates a regular place for his prayer,"** (Tractate Berachot 6b) namely, that he accepts the yoke of the Heavenly Kingdom, no longer repeats his foolishness, designates a place for his prayer that is the Shechinah, in the meaning of: "…but I am all prayer," (Psalms 109:4) a pleasant apartment in his heart, fine utensils in his limbs, and a beautiful wife that is his soul. Then, the God of Abraham will help him. Furthermore, "his enemies will fall under him." (Tractate Berachot 7b) **As the souls do, is the Shechinah accordingly present with them. A soul that is constantly in prayer or studying Torah** becomes **a permanent place for the Shechinah to reside. However, a soul that does not pray or study Torah regularly, but only occasionally, so too, is the presence** of the Shechinah **then only upon the soul occasionally.**

7. וְדָא אִיהוּ כִּי יְקָרֵא קַן צִפּוֹר לְפָנֶיךָ כו', דְּוַדַּאי נִשְׁמָתָא אִיהִי קַן צִפּוֹר. וְגוּפָא קַן דְּנִשְׁמָתָא. וְכֵן נִשְׁמָתִין דְּאִינּוּן עוּלֵימָן דִּילָהּ, דְּאִתְקְרִיאוּ בְּתוּלוֹת אַחֲרֶיהָ רֵעוֹתֶיהָ, יָתְבוּן בְּגוּפִין דְּאִינּוּן קַן דִּלְהוֹן, בְּאֲרוּ מִקְרֶה. בְּזִמְנָא דְלָאו

אִינוּן קְבוּעִין בְּבָתֵּי כְנֵסִיּוֹת וּבְבָתֵּי מֶדְרָשׁוֹת. וְדָא אִיהוּ כִּי יִקָּרֵא קַן צִפּוֹר לְפָנֶיךָ.

7. And this is the meaning of the verse: "If a bird's nest chance to be before you..." for surely the soul is a bird's nest, meaning a nest for the Shechinah, and the body is a nest for the soul. And thus are all the souls, which are maidens of the Shechinah, called: "...the virgins, her companions that follow her...." (Psalms 45:15) They occasionally dwell in bodies that are their nests, when they are not regular in the houses of prayer and Torah academies. And this is the meaning of: "If a bird's nest chance to be before you...."

8. וְעוֹד. קַן צִפּוֹר לְעֵילָא, אִיהוּ כָּרְסַיָּא. וְקַן דִּילָהּ לְתַתָּא, מטטרו"ן, וַעֲלֵיהּ אִתְּמַר, וְנַקֵּה לֹא יְנַקֶּה, דְּתַמָּן קַן. וְאִיהִי קַנָּא וְנוֹקֵם, בְּזִמְנָא דְּלָא אַשְׁכְּחַת קִינָא לְשַׁרְיָא.

8. It can **also** be explained as, **the nest** of the **bird above** that is Malchut of Atzilut, **is the throne,** meaning the World of Briyah, called "the throne;" **and her nest down below,** meaning in Yetzirah and Asiyah, **is Metatron,** of whom it is said: "...and he did not take revenge (*yenake*)..." (Numbers 14:18), **where the letters spelling *ken* (nest) are alluded to,** "He will remit those who repent, but not those who do not repent." (Tractate Yoma 86a) **And he,** Metatron is **"jealous and revenging (*kano venokem*)"** (Nahum 1:2) **when the Shechinah will not find a nest to nestle** in, as the above letters of *kano* and *venokem* hint to the letters of *ken*. According to the masters (Sanhedrin 38b) it was about Metatron: "...for he will not pardon your transgression...." (Exodus 23:21)

9. בַּדֶּרֶךְ: דָּא דְּאִתְּמַר בָּהּ, מֵתוּ בַמִּדְבָּר בַּדֶּרֶךְ בְּצֵאתָם מִמִּצְרָיִם. וְעוֹד בַּדֶּרֶךְ, דָּא קְבוּרַת רָחֵל, דְּאִיהִי בְּפָרָשַׁת אוֹרְחִין. וַעֲלָהּ אִתְּמַר, מִי יִתְּנֵנִי בַמִּדְבָּר מְלוֹן אֹרְחִים. וְאִינוּן תְּרֵין מְשִׁיחִין, דְּמִתַּמָּן קָא עָבְרִין כַּד אָתָאן לְמִפְרַק לְיִשְׂרָאֵל.

9. He explains the continuation of the verse: "If a bird's nest chance to be before you **in the way.**" **It was said of her,** of Malchut from the chest and above, which is called Leah, the wife of Jacob, and the generation of the wilderness: "**...died in the wilderness by the way, after they came forth from Egypt.**" (Joshua 5:4) **Another** explanation of "**in the way**" is that it **refers to the burial place of Rachel,** meaning Malchut from the chest and below, **which is in a crossroad.** This is what is meant by "in the way." **And about her it is said: "That I were in the wilderness, in a lodging place of wayfaring men...."** (Jeremiah 9:1) **The two Messiahs,** Messiah son of [ben] Joseph, and Messiah son of [ben] David, **will pass there,** by way of Rachel's tomb, **when they will come to redeem Israel.**

10. בְּכָל עֵץ, דָּא אִיהוּ עֵץ הַחַיִּים, דְּאִתְּמַר בֵּיהּ עֵץ חַיִּים הִיא לַמַּחֲזִיקִים בָּהּ. וַעֲלֵיהּ אִתְּמַר, כִּי הָאָדָם עֵץ הַשָּׂדֶה, וְעוֹד בְּכָל עֵץ, דָּא צַדִּיק. דְּאִתְּמַר בֵּיהּ עֵץ פְּרִי עֹשֶׂה פְּרִי לְמִינוֹ. וְדָא יוֹם הַשַּׁבָּת, דְּתַמָּן זִוּוּגָא דִשְׁכִינְתָּא עִם קוּדְשָׁא בְּרִיךְ הוּא. וְתַמָּן אִית לָהּ נַיְיחָא.

10. "...in any tree..." (Deuteronomy 22.6) **refers to the Tree of Life,** meaning Zeir Anpin from the chest and above, **which about it is said: "She is a tree of life to them who lay hold upon her...."** (Proverbs 3:18) **And about it,** Zeir Anpin, called" man," is said: "**...for the tree of the field is man....**" (Deuteronomy 20:19) **"...in any tree" could also** be explained **as referring to the Righteous,** meaning Yesod from the chest and below, **of which is said: "...and fruit tree yielding fruit after its kind...."** (Genesis 1:11) **This is the Sabbath day, when the mating of the Shechinah with the Holy One blessed be He, takes place, and then she has rest.**

11. וַעֲלֵיהּ אִתְּמַר, וְהָיָה כְּעֵץ שָׁתוּל עַל פַּלְגֵי מַיִם אֲשֶׁר פִּרְיוֹ יִתֵּן בְּעִתּוֹ, דָּא עִתּוֹ דְצַדִּיק, דְּאִיהִי לֵיל שַׁבָּת. דְּצַדִּיק מִנֵּיהּ פָּרְחִין נִשְׁמָתִין וַדְדָתִין בְּיִשְׂרָאֵל עֶרֶב שַׁבָּת, דְּאִתְקְרִיאוּ פָּנִים וַחֲדָשׁוֹת.

11. And about it, Yesod, the Righteous, is said: "**And he shall be like a tree planted by streams of water that brings forth its fruit in its season**

[lit. in its time]." (Psalms 1:3) **This is the righteous people's time to perform marital duty, the night of Shabbat, since from the Righteous,** that is Yesod, called the "sixth day," **new souls bloom in Israel on the eve of the Sabbath, referred to as "new faces."**

‫12. אִפְרוֹחִים: אִלֵּין תַּלְמִידֵי חֲכָמִים דִּבְגִינְהוֹן שַׁרְיָא שְׁכִינְתָּא עַל יִשְׂרָאֵל. אוֹ בֵּיצִים: אִלֵּין אִינּוּן תִּינוֹקוֹת שֶׁל בֵּית רַבָּן, דִּבְגִינְהוֹן שַׁרְיָא שְׁכִינְתָּא עַל יִשְׂרָאֵל, וְאִלֵּין אִינּוּן מָארֵי מִקְרָא.‬

12. "The young" are the students of the Torah who attained the Light of Ruach, **for whose sake the Shechinah dwells upon Israel. "Eggs" are the children in their rabbi's school, for whose sake the Shechinah dwells upon Israel, and they are the masters of the Scriptures,** who attained the Light of Nefesh.

‫13. וּבְזִמְנָא דְּאִינּוּן עָסְקִין בְּאוֹרַיְיתָא, אוֹ בְּמִצְוָה, דְּאִנּוּן קוּדְשָׁא בְּרִיךְ הוּא, וּשְׁכִינְתָּא, וְגַרְמֵי לְחַבְּרָא לוֹן כַּחֲדָא, יָרְתִין מִתַּמָּן נִשְׁמָתִין, וְאִתְקְרִיאוּ בָּנִים דְּקוּדְשָׁא בְּרִיךְ הוּא.‬

13. And when they are occupied with Torah or the precepts, which are the Holy One blessed be He, and His Shechinah, as the Holy One blessed be He, is called Torah, and His Shechinah is called a precept. And **when they cause them to connect together,** as there is no Torah without precepts, and no precept without Torah and the difference is only in the dominance, they **inherit from there,** from this union, **souls that are called children to the Holy One blessed be He.**

‫14. בְּגִין דְּמָארֵי מִקְרָא וּמָארֵי מִשְׁנָה, אִינּוּן גַּדְפִין דִּילָהּ, וּבְגִין דָּא וְהָאֵם רֹבֶצֶת עַל הָאֶפְרוֹחִים אוֹ עַל הַבֵּיצִים. אִיהִי רְבִיעָא עֲלַיְיהוּ בְּאַרְבַּע גַּדְפִין דִּילָהּ, דְּאִתְּמַר בְּהוֹן וְאַרְבַּע כְּנָפַיִם, יוֹנְקִין אַנְפֵּי זוּטְרֵי. וְאִינּוּן אַרְבַּע אַנְפִּין לְכָל חַד וְחַד. וּבְהוֹן אִימָּא רְבִיעָא עֲלַיְיהוּ. וְזִמְנִין אִסְתַּלְּקַת אֲבָל בְּגִין דְּאִינּוּן מִן מֵעוֹי, דְּאִתְּמַר בְּהוֹן, הֵמוּ מֵעַי לוֹ. בְּגִין דְּרַחֲמוֹי דְּהַבוּ מֵעָתָא עֲלַיְיהוּ,‬

דְּאִינּוּן מָארֵי קַבָּלָה, אִתְּמַר בְּהוֹן לֹא תִקַּח הָאֵם עַל הַבָּנִים. דְּאִימָּא לָא זָזָה מִנַּיְיהוּ לְעָלַם.

14. As the masters of the Scriptures and masters of Mishnah are wings to the Shechinah, **it is therefore said: "And the mother bird sitting upon the young, or upon the eggs...." She,** Malchut, **lies over them with her four wings, as said about them "...four wings."** (Ezekiel 1:6) **They are children, with their small faces,** which are the back Mochin, **four faces** of Chesed, Gevurah, Tiferet, and Malchut, **to each and every one,** as each and every one is composed of all four faces. **And over** the Mochin of Yenikah **the mother bird,** Malchut **reclines but sometimes** when they do not deserve it, **She is gone from them. However, sons** that merited the front Mochin **that are from her womb,** that is to say, that receive from inward parts of Malchut **about whom it is said: "...My innards yearn for him..."** (Jeremiah 31:20) **sons of love,** for whom her innards are moved, the masters of Kabbalah, it is said about them: **"...you shall not take the mother bird together with the young [lit. sons, *habanim*]..."** (Deuteronomy 26:2) **for this mother will never move away from them,** and She shines to them the illumination of the Upper Three Sefirot clothed with Chasadim.

15. דְּוַדַּאי קוּדְשָׁא בְּרִיךְ הוּא אִיהוּ אוֹרַיְתָא, וּשְׁכִינְתָּא הִיא מִצְוָה, זַכָּאָה מָאן דְּמִתְעַסֵּק בְּהוֹן, לְיַחֲדָא לוֹן. וְכֵן זָכוֹר וְשָׁמוֹר אִינּוּן קוּדְשָׁא בְּרִיךְ הוּא וּשְׁכִינְתֵּיהּ. זַכָּאָה אִיהוּ, מָאן דִּמְיַחֵד לוֹן בְּיוֹם שַׁבָּת דְּאִיהוּ יְסוֹד, בִּרְחִימוּ וּדְחִילוּ דְּיְ"הָ, דְּאִינּוּן אַבָּא וְאִימָּא אִינּוּן לְקַבֵּל תְּפִלִּין דְּרֵישָׁא י', וּתְפִלִּין דְּיָדָא ה'. דְּכַר וְנוּקְבָא.

15. Since the Holy One blessed be He, is surely the Torah, the aspect of Zeir Anpin, **and the Shechinah is a precept,** Malchut, the Female of Zeir Anpin. **Fortunate is he who is occupied with them,** the Torah and the precepts **to unite them. Similarly, "remember" and "keep" are the Holy One blessed be He, and His Shechinah. Fortunate is he who unites them on the Sabbath day,** which is Yesod, **with love and awe of**

the Yud and Hei of the Name of Yud-Hei-Vav-Hei, **which are Aba and Ima,** meaning Chochmah and Binah. **And they correspond to the head Tefilin, Yud, and the arm Tefilin, Hei, Male and Female.** On Shabbat, Zeir Anpin and Nukva, which are the Vav and Hei that correspond to the head and arm Tefilin, elevate to the Chamber of Aba and Ima. And any lower level that elevates to a higher level becomes like the higher level, and therefore Zeir Anpin and Nukva that are the secret of the Vav and Hei are considered like Yud and Hei on Shabbat. Zeir Anpin inherites the place of its father, and Nukva the place of the mother.

16. וְזַכָּאָה מָאן דִּמְיַחֵד לוֹן בִּקְרִיאַת שְׁמַע, בִּדְחִילוּ וּרְחִימוּ, דִּבְזִמְנָא דְּיִשְׂרָאֵל מִשְׁתַּדְּלִין בְּאוֹרַיְתָא דִּבִכְתַב, וּבְאוֹרַיְתָא דְּבְעַל פֶּה בִּרְחִימוּ וּדְחִילוּ, אִתְּמַר בְּהוֹן לֹא תִקַּח הָאֵם עַל הַבָּנִים. וּבְזִמְנָא דְּלָא מִשְׁתַּדְּלִין בְּהוֹן בִּרְחִימוּ וּדְחִילוּ אִתְּמַר בְּהוֹן שַׁלֵּחַ תְּשַׁלַּח אֶת הָאֵם.

16. **Fortunate is he who unites them,** the Male and the Female **with awe and love during the Shema reading.** As in the time when Israel study the Written Torah and the Oral Torah with love and awe, it says about them: "...you shall not take the mother bird together with the young...." But when they do not care to strive to study them with love and awe, it is said regarding them: "...but you shall surely let the mother go...." (Deuteronomoy 22:7)

17. בְּזִמְנָא דְּיִשְׂרָאֵל נָטְרִין שַׁבַּתָּא בְּזָכוֹר וְשָׁמוֹר, בִּדְחִילוּ וּרְחִימוּ, אִתְּמַר בְּהוֹן לֹא תִקַּח הָאֵם עַל הַבָּנִים. וְאִם לָאו, כְּתִיב בְּהוֹן שַׁלֵּחַ תְּשַׁלַּח וְגו', תְּרֵין תְּרוּכִין. וּבְזִמְנָא דְּיִשְׂרָאֵל מְיַחֲדִין לְקוּדְשָׁא בְּרִיךְ הוּא בִּתְפִלִּין דְּיָד, וּבִתְפִלִּין דְּרֵאשָׁא, בִּדְחִילוּ וּרְחִימוּ, אִתְּמַר בְּהוֹן לֹא תִקַּח הָאֵם עַל הַבָּנִים, וְאִם לָאו שַׁלֵּחַ תְּשַׁלַּח.

7. **When Israel keep the Sabbath, with "remember,"** that is Zeir Anpin, **and "keep,"** Malchut **with awe and love,** it says about them: "...you shall not take the mother bird together with the young...." But if not, it is written: "but you shall surely [lit. send away, you shall send away; שַׁלֵּחַ

תְּשַׁלַּח] let the mother go," with **two banishments;** one corresponds to the First Temple and one to the Second Temple, which are Binah and Malchut. **And when Israel unite the Holy One blessed be He, by the hand Tefilin and by the head Tefilin with awe and love, we learn about them: "…you shall not take the mother bird together with the young…" but if not, then "…you shall surely let the mother go…."**

18. וּבְזִמְנָא דִמְקַיְּימִין מִצְוַת בְּרִית מִילָה, וְאַעְבְּרָן מִנַּיְיהוּ עָרְלָה, וְעָבְדִין פְּרִיעָה, בִּדְוֹחִילוּ וּרְחִימוּ, אִתְּמַר בְּהוֹן לֹא תִקַּח הָאֵם עַל הַבָּנִים. וְאִם לָאו, שַׁלֵּחַ תְּשַׁלַּח אֶת הָאֵם. בְּזִמְנָא דְמִתְיַיחֲדִין בְּזִוּוּגַיְיהוּ בִּקְדוּשִׁין, וְשֶׁבַע בִּרְכָאן, דְּאִינוּן יִחוּדָא דִלְהוֹן בִּקְדוּשָׁא וּבְבִרְכָתָא, אִתְּמַר בְּהוֹן לֹא תִקַּח הָאֵם עַל הַבָּנִים. וְאִם לָאו שַׁלֵּחַ תְּשַׁלַּח וכו'.

18. During times when Israel observe the precept of circumcision; remove from them the foreskin, and uncover the membrane, with awe and love, it says about them: "…you shall not take the mother bird together with the young…" but if not: "…you shall surely let the mother go…." When they accomplish their union, by the marriage ceremony and the seven blessings, which is the unification of Zeir and Nukva, with holiness and benediction, since the groom is like the king, and is a chariot to Zeir Anpin, and the bride is a chariot to Malchut, **it says about them: "…do not take the mother bird together with the young…" but if not: "…you shall surely let the mother go…."**

19. וְאִינוּן יִשְׂרָאֵל בְּגָלוּתָא בִּרְשׁוּתָא אַוְחֲרָא, דְּכַד לָא מִתְיַיחֲדִין בְּזִוּוּגַיְיהוּ בִּקְדוּשִׁין וְשֶׁבַע בִּרְכָאן, דְּאִינוּן יִחוּדָא דִלְהוֹן, בִּקְדוּשָׁה וּבְרָכָה, בַּאֲתַר דִקְדוּשָׁה, שָׁרְיָא עֲלַיְיהוּ מְסָאֲבָא. וּבַאֲתַר דִבְרָכָה, שָׁרְיָא עֲלַיְיהוּ לְטוּתָא. וּבַאֲתַר דְיִחוּדָא, שָׁרְיָא עֲלַיְיהוּ פְּרוּדָא.

19. And Israel are in exile, under a different government. Since if they do not conclude their union by a marriage ceremony and seven blessings, which bring about **the union** between Zeir Anpin and Nukva **with holiness and blessing,** that is, with Chochmah and Chasadim, since

Chochmah is called "holiness" and Chasadim are called "blessing" then instead of holiness, impurity rests on them; instead of a blessing, a curse comes upon them; and in place of unity, dissention lies upon them.

20. וְדָא גְּרִים גָּלוּתָא לִשְׁכִינְתָּא, דְּאִתְתַּרְכַת מֵאַתְרָהָא וּמִקִּנָּהָא, דְּאִיהוּ יְרוּשָׁלַם. הָדָא הוּא דִכְתִיב, וּבְפִשְׁעֵיכֶם שֻׁלְּחָה אִמְּכֶם, תְּרֵין שִׁלּוּחִין: שַׁלֵּחַ תְּשַׁלַּח, חַד מִבַּיִת רִאשׁוֹן, וְחַד מִבַּיִת שֵׁנִי.

20. And it is a cause for exile of the Shechinah that is banished from Her place and Her nest, which is Jerusalem, as it is written: "And for your transgressions was your mother put away" (Isaiah 50:1) twice, in respect to Binah and Malchut. "...send away, you shall send away..." once from the First Temple, corresponding to Binah, and once from the Second Temple, corresponding to Malchut.

21. וְאִי תֵימָא דְקוּדְשָׁא בְּרִיךְ הוּא לָאו אִתְתָּרַךְ עִמֵּיהּ, בְּגִין דָּא אָמַר קְרָא, כְּצִפּוֹר נוֹדֶדֶת מִן קִנָּהּ כֵּן אִישׁ נוֹדֵד מִמְּקוֹמוֹ. בְּגִין לְנַטְרָא לָהּ בְּגָלוּתָא, מֵרְשׁוּ נוּכְרָאָה. הָדָא הוּא דִכְתִיב, אֲנִי יְ"יָ הוּא שְׁמִי וּכְבוֹדִי לְאַחֵר לֹא אֶתֵּן וְגוֹ'. לְאַחֵר: דָּא אֵל אַחֵר, דָּא סמא"ל. לַפְּסִילִים: אִלֵּין מְמַנָּן דְּעַל שַׁבְעִין אוּמִין.

21. Should you venture to think that the Holy One blessed be He, is not banished together with Her, do not think so because, for this reason the scripture says: "As a bird, that is Malchut that wanders from her nest, so is a man, that is Zeir Anpin who wanders from his place" (Proverbs 27:8) to protect Her in exile from a foreign government, as written "I am the Lord, that is My Name; and My Glory will I not give to another...." (Isaiah 42:8) "Another" is another God (El), and "graven images" (Sama"el) (Ibid.) are angels assigned over the seventy nations.

22. וּבְגִינָהּ קוּדְשָׁא בְּרִיךְ הוּא אִיהוּ, מֶלֶךְ אָסוּר בָּרְהָטִים. אִיהוּ אָסוּר עִמְּהוֹן בִּתְפִלִּין דְּרֵישָׁא, דְּאִינּוּן פְּאֵר דְּרֵישָׁא, דִּתְפִלִּין דְּרֵישָׁא אִינּוּן בַּאֲתַר דְּרַהֲטֵי דְמוֹחָא, וְדָא אִיהוּ אָסוּר בָּרְהָטִים.

22. And for the sake of the Shechinah, **the Holy One blessed be He, is as "a king held captive in the tresses thereof."** (Song of Songs 7:6) The "tresses" are vessels in relation to the Mochin, like the Tefilin's compartments are in relation to the portions, which are the Mochin. **He is caught together with them,** Israel, **in the head Tefilin, that are the adornment of the the head, as the head Tefilin is in the place of the tresses of man's brain. And this is meant by "held captive in the tresses."** And the Mochin only shine according to the characteristics of the vessels.

23. וְאִיהוּ וָלְבוּשׁ עִמְּהוֹן בִּתְפִלִין דְּיָד, בְּקֶשֶׁר שֶׁל יָד, וְדָא הוּא דִכְתִיב, פָּאֵרְךָ חֲבוֹשׁ עָלֶיךָ. וּבְגִין דְּאִיהוּ וָלְבוּשׁ עִמְּהוֹן בְּגָלוּתָא, אִתְּמַר בֵּיהּ, אֵין חָבוּשׁ מַתִּיר עַצְמוֹ מִבֵּית הָאֲסוּרִין. וּשְׁכִינְתָּא אִיהִי בֵּית הָאֲסוּרִין דִּילֵיהּ בְּגִין רְחִימוּ דִילָהּ, אִיהוּ אָסוּר בָּהּ. וְרָזָא דְמִלָּה, צְרוֹר הַמּוֹר דּוֹדִי לִי בֵּין שָׁדַי יָלִין.

23. And the Holy One blessed be He, is bound with Israel, **by the hand Tefilin** that are the Mochin over the Nukva's head, **by the knot on the hand,** which stands for Yesod of Zeir Anpin, that unites with Malchut. **And this is meant by the verse: "...bind on your turban...."** (Ezekiel 24:17) **And because He is bound with** Israel **in exile, it says in this respect, "A bound prisoner cannot extricate himself from the jailhouse."** (Tractate Berachot 5b) **The Shechinah is His jailhouse in which He is bound due to His love for Her.** And His illumination does not extend from Her downwards. **This is the secret meaning of: "My well beloved is to me a bag of myrrh that lies between my breasts."** (Song of Songs 1:13)

24. וּבְגִין דָּא, מַאן דְּבָעֵי לְאַשְׁגָּא לְמַלְכָּא, לֵית לֵיהּ רְשׁוּ לְאַשְׁגָּא לֵיהּ, אֶלָּא בִּשְׁכִינְתָּא. הָדָא הוּא דִכְתִיב, אַל יִתְהַלֵּל כוּ'. כִּי אִם בְּזֹאת וְגו'. וְאַהֲרֹן כַּד עָאל לְקֹדֶשׁ קָדְשִׁין בְּיוֹמָא דְכִפּוּרֵי, בָּהּ הֲוָה עָאל, דִּכְתִיב בְּזֹאת יָבֹא אַהֲרֹן אֶל הַקֹּדֶשׁ, דְּאִיהִי עֵת לַעֲשׂוֹת לַי"י.

24. Therefore, he who wishes to reach the King, Zeir Anpin, **has permission to reach Him only through the Shechinah,** Malchut. Because the attaining of Zeir Anpin in relation to Malchut is like the attaining of the Upper Three in relation to the Lower Seven. And because the Mochin are drawn from the Nukva, therefore only the Lower Seven of Chochmah are drawn. **This is the meaning of: "Let not the wise man glory in his wisdom…but only in this (zot)…"** (Jeremiah 9:22-23) as Malchut is called *Zot.* **And when Aaron entered into the Holy of Holies on Yom Kippur [Day of Atonement], he entered through** the Shechinah. **As is written:** "That he come not at all times (*et*) into the holy place… **"Thus [lit. and this; zot] shall Aaron come into the holy place."** (Leviticus 16:2-3) **As She,** the Shechinah that is connoted as E*t* is **"time (*et*) to act for the Lord…."** (Psalms 119:126)

.25 וּמֹשֶׁה בְּגִינָהּ אִתְקַיַּים בְּעָלְמָא, הֲדָא הוּא דִכְתִיב, וְזֹאת הַבְּרָכָה אֲשֶׁר וְגוֹ'. וּבָהּ עֲבִיד עֶשֶׂר מַכְתְּשִׁין לְפַרְעֹה. הֲדָא הוּא דִכְתִיב, וְאוּלָם בַּעֲבוּר זֹאת הֶעֱמַדְתִּיךָ, וְיַעֲקֹב בְּגִין דַּהֲוָה יָדַע דְּכָל רְעוּתָא דְמַלְכָּא בָּהּ, מַנִּי לִבְנוֹי עֲלָהּ, דְּלָא יַעֲלוּן קֳדָם מַלְכָּא אֶלָּא בָּהּ, וְכָל שְׁאֶלְתִּין דִּלְהוֹן בִּצְלוֹתִין וּבָעוּתִין לְמַלְכָּא, דִּיְהוֹן בָּהּ, הֲדָא הוּא דִכְתִיב, וְזֹאת אֲשֶׁר דִּבֶּר לָהֶם אֲבִיהֶם וְגוֹ'.

25. And Moses, for the sake of the Shechinah that he gave as an inheritance to Israel, **still lives in the world,** as the masters of blessed memory said, "Moses extends into each and every generation." **This is the meaning of: "And this (zot) is the blessing, with which…."** (Deuteronomy 33:1) **And through it he produced the ten plagues against Pharaoh, as is written: "But in very deed for this (zot) cause have I raised you up…"** (Exodus 9:16) **And concerning Her, because Jacob knew that the King's whole desire is concentrated on Her and instructed his children not to enter the presence of the King except through Her. And all their requests in prayers and pleadings shall pass to the King through Her. This is what is meant by: "And this (zot) is that which their father spoke unto them…."** (Genesis 49:28)

26. וְדָוִד, בְּגִין דַּהֲוָה יָדַע דְּכָל רְעוּתָא וְחֵילָא וְתוּקְפָּא דְּמַלְכָּא בָּהּ. אָמַר אִם
תַּחֲנֶה וְגוֹ', בְּזֹאת אֲנִי בוֹטֵחַ. דְּאִתְּמַר עֲלָהּ, וּמַלְכוּתוֹ בַּכֹּל מָשָׁלָה. וּמַאן דְּלָא
שָׁת לִבֵּיהּ גַּם לָזֹאת, עֲלֵיהּ אִתְּמַר, וּכְסִיל לֹא יָבִין אֶת זֹאת.

26. And David, who knew that the King's whole desire, power, and strength is for her, said: "Though a host should camp against me…in this (zot) I will be confident" (Psalms 27:3) of which is said: "And His Kingdom rules over all." (Psalms 103:19) And he who: "Neither did he set his heart even to this (zot)" (Exodus 7:23) which was said about Pharaoh, about him it says: "…nor does a fool understand this (zot)." (Psalms 92:7)

27. וּבְגִין דָּא, כַּד יִשְׂרָאֵל בָּעָאן בָּעוּתִין לְמַלְכָּא, אָמְרִין לָהּ אָנָה הָלַךְ דּוֹדֵךְ.
דְּאִתְּמַר בֵּיהּ, בְּרַח דּוֹדִי. אָנָה פָנָה דוֹדֵךְ וּנְבַקְשֶׁנּוּ עִמָּהּ, בְּכַמָּה בַּקָּשׁוֹת
דִּצְלוֹתִין וּבָעוּתִין. דִּבְגִינָךְ אִיהוּ נָחִית עֲלָן. דְּלָא זָז מִנָּנָא, אֶלָּא בְּגִין דְּלָא
נָהֲנָא יְקָרָא בָּךְ.

27. And since it is impossible to approach the King except through Her, when Israel submit their request to the King, they tell Her, the Shechinah: "Where is your beloved gone…" (Song of Songs 6:1) about whom is said: "Make haste, my beloved…" (Song of Songs 8:14); "Where has your beloved turned him, that we may seek him with you." (Song of Songs 6:1) with much beseeching of prayer and pleading. Since it is for your sake that He descends and dwells over us. But He moves away from us, meaning and that He departs from us only because we have not duly respected You.

28. דִּבְגִינָךְ הֲוָה אָסִיר עִמָּנָא כָּל שִׁית יוֹמִין, הֲדָא הוּא דִּכְתִיב יִהְיֶה סָגוּר
שֵׁשֶׁת יְמֵי הַמַּעֲשֶׂה וּבְיוֹם הַשַּׁבָּת יִפָּתֵחַ וְגוֹ'. דְּהָכִי אִיהִי שְׁכִינְתָּא סְתִימָא
עִמֵּיהּ בְּיוֹמָא דְּחוֹלָא, כְּשׁוֹשַׁנָּה דְּאִיהִי אֲטִימָא.

28. Since for Malchut's sake He is bound with us all the six days, meaning during the weekdays, when the external forces are able to draw from the

abundance of Mochin of Malchut, therefore He does not shine on her with the illumination of Chochmah during the weekdays. **Thus it is written: "...shall be shut for the six working days; but on the Sabbath day it shall be opened..."** (Ezekiel 46:1) **So then, the Shechinah is sealed in with Him during the weekdays, like this rose that is sealed** and closed.

29. וּבְיוֹמָא דְּשַׁבַּתָּא, וּבְיוֹמָא דְּוַזְדְעָא, וּבְיוֹמִין טָבִין, אִתְפָּתְוַת לְקַבְּלָא רֵיוִין וּבוּסְמִין, וּלְיַהֲרָתָא נַפְשִׁין וְעִנּוּגִין לִבְנַיְיהוּ. וַוי לוֹן לִבְנֵי נָשָׁא, דְּקוּדְשָׁא בְּרִיךְ הוּא אָסִיר עִמְּהוֹן בְּגָלוּתָא, וּשְׁכִינְתָּא אֲסִירַת עִמְּהוֹן. וְאִתְּמַר בָּהּ, אֵין וָבוּשׁ מַתִּיר אֶת עַצְמוֹ מִבֵּית הָאֲסוּרִים.

29. But on the day of Shabbat, and on the day of the New Moon and Holidays, when Zeir Anpin and Nukva ascend to Aba and Ima, whence the external forces and the Klipot cannot draw, Malchut **opens up to receive scents and fragrances, and to endow souls and pleasures for their children** of Zeir Anpin and Nukva, that are the souls of the righteous. **Woe to those people who the Holy One blessed be He,** Zeir Anpin, **is bound with in exile, and the Shechinah** that is Malchut **is bound with. It says regarding her, "the bound prisoner cannot extricate himself from the jailhouse."** (Tractate Berachot 5b)

30. וּפוּרְקָנָא דִּילָהּ דְּאִיהִי תְּשׁוּבָה, אִימָא עִלָּאָה, אִיהִי תַּלְיָא בִּידֵיהוֹן, דְּחַמְשִׁין תַּרְעִין דְּחֵירוּ עִמָּהּ, לְקָבֵל חַמְשִׁין זִמְנִין דְּאִדְכַּר יְצִיאַת מִצְרַיִם בְּאוֹרַיְיתָא דָּא הִיא וַיִּפֶן כֹּ"ה וָכֹ"ה, בְּאִלֵּין חַמְשִׁין אַתְוָן דִּמְיַוֲחַדִין לֵיהּ בְּכָל יוֹמָא פַּעֲמַיִם שְׁמַע יִשְׂרָאֵל, דְּאִית בְּהוֹן כֹּ"ה וְכֹ"ה אַתְוָן, וַיַּרְא כִּי אֵין אִישׁ דְּאִתְעַר לָהּ בְּגַוַּיְיהוּ.

30. And Her redemption, which is repentance, Supernal Ima, meaning Binah, **depends upon them,** meaning the elevating of Malchut to Binah, which represents correcting the Columns. **[Ima] has Fifty Gates of Freedom,** meaning Fifty Gates in Binah, **corresponding to the fifty times the exodus from Egypt is mentioned in the Torah. This is the meaning of "And he looked this way and that way (KoH and KoH)**

…" (Exodus 2:12) **using these fifty letters, with which one unifies the Holy One blessed be He, twice a day in the reading of "Hear Israel the Lord our God; the Lord is One," which contains KoH** 25 letters **plus KoH (25) letters. "He saw that there was no man"** (Ibid.) **to arouse Her** Binah **to shine into** Zeir Anpin and Nukva.

31. וְאִיהִי מַשְׁגִּיחַ מִן הַחֲלוֹנוֹת, דְּאִתְּמַר בְּהוֹן, וַלּוֹ נָא פְנֵי אֵ"ל וִיחָנֵּנוּ, לְהַהִיא דְּאִתְּמַר בָּהּ, אֵל נָא רְפָא נָא לָהּ, דְּאַסְוָותָא בִּידֵיהּ. דְּאִיהִי יָד פְּשׁוּטָה לְקַבֵּל שָׁבִים. וַיַּרְא כִּי אֵין אִישׁ.

31. And She, Binah: **"…looks in through the windows…"** (Song of Songs 2:9) **of which it is said: "And now, I pray you, entreat the favor of God…"** (Malachi 1:9) meaning they should elevate Feminine Water (Mayin Nukvin) by the Torah and the precepts **"that He will be gracious…"** (Ibid.) **to her, of whom it is said "Heal her now, God, I beseech You"** (Numbers 12:13) meaning Malchut, represented by Miriam. **For healing is in His hands, which is an outstretched hand to receive those who repent. "… and saw that there was no man…."** (Exodus 2:12)

32. וְאִיהִי בְּעַד הַחַלּוֹן נִשְׁקְפָה וַתְּיַבֵּב בִּתְרוּעָה, דְּאִיהוּ יְבָבָא, דְּאִתְּמַר בָּהּ וַיִּפְתַּח נֹחַ אֶת חַלּוֹן הַתֵּבָה אֲשֶׁר עָשָׂה, וְדָא יוֹם הַכִּפּוּרִים, דְּתֵיבַת נֹחַ הִיא אִימָא עִלָּאָה, חַלּוֹן דִּילָהּ הוּא עַמּוּדָא דְאֶמְצָעִיתָא, דְּבֵיהּ אוֹר, וְתוֹרָה אוֹר, וְאִיהוּ אוֹר הַגָּנוּז. וַיִּפֶן כֹּה וָכֹה, מֵצִיץ מִן הַחֲרַכִּים, אֵלּוּ עֲשֶׂרֶת יְמֵי תְשׁוּבָה. וַיַּרְא כִּי אֵין אִישׁ.

32. And she, Binah: **"Through the window she looked forth, and peered…"** (Judges 5:28) **with a Teru'ah, that is moaning. As is said** of Binah: **"Noah opened the window of the ark which he had made."** (Genesis 8:6) **This refers to Yom Kippur, as Noah's ark is the Supernal Ima,** Binah. **Her window is the Central Column,** Zeir Anpin, **in which there is Light,** according to the secret of: **"…and Torah is Light"** (Proverbs 6:23) since Zeir Anpin is considered Torah. **This is the Hidden Light (Or haGanuz),** in the secret of "the mother lends to her daughter from her own." "And he looked this way and that (*KoH* and *KoH*) way," to illuminate the Fifty Gates of Binah. "He peers through the lattices" are the ten intermediate days of repentance [between Rosh Hashanah and Yom Kippur], and "he saw that there was no man."

33. וְעוֹד, מַשְׁגִּיחַ מִן הַחַלּוֹנוֹת, אִלֵּין חַלּוֹנוֹת דְּבֵי כְנִשְׁתָּא, דְּאַבָּא וּבְנוֹי אִינוּן בְּבֵית אֲסִירָן וְאִיהוּ בְּכָל יוֹמָא אַשְׁגָּחוּתֵיהּ עֲלֵיהוּ, וְיָהִיב לוֹן מְזוֹנָא. וַיִּפֶן כֹּה וָכֹה, אִם אִית מָאן דְּיִתְעַר בְּתִיוּבְתָּא לְתַבְרָא בֵּית אֲסִירִין דִּלְהוֹן, הָדָא הוּא דִכְתִיב לֵאמֹר לַאֲסוּרִים צֵאוּ וְלַאֲשֶׁר בַּחֹשֶׁךְ הִגָּלוּ.

33. It could also be explained: "He looks through the windows," as referring to the windows of the synagogue because the father and the children, that is the Holy One blessed be He, and Israel are in the jailhouse during exile. And He watches over them daily and provides Israel their sustenance: "And he looked this way and that" to see if there is anyone awakened to repent in order to break down their own jailhouse, as is written: "Saying to the prisoners, 'Go forth;' to them that are in darkness, 'show yourselves.'" (Isaiah 49:9)

34. וַיִּפֶן כֹּה וָכֹה וַיַּרְא כִּי אֵין אִישׁ. אֶלָּא אִישׁ לְדַרְכּוֹ פָּנוּ, בַּעֲסָקִין דִּלְהוֹן, בְּאוֹרְחִין דִּלְהוֹן. אִישׁ לְבִצְעוֹ מִקְּצֵהוּ, בְּבִצְעָא דְּהַאי עָלְמָא, לְיָרְתָא הַאי עָלְמָא. וְלָאו אִינוּן מִסִּטְרָא דְּאִלֵּין, דְּאִתְּמַר בְּהוֹן, אַנְשֵׁי חַיִל יִרְאֵי אֱלֹקִי"ם אַנְשֵׁי אֱמֶת שֹׂנְאֵי בָצַע, אֶלָּא כֻּלְּהוּ צְוָוחִין בִּצְלוֹתִין בְּיוֹמָא דְכִפּוּרֵי, כִּכְלָבִים, הַב הַב כְּנָא מְזוֹנָא וּסְלִיחוּ וְכַפָּרָה וְחַיֵּי, כָּתְבֵנוּ לַחַיִּים. וְאִינוּן עַזֵּי נֶפֶשׁ, כִּכְלָבִים דְּאִינוּן אוּבִּין דְּעָלְמָא, דִּצְוָוחֵי לְגַבֵּיהּ, וְלֵית לוֹן בֹּשֶׁת אַנְפִּין.

34. "And he looked this way and that, and…he saw that there was no man," (Exodus 2:12) rather, each to his own way, bent on their own business, and their own ways: "each one to their own gain, one and all…." (Isaiah 56:11) All turn to their gain, from every quarter, to have profit in this world, in order to inherit this world, and they do not have qualities of these men of whom it says: "Able and God-fearing men, men of truth, hating unjust gain…." (Exodus 18:21) But they bark their

prayers on Yom Kippur (Day of Atonement), like dogs: "Give, give us sustenance, forgiveness, atonement, and longevity, record us for life." And they are insolent as those idol worshippers that scream to Him and are not ashamed to pray and plead just for their own benefit.

35. דְּלָא אִית מַאן דְּקָרָא לֵיהּ בִּתְיוּבְתָּא, לְמֶהֱדַר לְגַבֵּיהּ. וְאִדְּמִיָין לִכְלָבִים, דְּאִתְּמַר בְּהוֹן וַיִּתְעָרְבוּ בַּגּוֹיִם וַיִּלְמְדוּ מַעֲשֵׂיהֶם. וְאִינוּן עֵרֶב רַב, דְּכָל חֶסֶד דְּעָבְדִין, לְגַרְמַיְהוּ עָבְדִין.

35. For there is no one who calls to the Holy One blessed be He, **to repent and return to Him. And they are likened to dogs**, of whom is said: **"But mingled themselves with the nations, and learned their works."** (Psalms 106:35) **These are the mixed multitudes** (*erev rav*)**,** derived from "mingle," **that any kindness they do is for their own benefit** and not for the sake of their Creator.

36. וְעוֹד, אִינוּן שָׁאֲלִין מְזוֹנָא וְכִסּוּיָא וְעוֹנָה דְּאִיהוּ עוֹנַת וְגוֹ׳יְהוּ, דְּאִתְּמַר בָּהּ, שְׁאֵרָהּ כְּסוּתָהּ וְעוֹנָתָהּ לֹא יִגְרָע. וְלָא אִית מַאן דְּשָׁאִיל מְזוֹנָא, דְּאִיהוּ תּוֹרָה, שְׁאֵרָהּ דִּשְׁכִינְתָּא, וְאִיהִי אִימָא עִלָּאָה, דְּאִתְּמַר בָּהּ וְאַל תִּטּוֹשׁ תּוֹרַת אִמֶּךָ, כְּסוּתָהּ: דָּא כִסּוּיָא דְּצִיצִית, וְעַטִּיפוּ דִּילֵיהּ. וּתְפִלִּין דְּיָד, דְּאִתְּמַר בָּהּ תְּפִלָּה לְעָנִי כִי יַעֲטֹף. וְעוֹנָתָהּ: דָּא קְרִיאַת שְׁמַע בְּעוֹנָתָהּ. דְּאִם שְׁלשׁ אֵלֶּה לֹא יַעֲשֶׂה לָהּ לִשְׁכִינְתָּא, וְיָצְאָה חִנָּם אֵין כָּסֶף, לֵית לֵיהּ כִּסּוּפָא מִן שְׁכִינְתָּא, וְזָקוּף אִיהוּ. וְעוֹד אֵין כָּסֶף: לָא יְהֵא לֵיהּ כִּסּוּפָא לְעָלְמָא דְּאָתֵי.

36. Also, they request and plead for **their food, clothing, and mate** [lit. season]**,** meaning their time for mating, as is said **"...her food, her clothing, and her conjugal rights, shall he not diminish."** (Exodus 21:10) **But no one requests** spiritual **food, which is the Torah, the sustenance of the Shechinah, who is Supernal Ima,** Binah, **about whom it is said: "And do not forsake the teaching (Torah) of your mother."** (Proverbs 1:8) **"Her clothing" refers to the garment of Tzitzit and its enveloping,** with this fringed Tzitzit blessing: **"To envelope in Tzitzit," and also the arm Tefilin,** which are the Mochin of Malchut in the secret of "weak arm." [See Tikunei Zohar, Prologue 197] **Of it, it is said: "A prayer of the afflicted, when he faints [also: envelops]…."** (Psalms 102:1) **"And her conjugal rights [lit. season]" refers to the Shema reading on time.** Since by the Shema reading, the mating of Aba and Ima is made, in the secret of "her season" because from their union, Mochin flow to Zeir Anpin and Malchut so they could unite during the Amidah prayer, at "Bestow peace" (Sim shalom). **"And if he will not do these three to her,"** to the Shechinah: **"…then she shall go out for nothing, without money (kesef)."** (Exodus 21:11) **such a one has no humility before the Shechinah; he is impudent,** likened to impudent dogs. **Money (kesef) can also be interpreted as longing (kisuf) and craving: "…he will have no craving for the World to Come."** [See Zohar, Mishpatim 71 and 72]

37. וְהֵן כָּל אֵלֶּה יִפְעַל אֵ"ל פַּעֲמַיִם שָׁלשׁ עִם גָּבֶר, וּבְגִין דָּא, כִּי הִיא כְסוּתֹה לְבַדָּהּ, דָּא גִּלְגּוּלָא קַדְמָאָה. הִיא שִׂמְלָתוֹ לְעוֹרוֹ, דָּא גִּלְגּוּלָא תִנְיָינָא. בַּמֶּה יִשְׁכָּב, דָּא גִּלְגּוּלָא תְלִיתָאָה. וְאִלֵּין אִינּוּן תְּלַת לְבוּשִׁין, דִּתְלַת כִּסּוּיִין, דִּתְלַת גַּוְונִין דְּעֵינָא. דְּאִינּוּן לְבוּשִׁין לְבַת עַיִן, דְּאִיהִי נִשְׁמָתָא וּבְאִלֵּין תְּלַת אִתְּמַר, שָׁלשׁ פְּעָמִים בַּשָּׁנָה יֵרָאֶה כָּל זְכוּרְךָ.

37. **"Lo, God does all these things twice or three times with a man."** (Job 33:29) Meaning that the souls reincarnate to prepare for her three garments, which are the secret of the Three Columns. **Thus, it says: "For that is his only covering…"** (Exodus 22:26) **referring to the first incarnation, which stands for the Right Column, Chesed: "…it is his garment for his skin"** (Ibid.) **is the second reincarnation, the Left Column, Gevurah; "wherein shall he sleep"** (Ibid.) **is the third incarnation, the Central Column, Tiferet. And these are three garments of the three covers, in the three colors of the eye, which are covers for the pupil of the eye, which is the soul,** corresponding to Malchut that receives the Lights of the Three Columns, Chesed, Gevurah, and Tiferet. **And about these three we learned: "Three times in the year all your males shall appear (yera'eh)…"** (Exodus 23:17) and sight (re'iyah) is the secret of Chochmah.

לח. וְלָקֳבֵל תְּלַת גַּוְונִין אִינּוּן תְּלַת גַּוְונִין דְּשַׁרְגָּא, דְּאִתְּמַר בְּהוֹן וַיֵּרָא מַלְאַךְ
יְ"יָ אֵלָיו בְּלַבַּת אֵשׁ מִתּוֹךְ הַסְּנֶה. וַיֵּרָא, הָא גַּוְון חַד. בְּלַבַּת אֵשׁ מִתּוֹךְ הַסְּנֶה,
הָא גַּוְון תִּנְיָינָא. וַיֵּרָא וְהִנֵּה הַסְּנֶה בֹּעֵר בָּאֵשׁ, הָא תְּלִיתָא. וְאִינּוּן לָקֳבֵל שְׁלֹשָׁה
גַּוְונִין דְּעֵינָא. בְּלַבַּת אֵשׁ: דָּא בַּת עַיִן.

38. Corresponding to the three colors, Chesed, Gevurah, and Tiferet, **are the three colors in the candle light,** which are: a reddish, whitish and greenish flame, and sometimes black, in accordance with the meaning of, "black is red, really, except it is faulty." **About them it is said: "And the angel of the Lord appeared unto him in a flame of fire out of the midst of a bush…."** (Exodus 3:2) "And the angel of the Lord **appeared…" is one color,** Right, Chesed; **"…in a flame of fire out of the midst of a bush…" is a second color,** Tiferet, the Central Column that is from within. **"And he looked, and, behold, the bush burned with fire…"** (Ibid.) **is the third** color, the Left Column, Gevurah. **And they correspond to the three colors in the eye.** Chesed, Gevurah, and Tiferet; **"…a flame of fire…" is the pupil of the eye,** Malchut.

לט. בְּהַהוּא זִמְנָא דְּיִהוֹן נְהִירִין תְּלַת גַּוְונִין דְּעֵינָא, דְּאִינּוּן לָקֳבֵל תְּלַת גַּוְונִין
דְּקֶשֶׁת, מִיָּד וּרְאִיתִיהָ לִזְכֹּר בְּרִית עוֹלָם. וּבְהַהוּא זִמְנָא, כִּי עַיִן בְּעַיִן יִרְאוּ
בְּשׁוּב יְ"יָ צִיּוֹן.

39. During that time when all the three colors in the eye will illuminate, Chesed, Gevurah, and Tiferet of Chochmah, as eyes stands for Chochmah, **which correspond to three colors in the rainbow,** meaning Malchut, in which the Chochmah is revealed, **immediately: "And I will look upon it,"** by the Light of Chochmah called "seeing," **"…that I may remember the everlasting Covenant…."** (Genesis 9:16) **And about that time** is said, **"…for they shall see eye to eye, the Lord returning to Zion"** (Isaiah 52:8)

מ. אוֹר דְּעֵינָא, הוּא עַמּוּדָא דְּאֶמְצָעִיתָא. בַּת עַיִן, בֵּיתָא דִּילָהּ. בְּהַהוּא
זִמְנָא דְּיִתְפַּנֵּי עֲנָנָא מִן בַּת עֵינָא, דְּאִתְּמַר בָּהּ, סַכּוֹתָה בֶעָנָן לָךְ וְגוֹ' דְּאִיהִי

תְּבַלוּל דְּעֵינָא, דָּא רוּמִי רַבְּתָא, שְׁכִינְתָּא עִלָּאָה עֲתִידָה לְמֵימַר לְקוּדְשָׁא
בְּרִיךְ הוּא, לָמָּה תַעֲמוֹד בַּחוּץ, וְאָנֹכִי פִּנִּיתִי הַבַּיִת. אָנֹכִי, דִּיצִיאַת מִצְרַיִם.

40. The light of the eyes is the Central Column, Zeir Anpin. **The pupil of the eye,** Malchut, is **her house** of Chochmah, according to the meaning of: "Through wisdom, is a house built...." (Proverbs 24:3) **At that time, the cloud will clear out from the pupil of the eye, about which is said: "You have covered yourself with a cloud..."** (Lamentations 3:44) **which is a cataract in the eye,** something that confuses the eyesight (Tractate Bechorot 38b) **and this is greater Rome,** which is the Klipah that corresponds to Binah. Then, **the Supernal Shechinah,** Binah **will say to the Holy One blessed be He,** Zeir Anpin **"...why do you stand outside? For I (anochi) have prepared [lit. cleared] the house..."** (Genesis 24:31) meaning Malchut, **"I"** that is said **at the exodus of Egypt.** "I (anochi) am the Lord your God, who have brought you out of the land of Egypt..." (Exodus 20:2) meaning Binah, with the Light of Yechida.

41. וְאַף עַל גַּב דְּאֵין וָבוֹשׁ מַתִּיר עַצְמוֹ מִבֵּית הָאֲסוּרִים, דְּאִיהִי שְׁכִינְתָּא,
דְּאִיהִי אֲסוּרָה בְּגָלוּתָא, שְׁכִינְתָּא עִלָּאָה יִפְרוֹק לָהּ, הָדָא הוּא דִכְתִיב, אִם
יִגְאָלֵךְ טוֹב יִגְאָל וְאִם לֹא יַחְפֹּץ לְגָאֳלֵךְ וּגְאַלְתִּיךְ אָנֹכִי חַי יְ"יָ שִׁכְבִי עַד
הַבֹּקֶר. דְּאִיהִי יְמִינָא פְּשׁוּטָה לְקַבֵּל שָׁבִים, דְּלֵית מִלְּתָא דָא תַּלְיָא, אֶלָּא
בִּתְיוּבְתָּא. יְמִין עִלָּאָה דִּשְׁכִינְתָּא.

41. Even though our masters of blessed memory said, **"the bound prisoner cannot release himself from the jailhouse,"** which is the Shechinah, Malchut, **that is bound in exile, the Supernal Shechinah,** Binah, **will redeem her. This is the meaning of: "if he will act as a redeemer [lit. kinsman], let him redeem [lit. do the kinsman's part]. But if he is not willing to do the part of a redeemer [lit. kinsman] for you, I will do so myself, as the Lord lives; lie down until the morning"** (Ruth 3:13) **this is the right** hand called "morning" that is stretched to receive the penitent. As this matter of redemption **depends only on repentance, which is the right of the Supernal Shechinah,** which is Binah.

42. בְּהַהוּא זִמְנָא, שְׁכִינְתָּא עִלָּאָה כְּנֶשֶׁר יָעִיר קִנּוֹ, דְּאִיהִי יְרוּשָׁלַיִם, ק"ן ו', עַל גּוֹזָלָיו יְרַחֵף וְגוֹ', יְשָׂאֵהוּ עַל אֶבְרָתוֹ הָדָא הוּא דִכְתִיב, וָאֶשָּׂא אֶתְכֶם עַל כַּנְפֵי נְשָׁרִים וָאָבִיא אֶתְכֶם אֵלַי.

42. During that time of the redemption, **the Supernal Shechinah**, which is Binah, is "As an eagle stirs up her nest (*kino*, Kuf-Nun-Vav)..." (Deuteronomy 32:11) **which is Jerusalem,** Malchut, **the nest (*ken*, Kuf-Nun) of Vav,** Zeir Anpin, the Vav of the Name Yud-Hei-Vav-Hei. "...hover over her young...bears them on her pinions" (Ibid.) **is as written:** "...and how I bore you on eagles' wings, and brought you to Myself." (Exodus 19:4)

43. דְּבִזְמְנָא דִשְׁכִינְתָּא אִיהִי בְּגָלוּתָא אִתְּמַר בָּהּ, וְלֹא מָצְאָה הַיּוֹנָה מָנוֹחַ וְגוֹ'. אֶלָּא בְּשַׁבָּת וְיוֹמִין טָבִין, וּבְהַהוּא זִמְנָא אִתְיַיחֲדַת עִם בַּעְלָהּ. וְכַמָּה נִשְׁמָתִין יְתֵרִין קָא נָחֲתִין עִמָּהּ לְדַיְירָא בְּיִשְׂרָאֵל. הָדָא הוּא דִכְתִיב, וְשָׁמְרוּ בְנֵי יִשְׂרָאֵל אֶת הַשַּׁבָּת לַעֲשׂוֹת אֶת הַשַּׁבָּת לְדֹרֹתָם.

43. As when the Shechinah is in exile, in Briyah, Yetzirah, and Asiyah, **concerning her it is said, "And the dove found no rest for the sole..."** (Genesis 8:9) **except on Shabbat and Holidays,** when she elevates to Atzilut, **and during that period, She is united with Her husband** Zeir Anpin **and many extra souls descend with Her to dwell with Israel, as it is written: "Wherefore the children of Israel shall keep the Sabbath, to observe the Sabbath throughout their generations (*ledorotam*)..."** (Exodus 31:16) *ledorotam* is interpreted as: "their dwelling place (*lediratam*)."

44. זַכָּאָה אִיהוּ, מַאן דִּמְתַקֵּן לָהּ דִּירָה נָאָה, בְּלִבֵּיהּ. וְכֵלִים נָאִים, בְּאֵיבָרִים דִּילֵיהּ. וְאִשָּׁה נָאָה, דְּאִיהִי נִשְׁמָתָא. דְּבִגְנָהּ שַׁרְיָא שְׁכִינְתָּא עִלָּאָה, דְּאִיהִי נִשְׁמַת כָּל חַי עֲלֵיהּ. וְקוּדְשָׁא בְּרִיךְ הוּא אִיהוּ שַׁבָּת, בְּזֹד. וַיִּנָּפַשׁ, בְּזֹד. בִּשְׁכִינְתָּא עִלָּאָה אִיהוּ שַׁבַּת עֲלַיְיהוּ. וּבִשְׁכִינְתָּא תַּתָּאָה אִיהוּ וַיִּנָּפַשׁ עֲלַיְיהוּ. וְיָהִיב לוֹן נַפְשָׁאן יְתֵירָן, דְּאִינּוּן בְּתוּלוֹת אַחֲרֶיהָ רֵעוֹתֶיהָ, דְּקָא אַתְיָין עִמָּהּ.

44. Fortunate is he who prepares for Her, the Shechinah, **a pleasant abode in his heart, and nice vessels in his limbs, and a beautiful wife who is the soul, for whose sake the Supernal Shechinah will dwell upon it,** meaning Binah, **that is the soul of every living creature. And the Holy One blessed be He,** meaning Zeir Anpin, which stands for the Sabbath Day "rested (*shavat*), and was refreshed (*yinafash*)" (Exodus 31:17) **rested in one, and was refreshed in the other. With the Supernal Shechinah,** that is Binah, **He rests** upon Israel. **And with the lower Shechinah,** which is Malchut, **He prepares the Nefesh for them, providing them with extra souls, that are** called, **"…the virgins, her companions that follow her…."** (Psalms 45:15)

מה. וְכַמָּה מַלְאָכִים מִמַּנָּן וּמְשַׁמְּשִׁין דִּלְהוֹן, קָא אַתְיָין עִמְּהוֹן, דְּאִינוּן שַׁבְעִין דְּתַלְיָין מִן זָכוֹר וְשָׁמוֹר. וְדָא אִיהוּ וַיְכֻל"וּ, כְּלִיל שַׁבְעִין וּתְרֵין. וְאִתְקְרִיאוּ אִלֵּין נְפָשׁוֹת אוּשְׁפִּיזִין. בְּגִין דְּלָא שַׁרְיָאן בְּיִשְׂרָאֵל אֶלָּא בְּיוֹם הַשַּׁבָּת. וְכַד נָפִיק שַׁבָּת, כֻּלְּהוּ וְזֶרִין לְאַתְרַיְיהוּ.

45. And any ministering angels and their attendants come along with them, with these extra souls, **that are seventy,** like the numerical value of "wine" (*yayin*) [see Faithful Shepherd in Zohar, Pinchas 629], **which depend on "remember" and "keep"** that are Zeir Anpin and Malchut. **And this is the *Vayechulu*** [Friday Night Kiddush] **that includes 72,** corresponding to "remember" and "keep" plus the seventy words in the Kiddush. **These souls are called "guests" because they stay over Israel only on the day of Shabbat, and when Shabbat ends they all return** and elevate **to their place.**

מו. וְנִשְׁמָתִין דְּאִינוּן מִסִּטְרָא דִּשְׁכִינְתָּא עִלָּאָה, אִתְקְרִיאוּ בָּנִים. וְרוּוַח מט"ט דו"א דְּאִתְקְרִיאוּ אֶפְרוֹחִים. וְנַפְשִׁין מִסִּטְרָא דִּשְׁכִינְתָּא תַּתָּאָה, אִקְרוּן בֵּיצִים. וְדָא אִיהוּ רָזָא רֵשׁ סֻכַּת שָׁלוֹם עָלֵינוּ, אִימָא עִלָּאָה דְּאִיהִי סֻכַּת שָׁלוֹם, דְּמִסַּכֵּךְ עֲלַיְיהוּ, וְשָׁלוֹם עִמָּהּ. דְּאִתְּמַר בֵּיהּ הִנְנִי נוֹתֵן לוֹ אֶת בְּרִיתִי שָׁלוֹם.

46. The Neshamot, which are from the aspect of the Supernal Shechinah, Binah, **are called "sons;"** Ruach that is the aspect **of Metatron from Zeir Anpin** of Atzilut **are called "young chicks;" and Nefashot, which are from the aspect of the lower Shechinah,** Malchut, **are called "eggs." This is the meaning of** the benediction prayer [Friday Night Kiddush] on Shabbat eve, **"who spreads a Tabernacle of Peace upon us," referring to Supernal Ima,** Binah, **which is a Tabernacle of Peace that shields them and brings peace with it, concerning which it is said: "Behold, I give to him My Covenant of peace."** (Numbers 25:12)

47. וְאִית סוּכָּה לְתַתָּא, כ"ו ה"ס, דְּאִיהוּ יאקְדֹוּנק"י סוּכַּת שָׁלֹום. כּו"ס ת' דְּאִיהוּ תִּפְאֶרֶת. בְּהַהוּא זִמְנָא, יְהֹון בְּנִין בִּרְשׁוּתָא דְקוּדְשָׁא בְּרִיךְ הוּא, וְקָלָא נָפִיק וְיֵימָא, לֹא תִקַּח הָאֵם עַל הַבָּנִים. מִיָּד דְּנָפִיק זָכוֹר וְשָׁמוֹר דְּשַׁבָּת, וְיֵיתֵי לֵילְיָא דְּיוֹמָא קַמָּא דְשַׁבַּתָּא, קָלָא תִּנְיָינָא נָפִיק, שַׁלֵּחַ תְּשַׁלַּח.

47. There is a lower Tabernacle (Sukkah, Samech-Vav-Kaf-Hei), meaning Malchut. It equals **Kaf-Vav (26)** corresponding to Yud-Hei-Vav-Hei (26). Zeir Anpin, and **Samech-Hei (65)** is the numerical value of Adonai (65). **That is Yud-Alef-Hei-Dalet-Vav-Nun-Hei-Yud, a Tabernacle (Sukkat, Samech-Vav-Kaf-Tav) of Peace: cup (*kos, Kaf-Vav-Samech*),** Malchut, **plus Tav, which is Tiferet,** Zeir Anpin because Binah is called a Tabernacle of Peace since it shields her children, Zeir Anpin and Malchut, and protects them from the external forces. And on Shabbat, Malchut becomes one with Binah, and she, too, is called a Tabernacle of Peace. **At that time, the children will be under the rule of the Holy One blessed be He, and a voice goes forth and declares: "...you shall not take the mother bird together with the young...." And as soon as the "remember" and "keep" of Shabbat leave, and the night of the first day of the week arrives, a second voice emerges** and declares: "...but you **shall surely let the mother go."**

48. וְתוּ כִּי יִקָּרֵא קַן צִפּוֹר לְפָנֶיךָ, דָּא סוּכָּה, דְּאִיהִי אִימָא עִלָּאָה, בְּכָל עֵץ: הָדָא הוּא דִכְתִיב, וּלְקַחְתֶּם לָכֶם בַּיּוֹם הָרִאשׁוֹן פְּרִי עֵץ הָדָר. אֶפְרוֹחִים:

אִלֵּין שִׁבְעַת יְמֵי הַסֻּכּוֹת. אוֹ בֵּיצִים, דִּבְהוֹן עָבְדִין שֶׁבַע הַקָּפוֹת. וְרָזָא דְמִלָּה, נֻקְבָה תְּסוֹבֵב גָּבֶר. דָּא רָזָא וְהֶחֱזִיקוּ שֶׁבַע נָשִׁים בְּאִישׁ אֶחָד, דָּא קוּדְשָׁא בְּרִיךְ הוּא.

48. In addition, one should further explain the verse **"If a bird's nest chance to be before you…" This is the Tabernacle,** meaning the precept of Sukkah **that is** the Surrounding Light of **Supernal Ima,** Binah. "Bird" represents Aba in the secret of "…even a sparrow has found a home…" (Psalms 84:4) and Binah is the mother, in the secret of "If (*im*, which can be read as *em*, meaning mother) you call to understanding…" (Proverbs 2:3) and it is the secret of the precept of Sukkah, like a mother that hovers over her children, who are Zeir Anpin and Malchut. **"In any tree," refers to what is said** concerning Sukkot: **"And you shall take for yourselves on the first day the fruit of the citrus tree…"** (Leviticus 23:40) **"Young ones" are the seven days of Sukkot, in which seven encirclings (*hakafot*) are done,** one each day. The Lulav and its species stand for "young" (*efrochim*) because they bloom (*porchim*), and "eggs" stands for the Etrog, whose size is as an egg. **This is the secret meaning of: "…a woman shall court a man"** (Jeremiah 31:21) because the three festivals, Pesach, Shavuot, and Sukkot represent Chesed, Gevurah, and Tiferet. Pesach stands for the Right Column, Sukkot for the Left Column, the Female, and Shavuot for Tiferet. **And this is the secret meaning of "seven women** which stand for the Sukkot days **shall take hold of one man…"** (Isaiah 4:1) **this is the Holy One blessed be He,** signifying Tiferet and the holiday of Atzeret (Shavuot).

49. וּשְׁכִינְתָּא פְּרִי עֵץ הָדָר, אִימָא תַּתָּאָה. עֵץ: אִיהוּ לוּלָ"ב, לֹ"ו לֹ"ב נְתִיבוֹת דְּאִיהוּ אֶתְרוֹג. וְצָרִיךְ לְנַעְנְעָא בֵּיהּ לְשִׁית סִטְרִין, אַרְבַּע רוּחִין, וְעֵילָּא וְתַתָּא, לְאַתְעָרָא עֲלֵיהּ ו'.

49. And the Shechinah is "…the fruit of the citrus tree…" the lower Ima, Malchut. **The "tree" is the Lulav** and its species that stand for Zeir Anpin, **which has (*lo*, Lamed Bet; 32) paths** of Chochmah (Lulav is comprised of *lu*, which can be read as *lo*, meaning "it has," and *lav* equals 32, meaning "it has 32"), **which is the Etrog,** meaning Malchut, in which the Chochmah is revealed. Because from Supernal Chochmah until Malchut, which is called the lower Chochmah, none among the Sefirot can receive the illumination of Chochmah for itself. And this is the secret meaning of "Etrog is likened to the heart in which one contemplates." [See Zohar, Pinchas 822] **We need to shake it to the six sides, which are the four directions plus up and down, to awaken the Vav (6) over it** that stands for Da'at. [See the Gate of Meditations regarding Sukkot, discourse five]

50. וּתְכַלֵּת נְעֲנוּעִין לְכָל סִטְרָא, סָלְקִין חַ"י. וְצָרִיךְ אַרְבַּע זְמִנִין חַ"י, חַד בִּנְטִילַת לוּלָב וְחַד בְּאָנָא י"י, תְּרֵין אָחֲרָנִין בְּהוֹדוּ לַי"""י תְּחִלָּה וָסוֹף. וּבְאִלֵּין נְעֲנוּעִין, אִינּוּן מַשְׁפִּילִין מֵעֵילָא לְתַתָּא לְשַׁבְעִין וּתְרֵין. אוֹמִין פָּלְחֵי כּוֹכְבַיָא.

50. One needs **to shake three times to each side, and three times six equals eighteen. And four sets of eighteen are required,** which all together equals 72. And they are: **One when first taking the Lulav, one when saying "*Ana* (please) *Hashem;*" and the latter two, at the reading of the first and last "*Hodu* (praise) *laHashem.*" And during these shakings, one bestows to the 72 idol worshipping nations from above downward.** These are the seventy nations of the world and their root, Edom and Ishmael.

51. וּלְבָתַר דְּנָצְחֵי לוֹן אָמְרֵי אֲנִ"י וָה"ו הוֹשִׁיעָה נָא תְּרֵין זְמִנִין, דְּאִינּוּן וָא"ו מִן וה"ו. אֲנִ"י וה"ו מִן וַיִּסַּע וַיָּבֹא וַיֵּט, וּבְהַהוּא זְמְנָא, לֹא תִּקְוֹם הָאֵם עַל הַבָּנִים.

51. And after we conquer them, we say: *Ani Vahu Hoshia Na* **"We beseech You, help us"** twice. These are Vav-Alef-Vav from <u>Vav</u>-Hei-Vav, <u>Alef</u>-Nun-Yud, <u>Vav</u>-Hei-Vav (*vahu, ani, vahu*). Since besides the first *Ani* that is Malchut, there is Vav-Alef-Vav, from the acronym of Vav-Hei-Vav, Alef-Nun-Yud, Vav-Hei-Vav that is Zeir Anpin, **from** the verses: **"And the angel…removed…And it came…And Moses stretched out…"** (Exodus 14:19-21) from which the 72 Names are comprised, since the first of the 72 Names is the Name Vav-Hei-Vav. And in the middle, the 37 Name is

Alef-Nun-Yud. And towards the end, meaning the 49 Name, is the second Vav-Hei-Vav. **And during that time: "...you shall not take the mother bird together with the young...."**

בֵּיצִים, אִינוּן מִסִטְרָא דְאוֹפַנִים. אֶפְרוֹחִים, מִסִטְרָא דְנַעַר מטטרו"ן. .52 בָּנִים, מִסִּטְרָא דְכָרְסַיָּא, דְאִיהִי סֻכַּת שָׁלוֹם, דְאִיהִי קִנָּא דִשְׁכִינְתָּא.

52. Eggs are from the aspect of the wheels (*ofanim*) that are in the World of Asiyah. The young chicks are from the aspect of the young lad (*na'ar*), Metatron, meaning from the World of Yetzirah. **Sons are from the aspect of the throne,** meaning of the World of Briyah **that is the Tabernacle of Peace, which is the nest for the Shechinah.**

דְאִימָא עִלָּאָה מְקַנְּנָא בְּכָרְסַיָּא, בִּתְלַת סְפִירָן עִלָּאִין. עַמּוּדָא דְאֶמְצָעִיתָא, .53 כְּלִיל שִׁית סְפִירָן, מְקַנְּנָן בְּמטטרו"ן. אִימָא תַּתָּאָה, מְקַנְּנָא בְּאוֹפָן, דְאִתְּמַר בֵּיהּ, וְהִנֵּה אוֹפַן אֶחָד בָּאָרֶץ.

53. For Supernal Ima, meaning Tevunah of Atzilut, **is nestling in the Upper Three Sefirot,** Keter, Chochmah, and Binah of Atzilut that are clothed in her. She nestles **in the throne,** meaning in the World of Briyah. **The Central Column,** Zeir Anpin of Atzilut, **that includes Six Sefirot,** Chesed, Gevurah, Tiferet, Netzach, Hod, and Yesod of Atzilut, **nestles in Metatron, who is the secret of the World of Yetzirah. The lower Ima, Malchut of Atzilut, nestles in a wheel, the World of Asiyah, about which it is said: "behold one wheel upon the earth...."** (Ezekiel 1:15)

וְעוֹד שְׁכִינְתָּא מִסִּטְרָא דְכָרְסַיָּא, אִתְקְרִיאַת נֶשֶׁר. וּמִסִּטְרָא דְנַעַר יוֹנָה. .54 וּמִסִּטְרָא דְאוֹפָן, צִפּוֹר. וּשְׁכִינְתָּא דְמוּת אָדָם לָהֶנָּה.

54. It could be **further** discerned that **when the Shechinah,** Malchut of Atzilut, illuminates **in the aspect of the throne,** which is the World of Briyah, **She is called an "eagle." From the aspect of the young lad,** Metatron, the World of Yetzirah, She is called **a "dove." And from the**

aspect of the wheel, the World Asiyah, She is called **a "bird."** And all this is from the aspect of the Light of Chaya that comes from Malchut. **And the Shechinah,** meaning Malchut of Atzilut when it illuminates the Light of Yechida into Briyah, Yetzirah, and Asiyah is the secret of: **"…they had the likeness of a man"** (Ezekiel 1:5) because they receive from the aspect of the dot of Keter of Nukva that was diminished and descended to be the Atik of Briyah, Yetzirah, and Asiyah.

55. וְעוֹד, שַׁלֵּחַ תְּשַׁלַּח. תָּא וַחֲזֵי מַלְאָכָא אִית דִּמְמַנָּא עַל עוֹפִין, דְּאִינּוּן נַפְשִׁין, דְּאִתְקְרִיאוּ צִפָּרִין, וְסַנְדַלְפוֹ"ן שְׁמֵיהּ. וּבְזִמְנָא דְּיִשְׂרָאֵל מְקַיְּימֵי הַאי פִּקּוּדָא, וְאָזְלַת אִימָּא מִתְתָּרְכָא, וּבְנִין צָווֹחִין. אִיהוּ אוֹלִיף זְכוּ עַל עוֹפִין דִּילָהּ. וְאֵימָא לְקוּדְשָׁא בְּרִיךְ הוּא, וְהָא כְּתִיב וְרַחֲמָיו עַל כָּל מַעֲשָׂיו. אַמַּאי גְּזֵירַת עַל הַאי עוֹפָא דְּאִתְתָּרְכַת מִקִּנָּהּ.

55. There is more in the precept of dispatching the nest, as it says: **"But you shall surely let the mother go…"** Come and see, there is an angel assigned over birds, which are souls that are called "birds," whose name is Sandalfon, since he is at the end of the level stature and protects it from the external forces, like a sandal protects the feet. **And when Israel keep this precept** of dispatching the nest, **and the mother leaves and is banished, and the children cry, he advocates the merits of his birds** and pleads for mercy upon them, **and mentions to the Holy One blessed be He, what is written: "…and His tender mercies are over all His works."** (Psalms 145:9) **Wherefore then is this decree about this bird that was banished from its nest?**

56. וְכֵן מטטרו"ן אוֹלִיף זְכוּ עַל עוֹפִין דִּילֵיהּ, דְּאִינּוּן רוּחִין דְּפָרְחִין בִּבְנֵי נָשָׁא. דְּמִכֻּרְסְיָא אִינּוּן נִשְׁמָתִין, וּמֵהַאי חַיָּה רוּחִין, וּמֵאוֹפַן נַפְשִׁין, וְאִינּוּן בִּבְרִיאָה יְצִירָה עֲשִׂיָּה.

56. Likewise, Metatron pleads for the merits of his own birds, which are the spirits that fly into people, since from the throne, which is the World of Briyah, **come Neshamot, from this living creature** that is

Metatron **stem Ruchot, and from the Ofan, Nefashot. And they are in** the three Worlds: **Briyah** that is called the throne, from whence the Neshamot; **Yetzirah,** the World of the Angels, Metatron includes them all, from whence are the Ruchot; **and Asiyah,** the World of the Ofanim, from whence stem Nefashot.

57. בְּשַׁבָּת וְיוֹמִין טָבִין, נָחֲתִין עֲלַיְיהוּ נִשְׁמָתִין, וְרוּחִין וְנַפְשִׁין, בְּאֹרַח אֲצִילוּת, דְּאִינּוּן רוּחָא דְּקוּדְשָׁא מֵעֲשָׂר סְפִירָן. וְכָל מְמַנָּא אוֹלִיף זְכוּ עַל עוֹפִין דִּילֵיהּ, דְּאִינּוּן נִשְׁמָתִין דְּפָרְחִין בִּבְנֵי נָשָׁא. וּבְזִמְנָא דְּיִשְׂרָאֵל מְקַיְּימִין הַאי פִּקּוּדָא, כָּל מְמַנָּא אוֹלִיף זְכוּ עַל עוֹפִין דִּילֵיהּ.

57. On Shabbat and Holidays, Neshamot, Ruchot, and Nefashot descend on them through Atzilut, which are the Holy Spirit of the Ten Sefirot in Atzilut. **And each minister pleads the merits of his own birds,** which are the souls that fly into people. And when Israel observe this precept of dispatching the nest, **each minister pleads for the merits of his own birds.**

58. וְקוּדְשָׁא בְּרִיךְ הוּא מֶה עָבִיד, כָּנִישׁ לְכָל חַיָּלִין דִּילֵיהּ, וְיֵימָא הָא כָּל מְמַנָּא דְּעוֹפֵי דִלְתַתָּא אוֹלִיף זְכוּ עַל עוֹפִין דִּילֵיהּ דִּמְמַנָּא עֲלַיְיהוּ. וְלֵית בְּכוּ מָאן דְּאוֹלִיף זְכוּ עַל בְּנַי, דְּאִינּוּן יִשְׂרָאֵל, בְּנִי בְּכֹרִי יִשְׂרָאֵל. וְעַל שְׁכִינְתָּא דְּאִיהִי בְּגָלוּתָא, דְּקִנָּא דִּילָהּ דְּאִיהִי יְרוּשָׁלַיִם חֲרֵבָה. וּבְנוֹי בְּגָלוּתָא, תְּחוֹת יַד אֲדוֹנִים קָשִׁין אוּמִין דְּעָלְמָא וְלֵית מָאן דְּבָעֵי עֲלַיְיהוּ רַחֲמֵי, וְיוֹלִיף זְכוּ עֲלַיְיהוּ. בְּהַהוּא זִמְנָא צָווח קוּדְשָׁא בְּרִיךְ הוּא וְאָמַר לְמַעֲנִי לְמַעֲנִי אֶעֱשֶׂה. וְאֶעֱשֶׂה לְמַעַן שְׁמִי. וּבְדָא יִתְעַר עַל שְׁכִינְתֵּיהּ רַחֲמֵי וְעַל בְּנוֹי, דִּבְגָלוּתָא.

58. What does the Holy One blessed be He do? He gathers up all His hosts and says, "…each minister responsible for the birds below in Briyah, Yetzirah and Asiyah **pleads for the merits of the birds under his assignment. Is there no one among you to argue in favor of My children, Israel?"** As is said about them: **"Israel is My son, My firstborn."** (Exodus 4:22) **And the Shechinah that is in exile, whose nest is destroyed, which is Jerusalem, and His children are in exile** under the nations and no one to ask for mercy for them and argue in their favor. At that moment, the Holy One blessed be He cries out and declares: "For My own sake, for My own sake, will I do it…" (Isaiah 48:11) "…but I acted for My Name's sake…." (Ezekiel 20:14) And with this, mercy arouses towards His Shechinah and towards His children that are in exile.

59. קָם רַבִּי אֶלְעָזָר וְאָמַר, וְהָא קֳדָם דְּגָלוּ יִשְׂרָאֵל, וּשְׁכִינְתָּא, בַּמַּאי הֲווֹ מְקַיְּימִין שִׁלּוּחַ הַקֵּן. אָמַר לֵיהּ רַבִּי שִׁמְעוֹן, בְּרִי, בְּגִין לְאִתְעָרָא רַחֲמִין עַל אִינּוּן נַפְשִׁין וְרוּחִין וְנִשְׁמָתִין דַּהֲווֹ אָזְלִין בְּגָלוּתָא בְּגִלְגּוּלָא מִתְתַּרְכִין מִגּוּפַיְיהוּ דְּאִתְחֲרָבוּ, דַּעֲלַיְיהוּ אִתְּמַר, דְּקוּדְשָׁא בְּרִיךְ הוּא בּוֹנֶה עָלְמִין הֲוָה וּמַחֲרִיבָן, דְּאִשְׁתָּאֲרוּ חֲרֵבוֹן גּוּפַיְיהוּ מִנַּיְיהוּ.

59. **Rav Elazar rose,** asked and **said, "Yet before they went into exile, how did Israel keep** this precept of dispatching the nest?" Meaning if this precept is for the sake of awakening mercy for the unification of the Gadlut of Aba and Ima, face-to-face, then when the Israelites were not in exile and the unification of Aba and Ima, face-to-face with the Mochin of Gadlut, already existed both on Shabbat and weekdays, for what reason would they fulfill this precept? **Rav Shimon said to him, "My son,** the fulfillment of this precept was **to arouse compassion for those Nefashot, Ruchot, and Neshamot, that used to go** even then **into exile, banished from their ruined bodies, concerning which we learned that the Holy One blessed be He built worlds and destroyed them, and their bodies were left in ruins,** not being garments for the Nefesh, Ruach, and Neshama that disappeared **from them.**

60. וּמְנִיעוּ דְּבִרְכָאן לְעֵילָּא, גְּרִים וְנָהָר יֶחֱרַב וְיָבֵשׁ. וְהָכִי אוּקְמוּהוּ, אִתְחֲרַב בֵּיִת רִאשׁוֹן וְהָאָרֶץ הָיְתָה תֹהוּ וָבֹהוּ. אִתְחֲרַב בֵּית שֵׁנִי, וְחֹשֶׁךְ עַל פְּנֵי תְהוֹם. וּבְגִין אִלֵּין נִשְׁמָתִין, דְּאִתְבְּרִיאוּ קֳדָם דְּאִתְבְּרֵי עָלְמָא, וְלֵית לוֹן גּוּפִין. בְּגִין לְאִתְעָרָא רַחֲמֵי עָלַיְיהוּ, הֲווֹ מְקַיְּימֵי הַאי פִּקּוּדָא.

60. **And the withholding of blessings above,** which are the Lights of Chasadim, to the Zeir Anpin and Nukva of Atzilut **causes "…the river**

shall be drained dry" (Isaiah 19:5) and abundance will be prevented from flowing down to Briyah, Yetzirah, and Asiyah. **And it has been thus established that about the destruction of the First Temple** it is said: **"And the earth was without form and void"** (Genesis 1:2) **and concerning the destruction of the Second Temple** it is said: **"...and darkness was on the face of the deep..."** (Ibid.) **And for the sake of these souls that were created prior to the creation of the world, but have no bodies,** meaning that during the correction of the worlds, the vessels of the souls did not receive their correction, therefore **they used to fulfill this precept** of dispatching the nest **to arouse mercy for themselves** until we merit the Final Correction of "legs reached the legs" in a constant manner.

61. אָמַר לֵיהּ אַבָּא, אִם כֵּן תַּלְמִיד וְזָכָם, דְּאִיהוּ מִסִּטְרָא דְּמַחֲשָׁבָה, דְּאִתְּמַר בֵּיהּ, יִשְׂרָאֵל עָלָה בְּמַחֲשָׁבָה לִיבָּרְאוֹת, הַאי אוֹרַיְתָא אִיהוּ בֵן לְתַלְמִיד וְזָכָם, אִם כֵּן, אִתְּתָא דִּילֵהּ אַמַּאי צְרִיכָה יִבּוּם, דְּהָא לָא שָׁווּ אַפָּרְשׁוּתָא בְּאַרֵי מַתְנִיתִין לְתַלְמִיד וְזָכָם, מִשְּׁאָר בְּנֵי נָשָׁא.

61. Rav Elazar **said to** his father, Rav Shimon, **"Father, if** these souls that did not receive their correction during the correction of the worlds, get corrected by the precept of dispatching the nest, and not by the precept of Levirate Marriage (Yibum), and the secret of Yibum is to correct the soul of the deceased who did not leave a child, **a Torah scholar, who is in the aspect of thought (machshava),** which is broken up to *chashav* Mem-Hei (thought, 45), meaning he merited the Mochin of Gadlut of Atzilut, which is the secret of the Yud-Hei-Vav-Hei with Alef's that equals 45, **regarding whom is said, 'the thought arose to create Israel,' this Torah,** that he studied, **is like a son in relation to the Torah scholar, if so, why does his wife require a Levirate Marriage, seeing that the masters of the Mishnah did not make any differentiation between the Torah scholars and other people?** And if you say that it refers to other souls that did not receive their correction, have you not said, that those will be perfected by the precept of dispatching the nest?"

62. אָמַר לֵיהּ בְּרִי, וַדַּאי צְרִיכָה יִבּוּם לְאַלֵּין נִשְׁמָתִין, דְּאַזְלִין עַרְטִילָאִין מִשֵּׁשֶׁת יְמֵי בְּרֵאשִׁית. אָמַר לֵיהּ, וְהָא כְּתִיב לֹא יַחֲלִיפֶנּוּ וְלֹא יָמִיר אֹתוֹ וְגוֹ', וְכִי הַאי אִתְּתָא דְּאִיהִי קֹדֶשׁ קָדָשִׁין, תְּהֵא קִינָּא לְמַאן דְּלָאו אִיהוּ מִמִּינָהּ דְּהָא כְּתִיב תּוֹצֵא הָאָרֶץ נֶפֶשׁ חַיָּה לְמִינָהּ, וְלֵית לָהּ הַרְכָּבָה אֶלָּא מִמִּינָהּ.

62. Rav Shimon **said** to Rav Elazar, **"My son, she definitely requires a Levirate Marriage for** the benefit of **the souls that go naked ever since the six days of Creation."** Meaning for one who died without having children, and also did not have a brother to perform a Levirate Marriage with his wife. Rav Elazar **said to him, "Does it not say: 'He shall not alter it, nor change it…'?** (Leviticus 27:10) **Could then, this wife** of the Torah scholar **that is** considered **holy of holies, be a nest to someone not of her own kind,** who is not as holy as she is? **Is it not written: 'Let the earth bring forth living creatures after their kind'?** (Genesis 1:24) **And she can have no grafting except of her own kind,** the soul of a holy Torah scholar."

63. אָמַר לֵיהּ, בְּנִי גִּלְגּוּלִין אִינּוּן רָזָא דְּהַרְכָּבָה כְּגוֹן מָאן דְּמַרְכִּיב אִילָנָא דְּלָאו אִיהוּ מִמִּינֵיהּ, בְּאִילָנָא אָחֳרָא, כְּגוֹן מָאן דְּמַרְכִּיבִין אִלָּנִין דָּא בְּדָא, אֲבָל עִקָּרָא דְּאִם הָמֵר יְמִירֶנּוּ, צָרִיךְ דִּיהֵא קֹדֶשׁ בַּקֹּדֶשׁ.

63. Rav Shimon **said** to Rav Elazar, **"My son, incarnations are the secret of grafting, like someone who grafts one tree with another tree that is not its own kind** because the purpose of this inter-grafting of trees is to improve them. **But the principle of: 'And if he shall at all change,'** is to strive to draw a holy soul **that should be holy with holy** and not mundane in holy.

64. דְּאִילָנָא אִית מִסִּטְרָא דִּמְסָאֲבוּ, דְּאִיהוּ רַע. וּבְגִינֵיהּ אִתְּמַר, לֹא יָמִיר אֹתוֹ טוֹב בְּרַע וְרַע בְּטוֹב. דְּהַאי אִיהוּ רָזָא דְּצַדִּיק וְרַע לוֹ, רָשָׁע וְטוֹב לוֹ. אֲבָל אִם הָמֵר יְמִירֶנּוּ וְהָיָה הוּא וּתְמוּרָתוֹ יִהְיֶה קֹדֶשׁ. וּבְדָא מַרְכִּיבִין קֹדֶשׁ בַּקֹּדֶשׁ וּמְקַבְּלִין דֵּין מִן דֵּין. וְרָזָא דְּמִלָּה, מַקְבִּילוֹת הַלֻּלָאֹת. וּמִין בְּמִינוֹ הַאי אִיהִי צַדִּיק וְטוֹב לוֹ.

64. "As there is a tree from the aspect of impurity, which is bad, and about which it is said: '…nor change it, a good for a bad, or a bad for a good' (Leviticus 27:10) **which is the secret of 'the righteous for whom it is bad,'** meaning that he was evil in a previous incarnation. And similarly **'an evil man for whom it is good,'** meaning he was good in a previous incarnation. **However, 'And if he shall at all change…then both it and its substitute shall be holy' (Ibid.), and this way they graft holy with holy, and they benefit from each other,** according to the meaning of the verse: 'So I praised the dead that are already dead…' (Ecclesiastes 4:2) by their reincarnation into the living,' more than the living that are yet alive.' [See Zohar, Vayeshev 178] **It is the secret meaning of: '…the loops shall be opposite one another…'** (Exodus 26:5) meaning that the ties should all be on the part of holiness. **And a kind with its own kind refers to a righteous man for whom it is good.**

65. וְכַד הַהִיא נִשְׁמָתָא דְּאִיהִי קֹדֶשׁ, לָא אַשְׁכַּחַת מִינָהּ. אִתְּמַר בָּהּ, וְלֹא מָצְאָה הַיּוֹנָה מָנוֹחַ לְכַף רַגְלָהּ. וְהָכִי רָזָא דְּקֵן צִפּוֹר, דְּאִתְּמַר בָּהּ, שַׁלֵּחַ תְּשַׁלַּח אֶת הָאֵם, וְאָזְלָא מְנַדְּדָא מִן קִנָּהּ. וְהֶן כָּל אֵלֶּה יִפְעַל אֵל פַּעֲמַיִם שָׁלֹשׁ עִם גָּבֶר לָקֳבֵל תְּלַת שִׁלּוּחִים דְּיוֹנָה, וְכַד אַשְׁכַּחַת אֲתַר לְשַׁרְיָא תַּמָּן, אִתְּמַר בָּהּ, וְלֹא יָסְפָה שׁוּב אֵלָיו עוֹד. לְמֵיתֵי זִמְנָא אָחֳרָא בְּהַרְכָּבָה.

65. "But when that soul that is holy does not find its kind, it is said about her: 'But the dove found no rest for the sole of her foot….' (Genesis 8:9) **This is the secret of the bird's nest,** meaning the precept of dispatching the nest, **about which it is said: '…but you shall surely let the mother go….'** She goes and wanders from her nest, in the secret of the verse: "**Lo, God does all these things twice or three times with a man' (Job 33:29) corresponding to the three dispatches** said of the dove. **And when the soul finds a place to dwell there, it is said: 'and she did not return to him any more'** (Genesis 8:12) to come once more by grafting.

66. וּבְגִין דָּא, שִׁלּוּחַ הַקֵּן בְּכָל עוֹפִין קַדִּישִׁין אִיהוּ, דְּאִנּוּן נִשְׁמָתִין, דְּאָזְלִין מִתְתַּרְכִין, לְאִתְעָרָא רַחֲמֵי עֲלַיְיהוּ. וּמַה כְּתִיב בְּהוּ, גַּם צִפּוֹר מָצְאָה בַיִת,

דָּא גִּלְגּוּלָא קַדְמָאָה, דְּאִיהוּ נֶפֶשׁ. וּדְרוֹר קֵן לָהּ, דָּא גִּלְגּוּלָא תִּנְיָינָא, דְּרוּחָא. אֲשֶׁר שָׁתָה אֶפְרוֹחֶיהָ, דָּא גִּלְגּוּלָא תְּלִיתָאָה, דִּנְשָׁמָתָא.

66. "This is why the dispatching of the nest applies to all the holy birds, which are souls that wander around banished, to reawaken compassion upon them. And it is written about them: 'Even the sparrow has found a home….' (Psalms 84:4) This refers to the first incarnation, which is to correct the Light of **Nefesh.** '…and the swallow a nest for herself…' (Ibid.) is the second incarnation, of the Light of **Ruach;** '…where she may lay her young…' (Ibid.), is the third incarnation of the Neshama.'

67. וּבְגִין דָּא, שַׁלֵּחַ תְּשַׁלַּח, לְקַבֵּל נֶפֶשׁ וְרוּחַ. אֶת הָאֵם לְרַבּוֹת נְשָׁמָתָא. דְּאִתְּמַר בָּהּ, וּבְפִשְׁעֵיכֶם שֻׁלְּחָה אִמְּכֶם. אֶת הָאֵם, אֶת אָתָא לְרַבּוֹת, גִּלְגּוּלָא תְּלִיתָאָה.

67. "Therefore it is said: '…but you shall surely let go…' corresponding to Nefesh and Ruach: '…the mother' to include the Neshama, about which it is said: '…and for your transgressions was your mother sent away.' (Isaiah 50:1) [Concerning] **'the mother'** (et ha'em) the particle et is to add the third incarnation, to receive the Light of the Neshama called the "mother" (ha'em) that is Binah.

68. וּבְגִין דָּא, מָאן דִּמְקַבְּלִין אוֹשְׁפִּיזִין, דְּאִינּוּן נִשְׁמָתִין יְתֵרִין, דְּאִינּוּן מַרְכִּיבִין עֲלַיְיהוּ בְּעֶרֶב שַׁבָּת, בְּאַנְפִּין צְהוּבִין, בְּחֶדְוָה, בִּעֲנוּגָא בְּהַאי עָלְמָא. כַּד נִשְׁמָתָא וְרוּחָא וְנַפְשָׁא נָפִיק מִן גּוּפֵיהּ מֵהַאי עָלְמָא, הָכִי מְקַבְּלִין לוֹן בְּעָלְמָא דְּאָתֵי. וְאִתְּמַר בְּהוֹן, גַּם צִפּוֹר מָצְאָה בַיִת וכו'.

68." Consequently, those who receive the guests, which are the additional souls that are grafted on them on Shabbat eve, with a warm welcome and joy and pleasure in this world, when one's Neshama, Ruach, and Nefesh leave the body from this world, that is, at time of death, they are received similarly in the World to Come, with a joyous countenance. And it is said of them: 'Even the sparrow has found a home….'

69. זַכָּאָה אִיהוּ מָאן דִּמְקַבֵּל אוֹרְחִין בִּרְעוּ שְׁלִים, כְּאִלּוּ מְקַבֵּל אַפֵּי שְׁכִינְתָּא, דִּבְמִדָּה דְּמָדַד בַּר נַשׁ בָּה מוֹדְדִין לֵיהּ. אָתָא רַבִּי אֶלְעָזָר בְּרֵיהּ, וְנָשִׁיק יְדוֹי, וְאִשְׁתַּטְחוּ לֵיהּ כָּל חַבְרַיָּא, וְאָמְרוּ לֵיהּ, אִילוּ לָא אַתֵינָא לְעָלְמָא, אֶלָּא לְמִשְׁמַע מִלִּין אִלֵּין דַּיי.

69. "Happy is he who receives guests with complete desire, since it is as if he welcomes the face of the Shechinah, as 'the measure a person takes will be measured out to him.'" Rav Elazar approached and kissed his hand, and the rest of the friends prostrated themselves before him and said: "Had we come to this world just to hear this discourse, it would have been enough."

70. אַדְהָכִי, הָא אֵלִיָּהוּ קָא נָחֵית מֵעֵילָּא, בְּכַמָּה חֵילִין דְּנִשְׁמָתִין, וְכַמָּה מַלְאָכַיָּא סוֹחֲרָנֵיהּ וּשְׁכִינְתָּא עִלָּאָה עֲטָרָה עַל כֻּלְּהוּ, כֶּתֶר בְּרֵישׁ כָּל צַדִּיק. בְּהַהוּא זִמְנָא, קָלָא אִתְּעַר בְּאִילָנָא דִּלְעֵילָּא בְּנִגּוּנָא. וְכַמָּה עוֹפִין דְּנִשְׁמָתִין שַׁרְיָין תַּמָּן בְּעַנְפּוֹי. הָדָא הוּא דִכְתִיב, רְבָה אִילָנָא וּתְקִיף וכו'. וְיֵימָא הָכִי, רַבִּי רַבִּי, אַנְתְּ הוּא אִילָנָא דִּרְבָה, וּתְקִיף בְּאוֹרַיְיתָא. בְּעַנְפִּין דִּילָךְ, דְּאִינּוּן אֵבָרִין קַדִּישִׁין, כַּמָּה עוֹפִין שַׁרְיָין תַּמָּן, דְּנִשְׁמָתִין קַדִּישִׁין. כְּגַוְונָא דִּלְעֵילָּא, דְּאִתְּמַר בֵּיהּ, וּבְעַנְפּוֹהִי יְדוּרָן צִפֲּרֵי שְׁמַיָּא.

70. In the meanwhile Elijah descended from above, with many hosts of souls, surrounded by numerous angels, and the Supernal Shechinah, Malchut, a crown over all, a crown over the head of every righteous man. At that moment a melodic tune stirred in the Supernal Tree, Zeir Anpin, when many birds, souls, were residing there in the branches, as it is written: "The tree grew, and was strong...." (Daniel 4:8) And thus Elijah declared, "Rabbi, Rabbi, you are this tree that is great and strong in the Torah. In your branches, that are your holy limbs, there are many birds of souls holy like the souls above that dwell there, about which it is said: 'and the birds of the sky dwelt in its boughs.'" (Ibid. 9)

71. וְכַמָּה בְּנֵי נָשָׁא לְתַתָּא יִתְפַּרְנְסוּן מֵהַאי וֵזבּוּרָא דִּילָךְ, כַּד אִתְגַּלְיָא לְתַתָּאי. בְּדָרָא בַּתְרָאָה בְּסוֹף יוֹמַיָּא. וּבְגִינֵיהּ, וּקְרָאתֶם דְּרוֹר בָּאָרֶץ וגו'.

71. "And numerous people below, in this world, will be sustained from this compilation of yours that is the book of Zohar, when it will be revealed below in this world, in the final generation, in the end of days. And due to it, meaning by virtue of it, redemption will take place, as is said: '…and proclaim liberty throughout all the land….' (Leviticus 25:10)"

72. פָּתַח אֵלִיָּהוּ וְאָמַר כַּד נָפִיק שַׁבַּתָּא וְיוֹמִין טָבִין, וְיִשְׂרָאֵל אִינוּן תְּחוֹת מֶמְשָׁלָה דְסמא"ל וְשַׁבְעִין מְמַנָּן, וְדָחֲקִין לְיִשְׂרָאֵל, קָלָא נָפִיק מִן שְׁמַיָּא לְגַבֵּיהּ, וְיֵימָא הָכִי, יְרָ"א בֹּשֶׁ"ת. וְדָא בְּרֵאשִׁית, יְהֵא לָךְ כִּסוּפָא מִן שְׁמַיָּא, וְדָא [בְּרֵאשִׁית].

72. Elijah began and spoke, "At the end of Shabbat and festive days, when the additional soul departs, and Israel are under the dominion of Sama"el and the seventy ministers who distress Israel, a voice comes out from Heaven and declares to him as follows, 'awe, shame' (*yera boshet*), which is the anagram of **Beresheet,** meaning awe and shame will be appropriated to you from Heaven, and this is Beresheet."

For the fifth day of the month of Elul
Seventh Tikkun
Beresheet: *Yera Boshet* (Awe, Shame)

1. בְּרֵאשִׁית: יְרָ"א בּשֶׁ"ת. וַוי לֵיהּ לְסמָא"ל כַּד קוּדְשָׁא בְּרִיךְ הוּא יֵיתֵי לְמִפְרַק לִשְׁכִינְתָּא וּלְיִשְׂרָאֵל בְּנָהָא. וְתָבַע מִנֵּיהּ, וּמִשַּׁבְעִין אוּמִין וּמִמְּמַנָּן דִּילְהוֹן, כָּל עָאקוּ דְעָאקוּ לְיִשְׂרָאֵל בְּגָלוּתָא.

1. **Beresheet** is the anagram of *yera boshet* (awe, shame). Woe to Sama"el when the Holy One blessed be He will arrive to redeem the Shechinah and Israel, Her children, and prosecute him and the seventy nations and their ministers for every trouble they caused Israel in exile.

2. בְּגִין דְּקָדָם דְּגָלוּ יִשְׂרָאֵל, גַּלֵּי לֵיהּ קוּדְשָׁא בְּרִיךְ הוּא דַּהֲווֹ עֲתִידִין יִשְׂרָאֵל לְמֶהֱוֵי תְּחוֹת שִׁעְבּוּדַיְיהוּ. וְאַחֲזֵי לֵיהּ וּלְשַׁבְעִין מְמַנָּן דִּתְחוֹת יְדֵיהּ, אַגְרָא דִלְהוֹן, אִי הֲווֹ אוֹקְרִין לְיִשְׂרָאֵל בְּגָלוּתָא. הָדָא הוּא דִכְתִיב, וַיְבָרֶךְ יְ"יָ אֶת בֵּית הַמִּצְרִי בִּגְלַל יוֹסֵף.

2. Because before Israel went into exile, the Holy One blessed be He revealed to him that Israel will be under their yoke, and showed him, Sama"el, and the seventy ministers under him, their recompense if they would honor Israel in exile, as it says: "...the Lord blessed the Egyptian house for Joseph's sake..." (Genesis 39:5)

3. וְאִיהוּ וּמְמַנָּן דִּילֵיהּ לָא עָבְדִין לְהוֹן יְקָרָא, אֶלָּא עָבְדִין בְּהוֹן וּבִשְׁכִינְתָּא קְלָנָא, דְּאָמְרִין לוֹן כָּל יוֹמָא, אַיֵּה אֱלֹקֵי"ךְ. וּבְגִין דָא, קָלָא נָפִיק לְגַבֵּיהּ כָּל יוֹמָא מִן שְׁמַיָּא וְאָמַר. יְרָ"א בּשֶׁ"ת, יְהֵא לָךְ כִּסּוּפָא מִן שְׁכִינְתָּא. יְרָא שָׁמַיִם, יְהֵא לָךְ כִּסּוּפָא מִקּוּדְשָׁא בְּרִיךְ הוּא, דְּאִיהוּ שָׁמַיִם. הָדָא הוּא דִכְתִיב, וְאַתָּה תִּשְׁמַע הַשָּׁמַיִם, וְדָא בְּרֵאשִׁית.

3. But he and his ministers, not only do they not respect Israel, but cause them and the Shechinah disgrace, telling them daily: "Where is your God?" Therefore, a Voice comes out from Heaven, daily, to Sama"el

declaring "*Yera boshet,* you shall be ashamed of the Shechinah, *yere shamayim,* you shall have the awe of Heaven and ashamed before the Holy One blessed be He, called Heaven (*Shamayim*)," as it is written: "then hear You in Heaven...." (I Kings 8:34) And this is Beresheet the anagram of *yera Shamayim* (awe of Heaven), *yera bayit* (awe of house), as further explained in the eighth correction.

For the fifth day of the month of Elul
Eighth Tikkun
Beresheet: *Rosh Bayit* (Head of the House)

1. בְּרֵאשִׁית: ש', שָׁמַיִ"ם. יֵרֵ"א שָׁמַיִ"ם יֵרֵ"א בַּיִ"ת דִּילֵיהּ. דְּאִיהוּ רֹא"שׁ
בַּיִ"ת, דְּחִיל לֵיהּ בְּבֵיתֵיהּ, דָּא הוּא בְּרֵאשִׁי"ת. וְאִיהוּ וּמְמַנָּן דִּילֵיהּ לָא דְּחִילוּ
מִנֵּיהּ, וְחָרִיבוּ בֵּיתֵיהּ, בַּיִת רִאשׁוֹן וּבַיִת שֵׁנִי.

1. **Beresheet:** the letter **Shin** of the word *beresheet* hints to **Heaven** (*Shamayim*), namely Zeir Anpin. **His house** (*bayit*) **is awe** (*yir'ah*), which is Malchut. **For He is the head of the house** (*rosh bayit*); Zeir Anpin is Rosh, the Upper Nine Sefirot, and Malchut that is the house is his Female. [Meaning], **have awe of Him in His house, and this is** the anagram of **Beresheet. But he,** Sama"el **and his ministers, did not have awe of Him, and they destroyed the First Temple** [lit. house] **and the Second Temple.**

2. וּבְגִין דָּא, וְחָפְרָה הַלְּבָנָה דְּאִיהוּ נָחָשׁ אֵשֶׁת זְנוּנִים. וּבוֹשָׁה הַחַמָּה, דְּאִיהִי
גֵּיהִנָּם. דְּנָחָשׁ אֵשֶׁת זְנוּנִים חָרִיבַת בֵּיתָא דִּשְׁכִינְתָּא. וְחַמָּה דְּאִיהוּ גֵּיהִנָּם סַם
הַמָּוֶת, אוֹקִידַת הֵיכָלָא.

2. **Therefore** it says: **"Then the moon shall be confounded"** (Isaiah 24:23) **which is the serpent, a wife of harlotry. "And the sun ashamed"** (Ibid.) **is Gehenom,** meaning the Male and the Female of the Klipot. **Because the serpent, a wife of harlotry, destroyed the home of the Shechinah, and the sun, which is Gehenom, and the potion of death, burned the sanctuary.**

3. וּבְזִמְנָא דְּקוּדְשָׁא בְּרִיךְ הוּא בָּנֵי לוֹן כְּמִלְּקַדְּמִין הָדָא הוּא דִכְתִיב, בּוֹנֵה
יְרוּשָׁלַיִם יְ"י, בְּהַהִיא זִמְנָא וְחָפְרָה הַלְּבָנָה וּבוֹשָׁה הַחַמָּה. אֵימָתַי. בְּזִמְנָא דְּכִי
מָלַךְ יְ"י צְבָאוֹ"ת.

3. **At the time, when the Holy One blessed be He will reconstruct them as in the beginning, as is written: "The Lord builds Jerusalem"** (Psalms 147:2) **"Then the moon shall be confounded, and the sun ashamed...."**

When will this happen? "**When the Lord of Hosts will reign....**" (Isaiah 24:23)

4. דְּבִנְיָינָא קַדְמָאָה אִתְעֲבִיד עַל יְדֵי דְבַר נַשׁ, וּבְגִין דָּא שַׁלִּיטוּ עֲלַיְהוּ, בְּגִין דְּאָם יְ"י לֹא יִבְנֶה בַּיִת שָׁוְא עָמְלוּ בוֹנָיו בּוֹ. וּבְגִין דְּבִנְיָינָא בַּתְרָאָה יְהֵא עַל יְדָא דְקוּדְשָׁא בְּרִיךְ הוּא, יִתְקַיַּים. וְעַל דָּא אָמַר קְרָא, גָּדוֹל יִהְיֶה כְּבוֹד הַבַּיִת הַזֶּה הָאַחֲרוֹן מִן הָרִאשׁוֹן.

4. **Because the first building** of the two Temples **was constructed by man's hands, therefore the nations were able to dominate them, as is written: "Except the Lord build the house, they labor in vain that build it."** (Psalms 127:1) **The latter Temple will endure because it will be by the Holy One blessed be He, and about this, the verse says: "The glory of this latter house shall be greater than that of the former...."** (Haggai 2:9)

5. וּבְהַאי זִמְנָא דְּיִתְבְּנֵי בִּנְיָינָא עַל יְדָא דְקוּדְשָׁא בְּרִיךְ הוּא לְעֵילָא וְתַתָּא, אִתְּמַר בִּשְׁכִינְתָּא עִלָּאָה וְתַתָּאָה, וְהָיָה אוֹר הַלְּבָנָה כְּאוֹר הַחַמָּה. וְזָהֲרָה הַלְּבָנָה וּבוֹשָׁה הַחַמָּה דָּא סמא"ל וְנוּקְבָא דִילֵיהּ. וּבְגִין דְּלָא דְחִיל סמא"ל מִן קוּדְשָׁא בְּרִיךְ הוּא דְּאִיהוּ שָׁמַיִם. וּבַת זוּגֵיהּ לָא דְּחִילַת מִשְּׁכִינְתֵּיהּ, דְּאִיהִי אַרְעֵיהּ, אִתְּמַר בְּהוֹן, כִּי שָׁמַיִם כֶּעָשָׁן נִמְלָחוּ וְהָאָרֶץ כַּבֶּגֶד תִּבְלֶה, הוּא סמא"ל וּבַת זוּגֵיהּ.

5. **When the** Temple **structure will be rebuilt by the Holy One blessed be He above** in Atzilut, **and below** in this world, **it is said about the Supernal Shechinah,** Binah, **and the lower Shechinah,** Malchut, **"Moreover the light of the moon,** Malchut **shall be as the light of the sun..."** (Isaiah 30:26) that is Zeir Anpin with the Mochin of Gadlut from Binah. And it is also said: **"Then the moon shall be confounded, and the sun ashamed" which refers to Sama"el and his female,** which are the Male (Zeir Anpin) and the Female (Nukva) of the Klipot. **And because Sama"el,** the Male of the Klipah, **showed no awe towards the Holy One blessed be He, who is called Heaven,** Zeir Anpin, **and his mate** the Female of the Klipah,

had no awe towards the **Shechinah,** Malchut, **that is** called **Earth, it is said regarding them,** the Male and the Female of the Klipot: **"...for the Heavens shall vanish away like smoke, and the Earth shall grow old like a garment...."** (Isaiah 51:6) **This refers to Sama"el and his mate.**

For the sixth day of the month of Elul
NINTH TIKKUN
Beresheet: *Yera Shabbat* (Awe of Shabbat)

1. בְּרֵאשִׁית: יָרֵ"א שַׁבָּ"ת, דְּאִיהִי שְׁכִינְתָּא. דַּעֲלָהּ אִתְּמַר, מְחַלְלֶיהָ מוֹת יוּמָת. דְּעָאלוּ אוֹיְבִים בְּחָלָל דִּילָהּ, דְּאִיהוּ קֹדֶשׁ קָדָשִׁים. וְאִתְּמַר בְּהוֹן אֶת מִקְדַּשׁ יְ"יָ טִמֵּא. וְזֹלֵל מַמְלָכָה וְשָׂרֶיהָ.

1. The anagram of **Beresheet** is *yareh Shabbat,* fearful of desecrating the Shabbat, **which is the Shechinah,** meaning Malchut with the Mochin of the Upper Three Sefirot, **about which is written: "...everyone that profanes it shall surely be put to death...."** (Exodus 31.14) Because during the time of the destruction of the Temple **the enemies entered into her inner space,** which was established to be in the aspect of *avira dela ityada* [lit. air that is not known], **which is the Holy of Holies,** meaning the Upper Three Sefirot, since Kodesh is the secret of Keter and Kodashim is Aba and Ima. One who wants to draw Light to her space shall surely be put to death, **and it is said about them: "...because he has defiled the sanctuary of the Lord..."** (Numbers 19:20) **and also: "...he has profaned the kingdom and its princes."** (Lamentations 2:2)

2. וְשִׁפְחָה עָאלַת בַּאֲתַר דִּגְבִירָה, דְּאִיהִי נִדָּה שִׁפְחָה גּוֹיָה זוֹנָה. וְסָאִיבַת אַתְרָהָא, דְּתַמָּן הֲוָה נַיְיחָא דִּשְׁכִינְתָּא. וְקָלָא הֲוָה נָחִית וְאָמַר, יְרֵא שַׁבָּת, וְאִיהִי לָא עָבְדַת כָּךְ, אֶלָּא וְזֹלֵל מַמְלָכָה וְשָׂרֶיהָ. וּבְרַוַּות שְׁכִינְתָּא מִתַּמָּן.

2. And the maid, who is unclean (*niddah*), a handmaid, a heathen woman, a harlot, entered in place of the Shechinah that is **the Mistress, and defiled Her place, where the Shechinah dwelt. And a Voice came down and declared, "Fear Shabbat." But she,** the Female of the Klipah did not do so, but **"...profaned the kingdom and its princes."**

3. בְּהַהוּא זִמְנָא, עֲוֹנָקוּ עַל מִשְׁבַּתֵּיהָ, וְאָמְרַת שִׁפְחָה, לַאו הַאי, כְּגַוְונָא דְּעָבְדַת שָׂרֵי לְשִׁפְחָה דִּילָהּ, הָדָא הוּא דִּכְתִיב שָׂרֵי מִפְּנֵי שָׂרַי גְּבִרְתִּי אָנֹכִי בֹּרַחַת.

3. During that time of the destruction of the Temple **they "...gloated at her destruction."** (Lamentations 1:7) because they kept the Sabbath. **And the maid said, this is like what my mistress Sarai did to her maid,** in banishing her, **as is written: "I flee from the face of my mistress Sarai"** (Genesis 16:8)

4. אָמַר קוּדְשָׁא בְּרִיךְ הוּא, בְּרַתָּא דְרָשָׁע וַיָּיבָא. וְהָא אַף עַל גַּב דְּשָׂעֲרֵי תָּרְכַת לָהּ אֲנָא רְוִזימְנָא עֲלָהּ וְעַל בְּנָהּ, וְאַתּוּן לָא עֲבַדְתּוּן הָכִי אֶלָּא גְרַמְתּוּן בִּישׁ תְּחוֹת טָב. אֲנָא אוֹמֵינָא, לְאַעֲבָרָא מַלְכוּתָא וַיָּיבָא מֵעָלְמָא. וְלָא יְהֵא חֶדְוָה קֳדָמַי עַד דְּיִתְאֲבִידוּ מֵעָלְמָא. וּבְהַהוּא זִמְנָא, יְהֵא חֶדְוָה קֳדָמַי. הָדָא הוּא דִכְתִיב, וּבַאֲבֹד רְשָׁעִים רִנָּה.

4. The Holy One blessed be He said, "Even though Sarai banished this daughter of a sinful evil man, I had compassion for her and her son, but you did not behave like this, but you repayed good with evil. I swear to remove the evil kingdom from the world. And no joy will emanate from before Me until they perish. And at that time there will be joy before Me, as is written: "...and when the wicked perish, there is joy." (Proverbs 11.10)

For the sixth day of the month of Elul
Tenth Tikkun
Beresheet: *Shir Ta'ev* (Song of Longing)

‎1. בְּרֵאשִׁית: שִׁיר תָּאֵב. וְהָא אִיהוּ שִׁיר מְשׁוּבָּח מִכָּל הַשִּׁירִים. תָּאֵב מִכָּל
‎הַשִּׁירִים. וַעֲלֵיהּ אִתְּמַר, שִׁיר הַשִּׁירִים אֲשֶׁר לִשְׁלֹמֹה: לַמֶּלֶךְ שֶׁהַשָּׁלוֹם שֶׁלּוֹ,
‎הָכִי אוּקְמוּהוּ. וְהַאי שִׁיר מָתַי יִתְעַר. בְּזִמְנָא דְּיִתְאַבְּדוּן סמא"ל וּמְמַנָּן דִּילֵיהּ
‎וַיֵּיבַיָּא מִן עָלְמָא.

1. Beresheet is the anagram of *shir ta'ev* (**song of longing**), namely, the song
about which it says "…but when the wicked perish, there is joy." (Proverbs
11:10). **This hymn is the most praiseworthy of all songs, and about it is
said: "The Song of Songs, which is Solomon's"** (Song of Songs 1:1) **of the
King that peace (***shalom***) is his,** meaning Zeir Anpin. **Thus it has been
interpreted.** He asks, **"When will this song take effect?"** and replies,
"When Sama"el and his evil ministers will be removed from the world."

‎2. וּבְהַהוּא זִמְנָא, אָז יָשִׁיר מֹשֶׁה. אָז שָׁר לָא כְּתִיב, אֶלָּא יָשִׁיר. וְהָא אוּקְמוּהוּ.
‎וְהַאי שִׁיר בְּאָז, סָלִיק בְּפוּמָא. אֲבָל שִׁיר אִיהוּ וַדַּאי חָכְמַת שְׁלֹמֹה. בְּהַהוּא
‎זִמְנָא, וַתֵּרֶב חָכְמַת שְׁלֹמֹה. דִּבְהַהוּא זִמְנָא, וּמָלְאָה הָאָרֶץ דֵּעָה אֶת י"י כו'.

2. And at that time it is written "Then Moses sang [lit. will sing]…"
(Exodus 15:1); **it is not written "sang," but rather "will sing," and this
was explained** that Israel will recite this song in the future. [See Zohar,
Terumah 98] **And his song** that begins **with "Then,"** such as "Then
spoke Solomon…" (I Kings 8:12) or "Then spoke Joshua…" (Joshua 10:12)
is sung with the mouth, meaning Malchut that is called "mouth" and is
called the "spirit of holiness." **However, a** regular **song definitely refers to
the wisdom of Solomon,** meaning Malchut that is called "holy" like the
Supernal Chochmah. **At that time** it is said: **"And Solomon's wisdom
excelled"** (I Kings 5:10) **since of that time,** at the Final Correction, it is said
"for the earth shall be full of the knowledge of the Lord…." (Isaiah 11:9)

3. וּמָאן סָלִיק לָהּ לְאַתְרָהּ, דָּא מֹשֶׁה. וְרָזָא דְּמִלָּה, אָז יָשִׁיר מֹשֶׁה. בְּאָן סָלִיק לָהּ בְּזַרְקָא, הַאי תַּגָּא דְזַרְקָא, אִיהִי י' יָשִׁיר. וְתָקוּם מִן ה' דְּמֹשֶׁה, וְשַׁרְיָא עַל רֵישָׁא דְו'. וְאִתְעֲבִידַת תַּגָּא, וְסָלִיק לָהּ עַד אֲתַר דְּאִתְגְּזָרַת מִתַּמָּן.

3. And who will raise her, Malchut, to her place? Moses will, according to the secret meaning of: "Then Moses will sing (*yashir*)." He asks "Where will he raise her?" and responds, "With the Zarka of the cantillation marks, and the crownlet of Zarka is the Yud of *yashir*. And she will rise up by the Hei of Moses, reside on the head of the Vav and become a crownlet over the Vav to mean Zayin, and raise her to the place whence she was originally hewn from.

4. כַּד סָלְקָא לְגַבֵּי י' עִלָּאָה, אִתְקְרִיאַת שִׁיר. וְכַד נָחֲתָא לְגַבֵּי ה', אִתְקְרִיאַת שִׁירָה. הָדָא הוּא דִכְתִיב, אָז יָשִׁיר מֹשֶׁה וּבְנֵי יִשְׂרָאֵל אֶת הַשִּׁירָה הַזֹּאת לַי"י וְגו'.

4. "When she rises to the Yud that is the secret of Supernal Aba and Ima, in the secret of 'A virtuous woman is a crown to her husband...' (Proverbs 12:4) she is called *shir* (song, in the masculine), as in the verse '...the ark of the the Lord, the Lord of all the Earth...' (Joshua 3:13) where the verse refers to Malchut, which is the Ark of the Covenant, by the name 'master' (*adon*), a masculine term. And when she descends to the lower Hei to become the Female to Zeir Anpin, she is called *shirah* (song, in the feminine), as is written: 'Then will Moses and the children of Israel sing this *shirah* to the Lord....'

5. דַּעֲלָהּ אִתְּמַר, אֶבֶן מָאֲסוּ הַבּוֹנִים וְגו' דְּאִיהִי אַבְנָא דִי מְחָת לְצַלְמָא דַּעֲבוֹדָה זָרָה. בְּהַהִיא זִמְנָא דִּמְחָת לְצַלְמָא דַּעֲבוֹדָה זָרָה אִתְּמַר בָּהּ, וְאַבְנָא דִי מְחָת לְצַלְמָא הֲוָת לְטוּר רַב וּמְלָאַת כָּל אַרְעָא. הָדָא הוּא דִכְתִיב, מְלֹא כָל הָאָרֶץ כְּבוֹדוֹ.

5. "Concerning her it is said: 'The stone which the builders rejected...' (Psalms 118:22) which is the stone that struck the image of idol worship.

At that time when it strikes down the image of idolatry, it is said about it: 'and the stone that smote the image became a great mountain, and filled the whole earth.' (Daniel 2:35) This is the meaning of: 'the whole earth is full of His glory' (Isaiah 6:3) in the secret of the verse 'for the earth shall be full of the knowledge of the Lord....'

‫6. וְהָכִי סְלִיקַת, עַד דְּלָא אַשְׁכְּחִין לָהּ אֲתַר, וְשָׁאֲלִין מַלְאָכִין בְּגִינָהּ, אַיֵּה מְקוֹם כְּבוֹדוֹ לְהַעֲרִיצוֹ. וְלָא אַשְׁכְּחִין לָהּ שִׁיעוּרָא, עַד דְּאָמְרִין בָּרוּךְ כְּבוֹד יְ"יָ מִמְּקוֹמוֹ. בְּגִין דְּסָלְקָא לֵיהּ עַד אֵין סוֹף, דְּאִיהוּ י', רֵישָׁא דָא'.‬

6. "And thus, she ascends upwards until she can not be found, meaning to say, her place can not be reached. And the angels ask of her: 'Where is the place of His glory to adore Him,' but do not find her or comprehend the size of her stature, so they say: 'Blessed be the glory of the Lord from His place' (Ezekiel 3:12) because she ascended up to the Endless Light, which is Yud, the top of Alef, which signifies Keter. Therefore it is impossible to comprehend her."

‫7. וּבְאָן סְלִיקַת. בְּעַמּוּדָא דְּאֶמְצָעִיתָא, דְּאִיהוּ ו', עֲטָרָה עַל רֵישֵׁיהּ. כַּד סְלִיקַת עֲטָרָה עַל רֵישֵׁיהּ, אִתְּמַר בָּהּ, אֵשֶׁת חַיִל עֲטֶרֶת בַּעְלָהּ. וְכַד נְחִיתַת תְּחוֹתֵיהּ, אִתְקְרִיאַת בַּת זוּגֵיהּ, יְחוּדֵיהּ.‬

7. He asks, "To which level does she ascend?" And he replies, "To the Central Pillar—meaning to the Central Column because in the stature of Ibur she elevates to Yesod and she has the stature of Netzach, Hod, and Yesod. In Yenikah, she elevates to Tiferet and has the stature of Chesed, Gevurah, and Tiferet, and in Gadlut she elevates to Da'at and has the stature of Chochmah, Binah, and Da'at until she elevates to Keter—which is Vav, Zeir Anpin and she becomes a crown over His head. When He rises up to Keter and She has become a crown to His head, it is said about her: 'A virtuous woman is a crown to her husband...' (Proverbs 12.4) and when she descends under Him, she is called his spouse, meaning his wife and unity."

8. אִיהוּ תַּגָּא לְעֵילָא, תַּגָּא דְּסֵפֶר תּוֹרָה. בְּגִינָהּ אִתְּמַר, וּדְאִשְׁתַּמֵּשׁ בְּתַגָּא חֲלָף, וְאִיהִי נְקוּדָה דְּקָמֵ"ץ לְתַתָּא, יְחוּדֵיהּ. לְעֵילָא אִיהוּ כְּגַוְונָא דָּא א, תַּגָּא עַל סֵפֶר תּוֹרָה. לְתַתָּא כְּגַוְונָא דָּא א, נְקוּדָה דְּאוֹרַיְתָא, בְּגִינָהּ אִתְּמַר, מַגִּיד מֵרֵאשִׁית אַחֲרִית.

8. **Malchut is a crownlet above, the crownlet of the Torah scroll, about which it is said, "he who exploits the crown of the Torah for his own ends shall perish"** (Tractate Avot 1:13), since one should not keep her with the Mochin of the back. **[He] is the Kametz vowel below,** meaning the Mochin of the face, where she **unites** with him. **When she is above, she is like this: א, a crownlet of the Torah scroll,** which is the secret of Zeir Anpin. When she is **below,** with Mochin of the face, she is **like this: א, the vowel of the Torah,** since the cantillation marks are Keter, and the vowels are Chochmah. **About it, it is said: "Declaring the end from the beginning..."** (Isaiah 46:10) as Malchut is what is referred to in: "I am the first, and I am the last..." (Isaiah 44:6)

9. כַּד אִיהִי וַיָּה בֵּינַיְיהוּ, אוֹמְרִים מִמְּקוֹמוֹ, הוּא יִפֶן בְּרַחֲמָיו לְעַמּוֹ. כַּד אִסְתַּלִּיקַת מִינַיְיהוּ, שׁוֹאֲלִים אַיֵּה מְקוֹם כְּבוֹדוֹ לְהַעֲרִיצוֹ. וּבְהַהוּא זִמְנָא דְּסָלְקָא אִיהִי, כֻּלְּהוּ חֵיוָן תְּרַפֶּינָה כַּנְפֵיהֶם.

9. **When she is a living creature among them,** among the living creatures, as it is written: "...It flashed up and down among the living creatures..." (Ezekiel 1:13) meaning with the Shuruk vowel that is the aspect of Chochmah, which is called Chaya (Living Creature), and she is without Chasadim, **they say: "May He turn from His place in compassion toward His people,"** to clothe Chochmah with Chasadim. **And when she goes up from them,** meaning when she elevates to Aba and Ima to receive Mochin of the face, **they ask: "Where is the place of His glory to adore Him."** **And at the time she ascends, all the holy living creatures "let down their wings."** (Ezekiel 1:25)

10. וְאֵימָתַי סָלְקָא אִיהִי לְעֵילָא, בְּעָמְדָם יִשְׂרָאֵל בַּעֲמִידָה. הה"ד, בְּעָמְדָם
תְּרַפֶּינָה כַנְפֵיהֶם. דִּסְלִיקַת עַד אֵין סוֹף, לְמִשְׁאַל מְזוֹנָא מֵעִלַּת הָעִלּוֹת, וְכַד
נְחִיתַת, נְחִיתַת מַלְיָא מִכָּל טָבִין, בְּהַהוּא זִמְנָא חֵיוָן פָּתְחִין גַּדְפַּיְיהוּ לְגַבָּהּ,
לְקַבְּלָא לָהּ בְּחֶדְוָה בְּכַמָּה שִׁירוֹת וְתוּשְׁבְּחָן.

10. **When does she ascend above? When Israel stand upright** meaning in the Amidah prayer, as it is written: **"When they stood still, they let down their wings," because she ascends upward to the Endless Light to request food from the Cause of Causes. And when she descends, she comes down replete with every goodness,** meaning both Chochmah and Chasadim, **and at that moment the living creatures open up their wings towards her,** as is written: "And their wings were divided upwards" (Exekiel 1:11), **with many songs and praises.**

11. וּבְאָן אֲתַר נָחֲתַת. בָּאָת ו' דְּאִיהִי עַמּוּדָא דְּאֶמְצָעִיתָא בֵּיהּ קָרָאן לֵיהּ
שְׁמַע יִשְׂרָאֵל, שִׁי"ר אֵ"ל. וּבְהַהוּא זִמְנָא דְּנָחֲתַת, מַה כְּתִיב בְּחֵיוָן. וָאֶשְׁמַע
אֶת קוֹל כַּנְפֵיהֶם.

11. **He asks, "And where** that is to say, in which level, **does she come down?"** and answers, **"In the letter Vav,** which is the level of Zeir Anpin, **the Central Column,** that shines with Chasadim with which she is clothed. And Israel **call Him** and invite **Him** to receive her, **and say:** *Shema Yisrael,* an anagram—*shir El*—that is comprised of Chochmah and Chasadim, *El* from His Right and *shir* from His Left. **And when she descends, it is written about the living creatures: 'I heard the noise of their wings....'** (Ezekiel 1:24)"

12. קָם אֵלִיָּהוּ וְאָמַר. רַבִּי רַבִּי, וַחֲזוֹר בָּךְ. בְּוַדַּאי כַּד אִיהִי סָלְקַת, כֻּלְּהוּ
חֵיוָן מִצַּפְצְפִין לְגַבָּהּ, בְּכַמָּה שִׁירִין וְתוּשְׁבְּחָן, וְאִיהִי סָלְקָא עַל כֻּלְּהוּ, עַד אֵין
סוֹף. הֲדָא הוּא דִכְתִיב, רַבּוֹת בָּנוֹת עָשׂוּ חָיִל וְגוֹ'.

12. Elijah stood up and said, "Rabbi, Rabbi, recall your words, since Rav Shimon said that at the time of her ascent to Aba and Ima the living creatures let down their wings, and during her descent, to unite, it is written: 'And I heard the noise of their wings' (Ibid.). Elijah told him that the order was in reverse, that **surely, when she ascends, all the living creatures chirp to her with all kinds of songs and praises, and she rises above all to the Endless Light, as is written: 'many daughters have done virtuously....'** (Proverbs 31:29)

13. עַד דְּקָרְאן לָהּ יִשְׂרָאֵל לְתַתָּא בִּקְרִיאַת שְׁמַע, דְּתֵיחוֹת לְגַבַּיְהוּ. וּבְאָן קָרְאן לָהּ. בְּבֶן זוּגָהּ, דְּאִיהוּ ו', יִשְׂרָאֵל סָבָא. וְאִיהוּ שִׁיר אֵל, שִׁיר דִּילֵיהּ. דְּאִם לָא קָרְאן לָהּ בֵּיהּ, לָא נַחֲתָא עֲלַיְהוּ.

13. "This is until Israel below, in this world, raise Feminine Water (Mayin Nukvin), and **call to her in the Shema reading to come down to them."** He asks, **"And at which** level **do they call on her,** to reveal her illumination, either in her own aspect, which is the illumination of Chochmah or in the aspect of Zeir Anpin, which is the illumination of Chasadim?" He answers, **"Her spouse, which is Vav, Israel-Saba,** so she would illuminate by mating with Zeir Anpin, **and he is** called *shir El,* as the Female is included in him, **and she is his song, and if she is not called,** if her Chochmah is not clothed with his Chasadim, **she does not descend** to dwell **upon them.**

14. וּבְהַהוּא זִמְנָא דִּנְחִיתַת, קָשְׁרִין לָהּ בִּתְפִלָּה דְּיָד לְתַתָּא, דִּתְהֵא קְשׁוּרָה עִמֵּיהּ. וְרָזָא דְּמִלָּה וְנַפְשׁוֹ קְשׁוּרָה בְנַפְשׁוֹ.

14. "When Malchut **comes down, she is bound below** by diminishing Her Upper Three Sefirot to be the Lower Six Sefirot **with the hand Tefilin,** meaning to unite the small Zeir Anpin and Nukva that are below the chest, **so that She will be tied to Him** to clothe Her illumination of Chochmah with His Chasadim, **which is the meaning of: '...his soul (Nefesh) is bound up in the lad's soul (Nefesh).'** (Genesis 44:30)

15. וְקֶשֶׁר דְּתַרְוַוְיְהוּ, אִיהוּ שֶׁ"ר קְ לְתַתָּא. וּלְעֵילָּא שַׁלְשֶׁ"ת, תְּפִלִּין עַל רֵישֵׁיהּ. בְּרָזָא דְּטַעֲמֵי אִתְקְרִיַּת תְּנוּעָה. מִסִּטְרָא דִּנְקוּדָה יְוֹוּדָא.

15. "**The bond of both** Zeir Anpin and Nukva **is the Shuruk** meaning Vav and a dot. Vav hints to Zeir Anpin, and the dot hints to Nukva below, meaning to the place of the small Zeir Anpin and Nukva that receive from Yisrael-Saba and Tevunah, which are from the chest and below. **And above,** meaning the large Zeir Anpin and Nukva that are from the chest and above, and receive from the Supernal Aba and Ima, **is a Shalshelet** of the cantillation marks, **Tefilin on his head,** which are the Mochin of the large Zeir Anpin and Nukva. **In relation to the cantillation marks,** which are the Mochin of the back, Malchut **is called movement,** since She cannot receive Chochmah without Chasadim, and She is moved back and forth from Judgment to Mercy, and from Mercy to Judgment. **In relation to the vowels,** which are the Mochin of the face, Malchut **is called union** because She unites with Zeir Anpin and illuminates with Chasadim like Her husband Zeir Anpin.

16. וְצָרִיךְ לְאַרְכָא לָהּ בִּתְנוּעָה, דְּאִיהוּ רְבִיעַ, עַד אֵין סוֹף לְעֵילָּא. וְצָרִיךְ לְנַחֲתָא לָהּ בְּחִיר״ק עַד אֵין תַּכְלִית, לְאַמְלְכָא לָהּ עַל תַּתָּאִין, וּבְשׁוּרֶק צָרִיךְ לְיַחֲדָא לָהּ בְּבַעְלָהּ.

16. "**One should extend her by the movement, which is Ravi'a** of the cantillation marks that hints to Chasadim, which are the Right of the cantillation marks, **until** she will rise to the Light of **the Endless above** to receive Mochin of the Face, **and one should bring Her back down,** meaning draw the illumination of unification **by the Chirek,** which is the Light of Chasadim that comes out on the Masach of the lower level that is included in the level above it, signified by the Chirek that is under the letters, **without end, to have her reign over the lower beings** because there is no contraction (*tzimtzum*) at all on the Light of Chasadim, and it spreads from above downward. **And by the Shuruk that is the Left Column, one should unite her with her husband,** so that She will illuminate from below upward.

‎17. וּבְחוֹלֶ״ם אִיהִי תַּגָּא עַל רֵישֵׁיהּ. וּבְחִירֵ״ק אִיהִי כָּרְסַיָּא תְּחוֹתֵיהּ. וּבְשׁוּרֵ״ק אִיהוּ יִחוּדָא לְגַבֵּיהּ. כְּגַוְונָא דָא ו. וְכַד אִיהִי לְעֵילָּא תַּגָּא עַל רֵישֵׁיהּ, וְאִיהִי בְּרַתָּא תְּחוֹת רַגְלוֹי, וְאִיהוּ בְּיִחוּדָא דִּילֵהּ, בְּחֵיקֵיהּ, אִתְעֲבִידַת שׁוֹרֵ״ק קְשׁוּרָא דִּילֵהּ.

17. "And when She is as **Cholem**, which is **Right, She is a Crown over His head, and as the Chirek**, which is the Central Column, **She is a Throne beneath Him, and as the Shuruk**, which is the Left Column, **She unites with him**, to include Her illumination with His Chasadim **like a Vav with a dot. And when She is above, a Crown on His head descends down beneath his feet, and is united with Him to his Bosom**, meaning when She comprises the Three Columns, Right, Left and Central, that are the three vowels, Cholem, Chirek, and Shuruk, then Nukva **becomes a Shuruk** of three dots, which hint at all his three parts—beginning, middle, and end—that are included in Her, as She is **His bond** because He ties all Three Columns together by the Masach of Nukva that is included in Him.

‎18. וְכַד בָּעֵי לְתַבְּרָא קְלִיפִין, דְּאִינּוּן צְלָמִים. בָּהּ אִתְקְרֵי שְׁבָ״א, תְּבִי״ר. וּבָהּ עֲבַר תְּעַבֵּר מַצֵּבוֹתֵיהֶם. אֲבָל יִחוּדָא דִּילָהּ בִּנְקוּדַת שׁוּרֵ״ק ו דְּאִיהוּ יְסוֹד, חַ״י עָלְמִין, חַ״י בִּרְכָאן דִּצְלוֹתָא.

18. "And when She wishes to break down the Klipot, which are the images (idols), She is called Sh'va (Shin-Bet-Alef)**, meaning the Gevurah vowel, as in the verse: '…by fire (b'esh; Bet-Alef-Shin) will the Lord execute judgment…' (Isaiah 66:16) And from the Left of the cantillation marks She is called **Tevir, and by Her** attribute of Gevurah **'and break in pieces their images.'** (Exodus 23:24) **However Her union** with Zeir Anpin **is through the vowel Shuruk in Vav,** namely, Melopum, **which is Yesod, the Life** (*Chai*) of the worlds, the eighteen (*chai*) blessings of the Amidah prayer.

‎19. בְּזִמְנָא דְּאִינּוּן בְּיִחוּדָא וַדָּא, צְרִיכִין יִשְׂרָאֵל לְמֵיקַם בִּצְלוֹתָא, בַּחֲשַׁאי. וְרָזָא דְּמִלָּה, הָבִיאוּ לָהּ בַּחֲשַׁאי. וּבְגִין דָּא, בְּעָמְדָם יִשְׂרָאֵל בַּעֲמִידָה, לְאִתְעֲרָא לְגַבָּהּ חַ״י בִּרְכָאן בַּחֲשַׁאי, לַאֲרָקָא לָהּ בִּרְכָאן, אִתְּמַר בְּחֵוָין,

בְּעָמְדָם תְּרַפֶּינָה כַּנְפֵיהֶם. דְּלָא צָרִיךְ לְמִשְׁמַע גַּדְפַיְהוּ, כְּגַוְונָא דְּחַיָּה,
דְּאִתְּמַר בָּה וְקוֹלָהּ לֹא יִשָּׁמֵעַ.

19. "When Zeir Anpin and Nukva **are in union, Israel need to stand silent in prayer, and this is the meaning of** 'her servants **brought to her in silence.'** (Tractate Pesachim 56a) **Consequently, when Israel are standing** during the Amidah prayer **to silently stir towards Her the eighteen blessings, to pour on Her the benedictions, it is said regarding the living creatures: '...when they stood still, they let down their wings...'** since the sound of **their wings must not be heard. This is like Hannah's prayer: '...but her voice was not heard.'** (I Samuel 1:13)

20. וְהָכִי צְרִיכִין יִשְׂרָאֵל לְיַחֲדָא בְּבַת זוּגַיְיהוּ, בַּחֲשַׁאי בַּעֲנָוָה, בְּאֵימָה,
בִּרְתֵת, בְּזִיעַ, בִּכְסוּפָא כְּמָה דְּאוּקְמוּהוּ קַדְמָאִין, כְּמִי שֶׁכְּפָאוֹ שֵׁד, דְּאִיהִי
שֵׁד מָן עד"י. הִדְּבָהַהוּא זִמְנָא אִתְעֲבַר מִתַּרְעָא. וְדָא רָזָא דִּמְזוּזָה, דְּאִתְּמַר
בָּהּ וּכְתַבְתָּם עַל מְזוּזוֹת בֵּיתֶךָ, מְזוֹ"זַת כְּתִיב, זָ"ז מָוֶ"ת.

20. "And so should Israel unite **themselves with their wives, in secrecy, with humility, awe, trembling, quaking, and modesty as established by the earlier masters '...as one who is forced by a demon (**shed**),'** (Tractate Nedarim 20b) **that is the Shin-Dalet of the Name Shadai, which in that moment,** meaning at the time of unification, **is removed from the Gate,** namely, Malchut that is called '...the Gate of the Lord....' (Psalms 118:20) **And this is the secret of the Mezuzah, of which it is said: 'And you shall write them upon the doorposts of your house....'** (Deuteronomy 6:9) Mezuzot (מְזוּזוֹת) **is spelled with the same letters as** zaz mavet (זָ"ז מָוֶ"ת; death is moved away).

21. וְאִם הוּא אִשְׁתְּמַּע קָלֵיהּ, מִיָּד לַפֶּתַח חַטָּאת רֹבֵץ. וְלָא עוֹד, אֶלָּא דְּאִיהוּ
זָעִיר בִּמְהֵימָנוּתָא, וְלָא לְמַגָּנָא אוּקְמוּהָ קַדְמָאִין, כָּל הַמַּשְׁמִיעַ קוֹלוֹ בִּתְפִלָּתוֹ
הֲרֵי זֶה מִקְּטַנֵּי אֲמָנָה.

21. "**And if he raises his voice to be heard,** in the Amidah prayer, which is the time of unification, and wants to draw down her illumination from above downward, **instantly: '…sin crouches at the door….'** (Genesis 4:7) **Furthermore, he is of little faith,** which is the secret of the correction of the vessels, and he is drawn to the large Lights that cause the shattering of the vessels and the sin of the Tree of Knowledge. **And it was not in vain that the earlier masters have established, 'anyone who raises his voice to be heard in his prayer is of those of little faith.'** (Tractate Berachot 24b)"

22. בְּהַהוּא זִמְנָא דְמִיַחֲדָא קוּדְשָׁא בְּרִיךְ הוּא בִּשְׁכִינְתֵּיה, כֻּלְהוּ חַיָּוָן מְקַבְּלִין דֵּין מִן דֵּין בִּרְכָאן, וְכֻלְהוּ בִּקְדוּשָׁה. וּבְגִין דָּא, תַּקִּינוּ קְדוּשִׁין וּבִרְכָאן לְכַלָּה. וְלָקֳבֵל בְּרָכָה וּקְדוּשָׁה וְיִחוּד דְקוּדְשָׁא בְּרִיךְ הוּא. הָכִי צְרִיכִין יִשְׂרָאֵל דְּיֶהֱא יִחוּדָא דִּלְהוֹן בִּקְדוּשָׁה וּבִרְכָה, וְהָכִי כָּל מְזוֹנַיְיהוּ בְּבִרְכָה וּקְדוּשָׁה. וְלֵית קְדוּשָׁה פָּחוֹת מֵעֲשָׂרָה. דְאִיהִי י'.

22. When the Holy One blessed be He, is in union with His Shechinah, during the blessing of "Bestow peace" (*Sim shalom*) **all the living creatures receive blessings from each other, and everything is in a state of sanctity, and therefore the marriage ceremony** (*kidushin*) **and benedictions of the bride have been composed. And corresponding to the blessing, sanctity and unison of the Holy One blessed be He, Israel must perform their union with holiness and blessing. And similarly should be their eating,** which is the secret of union and mating, **with blessing and sanctity.** [See Zohar, Ekev 37] **And no holiness dwells upon less than ten people,** which hints to Yud of the Holy Name, namely Chochmah.

23. וּבְגִין דְּטַבַּעַת אִיהִי י', כְּגַוְונָא דָא ם, בָּה אִתְקַדְּשַׁת כַּלָּה. וְצָרִיךְ לְאַעֲלָא לָה בְּאֶצְבְּעָא דִילָה, דְאִיהוּ דְיוֹקְנָא דְאָת ו', וְאִתְעֲבִידַת ז'. וְצָרִיךְ תְּרֵין סַהֲדִין, דְּאִינּוּן לָקֳבֵל ה"ה. וְכַד אִיהִי טַבַּעַת בְּרֵישָׁא דְאֶצְבְּעָא, וְאִתְעֲבִידַת ז', בְּהַהוּא זִמְנָא צָרִיךְ לְבָרְכָא לָה בְּשֶׁבַע בִּרְכָאן דְּיַרְתָּא כַּלָּה.

23. And since the ring is in the shape of Yud that hints to Chochmah, which is "sanctity" **like [the final mem]** ם, which is all round, signifying

Supernal Aba and Ima that illuminate with covered Chasadim, **the bride,**
Malchut, **is sanctified by it.** And that ring **should be put on her finger
that is shaped like Vav, and it becomes Zayin,** in the secret of the verse:
"A virtuous woman is a crown to her husband…" (Proverbs 12:4) above the
chest, and "Blessings are upon the head of the righteous…" (Proverbs 10:6)
below the chest. [See the Third and Fourth Tikkun] **And two witnesses
are required, who correspond to the two Hei's** of the Name Yud-Hei-
Vav-Hei, which then completes the ring and the finger that are Yud and
Vav, and the two witnesses are the two Hei's. **And when that ring is at the
tip of her finger and becomes Zayin (7), she needs to be blessed by the
seven blessings, which are the inheritance of the bride** from Zeir Anpin
and Binah. [See Zohar, Terumah 791]

24. בְּהַהוּא זִמְנָא דְּמִתְיַחֲדִין, יִשָּׁקֵנִי מִנְּשִׁיקוֹת פִּיהוּ. מַאי נְשִׁיקוֹת פִּיהוּ. תְּרֵין
שִׂפְוָון דִּילֵיהּ, וּתְרֵין דִּילָהּ, אִינּוּן אַרְבַּע גַּדְפִין דְּחֵיוָון, דְּאִתְּמַר בְּהוֹן וְאַרְבַּע
כְּנָפַיִם לְאַחַת לָהֶם.

24. During the time of unification, it is said: **"Let him kiss me with the
kisses of his mouth** (*pihu*, Pei-Hei-Vav)…." (Song of Songs 1:2) **Why is it
written: "kisses of his mouth,"** it should read "your mouth."? He answers,
"Rather, **two of his lips and two of her** lips, meaning to say the mouth
of (*pi*) Hei-Vav, which are Zeir Anpin and Nukva. And the lips **are the
four wings of the living creatures,** concerning which is said about them:
'…and every one of them had four wings.' (Ezekiel 1:6) which are made
into one.

25. וְכַד אִתְכְּלִילָן תְּרֵין אַנְפִּין דִּילֵיהּ וּתְרֵין דִּילָהּ, וְאַרְבַּע דְּרוֹעִין דְּתַרְוַויְהוּ,
אִתְּמַר בְּהוֹן וְאַרְבָּעָה פָּנִים לְאֶחָת וְאַרְבַּע כְּנָפַיִם לְאַחַת לָהֶם. וְאִינּוּן אַרְבַּע
אַנְפִּין יהֹו"ה, אַרְבַּע גַּדְפִין אדנ"י, בְּחוֹבּוּרָא חֲדָא יאהדונה"י.

25. "And when his two faces and her two faces, **and the four arms of
both** are included, it is said regarding them: "And every one had four
faces, and every one had four wings." **And the four faces are** the four

letters of **Yud-Hei-Vav-Hei, and the four wings are** the four letters **Adonai. And when combined together they are Yud-Alef-Hei-Dalet-Vav-Nun-Hei-Yud.**

כו. כַּד מִתְחַבְּרָן אַתְוָון, אִקְרֵי חַשְׁמַל: חַיּוֹת אֵשׁ מְמַלְּלָן, וְזִמְנִין חָשׁוֹת וְזִמְנִין מְמַלְּלוֹת. וּבְגִינַיְהוּ אִתְּמַר, גָּדוֹל הָעוֹנֶה אָמֵן יוֹתֵר מִן הַמְבָרֵךְ. בְּגִין דְּבִמְתְחַבְּרִין חָתָן וְכַלָּה, תְּמַנְיָא אַתְוָון כַּחֲדָא.

26. "When the letters of Yud-Hei-Vav-Hei and Adonai **are joined together,** it is called *chash'mal,* which means *chayot esh memalelot* (muttering beasts of fire); sometimes they whisper (*chashot*) and sometimes they speak (*memalelot*) (See Tractate Chagigah 13b), meaning Zeir Anpin and Malchut that are the secret of "voice" and "speech" are in unification during the Amidah prayer, and then is the main dominion of Zeir Anpin, which is the aspect of Chasadim. And the illumination of Chochmah that is the secret of Adonai and speech, even though it also shines, it is considered a whispering speech, which does not dominate—and this is the meaning of 'sometimes they whisper.' When there is no unification, then the dominion of Malchut is noticed, which is the secret of speech and the illumination of Chochmah, and then 'sometimes they speak.' **About this it was said: 'Greater is he who answers "Amen,"** which is the secret of the unification of Yud-Alef-Hei-Dalet-Vav-Nun-Hei-Yud that equals the numerical value of Amen (91), **than one who recites the blessing'** because the unification and integration of Yud-Hei-Vav-Hei and Alef-Dalet-Nun-Yud only happens when the cantor repeats the Amidah and people answer 'Amen,' and not during the blessings of the prayer or the silent Amidah. He is greater **because the bride and groom,** Zeir Anpin and Malchut **are joined together,** which are **the eight letters** of Yud-Hei-Vav-Hei and Adonai **in unison,** which equal the numerical value of Amen (91)."

כז. אִינּוּן אַרְבַּע חֵיוָון אִינּוּן אדנ״י, וְאִינּוּן אַרְיֵה שׁוֹר נֶשֶׁר אָדָם. אַרְיֵה מְקַבֵּל עֲלֵיהּ י׳ בְּמוֹחָא. וּבְזִמְנָא דְּאִיהוּ בִּימִינָא, דְּאִתְּמַר בֵּיהּ וּפְנֵי אַרְיֵה אֶל הַיָּמִין לְאַרְבַּעְתָּם, הָרוֹצֶה לְהַחְכִּים יַדְרִים. שׁוֹר לִשְׂמָאלָא, לָקֳבֵל לִבָּא. ה׳ הֶבֶל

דְּלִבָּא תַּמָּן ה׳, מִצָּפוֹן זָהָב יֶאֱתֶה. בְּהַהוּא זִמְנָא דְּאִיהִי ה׳ בְּלִבָּא, הָרוֹצֶה
לְהַעֲשִׁיר יַצְפִּין.

27. These four living creatuers are the four letters of the Name **Adonai**,
which is Malchut, **and they are: a lion, an ox, an eagle, and a man.** And
he explains how they unite with the four letters Yud-Hei-Vav-Hei: **the lion
receives upon it the Yud in the brain** because each aspect of the Name
Adonai receives from the part corresponding to it in the Name Yud-Hei-
Vav-Hei. **And when it is** under the rule of **the Right,** which is Chasadim,
as said about it: "And they four had the face of a lion, on the right side"
(Ezekiel 1:10) then **"whoever wishes to get wiser should turn south,"** and
receives Chochmah of the Right from Supernal Aba and Ima, which is the
secret of the Yud in Yud-Hei-Vav-Hei. **The ox is to the left, corresponding
to the heart,** meaning Chochmah of the Left, **Hei** of Yud-Hei-Vav-Hei,
which is the secret of Yisrael-Saba and Tevunah, **the vapor (**hevel**)** that
rises **from the heart** to the brain **where Hei is,** which is Binah. **"Out of
the north comes golden splendor"** (Job 37:22) refers to Chochmah of
the Left that is called "gold." **When Hei is in the heart,** meaning under
the dominance of the Left Column, then, **"he who wishes to get wealthy
should turn north."**

28. יֽ״ה: דְּוֹחִילוּ, וּרְוֹוִימוּ. אַבָּא וְאִימָּא. דְּרוֹעָא יְמִינָא, וּשְׂמָאלָא. וַיַּעֲבֹ״ר:
חֶסֶד וּגְבוּרָה, דְּסַלְקִין לְחוּשְׁבַּן ע״ב תֵּיבִין, וְרִי״וּ אַתְוָון דְּע״ב שְׁמָהָן, וְדָא
רָזָא דְוַיַּעֲבֹ״ר, עִיבּוּר כְּלָל תַּרְוַויְיהוּ.

28. Yud and Hei of the Name Yud-Hei-Vav-Hei **are awe and love,** and
Aba and Ima, since Aba is the secret of the Supernal Aba and Ima, since
it relates to the simple Yud of Yud-Hei-Vav-Hei, which is Supernal Aba
that stores concealed Chochmah of Arich Anpin, and the Supernal Ima
is the secret of the filling of Yud (Vav-Dalet) and is the secret of Yisrael-
Saba and Tevunah, which is the first Hei of Yud-Hei-Vav-Hei. **The right
and left arms** are Chesed and Gevurah of Arich Anpin; Aba is linked
and depends on Chesed, and Ima is linked and depends on Gevurah.

"...passed by (*vaya'avor*, Vav-Yud-Ayin-Bet-Resh)..." (Exodus 34:6) equals the numerical value **of Chesed and Gevurah, which are 72 (Ayin-Bet) words and 216 (Resh-Yud-Vav) letters** from three times 72 letters that numerically are 216 **from the 72 Names,** extracted from the permutations of the three verses "And the angel of God..." (Exodus 14:19-21). Each verse has 72 letters totaling 216 letters. By the combination of the three verses together, they become 72 Names, three letters in each Name. **And this is the secret meaning of *vaya'avor*, denoting impregnation (*ibur*, Ayin-Yud-Bet-Vav-Resh), that includes both 72** Names and 216 letters.

29. ו', דָּא אוֹרַיְתָא, דְּשַׁרְיָא בְּפוּמָא. וּבְרוּחָא דְּפוּמָא פָּרְחַת עַל נֶשֶׁר, דְּנֶשֶׁר אִיהוּ חוֹטָמָא, תְּרֵין גַּדְפוֹי דִּילֵיהּ, תְּרֵין שִׂפְוָון. וַעֲלָהּ אִתְּמַר, כִּי עוֹף הַשָּׁמַיִם יוֹלִיךְ אֶת הַקּוֹל וּבַעַל כְּנָפַיִם יַגֵּיד דָּבָר. וְדָא עַמּוּדָא דְּאֶמְצָעִיתָא, דְּחָכְמָה וּבִינָה אִינּוּן נִסְתָּרוֹת בְּמוֹחָא וְלִבָּא, בִּרְחִימוּ וּדְחִילוּ, וְאוֹרַיְתָא בְּלָא דְחִילוּ וּרְחִימוּ, לָא פָּרְחַת לְעֵילָא.

29. Vav of the Name Yud-Hei-Vav-Hei **is Torah,** which is the secret of the Light of Ruach **that dwells in the mouth,** which is Malchut, Nefesh of Ruach. **And by the breath or wind (ruach) of the mouth,** in the secret of the verse: "For they are life to those who find them..." (Proverbs 4:22) the Returning Light **soars** from below upward **with the eagle, as the eagle is the nose, and the two lips are its two wings, and about it is said "...a bird of the air..."** (Ecclesiastes 10:20) namely the eagle, as is said "...the way of the eagle in the air..." (Proverbs 30:19) **"...shall carry the voice, and that which has wings shall tell the matter."** (Ecclesiastes 10:20) **And this** eagle, which signifies the nose **is the Central Column because Chochmah and Binah** that are the aspects of the lion and the ox **are hidden in the brain and the heart, with love and awe.** And the eagle is the secret of Torah and the Central Column that reconciles between Chochmah and Binah that are love and awe, and is composed of them. **And Torah without love and awe,** which are Chochmah and Binah, **does not fly upwards.**

30. וְכֶתֶר, בֵּיהּ תַּלְיָין בְּנֵי וַחַיֵּי וּמְזוֹנֵי. דְּאִיהוּ מַזָּלָא דְּכֻלְּהוּ. וְאִיהוּ לָא תַּלְיָא בְּמַזָּלָא. וּבְגִין דָּא אוּקְמוּהוּ, בְּנֵי וַחַיֵּי וּמְזוֹנֵי לַאו בִּזְכוּתָא תַּלְיָא מִלְתָא, אֶלָּא בְּמַזָּלָא תַּלְיָא מִלְתָא, דְּחֶסֶד אִיהוּ זְכוּתָא.

30. And upon Keter, meaning the beard of Arich Anpin, **depend children, longevity, and sustenance, which makes them all thrive. But it,** Keter, **is not dependent on luck** (*mazal*), **and therefore they established that "Children, longevity, and sustenance do not depend on merit but upon** *mazal* **does this matter depend"** (Tractate Mo'ed Katan 28a) **because Chesed is merit.**

31. ה' זְעֵירָא, דְּמוּת אָדָם, בָּהּ אִשְׁתַּלִּים יהו"ה וְהִיא מַלְכוּתָא קַדִּישָׁא, אִיהִי מִצְוָה, עֲשִׂיַּית פִּקּוּדִין. דְּאִיהִי שַׁרְיָא בְּרמ"ח אֵבָרִים. וְתוֹרָה וּמִצְוָה עֲלַיְיהוּ אִתְּמַר וְהַנִּגְלֹת לָנוּ.

31. The small Hei, meaning the last Hei of the Name Yud-Hei-Vav-Hei that is the secret of the small Hei in *behibar'am* "...when they were created..." (Genesis 2:4) is **the image of man,** as in the verse: "As for the likeness of their faces, they had the face of a man...." (Ezekiel 1:10) **With it, the Name Yud-Hei-Vav-Hei is perfected,** that is awe and love, Torah and precepts (*mitzvot*). **And She,** meaning the Hei, **the Holy Malchut, is the precepts, the performing of commandments. As She,** Malchut, **dwells in the 248 members of the body,** which correspond to the 248 positive precepts, **about the Torah and the precepts is said: "...but those things that are revealed belong to us...."** (Deuteronmoy 29:28) See what it says in Zohar, Naso 50 and 51: "If a person is in awe of the Holy One blessed be He or loves Him, no one else knows, for it is unknown except to himself and his Master. However, if a person studies the Torah and pursues positive commandments, it is known to everyone."

32. וְתוֹרָה וּמִצְוָה בְּלָא דְּחִילוּ, וּרְחִימוּ לָא יְכִילַת לְסַלְּקָא וּלְמֵיקַם קֳדָם י"ה, אִיהִי כְּלִילָא דְּכֹלָּא. וְעַל כֹּלָּא אָדָ"ם: יוּ"ד ה"א וא"ו ה"א. דָּא מַחֲשָׁבָה. דְּסָלִיק כֹּלָּא עַד אֵין סוֹף.

32. The Torah and the precepts, without an awakening of **awe and love, cannot rise and stand up before Yud-Hei.** Meaning to unify the Name Yud-Hei in Vav-Hei, to draw the Mochin of Aba and Ima to Zeir Anpin and Malchut. **She,** Malchut, **includes all of them** because all the Sefirot are included in Her, **and over all is man: Yud-Vav-Dalet, Hei-Alef, Vav-Alef-Vav, Hei-Alef.** [Yud-Hei-Vav-Hei spelled with Alef's, which equals 45 and is the same numerical value of *adam* "man"] **This is thought,** Zeir Anpin with the Mochin of Gadlut **that raises all of them to the Endless** because with the ascent of Zeir Anpin and Nukva, all ascend.

33. בְּמַלְכוּתָא אִשְׁתַּכְלִים כֹּלָּא, עֵילָא וְתַתָּא. וְאִיהִי כְּלִילָא מֵאַרְבַּע פַּרְשִׁיִּין דִּקְרִיאַת שְׁמַע, דְּאִינּוּן רמַ"ח תֵּיבִין עִם אַ"ל מֶלֶךְ נֶאֱמָן. וּבְגִין דְּלָא יַעַבְדוּן הַפְסָקָה תַּקִּינוּ לְמֶהְדַּר שְׁלִיחָא דְּצִבּוּרָא, יְ"י אֱלֹקֵיכֶ"ם אֱמֶת.

33. All are completed with the Sefira of **Malchut, above and below** because the upper Malchut is the Keter to the lower Malchut, and therefore they are considered complete. [See Zohar, Pinchas 839] **And she is composed of the four passages of the Shema reading.** The first passage is *Shema Yisrael...* "Hear Israel..." (Deuteronomy 6:4) and *Baruch Shem Kevod Malchuto Le'olam Va'ed.* "Blessed be the Name of the glory of His Kingdom forever and ever;" the second is "And you shall love..." (Ibid. 5); the third is "And it shall come to pass, if you hearken..." (Deuteronomy 11:13); the fourth is the section about the Tzitzit. **Together they contain 248 words.** In the first passage, 12 words, in the second, 42, in third 122, in the fourth 69, which add up to 245, **plus the three** words *El Melech Ne'eman* "God is a trusted King" totals 248 words. **And so as not to create a break** between the blessing of "who chooses his people Israel with love," and the Shema reading **it has been established that the cantor repeats "The Lord, your God is true"** again. [See Zohar Chadash, Ruth 714-717]

34. וְכַד יִשְׂרָאֵל אָמְרִין שְׁמַע, וַדַּאי חֵיוָון שָׁמְטִין גַּדְפַּיְיהוּ. בְּאָן אֲתַר. בְּכַנְפֵי מִצְוָה, דְּאִתְּמַר בְּהוֹן עַל אַרְבַּע כַּנְפוֹת כְּסוּתְךָ אֲשֶׁר תְּכַסֶּה בָּהּ, דְּאִיהוּ

כְּגַוְונָא דִּמְעִיל הָאֵפוֹד, דְּפַעֲמוֹנִים וְרִמּוֹנִים אִינוּן לָקֳבֵל זַלְזַלִין וְקִשְׁרִין. שׁוּלֵי הַמְּעִיל, אִינוּן לָקֳבֵל כַּנְפֵי מִצְוָה.

34. And when Israel recite the Shema, the living creatures certainly spread out their wings, as is written: "...and I heard the noise of their wings...." (Ezekiel 1:24) He asks, **"In which area** do we indicate this?" and answers, **"In relation to the precept concerning the corners [lit. wings] of the garment,** meaning the Talit, **about which it is said: '...upon the four corners [lit. wings] of your covering, with which you cover yourself.'** (Deuteronmoy 22:12) The Talit **is like the robe of the Efod. The bells and pomegranates,** about which it is said: "...the sound thereof shall be heard when he goes in to the holy place..." (Exodus 28:35) **correspond to the segments and knots** of the Tzitzit tassels [see Zohar, Balak 435]; **the lower borders of the robe correspond to the corners [lit. wings] of precept (*mitzvah*).**

35. וְאִינוּן חָמֵשׁ קִשְׁרִין, לָקֳבֵל שְׁמַע יִשְׂרָאֵל יְ"יָ אֱלֹקֵי"נוּ יְ"יָ. דְּאִינוּן לָקֳבֵל חָמֵשׁ נִימִין דְּכִנּוֹר דְּדָוִד, דַּהֲוָה מְנַגֵּן מֵאֵלָיו. י"ג חֻלְיָין כְּחוּשְׁבַּן אֶחָ"ד דְּקָלָא דְּנִגּוּנָא סָלְקָא בְּאֶחָד.

35. "And there are five knots that correspond to the five words: **'Hear, Israel, the Lord our God the Lord...'** (Deuteronomy 6:4) **which also corresponds to the five strings of David's harp that would play by itself,** and its sound was heard. **[There are] thirteen segments,** since there are 39 coils and each section of three coils is considered one segment, **like the numerical value of *echad* (one; 13) since the sound of the melody ascends** at the word *echad*, as the masters of blessed memory said 'anyone who lengthens the pronunciation of *echad*, his life is prolonged.'"

36. וְדָא וַ"י בֵּין חֻלְיָין וְקִשְׁרִין לְכָל סְטַר, סָלְקִין ע"ב. וְדָא אִיהוּ וְהוּכַן בַּחֶסֶד כִּסֵּ"א. חֶסֶ"ד: ע"ב. כָּל מָאן דְּאִתְעַטַּף בְּעִטּוּפָא דְּמִצְוָה, כְּאִלּוּ אַתְקִין כֻּרְסְיָיא לְקוּדְשָׁא בְּרִיךְ הוּא. וְאִינוּן יאהדונה"י, לְכָל חַד אַרְבַּע אַנְפִּין, וְאַרְבַּע גַּדְפִין סָלְקִין ס"ד, וּתְמַנְיָא אַתְוָון יאהדונה"י סָלְקִין ע"ב. וְכַנְפֵי מִצְוָה

אוֹלְפִין רָזָא, דְּאִינּוּן ח' חוּטִין לְכָל סְטַר, לָקֳבֵל אַרְבַּע אַנְפִּין וְאַרְבַּע גַּדְפִין, דְּכָל חַיָּה. וּבְחוּשְׁבַּן זְעֵיר דַּחֲנוֹךְ, אָ"ז אִיהוּ שד"י. אָז יָשִׁיר בְּכָל אֲתַר.

36. "And these eighteen, between the thirteen segments and five knots that together add up to eighteen, to each side of a Talit at the four corners, amount to 72, and this is what is meant by: 'And a throne is established in mercy (chesed)...' (Isaiah 16:5) Chesed equals 72. And anyone who envelopes himself with the garment prescribed by a precept is considered as if he established a throne for the Holy One blessed be He. And these four corners (wings) of the Talit and the four living creatures of the Throne are integrated from the two Names Yud-Alef-Hei-Dalet-Vav-Nun-Hei-Yud, each having four faces and four wings, as when multiplied by eight they equal 64, and together with the basic eight letters Yud-Alef-Hei-Dalet-Vav-Nun-Hei-Yud they total 72. And the corners of the garment, meaning the fringed tassels, teach us a secret. They consist of eight threads to each side of the Talit, corresponding to the four faces and four wings of each living creature. And according to the reduced numbers of Enoch, az (then; 8) equals Shadai (314; 3+1+4=8), through which all the Lights are revealed. Az yashir 'Then he will sing...' comes from 'singing' and 'gazing,' as is the secret meaning of Tzitzit, from the term 'peeking and peeping' (tziz umatzitz), which is the illumination of Chochmah, everywhere, without fear of the external forces."

37. וְאָמְרוּ מָארֵי מַתְנִיתִין כָּל מָאן דְּפָחֲוַית, לָא יִפָחוֹת מִשֶּׁבַע וְכָל מָאן דְּאוֹסִיף, לָא יוֹסִיף עַל י"ג. וְאִינּוּן שֶׁבַע, לָקֳבֵל שֶׁבַע יְמֵי בְּרֵאשִׁית דִּרְבִיוִין לְשֶׁבַע שִׁמְהָן אֲבֵנֵ"ד אבגית"ץ כו'. וַעֲלַיְיהוּ אִתְּמַר, שְׂרָפִים עוֹמְדִים מִמַּעַל לוֹ שֵׁשׁ כְּנָפַיִם שֵׁשׁ כְּנָפַיִם לְאֶחָד. דִּבְהוֹן פָּרְחַת צְלוֹתָא לְעֵילָא. וְאִינּוּן תַּמָּן מ"ב, לָקֳבֵל מ"ב אַזְכָּרוֹת, דְּאִינּוּן בִּתְפִלִּין דְּיָד וּתְפִלִּין דְּרֵישָׁא. וַעֲלַיְיהוּ אִתְּמַר, וְרָאוּ כָּל עַמֵּי הָאָרֶץ כִּי שֵׁם י"י וְגוֹ'.

37. The masters of the Mishnah said, "One who minimizes the sets of windings may not have fewer than seven sets, and one who adds to this number of sets may not have more than thirteen sets of windings."

(Tractate Menachot 39a) **And the seven correspond to the seven days of Creation,** of which Malchut is composed, **that hint to the seven Names: Alef-Bet-Gimel-Yud-Tav-Tzadik, etc.,** as in each Name comprises six letters, **and regarding them is said: "And above him stood the seraphim; each one had six wings"** (Isaiah 6:2) **with which the prayer,** which is Malchut, **soars up** and rises **above. And they are the 42-letter Name,** (6x7), **corresponding to the 42 Names in the arm Tefilin and the head Tefilin. And about them was said: "And all people of the earth shall see that the Name of the Lord is called upon you..."** (Deuteronomy 28:10) Thirteen stands for the Thirteen Attributes of Mercy, and Malchut is the opening to all of them and includes all of them. [See Zohar, Shlach Lecha 341]

38. וְאִינּוּן תַּכְשִׁיטִין דְּכַלָּה, תְּפִלִּין דְּרֵישָׁא עֲטֶרֶת זָהָב בְּרֵישָׁא דְּכַלָּה. וּתְפִלִּין דְּיָד, טַבַּעַת הַדְּרוֹעָא. הָא כַּלָּה מִתְתַּקְּנָא בְּתַכְשִׁיטִין דִּילָהּ, צָרִיךְ לְִקְרָא לְחָתָן דִּילָהּ. הָדָא הוּא דִכְתִיב שְׁמַע יִשְׂרָאֵל, וְהָא אִינּוּן בְּחוּפָּה.

38. And the Tefilin are the ornaments of the bride Malchut; **the head Tefilin is a gold crown on the brides head, and the arm Tefilin is the ring on the arm. And thus when the bride is ready with her jewels, her groom needs to be summoned, as is written: "Hear, Israel..."** (Deuteronomy 6:4) **and thus they are under their bridal canopy.**

39. צְרִיכָה עַמָּא קַדִּישָׁא לְמֵיקַם בַּעֲמִידָה קֳדָמֵיהוֹן, עִם חַזָּן לְבָרְכָא לוֹן בְּשֶׁבַע בִּרְכָאן, וּלְקַדְּשָׁא חֲתָן וְהַכַּלָּה בְּקָדְמֵיתָא בְּקִדּוּשִׁין. וּבְעָמְדָם עַמָּא קַדִּישָׁא, וְחַזָּן לְבָרְכָא לוֹן. חֵיָוָן קַדִּישִׁין דַּהֲווֹ מְנַגְּנִין בְּגַדְפַּיְיהוּ, תְּרַפֶּינָה כַּנְפֵיהֶן.

39. The Holy Nation, Israel, **need to stand upright in their presence, with a cantor to bless them with seven blessings after he sanctifies the groom and bride,** Zeir Anpin and Malchut, **in the marriage ceremony of Kidushin. "When they stood still,"** the holy nation and the cantor, **to bless them, the living creatures that were making music with their**

wings during the Shema reading: "…let down their wings" (Ezekiel 1:25) at the silent Amidah prayer.

40. שֶׁל תְּפִלִּין, דָּא אִימָא עִלָּאָה. עֲלָהּ אִתְּמַר, וְרָאוּ כָּל עַמֵּי הָאָרֶץ כִּי שֵׁם יְהֹוָ"ה נִקְרָא עָלֶיךָ וְיָרְאוּ מִמֶּךָ. שִׁי"ן סָלִיק אַתְווֹי ש"ס, ה' דְּיַד כֵּהָה שִׂא"ה. וְרַמַ"ח פִּקּוּדִין דְּכְלִילָן בְּרַמַ"ח תֵּיבִין דִּקְרִיאַת שְׁמַע בְּאַרְבַּע פָּרְשִׁיָּין, הָא תַּרְי"ג. עֲלַיְיהוּ אִתְּמַר, זֶה שְׁמִי לְעוֹלָם וְזֶה זִכְרִי לְדֹר דֹּר. שְׁמִ"י עִם י"ק שִׂא"ה, זִכְרִ"י עִם ו"ק רַמַ"ח, וְכֹלָּא תַּרְי"ג. אוֹרַיְתָא אִיהִי שְׁמָא דְּקוּדְשָׁא בְּרִיךְ הוּא.

40. The Shin of Tefilin is the Supernal Ima, Binah that shines with the Upper Three Sefirot of Chochmah, which are the secret of Shin (300) because the Sefirot of Binah are in hundreds. About her it is said: "And all the people of the earth shall see that the Name of the Lord is called upon you; and they shall be afraid of you." (Deuteronomy 28:10) The letters of Shin (Shin-Yud-Nun) equal 360; the Hei (5) of the weak hand is Malchut, and Malchut and Binah together equal 365. Plus the 248 precepts that are included in the 248 words of the four passages of the Shema reading, are together 613. About them is said: "This is My Name (Shmi) forever, and this is My Memorial (Zichri) to all generations." (Exodus 3:15) Shmi plus Yud-Hei equals 365 because the 365 negative precepts are the corrections of Chochmah, which is the secret of the Upper Three Sefirot, and therefore they are in the secret of Yud-Hei. Zichri plus Vav-Hei is 248, as the 248 positive precepts are the corrections of Chasadim, which are Zeir Anpin, and thus they are Vav-Hei. And all of them together equal 613. The Torah, which is the secret of Zeir Anpin with the Mochin of Gadlut, is the Name of the Holy One blessed be He in the secret of: "…the Name of the Lord…" (Deuteronomy 28:10) because awe and love stand for Yud-Hei, and the Torah and precepts stand for Vav-Hei.

41. וְעוֹד, צִיצִית אִיהִי כָּרְסַיָּא. תְּפִלִּין, קוּדְשָׁא בְּרִיךְ הוּא דְּנָחִית עַל כָּרְסַיָּא, דְּקָרְאָן לֵיהּ בִּקְרִיאַת שְׁמַע, הָא קוּדְשָׁא בְּרִיךְ הוּא יָתִיב עַל כָּרְסַיָּא. צְרִיכִין

לְמֵיקָם בְּגִינֵיהּ בִּצְלוֹתָא דַעֲמִידָה. תְּלַת וְזַיְלִין הֵיכָה אַתְיָין בְּזִמְירוֹת שִׁירוֹת
וְתִשְׁבָּחוֹת. בְּהַהוּא זִמְנָא דְאִיהוּ עַל כָּרְסְיֵיהּ, מַה אָמְרִין, אֵל מֶלֶךְ יוֹשֵׁב עַל
כִּסֵּא רַחֲמִים וּמִתְנַהֵג בַּחֲסִידוּת.

41. Furthermore, the precept of Talit and **Tzitzit is the throne. The Tefilin,** which are the Mochin of the Upper Three Sefirot, **by which the Holy One blessed be He comes down upon the Throne, when He is invited at the Shema reading,** by the clothing of the illumination of Chochmah of the Tefilin in the Chasadim of the Shema reading. **Thus the Holy One blessed be He sits upon the Throne,** which is the secret of the canopy, the Lower Six Sefirot, as mentioned. Therefore, **one needs to stand up in His honor in the Amidah prayer** to draw the Upper Three Sefirot of Mochin. This is because sitting is the secret of the Lower Six, since Netzach, Hod, and Yesod are not matured, and if the Netzach, Hod, and Yesod of the vessels are missing then the Upper Three Sefirot of Lights are also missing. Standing is the secret of the Upper Three Sefirot, like one who stands and reveals his entire stature. **Three camps from the hosts** of Malchut that are Ofanim from Asiyah, Chayot (Holy Living Creatures) from Yetzirah, and Seraphim from Briyah **arrive with melodies, songs, and praises** of the Amidah prayer. **When He sits on the Throne,** meaning after the Amidah, **they say: "God (El), the King sits on a throne of mercy and conducts Himself with kindness."**

42. הַאי תִּקּוּנָא אִיהוּ לְגַבֵּי צַדִּיקִים גְּמוּרִים, דִּמְתַקְּנִין כָּרְסַיָּא לְקוּדְשָׁא בְּרִיךְ
הוּא בְּצִיצִית, וְנָחֲתִין לֵיהּ בִּתְפִלִּין, וְקַיְימִין קֳדָמוֹהִי בִּצְלוֹתָא. לְבֵינוֹנִיִּים צִיצִית
וּתְפִלִּין אִינּוּן כַּשִּׁיעוּר לְעוֹל וְכַחֲמוֹר לְמַשְׂאוֹי. וּבְשַׁבָּת אִתְּמַר בְּהוֹן, לְמַעַן יָנוּחַ
שׁוֹרְךָ וַחֲמוֹרֶךָ. לָרְשָׁעִים אִינּוּן קְשִׁיעוּרָא לְכָל מְקַטְרְגִין דִּלְהוֹן.

42. This correction belongs to the completely righteous, who establish the Throne of the Holy One blessed be He through the precept of **Tzitzit, and they draw down** Mochin of the illumination of Chochmah with the precept of **Tefilin, then stand before Him in prayer. For the average [not completely righteous or wicked], the precepts of Tzitzit and**

Tefilin are like an ox that carries a yoke and a donkey that carries a burden. And on Shabbat, which is a day of rest, it is said about them: "... that your ox and your donkey may rest...." (Exodus 23:12) As for the wicked ones, by the precept of Tzitzit and Tefilin they tie up all their denouncers.

43. דְּהָכִי אִינּוּן עֲשָׂרָה כִּתְרִין עִלָּאִין, דְּמִתְלַבְּשִׁין בְּהוֹן עֲשַׂר אַתְוָון, דְּהָא לָקֳבֵל דָּא בְּרָא קוּבָּ"ה. אֲבָל כִּתְרִין תַּתָּאִין, אִינּוּן קְלִיפִין לְגַבֵּי כִּתְרִין עִלָּאִין, דְּמִתְלַבְּשִׁין בְּהוֹן עֲשַׂר אַתְוָון, בִּצְלוֹתָא, לְמֶהֱוֵי כְּפוּיִין תְּחוֹתוֹי כִּתְרִין תַּתָּאִין.

43. For such are the Ten Supernal Sefirot of Malchut, in which are clothed the ten letters Yud-Vav-Dalet, Hei-Alef, Vav-Alef-Vav, Hei-Alef [the spelling out of Yud-Hei-Vav-Hei that equals 45], which is Zeir Anpin with the Mochin of Gadlut, as the Holy One blessed be He created corresponding ones so each aspect will receive from the corresponding higher aspect, and therefore, the ten letters that are the Ten Sefirot of Zeir Anpin are clothed in the Ten Sefirot of Malchut. (Zohar, Pinchas 287) However, the lower Sefirot are like outer shells in relation to the upper Sefirot, in which the ten letters of the Yud-Hei-Vav-Hei that equals 45 are clothed during the prayer, so that the lower Sefirot should be subordinate under it.

44. וּבְזִמְנָא דְּצַדִּיקַיָּא מְתַקְּנִין בְּכַנְפֵי מִצְוָה וּבִתְפִלִּין, אִתְכַּפְיָין תְּחוֹתַיְיהוּ כִּתְרִין תַּתָּאִין. בְּהַהוּא זִמְנָא יֵעוּל מַלְכָּא בְּהֵיכָלֵיהּ, דְּאִיהוּ אדנ"י, כְּגַוְונָא דָּא יאהדונה"י, הָא מַלְכָּא בְּהֵיכָלֵיהּ, מַאן דְּבָעֵי לְמִשְׁאַל שְׁאֶלְתּוֹי, יֵעוּל. וּבְגִין דָּא אדנ"י שְׂפָתַי תִּפְתָּח.

44. And when the righteous make corrections by the fringed garment that is Tzitzit and by the Tefilin, the lower Sefirot become subordinate to them. At that moment the King, Zeir Anpin enters into His sanctuary, which is Adonai that is Malchut, and unification is accomplished, such as this Yud-Alef-Hei-Dalet-Vav-Nun-Hei-Yud, and then whoever wishes to

enter and make his requests, let him enter and ask. **And for this reason it is said, "God (Adonai), open my lips."** (Psalms 51:17)

45. בִּתְלַת קַדְמָאִין, יְסַדֵּר בַּר נַשׁ שְׁבָחוֹי כְּעַבְדָּא דִּמְסַדֵּר שְׁבָחוֹי קֳדָם רַבֵּיהּ. דְּאִלֵּין תְּלַת כָּתְבִין כָּל זַכְוָן. וּתְלַת בַּתְרָאִין חָתְמִין. וּבְגִין דָּא צָרִיךְ בַּר נַשׁ לְמֶעֱבַד בְּהוֹן כְּעַבְדָּא, דִּמְקַבֵּל פְּרָס מֵרַבֵּיהּ, וְהָלַךְ לֵיהּ. דְּהַתָּם אִיהִי בֵּית קִבּוּל, וְחוֹתָמָא דִּקְשׁוֹט. וְאִיהִי מַלְכוּתָא קַדִּישָׁא.

45. In the first three blessings of the Amidah prayer, called the Patriarchs, Gevurot, and the sanctification of the Holy Name, **one should prepare the praise** of the Lord, **like a servant that reads praises before his master. All the merits are inscribed in these three** blessings because they are the secret of Chesed, Gevurah, and Tiferet that are the hands that ascend to become Chochmah, Binah, and Da'at with which one writes, **and the last three** blessings, called desire (*retzeh*), thanksgiving (*hoda'ah*) and bestow peace (*sim shalom*), **seal. It is therefore appropriate for a person to conduct himself as a servant that receives a gift from his master, and goes on his way, since there,** in *sim shalom*, **is the receptacle,** a vessel that holds blessing, as the masters of blessed memory said, "The Holy One blessed be He found no vessel to hold blessing for Israel but peace," **the seal of truth** because they are the secret of Netzach, Hod, and Yesod that rise to become Chesed, Gevurah, and Tiferet. And Tiferet is the secret of Jacob, in the secret of the verse: "You will show truth to Jacob...." (Micah 7:20) And there **is the Holy Malchut,** which is the ring of the King.

46. בְּאֶמְצָעִיּוֹת צָרִיךְ לְמִשְׁאַל, דְּהַתָּם ו"ו, חַד מָארֵי כְּתִיבָה, וְחַד מָארֵי חֲתִימָה. וְאִינּוּן ו' עִלָּאָה, ו' תַּתָּאָה, כְּלִילָן תְּרֵין עֲשַׂר פִּרְקִין. תְּלַת קַדְמָאִין, רֵישָׁא וּתְרֵין דְּרוֹעִין. תְּלַת בַּתְרָאִין, גּוּפָא וּתְרֵין שׁוֹקִין. הָא אִתְפַּטַּר מִמַּלְכָּא, בְּגִין דָּא צָרִיךְ לְמֵיתַב תְּלַת פְּסִיעָן לַאֲחוֹרָא. וְרָזָא דְּמִלָּה, וַיֶּאֱסוֹף רַגְלָיו אֶל הַמִּטָּה.

46. In the middle blessings **one should ask** for personal needs **because there** are **two Vav's, one for the scribes and one for those who seal,**

which are the upper Vav, meaning Tiferet, and the lower Vav, Yesod. They are made of twelve sections that correspond to the twelve middle blessings. The first three blessings are the head and the two arms, up to the chest. The last three are the body and the two legs, namely from the chest down. And now when it is time for unication he hereby takes leave from the King and goes on his way so as not draw the illumination of the unification from above downward. Therefore, he should take three steps back, and the secret meaning of it is "…he gathered up his feet into the bed…." (Genesis 49:33)

For the seventh day of the month of Elul
Eleventh Tikkun
Beresheet: *Bara Sheet* (He created Six)

1. בְּרֵאשִׁית: בָּרָ"א שִׁי"ת. וּמַאי נִיהוּ. שִׁית הֵיכָלִין. אֱלֹקִי"ם: אִימָא עִלָּאָה,
דְּאִיהִי הֵיכָלָא שְׁבִיעָאָה, עֲלַיְיהוּ. וּכְמָה דְּאִימָא עִלָּאָה אַפִּיקַת שִׁית, הָכִי
אִימָא תַּתָּאָה אַפִּיקַת שִׁית, וּמַאי נִיהוּ. אֶת הַשָּׁמַיִם וְאֶת הָאָרֶץ. וְאִינּוּן שִׁית
מָאנִין, דְּאִתְּמַר בְּהוֹן כִּי שֵׁשֶׁת יָמִים עָשָׂה יְ"יָ אֶת הַשָּׁמַיִם וְאֶת הָאָרֶץ,
וְהֵיכָלִין תַּתָּאִין, אִינּוּן מָאנִין לְהֵיכָלִין עִלָּאִין.

1. **Beresheet** is the anagram of *Bara sheet* (He created six). He asks, **"Who they are they?"** and answers, **"Six chambers. Elokim is the Supernal Ima,** namely Binah, **which is the seventh chamber** because 'chamber' is a name of Malchut, and as each Sefira is composed of seven Sefirot, there is a chamber that acts as Malchut in each Sefira. **And like the Supernal Ima,** Binah **produced six chambers, so too the lower Ima,** Malchut, **produced six. Who are they? [They are] '...the Heavens and the Earth...'** (Genesis 1:1) that are Zeir Anpin and Malchut, since the Supernal Chamber includes the Upper Three Sefirot, and Yesod includes Malchut as well, which is the chamber called Livnat Hasapir (Chamber of Sapphire Stone [lit. brick]). **They are also six vessels, about which was said:'For in six days the Lord made Heaven and Earth...'** (Exodus 20:11) and the Sabbath Day is Malchut that shines with the illumination of the Upper Three Sefirot, and completes the six working days. **And the lower chambers are vessels for the upper chambers,** and each lower chamber receives from its corresponding upper chamber.

2. וְכַד יִשְׂרָאֵל הֲווֹ מְצַלָּאן, כָּל הֵיכָלִין אִלֵּין הֲווֹ מִתְפַּתְּחָן לְגַבַּיְיהוּ. וּכְעַן
בְּגָלוּתָא אִתְחֲמַר בְּהוֹן, כָּל הַשְּׁעָרִים נִנְעֲלוּ, וּשְׁכִינְתָּא לְבָר מֵהֵיכָלָה וְקוּדְשָׁא
בְּרִיךְ הוּא לְבָר מֵהֵיכָלֵיהּ. וּמַלְאֲכַיָּא דִּמְמַנָּן עַל צְלוֹתִין, לְבָר מֵהֵיכָלֵיהוֹן.
הֲדָא הוּא דִּכְתִּיב הֵן אֶרְאֵלָּם צָעֲקוּ חוּצָה. וְלָא אִית לוֹן לִצְלוֹתִין אֲתָר
לְעֵלָּא. וְדָא אִיהוּ כָּל הַשְּׁעָרִים נִנְעֲלוּ.

2. "When Israel were praying, all these chambers were opened towards them, to receive their prayers. But now, in exile, we studied about them that 'all the gates, namely the Malchut of Malchut of each chamber were locked,' (Tractate Berachot 32b) and the Shechinah, meaning the general Malchut, is outside Her chamber. And the Holy One blessed be He, Zeir Anpin, is outside His chamber, and the angels appointed over the prayers are outside their chambers. This is the meaning of: 'Behold, the mighty ones shall cry outside…' (Isaiah 33:7) and there is no place for the prayers to enter. And this is what is meant by 'and all the gates were locked.'

3. אֲבָל שַׁעֲרֵי דִמְעָה לֹא נִנְעֲלוּ, וְלֵית מָאן דְּאַפְתַּח לוֹן לְאִלֵּין שַׁעֲרִים עַד דְּיֵיתֵי מָארֵי דְּדִמְעָה, דְּאִתְּמַר בֵּיהּ, וַתִּפְתַּח וַתִּרְאֵהוּ אֶת הַיֶּלֶד וְהִנֵּה נַעַר בֹּכֶה, וְלֵית הֵיכְלָא מִתְפַּתְּחָא אֶלָּא בֵּיהּ. וְדָא אִיהוּ וַתִּפְתַּח, וַתִּפְתַּח וַדַּאי הֵיכְלָא לְגַבֵּיהּ. בְּמַאי אִתְפַּתַּח לֵיהּ בְּדִמְעָה. הֲדָא הוּא דִכְתִיב וְהִנֵּה נַעַר בֹּכֶה, וּמִיַּד וַתַּחְמֹל עָלָיו. וְעוֹד וַתִּפְתַּח, כַּד יִשְׂרָאֵל פָּתְחִין בִּתְיוּבְתָּא, בִּבְכִיָּה, מִיָּד וַתַּחְמֹל עָלָיו. וְדָא אִיהוּ בִּבְכִי יָבֹאוּ, בִּזְכוּת בְּכִיָּה דִילָהּ, יִתְכַּנְּשׁוּן מִן גָּלוּתָא.

3. "However, the Gates of Tears were not locked, for no one opens these gates of the chambers until those who shed tears arrive, of whom it is said: 'And she opened it, she saw the child, and behold, a boy that wept…' (Exodus 2:6) and the chamber is opened only through him. This is the meaning of '…she opened…' since that chamber is surely opened for his sake." He asks, "With what did he open it?" and replies, "With tears, as said: '…and behold, a boy that wept,' and immediately '…she had pity on him.' (Ibid.) It could also be explained: '…she opened…' refers to the Shechinah, when Israel begin their repentance with crying, she instantly '…had pity on him….' And this is the meaning of 'They shall come with weeping….' (Jeremiah 31:8) By virtue of his crying they will be gathered from the exile. [See Zohar, Shemot 203]

4. דְּאִית הֵיכְלָא דְּדִמְעָה, דְּלֵית לָהּ רְשׁוּ לְמִפְתַּח, אֶלָּא בְּדִמְעָה. וְאִית הֵיכְלָא דְּנִגּוּנָא, דְּלֵית לָהּ רְשׁוּ לְמִפְתַּח, אֶלָּא בְּנִגּוּנָא. וּבְגִין דָּא, דָּוִד מִתְקָרֵב

לְהַהוּא הֵיכְלָא בְּנִגּוּנָא. הָדָא הוּא דִכְתִיב, וְהָיָה כְּנַגֵּן הַמְנַגֵּן. וְאִית הֵיכְלָא
דִּנְהוֹרָא, דְּלָא מִתְפַּתְּחָא אֶלָּא לְבַר נַשׁ דַּהֲוָה מִתְעַסֵּק בִּנְהוֹרָא דְאוֹרַיְתָא.

4. "For there is a Chamber of Tears, which Malchut **is only allowed to
open by tears. And there is a Chamber of Melodies that she may open
only with a melody. It is for this reason that David approached that
chamber with melodies, as is written: 'And it came to pass, when the
minstrel played** that the hand of the Lord came upon him.' (II Kings 3:15)
**There is also a Chamber of Light that opens only to a person engaged in
the Light of Torah.**

5. וְאִית הֵיכְלָא דִנְבוּאָה, דְּלָא מִתְפַּתְּחָא אֶלָּא לְבַר נַשׁ, דַּהֲוָה וְחָכַם גִּבּוֹר
וְעָשִׁיר. וְאִית הֵיכְלָא דְיִרְאָה, דְּאִתְקְרֵי הֵיכַל הַיִּרְאָה, דְּלָא מִתְפַּתְּחָא אֶלָּא
לְמַאן דְּאִית בֵּיהּ דְּוֹזִילוּ. וְאִית הֵיכְלָא דַעֲנִיִּים, דְּלָא מִתְפַּתְּחָא אֶלָּא לַעֲנִיִּים,
דַּהֲווֹ מִתְעַטְּפִים קֳדָם י"י בִּצְלוֹתָא. וַעֲלֵיהוֹ אִתְּמַר, תְּפִלָּה לְעָנִי כִי יַעֲטֹף.

**5. "And there is a Chamber of Prophecy that opens only to a person who
is wise,** referring to Chochmah of the Right that is Chasadim, **mighty,**
referring to Chochmah of the Left called Gevurot, **and wealthy,** which is the
Central Column, Tiferet, Chochmah, and Chasadim together. The humble
and of high stature that is mentioned in the Talmud (Tractate Shabbat 92a,
and Nedarim 38a) are the secret of the corrections of the Masach. They are
both one, in the secret of 'he who is small is great' (Zohar, Shlach Lecha
210) because according to the density, Masach is the measurement of the
stature. **There is also the chamber called the Chamber of Awe, since it
is opened only to one who has awe. There is the Chamber for the Poor
that only opens to the poor, who delay** all prayers from entering **before
the Lord during the prayer service,** meaning that the pauper delays all the
previous prayers [of others] until his prayer enters, **and about them it is
said: 'A prayer for the afflicted when he faints....'** (Psalms 102:1)

6. וְאִית תַּרְעָא דְּצַדִּיקַיָּא, דְּלָא מִתְפַּתְּחָא אֶלָּא לְצַדִּיקַיָּא. הָדָא הוּא דִכְתִיב, זֶה הַשַּׁעַר לַי"ְ צַדִּיקִים יָבֹאוּ בוֹ. וְהַאי אִיהוּ תַּרְעָא דְּצַדִּיק חַ"י עָלְמִין, דְּאִתְּמַר בֵּיהּ וְלֹא רָאִיתִי צַדִּיק נֶעֱזָב וְזַרְעוֹ מְבַקֶּשׁ לָחֶם.

6. "And there is the Gate of the Righteous, referring to the crown of Yesod, which is Malchut, since Yesod and Malchut are one chamber, in the secret of Livnat Hasapir (Sapphire Stone), **that is opened only to righteous people, as is written: 'This is the Gate of the Lord, into which the righteous shall enter.'** (Psalms 118:20) **this is the Gate of Righteous Life of the World** (*tzadik chai olamim*)**,** meaning Yesod, of whom it is said: **'yet I have not seen the righteous forsaken nor his seed begging for bread.'** (Psalms 37:25) and it is also said pertaining to him 'Blessing are upon the head of the righteous….' (Proverbs 10:6)

7. וּכְעַן בְּגָלוּתָא, אִתְּמַר בֵּיהּ הַצַּדִּיק אָבָד. מַאי אָבָד. אָבַד לְמַטְרוֹנִיתָא. וְאִתְּמַר בֵּיהּ, וְנָהָר יֶחֱרַב וְיָבֵשׁ. יֶחֱרַב בְּבֵית רִאשׁוֹן, וְיָבֵשׁ בְּבַיִת שֵׁנִי.

7. "But now in exile it is said of him: 'The righteous perish….'" (Isaiah 57:1) He asks, **"What did he lose?"** Since it does not use the passive of "lose," what then did he lose? And he answers, **"He lost the Queen. About him it is said: 'And the river shall be drained dry.'** (Isaiah 19:5) because during the unification of Yesod and Malchut the Masach is fixed, in the secret of 'a river that flows and comes out,' so that the Supernal Light is drawn by them like the water of a river that continue to flow without end. Now that the correction of the Masach has ceased, it is **'drained' in the First Temple and 'dry' in the Second Temple.**

8. וּבְגִין דְּלֵית לֵיהּ מִדִּילֵיהּ, עֲנִיִּין צָוְוחִין בְּחַ"י בִּרְכָאן דִּצְלוֹתָא לְגַבֵּי חַ"י עָלְמִין, וְהָא אִסְתַּלַּק מִתַּמָּן נְבִיעוּ וּבִרְכָאן. וְלֵית מָאן דְּיָהִיב לוֹן. וְתַרְעִין אוֹחֲרָנִין סְתִימִין. וְתַרְעָא דְּצַדִּיק חֲרָבָא וִיבֵשָׁה, כְּמָה דְּעָנִי חָרֵב וְיָבֵשׁ. וְרָזָא דְּמִלָּה, יִקָּווּ הַמַּיִם מִתַּחַת הַשָּׁמַיִם אֶל מָקוֹם אֶחָד וְתֵרָאֶה הַיַּבָּשָׁה.

8. "**And since it has nothing of its own** because the union with the Supernal Light ceased, **the poor and destitute scream during the eighteen blessings of the Amidah prayer to the Life of the Worlds (*Chai* (18) *Olamim*),** Yesod, **and thus the wellspring,** which is the secret of the Masach, **and blessings,** which are the secret of the abundance of the unification **have ceased from him, and there is no one to give to them. Also the rest of the gates** of the other Sefirot **are sealed, and the Gate of the Righteous, which is the secret of the Crown of Yesod, is wasted and dried up, like the poor are wasted and dried up. This is the meaning of: 'let the waters under the heaven be gathered together to one place, and let the dry land appear.'** (Genesis 1:9)

9. וְלֵית תַּרְעָא פְּתִיחָא, אֶלָּא תַּרְעָא דְדִמְעָה. וּמַאי אִיהִי, בַּת עַיִן, דְּדִמְעָה מִינָּהּ נַפְקָא. וַעֲלָהּ אִתְּמַר, שָׁמְרֵנִי כְּאִישׁוֹן בַּת עָיִן. וּבָהּ וְהִנֵּה נַעַר בֹּכֶה לְגַבֵּי קוּדְשָׁא בְּרִיךְ הוּא, דִּירַחֵם עֲלֵיהּ בְּגָלוּתָא. הָדָא הוּא דִכְתִיב, אַתָּה תָקוּם תְּרַחֵם צִיּוֹן. בְּגִין דְּאִיהִי לַבַּת אֵשׁ, דְּאִתְחֲזְיָיא לְמשֶׁה בַּסְּנֶה, דִּכְתִיב וַיֵּרָא מַלְאַךְ יְ"י אֵלָיו בְּלַבַּת אֵשׁ מִתּוֹךְ הַסְּנֶה. אִיהִי בַּ"ת מִן בְּרֵאשִׁי"ת. וְדָא תִּקּוּנָא תְּרֵיסַר.

9. "And no Gate is open because all the Gates were locked, **except for the Gate of Tears** that is open." He asks, **"And which it is?"** And answers, **"The apple [lit. daughter] of the eye,** meaning Malchut that rose up to the eyes **from which tears flow out, and about it is said: 'protect me like the apple of the eye....'** (Psalms 17:8) **And pertaining** to Malchut that is sweetened by the Chasadim of Binah is said: **'...and behold, a boy wept...' to the Holy One blessed be He, to have pity on him in exile. That is** the meaning of **what is written: '....you will rise and have mercy upon Zion...'** (Psalms 102:14) **because She,** Malchut, **is a flame of fire** because in Her is revealed the Thirty-Two Paths of Wisdom (Chochmah), which start to be revealed when the Yud exits *avir* (air) in the secret of the Shuruk vowel, when the Left rules without the Right that is 'fire,' **which was shown to Moses at the burning bush,** which is Gevurot because Chochmah is revealed together with Gevurot to those who want to draw [Chochmah] from above downward, **as is written: 'And the angel of the Lord appeared to him in a flame (*labat*) of fire out of the midst of the bush....'** (Exodus 3:2) **This is the daughter (*bat*)** Malchut **of Beresheet,** which elevated to the head of Arich Anpin that is call *resheet* (beginning), and this is the Twelfth Tikkun."

For the seventh day of the month of Elul

TWELFTH TIKKUN

"And the Lord's angel appeared to him in a flame of fire"

1. בְּרֵאשֵׁי"ת מַאֲמַר קַדְמָאָה דְכֹלָּא, כְּלִילָא מֵעֲשָׂר אֲמִירָן, וְאִיהִי ל"ב אֱלֹקִי"ם דְּעוֹבָדָא דִּבְרֵאשִׁית. וּמִסִּטְרָא דִשְׂמָאלָא אִתְיְיהִיבַת, דְּאִיהִי גְּבוּרָה, אֶשָׁא סוּמְקָא. וּבְגִין דָּא בְּלַבַּת אֵשׁ. וּמֹשֶׁה הֲוָה מִסִּטְרָא דְלֵיוָאֵי, מִסִּטְרָא דִּילֵיהּ מַמָּשׁ.

1. The word **Beresheet** is **the first saying of all** sayings. Beresheet refers to the Partzuf of Arich Anpin of Atzilut that is called *resheet* (first), since it is the first Partzuf from which come out all of the Mochin of the Worlds, and from the Partzufs that are above it, meaning the Partzufs of Adam Kadmon (Primordial Adam) and the Male and Female of Atik, no Mochin reach the Worlds because they are established with the Malchut of the attribute of Judgment (Gevurah), which has not been sweetened with Mercy (Chasadim). The first Partzuf, which is the root of comprehension, is Arich Anpin, since it is established with the Malchut that is sweetened with mercy. And because it is only the root of comprehension it is called *resheet*, which is the first word in the Torah, since Torah represents comprehension. It is with Bet, which is Malchut that elevated to the head of Arich Anpin, which is called *resheet*, and this is Beresheet (Bet-*resheet*). By the elevation of Malchut, Binah of Arich Anpin exited the head of Arich Anpin, and **it comprises ten sayings,** which is the secret of the Ten Sefirot of Supernal Aba and Ima, which are the Upper Three of Binah, **and** it includes **the 32** mentions of **Elokim** stated **in the works of Creation,** which is the secret of the Ten Sefirot of Yisrael-Saba and Tevunah, which include the 22 letters of Zeir Anpin and Malchut, which together are 32 and are included in the Lower Seven of the Binah of Arich Anpin. **It was given from the Left side,** which is the secret of the Shuruk vowel, **which is Gevurah, red fire,** meaning the Judgments of the male, which are red, **and therefore** it says: **"…in a flame of fire…."** (Exodus 3:2) **And Moses was from the side of**

the tribe **Levi,** which is Left, and therefore He appeared to him **from his own actual aspect.**

2. וְאַמַּאי אִתְגַּלְיָא לֵיהּ בַּסְנֶה. לְאַחֲזָאָה דַּהֲוַת בְּדוֹחֲקָא בֵּין הַקּוֹצִים, וְעִם כָּל דָּא וְהַסְּנֶה אֵינֶנּוּ אֻכָּל, בְּגִין שׁוֹשַׁנִּים דְּאִינּוּן בְּנָהָא, דְּאִינּוּן יִשְׂרָאֵל, דַּהֲווֹ עֲתִידִין לְמֶהֱוֵי בְּגָלוּתָא בֵּין עֵרֶב רַב, דְּאִינּוּן קוֹצִים. וְדָא אִיהוּ רָזָא, כִּי אֶעֱשֶׂה כָלָה בְּכָל הַגּוֹיִם אֲשֶׁר הִדַּחְתִּיךָ שָׁמָּה וְאוֹתְךָ לֹא אֶעֱשֶׂה כָלָה.

2. He asks, **"And why did He appear to him in the bush** that alludes to judgments? **To show him that** the Shechinah **was distressed among the thorns, and yet: '...the bush was not consumed'** (Ibid.) **because of the roses among them, which are Israel who were to be in exile among the mixed multitudes who were thorns,** and are not consumed. **And this is the secret of the verse: 'for I will make a full end (***kalah***) of all the nations where I have driven you; but I will not make a full end of you.'** (Jeremiah 46:28)"

3. אַחֲזֵי לֵיהּ אַגְרָא דְכַלָּה, וְאִיהִי לַבַּת אֵשׁ, בֵּין הַקּוֹצִים, דְּאִינּוּן וַיְיבַיָּא כַּד דָּחֲקִין לִשְׁכִינְתָּא וְיִשְׂרָאֵל, אַגְרָא דִלְהוֹן כַּלָּה. נָפְקָא שְׁכִינְתָּא כַּלָּה מִבֵּינַיְיהוּ וְיֵיתֵי חָתָן בְּגִינָהּ, וְדָא אִיהוּ אַגְרָא דְכַלָּה דוֹחֲקָא, וְיִפְרוֹק לוֹן מִן גָּלוּתָא בְּגִינָהּ.

3. He showed him the reward of **end (***kalah***,** which can also mean "bride"), which is Malchut, **who is a flame of fire among the thorns,** to say, **when the wicked oppress the Shechinah and Israel,** Israel's **reward is ***kalah***,** for through the oppression they merit the Supernal Bride (*kalah*). **The Shechinah** that is **the bride emerges from among** the thorns, **and the groom,** who is Zeir Anpin, **will come for her** to join her, **and this is what** our masters said *agra dekalah dochaka*—that the reward for going to public lectures (*kalah*) is for the pressure [and effort], meaning the reward for pressure [and effort] is the bride, **and He will redeem them from exile for Her sake.**

4. וְדוֹחֲקָא דְּצַלוּתָא דְּעֵרֶב רַב לְיִשְׂרָאֵל, מְבַהֵר לוֹן פּוּרְקָנָא. וְרִפְיוֹן דִּילְהוֹן, מְעַכֵּב לוֹן לְיִשְׂרָאֵל פּוּרְקָנָא. בְּגִין דָּא אִתְחֲזֵי לֵיהּ לְמֹשֶׁה בְּלַבַּת אֵשׁ מִתּוֹךְ הַסְּנֶה, מִגּוֹ כּוּבִין.

4. The more the mixed multitudes oppress [and pressure] Israel in exile, the more they speed up their redemption. And when they give up, meaning if they do not oppress, **Israel's redemption is delayed. Therefore, He appeared to Moses in a flame of fire in the bush from among thorns.**

5. כַּד אִתְקָרִיב תַּמָּן לְמֶחֱזֵי עוֹבָדָא דָא, אָמַר לֵיהּ הַקָּדוֹשׁ בָּרוּךְ הוּא, אַל תִּקְרַב הֲלוֹם שַׁל נְעָלֶיךָ. הָכָא רֶמֶז, דְּאִתְפַּשַּׁט מִן גּוּפָא דִּילֵיהּ, דְּאִיהוּ נַעַל לְגַבֵּי גּוּפָא אָחֳרָא דְּאִתְלַבַּשׁ כַּד אִתְקָרִיב. וְאִית מָאן דְּיֵימָא דְּאִיהוּ אִתְּתֵיהּ, וְכֹלָּא קְשׁוֹט דָּא וְדָא.

5. When he approached to see this occurrence, the Holy One blessed be He said to him, "Do not come near; put off your shoes...." (Exodus 3:5) **Here is an allusion that Moses was disrobed from his body, which he slipped off like a shoe,** which hints to his foot that keeps him up, **to another body with which he became attired,** from the *chashmal* [lit. electricity] of the clear and pure body that Moses merited at the bush, **when he approached. Some say** that "put off your shoes" **refers to his wife,** who he was commanded to separate from. **They are both true;** it refers both to his body and his wife.

6. וְכֵן אַחֲזֵי לֵיהּ, דְּבֵי מַקְדְּשָׁא דְּאִיהִי בִּנְיָנָא דְּבַר נַשׁ, דְּעָתִיד לְאִתְחֲרְבָא. וְיִתְבְּנֵי זִמְנָא אָחֳרָא עַל יְדָא דִּקְבָּ"ה. הַהַ"ד, מְעוֹנָה אֱלֹקֵ"י קֶדֶם. וּכְתִיב מִקְדָּשׁ יְ"יָ כּוֹנְנוּ יָדֶיךָ. גָּדוֹל יִהְיֶה כְּבוֹד הַבַּיִת הַזֶּה הָאַחֲרוֹן מִן הָרִאשׁוֹן. בְּגִין דְּאִתְּמַר בּוֹ, וַאֲנִי אֶהְיֶה לָהּ נְאֻם יְ"יָ חוֹמַת אֵשׁ סָבִיב.

6. And He also showed Moses that the Temple, which is built by man, will eventually be destroyed, and it will be built again by the Holy One blessed be He. This is what is meant by: "The eternal God is a dwelling place" (Deuteronomy 33:27) **and: "...the sanctuary, Lord, which Your**

hands have established" (Exodus 15:17) and: "The glory of this latter house shall be greater than that of the former..." (Haggai 2:9) because it is said of it "'For I,' says the Lord, 'will be to her a wall of surrounding fire'...." (Zechariah 2:9)

7. אִתְּמַר בְּבֵי מִקְדְּשָׁא בּוֹנֵה יְרוּשָׁלַיִם יְ"יָ, וְאִתְּמַר הָתָם לְגַבֵּי אָדָם, וַיִּבֶן יְ"יָ אֱלֹקִי"ם אֶת הַצֵּלָע אֲשֶׁר לָקַח מִן הָאָדָם, דָּא וְזִכְמָה. וַיְבִיאֶהָ אֶל הָאָדָם, דָּא עַמּוּדָא דְּאֶמְצָעִיתָא, דַּרְגָּא דְּמֹשֶׁה. וְהַאי צֵלָע, אִיהוּ וַדַּאי כַּלַּת מֹשֶׁה. וַעֲלָהּ אִתְּמַר, וַיֵּרָא אֵלָיו מַלְאַךְ יְ"יָ בְּלַבַּת אֵשׁ. דְּאִיהִי בַּת יְחִידָה, דְּמִנָּהּ נָפִיק נְהוֹרָא דְּאוֹרַיְיתָא.

7. It was said about the Holy Temple: "The Lord does build up Jerusalem...." (Psalms 147:2) Meaning that Malchut, whose interior is the Temple, and whose exterior is Jerusalem, is built by the four letters of the Name Yud-Hei-Vav-Hei. And it is said by Adam: "the rib, which the Lord God Aba and Ima had taken from the man..." which is Chochmah. The side (tzela) is the curtain of the Netzach, Hod, Yesod of Zeir Anpin, where the illumination of Chochmah gets revealed, which is behind Zeir Anpin, since the face of Zeir Anpin shines with Chasadim. "...And brought her unto the man" (Genesis 2:22) is the Central Column, which is the level of Moses. Meaning that they corrected it with the Mochin of face-to-face so that it shines with both Lights, Chochmah, and Chasadim, and the Yesod of Aba that shines with the illumination of Chochmah to Zeir Anpin is called Moshe. The side, upon which are revealed the Thirty-Two Paths of Widsom (Chochmah), is most certainly the bride of Moses, and about it is said "And an angel of the Lord appeared to him in a flame (labat) of fire..." (Exodus 3:2) for she is an only daughter (bat), in the secret of "the father establishes the daughter," from which emerges the Light of the Torah, since she reveals the Light of the Supernal Chochmah and all the Supernal Mochin in all the worlds.

‫8. כְּגַוְונָא דָא אִתְּמַר, וַתִּפְתַּח וַתִּרְאֵהוּ אֶת הַיֶּלֶד. וַתִּרְאֵהוּ, דָא שְׁכִינְתָּא.‬
‫דַּהֲוָה בָכֵי בְּגִינָהּ, מִיָּד וַתַּחְמוֹל עָלָיו. וְדָא הוּא בִּבְכִי יָבֹאוּ וּבְתַחֲנוּנִים אוֹבִילֵם‬
‫בְּתַחֲנוּנִים וַדַּאי, לְקַיְּימָא וּבְרַחֲמִים גְּדוֹלִים אֲקַבְּצֵךְ.‬

8. **Similarly it is said** concerning Moses: "And when she had opened it,
and saw it, even the child...." (Exodus 2:6) "...she saw... the child," **refers
to the Shechinah,** Malchut, **"...a boy that wept"** for her to reveal Her
illuminations. **Immediately: "And she had compassion on him"** (Ibid.).
This is what is meant by: **"They shall come with weeping, and with
supplications will I lead them...."** (Jeremiah 31:8) **with supplications
assuredly,** to uphold the verse: **"...but with great compassion will I
gather you."** (Isaiah 54:7)

‫9. בְּהַהוּא זִמְנָא, כָּל חֵיוָן יִתְעָרוּן בְּקָלָא. וְעוֹפִין מְצַפְצְפִין בְּשִׁיר, לְקַבְּלָא‬
‫בְּרַתָּא, בְּחֶדְוָה בִּנְגּוּנָא. לְקַבְּלָא קִדּוּשִׁין מֵחֲתָנָא, דְּאִינוּן קָדוֹשׁ קָדוֹשׁ קָדוֹשׁ‬
‫וכו'.‬

9. **At that time,** when Zeir Anpin and Nukva ascend and are built with
the great Mochin of Aba and Ima, **all the living creatures** of the Chariot,
rouse with a great sound, and birds who are the souls of the righteous
chirp with song to welcome the daughter, who is Malchut, **with joy and
melody to receive the marriage rites** (*kidushin*), which are the Mochin of
the Upper Three Sefirot, **from the groom,** who is Zeir Anpin, **which are
"Holy, Holy, Holy** (*Kadosh, Kadosh, Kadosh*)...." (Isaiah 6:3)

‫10. וְלֵית קְדוּשָׁה פָּחוֹת מֵעֲשָׂרָה, וְקִדּוּשִׁין אִינוּן מִסִּטְרָא דְּחָכְמָה, דְּאִיהוּ‬
‫י', קֹדֶשׁ יִשְׂרָאֵל לַיְיָ רֵאשִׁית תְּבוּאָתֹה, רֵאשִׁית וַדַּאי. וּמִתְבָּרְכִין בְּשֶׁבַע‬
‫בִּרְכָאן, מִסִּטְרָא דְּאִימָא עִלָּאָה, דְּאִיהִי בְּרָכָה. וַעֲלָהּ אִתְּמַר, לְהָנִיחַ בְּרָכָה‬
‫אֶל בֵּיתֶךָ.‬

10. **There is no Holiness** (*Kedushah*) **with less than ten people,** meaning
a complete stature of Ten Sefirot. **And the marriage ceremony** (*kidushin*)
is from the side of Chochmah, which is Yud of the Name Yud-Hei-Vav-

Hei, according to the secret of the verse: **"Israel is holy to the Lord, His first-fruits of the increase...."** (Jeremiah 2:3) **"First" assuredly,** since "first" refers only to Chochmah. **They are blessed with seven blessings,** which are the Lights of Chasadim that clothe Chochmah, **from the side of Supernal Ima,** meaning Binah, **who is a blessing.** The Lights of Chasadim are called "blessing" since no restriction (*tzimtzum*) is on them. **And concerning it is written: "...to cause a blessing to rest on your house."** (Ezekiel 44:30)

11. וְשֶׁבַע בִּרְכָאן אִינּוּן, בְּשַׁחֲרִית שְׁתַּיִם לְפָנֶיהָ וְאַחַת לְאַחֲרֶיהָ. וּבְעַרְבִית, שְׁתַּיִם לְפָנֶיהָ וּשְׁתַּיִם לְאַחֲרֶיהָ. וְאִינּוּן שֶׁבַע סְפִירָן דִּכְלִילָן בְּחָתָן וְכַלָּה, וְדָא אִיהוּ שְׁמַע יִשְׂרָאֵל וְגוֹ'. הָא הָכָא קְדוּשָׁה, וּבְרָכָה, וְיִחוּד. בְּהַהוּא זִמְנָא אִתְעַר דָּוִד בְּכִנּוֹר דְּאִיהוּ מְנַגֵּן מֵאֵלָיו, בַּעֲשָׂרָה מִינֵי נִיגוּנִין. קַדְמָאָה בְּאַשְׁרֵי, וְדָא תִּקּוּנָא תְּלֵיסַר.

11. And there are seven blessings in the Shema reading. **In Shacharit (the Morning Prayer)** one recites **two blessings before and one after it, and in Arvit (the Evening Prayer) two before and two after it. They are seven Sefirot,** the Lower Six of Gadlut from Aba and Ima **that are included in the groom and bride,** Zeir Anpin and Nukva. **And this is** the unity of *Shema Yisrael* **"Hear Israel...."** We have here sanctity (*kedusha*)–the Mochin of Chochmah, **a blessing** (*beracha*) the Mochin of Binah, **and unity** (*yichud*)–meaning Da'at that includes Chochmah and Binah. **At that time David,** meaning Malchut, **is awakened by the violin,** in which blew a north wind that represents the illumination of Chochmah from the Left, **that used to play by itself,** meaning from below upward, **with ten different types of melody,** which will now be explained. **The first one is** *Ashrei,* **and this is the Thirteenth Tikkun.**

For the eighth day of the month of Elul
Thirteenth Tikkun
Ten types of melodies King David used to sing

1. בְּרֵאשִׁית, תַּמָּן אַשְׁרֵ"י, וְדָא אִיהוּ אַשְׁרֵי הָאִישׁ. וְאִיהוּ אהי"ה אֲשֶׁר אהי"ה, רֵישָׁא לְכָל רֵישִׁין. וַעֲלָהּ אִתְּמַר, רֹאשֵׁךְ עָלַיִךְ כַּכַּרְמֶל, וְדָא תְּפִלִּין דְּרֵישָׁא. וְדַלַּת רֹאשֵׁךְ כָּאַרְגָּמָן, דָּא תְּפִלִּין דְּיָד. וּבֵיהּ מְשַׁבְּחִין לְבַת, בְּהַאי אַשְׁרֵי. הֲדָא הוּא דִכְתִיב, בְּאָשְׁרִי כִּי אִשְּׁרוּנִי בָּנוֹת.

1. The word **Beresheet contains** *ashrei bat* [lit. "praise [bless] the daughter"]. **This is the meaning of the verse: "Blessed [happy] is the man…"** (Psalms 1:1) **and also:** *Eheye Asher Eheye* **(Alef-Hei-Yud-Hei)** "I am that I am" (Exodus 3:14) **the head of all heads, of which it is said: "Your head upon you like Carmel …"** (Song of Songs 7:6) spelled the same as *kar maleh* (full meadow), full of goodness of both Chochmah and Chasadim. **And this is the head Tefilin. "And the hair of your head like purple"** (Ibid.) **is the hand Tefilin. With these Mochin they praise the daughter (bat),** who is Malchut, **with this** *ashrei* **as is written: "Happy am I, for the daughters will call me happy (blessed)…."** (Genesis 30:13)

2. מָאן זָכֵי לְאַעֲלָא תַּמָּן. אֲשֶׁר לֹא הָלַךְ בַּעֲצַת רְשָׁעִים, דְּאִיהִי עֵצָה בִּישָׁא מִסִּטְרָא דְּעֵץ הַדַּעַת טוֹב וָרָע. וּבְדֶרֶךְ חַטָּאִים לֹא עָמָד, מָאן דֶּרֶךְ חַטָּאִים. הַהִיא דְּאִתְּמַר בָּהּ, כֵּן דֶּרֶךְ אִשָּׁה מְנָאָפֶת אָכְלָה וּמָחֲתָה פִיהָ וְגוֹ'. וּבְמוֹשַׁב לֵצִים לֹא יָשָׁב, מָאן מוֹשַׁב לֵצִים. דָּא לִילִי"ת, אִימָן דְּעֵרֶב רַב, דְּאִיהִי מְטַמְּאָה כְּנֶדָה בְּמוֹשָׁבָהּ. וְכֵן עֵרֶב רַב מְטַמְּאִין בְּמוֹשָׁבָם, לְצַדִּיקַיָּא דְּיָתְבִין בֵּינַיְיהוּ, כְּנֶדָה.

2. **He asks, "Who merits to enter there?"** Meaning that his good deeds will ascend as Mayin Nukvin (Feminine Waters) through which those Mochin will become revealed, and answers: **"The man who (asher) does not walk in the counsel of the wicked."** (Psalms 1:1) **This is a bad counsel from the side of the Tree of Knowledge of Good and Evil,** to draw Chochmah from above downward, which is the sin of the Tree of

Knowledge, Good and Evil. 'Nor stands in the way of sinners.'" (Ibid.)
He asks, "What is: 'the way of sinners,'?" and answers, "The one about
which it is said: 'So is the way of an adulterous women, she eats, and
wipes her mouth....' (Proverbs 30:20) Meaning the Female Klipah called
'the wife of harlotry.' 'Nor sits in the seat of scorners.'" (Psalms 1:1) He
asks, "What is 'the seat of scorners,'?" and answers, "This refers to Lili"t,
the matriarch of the mixed multitude who defiles a dwelling place like
a niddah (menstruating woman). So do the mixed multitude make their
dwelling ritually impure for the righteous who dwell among them, like
a niddah."

3. וּמַאן דְּאִתְחַדְבַּק בְּהַאי אַשְׁרֵי, דְּאִיהוּ כִּתְרָא וְרֵישָׁא דְּאוֹרַיְיתָא, אִתְּמַר
בֵּיהּ, וְהָיָה כְּעֵץ שָׁתוּל עַל פַּלְגֵי מָיִם. וְדָא עֵץ וַחַיִּים, דְּאִתְּמַר בֵּיהּ וְעָלֵהוּ לֹא
יִבּוֹל. וְהַאי תִּקּוּנָא קַדְמָאָה.

3. And whoever joins Ashrei, meaning whoever causes by their action for
Malchut to elevate until Binah of Arich Anpin, which is the crown and
the head of the Torah, which is the secret of Zeir Anpin, with the Mochin
of Aba and Ima, in the secret of the verse: "But his delight is in the Torah of
the Lord..." (Psalms 1:2), about him it is said: "And he shall be like a tree
planted by streams of water...." (Psalms 1:3) And this tree is the Tree
of Life, about which it is said "...whose leaf does not wither...." (Ibid.)
This is the first correction of the ten corrections that David composed
in Psalms.

4. תִּנְיָינָא בְּשִׁיר, דָּא חָכְמָה, שָׁר י' וּתְכַלַת יוּדִין אִנּוּן, י'י'י'. וְאִינּוּן רֵישָׁא
וְסוֹפָא וְאֶמְצָעִיתָא דְּאָת י'. וְאִינּוּן רְמִיזִין בִּשְׁמָא סְתִים, דְּאִיהוּ יוֹד הֵי וָאו הֵי.

4. The second correction is with song (shir; Shin-Yud-Resh), referring
to Chochmah. Shar (Shin-Resh) derives from seeing and gazing, which
is both Chochmah and Yud. There are three Yud's, which are the top,
bottom and center of the letter Yud, meaning the top point, the bottom
point and the dot itself. They are hinted at in the concealed Holy Name

Yud-Vav-Dalet, Hei-Yud, Vav-Alef-Vav, Hei-Yud, which is the Name of Samech-Gimel (63) that shines from the chest of Arich Anpin and above, where the lights are concealed, which is not the case by the Name of Mem-Hei (45) that shines from the chest of Arich Anpin and below, where the lights are revealed, and therefore [the Name of 45] is called the *Shem haMeforash* (the Explicit Name).

5. בְּאִלֵּין תְּלַת, עַבֵּוֹ דָּוִד מַלְכָּא לִבְרַתָּא דְּמַלְכָּא. הָדָא הוּא דִּכְתִיב שִׁיר לַמַּעֲלוֹת. ל׳ מַעֲלוֹת אִינּוּן וַדַּאי. אִינּוּן תְּלָתִין דַּרְגִּין דִּבְהוֹן בְּרַתָּא סָלְקָא לְגַבֵּי אַבָּא.

5. With these three Yud's, **King David used to sing to the King's daughter,** which is Malchut that ascends to Chochmah. **This is what is meant by: "A Song of Ascents (*Shir Lama'alot*)"** (Psalms 121:1) **Lamed** *ma'alot* **(30 steps)** because surely three times Yud (10) is 30. **And they are thirty levels,** namely Binah, Tiferet, and Malchut each comprised of Ten Sefirot, **with which the daughter,** which is Malchut, **ascends to Aba** of Atzilut, which is the secret of the Name of 63, the Binah of 45, since Atik took the Keter of 45, Arich Anpin took the Chochmah of 45, and Aba took the Binah of 45, which is 63.

6. בְּחָמֵשׁ נִימִין דְּכִנּוֹר, דְּאִינּוּן וְחָמֵשׁ אַזְכָּרוֹת דְּאַדְכִּיר וְחָמֵשׁ זִמְנִין י״י בְּהַאי מִזְמוֹר. וַד, עֶזְרִי מֵעִם יְיָ. ב׳, י״יָ שֹׁמְרֶךָ. ג׳, י״יָ צִלְּךָ. ד׳, י״יָ יִשְׁמָרְךָ מִכָּל רָע. ה׳, י״יָ יִשְׁמָר צֵאתְךָ וּבוֹאֶךָ.

6. With the five strands of the violin, which are Keter, Chochmah, Binah, Tiferet, and Malchut, namely a complete stature of Ten Sefirot that shine with the illumination of Chochmah, **which are five Names of the Lord that are mentioned in the Psalm [Psalms 121]. One is: "My help comes from the Lord," the second: "the Lord is your keeper;" the third: "the Lord is your shade;" the forth: "the Lord shall keep you from all evil;" and the fifth: "the Lord shall guard your going out and your coming in."**

7. וּבְהוֹן מַלְכָּא אָמַר לְגַבֵּי כַלָּה, צַהֲלִי קוֹלֵךְ בַּת גַּלִּים, בַּת עֲשָׂרָה גַּלְגַּלִּים דְּסַלִּיק בְּהוֹן יוֹ"ד הָא וְאו הָא בַּעֲשָׂרָה מִינֵי נְגוּנִין, וּבְאַרְבַּע חֵיוָן דְּאִינּוּן יהו"ה בְּשִׁיר פָּשׁוּט, כָּפוּל, מְשׁוּלָשׁ, מְרוּבָּע, דְּאִיהוּ יהו"ה דְּקוֹלוֹ סָלְקָא כְּגַלֵּי יַמָּא. וְגַלֵּי יַמָּא דִּלְעֵילָא, אִינּוּן עֲשָׂרָה גַּלְגַּלִּין.

7. **And with them the King,** Zeir Anpin, **said to the bride,** meaning Malchut: **"Lift up your voice, daughter of waves (galim)"** (Isaiah 10:30) because when Malchut has the Mochin of Aba she is called the daughter of *Galim*, the daughter of Abraham the patriarch, which is Chesed that rose to become Chochmah. **Ten wheels (galgalim),** meaning Ten Sefirot, as every Sefira that shines with the Light of Chochmah is called a "wheel" (*galgal*) because it shines from below upward, **with which to raise Yud-Vav-Dalet, Hei-Alef, Vav-Alef-Vav, Hei-Alef with ten types of melody,** which represent the Ten Sefirot of Zeir Anpin with the Supernal Mochin of Aba and Ima, **and the four living creatures, which are** the four letters of simple **Yud-Hei-Vav-Hei** of Malchut, that elevate to the Name of Ayin-Bet (72) **with a simple song,** which is Yud, **double,** meaning Yud-Hei, **triple,** meaning Yud-Hei-Vav, **quadruple, which is the Name Yud-Hei-Vav-Hei. Its voice rises like the waves of the sea,** when Malchut has the great Mochin that are called waves, which are the Mochin of Aba. **And the waves of the Celestial Sea are ten wheels** meaning the ten letters in the *ribua* [lit. four] of the Name Yud-Hei-Vav-Hei: Yud, Yud-Hei, Yud-Hei-Vav, that together equal 72.

8. וַעֲלַיְיהוּ אִתְּמַר, יָדָיו גְּלִילֵי זָהָב מְמֻלָּאִים בַּתַּרְשִׁישׁ, בִּתְרֵין דְּרוֹעִין דִּבְרַתָּא, וּבְהוֹן שִׁית פִּרְקִין, וְאִינּוּן שִׁית דַּרְגִּין דְּכָרְסַיָּא, שֵׁשׁ מַעֲלוֹת לַכִּסֵּא. וְכַד סָלִיק ו' בְּהוֹן, יִתְעָרוּן לְגַבֵּיהּ לְקָבְלָא לֵיהּ שְׂרָפִים בְּגַדְפַיְיהוּ. הֲדָא הוּא דִּכְתִיב, שְׂרָפִים עוֹמְדִים מִמַּעַל לוֹ שֵׁשׁ כְּנָפַיִם וְגוֹ'.

8. **And about them is said: "His hand are like rods of gold set with beryl (tarshish)..."** (Song of Songs 5:14) meaning twice six (*trei shesh*), six of Zeir Anpin and six of Malchut, **in the two arms of the daughter,** who is Malchut. **They contain six segments,** three segments in the Right and

three in the Left. **They are six steps,** Chesed, Gevurah, Tiferet, Netzach, Hod, and Yesod **of the throne,** in the secret of **"there were six steps to the throne…."** (I Kings 10:19) **And when Vav,** which is Zeir Anpin, **ascends to them, the Seraphim are roused to receive him with their wings, as it is written, "Above Him stood the Seraphim; each one had six wings…."** (Isaiah 6:2)

9. וּמָאן דְּסָלִיק עַל גַּדְפַּיְיהוּ וּפָרַח בְּהוֹן. אִיהוּ ו', כְּלִיל שִׁית תֵּיבִין דְּיִחוּדָא, שְׁמַע יִשְׂרָאֵל. וּבְגִינֵיהּ אִתְּמַר, כִּי עוֹף הַשָּׁמַיִם וְגוֹ'. וְכַד סָלְקָא בְּרַתָּא, סָלְקָא בִּתְרֵין דְּרוֹעוֹי, דְּאִינּוּן חֶסֶד וּגְבוּרָה דְּבְהוֹן שִׁית פִּרְקִין דְּאִיהִי ו'. וְרָזָא דְמִלָּה, שְׂמֹאלוֹ תַּחַת לְרֹאשִׁי וִימִינוֹ תְּחַבְּקֵנִי.

9. He asks, **"Who mounts the wings and flies with them?"** He answers, **"It is Vav,** meaning Zeir Anpin, **that includes the six words of the unification: 'Hear, Israel,** the Lord our God the Lord is one,' **and about him is said: 'for a bird of the air** shall carry the voice' (Ecclesiastes 10:20), meaning the sound of the Shema reading. **And when the daughter,** Malchut, **ascends, she ascends with his two arms, which are Chesed and Gevurah—wherein there are six segments, meaning Vav (6). And the secret of the matter is in the verse: "Let his left hand be under my head, and his right hand embrace me"** (Song of Songs 2:6) since Gevurah is Left and Chesed is Right.

10. כַּד סָלְקָא הַאי שִׁיר, סָלְקָא בְּשִׁית תֵּיבִין, דְּאִינּוּן שְׁמַע יִשְׂרָאֵל וְגוֹ'. וְכַד נָחֲתָא, נָחֲתָא בְּשִׁית, דְּאִינּוּן בָּרוּךְ שֵׁם כְּבוֹד מַלְכוּתוֹ לְעוֹלָם וָעֶד. וְגַוְונָא כַּד סָלִיק, סָלִיק בְּשִׁית. וְכַד מָאִיךְ, מָאִיךְ בְּשִׁית. וַעֲלַיְיהוּ אִתְּמַר עוֹקָיו עַמּוּדֵי שֶׁשׁ.

10. When this song, meaning Malchut with the illumination of Chochmah called "song," **rises** to become included in the unification that is above the chest, **it does so with the six words of "Hear, Israel…"** (Deuteronomy 6:4), meaning that she is included with Chasadim of Zeir Anpin in the secret of the Supernal Unity. **And when she descends** below the chest **she**

descends with six words, which are, **"Blessed is the Name of the glory of His Kingdom forever"** which is the lower unification. **When the melody** of the cantillation marks, which are the Mochin of the back, **ascends, it ascends with six** which are Chesed, Gevurah, Tiferet, Netzach, Hod, and Yesod, **and when it descends it descends with six.** "The head of the king is established in Chesed and Gevurah" [Zohar, Mishpatim 520], since the Mochin of Chochmah, Binah, and Da'at that illuminate in Zeir Anpin and Nukva are not constant, but they only [exist] during the prayer, Shabbats and Holidays. Therefore, they are not considered like Chochmah and Binah, but rather like Chesed and Gevurah, which are the Lower Six. This is the major difference between Arich Anpin, whose Upper Three is constant and qualify as Upper Three, and Zeir Anpin, whose Upper Three is not constant. This is why even when [Zeir Anpin] has the Upper Three, which are Chochmah, Binah, and Da'at, they are considered Chesed, Gevurah, and Tiferet. Therefore, "it ascends with six and descends with six," which refer to the Chesed, Gevurah, and Tiferet that ascended and became Chochmah, Binah, and Da'at, but are not actually the Upper Three. **About them is said "his legs are pillars of marble [*shesh*, which also means "six"]..."** (Song of Songs 5:15) since drawing the Mochin of the back cause a unification in the lower Zeir Anpin and Nukva, and drawing the Mochin of the face cause a unification in the Supernal Zeir Anpin and Nukva.

11. וַעֲשָׂרָה גַּלְגַּלִּין אִינוּן י', דְּאִינוּן לָקֳבֵל עֶשֶׂר אֶצְבְּעָן דְּבָטְשִׁין בִּנְגּוּנָא. חָמֵשׁ בַּחֲמֵשׁ, וְאִינוּן ה"ה. דְּסָלְקִין בֵּיהּ בְּשִׁית דַּרְגִּין דְּאִיהוּ ו', בֵּיהּ סָלְקִין וְנַחֲתִין. וְאִיהוּ כְּגַוְונָא דְּסֻלָּם, דְּאִתְּמַר בֵּיהּ, וְהִנֵּה סֻלָּם מֻצָּב אַרְצָה וְגוֹ', וְהִנֵּה מַלְאֲכֵי אֱלֹקִ"ם עֹלִים וְיֹרְדִים בּוֹ.

11. And the ten wheels are the Yud of the Name Yud-Hei-Vav-Hei that is Chochmah, **which corresponds to the ten fingers that strum** when **playing music; five and five** of the two hands, **which are Hei and Hei** of the Name Yud-Hei-Vav-Hei, namely Binah and Malchut, **that ascend its six steps** Chesed, Gevurah, Tiferet, Netzach, Hod, and Yesod, **which is**

the **Vav** of the Name Yud-Hei-Vav-Hei, which is Zeir Anpin. **It is like the**
ladder about which it is said: "And behold a ladder set up on the earth…
and behold the angels of God ascending and descending on it" (Genesis
28:12) and this Yud-Hei-Vav-Hei is the secret of the Ten Sefirot that are
included in Malchut.

12. וְכֹלָּא יהו"ה יו"ד ה"א וא"ו ה"א, יָ"ד, וְדָוִד מְנַגֵּן בְּיָד. ו' אִיהוּ גּוּפָא,
גַּדְפוֹי ה"ה רֵישָׁא דִילֵהּ י'. בֵּהּ סָלִיק קָלָא דִנְגּוּנָא.

12. It is all Yud-Hei-Vav-Hei; Yud-Vav-Dalet, Hei-Alef, Vav-Alef-Vav,
Hei-Alef, which is the secret of Zeir Anpin and Malchut, **a hand** (*yad;*
14), fourteen letters. "…and David played with his hand" (I Samuel 19:9)
raising Zeir Anpin and Nukva to receive the Mochin of Aba and Ima,
when they are completed with the aforementioned fourteen letters. **Vav is**
the secret of **the torso,** Tiferet, **its wings** with which it rises and flies to
Aba and Ima to receive the Mochin **are Hei-Hei,** Binah and Malchut. **Its**
head is Yud, Chochmah, and this Yud-Hei-Vav-Hei is the secret of the Ten
Sefirot of Zeir Anpin. **With** the Name Yud-Hei-Vav-Hei of Zeir Anpin,
the sound of the melody rises to clothe Aba and Ima and to receive the
Upper Three Sefirot, which are the Mochin.

13. וְעוֹד ו' אִיהִי מְנַרְתָּא. ה ה שְׁלֹשָׁה קְנֵי מְנוֹרָה מִצִּדָּהּ הָאֶחָד וְגו' ו' מְנוֹרָה
בְּאֶמְצַע נֵר עַל רֵישֵׁיהּ י'.

13. And we can **also** explain the verse: "…and David played with his hand"
that **Vav is the candelabra,** meaning Zeir Anpin; **Hei and Hei are the "…**
three branches of the candelabra…" (Exodus 25:32) which are three Vav's
like the shape of Hei: **"…out of the one side,** and three branches of the
candelabra out of the other side." (Ibid.) **Vav, Zeir Anpin, is the candelabra**
in the center and **Yud is the candle on the top of it.**

14. כַּד שַׁרְיָא בְּאָת ו', אִתְעֲבִיד ז'. וְרָזָא דְמִכְלָה יָאִירוּ שִׁבְעַת הַנֵּרוֹת. לָקֳבֵל
מְנַרְתָּא דְאִיהִי ו' וְשִׁית קְנֵי מְנַרְתָּא דְאִינוּן ה ה שִׁיּת וָי"ן. וְרָזָא דְמִכְלָה,

שִׁבְעָה וְשִׁבְעָה מוּצָקוֹת, עַד דְּסָלְקִין לְי"ּד, דְּאִיהוּ יְהֹו"ּה יֹו"ּד הֵ"ּא הֵ"ּה וָא"ּו
הֵ"ּא. וְדָא אִיהוּ וְדָוִד מְנַגֵּן בְּיָד. יָ"ּד לְקָבֵל יָ"ּד.

14. When Malchut, which is the secret of Yud, **dwells on the letter Vav,** which is the secret of Zeir Anpin, in the secret of "A virtuous woman is a crown to her husband..." (Proverbs 12:4) **it becomes** the letter **Zayin (7). This is the secret of: "...the seven lamps shall give light** in front of the candelabra..." (Numbers 8:2) **which is Vav, and the six branches of the candelabra, which are Hei and Hei,** each in the shape of three Vav's, are altogether **six Vav's. The secret of the matter** is hinted in the verse: **"seven ... and seven pipes..."** (Zechariah 4:2) since Zeir Anpin is split in his chest that Chesed, Gevurah, and Tiferet are from his chest and above, and Netzach, Hod, and Yesod are from his chest and below. And there are Netzach, Hod, and Yesod that are included in Chesed, Gevurah, and Tiferet that are above the chest, and there are Chesed, Gevurah, and Tiferet that are included in Netzach, Hod, and Yesod that are below the chest. This is the secret of the two Vav's in the annunciation of Vav (Vav-Vav); the upper Vav is the secret of Tiferet, and the lower Vav is Yesod. Malchut that elevated in the secret of "a candle on top of it" shines to both of them; in Tiferet it is the secret of "A virtuous woman is a crown to her husband..." (Proverbs 12:4) and [also] the seventh day, which is Shabbat, and in Yesod that is below the chest it is the secret of "a crown for the head of the righteous." Therefore, there are seven above the chest and seven below the chest, **that equal "hand"** (*yad*; Yud-Dalet; 14) **which is Yud-Vav-Dalet, Hei-Alef, Vav-Alef-Vav, Hei-Alef,** which are fourteen letters that allude to the illumination of the candelabra. **And this is the meaning of: "...David played with his hand..."** (I Samuel 19:9) since he rose and became a chariot for Zeir Anpin, **the hand** (*yad*; 14) of David **corresponds to the fourteen** of Zeir Anpin, and every aspect below receives from the corresponding aspect above.

15. וְסָלְקָא ה' בְּאָת ו', וּלְבָתַר סָלִיק ו' בְּי' שִׁית זִמְנִין עֶשֶׂר, עַד דְּסָלִיק לְשִׁתִּין וְאִינוּן אַתְוָון הַדְּבֵקוֹת בִּקְרִיאַת שְׁמַע, דִּבְגִינַיְיהוּ אִתְּמַר, כָּל הַמֵּשִׂים רֶיוַח בֵּין הַדְּבֵקִים, מְצַנְּנִים לֵיה גֵּיהִנָּם.

15. By the illumination of these Mochin, **Hei**, which is Malchut, **ascends** and is included **in the letter Vav**, which is Zeir Anpin. **Afterwards Vav ascends**, which is Zeir Anpin, together with Malchut **to Yud**, since every Sefira of Zeir Anpin has Upper Three Sefirot, **which are six times ten, so they equal sixty,** which is the secret of the Lower Six of Gadlut that shine to Zeir Anpin and Nukva from the unification of Aba and Ima during the Shema reading. **They are the joined letters in the Shema reading,** which are the secret of Zeir Anpin and Nukva that are called "letters." **Of them we learned "Whoever leaves space between the adjacent words,"** which is the secret of the Nesirah (sawing) to separate them from the unification of back-to-back to unite them face-to-face: **Gehenom (Hell) is cooled down for his sake."** (Berachot 15b)

16. וּשְׁלֹמֹה עֲלַייהוּ אָמַר, הִנֵּה מִטָּתוֹ שֶׁלִּשְׁלֹמֹה שִׁשִּׁים גִּבּוֹרִים סָבִיב לָהּ. וְאִינוּן נָטְרִין עַרְסֵיהּ. וּלְקָבְלַייהוּ שִׁשִּׁים הֵמָּה מְלָכוֹת. אִלֵּין דְּכוּרִין, וְאִלֵּין נוּקְבִין. אִלֵּין הִקְרִיאַת שְׁמַע דְּתַקִּין מֹשֶׁה, דְּכוּרִין. אִלֵּין דִּשְׁלֹמֹה, נוּקְבִין. וְאִלֵּין בֵּית קָבוֹל לְאִלֵּין. דַּרְגִּין דִּשְׁלֹמֹה, אִינוּן בֵּית קָבוֹל לְדַרְגִּין דְּמֹשֶׁה. וְכַד מִתְחַבְּרָן כֻּלָּא כְּאֶחָד, שְׁלֹמֹ"ה אִתְהַפַּךְ לְמֹשֶׁ"ה.

16. And concerning them Solomon said: **"Behold it is the bed of Solomon; sixty valiant men are about it..."** (Song of Songs 3:7) namely the Lower Six Sefirot of Zeir Anpin that shine to Malchut with the illumination of the Upper Three Sefirot, **and they guard his bed,** because the illumination of the Upper Three Sefirot are a protection against the external forces. **And corresponding to them** is said: **"There are sixty queens..."** (Song of Songs 6:8) meaning the Lower Six of Gadlut that illuminate in Malchut herself. **These** of Zeir Anpin **are male, and those** of Malchut **are female. These of the Shema reading that Moses composed,** who was a chariot to Zeir Anpin, **are male, and these of Solomon,** who was a Chariot to Malchut, **are female. And those** of Malchut **are receptacles to those** of Zeir Anpin. **The levels of Solomon,** representing Malchut, **are receptacles to the levels of Moses,** who is the secret of Zeir Anpin. **And when they join, they all become as one.** Solomon (Shlomo), who is the secret of the Chariot of Malchut, ascends and **becomes** a chariot for Zeir Anpin, namely **for Moses (leMoshe),** spelled the same as Solomon (Shlomo).

17. בְּתִיקוּנִין דְּאַרְבַּע אַתְוָון אִתַּקַּן שִׁיר וַעֲלַיְיהוּ אִתְּמַר, וְהִנֵּה מַלְאֲכֵי אֱלֹקִי"ם וְגוֹ', סָלְקִין תְּרֵין, וְאִינּוּן י"ה. וְנָחֲתִין תְּרֵין, וְאִינּוּן ו"ה. וְכֵן, גַּלְגַּלֵּי יַמָּא סָלְקִין בְּעֶשֶׂר, וְאִינּוּן יוֹד הֹא ואו הֹא, וְאַרְבַּע חֵיוָון.

17. Among the compositions with the four letters of Yud-Hei-Vav-Hei, **a song was composed;** "song" meaning Malchut with the illumination of Chochmah. **And about them,** the four letters of the Holy Name **is said:** **"and behold the angels of God..."** (Genesis 28:12) **two ascend, which are Yud-Hei** that shine with covered Chasadim, since their way is to illuminate from below upward, **and two descend, which are Vav-Hei,** that shine with revealed Chasadim, since their way is to illuminate from above downward. [See Zohar, Beresheet A 134] **The waves of the sea,** which signify the Ten Sefirot of Zeir Anpin that are like the aqueduct that moves the wheel [see Zohar, Pinchas 46] **also rise with ten, which are Yud-Vav-Dalet, Hei-Alef, Vav-Alef-Vav, Hei-Alef and the four living creatures,** which are the four letters of the simple Yud-Hei-Vav-Hei.

18. כַּד סָלְקָא בְּרַתָּא בְּשִׁיר, נִשְׁרָא נָטִיל י' בְּפוּמָא, וְעַל רֵישָׁתָא. ו' בְּגוּפָא. ה"ה בְּגַדְפָהָא. אָדָ"ם יו"ד ה"א וא"ו ה"א, רְכִיב עַל כֹּלָּא. וּדְמוּת פְּנֵיהֶם פְּנֵי אָדָם, דָּא סָלִיק עַל כֹּלָּא. וּפְנֵי אַרְיֵה אֶל הַיָּמִין לְאַרְבַּעְתָּם, דָּא יְהֹו"ה. וּפְנֵי שׁוֹר וּפְנֵי נֶשֶׁר אִינּוּן מֶרְכָּבָה לִשְׁמָא דִיהוֹ"ה וְאָדָם עַל כֹּלָּא.

18. When the daughter, Malchut, **ascends with a song,** meaning with the illumination of Chochmah, **the eagle** that is the Central Column, Tiferet, **takes Yud in his mouth and on his head, Vav in the body, and Hei-Hei with the wings,** meaning the simple Yud-Hei-Vav-Hei that is the secret of the Light of Nefesh. **Man** (*adam;* **45),** which is the secret of the Yud-Hei-Vav-Hei fully spelled out: **Yud-Vav-Dalet, Hei-Alef, Vav-Alef-Vav, Hei-Alef,** which is the secret of the Light of Ruach, **rides upon all** the living creatures, in the secret of the verse: **"as for the likeness of their faces, they had the face of a man…."** (Ezekiel 1:10) Meaning the face of man **rises above all** the living creatures. **"…the face of lion, on the right side…"** (Ibid.) which is the secret of Chesed, **"…and they four…" refers to Yud-Hei-Vav-Hei,** meaning simple Yud-Hei-Vav-Hei, **and so also the "face of an ox"** and the **"face of an eagle" are a Chariot of the Name Yud-Hei-Vav-Hei** of only four letters, which is the meaning of "and they four," which is the secret of the Light of Nefesh of Chochmah. **And man** (*adam*), who is the secret of the Yud-Hei-Vav-Hei that equals 45 that is the secret of the Ruach of Chochmah, **is above all.**

19. בְּזִמְנָא דְאִיהִי סָלְקָא בְּכָל אִלֵּין תִּקּוּנִין, אִיהוּ מְשַׁבַּח לָהּ. הָדָא הוּא דִכְתִיב, כְּחוּט הַשָּׁנִי שִׂפְתוֹתַיִךְ וּמִדְבָּרֵךְ נָאוֶה. הָא תְּרֵין מִינֵי נִגּוּנִין דְּשַׁבַּח דָּוִד מַלְכָּא, בְּאַשְׁרֵי. בְּשִׁיר.

19. At the time she, Malchut, **ascends with all these compositions** that reveal the Light of Chochmah, **he,** Zeir Anpin, **praises her, as is written: "Your lips are like a thread of scarlet and your mouth is comely…."** (Song of Songs 4:3) **Thus, these are two kinds of melody,** of the ten melodies **with which King David praised with "Praise"** (*Ashrei*) which is the secret of Keter, **and "Song"** (*Shir*), which is the secret of Chochmah.

20. תְּלִיתָאָה בַּבְּרָכָה, וְדָא שְׁכִינְתָּא עִלָּאָה. וַעֲלָהּ אִתְּמַר, בָּרְכִי נַפְשִׁי אֶת יְ"י. מֵהַאי אִתְיְהִיבַת בְּבַר נָשׁ נִשְׁמַת חַיִּים, דְּאִתְּמַר בָּהּ וַחֲמִשָּׁה תִּקּוּנִין. מַה הַקָּדוֹשׁ בָּרוּךְ הוּא זָן כָּל עָלְמָא, הָכִי נִשְׁמָתָא זָנַת כָּל גּוּפָא. מַה הַקָּדוֹשׁ בָּרוּךְ הוּא רוֹאֶה וְאֵינוֹ נִרְאֶה, הָכִי נִשְׁמָתָא רוֹאָה וְאֵינָהּ נִרְאֵית. מַה הַקָּדוֹשׁ בָּרוּךְ הוּא יוֹשֵׁב בַּחֲדָרֵי חֲדָרִים, הָכִי נִשְׁמָתָא יוֹשֶׁבֶת בַּחֲדָרֵי חֲדָרִים. מַה הַקָּדוֹשׁ בָּרוּךְ הוּא מָלֵא כָּל הָעוֹלָם, הָכִי נִשְׁמָתָא מְלֵאָה אֶת כָּל הַגּוּף. מַה הַקָּדוֹשׁ בָּרוּךְ הוּא דָּן אֶת כָּל הָעוֹלָם, הָכִי נִשְׁמָתָא דָּנָה אֶת גּוּפָא.

20. The third melody **is with a blessing. This is the Supernal Shechinah,** namely Binah, **about which it is said: "Bless the Lord, my soul"** (Psalms 104:1), as our masters said (in Beresheet Rabbah, 14:9) that [the soul] is called by five names Nefesh, Ruach, Neshama, Chaya, and Yechida. **The breath of life (nishmat chayim) was given into man from this,** namely Binah, since Nefesh comes from Malchut, Ruach from Zeir Anpin and Neshama from Binah, **for five qualities were related** to the Neshama: **Just as the Holy One blessed be He sustains the entire world so does the Neshama sustain the entire body. Just as the Holy One blessed be He sees yet is not seen, so does the Neshama see yet is not seen. Just as the Holy One blessed be He sits in the inner sanctum so does the Neshama sit in the inner sanctum; just the Holy One blessed be He fills the whole world, so does the Neshama fill the entire body. Just as the Holy One blessed be He judges the whole world so does the Neshama judge the body.**

‏21. וְרָזָא דְנִשְׁמָתָא דְּאִיהִי שָׁוָה לְקוּדְשָׁא בְּרִיךְ הוּא, דָּא בִינָה, מִ"י. וַעֲלָהּ אִתְּמַר, וְאֶל מִי תְדַמְּיוּנִי וְאֶשְׁוֶה, אֶל מִי וַדַּאי וְהָא אוּקְמוּהָ מָארֵי מַתְנִיתִין וַחֲמִשָּׁה דְבָרִים אִלֵּין.

21. And the secret of the Neshama being likened to the Holy One blessed be He is that it is Binah, called "who" (mi; 50) referring to the Fifty Gates of Binah, **of which it is said: "To whom (mi) then will you liken Me, that I should be his equal?"** (Isaiah 40:25) **"To whom" (mi) certainly,** meaning Binah. **The scholars of the Mishnah already established these five qualities.**

‏22. וַחֲמִשָּׁה וַדַּאי, בְּגִין דְּאִינוּן מִסִּטְרָא דְה' עִלָּאָה. וְאִינוּן כֻּלְּהוּ תִּקּוּנִין בְּלֵב, כְּמָה דְאוּקְמוּהוּ מָארֵי מַתְנִיתִין, הַלֵּב מֵבִין. הַלֵּב רוֹאֶה. הַלֵּב שׁוֹמֵעַ, הָא תְּלַת. ה' אִיהִי מַמָּשׁ הֶבֶל, וְרוּוְחָא דְפוּמָא, דְּסַלִּיק בֵּיהּ קָלָא וַאֲמִירָה וְדִבּוּרָא.

22. There are surely five qualities because they come from the aspect of Supernal Hei, which is Binah that spreads to five levels, as it is known that

Binah spreads down to Hod. **And they are all qualities of the heart, as established by the scholars of the Mishnah that the heart understands, the heart sees, the heart hears; these are three. Hei is actually breath,** for it is a Light letter containing only breath (*hevel*), which are the same letters that spell the word "the heart" (*halev*). And from it comes **breath from the mouth, with which are fashioned sound, utterance and speech.** The fifth quality is the thought of the heart, as it says "Many thoughts are in the heart of man…" (Proverbs 19:21), as it will say in verse 25.

23. עַרְקִין דְּלִבָּא אִינּוּן כַּחֲיָילִין בָּתַר מַלְכְּהוֹן, וְרָזָא דְמִלָּה, אֶל אֲשֶׁר יִהְיֶה שָׁמָּה הָרוּחַ לָלֶכֶת יֵלֵכוּ, הָכִי מִתְנַהֲגִין עַרְקִין דְּלִבָּא לְגַבֵּי רוּחָא. כְּגַוְונָא דִעֵלָּאִין.

23. The arteries of the heart are like soldiers that follow their king, and the secret of the matter is in: "…wherever the spirit (*ruach*) was to go, they went…." (Ezekiel 1:12) So are the arteries of the heart led towards the air [lit. spirit] that comes from the heart, **just as in the upper** levels.

24. הֲרֵי לָךְ רוּחַ בְּלֵב, דְּנָפִיק מֵאָן שְׂמָאלָא דְלִבָּא, וְאִיהוּ הֲוָה רוּחַ צְפוֹנִית דְּבָטַשׁ בְּכִנּוֹר דְּדָוִד, וּבְהַאי רוּחָא הֲוָה בָטַשׁ בְּחָמֵשׁ נִימִין דְּכִנּוֹר, דְּאִינּוּן חָמֵשׁ כַּנְפֵי רֵיאָה. וּבְקָנֶה סָלִיק קוֹל לְלִבָּא.

24. So we see that the Ruach is in the heart in accordance with the secret of the verse: "for the blood is the life (*nefesh*)…" (Deuteronomy 12:23) **that emerges from the left ventricle of the heart,** meaning the left cavity. **And it was the north wind that beat upon David's harp,** which is the secret of the lung (*re'ah*; רוּחָא), which are the same letters that spell "sight" (*re'iyah*; רִיאָה) since the Light of Chochmah included with Chasadim, which is called "sight," illuminates there. **And with this wind he strummed upon the five strands of the harp, which are the five wings,** lobes, **of the lungs. Through the windpipe** that breathes air into the heart **the voice rises to the heart,** in the secret of the verse, "Hark, my beloved knocks…." (Song of Songs 5:2)

25. וְאִיהוּ אֵשׁ אוֹכְלָא מֵאוּדְנָא יְמִינָא דְלִבָּא, דְאִיהִי כְּלַפֵּי כָּבֵד. וּמִנֵּיהּ נָפִיק דִּבּוּר. הָדָא הוּא דִכְתִיב, הֲלֹא כֹה דְבָרִי כָּאֵשׁ, וְאִי לָאו כַּנְפֵּי רֵיאָה דְנָשְׁבִין עַל לִבָּא, הֲוָה אוֹקִיד כָּל גּוּפָא. מַחֲשָׁבָה בְּלִבָּא דָא י', וְה"ה ה' אִנּוּן אֲמִירָה וְדִבּוּרָא, ו' קָלָא, כְּלִיל כֹּלָּא.

25. **And it,** meaning the heart, **is a consuming fire from the right ventricle of the heart,** the right cavity, **located against the liver,** which is also on the right side, **and from there comes out speech. This is what is meant in the verse: "Is not My word like fire?"** (Jeremiah 23:29) **And if not for the wings of the lungs that blow** the Light of Chasadim, which is the secret of air (*ruach*) **on the heart, the whole body would be burnt. The "thought in the heart" is Yud** of the Name Yud-Hei-Vav-Hei, meaning Chochmah, **and Hei-Hei are "utterance" and "speech,"** meaning Binah and Malchut in the secret of Leah and Rachel. **Vav,** Zeir Anpin, **is "voice" that includes everything,** utterance and speech.

26. רְבִיעָאָה בְּמִזְמוֹר, וְדָא הוּא דְרוֹעָא יְמִינָא. הָדָא הוּא דִכְתִיב, מִזְמוֹר שִׁירוּ לַי"י שִׁיר חָדָשׁ כִּי נִפְלָאוֹת עָשָׂה הוֹשִׁיעָה לּוֹ יְמִינוֹ. וַעֲלָהּ אִתְּמַר, הוֹשִׁיעָה יְמִינְךָ.

26. **The fourth** composition **is with "Psalm"** (*Mizmor*), **which is the right arm** meaning Chesed, **as is written: "A psalm, sing unto the Lord a new song; for He has done marvelous things. His right hand...have wrought salvation for Him"** (Psalms 98:1) which is Chesed. **It is said about it: "...save with Your right hand...."** (Psalms 60:7)

27. וְאִיהוּ בְּגָלוּתָא עִם שְׁכִינְתָּא, וְאִיהוּ תָּמִיךְ לָהּ. וְרָזָא דְמִלָּה, וּזְרוֹעַ י"י עַל מִי נִגְלָתָה. וּבֵיהּ אוּמָאָה דְפוּרְקָנָא, הָדָא הוּא דִכְתִיב נִשְׁבַּע י"י בִּימִינוֹ וּבִזְרוֹעַ עֻזּוֹ. וְעוֹד וַי"י י"י שִׁכְבִי עַד הַבֹּקֶר.

27. **And it,** meaning Chesed, **is in exile with the Shechinah, and supports Her. And the secret meaning of the matter is: "And to whom..."** (Isaiah 53:1), meaning Binah, about which it is said: "...He delights in

mercy" (Micah 7:18) "**is the arm of the Lord revealed**" (Ibid.) during the redemption. **And with it,** Chesed, **the oath to redeem is taken, as is written: "The Lord has sworn by His right hand and by the arm of His strength...."** (Isaiah 62:8) **and: "...as the Lord lives, lie down until the morning"** (Ruth 3:13) which is the secret of Chesed, the morning of Abraham.

28. וְאַמַּאי אִתְקְרֵי וְרוֹעַ י"יָ, בְּגִין דְּכַף הַיָּד בֵּיהּ י'. וְחָמֵשׁ אֶצְבְּעָאן ה'. קָנֶה דִּימִינָא דְּאִיהוּ דְּרוֹעָא ו', כָּתֵף בֵּיהּ ה'.

28. He asks, "**Why** is the arm **called the "arm of the Lord (Yud-Hei-Vav-Hei)?**" and answers, "**Because the palm of the hand contains Yud** of the Yud-Hei-Vav-Hei, namely Chochmah 'thought,' like the closed fist that does not permit what it contains to be known. **Five fingers,** meaning an open hand, **are Hei**, Binah. **The right arm-bone, which is the arm, is Vav,** meaning Zeir Anpin. **The shoulder,** meaning that part of the arm that is attached to the body **has** the lower **Hei,** meaning Malchut. It is in the secret of 'raise up your hands in holiness,' that the hands are raised upwards in the secret of the Upper Three, and therefore *katef* (shoulder) equals 500, which is a hint to the Hei. It turns out that the hand contains the Yud-Hei-Vav-Hei, and therefore it is called 'the arm of the Lord' (Yud-Hei-Vav-Hei).

29. וְדָא עַמּוּדָא דְּאֶמְצָעִיתָא, דְּאִתְהַקְשַׁר בִּימִינָא, לְאַקְמָא בֵּיהּ שְׁכִינְתָּא, מִגָּלוּתָא. וּמֹשֶׁה דְּאִיהוּ דְּיוֹקְנָא דְּעַמּוּדָא דְּאֶמְצָעִיתָא, אִתְּמַר בֵּיהּ, מוֹלִיךְ לִימִין מֹשֶׁה זְרוֹעַ תִּפְאַרְתּוֹ.

29. "And this, namely the Name Yud-Hei-Vav-Hei is the secret of **the Central Column,** meaning Tiferet, Zeir Anpin, **that is attached to the Right,** which is Chesed, **to raise with it the Shechinah from exile. And concerning Moses, who is in the image of the Central Column,** meaning the level of Tiferet in the secret of 'you placed on his head a glorious (*tiferet*) crown' it is said: '**That caused His glorious (*tiferet*) arm to go at the right [hand] of Moses.'** (Isaiah 63:12)

30. וְאִיהוּ בּוֹקֵעַ מַיָּא דְאוֹרַיְיתָא, לְגַבֵּי זֶרַע אַבְרָהָם, דְאִיהוּ יְמִינָא, לְמֶהֱוֵי לֵיהּ שֵׁם עוֹלָם. וְאִתְקַשַּׁר בָּהּ' דְאַבְרָהָם, דְאִיהִי וַחֲמִשָּׁה חוּמְשֵׁי תוֹרָה, וּבָהּ אִשְׁתַּלִּים מֹשֶׁה. וּמִיָּד דְּאִשְׁתַּלִּים, אִתְגַּלְיָא עֲלֵיהּ יְמִינָא, וְדָא הוּא וּזְרוֹעַ יְ"יָ עַל מִי נִגְלָתָה.

30. "He divides the waters of Torah for the seed of Abraham, who is the Right, so he would have eternal renown. He is attached to the Hei of Abraham that is made with the aspect of Chasadim of Binah. It is the Hei of *behibaram* '...when they were created...' (Genesis 2:4) And it is the five books of the Torah, and Moses was perfected with it, meaning with the Hei of the aspect of Chasadim. As soon as he was perfected, the Right was revealed to him. This is the secret of the Torah, in the secret of '... at His right hand was a fiery law unto them.' (Deuteronomy 33:2) And this is: 'and upon whom (*mi*; 50) has the arm of the Lord been revealed,' (Isaiah 53:1) meaning it was revealed because of 'whom' (*mi*), which is Binah."

31. וַחֲמִשָּׁאָה בְּנִגּוּן, דְאִיהִי גְּ"ן, דְסָלִיק מִנֵּיהּ כַּמָּה נְגִינוֹת עוֹלֵימָן, מִסִּטְרָא דִשְׂמָאלָא דְּמִתַּמָּן רוּחַ צָפוֹן הֲוָה נָחֲתָא בְּכִנּוֹר דְּדָוִד, וַהֲוָה מְנַגֵּן מֵאֵלָיו. הָדָא הוּא דִכְתִיב, וְהָיָה כְּנַגֵּן הַמְנַגֵּן וְגוֹ'.

31. The fifth composition is with melody (*nigun*), meaning Gevurah, which is the secret of the singing of the Levites. It contains the letters of Gan גַּ"ן, meaning Malchut that suckles from Gevurah. From it emerge several melodies, maidens (*alamot*) derived from concealment (*he'elem*), which are from the Left side, and they need to be united with Chasadim so that Chochmah can be revealed, from which a north wind would descend, which is Gevurah, the Left side, on David's harp, thus being united with Chasadim, in the secret of "...the trustworthy mercies of David." (Isaiah 55:3) And it played by itself, meaning from below to above, as it says: "...when the minstrel played..." (II Kings 3:15)

32. וּמִתַּמָּן רַעֲמִין נָפְקִין, הָדָא הוּא דִּכְתִיב וְרַעַם גְּבוּרוֹתָיו מִי יִתְבּוֹנָן. וּמִתַּמָּן רְעָה הִתְרוֹעֲעָה הָאָרֶץ, בִּתְרוּעָה מִסִּטְרָא דְּמַטָּה כְּלַפֵּי וֶחֶסֶד. מוֹט הִתְמוֹטְטָה אֶרֶץ בִּתְקִיעָה. פּוֹר הִתְפּוֹרְרָה אֶרֶץ, בִּשְׁבָרִים.

32. And from there, from the Left side, when it unites with the Right, **thunders,** which are the sounds of judgment, **come out** and are heard and known for their importance, **as it says: "But the thunder of His mighty deeds, who can understand?"** (Job 26:14) **And from there,** from the side of Gevurah: **"The earth is utterly broken down…"** (Isaiah 24:19) **by Teruah,** which is the secret of the Gevurot (Judgments) of the Female that is in the Central Column, Tiferet, **from the side that turns towards Chesed,** which is Right because the Gevurot (Judgments) of the Female are on the Right: **"…the earth is crumbled in pieces…"** (Ibid.) **with Tekiah,** where the Gevurot (Judgments) of the Female are **"…the earth is violently shaken"** (Ibid.) **by Shevarim,** which is on the Left, and Gevurot (Judgments) of the Male are there.

33. בְּהַהוּא זִמְנָא תְּלַת אֲבָהָן מִתְקַשְּׁרִין בִּגְבוּרָה, וְאִתְעֲבִידוּ בָהּ תְּרוּעָה שְׁבָרִים תְּקִיעָה. וּבְהוֹן, רְעָה הִתְרוֹעֲעָה וְגוֹ' וְדָא יְהֵא בְּסוֹף יוֹמַיָּא. וְכָל אָתִין אִלֵּין, בְּאַרְעָא דְיִשְׂרָאֵל יְהוֹן, בְּגִין דְּתַמָּן חֶבְרוֹן דַּאֲבָהָן תַּמָּן קְבוּרִים.

33. At that time of the above mentioned blowings **the three Patriarchs,** who are Chesed, Gevurah, and Tiferet, **connect with Gevurah, and produce in it Teruah, Shevarim, and Tekiah, and through them,** meaning with the blowings of Teruah, Shevarim, Tekiah: **"…the earth is crumbled in pieces.…"** This will take place at the End of Days. And all these signs will be in the land of Israel because Hebron is there, where the Patriarchs are buried.

34. שְׁתִיתָאָה הַלְלוּיָהּ הַלְלוּהוּ, וְדָא ה"ו. עֲלֵיהּ אִתְּמַר, לֵיל שִׁמּוּרִים הוּא לַ"יְיָ. וְדָא אִיהוּ עַמּוּדָא דְאֶמְצָעִיתָא. וְרָזָא דְמִלָּה, הַשְׁמִיעוּ הַלְלוּ וְאִמְרוּ הוֹשַׁע יְ"יָ אֶת עַמְּךָ אֶת שְׁאֵרִית יִשְׂרָאֵל, לְקַיֵּם קְרָא, כִּימֵי צֵאתְךָ מֵאֶרֶץ מִצְרָיִם אַרְאֶנּוּ נִפְלָאוֹת.

34. The sixth composition **is "Praise Yah"** (*Haleluyah*), **"Praise Him"** (*Haleluhu*), **which is Hei-Vav,** namely Zeir Anpin and Nukva, since all the compositions until here are in the aspect of the Upper Three, because Chesed and Gevurah are the Upper Three of the Chasadim, and from Tiferet and below the Lower Three begin. **About him,** meaning Zeir Anpin, it is said: **"It was a night of watchfulness (*leil shimurim*) unto the Lord..."** (Exodus 12:42) The word "night" (*leil*) assumes a masculine suffix, and "watchfulness" (*shimurim*) is in plural because the Female is included in the Male, "and wherever male and female are together, the praise is directed only to the male." (Zohar, Bo verse 132) **That is the Central Column,** meaning Zeir Anpin, Tiferet, **and the secret of the matter is in: "... announce you, praise you, and say, 'Lord save Your people, the remnant of Israel.'"** (Jeremiah 31:6) **so as to fulfill the verse: "As in the days of your coming forth out of the land of Egypt will I show him marvelous things."** (Micah 7:15)

35. וְרָזָא דְמִלָּה, מַ״ה שֶׁ״הָיָה ה״וּא שֶׁ״יִּהְיֶה. וּבֵיהּ מִ״מְּכוֹן שִׁ״בְתּוֹ ה״שְׁגִּיחַ. בְּגִין דְּאִיהוּ דְּיוּקְנָא דְּעַמּוּדָא דְּאֶמְצָעִיתָא.

35. The secret of the matter is in: "That which has been, it is that which shall be..." (Ecclesiastes 1:9) the acronym of *ma shehay hu sheyihiye* is "Moshe" (Mem-Shin-Hei), who represents Tiferet. **Through him: "From the place of His habitation He looks intently upon..."** (Psalms 33:14) is also the acronym of *Mimechon shivto hishgi'ach*, "Moshe" **since he bears the image of the Central Column** because Moses is the chariot of the inner Tiferet.

36. בְּהַהוּא זִמְנָא אִתְקַיַּים רָזָא דְּמַתְנִיתִין דְּאָמַר, אוֹכְלִין כָּל אַרְבַּע, וְתוֹלִין כָּל חָמֵשׁ, דְּהַיְינוּ אֶלֶף וַחֲמִשָּׁאָה. וְשׁוֹרְפִין בִּתְחִלַּת שֵׁשׁ, דְּאִיהוּ אֶלֶף שְׁתִיתָאָה.

36. At that time the secret of the following Mishnah will be fulfilled: **"One may eat [Chametz] the entire fourth hour,"** (Tractate Pesachim 11b) meaning Keter, Chochmah, Binah, and Chesed of the vessels, which contain the Illuminations of Chesed, Gevurah, Tiferet, and Netzach during Katnut, which illuminate with concealed Chasadim, and "eating" is the secret of Chasadim, **"and one places it in abeyance for the entire fifth hour," which is the fifth millennium,** meaning Gevurah of the vessels and Hod of Illuminations, which does not come from above downward and its illumination hangs from below upward, and we do not eat or burn, **"and one burns it at the beginning of the sixth hour,"** meaning Tiferet of vessels and Yesod of Lights, **which is the sixth millennium,** and the stature of Malchut begins from Tiferet and below, which is called "seven," where the revealed Chasadim shine with Chochmah that burn and demolishes the external forces.

37. וּבְגִין דְּלָא יַפְרִישׁוּ בֵּין שֵׁשׁ דְּאִיהוּ עַמּוּדָא דְּאֶמְצָעִיתָא, וּבֵין שֶׁבַע דְּאִיהִי בַּת זוּגֵיהּ. צָרִיךְ לְבַעֲרָא שְׂאוֹר וְחָמֵץ דְּאִינּוּן עֵרֶב רַב, דְּלָא יִתְחֲזוּן בֵּין שֵׁשׁ דְּאִיהוּ ו', וּבֵין שֶׁבַע. דְּאִתְּמַר בָּהּ, שֶׁבַע בַּיּוֹם הִלַּלְתִּיךְ.

37. And so as not to separate between the six, which is the Central Column, meaning Zeir Anpin that includes the Lower Six Sefirot, **and seven,** meaning Malchut, **which is his spouse, it is necessary to burn Se'or and Chametz, for they are** a hint **to the mixed multitude, so that they should not be seen between six, which is Vav,** Zeir Anpin, **and seven** that is Malchut, **for it is said: "Seven [times] a day I praised You...."** (Psalms 119:164)

38. בְּגִין דְּעֵרֶב רַב אַפְרִישׁוּ בֵּין שֵׁשׁ לְשֶׁבַע בְּמַתַּן תּוֹרָה. כְּמָה דְּאַתְּ אָמַר, וַיַּרְא הָעָם כִּי בֹשֵׁשׁ מֹשֶׁה. וְאוּקְמוּהוּ בַּשֵּׁשׁ, בְּאִלֵּין שִׁית שַׁעְתִּין עֲבַדוּ יָת עֶגְלָא, וְאַפְרִישׁוּ בֵּין ו"ה, דְּאִינּוּן שֵׁשׁ לְשֶׁבַע. הָכִי יַפְרִישׁ לוֹן קוּדְשָׁא בְּרִיךְ הוּא בֵּין שֵׁשׁ לְשֶׁבַע.

38. Because the mixed multitude separated six and seven, meaning Zeir Anpin and Malchut, **at the Giving of the Torah, as it says: "When the people,** which are the mixed multitude [See Zohar, Pinchas 473] **saw that Moses delayed (boshesh)..."** (Exodus 32:1) **they established** that it meant

with six (*beshesh*) because they saw that the level of Moses is the Lower Six
Sefirot. [See Zohar, Ki Tisa 63] **In these six hours they made the Golden
Calf, and separated Vav and Hei, which are six,** the level of Moses, **and
seven,** which is Malchut. **Thus will the Holy One blessed be He separate
them** at that time of redemption as is written: "...and the unclean spirit
to pass out the land." (Zachariah 13:2) **between six,** meaning the sixth
millennium, Yesod, **and seven,** meaning Malchut.

39. דִּבְגִינַיְיהוּ הֲוַת מַצָּה פְּרוּסָה, לֶחֶם עֹנִי עֹנִי וַדַּאי. וּבְהַהוּא זִמְנָא תְּהֵא
שְׁלֵימָה כְּמַוְונָא דַּחֲבֶרְתָּה, דְּאִיהִי מַצָּה שְׁלֵימָה. הָדָא הוּא דִכְתִיב וְהָיָה אוֹר
הַלְּבָנָה כְּאוֹר הַחַמָּה.

39. Because of the mixed multitude, Malchut **was a piece of Matzah,
the bread of poverty,** as our masters have said "the way of a poor man is
to eat a piece of bread" (Pesachim 115b) **poverty assuredly** because the
abundance of Malchut while it is in the aspect of Left without Right,
meaning Chochmah without Chasadim, it considered like bread of poverty,
since Chochmah does not illuminate without Chasadim, and the mixed
multitudes give strength to the Left. **And at that time** of the redemption,
Malchut **shall be whole,** and will again shine in the aspect of Chasadim
with the Mochin of Gadlut, **like her companion the whole Matzah,**
that alludes to Zeir Anpin that illuminates with Chasadim, **as it says:
"Moreover the light of the moon shall be as the light of the sun...."**
(Isaiah 30: 26)

40. וְאַמַּאי הֲוַת מַצָּה פְּרוּסָה בְּגִין דְּאִסְתַּלַּק מִנָּהּ ו' רֶגֶל דִּילָהּ, לְמֶהֱוֵי לָהּ
כִּמְצֹרָע. וּמַצָּה פְּרוּסָה אִשְׁתְּאָרַת ד'. וּבְגִין דָּא מַצָּה פְּרוּסָה ד', מַצָּה שְׁלֵימָה
ה' וּבְגִין דָּא אָמְרִין הַלֵּל גָּמוּר וְהַלֵּל שֶׁאֵינוֹ גָּמוּר בַּפֶּסַח, לְקָבֵל מַצָּה שְׁלֵימָה
וּמַצָּה פְּרוּסָה.

40. He asks, **"And why was it a piece of Matzah?"** and answers, **"Because
the Vav was removed from it,"** which alludes to the Light of Chasadim,
her foot upon which she stands because Chochmah cannot illuminate

without Chasadim, **to become for her as a precept (***mitzvah***),** [which is Matzah] with the addition of Vav that alludes to Zeir Anpin. **Therefore, a piece of Matzah is called Dalet,** which comes from *dalah* (poor), and **a whole Matzah is** called **Hei. Therefore, we recite both the complete Halel and the half Halel during Pesach, corresponding to the whole Matzah,** which is the secret of Malchut with Mochin of Gadlut, **and a piece of Matzah,** which is the secret of the bread of poverty.

41. וְאָמְרִין מָרוֹר עַל שֵׁם ו' דְּאִתְפָּרַשׁ מִן ה', וְדָא גָּרִים לוֹן דְּוַיְמָרֲרוּ אֶת חַיֵּיהֶם אִיהוּ מָרוֹר. וְאִיהִי מָרָה הֲדָא הוּא דִכְתִיב, קְרָאן לִי מָרָה כִּי הֵמַר שַׁדַּי לִי. בַּעֲבוֹדָה קָשָׁה: בְּקַשְׁיָא בְּחוֹמֶר: קַל וָחוֹמֶר, בֵּין אוּמִין דְּעָלְמָא.

41. "**And we say, '**This **bitter herb (Maror)'** on Pesach eve, **representing Vav,** is the secret of Zeir Anpin **that is separated from the Hei,** the secret of Malchut. **And this caused** what it says in the verse: '**They made their lives bitter....'** (Exodus 1:14) Zeir Anpin was revealed with Judgments (Gevurot) from the Left without sweetening. **This is the bitter herb (Maror). And She,** meaning Malchut**, is bitter,** which is the judgments of locks **as it says: 'Call me Mara (bitter) for the Almighty has dealt very bitterly with me.'** (Ruth 1:20) **'...with hard service...'** (Exodus 1:14)**: with hard questions** about the Blessed One's actions, **'...in mortar (***chomer***)...'** (Ibid.)**; an inference from minor to major (***chomer***),** light and grave injunctions **among the nations,** as our masters have said, 'If one does not merit, then the Torah becomes for him a potion of death.' (Tractate Yoma 72b)"

42. וּמַאן גָּרִים דָּא. י' מִן שַׁדַּי, רְשִׁימוּ דִּבְרִית, דְּיָהִיב מֹשֶׁה בְּעֵרֶב רַב. בְּגִין דָּא נָחִית מֹשֶׁה בְּמַדְרֵגֵיהּ, הֲדָא הוּא דִכְתִיב לֶךְ רֵד כִּי שִׁחֵת עַמְּךָ. עַמְּךָ וְלֹא עַמִּי.

42. He asks, "**Who caused this?**" and answers, "**Yud of** the Name **Shadai 'Almighty,' a mark of** the sign of **the Covenant that Moses placed on the mixed multitude,** and converted them. Yet they caused Israel to sin by the

golden calf. **Because of this Moses descended from his level, as it says:**
'**Go, get you down, for your people…have dealt corruptly.**' (Exodus 32:7)
'**your people,**' which are the mixed multitude, **not My own.**

43. וְעַל יְדֵיה עֲתִידָה שְׁכִינְתָּא לְיַחֲדָא עִם קוּדְשָׁא בְּרִיךְ הוּא, בְּגִין דְּאִיהוּ
אַפְרִישׁ לוֹן, צָרִיךְ לְיַחֲדָא לוֹן, לְתַקְנָא בַּמֶּה דְּוָאב. קָמוּ כָּלְהוּ חַבְרַיָּא וְנָשְׁקוּ
לֵיהּ, וְאָמְרוּ אִי לָא אָתֵינָא לְעָלְמָא, אֶלָּא לְמִשְׁמַע דָּא, דַּי.

43. "And through Moses the Shechinah Malchut **will unite with the Holy
One blessed be He** Zeir Anpin. **Since he caused the separation between
them, he must unite them; to repair what he damaged."** All the friends
got up and kissed Rav Shimon, and said, "If we came to this world only
to hear this, it is sufficient."

44. שְׁבִיעָאָה בְּנִצּוּחַ, דְּאִיהוּ נֵצַח יִשְׂרָאֵל. וַעֲלֵיה אִתְּמַר, וְגַם נֵצַח יִשְׂרָאֵל לֹא
יְשַׁקֵּר. וַעֲלֵיה אִתְּמַר, לַמְנַצֵּחַ עַל אַיֶּלֶת הַשַּׁחַר. לַמְנַצֵּחַ עַל הַשְּׁמִינִית. מָאן
שְׁמִינִית הוֹד. וְאִיהוּ נֵצַח עֲלֵיה.

44. The seventh melody **is with conducting** (*nitzuach*) derived from
victory and eternity, **for He is the Eternal One (Netzach) of Israel,**
namely Netzach, the right leg of Zeir Anpin called Israel, as in the verse:
"At Your right hand are pleasures for evermore (*netzach*)." (Psalms 16:11)
**And about Him is said: "And also the Eternal One (*Netzach*) of Israel
will not lie"** (I Samuel 15:29) **and, "To the chief musician upon Ayelet
Hashachar"** (Psalms 22:1); **"To the chief musician of the Shminit [lit.
eighth]."** (Psalms 12:1) He asks, **"Who is the Shminit?"** and answers,
"Hod, the Sefira of Hod is the eighth Sefira, **and above it is Netzach** the
seventh Sefira."

45. תְּמִינָאָה בְּהוֹדָאָה, וּבֵיהּ הֲוָה מְשַׁבַּח דָּוִד הוֹדוּ לַי"יָ. וְדָא הוֹד וַדַּאי.
לַמְנַצֵּחַ הוֹדוּ, בְּהוֹן רְמִיזִין נֵצַח וְהוֹד. וְאִינּוּן נִסִּין. וּבֵיהּ שַׁבַּח מֹשֶׁה אָז, הָדָא
הוּא דִּכְתִיב אָז יָשִׁיר מֹשֶׁה. בְּגִין דְּאִיהִי הוֹד דְּיָהִיב לְמֹשֶׁה. אָז תִּקְרָא וַי"יָ

יַעֲנֶה. וְאִיהוּ תְּמַנְיָא יוֹמִין דִּמְילָה. וּבַתְרֵיהּ בְּרִית, דְּאִיהוּ יְסוֹד צַדִּיקָא דְּעָלְמָא. וּבֵיהּ אִתְגַּלְיָא י' דִּמְילָה, עֲשִׂירָאָה לְעֶשֶׂר סְפִירָן.

45. The eighth melody is thanksgiving, and with it David would sing and say: "**Give thanks unto the Lord….**" (Psalms 107:1) This is definitely the Sefira of **Hod. "To the conductor (*lamenatze'ach*)" and "Give thanks (*hodu*)" both allude to** the two Sefirot **Netzach and Hod. And they are miracles** because the revealed Chasadim illuminate in them, **and about the eighth Sefira, which is Hod, Moses sang, as is written: "Then (*Az; 8*) sang Moses…."** (Exodus 15:1) **Because** the Sefira of **Hod was the one given to Moses,** as is written "And you shall put some of your honor (*hod*) upon him…." (Numbers 27:20) See what is written in Zohar, Pinchas 194-195, where Rav Shimon asked "If that is so…then Binah is your level." The Faithful Shephard replied: "That is a good question that you have asked. The reason is that the letter Hei of Yud-Hei increases and is multiplied by the Yud of Yud-Hei, making five times ten, which are the Fifty Gates of Binah, whose extension is from Chesed to Hod, namely five Sefirot. And there is, therefore, just one extension from Binah to Hod." Therefore, when we say Hod we include Binah. **"Then (*Az*) shall you call, and the Lord will answer…."** (Isaiah 58:9) And the Sefira of Hod includes **the eight days of circumcision, followed by the Covenant (*Brit*; circumcision), which is the ninth Sefira, the Righteous, the foundation (*yesod*) of the world. And in it,** in Yesod, **is revealed the Yud of circumcision,** which is the secret of the crown of Yesod, meaning Malchut, **the tenth** Sefira that completes **the Ten Sefirot.**

46. וְאִיהוּ הוֹד תְּמַנְיָא יוֹמֵי דַחֲנוּכָה, לְאַרְבְּעָה וְעֶשְׂרִין יוֹמִין, דְּאִינוּן בשכמל"ו. וּמִיָּד דַּעֲלֵהּ זַיִת טָרָף בְּפִיהָ, שַׁרְיָא כ"ה עַל יִשְׂרָאֵל, בְּכ"ה בְּכִסְלֵו וְאִלֵּין אִינוּן כ"ה אַתְוָון דִּיְחוּדָא, דְּאִינוּן שְׁמַע יִשְׂרָאֵל וגו'. וְדָא אִיהוּ וַחֲנוּכַ"ה: חֲנ"וּ כ"ה. אֲבָל נֹצֵחַ, אִתְּמַר בֵּיהּ וַתָּנַח הַתֵּיבָה בַּחֹדֶשׁ הַשְּׁבִיעִי. בְּגִין דְּנֹצַח בֵּיהּ רְמִיזוֹ נֹחַ צַדִּיק. וּבֵיהּ וְהַמַּיִם גָּבְרוּ מְאֹד.

46. And Hod is the Sefira that shines during **the eight days of Chanukah, on the 24th day** of the month Kislev, until Chanukah, **which correspond to** the twenty four letters of **"Blessed be the Name of the glory of His Kingdom forever and ever"** *Baruch Shem Kevod malchuto le'olam va'ed,* which is the correction of the Judgments (Gevurot) of Malchut in the secret of the lower unification. **And as soon as "...in her mouth an olive leaf freshly plucked..."** (Genesis 8:11) and the perfection in the root of Malchut was revealed, by the candles of Chanukah that are lit with olive oil, **the 25th dwells upon Israel, on the 25th day of Kislev.** Meaning a complete structure of five Partzufs, each one composed of five, which together equal 25, which complete the 25 levels of Light. **These are the 25 letters of** the Supernal Unity of Zeir Anpin, which are: **"Hear, Israel..."** (Deuteronomy 6:4) because after the root of Malchut turned into Light, she is equal in purity to Zeir Anpin and has 25 aspects of Light like Zeir Anpin. **This is Chanukah: ChaNu Caf-Hei [lit. they rested on the 25th]. But about Netzach, the seventh Sefira, is said: "And the ark rested in the seventh month..."** (Genesis 8:4), **since Noach (Nun-Chet) the righteous (***tzadik***) is alluded to in Netzach (Nun-Tzadik-Chet), and about it is said: "And the waters prevailed exceedingly...."** (Genesis 7:19)

47. וְכַד לָא נָטְרִין יִשְׂרָאֵל בְּרִית מִילָה, מִתְגַּבְּרִין אוּמִין דְּעָלְמָא וְכַד נָטְרִין לָהּ, אִתְּמַר בְּהוֹן וְהַמַּיִם הָיוּ הָלוֹךְ וְחָסוֹר עַד הַחֹדֶשׁ הָעֲשִׂירִי. דָּא י' דִּמִילָה, דְּאִיהִי מַלְכוּת. עֲשִׂירָאָה לְעֶשֶׂר סְפִירָן. וְדָא אִיהוּ אֶת קַשְׁתִּי נָתַתִּי בֶּעָנָן, דְּאִיהוּ בְּרִית.

47. But when Israel do not observe the precept of Circumcision, which is the secret of the correction of the legs, because the legs are mainly corrected by Yesod that regulates Netzach and Hod, **the nations** called "...the proud waters..." (Psalms 124:5) **prevail** [See Zohar, Noah 96]**, and when they do observe it, it says about them: "And the waters decreased continually until the tenth month..."** (Genesis 8:5), which **is the Yud of circumcision (***milah***), which is Malchut,** meaning the crown of Yesod, **tenth to the Ten Sefirot. This** what is meant by **"...My rainbow..."** (Genesis 9:13) which is the Yesod of Malchut "**...in the cloud...**" which is the secret of the Malchut of Yesod, and the two sweeten each other in the secret of the opening (*maftecha*), and then all the Mochin are revealed on her to sustain the world, which is the meaning of: "And I will look upon it, that I may remember the everlasting Covenant...." (Genesis 9:16)

48. וְיַעֲקֹב בְּהַהִיא יַרְכָא, אִתְּמַר בֵּיהּ וְהוּא צוֹלֵעַ עַל יְרֵכוֹ, דְּפָרְחוּ מִנֵּיהּ י', וְאִשְׁתְּאַר עָקֵב, וְרָזָא דְמִלָּה, הוּא יְשׁוּפְךָ רֹאשׁ וְאַתָּה תְּשׁוּפֶנּוּ עָקֵב. כַּד אִשְׁתַּלִּימַת סוּכָּה בְּיֶרֶךְ דִּילָהּ, אִתְּמַר בְּיַעֲקֹב, וַיָּבֹא יַעֲקֹב שָׁלֵם.

48. It is said about Jacob's thigh, meaning Netzach: "**...and he limped upon his thigh...**" (Genesis 32:32), [See Zohar, Beresheet A 142] because until then he did not get corrected with the correction of the Columns, except for the chest of Zeir Anpin and above, which is Chesed, Gevurah, and Tiferet, and he did not get corrected at all in the aspect of Netzach, Hod, and Yesod, which are from the chest and below. Therefore, after the angel touched the aspect of the chest and below, he touched the hollow of the thigh of Jacob, **because the Yud flew away from Jacob,** which is the secret of Malchut since from the chest and below is the place of Malchut, **and the heel (*akev*) remained, and the secret meaning of this matter is: "...they shall bruise your head, and you shall bruise their heel."** (Genesis 3:15) meaning that the external forces infiltrated Malchut that is called *akev*, since it is in the end of all the Sefirot, in the secret of "her legs go down to death..." (Proverbs 5:5) which are the Klipot. **And when the Sukkah was completed with his thigh,** meaning when a curtain (*masach*) was established, since Sukkah comes from the word *masach*, so that the Light is not drawn from above downward, since with this [curtain] the grasp of the external forces is nullified, **then it is said of Jacob: "And Jacob came to Shalem [lit. whole]..."** (Genesis 33:18) since this is the meaning of "...and God fashioned the side (*hatzela*)..." (Genesis 2:22), since *tzela* comes from *tzolea* (limping).

49. וְיַעֲקֹב וַדַּאי אִיהוּ דִּיוֹקְנָא דְעַמּוּדָא דְאֶמְצָעִיתָא, מִסִּטְרָא דִלְבָר. וְהָא מֹשֶׁה תַמָּן הֲוָה. אֶלָּא, מִסִּטְרָא דִלְגָאו הֲוָה. דָּא מִגוּפָא, וְדָא מִנִּשְׁמְתָא.

49. And Jacob certainly is the image of the Central Column, meaning a chariot of Zeir Anpin, **from the external aspect.** He asks, **"But Moses is there?"** and answers, **"Rather** Moses is a chariot of Zeir Anpin **from the inner aspect** of Zeir Anpin. **This one,** Jacob is a chariot to **the bodily** aspect of Zeir Anpin, which is outer, **and the other,** Moses, **is** of the aspect **of the soul,** which is inner.

50. וּבְגִין דָּא תְּרֵין יַרְכִין דְּעַמּוּדָא דְאֶמְצָעִיתָא אִינּוּן נֵצַח וְהוֹד. וּמָתַי יִהְיֶה עַמּוּדָא דְאֶמְצָעִיתָא שְׁלִים, כַּד אִתְחַוַּבר בִּשְׁכִינְתָא. הָדָא הוּא דִּכְתִּיב, וְיַעֲקֹב נָסַע סֻכֹּתָה וַיִּבֶן לוֹ בָּיִת. הָדָא הוּא דִּכְתִּיב, וַיִּבֶן יְ"יָ אֱלֹקִי"ם אֶת הַצֵּלָע. בְּהַהוּא זִמְנָא דְּאִתְחַוַּבר עִמָּה, וַיָּבֹא יַעֲקֹב שָׁלֵם. בְּהַהוּא זִמְנָא תְּהֵא סוּכָּה שְׁלֵימָתָא, כ"ו ה"ס. יאהדונה"י.

50. "Therefore, because Jacob is the outer aspect of Tiferet, in the aspect of the body, **Netzach and Hod,** which are outside the body**, are the two legs of the Central Column,** Jacob, that support him. **And when will the Central Column be complete? When it joins with the Shechinah,** which is Malchut. **This is what is written: 'and Jacob journeyed to Sukkot, and built himself a house'** (Genesis 33:17) **and it is also written: 'which the Lord God fashioned** (hatzela) **from man....'** (Genesis 2:22) **It is written concerning the time he joined with her: 'And Jacob came to Shalem....'** (Genesis 33:18) **And at that time it will be a complete Sukkah,** meaning the spelling of Sukkah will be full, with Vav, whose numerical value is **Kaf-Vav (26),** namely Yud-Hei-Vav-Hei, which is the secret of Zeir Anpin, and **Hei-Samech (65)** the numerical value of Adonai, Malchut, combined into **Yud-Alef-Hei-Dalet-Vav-Nun-Hei-Yud."**

"And you shall take for yourselves on the first day
the fruit of the Hadar Tree"

51. קָם רַבִּי אֶלְעָזָר וְאָמַר, אַבָּא אַבָּא אַמַּאי אִתְּמַר בְּיוֹמָא קַדְמָאָה דְּסֻכּוֹת, וּלְקַחְתֶּם לָכֶם בַּיּוֹם הָרִאשׁוֹן פְּרִי עֵץ הָדָר. אָמַר לֵיהּ, בְּרִי, מָאנֵי קְרָבָא בִּימִינָא נָטְלִין לוֹן.

51. Rav Elazar got up and said to Rav Shimon, **"Father, father, why does it say about the first day of Sukkot,** which takes place exactly on the fifteenth of the month, as mentioned, **'And you shall take for yourselves on the first day the fruit of the Hadar tree....'** (Leviticus 23:40), meaning what is the verse alluding to with the words 'on the first day.'?" **He,** Rav Shimon, **said** to Rav Elazar, **"My son,** the verse alludes to **the weapons of war,** which are the four species that represent the four letters Yud-Hei-Vav-Hei. **We take them with the right hand,** and the first day is the secret of the Right Column, Chesed—the first day that accompanies all days.

52. וּבְאִלֵּין מָאנֵי קְרָבָא, אִינּוּן יִשְׂרָאֵל רְשִׁימִין, דְּנָצְחִין דִּינָא מְתַל לְמַלְכָּא, דַּהֲוָה לֵיהּ דִּינָא וּקְרָבָא בְּשַׁבְעִין אוּמִין, וְלָא הֲוֹו יַדְעִין מָאן נָצַח דִּינָא, וְשָׁאֲלִין לֵיהּ מָאן נָצַח דִּינָא. אָמַר, תִּסְתַּכְּלוּן בְּאִלֵּין דִּרְשִׁימִין בְּמָאנֵי קְרָבָא בִּידַיְיהוּ, וְתִנְדְּעוּן מָאן נָצַח דִּינָא.

52. "And by these weapons, namely the four species, **are Israel marked to have won the trial. This is likened to a king who had a trial and war against seventy nations, but it was not known who won the trial. And they asked him who won the trial.** The king **said, 'Look at who has weapons in their hands and you will know who won the trial.'**

53. וּלְקַחְתֶּם לָכֶם בַּיּוֹם הָרִאשׁוֹן פְּרִי עֵץ הָדָר: דָּא אֶתְרוֹג, דְּאִיהִי שְׁכִינְתָּא, לִבָּא. דְּאִיהִי עִקָּרָא דְּכָל אַבְרִין דְּגוּפָא, דְּאִינּוּן תְּלַת הַדַּסִּים, וְלוּלָב, וּתְרֵי בַּדֵּי עֲרָבָה. לִבָּא בְּאֶמְצָעִיתָא, וְאַבְרִין סְחוֹר סְחוֹר לֵיהּ.

53. "'And you shall take for yourselves on the first day the fruit of the Hadar tree....' This is the Etrog, which is the Shechinah, namely Malchut, which is the fruit of Zeir Anpin that is called 'hadar tree.' And it corresponds to the heart, which is the main [organ] among all the organs in the body, which are three myrtles, Chesed, Gevurah, and Tiferet, the Lulav, Yesod, and two willow branches, Netzach and Hod. The heart, which is the Etrog, Malchut, is in the center, and the organs are all around it.

54. וּבְגִין דָּא, אֶתְרוֹג דָּא שְׁכִינְתָּא. וְהָכִי אוּקְמוּהָ מָארֵי מַתְנִיתִין, אִי נִטְלָה בּוּכְנָתוֹ וְאִי עָלָה חֲזָזִית עַל רֻבּוֹ פָּסוּל. בְּגִין דְּאִיהוּ דָּמֵי לִשְׁכִינְתָּא, דְּאִתְּמַר בָּהּ, כֻּלָּךְ יָפָה רַעְיָתִי וּמוּם אֵין בָּךְ.

54. "Therefore, the Etrog that corresponds to the heart is the Shechinah. And this is the meaning of what the masters of the Mishnah established; that if its upper stem was removed or if lichen grew over most of it, it would be unfit to use, because it is compared to the Shechinah, about whom is said: 'You are all fair, my love, and there is no blemish in you.' (Song of Songs 4:7)

55. כַּפֹּת תְּמָרִים, דָּא לוּלָב. וַעֲלֵיהּ אִתְּמַר נִפְרְצוּ עָלָיו פָּסוּל בְּגִין דְּדָא אִיהוּ מְקַצֵּץ בִּנְטִיעוֹת מָאן דִּמְבָרֵךְ עֲלָהּ בְּיוֹמָא קַדְמָאָה דְּסֻכּוֹת, בְּגִין דְּאִיהוּ קְשׁוּרָא וְיִחוּדָא דְּכֹלָּא, חַ"י עָלְמִין, דְּאִיהוּ לְקַבֵּל חַ"י חוּלְיָין דְּשִׁדְרָה.

55. "'...branches of palm trees...' (Leviticus 23:40) refers to the Lulav, of which we learned that, 'if its leaves are severed it is unfit to recite a blessing over it.' Therefore, whoever makes a blessing over a Lulav whose leaves are severed on the first day of Sukkot, he cuts down the young trees, which are the Sefirot, since his actions below awaken corresponding actions above, because it, meaning the Lulav, which is Yesod, is the bond and unity of all the Sefirot. And it is called the Life (chai; 18) of the Worlds, since it includes nine Sefirot of Returning Light from below upward, and 18 in the

two worlds, which are Zeir Anpin and Malchut, **which correspond to the eighteen vertebrae of the spinal column.**

56. וּבְגִין דָּא אוּקְמוּהוּ מָארֵי מַתְנִיתִין, לוּלָב דּוּמֶה לְשִׁדְרָה, וְרָזָא דְלוּלָב, צַדִּיק כַּתָּמָר יִפְרָח. וְדָא אִיהוּ כִּי כֹל בַּשָּׁמַיִם וּבָאָרֶץ, וְתִרְגֵּם אֻנְקְלוֹס, דַּאֲחִיד בִּשְׁמַיָּא וּבְאַרְעָא.

56. "Therefore, the masters of the Mishnah established that the Lulav is compared to the spine, which is the foundation of all the bones. [See Zohar, Pinchas 422] The secret of the Lulav is 'The righteous shall flourish like the palm tree...'** (Psalms 92:13) because 'the righteous' is Yesod, and the "palm tree" is the Lulav, [as it says] '...branches of palm trees....' **This is** the meaning of what is said: **'for all that is in Heaven and on Earth'** (I Chronicles 29:11) and 'all' alludes to Yesod. **And Onkelos translates: 'That is attached to Heaven and Earth,'** namely Yesod that is attached to Heaven and Earth, which are Zeir Anpin and Malchut.

57. וְצָרִיךְ לְנַעְנְעָא ח"י נִעְנוּעִין, בְּשִׁית סִטְרִין. דְּאִינּוּן וֹזוּתָם מִזְרָח בֵּיה"ו וכו'. שִׁית הֲוַיּוֹ"ת דְּאִית בְּהוֹן תַּמְנֵי סְרֵי אַתְוָן. וְכֻלְּהוּ רְמִיזִין בְּסֵפֶר יְצִירָה.

57. "We must shake eighteen times in six directions, three in every direction, **which are the seal of the east with Yud-Hei-Vav** because by the precept of the Taking of the Lulav while facing east we awaken the unification of Chochmah and Binah above, in the Chochmah and Binah of Yisrael-Saba and Tevunah, which are Yud and Hei, and Zeir Anpin that elevates and regulated between Chochmah and Binah is the secret of Vav, which is Da'at. In this way, the east, which is the secret of Zeir Anpin, sealed the Mochin, which are Yud-Hei-Vav that are Chochmah, Binah, and Da'at, up in Yisrael-Saba and Tevunah, in the secret of 'three come out of one.' Afterwards, with the shaking of each direction, the Mochin get revealed and sealed below in Zeir Anpin and Nukva, in the secret of 'one is sustained by three,' in the six combinations of Yud-Hei-Vav, each side according to its governing attribute. For example, Yud-Hei-Vav in the south, Hei-Vav-Yud in the north, etc. [as is explained in the Ari's Gate of Meditations, Volume II regarding Sukkot, discourse five] **There are six permutations of Yud-Hei-Vav, which contain eighteen letters, and they are all alluded to in the Book of Formation (Sefer Yetzirah).**

58. וְהָכִי אוּקְמוּהוּ מָארֵי מַתְנִיתִין, מוֹלִיךְ וּמֵבִיא לְמָאן דְּאַרְבַּע רוּחוֹת הָעוֹלָם דִּילֵיהּ, מַעֲלֶה וּמוֹרִיד, לְמָאן דִּשְׁמַיָּא וְאַרְעָא דִילֵיהּ.

58. "And so have the masters of the Mishnah established (Tractate Sukkah 37b) that it is necessary to shake to the six directions. **One extends and returns** the Lulav and its species **to He to Whom the four directions of the world belong, and he raises and lowers to He to Whom Heaven and Earth belong.**

59. תְּלַת הֲדַסִּין: גּוּף וּתְרֵין דְּרוֹעִין. וְאִינּוּן לָקֳבֵל עֵינָא, וְכַנְפֵי עֵינָא. תְּרֵי בַּדֵּי עֲרָבוֹת, לָקֳבֵל תְּרֵין שׁוֹקִין, וְלָקֳבֵל תְּרֵין שִׂפְוָון.

59. "The three branches of **myrtle** are Chesed, Gevurah, and Tiferet, which are **the body,** Tiferet, **and two arms,** which are Chesed and Gevurah; **they correspond to the eye and the two eyelids. Two boughs of willow,** which are Netzach and Hod, **correspond to the two legs,** which are Netzach and Hod of the body, **and to the two lips,** which are Netzach and Hod of the head.

60. וְכַד אִינּוּן כֻּלְּהוּ אֲגוּדָה וַחֲדָא בְּלוּלָב דְּאִיהוּ שִׁדְרָה, מַה כְּתִיב אָמַרְתִּי אֶעֱלֶה בְתָמָר: א' אֶתְרוֹג. ע' עֲרָבָה. כ' לוּלָב. ה' הֲדַס. כֻּלְּהוּ אִתְעֲבִידוּ לָקֳבֵל אַרְבַּע מִינִין. דִּמְרַכַּבְתָּא, הָרוֹכֵב בְּהוֹן אִיהוּ יהו"ה. וְצָרִיךְ לְסַדְּרָא בְּהוֹן בְּהַקָּפָה, כְּגַוְונָא דְמִזְבֵּחַ.

60. "And when all the species are in a bundle with the Lulav, namely Yesod, **which is the spine** that rises up to the brain, **it is written: 'I said, I will climb up** (e'eleh, Alef-Ayin-Lamed-Hei) **into the palm tree....'** (Song of Songs 7:9) The initials of e'eleh are **Alef–Etrog, Ayin–Arava (willow),**

Lamed–Lulav, Hei–Hadas (myrtle). All of them, all the hosts of Heaven, **are formed** in lines and are organized under the Three Columns and Malchut, **corresponding to the four species of the chariot** of the Lulav. See Zohar, Va'etchanan verse 62, where it says 'When man is about to unite the Name of the Holy One blessed be He, all the hosts of Heaven stand in rows so as to be established and reach perfection by means of that unification.' **The one who rides them,** meaning the four species, **is Yud-Hei-Vav-Hei** because the myrtle is the secret of Yud, the willows are the first Hei, the Lulav is Vav, and the Etrog is the last Hei. **And they,** the Lulav and its species, **must be set in a circle** around the table or the platform in the synagogue, which are **like the altar** of the Temple." [The concept of the shakings and encircling are found in the Gate of Meditations, Volume II of the Ari, in the aforementioned discourse.]

61. וּלְמָאן. לְמַן דְּאִתְנְטָעוּ אִלֵּין נְטִיעִין בֵּיהּ. וְרָזָא דְמִלָּה, נְקֵבָה תְּסוֹבֵב גֶּבֶר. נְקֵבָה, נ' מִן גַּן. גֶּבֶר גּ' מִן גַּן: הוּא כְּלִיל תְּלַת וְחַמְשִׁין סִדְרִין דְּאוֹרַיְיתָא דִּבִכְתָב. וְשֶׁבַע יוֹמִין דְּסוּכּוֹת, הָא שִׁתִּין. לָקֳבֵל שִׁתִּין מַסֶּכְתּוֹת.

61. He asks, **"For whom are they?"** all of the great Mochin that are drawn in the seven days of the Holiday, by the shakings and by the encirclings, and answers, **"For the Garden** (*gan*, Gimel-Nun), namely Malchut, **since the young trees,** which are the Sefirot of Zeir Anpin and Malchut, **were planted in it. The secret of the matter is: 'a woman shall court a man'** (Jeremiah 31:21) **A woman** (*nekevah*), which is Malchut, **is alluded to in the Nun of *gan*** (garden), and **man** (*gever*), namely Zeir Anpin, **is alluded to in the Gimel of *gan*. *Gan* is the inclusive** number **of the 53 weekly portions of the Written Torah,** which is Zeir Anpin, **plus the seven days of Sukkot** it is **sixty, corresponding to the sixty tractates** of the Oral Torah, which is Malchut.

62. שְׁמִינִי עֲצֶרֶת, חַג בִּפְנֵי עַצְמוֹ, בֵּיהּ נְבִיעוּ דְּאוֹרַיְיתָא, לְאַשְׁקָאָה אִילָנָא, דְּאִיהוּ נָטוּעַ בְּגַן, וְשָׁרָשׁוֹי וְעַנְפוֹי, אִיהוּ כְּגַוְונָא דְּחוּג הָאָרֶץ, דְּכָל חַגִּין מִתְחַגְּגִין בֵּהּ.

62. "Shmini Atzeret is a holiday by itself. In it illuminates a wellspring of the Torah, namely the Chasadim from the Central Column, to water the tree, namely Zeir Anpin, which is planted in the Garden, and its roots and branches. The holiday of Shmini Atzeret is like '…the circle of the earth…' (Isaiah 40:22) around which all the holidays are celebrated because from the union of Zeir Anpin and Malchut on the day of Shmini Atzeret blessings are drawn, which are the Lights of the Chasadim, flow to Israel for the entire year. [See Zohar, Tzav 119]

63. תְּשִׁיעָאָה בְּרִנָּה, וְדָא אִיהוּ רַנְּנוּ צַדִּיקִים בַּיְ"יָ. וְדָא דַרְגָּא דְּצַדִּיק חַ"י עָלְמִין. מִתַּפָּן רִנָּה. וּבֵיה פּוּרְקָנָא. הָדָא הוּא דִכְתִיב, צֶמַח צַדִּיק, וּמִתַּוְוֹתָיו יִצְמָח. מִתַּוְוֹתָיו, וַדַּאי, הַהִיא דְּאִיהִי עֲשִׂירִית לְכֹלָא, וְצַדִּיק נָטִיל מִשְׂמָאלָא, וְעַמּוּדָא דְּאֶמְצָעִיתָא מִימִינָא. הָדָא הוּא דִכְתִיב מִימִינוֹ אֵשׁ דָּת לָמוֹ.

63. "The ninth melody is rejoicing (rinah), and that is what is said 'Rejoice in the Lord, you righteous….'" (Psalms 33:1) This is the level of the Righteous, the life of the worlds, namely Yesod. From there emanates joy (rinah, Resh-Nun-Hei) spelled with the letters of river (nahar, Nun-Hei-Resh) as in the verse: 'And a river went out from Eden…' (Genesis 2:10) which is Yesod. And contains redemption, which is what is meant by: 'a righteous offshoot' (Jeremiah 23:5) [see Zohar, Pinchas 271 and 339] in the accordance with the secret meaning of the verse: 'But when the wicked perish there is joy (rinah).' (Proverbs 11:10); 'who shall grow up out of his place…' (Zechariah 6:12), literally under him, namely Malchut that is under Yesod, which is the tenth to all the Sefirot. The righteous, Yesod, takes from the Left, and the Central Column, Tiferet, takes from the Right, as is written: '…at His right hand was a fiery law unto them.' (Deuteronomy 33:2)

64. בְּהַהוּא זִמְנָא דִּיהוֹן תְּרֵין שְׁמָהָן כַּחֲדָא, אִתְּעָרָא בְּרַתָּא דְּמַלְכָּא, בְּשִׁיר הַשִּׁירִים, וּמִשְׁלֵי, וְקֹהֶלֶת. דְּאִינּוּן שְׁלֹשֶׁת אֲלָפִים מָשָׁל, תְּלַת יוֹדִי"ן, דְּאִינּוּן תְּלַת טִפִּין דְּמוֹחָא, דְּנָחֲתִין מִן י'. וּלְאָן אִתְמַשְׁכוּ. לְגַבֵּי צַדִּיק, דְּאִיהוּ קֶשֶׁת

וּבַה דַּהֲוָה קָטָן, אִתְעֲבִיד גָּדוֹל. וְרָזָא דְמִלָּה שׂוֹפָר הוֹלֵךְ פָּזֵר גָּדוֹל. מַה יְהֵא זָרִיק חֵץ בְּדִיוּקְנָא דָא ׳׳.

64. Here is missing the beginning of the matter, and the beginning is found in the Tikkunim Chadashim, page 131a, where it says the following: **This is the secret of Amen,** which equals 91 like the numerical value of Yud-Hei-Vav-Hei plus Alef-Dalet-nun-Yud, which are Zeir Anpin and Malchut, unified as one, **Yud-Alef-Hei-Dalet-Vav-Nun-Hei-Yud, which is the combination of two Names. Therefore, the one who says "amen" is greater,** since he unities and combines the two Names, **than the one who makes the blessing,** since in the other blessings of the prayer the two Names are not united. [See Zohar, Pinchas 312] **"At that time, when the two Names** Yud-Hei-Vav-Hei and Adonai **are one, the King's daughter,** Malchut, **will be aroused with Song of Songs, Proverbs, and Ecclesiastes,** which correspond to the Three Columns: Song of Songs– Right, Lovingkindness; Ecclesiastes–Left, Judgment; Proverbs–Central Column, Mercy. [See Zohar, Bo 142] **They are three thousand parables,** corresponding to the Three Columns, **which are three Yud's,** which hint to the Chochmah, Binah, and Da'at of Chochmah, **that are the three drops of the brain that descend from Yud,** which is the secret of the Supernal Aba and Ima whose Sefirot are all in the secret of "thousand." **And to where are they drawn; to the Righteous who is rainbow,** namely the crown of Yesod. **And whoever was small,** meaning Zeir Anpin with the Mochin of the Lower Six, which are Chesed, Gevurah, Tiferet, Netzach, Hod, and Yesod of Lights in the Chochmah, Binah, Da'at, Chesed, Gevurah, and Tiferet of vessels, due to the opposite relation between the lights and vessels, **becomes great** because by the acquisition of the Chochmah, Binah, and Da'at of Lights it is considered that it acquired the vessel of Yesod of Gadlut, which includes Netzach and Hod. **This is indicated in** *Shofar Holech* [lit. forward horn], *Pazer Gadol* [lit. great scatter]." He asks, **"What does he throw (*zarik*)?"** and answers, **"An arrow shaped in this form** ׳׳, namely *Pazer* of the cantillation marks."

The one who slays that serpent shall
be given the King's daughter

65. פָּתַח רַבִּי שִׁמְעוֹן וְאָמַר, עֶלָאִין, אִתְתַּקְנוּ וְאוֹזְדַרְזוּ בְּמָאנֵי קְרָבָא, לְגַבֵּי חִוְיָא דְאִיהוּ מְקַנְּנָא בְּטוּרִין וְאִיהוּ קָטִיל לְאָדָם קַדְמָאָה, וּלְכָל דָּרִין דַּהֲווֹ אֲבַתְרֵיהּ.

65. Rav Shimon opened and said, "Celestial beings, hurry and prepare yourselves with weapons against the serpent that nests in the great mountains, he who killed Primordial Adam and all the generations after him."

66. וּבְגִין דָּא כָּרוֹזָא נָפִיק בְּכָל יוֹמָא, מָאן דְקָטִיל הַהוּא חִוְיָא, דְאִיהוּ מְקַנְּנָא בְּטוּרִין, יָהֲבִין לֵיהּ בְּרַתָּא דְמַלְכָּא. דְאִיהוּ צְלוֹתָא, דְיָתִיב עַל מַגְדְלָא. דְאִתְּמַר בָּהּ מִגְדַל עֹז שֵׁם יְ"יָ בּוֹ יָרוּץ צַדִּיק וְנִשְׂגָּב.

66. Therefore, a proclamation comes out daily and proclaims that whoever slays that serpent, which nests in the mountains, shall be given the King's daughter, namely Malchut, which is prayer, in the secret of: "...I am all prayer." (Psalms 109:4) She sits on a tower, about which is written "The Name of the Lord is a strong tower, the righteous man runs into it and is set up high." (Proverbs 18: 10)

67. אַדְהָכִי, הָא רַעְיָא מְהֵימְנָא קָא אָתֵי, בְּכַמָּה עָאנִין וְתוֹרִין וְאִמְרִין, וְחוּטְרָא בִּידֵיהּ, סָלִיק עֵינֵיהּ לְמַגְדְלָא, וְאָתָא חַד בַּר נַשׁ עוּלֵימָא, צַדִּיק שְׁמֵיהּ, דַּהֲוָה יָתִיב עַל מַגְדְלָא, הַשְׁתָּא בִּידוֹי וַהֲוָה זָרִיק חִצִּים לְגַבֵּי חִוְיָא, וְדָא אִיהִי פָּזֵר גָּדוֹל ל. וְחִוְיָא לָא הֲוָה חָשִׁיב לוֹן.

67. In the meantime, the Faithful Shepherd arrived, namely Moses, with many sheep, oxen, and lambs, who are the souls of the righteous who are mentally crafty yet consider themselves like animals with his staff in his hand. He raised his eyes to the tower and saw there a young man whose name was *tzadik* (righteous), namely Yesod, who was sitting on the tower,

as explained in the previous verse, **with his bow in his hand,** namely his wisdom and prayer. **He was shooting arrows at the serpent, which is the great Pazer** ׀**. But the serpent paid them no attention,** meaning it was not slain by his arrows.

68. וְקַשְׁתָּא, אִיהִי לִישָׁנָא דְּפוּמָא, אֲגוֹזָא דְּקַשְׁתָּא, פּוּמָא. וְחוּט הַשָּׁנִי, דָּא שָׂפָה, חוּט שֶׁל חֶסֶד, דְּבֵיהּ הֲוָה צַדִּיק זָרִיק חִצִּין, דְּאִינוּן מִלּוּלִין דִּצְלוֹתָא, לְגַבֵּי חִוְיָא. וְחִוְיָא לָא הֲוָה חָשִׁיב לוֹן.

68. He explains, "The Chochmah, Binah, and Da'at of Malchut that is called 'mouth,' **the bow is the tongue in the mouth,** which alludes to Chochmah**, the nut of the bow is the mouth,** meaning the Central Column, Da'at, in the secret of the correction of the dividing line (*parsa*), and nut (*egoz*) comes from *ektzotz* (I will cut), **the Scarlet thread is the lip,** as in the secret meaning of: 'Your lips are like a scarlet thread…' (Song of Songs 4:3) and it is Binah, **a thread of Chesed,** in the secret of the verse: 'Because He delights in mercy.' (Micah 7:18) which refers to Binah. **For with** this thread **the righteous one was shooting arrows, [which are like the words of prayer towards the serpent], but the serpent ignored them.**

69. עַד דְּאָתָא רַעְיָא מְהֵימְנָא, וְנָטִיל חֵין חַד, וְזָרִיק לְגַבֵּיהּ, דָּא בָּתַר דָּא, בִּצְלוֹתֵיהּ, הָדָא הוּא דִּכְתִיב, עַד יְפַלַּח חֵץ כְּבֵדוֹ דְּחִוְיָא, דְּאִיהוּ סמא"ל, אֵל אַחֵר, דְּתַמָּן יְסוֹדֵיהּ וְעִקָּרֵיהּ.

69. "**Until the Faithful Shepherd,** namely Moses, **came and took an arrow and shot it at** the serpent, **one after another, with his prayer,** which was the bow, **as it says: 'until an arrow pierced his liver'** (Proverbs 7:23), **of the serpent, who is Sama"el, a strange God (***El***), for there** in the liver **is his base and essence.**

70. וּבְגִין דָּא, הַכָּבֵד כּוֹעֵס. בְּמַאי כּוֹעֵס בְּמָרָה, דְּאִיהִי דְּבוּקָה בֵּיהּ, וְדָא סַם הַמָּוֶת. נוּקְבָא דִּילֵיהּ. וְנָבָא דִּילֵיהּ, יוֹתֶרֶת הַכָּבֵד. יוֹתֶרֶת אִתְקְרִיאַת,

דִּבְתַר דַּעֲבִידַת נְאוּפִין, יָהִיבַת שְׁיּוּרִין לְבַעְלָהּ. וּזְנָבָא אִיהִי שִׁפְחָה דִּילֵיהּ,
בְּמִרָה כָּעִיס, וּבְזְנָבָא קָטִיל.

70. "Therefore, the liver becomes angry, and anyone who gets angry is as
though he worships idols (Tractate Shabbat 105b). **How does it become
angry? With the gall that is attached to it, which is a potion of death,**
which is the meaning of what our scholars said: 'that a drop of gall hangs
from the sword of the Angel of Death.' (Tractate Avoda Zara 20a) **Its
female is its tail, the lobe of the liver. It is called** *yoteret* [lit. addition
or leftover], **because after she commits adultery, she gives the remains
to her husband,** since *yoteret* (lobe) comes from 'leftover.' **The tail is his
maidservant,** because she runs errands for him. **He gets angry with the
gall and kills with his tail,** which is the lobe that is extra like the tail.

71. מִרָה אִיהִי פַּרְצוּף דִּילֵיהּ. יוֹתֶרֶת זָנָב דִּילֵיהּ. כְּגַוְונָא דְּאָדָם, דְּעָבִיד לֵיהּ
פַּרְצוּף, וּלְבָתַר זָנָב, דְּהַאי אָדָם רָע אִתְקְרֵי. וְדָא כְּגַוְונָא דְּדָא, דָּא אָדָם
דְּאִתְנְטִיל מֵאִילָנָא דְּחַיֵּי. וְדָא אָדָם, דְּאִתְנְטִיל מֵאִילָנָא דְּמוֹתָא.

71. "The gall is its face, meaning a complete Partzuf of the attribute if
Judgment, and includes four galls: white gall, red gall, green gall, and black
gall. [See Zohar, Pinchas 420] **The lobe is its tail,** and was cut out from
him to be his female part, and she is a harlot, **like Primordial Man, for
whom He made a face,** in the secret of them being created with two faces,
and then a tail in the secret of 'and God fashioned the side.' [See Tractate
Berachot 61a, where Rav and Shmuel hold two different opinions, and
both are words of God] **For this one is called an evil man, and one** was
created **as the other,** in the secret of: 'God made the one as well as the
other....' (Ecclesiastes 7:14) **The** Primordial **Man was taken from the Tree
of Life,** which is Zeir Anpin, **and this man of** wickedness **was taken from
the Tree of Death,** which is Malchut of the attribute of Judgment.

72. לְבָתַר דְּיִפָּלֵוּ חֵץ כִּבְדוֹ. זֶרַע יוֹרֶה כַּחֵץ לְגַבֵּי כַלָּה. יו"ד זֶרַע דְּאִתְמַשֵׁךְ מִינֵיהּ, וְדָא ז', וְאִתְּמַר בָּהּ לְשַׁלְּחוּ לִי לְמַטָּרָה. וְדָא בַּת עַיִן, בֵּית קְבוּל לְזֶרַע, דְּאִיהוּ ז' וַדַּאי.

72. **"After the arrow pierces the liver** of Sama"el, **a seed shoots like an arrow to the bride,** namely Malchut, since all the judgments that are found in holiness, in a way of battling the Other Side, are before the unification of Yud-Hei-Vav-Hei and Adonai. But after the unification, all the battles are already finished (as it says later in the Twenty-First Tikkun). **Yud is the secret of a drop of seed,** the Mochin that come from Chochmah that is Yud, which flows to Yesod, Vav. **This is** Zayin, which is the secret of Yud over Vav. **And it is said about it,** the drop from the brain: '...**I shot at a mark.**' (I Samuel 20:20) **And this** Malchut **is the pupil of the eye** (*bat ayin*), since each Sefira is composed of Ten Sefirot, and seven times ten is seventy (Ayin), and Malchut that receives them is called 'daughter' (*bat*) of Ayin (70). **She is a receptacle for the seed, which is surely Zayin."**

73. מַאי מַטָּרָה. דָּא יָרֵחַ ⅄ בֶּן יוֹמוֹ, סִיהֲרָא קַדִּישָׁא מַטָּרָה אִיהִי וַדַּאי לְבַת עַיִן. נְקוּדָה זְעֵירָא מִלְּגָיו. לְגַבָּהּ הוּא שָׁלַח וَצֵּים בִּרְחִימוּ דְּעַיְנִין.

73. He explains, **"What is 'a mark'** that Jonathan told David: 'I shot at a mark (or: guard).' **This is** *yare'ach ben yomo* ⅄ **(day-old Moon), the Holy Moon,** namely Malchut at the beginning of her renewal, on the first day of the month. **She certainly guards the pupil of the eye, which is a tiny dot within,** which is the pupil that is the essence of the eye, where only there is Chochmah revealed. **This is where he shot his arrows with love of the eyes,** which is the Light of Chochmah, called 'eyes.'

74. מַטָּרָה: וַדַּאי שְׁכִינְתָּא, דְּאִיהִי אֲגִינַת עַל יִשְׂרָאֵל, מֵחִוְיָא, בִּישָׁא, סמא"ל. וּלְמַאן דְּאִיהִי אֲגִינַת עֲלֵיהּ, אִתְּמַר בֵּיהּ, לֹא תִירָא מִפַּחַד לָיְלָה מֵחֵץ יָעוּף יוֹמָם.

74. "The mark is surely the Shechinah that guards Israel against the evil serpent, Sama"el. And about those she is guarding is said: 'You shall not be afraid of the terror by night, nor of the arrow that flies by day.' (Psalms 91:5)

‫75. בְּאֶבְרָתוֹ יָסֶךְ לָךְ. דָּא אֵבֶר מִן הַחַי צַדִּיק. וְתַחַת כְּנָפָיו תֶּחְסֶה: אִינּוּן‬
‫ה"ה. דְּאָת ז', ו' אִיהוּ אֶבְרָתוֹ. כָּלוּל י"ו. גּוּפָא דִּילֵיהּ ו'. רֵישָׁא דִּילֵיהּ י'.‬
‫גַּדְפוֹי ה"ה.‬

75. "'He shall cover you with His pinions (*evrato*)....' (Psalms 91:4) He explains that *evrato* refers **to flesh torn from the living [animal],** namely Yesod, that is called **the Righteous** life of the world, which is comprised of nine Sefirot of Direct Light and nine Sefirot of Returning Light, which together equal *chai* (life; 18). **'And under His wings shall you take refuge....'** (Ibid.) His wings **are the two Hei's,** Binah and Malchut **because the letter Zayin is His pinion, which includes Yud-Vav,** namely Yesod and the crown, **its body is Vav and its head is Yud,** as in, a crown over the head of the righteous. **His wings are Hei and Hei,** meaning a complete stature of Chochmah, Binah, Tiferet and Malchut, which is included in Yesod.

‫76. וּבְגִין דָּא, וְתַחַת כְּנָפָיו תֶּחְסֶה צִנָּה וְסוֹחֵרָה אֲמִתּוֹ. צִנָּה וְסוֹחֵרָה: שְׁכִינְתָּא‬
‫עִלָּאָה וְתַתָּאָה. אֲמִתּוֹ: דָּא עַמּוּדָא דְּאֶמְצָעִיתָא. רֵישָׁא דִּילֵיהּ, וְחָכְמָה עִלָּאָה.‬
‫צַדִּיק אִיהוּ בְּצַלְמוֹ כִּדְמוּתוֹ. זַכָּאָה אִיהוּ מָאן דְּנָטִיר בְּרִית מִילָה, וְאוֹרַיְיתָא‬
‫דְּאִיהוּ עַמּוּדָא דְּאֶמְצָעִיתָא דְּתַרְוַויְיהוּ, מְגִינִין עֲלֵיהּ, חַד בְּעָלְמָא דָּא, וְחַד‬
‫בְּעָלְמָא דְּאָתֵי.‬

76. "Because Yesod is comprised of the entire stature of Zeir Anpin, therefore: 'and under His wings shall you take refuge; His truth shall be your shield and buckler.' (Ibid.) 'Shields and buckler' are two shields, which **are the Upper Shechinah**–Binah, **and the lower**–Malchut; 'His truth' is the Central Column–Tiferet, Jacob, according to the meaning of: 'You will show truth to Jacob....' (Micah 7:20) **His head is Supernal**

Chochmah. The Righteous, namely Yesod, **is in his image, after His likeness** because every aspect receives from its corresponding higher aspect. **Praised is he who guards the circumcision,** which is the aspect of Yesod, **and the Torah, which is the aspect of the Central Column,** Tiferet. **Both protect him, one in this world,** meaning that he merits all the Revealed Lights, which are Chochmah that are called 'this world,' **and one in the World to Come,** and he merits all the Concealed Lights, which are Chasadim, called 'the World to Come.'"

For the eighth day of the month of Elul
Fourteenth Tikkun
"The first of the first-fruits of your land… You shall not boil a kid in its mother's milk"

1. בְּרֵאשִׁית, עֲלָהּ אִתְּמַר, רֵאשִׁית בִּכּוּרֵי אַדְמָתְךָ תָּבִיא בֵּית יְ"יָ אֱלֹקֶי"ךָ, לֹא תְבַשֵּׁל גְּדִי בַּחֲלֵב אִמּוֹ. תָּא וְחֲזֵי, וְחָכְמָה עִלָּאָה, עֲלָהּ אִתְּמַר קַדֶּשׁ לִי כָל בְּכוֹר, דְּכָל בְּכוֹרִים עַל שְׁמָהּ אִתְקְרִיאוּ. וּשְׁכִינְתָּא מִתַּמָּן אִתְקְרִיאַת בְּכוֹרָה.

1. **It is said about Beresheet,** meaning Chochmah, as is written: "…the beginning of wisdom…" (Psalms 111: 10) **"The first (*resheet*) of the first-fruits of your land you shall bring into the house of the Lord your God. You shall not boil a kid in its mother's milk."** (Exodus 23:19) **Come and see, concerning Supernal Chochmah: "Sanctify to Me all the firstborn…"** (Exodus 13:2) Because Chochmah is called holiness (*kodesh*), **all firstborns,** meaning all Sefirot that have the Upper Three, **are named after it,** since it shines with the illumination of the Upper Three Sefirot. **And the Shechinah,** meaning Malchut, **from there,** meaning when She contains the Light of Chochmah, **is called Firstborn.**

2. וְחָכְמָה וַדַּאי עֲלָהּ אִתְּמַר, וְרֵאשִׁית כָּל בִּכּוּרֵי כֹל. וּבְרָא בּוּכְרָא דִּילָהּ קַדְמָאָה דְּכֹלָּא דָּא ו', עַמּוּדָא דְּאֶמְצָעִיתָא. בִּכּוּרֵי אַדְמָתְךָ, תְּרֵי סַמְכֵי קְשׁוֹט. מַאי אַדְמָתְךָ, שְׁכִינְתָּא תַתָּאָה. וְאִנּוּן כָּל בִּכּוּרֵי כֹל, מִסִּטְרָא דְּצַדִּיק דְּאִיהוּ כֹל.

2. **About Chochmah,** meaning Supernal Aba and Ima, **is certainly said: "And the first of all the first-fruits of all things…."** (Ezekiel 44:30) **And its firstborn son, which is the first of all, is Vav, the Central Column,** meaning Zeir Anpin. **"…the first-fruits of your land…" are the two supports of truth,** namely Netzach and Hod. He asks, **"What is 'your land,'?"** and answers, **"The lower Shechinah,** namely Malchut. **And they,** Netzach and Hod, **are 'all the first-fruits of all things' from the aspect of the Righteous,** Yesod, **that is** called **'all,'** because it comprises the five

Sefirot Chesed, Gevurah, Tiferet, Netzach, and Hod, each containing Ten
Sefirot, so they are fifty like the numerical value of *kol* (all).

‫3. וּשְׁכִינְתָּא אִיהִי אַרְעָא, דְּבֵיהּ גָּדְלִין וְצָמְחִין אִלָנִין. דַּעֲלָהּ אִתְּמַר, צֶמַח‬
‫צַדִּיק, דְּאִיהוּ עֵץ פְּרִי, אִילָנָא רַבָּא וּתְקִיף, עַמּוּדָא דְּאֶמְצָעִיתָא. עֲשָׂבִין‬
‫וְדִשְׁאִין, דְּאִינוּן תַּלְמִידֵי חֲכָמִים, מִתַּפָּן צָמְחִין. בְּגַן, בְּגִין דְּאִיהִי אוֹרַיְיתָא‬
‫דְּבַעַל פֶּה.‬

3. "And the Shechinah, namely Malchut, **is** called 'land,' for in Her,
meaning in the Returning Light that ascends from Malchut, **trees sprout
and grow,** which are the Sefirot. **For about her is said '…a righteous
off shoot…'** (Jeremiah 23:5) **which is a fruit tree, a big strong tree, the
Central Column,** Zeir Anpin, in which are included six Sefirot. **Grasses
and herbs, who are Torah scholars, grow from there,** from Malchut, **in
the garden, since she is the Oral Torah."**

‫4. וּמַאן אַשְׁקֵי וְרַוֵּי בָּהּ אִלָנִין וְעֲשָׂבִין וְדִשְׁאִין, מַעְיַן גַּנִּים, דְּאִיהִי חָכְמָה,‬
‫רֵאשִׁית כָּל, בִּכּוּרֵי כֹל. וּמֵאַיִן נַפְקָא מַעֲיָנָא דְּמַיָּא, מִבֵּית יְ"יָ. הָדָא הוּא‬
‫דִּכְתִיב, וּמַעְיָן מִבֵּית יְ"יָ יֵצֵא.‬

4. He asks, **"Who waters and saturates her trees, grasses and herbs?"**
and answers, **"…a fountain of gardens…"** (Song of Songs 4:15) **which is
Chochmah, 'the first of all the first-fruits of all things.'"** He asks, **"And
from where does the fountain of water come out,** refering to Zeir Anpin
that shines with Chasadim that are called water?" and answers, **"From the
house of the Lord,** which is Binah, **as is written: 'and a fountain shall
come forth of the house of the Lord….'** (Joel 4:18)

‫5. וּבְגִין דָּא, רֵאשִׁית בִּכּוּרֵי אַדְמָתְךָ תָּבִיא בֵּית יְ"יָ אֱלֹקֶי"ךָ. וְכֵן רֵאשִׁית‬
‫דְּעָאנֵי וְאִמְּרֵי. הָדָא הוּא דִּכְתִיב, וְרֵאשִׁית גֵּז צֹאנְךָ תִּתֶּן לוֹ.‬

5. "Therefore, because the first-fruits are the illumination of the Upper
Three Sefirot: **'The first of the first-fruits of your land you shall bring**

to the house of the Lord your God…' (Exodus 23:19) so they shall be sanctified unto the Lord, instead of drawing the illumination of the Upper Three Sefirot from above downward. **And so with the first of the sheep and lambs,** namely the first fleece, **as it is written: '…and the first of the fleece of your sheep shall you give to Him.'** (Deuteronomy 18:4)"

6. וּסְמִיךְ לֵיהּ לְרֵאשִׁית בִּכּוּרֵי אַדְמָתְךָ וכו', לֹא תְבַשֵּׁל גְּדִי בַּחֲלֵב אִמּוֹ. מַאי הַאי לְגַבֵּי הַאי. קָם רַבִּי שִׁמְעוֹן עַל רַגְלוֹי, פָּתַח בְּקָלָא סַגִּיא וְאָמַר, אֵלִיָּהוּ אֵלִיָּהוּ, נְחֵית הָכָא בִּרְשׁוּתָא דְמָארָךְ, וְאַנְהִיר, עֵינַיְיהוּ דְאִלֵּין סָבִין בְּהַאי מִלָּה, דְּלָא יֵתוּן לְמֵיכַל בָּשָׂר בֶּחָלָב.

6. He asks, "In the verse following '…the first-fruits of your land…' is said, 'You shall not boil a kid in its mother's milk.' Why are they adjacent?" Meaning what connection is there between the precept of first-fruits and the prohibition of eating meat and dairy." **Rav Shimon rose on his feet and opened with a loud voice, saying: "Elijah, Elijah. With permission of your Master, descend here and enlighten the eyes of these elders on the matter so that they will not come to eat meat with dairy."**

7. אַדְהָכִי, הָא אֵלִיָּהוּ קָא נָחֵית, וְלָא אִתְעַכַּב. אָמַר בּוֹצִינָא קַדִּישָׁא, וְהָא רָזָא דָא וַדַּאי, אִיהוּ רָזָא דְלָא תַחֲרוֹשׁ בְּשׁוֹר וּבַחֲמוֹר יַחְדָּיו. כַּד בּוּכְרָא דְאִיהוּ יִשְׂרָאֵל, עַמּוּדָא דְּאֶמְצָעִיתָא, לָא אַתְיָין לֵיהּ לְבֵית י"י, וְחָלָב אִתְעָרַב בְּבִשְׂרָא, וְגָרְמִין לְאִתְעָרְבָא שׁוֹר בַּחֲמוֹר. וְדָא אִיהוּ כִּלְאַיִם, מִין דְּלָאו בְּמִינֵיהּ.

7. **In the meantime, Elijah descended and was not delayed.** Elijah said to Rav Shimon, **"Holy Luminary! The secret** of the prohibition of meat with milk **is certainly the secret meaning of: 'You shall not plough with an ox and a donkey together.'** (Deuteronomy 22:10) **When the firstborn, which is Israel, the Central Column,** meaning Zeir Anpin with the Mochin of Gadlut, **is not brought to the house of the Lord,** meaning if it does not go up with Malchut to the place of Aba and Ima, then **milk** that is internal **becomes mixed with meat,** which is external, **and causes the ox,** which is

the Left side of holiness, **to be mixed with the donkey,** which is the Klipah of the Right, **and this is a hybrid (*kilayim*) of two different species."**

8. אָמַר רַבִּי שִׁמְעוֹן, אֵלִיָּהוּ אֵלִיָּהוּ וְהָא שׁוֹר אִיהוּ מִסִּטְרָא דְּדַכְיוּ, וַחֲמוֹר מִסִּטְרָא דִּמְסָאֲבוּ, דָּא אִיהוּ כִּלְאַיִם טוֹב וּבִישׁ אֲבָל וְחָלָב אִיהוּ מִסִּטְרָא דְּדַכְיוּ, וּבִשְׂרָא מִסִּטְרָא דְּדַכְיוּ.

8. Rav Shimon said to Elijah, **"Elijah, Elijah, but the ox is from the side of purity and donkey is from the side of defilement. This is** understandably **a mixture of good and evil,** meaning defilement and purity, **but** as for meat and milk, **milk is from the pure side and meat is from the pure side.** So how can you compare meat and milk to ox and donkey?"

9. אָמַר לֵיהּ, וַדַּאי הָכִי הוּא, אֲבָל הַאי רָזָא אִשְׁתְּמוֹדְעָא בִּקְרָא דָא, תּוֹצֵא הָאָרֶץ נֶפֶשׁ חַיָּה לְמִינָהּ. דְּאַף עַל גַּב דְּאִינּוּן מִסִּטְרָא דְּדַכְיוּ, כֻּלְּהוֹן אִינּוּן דְּכַר וְנוּקְבָא, וְאִינּוּן זוּגִין וּמָאן דְּנָטִיל מִמַּה דְּלָאו אִיהוּ מִינֵיהּ, הַהוּא בַּר דְּאִתְדַּרְכִּיב מִתַּרְוַויְיהוּ, עֲלֵיהּ אִתְּמַר לֹא תְבַשֵּׁל גְּדִי בַּחֲלֵב אִמּוֹ.

9. Elijah **said to** Rav Shimon, **"Certainly, it is so** that there is a similarity between the prohibition of meat and dairy, and 'You shall not plough with an ox and donkey together.' **But this secret** of the prohibition of meat and milk **is known from this verse,** as is said: **'Let the earth bring forth living creatures after their kind…'** (Genesis 1:24), meaning with its own pair and kind. [See Zohar, Vayikra 186] **Thus even though they are of the pure side they are all male and female** of their own species, **and are pairs. But whoever takes from that which is not his kind,** then **the child that is crossbred from both,** meaning from a mixed pair, **about** that child **is said: 'You shall not boil a kid baby goat in its mother's milk.'"**

10. אָמַר בּוֹצִינָא קַדִּישָׁא, בְּוַדַּאי כְּעַן אִיהוּ מִלָּה בְּדוּכְתָּהָא, וְדָא אִיהוּ בְּרִירָא דְּמִלָּה. וְדָא אִיהוּ מִלֵּאתְךָ וְדִמְעֲךָ לֹא תְאַחֵר, כְּמָה דְּאַתְּ אָמַר, שְׂמֹאל יְקַדְּמֶנּוּ אַחֵר בְּרַחֲמִים. חוֹבָא דָא, דְּעֵרֶב בַּר נָשׁ טִפָּה בּוּכְרָא, בְּזוּוּגָא

גְּדָה, שִׂפְחָה, גּוֹיָה, זוֹנָה, דָּא גְּרִים, דְּנָטִיל אַחֵר בַּת זוּגֵיהּ. וְאִיהוּ מִדָּה
לָקֳבֵל מִדָּה.

10. The Holy Luminary, namely Rav Shimon, **said, "Certainly now the matter is in place,** the reason why 'The first of the first-fruits of your land...' is adjacent to, 'You shall not boil a kid in its mother's milk,' **and this is the clarification of the matter. And this is the meaning of** what is said by, **'You shall not delay** to offer **the fullness** of your first-fruit harvest, **and of the outflow of your presses.** The firstborn of your sons shall you give to Me.' (Exodus 22:28) By fulfilling the precept of 'the firstborn of your sons shall you give to Me,'—and if the first and most important shall be for the sake of the Lord—then 'the fullness [of your first-fruit harvest],' namely the woman that is his soul mate, is by whom the man becomes full and complete. 'And of the outflow of your presses (*dimacha*),' is the drop of semen, which comes from the phrase *ma'alin et hameduma* (lifts the mixture) (Tractate Shabbat 141b) or like 'tear' (*dema'ot*) that are alluded to in the wine press and oil press, where when the oil and wine flow down they are like tears. 'Do not delay' **is as you say: 'Lest another receives her first through mercy.' The sin of mixing his first drop in an intercourse with a Niddah, maid servant, foreign woman or a harlot causes that another person will take his soul mate. And that is measure for measure,** since he gave his drop to the external forces instead of his soul mate, therefore another person will take his wife.

11. וּבְגִין דָּא, רֵאשִׁית בִּכּוּרֵי אַדְמָתְךָ תָּבִיא בֵּית יְ"יָ אֱלֹקֶי"ךָ, לֹא תְבַשֵּׁל
גְּדִי בַּחֲלֵב אִמּוֹ. דְּהַהוּא בַּר, אִיהוּ עִרְבּוּבְיָא דְּנָפִיק כִּלְאַיִם, מֵאִתְּתָא דְּלָאו
מִינֵיהּ, דְּאִיהִי כְּגַּוְנֵיהּ.

11. "Therefore it says: **'The first of the first-fruits of your land you shall bring to the house of the Lord your God...'** because by the merit of this precept you are assured that **'you shall not boil a kid in its mother's milk'** (Exodus 23:19); that the exterior will not mix with the interior. **Since that child** born from a prohibited woman is called a kid (baby goat), and **is a**

mixture of opposite species, from a woman that is not of his kind, who is opposite to him (*kenegdo*).

12. וּבְגִין דָּא, זָכָה עֵזֶר, בַּת זוּגֵיהּ, דְּאִיהִי עֵזֶר לֵיהּ בְּאוֹרַיְיתָא, בְּפִקּוּדָא, בִּדְחִילוּ, וּבִרְחִימוּ. עֵזֶר לוֹ בְּעָלְמָא דֵין, וּבְעָלְמָא דְאָתֵי. וְאִם לָאו, אָחֳרָא דְּלָאו אִיהוּ מִינֵיהּ, אִיהִי כְּנֶגְדּוֹ, לְאוֹבָדָא לֵיהּ מִתְּרֵין עָלְמִין. וְכָל דָּא גְּרִים לֵיהּ, בְּגִין דְּלָא נָטִיר טִפָּה קַדְמָאָה לְבַת זוּגֵיהּ.

12. "**Therefore** our masters said about the verse: 'I will make for him a fitting helper (*ezer kenegdo*).' (Genesis 2:18) 'If he merits, she helps him,' (Tractate Yevamot 63a), meaning he merits **his spouse,** meaning his soul, since the woman is the soul,]see Sixth Tikkun, 44[**for she helps him with Torah and precepts, and with fear and love.** [See Sixth Tikkun, 16] **She is a help to him in this world and in the World to Come. And f he does not** merit, and he has **another who is not his own kind, she will be against him (***kenegdo***), causing him to lose both worlds. And all this was brought on him because he did not keep his first drop for his spouse.'**

13. וְעִם כָּל דָּא, אִם וְזַר בִּתְיוּבְתָּא, עֲלֵיהּ אִתְּמַר וְשָׁב וְרָפָא לוֹ. וְיָהִיב לֵיהּ בַּת זוּגֵיהּ, דְּאִתְּמַר בָּהּ רִפְאוּת תְּהִי לְשָׁרֶךָ. וְאִיהִי דְּיוּקְנָא דְּאוֹרַיְיתָא, דְּאִיהִי אַסְוּוּתָא, וְאִיהִי חַיִּים. הָדָא הוּא דִּכְתִיב, עֵץ חַיִּים הִיא לַמַּחֲזִיקִים בָּהּ. וְאִתְּתֵיהּ אִיהִי בְּדִיוּקְנָהָא, הָדָא הוּא דִּכְתִיב רְאֵה חַיִּים עִם אִשָּׁה אֲשֶׁר אָהַבְתָּ.

13. "**Nevertheless, if he repents, it is said about him: '...return, and be healed.' (Isaiah 6:10) And his soul mate is given to him, as is said: 'it shall be healing to your navel....' (Proverbs 3:8) And she is in the form of Torah, which is healing and is life, as is written: 'She is a Tree of Life to them who lay hold upon her....' (Ibid. 18) And his wife,** meaning his soul mate as mentioned, **is in the form** of Torah **as written: 'Enjoy life with the wife whom you love....'** (Ecclesiastes 9:9)

14. אוֹרַיְיתָא אִיהִי טוֹב. הָדָא הוּא דִכְתִיב, כִּי לֶקַח טוֹב נָתַתִּי לָכֶם. וְאִתְּתֵיהּ
אִיהִי בְּדִיּוּקְנָהָא, הָדָא הוּא דִכְתִיב מָצָא אִשָּׁה מָצָא טוֹב. טוֹב סוֹף סוֹף, עֲשַׂר
מִלִּין אִתְּמַר בְּהַאי, וַעֲשַׂר בְּהַאי. וְהָא אוּקְמוּהָ חַבְרַיָּא.

14. "The Torah is called **good**, **as is written: 'For I give you good
doctrine...'** (Proverbs 4:2), **and his wife,** meaning his soul mate, **is in her
image, as is written: 'He who finds a wife finds a great good...'** (Proverbs
18:22) **Finally, ten words were said by this one,** meaning the Torah, **and
ten** kinds of joy were said **by the other,** meaning the wife, namely delight
and gladness, bridegroom and bride, rejoicing, joy, love, and brotherhood,
peace and friendship." This was already established by the friends in Zohar,
Terumah, 798.

For the ninth day of the month of Elul
Fifteenth Tikkun
Beresheet is Yisrael

1. בְּרֵאשִׁית: דָּא יִשְׂרָאֵל. הָדָא הוּא דִכְתִיב, קֹדֶשׁ יִשְׂרָאֵל לַי"יָ רֵאשִׁית תְּבוּאָתֹה. רֵאשִׁית, בְּלָא עִרְבּוּבְיָא אָחֳרָא. וּמַאן דְּאִיהוּ קֹדֶשׁ, לָא הֲוָה לֵיהּ הַרְכָּבָה מִמִּינָא אָחֳרָא.

1. Beresheet, this is Israel, which is the letters of *li rosh* "I have a head," meaning Zeir Anpin called Israel with the Mochin of Supernal Aba and Ima, **as it says: "Israel is holy to the Lord…."** (Jeremiah 2:3) And holy is Chochmah of the Right, which are Supernal Aba and Ima. **"….the first-fruits of His increase;"** (Ibid.) **"first" with nothing else mixed in,** for it is all Chasadim, **because one who is holy does not have a mixture of another species** of Judgments.

2. וּבְגִין דְּאִיהִי קֹדֶשׁ לֵית לֵיהּ הַרְכָּבָה, צָרִיךְ בֵּיהּ נְטִירוּ לְגַבֵּי בַּת זוּגֵיהּ. דְּאִיהִי ה'. וּבְגִין דָּא, רֵאשִׁית תְּבוּאָת"ה ה', לֵית בֵּיהּ פְּגִימוּ. הָדָא הוּא דִכְתִיב, וְיַעֲקֹב אִישׁ תָּם, לֵית בֵּיהּ פְּסוֹלֶת, אִיבָּא דָּא לְמַלְכָּא אִתְחֲזֵי. וּבְגִין דָּא, כָּל אוֹכְלָיו יֶאְשָׁמוּ רָעָה תָּבֹא אֲלֵיהֶם נְאֻם י"יָ.

2. And because he is holy, and was not grafted, he must be guarded so that his abundance does not flow to the external forces, as it pertains to **his spouse,** which is Hei, Malchut. **Therefore, "…the first-fruits of His increase (*tevuato*)" spelled with Hei,** meaning the root of the souls of the righteous **is without blemish. This is the meaning of: "And Jacob was a simple [or perfect; *tam*] man"** (Genesis 25:27) **without refuse. This fruit,** namely the soul of the righteous, **belongs to the King, and therefore: "… all that devour him shall be held guilty; evil shall come upon them, says the Lord."** (Jeremiah 2:3)

3. הָדָא אִיהוּ עֵץ הַחַיִּים, דְּאִיבָּא דִּילֵיהּ סַם חַיִּים, בַּת זוּגֵיהּ נְטִירָא לֵיהּ, בְּעָלְמָא דֵין וּבְעָלְמָא דְּאָתֵי. עֲלָהּ אִתְּמַר, וְלָקְחוּ גַּם מֵעֵץ הַחַיִּים וְאָכַל וָחַי

לְעוֹלָם. גַּם לְרַבּוֹת בַּת זוּגֵיהּ, סַם וַחַיִּים דִּילֵיהּ, וְאִיהוּ נָטִיר לֵיהּ בְּעָלְמָא דֵין וּבְעָלְמָא דְאָתֵי.

3. Because this, namely the righteous one who is a chariot to Zeir Anpin, **is the Tree of Life, whose fruits,** meaning souls, **the elixir of life,** namely Malchut, **his spouse, guards him in this world and in the World to Come. About her is said: "...and take also from the tree of life and eat, and live forever!"** (Genesis 3:22) "Also" comes to include his spouse, his elixir of life, who guards him in this world and in the World to Come.

4. וּמָאן דְּבָעֵי לְנַטְלָא בַּת זוּגֵיהּ כְּגוֹן אוּרִיָּה דְּאַקְדִּים לְדָוִד, אִתְּמַר בֵּיהּ כָּל אוֹכְלָיו יֶאְשָׁמוּ רָעָה תָּבֹא אֲלֵיהֶם נְאֻם יְיָ. דְּבַת זוּגֵיהּ דְּצַדִּיק אִיהוּ מַצָּה שְׁמוּרָה, לְגַבֵּי מַצָּה שְׁלֵימָה עֲשִׁירָה.

4. And he who wishes to marry the soul mate of a righteous man, **like Uriah who preceded David** and married Batsheva, who was destined for David, **it is said about him: "...all that devour him shall be held guilty; evil shall come upon them, says the Lord"** because the spouse **of a righteous man** is a chariot for Malchut and **is a Matzah guarded for a whole Matzah,** namely her husband, who is a chariot for Zeir Anpin, **that is rich** that illuminates with Chochmah and Chasadim. [See Zohar, Pinchas 609; "bread" is Vav]

5. וּמָאן גְּרִים דָּא לְמֶהֱוֵי בַּת זוּגֵיהּ, מַצָּה שְׁמוּרָה לְגַבֵּהּ בְּגִין דְּנָטַר טִפָּה דִּילֵיהּ וּמָאן דְּפָגִים טִפָּה דִּילֵיהּ, אִתְקְרֵי בַּת זוּגֵיהּ מַצָּה פְּרוּסָה, לֶחֶם עֹנִי. וְרָזָא דְמִלָּה, כָּל מָאן דִּמְזַלְזֵל בְּנַהֲמָא, אוֹ בִּפֵירוּרִין דְּנַהֲמָא, דְּאִינוּן טִפִּין בְּכַוַּיִת עֲנִיּוּת קָא רָדִיף אַבַּתְרֵיהּ, אֶלָּא צָרִיךְ לְנַטְרָא טִפִּין דִּילֵיהּ, דְּלָא יְזָרִיק לוֹן בַּאֲתַר דְּלָא אִצְטְרִיךְ.

5. What causes his soul mate to be a Matzah guarded for him? It is by reserving his drop. And whoever blemishes his drop, by spilling it on the ground, as is written: **"...for all flesh has corrupted its way on the earth"** (Genesis 6:12) **his soul mate is called a piece of Matzah, the bread of**

poverty. And the secret of the matter is that whoever degrades bread or bread crumbs, which are (like) drops like an olive-size measurement, poverty pursues him. Rather, he has to keep his drops, namely the crumbs that are likened to drops of semen, from throwing them where he should not. Meaning there is nothing in this world that does not have an important source in the Upper Worlds, and especially bread on which our lives depend. Therefore, one who degrades his bread causes a blemish in the root of his life above. The crumbs of bread are likened to the crumbs of the brain, which are the drops of semen, which one must not throw away on the ground, as it says "...for all flesh has corrupted its way on the earth," and so too whoever degrades the crumbs of the "bread of the Torah," which are the secrets. [See Zohar, Pinchas 620]

6. וּבְגִין דָא אוּקְמוּהוּ מָארֵי מַתְנִיתִין אוּקִירוּ לִנְשַׁיַיכוּ, כִּי הֵיכִי דְתִתְעַתָּרוּ וְאוֹקִירוּ דִלְהוֹן, לְנַטְרָא טִפָּה קַדְמָאָה, דְלָא יַעֲבִיד בָּהּ פְּסוֹלֶת. דִפְסוֹלֶת דְאַבְרָהָם וְיִצְחָק, גְּרִים דְאוּמָּה דְעֵשָׂו וְיִשְׁמָעֵאל, יִשְׁתַּעְבְּדוּן בִּבְנֵיהוֹן בְּגָלוּתָא. וְנִסִיוֹנָא דִלְהוֹן בָּאֶשָׁא וְסַכִּינָא. שֵׁזִיב לוֹן מִשְׂרֵיפָה וַהֲרֵג דִלְהוֹן.

6. Therefore, the scholars of the Mishnah established and said, "Honor your wives so that you will become rich," (Bava Metzia 59a) because he who degrades his wife causes poverty, and he who honors her acquires wealth. Honoring them is to guard the first drop so that it will not turn into refuse, namely a mixture of Judgments. Because the refuse of Abraham, that is, the dross of the silver, because Abraham is Chesed called "silver," and Ishmael and the children of Keturah are his refuse and Isaac who is Gevurah, called "gold," whose refuse is the dross of gold, namely Esau caused that the nation of Esau and Ishmael would enslave their descendants in exile. And their test, meaning the test of Abraham and Isaac, of the fire, namely Ur Casdim, and the knife, namely the binding, saves them, the seed of Abraham and Isaac, from burning and slaughter by Ishmael and Esau.

‫7. יַעֲקֹב בְּגִין דְּלָא הֲוָה בֵיה פְּסוֹלֶת, אִתְּמַר בְּזַרְעֵיה בְּגָלוּתָא, וַיִּשְׁכֹּן יִשְׂרָאֵל‬
‫בֶּטַח בָּדָד עֵין יַעֲקֹב. אִתְּמַר הָכָא בֶּטַח בָּדָד, וְאִתְּמַר הָתָם בְּמַפְּקָנוֹ דְּגָלוּתָא,‬
‫יְיָ בָּדָד יַנְחֶנּוּ וְאֵין עִמּוֹ אֵל נֵכָר. לָא אִתְעָרְבוּן בִּבְנוֹי עִרְבוּבְיָא דְּגִיּוֹרִים, וּבְגִין‬
‫דָּא אֵין מְקַבְּלִים גֵּרִים לִימוֹת הַמָּשִׁיחַ.‬

7. Because Jacob did not have any refuse, it is said of his descendants
in exile: "Israel shall dwell isolated in safety; the fountain of Jacob."
(Deuteronomy 33:28) It says here "isolated in safety" and elsewhere,
concerning them going out of exile: "so the Lord alone did lead him, and
there was no strange god with him." (Deuteronomy 32:12) No converts
shall mix with his descendants. Therefore, in the time of the Messiah,
no converts will be accepted.

‫8. דַּעֲלַיְיהוּ דְּזַרְעָא יַעֲקֹב אִתְּמַר, גֶּפֶן מִמִּצְרַיִם תַּסִּיעַ מַה גֶּפֶן לָא מְקַבְּלָא‬
‫הַרְכָּבָה מִמִּין אָחֳרָא, כֵּן זַרְעֵיה הֲווֹ נָטְרִין אוֹת בְּרִית, וְלָא מְקַבְּלִין הַרְכָּבָה‬
‫מִמִּין אָחֳרָא.‬

8. For about the seed of Jacob is said: "You have plucked a vine out
of Egypt..." (Psalms 80:9) Just as a vine does not accept a graft from
another kind, so too the seed of Jacob guarded the sign of circumcision
and do not accept a hybrid from another kind.

‫9. וְכָל מָאן דְּנָטִיר אוֹת בְּרִית, זָכֵי לְמַלְכוּ. כְּגַוְונָא דְּיוֹסֵף. וְיִשְׂרָאֵל בְּגִין‬
‫דְּנָטְרִין בְּרִית, זָכוּ לְמַלְכוּתָא. וְאִתְּמַר בְּהוֹן, כָּל יִשְׂרָאֵל בְּנֵי מְלָכִים. וּמֹשֶׁה‬
‫בְּגִין דְּנָטַר אוֹת בְּרִית, אִתְּמַר בֵּיה, וַיְהִי בִישׁוּרוּן מֶלֶךְ. זַכָּאָה אִיהוּ מָאן‬
‫דְּנָטַר בְּרִית.‬

9. And all who guard the sign of the Covenant merit the Kingdom, like
Joseph did. And because Israel guard the Covenant they merited the
Kingdom, as is written: "Your people also shall be all righteous; they shall
inherit the land forever..." (Isaiah 60:21) which is Malchut. And it is said
of them, "all Israel are the children of kings" (Mishnah Shabbat 14:4)
Because Moses guarded the Covenant, it is said of him; "And he became

king in Jeshurun...." (Deuteronomy 33:5) Happy is he who guards the
Covenant.

For the ninth day of the month of Elul
Sixteenth Tikkun
Beresheet is *challah* (first piece of bread's dough)

‫1. בְּרֵאשִׁית: דָּא חַלָּה. הָה"ד, רֵאשִׁית עֲרִיסוֹתֵיכֶם חַלָּה תָּרִימוּ תְרוּמָה.‬
‫וְהָא אוּקְמוּהוּ, דְּאָדָם חַלָּתוֹ שֶׁל עוֹלָם הֲוָה. וּמְנָא לָן דְּחַלָּה אִיהִי רֵאשִׁית.‬
‫דִּקְרָא אוֹכַח, הָדָא הוּא דִּכְתִיב רֵאשִׁית עֲרִיסוֹתֵיכֶם חַלָּה תָּרִימוּ תְרוּמָה.‬

1. Beresheet is *challah,* as is written: "Of the first yield of your dough,
you shall set aside a cake (*challah*) for a gift…." (Numbers 15:20) He asks,
"They have established that Adam after he sinned was the *challah* of the
world, as is written that '…but he who exacts gifts overthrows it' (Proverbs
29:4) which refers to Adam who was the final sanctification (*challah*) of
the world. How do we know that *challah* is first? The Torah proves it,
as is written: 'Of the first yield of your dough, you shall set aside a cake
(*challah*) as a gift…' (Numbers 15:20) If so, what is *challah*?"

‫2. מַאי חַלָּה. אֶלָּא שִׁבְעָה מִינִין אִינוּן: חִטָּה, וּשְׂעוֹרָה, וְגֶפֶן, וּתְאֵנָה, וְרִמּוֹן,‬
‫אֶרֶץ זֵית שֶׁמֶן, וּדְבָשׁ, דְּהוּא דְּבַשׁ תְּמָרִים. חִטָּה, אִילָנָא אִיהוּ דְּאָכִיל מִנֵּיהּ‬
‫אָדָם קַדְמָאָה, וְאִיהוּ לָא אַפִּיק מִתַּמָּן חַלָּה, וּבְגִין דָּא לָא חָל בֵּיהּ ה', וְשַׁרְיָא‬
‫בֵּיהּ ח', ט', וְגָרִים לֵיהּ מוֹתָא. וְחַלָּה. אִיהוּ שְׁכִינְתָּא, כְּלִילָא מִשִּׁבְעָה מִינִין‬
‫אִלֵּין. וּבָהּ חָב אָדָם קַדְמָאָה.‬

2. He answers, "The seven species, which the land of Israel is praised for,
which is Malchut, are: '…wheat, and barley, and vines, and fig trees, and
pomegranates; a land of olive trees, and honey…;' (Deuteronomy 8:8)
'honey' being date honey that comes from the tree that grows from the
ground. 'Wheat' is the tree that the Primordial Man (Adam) ate from,
since an infant does not know to call 'father' or 'mother' until he tastes
grain, and this is called the Tree of Knowledge of Good and Evil (Tractate
Berachot 40a). But he did not separate *challah* (the priest's share of the
dough) from it, therefore the Hei, which is Malchut, did not rest on him,
and the letters Chet and Tet settled on him, which denote the grasp of

the external forces, **and brought death on him. *Challah* is the Shechinah that is composed of the seven species, and against her Primordial Man sinned.”**

3. טִפָּה דָא י'. עִסָּה צָרִיךְ לְאַפָּקָא מִינָהּ חַלָּה. וּמִיָּד חָל עַל הַהִיא טִפָּה, וְיָהִיב לֵיהּ זֶרַע כְּלִיל מִתַּרְוַיְיהוּ, דְּאִיהוּ ו'. וְרָזָא דְּמִלָּה, הֵ"א לָכֶם זֶרַע.

3. This drop is Yud, namely Chochmah, which is **the *challah* that needs to be separated from the dough, and then immediately the Hei settles** (*chal*-Hei, which spells out *challah*), this Hei is Binah that shines with Chasadim, **on this drop** that is Chochmah, **and he is given seed composed of both,** Chochmah and Chasadim, **which is Vav (6). The secret of it is: “Lo, here is seed [grain] for you…”** (Genesis 47:23) which in Hebrew is *heh lachem zera*, and *heh* is spelled Hei-Alef, which equals six, and the word for “grain” literally means “seed.”

4. וּבְגִין דָּא, חַלָּה וַדַּאי אִיהִי פִּקּוּדָא דְּאִתְמַנֵּי לְאִתְּתָא, הִבְגִינָהּ מֵת אָדָם, דְּאִיהוּ חַלָּתוּ שֶׁל עוֹלָם, צְרִיכָה אִיהִי לְאַפְרָשָׁא חַלָּה, וּלְאַפָּקָא לָהּ מֵעִסָּתָהּ, דְּאִיהִי טִפָּה דִּילָהּ, לְהַחֲזִירָהּ עַל אָדָם.

4. Therefore, certainly *challah* is a precept of which the woman is commanded, and since due to her Adam died, who was the sanctification (*challah*) **of the world, she needs to set aside a part of the *challah* and to remove it from her dough, which is her drop** that hints to the Upper Three of the Upper Three, **and return it to Adam,** meaning to return the Light of the *challah*, in the secret of *chal*-Hei (Hei settles).

5. אִיהִי אַטְפַת שְׁרָגָא דִּילֵיהּ, דְּאִתְּמַר בֵּיהּ נֵר יְ"יָ נִשְׁמַת אָדָם, צְרִיכָה לְאוֹקְדָא לֵיהּ בְּלֵיל שַׁבָּת, בְּאִתְעָרוּ דְּשַׁלְהוֹבִין דְּאֶשָּׁא דִּרְחִימוּ לְגַבֵּי בַּעְלָהּ. וְרָזָא דְּמִלָּה, מַיִם רַבִּים לֹא יוּכְלוּ לְכַבּוֹת אֶת הָאַהֲבָה. וְאִתְעָרוּ דְּחַוְּבִּימוּתָא דְּלֵיל שַׁבָּת מֵאִתְּתֵיהּ, צְרִיכָה בִּרְחִימוּ וּדְחִילוּ. וְדָא אִיהוּ אִשָּׁה כִּי תַזְרִיעַ וְיָלְדָה זָכָר.

5. **She extinguished his candle, of which is said: "The spirit [soul] of man is the lamp [candle] of the Lord...."** (Proverbs 20:27) **So she needs to light it on the eve of Shabbat,** since on Shabbat the Mochin of Chaya shine, **by the arousal of the flames of fire of love for her husband. The secret of the matter is "Many waters cannot quench [lit. extinguish] love..."** (Song of Songs 8:7), since when the Light of Chochmah of the Left Column of Ima illuminates to Nukva it is a burning flame, since it is without Chasadim. And when the Right Column comes with its Chasadim, which are called "water," to extinguish the fire, it does not extinguish the illumination of Chochmah, on the contrary, it adds and completes its illumination since it clothes Chochmah with Chasadim, and [Nukva] shines with all of its completion. **And the arousal of the warmth from his wife on the eve of Shabbat must be with love and awe. This is: "If a woman be delivered and bare a male child...."** (Leviticus 12:2)

6. עַל שְׁפִיכַת דָּמִים, דְּאָדָם אִזְדְּרִיקַת דְּמָהּ. וְעַל דָּא, צְרִיכָה לְנַטְרָא לֵיהּ מִדַּם נִדָּה. וּבְגִין דָּא, עַל תְּלַת מִלִּין אִלֵּין נָשִׁים וְהִירוֹת, בַּנִּדָּה, וּבַחַלָּה, וּבְהַדְלָקַת הַנֵּר. עַד כָּאן רָזָא דְחִטָּה, דְּמִתַּמָּן חַלָּה. וְחִטָּ"ה, אִיהוּ רָזָא דְעֶשְׂרִין וּתְרֵין אַתְוָון דְּאוֹרַיְיתָא.

6. **For this,** for bringing **bloodshed on Adam,** since he was sentenced to death and to having his limbs drop off, as mentioned before, **her blood is thrown away,** meaning the five bloods of impurity, in the secret of Niddah (menstruating woman), which is spelled Nun-Dalet-Hei, Hei being five. **Therefore, she has to guard him from the menstruation blood. Therefore, women need to be careful to observe three things,** namely, **Niddah (Laws of menstruation), Challah (setting aside a part of the dough) and lighting the Shabbat candles. Up to here is the meaning of wheat (chitah) from which** challah **is separated. Wheat (**chitah**, Chet-Tet-Hei, which equals 22) is the secret of the 22 letters of the Torah.**

For the tenth day of the month of Elul
Seventeenth Tikkun
The first of the tithe of your grain

1. בְּרֵאשִׁית, עֲלָהּ אִתְּמַר רֵאשִׁית מַעֲשַׂר דְּגָנְךָ. וְדָא מַלְכוּת, דְּאִיהִי מַעֲשַׂר. וְאִיהִי עֲשִׂירִית לְעֶשֶׂר סְפִירוֹת. וּבְגִינָהּ מְעַשְּׂרִין וּמוֹץ וְתֶבֶן, דְּאִינּוּן לְבוּשִׁין דְּחִטָּה בְּהַאי עָלְמָא, פְּטוּרִין מִמַּעֲשַׂר.

1. It is said about Beresheet, the tithe of "the first of your grain...." (Deuteronomy 18:4) **This is Malchut** called "tithe" (*ma'aser*), **since it is the tenth among the Ten Sefirot, and for her sake,** meaning to perfect her, **we tithe,** in the secret of "the tenth is holy," which is Malchut that is perfected with a curtain (*masach*). No Light is drawn from the Endless, blessed be He, except by a Binding by Striking (*zivug dehaka'ah*) from the Supernal Light on the *masach* that is in the vessel of Malchut, and for this reason Malchut is considered to be the building of all the worlds. **Chaff and straw in this world,** which allude to the male and female of the Klipot, **which are the garments of wheat, are exempted from tithing.**

2. וּמַאן דְּבָעֵי לְאַפָּקָא מַעֲשַׂר מֵחִטָּה בָּעֵי לְנַקְיֵיהּ מִן מוֹץ וְתֶבֶן, דְּאִינּוּן ח"ט, וְאִשְׁתָּאֲרַת אִיהִי ה' נְקִיָּה, בְּהַהוּא זִמְנָא יְהֵא זָרִיק בָּהּ טִפָּה, דְּאִיהִי יו"ד.

2. And he who wishes to separate a tithe from wheat, meaning to correct Malchut, **has to clean it from chaff and straw, which are Chet-Tet** that allude to Klipot, **so she,** Malchut, **remains a clean Hei,** in the secret of establishing the curtain (*masach*) to elevate Returning Light, which is Chasadim. **At that time he will inject a drop into her,** meaning to unite her with a Supernal Light, which is the secret of Direct Light, Chochmah, **which is Yud.**

3. וּכְגַוְונָא דָא, בְּזִווּגָא דְּבַר נָשׁ, צָרִיךְ לְנַקָּאָה טִפָּה מֵחֵט"א דְּאִיהוּ יֵצֶר הָרָע לְמֶהֱוֵי זַרְעָא נְקִיָּה בָּהּ. הֲדָא הוּא דִכְתִיב, ה"א לָכֶם זֶרַע.

3. Similarly when one mates, the man **needs to** sanctify himself, **cleanse the drop** of mating **from sin** (*chet*, Chet-Tet-Alef), **which is the Evil Inclination, so that the seed will be clean with a Hei,** meaning for the sake of Heaven. **This is the meaning of: "here** (*heh*, Hei-Alef) **is grain (also 'seed') for you...."** (Genesis 47:23)

4. אֲבָל בְּעָלְמָא דְּאָתֵי, וְחִטָּה אִיהִי נְקִיָּה, אִיהִי וּלְבוּשָׁהּ, וְאִיהִי עֶשְׂרִין וּתְרֵין אַתְוָון דְּאוֹרַיְתָא. וּבְגִין דָּא, בְּהַמּוֹצִיא, בַּעַל הַבַּיִת צָרִיךְ לְדַקְדֵּק בָּהּ׳, לְמֶהֱוֵי אִיהִי נְקִיָּה בְּלָא פָּסוֹלֶת.

4. But in the World to Come, meaning when Malchut has risen to Binah that is called the World to Come, **wheat,** which is Malchut, **is clean, it and its garment,** which are Zeir Anpin and Nukva, **and is the 22 letters of the Torah,** since Zeir Anpin and Nukva, which are called the 22 letters, would not be ready to receive all this correction and Light without this sweetening of Malchut in Binah, and all the 22 letters come out of this sweetening of Malchut in Binah, whether in Zeir Anpin or Nukva, which are the collective of all the illuminations. Therefore, **in the Hamotzi,** the blessing over the bread, **the master of the house,** who breaks the bread (Tractate Berachot 46a), **must take special care in pronouncing the Hei** of Hamotzi, which is the hint to Malchut that elevates to Binah, **because she is clean of any refuse.**

5. וּתְרֵין עֶשְׂרוֹרִין אִינּוּן דְּאָמַר קְרָא עַשֵּׂר תְּעַשֵּׂר אַמַּאי. אֶלָּא בְּגִין לְקַשְּׁרָא לָהּ בִּתְרֵין דְּרוֹעִין, דְּאִינּוּן כֹּהֵן לֵוִי, דְּאִינּוּן מַעֲשֵׂר רִאשׁוֹן לְלֵוִי, מַעֲשֵׂר מִן הַמַּעֲשֵׂר לַכֹּהֵן.

5. And there are two tenths meaning two tithes **that the verse describes,** as is written: **"Tithe shall you tithe...."** (Deuteronomy 14:22) He asks, **"Why** are there two? Does the tithe not allude to the correction of Malchut, and there is only one Malchut?" He answers, **"To connect her with the two arms, which are,** Chesed and Gevurah, **Cohen and Levi, which are the first tithe for the Levite,** which is in the Left Column of Zeir Anpin, in the secret of the verse: '...his left hand be under my head...' (Song of Songs 2:6) **and the tithe of the tithe goes to the Cohen,** which is in the Right Column, in the secret of the verse: '...and his right hand embraces me' (Ibid.) This way, she is composed of Chochmah of the Left and Chasadim of the Right.

6. דְּכָל סְפִירָן סָלְקִין לְעֶשֶׂר, עַד דְּסָלְקִין לְמֵאָה, וְאִיהִי אִתְעֲבִידַת תְּרוּמָה, לְכָלְהוּ מֵאָה. וּבְגִין דָּא, שִׁיעוּר תְּרוּמָה תְּרֵי מִמֵּאָה. לְקָבֵל תְּרֵין לוּחִין דְּאוֹרַיְיתָא, דְּאִיהִי תוֹרָה דְּאִתְיְהִיבַת בְּאַרְבְּעִין יוֹמִין. וְדָא אִיהוּ תּוֹרָ"ה מ'. וּבָה אִתְעֲבִידוּ סְפִירָן כָּלְהוּ, עֶשְׂרוֹנִים. תְּלַת אֲבָהָן תְּלַת עֶשְׂרוֹנִין. תְּרֵי נְבִיאֵי קְשׁוֹט אִינּוּן עֶשָׂרוֹן עֶשָׂרוֹן.

6. Because all the Sefirot equal ten, with Malchut, because Malchut completes the ten, as is written in the *Sefer Yitzirah* ("Book of Formation") "ten, and not nine." And since every Sefira is composed of ten Sefirot, **until they add up to one hundred. And she becomes the Trumah out of every one hundred** Sefirot, because the illumination of all are revealed by the Returning Light that elevates from Malchut. **Therefore, the amount for the priest's gifts (*trumah*) is two out of a hundred** or, if one is generous, one out of forty, **corresponding to the Two Tablets of the Torah, for the Torah was given in forty days. This is** Trumah, spelled with the letters **Torah-Mem (Torah-40). With her all the Sefirot become units of ten; three Patriarchs,** who are Chesed, Gevurah, and Tiferet, are **three tens; the two Prophets of truth,** which are Netzach and Hod, **are ten each.**

Appendix A
Ten Sefirot—Tree of Life

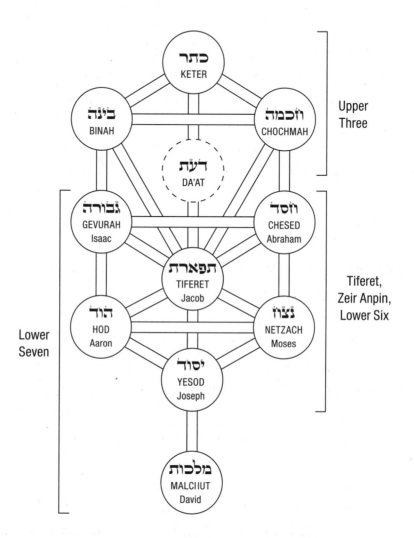

According to kabbalistic teaching, the creation of the universe was made possible by a withdrawal of the Light of the Creator, which was otherwise present everywhere. The reason for this withdrawal was for our own sake. Therefore we are separated from the Light of the Creator by a sequence of ten energy fields known as the Sefirot (singular, Sefira), which essentially are packets of bottled-up energies, each with its own intelligence and individual attributes. The Sefirot may be thought of as spiritual transformers, successively downgrading the Creator's Infinite Light until it reaches us in a manageable intensity.

Arranged in three columns—Right, Left, and Central—these Ten Sefirot make up what kabbalists call the Tree of Life. The Ten Sefirot are not simply external to ourselves as they are both levels to be attained and also are all contained within us in potential form, ready to be awakened and mastered through our transformative spiritual work. As we transform our natures, we increase the capacity of our spiritual vessel to hold more Light, thus giving us the ability to draw ever nearer to the Creator.

1. Keter

Keter (Crown) is the pinnacle of the Central Column. This Sefira is located just below the Endless World of Limitless Light (Or Ein Sof), far beyond mortal comprehension. Keter is the source of everything but only in an undifferentiated potential, and channels the Light of the Creator to the rest of the Sefirot. It functions as a supercomputer, containing the total inventory of what each of us is, ever has been, or ever will be. As such, it is the genesis not only of our lives in this Earthly realm but of every thought, idea, or inspiration we ever will have while we sojourn here, and that includes lifetimes of the past, the present, and the future.

2. Chochmah

As the highest level of the Right Column, Chochmah (Wisdom) is the first Sefira to receive the Light of the Creator that flows from the Endless World through Keter. Chochmah, the universal masculine principle, is recognized as the primordial point of Creation from which all knowable reality originates. It is pure wisdom. Chochmah bestows this Light to the Sefira of Binah.

3. Binah

As the highest level of the Left Column, the Sefira of Binah (Intelligence/ Understanding)—the universal feminine principle—is the recipient of Chochmah's Light of Wisdom, and embodies intelligence and understanding. Binah is a reservoir of all energy, ranging from that which motivates human endeavor to that which keeps galaxies spinning.

As Chochmah and Binah meet, thought becomes manifest into action. Their combined energies are funneled through the Sefira of Da'at (Knowledge), which lies on the Central column below Keter and slightly above Zeir Anpin. Even to kabbalists, Da'at is enigmatic, but while not regarded as a true Sefira, it functions as an interface to unify the energies of Chochmah's Wisdom and Binah's Understanding, transmitting them as Knowledge to the Lower Seven Sefirot.

4. Chesed
The Sefira of Chesed, the most expansive of the Sefirot, sits below Chochmah on the Right Column representing Mercy and Lovingkindness. Chesed holds the Light emanated from Chochmah and Binah through Da'at, and represents the complete Desire to Share. Abraham the Patriarch is the Chariot of Chesed,

5. Gevurah
The Sefira of Gevurah represents Justice and Judgment. Where Chesed expands, Gevurah contracts. Where Chesed says, "Share," Gevurah says, "Restrict." It is here that the process of differentiation, the beginning of physicality originates. Isaac the Patriarch is the Chariot of Gevurah.

6. Tiferet
The Sefira of Tiferet, representing Beauty and the ideal balance between Gevurah (Justice) and Chesed (Mercy), rests below Keter on the Central Column, and at the midpoint beneath Chesed on the Right and Gevurah on the Left. Tiferet may be thought of as the heart of the Tree of Life. As a balance between judgment and mercy, Jacob the Patriarch is the Chariot for Tiferet.

7. Netzach

The Sefira of Netzach (Victory) resides on the Right Column, just below Chesed. A repository of positive energy from Chesed, Netzach radiates the Desire to Share and becomes the channel of that energy as it approaches the physical world in which we live. It is associated with Moses, who as a link between the Creator and humankind personifies these enduring qualities. Netzach is also known as Eternity, and it represents involuntary processes as well as the right brain, where the creative process takes place. Netzach is the artist, the poet, the musician, the dreamer, and the masculine fertilizing principle. Its feminine counterpart, directly across the way on the Left Column, is Hod.

8. Hod

The Left Column counterpart to Netzach is the Sefira of Hod (Glory). Hod is the feminine or manifesting principle. It is here that the potentials held in the male aspects of Chesed and Netzach begin to become materialized and dreams concrete. Hod is also associated with prophecy, controlling voluntary processes and left-brain activity, as well as channeling the practicality of Gevurah into the human psyche. Hod is associated with Aaron, the High Priest.

9. Yesod

At the base of the Tree of Life is Yesod (Foundation). This Central Column Sefira sits like a great reservoir. All the Sefirot above pour their attributes into Yesod's vast basin where they are funneled into the World of Action—Malchut. Yesod is associated with Yosef haTzadik (Joseph the Righteous).

10. Malchut

Malchut (Kingdom) is the lowest of the Sefirot, and is the world of our material universe. It is associated with King David. It is the only Sefira on the Tree of Life where physical matter exists as a minuscule percentage of the whole, and where the Tree of Knowledge sinks its roots. And it is here that a divergence in human attitude spells the difference between individual lives lived in the Light and those lived in darkness.

Partzuf (Face/Countenance)

Partzuf is a complete spiritual structure of the Ten Sefirot. Partzuf represents the Head—the Upper Three Sefirot or potential, and the Body—the Lower Seven Sefirot or actual. There are five Partzufim (plural of Partzuf) in the metaphysical world:

1. Arich Anpin (Long Face)—also referred to as: Atik, Atik Yomin, Atika Kadisha

2. Aba (Father)—contains two parts:
   a. Chochmah
   b. Yisrael-Saba

3. Ima (Mother)—contains two parts:
   a. Binah
   b. Tevunah

3. Zeir Anpin (Small Face)

4. Nukva (Female)—also referred to as Malchut

The chief Partzufim we interact with are Chochmah, Binah, Tiferet (Zeir Anpin), and Malchut (Nukva), and they correspond to the four letters of the Tetragrammaton: Yud-Hei-Vav-Hei.

Five Worlds

All of the above Spiritual Structures (Partzufim) create one spiritual world. There are Five Worlds in total that comprise all reality.

Adam Kadmon (Primordial Man) – The first and highest spiritual World. There are four spiritual Worlds through which our soul ascends and descends during the course of the day as we make our spiritual connections. However, this fifth World that is even higher than these four—a World that we cannot reach through our connections—is called Primordial Man.

Atzilut (World of Emanation) – The second (from above downward) of the five spiritual Worlds that appeared after the Tzimtzum (Contraction). In this high and most exalted World, the Vessel is passive in relation to the Light, allowing the Light to flow without any agenda. This World is related to the Sefira of Chochmah (Wisdom) and is completely protected from the Klipot (shells).

Briyah (World of Creation) – The third (from above downward) of the five spiritual Worlds that appeared after the Tzimtzum (Contraction). This World is related to the Sefira of Binah (Understanding) and is a universal energy store. It is also related to the Shechinah (Supernal Mother) and almost completely protected from the Klipot (shells).

Yetzirah (World of Formation) – The fourth (from above downward) of the five spiritual Worlds that appeared after the Tzimtzum (Contraction). Whereas in the lowest World, the World of Action, evil is the predominant force, in the World of Formation, goodness is the predominant force. Yetzirah is related to the Sefira of Zeir Anpin (Small Face) and to the energy of the Shield of David.

Asiyah (World of Action) – The lowest of the five spiritual Worlds that emerged after the Tzimtzum (Contraction) of the Vessel. The World of Action is the dimension where the least amount of Light is revealed. This enables human beings to exercise their free will in discerning between good and evil. This World is also related to the Sefira of Malchut (Kingdom) and is referred to as the Tree of Knowledge of Good and Evil.

Five Levels of the Soul

Nefesh – The lowest part of our soul that every person is born with. It allows the Klipot to connect to us. Nefesh is usually fueled by the Desire to Receive for the Self Alone; it is the animal instinct and psyche that we all have. The Torah teaches us that the connection to Nefesh is through the blood, and this is why we do not eat or drink anything that has animal blood in it: We do not want to connect to the raw instinct of that animal.

At certain age-related milestones in our lives, we receive additional parts of the soul.

Ruach (Spirit) – Of the five parts that make up the soul, Ruach is the next level up from Nefesh. It is an additional part of our soul that enters us when we reach Bar/Bat Mitzvah (age 13 for a boy, 12 for a girl), and activates our free will to choose between Light and darkness.

Neshama (Soul) – This is the third part of our soul, which we receive when we reach the age of 20. It is called "Soul" because until we receive this third part, our own soul is not yet complete. This third part of the soul allows us to connect directly to the Light of the Creator. It is the Light that is contained in Binah.

Chaya (Life-Sustaining) – The fourth part of our soul, called Chaya, is very rarely received because it denotes that an individual has achieved such a high level of spirituality that they no longer have the evil inclination within them. Chaya is the Light of the Sefira of Chochmah, which provides life and sustains the soul.

Yechida (Oneness) – The fifth and highest part of a person's soul, when the individual unites completely with the Light of the Creator.

Names of God

Just as a single ray of white sunlight contains the seven colors of the spectrum, the one Light of the Creator embodies many diverse spiritual forces. These different forces are called Names of God. Each Name denotes a specific attribute and spiritual power. The Hebrew letters that compose these Names are the interface by which these varied Forces act upon our physical world. The most common Name of God is the Tetragrammaton (Yud-Hei-Vav-Hei; יהוה). Because of the enormous power the Tetragrammaton transmits, we do not utter it aloud. The Tetragrammaton is spelled one way (Yud-Hei-Vav-Hei) but is pronounced another way, namely "Adonai" (Alef-Dalet-Nun-Yud, אדני). Because the pronunciation of "Adonai" has a tremendous amount of Light, we only pronounce it when we make a blessing, when we recite a kabbalistic prayer or when we read from the Torah. (See chart below for the pronunciations of the Names and which Sefira it corresponds to).

Name (Hebrew)	Name (English)	Pronunciation	Corresponding Sefira
אהיה	Alef-Hei-Yud-Hei	Alef-Kei-Yud-Kei	Binah
אל	El	Kel	Chesed
אלהים	Elohim	Elokim	Gevurah, also Malchut
יהוה	Yud-Hei-Vav-Kei	Yud-Kei-Vav-Kei or Adonai	Tiferet, Zeir Anpin
צבאות	Tzeva'ot	Tzevakot	Netzach and Hod
שדי	Shadai	Shakai, Shin-Dalet-Yud	Yesod
אדני	Adonai	Alef-Dalet-Nun-Yud or HaShem	Malchut/Nukva

Holidays – Days of Power

In Kabbalah, Holidays are known not as days of remembering, memorializing, and paying homage to some event in the past, instead these Holidays are cosmic times of connection. Holidays are opportunities to tap into and access the unique energies that exist at these specific points in time using the technology and tools of Kabbalah.

Rosh Hashanah – Seed level of the year

Yom Kippur – At-one-ment with the Light

Sukkot – Surrounding ourselves with the Light of kindness, protection and certainty

Simchat Torah – Joy of the Torah and the beginning of the Torah reading cycle

Chanukah – Lighting candles for eight days and connecting to the Or haGanuz (Concealed Light)

Purim – Joy and certainty beyond logic

Pesach – Freedom from the bondage of the ego

Shavuot – Accepting the spiritual system of the Torah, thus breaking free from death

Appendix B
Glossary

248 – There are 248 bone segments of the human body as well as 248 words in the *Shema* prayer and 248 positive Precepts. These positive Precepts are the proactive "to-do" actions, and each one relates to a different part of the body. When we perform these Precepts, we strengthen our body. See also: 365, 613

365 – There are 365 tendons and sinews in the human body as well as 365 negative Precepts. These negative Precepts are the proactive "do not do" actions, referring to acts of restriction and refraining from acting on our negative and selfish impulses. Each Precept corresponds to a different sinew and tendon, and to each of the 365 days of the year. See also: 248, 613

613 – The number of Precepts—spiritual actions—that we can do to get spiritually closer to the Light of the Creator. There are 613 Precepts, and all can be found within the Five Books of Moses. These Precepts are divided into two categories: 248 Precepts of positive "to-do" actions, and 365 Precepts of negative "do not do" actions. Performing both types of Precepts will bring us closer to the Creator. See also: Precept, 248, 365

Abraham the Patriarch – An important figure in the Book of Genesis, Abraham is one of the three patriarchs of the Torah and the father of Isaac the Patriarch. Abraham's life and actions were the epitome of absolute sharing. Abraham is a chariot and the link to the Sefira of Chesed (Mercy) and represents Right Column. Connecting to him give us the energy of mercy and unconditional sharing.

Amen – The word Amen literally means "true" or "trustworthy." When one makes a blessing or says Kaddish, the listeners answer "Amen." The Zohar explains that saying "Amen" is not really about validating a blessing or praise, rather the word Amen has the numerical value of 91, which is the sum of two Names of God: Alef-Dalet-Nun-Yud (65) and Yud-Hei-Vav-Hei (26). Alef-Dalet-Nun-Yud represents the World of Malchut, or the physical world, and Yud-Hei-Vav-Hei represents Zeir Anpin or the metaphysical, Upper World. Saying "Amen" unifies the Upper and Lower Worlds, Light and Vessel, as well as the fulfilment of desire. Therefore, the sages said "greater is the one who says 'Amen' than the one who makes the blessing."

Amidah – Literally translates as "standing," the Amida is the silent prayer we recite standing up. There are 18-19 blessings during the weekday Amida, and seven during Shabbat and Holidays. We say Amida three times a day: Shacharit in the morning, Mincha in the afternoon, and Arvit at night.

Angels – Frequencies or packets of spiritual energy-intelligence that constantly roam and move about among us, acting as messengers from the Creator and affecting things that happen in our daily life. We can imagine an angel as being a conduit or channel that transports cosmic energy or thoughts from one place to another or from one spiritual dimension to the other. Angels have no free will, and each angel is dedicated to one specific purpose. When reading about an Angel in the Zohar, we do not pronounce its name, since saying the name aloud draws too much energy. However, names of Angels that are also names of humans are okay to pronounce, like Michael, Gabriel, and Rafael.

Awe – A term usually related to "wonder" or "fear." In Hebrew, the words "awe" and "see" have the same letters, teaching us that the true meaning of awe is related to "seeing" the Almightiness of the Creator rather than fearing it. Awe is often used in the phrase "Awe/Fear of the Creator." It is only when we "see" the future negative outcome of our past or present actions and perceive the Divine Wisdom that we stand in awe in front of our Maker.

Brit – Brit (Circumcision) means "Covenant" and represents the contract we have with the Creator to perform good deeds in this world and work on ourselves to become like the Light. The original Covenant was when Abraham performed the Circumcision as a sign and stamp to the Covenant and bond with the Creator. Therefore, when a baby boy is eight days old we perform a Brit Milah, which is the Covenant of the Circumcision, as a way to assist the child in his connection to the Creator and the spiritual work.

Cantillation Marks (*Te'amim*) – the musical notes in the Torah that tell the reader how to sing the Torah reading. Kabbalists have also learned many secrets from the cantillation marks, and why some words have specific notes and others not. In the Zohar it speaks of the Torah having three levels: letters, vowels and cantillation marks.

Central Column – The force that regulates between Right and Left, mercy and judgment. Central Column represents the concept of restricting our reactive nature and regulating mercy and judgment with balance. Jacob the Patriarch was the embodiment of Central Column, and therefore an Israelite is one who aligns themselves with the Central Column concept. Central Column also represents the Sefirot that are in the center of the Tree of Life: Da'at, Tiferet, Yesod.

Chai haOlamim – Meaning "Life of the Worlds" or "eternal life," both concepts relate to the Light of the Creator. *Chai* (life) also has the numerical value of 18.

Chariot – A Chariot is a conduit or vehicle. Like the saddle on a horse, which connects the rider and the horse, Chariots help us to connect to the Upper Worlds. The patriarchs, along with Moses, Aaron, Joseph the Righteous, and King David are all considered Chariots for the Lower Seven Sefirot. When we connect to a specific Chariot, we elevate our consciousness and give ourselves a spiritual boost.

Chasadim, Light of – When we awaken in ourselves a desire for the Light of the Creator through transforming our Desire to Receive into the Desire to Receive for the Sake of Sharing, we create a new Light that is called the Light of Chasadim. This Light clothes the Light of Chochmah (Wisdom), which is the essence of the Light of the Creator, and thus enables the Vessel (us) to contain and hold it.

Clothing – All spiritual energy, like the Lightforce of the Creator, needs to be concealed to be revealed. This concealment is referred to as "clothing." Our thoughts, words, and actions are clothing for the Lightforce of the Creator. Our body is the clothing for our soul. The Torah is the clothing for the Creator. When a Partzuf receives assistance from a lower Partzuf, then the lower one is a garment or clothing to the upper Partzuf.

Ein Sof (Endless) – Before the creation of this world, the Endless Light of the Creator filled all existence. There was no lack of any kind. All desires were completely fulfilled, and the Vessel, which is the Desire to Receive, was not blemished by the Desire to Receive for the Self Alone.

Etrog – The fruit of the citron tree that is used on the Holiday of Sukkot. Leviticus 23:40 says, "On the first day you shall take the fruit of majestic trees, branches of palm trees, boughs of leafy trees, and willows of the brook; and you shall rejoice before the Lord your God for seven days."

Evil Inclination – Each of us always has two inner voices that guide us to do everything, whether positive (proactive) or negative (reactive). The evil inclination is the voice that pushes us to be reactive and negative. It is sometimes referred to as Satan, which in Hebrew simply means "adversary." The evil inclination is our internal opponent that always tells us to act selfishly and reactively.

Exile – The state of existence where we are less connected and less in tune with the Light; a state where chaos rules and miracles are rare. This state was brought about by the destruction of both Holy Temples. The Hebrew word for "exile" is *Galut*, which is related to the word *hitgalut* "reveal," because this state of existence will change permanently once the wisdom of Kabbalah is revealed to everyone.

Gadlut – Literally meaning "greatness" or "maturity," Gadlut refers to having expanded consciousness and being spiritually mature.

Gehenom (Hell) – A purgatory-like place where souls that have passed on but require cleansing from the negativity they revealed while alive go; here all their negativity is purified. The souls remain in Gehenom no longer than 12 months to complete the purification process.

Halachah – Spiritual laws of the universe based on the 613 Precepts in the Torah and the later Talmudic laws, along with customs and traditions (*minhagim*). The literal meaning of Halachah is "the path," it is a way of connecting to the path of life through the actions that we do.

Holy One blessed be He – The Light, the Creator, God. Representing the force of Zeir Anpin, He is the male aspect of the Light of the Creator that fills the Vessel.

Impurity – A term used to describe the level where a person is failing to resist his ego and the evil inclination, and thus is sinking lower and lower into selfishness.

Isaac the Patriarch – One of the three patriarchs of the Torah, Isaac was the son of Abraham and the father of Jacob. We learn about the spirit of Isaac from the biblical story of the Binding of Isaac where he showed courage and completely let go of his personal agenda. Isaac is a chariot for the Sefira of Gevurah and represents Left Column. Connecting with Isaac can give us the courage and ability to overcome challenges and hardship.

Israelite – A code name for anyone following a spiritual path, working on their negative traits, and constantly striving to transform them to positive ones. Israelites are people who take upon themselves the responsibility of spreading the Light and for putting other people's needs before their own. They also understand and follow the spiritual rules of cause and effect, and do not take the Torah literally but rather as a coded message.

Jacob the Patriarch – One of the three patriarchs of the Torah, Jacob was the son of Isaac and the father of the twelve tribes of Israel. Having to hide from his brother for 20 years and facing other grave challenges for most of his life, Jacob lived a life of restriction. Nevertheless, he kept absolute trust in the Creator and therefore never disconnected from the Light of the Creator. Jacob is a Chariot to the Sefira of Tiferet and Central Column, which represents balance and absolute certainty.

Katnut – Literally meaning "smallness" or "immaturity," Katnut represents the state of our consciousness when we are reactive, selfish, and spiritually immature.

Kavanah (Intention, Meditation) – The act of centering our consciousness with focused attention appropriate to a situation or connection.

Leah – Name of the Partzuf of the upper part of Nukva, known as the Hidden World.

Left Column – The force that draws energy like a magnet and starts the flow of Light to a vessel or desire. The attributes of Left Column are found in the following characteristics: strength, desire to receive, setting boundaries, discipline, and the rejection of that which is bad. Left Column also represents the Sefirot that are on the Left Column of the Tree of Life: Binah, Gevurah, Hod.

Lower Seven – In each of the Four Spiritual Worlds there are ten levels or Sefirot. The Lower Seven Sefirot are Chesed (Mercy), Gevurah (Judgment/Might), Tiferet (Beauty), Netzach (Eternity/Victory), Hod (Glory), Yesod (Foundation), and Malchut (Kingdom). Collectively, the Lower Seven Sefirot represent the six directions: south, north, east, up, down, and west. See also: *Vav Ketzavot*, Upper Three

Lulav – The date palm branch bound together with willows and myrtle is used on the Holiday of Sukkot. Leviticus 23:40 says, "On the first day you shall take the fruit of majestic trees, branches of palm trees, boughs of leafy trees, and willows of the brook; and you shall rejoice before the Lord your God for seven days."

Masach (Curtain) – A spiritual curtain that delays the Vessel from receiving the Light and also delays the Light from entering the Vessel.

Mayin Duchrin (Masculine Waters) – Awakening from Above to give energy for the Unification.

Mayin Nukvin (Feminine Waters) – Awakening from Below to give energy to the Female for the Unification. There are two kinds of Mayin Nukvin: The first is the effort that the Female makes to be unified with Her Male. The second is when the Lower Partzuf will make an extra effort to give this energy to the Upper Partzuf and thereby the Upper Partzuf will be able to be unified and give back higher illuminations to this Lower Partzuf.

Merit – In Hebrew, this word is *zechut*, which is derived from the root word for "pure," meaning that when we transform our selfish nature into one of selflessness and sharing with others, we become pure. In doing so, we will attain the merit of a spiritual lifeline, which will be there when we most need it to remove the chaos, pain, and suffering we are experiencing.

Messiah (Mashiach) – Often described as a person, the concept of Messiah simply means the collective consciousness of humanity where everyone cares about others' needs ahead of their own, in this way emulating the complete selflessness of the Light. The concept of death (in health, business, relationships, or anything else) cannot exist within the realm of this consciousness.

Milui (Spelled out) – When a Name or a word is written or named by the letters that comprise the conventionally accepted form of it, it is called *milui*. When a name is spelled out this diminishes some of its power and represents a spiritual thickness. There are four ways to spell out the Name of Yud-Hei-Vav-Hei and three ways to spell out the Name of Alef-Hei-Yud-Hei.

Mochin – Literally means "brains" and represents quality of consciousness. When we sleep, our Mochin go up, and that is why we are unconscious. When Zeir Anpin has Mochin, it means Zeir Anpin has attained the Upper Three Sefirot (Chochmah, Binah, Da'at) and is now complete.

Nations – Nations actually represent the inner attributes and character traits of our individual self. The nation of Amalek refers to the doubt and uncertainty that dwells within us when we face hardship and obstacles. Moab represents the dual nature of man. *Nefilim* refers to the sparks of Light that we have defiled through our impure actions, and to the negative forces that lurk within the human soul as a result of our own wrongful deeds.

Numerical Value – There are 22 Hebrew letters, each with a numerical value ranging from 1 to 400, which when combined produce words and phrases with their own numerical values. Hebrew words or phrases that have the same value are usually another form of providing us with spiritual insight for our lives through the Torah. The main sources for deciphering these combinations are *Sefer Yetzirah* ("Book of Formation"), the Zohar, and the Writings of the Ari.

Or Pnimi (Inner Light) – The Light that we have earned through our proactive actions. This Light is who we are and what we are; it is our life experience and wisdom.

Or Makif (Surrounding Light) – The Light that pushes us to grow and reveal our potential Light. Or Makif refers to our potential and to everything we were meant to accomplish throughout our lifetime. Or Makif is connected to the quantum Light of the Creator that is waiting to be revealed through our proactive actions.

Or Yashar (Direct Light) – The Light of the Creator before it has any interaction with a vessel. Or Yashar is Light in its raw, naked form; it has no manifestation as yet.

Or Chozer (Returning Light) – When the Direct Light reaches our level of Malchut (Fourth Phase) and strikes the Curtain, due to the restriction of the Vessel, the Light revealed is called the Returning Light.

Other Side (Sitra Achra) – According to Kabbalah, the world is made of opposites: positive and negative, good and evil. The Light of the Creator represents the side of positivity, order, and clarity, while the Other Side represents negativity, darkness, and chaos. The Other Side needs a source of energy but cannot feed directly from the Light of the Creator. Every time we make a wrong choice or get upset and act reactively, the Other Side can take advantage of this and suck the Light away from us.

Patriarchs – Abraham, Isaac, and Jacob, who are the three pillars of the Torah. They are referred to as the Chariots and channels for the Sefirot of Chesed (Right column), Gevurah (Left column), and Tiferet (Central columns) that we can use to achieve balance in our day-to-day life.

Precept – One of the 613 spiritual actions we can do to connect to the Light of the Creator. There are two types of Precepts: those between man and his fellow man, and those between man and the Creator. In Hebrew, the word for precept is *mitzvah*, meaning "unity" or "bonding" because the Precepts create unity between the Creator and ourselves.

Pure – Without spiritual blemish. Someone or something that is completely cleansed of negativity. Someone who has less of a Desire to Receive and more of a Desire to Share. The purer a person is, the more Light can shine through him and illuminate his life and the lives of others around him.

Rachel – Name of the Partzuf of the Lower part of Nukva, known as the "revealed world".

Right Column – The positive force of Light that wants to fill the vessel. The attribute of Right Column is found in the following characteristics: giving, imparting, mercy, letting go, going with the flow, love, and accepting with love that which is good. Right Column also represents the Sefirot that are on the right side of the Ten Sefirot or Tree of Life: Chochmah, Chesed, Netzach.

Sages – Kabbalists from the time of the Second Temple who were very wise individuals that left us with deep wisdom and many lessons found in the Mishnah and Talmud.

Shechinah (Divine Presence) – The Light of the Creator's closest frequency to the physical world. The Shechinah corresponds to the female aspect of the Light of the Creator, and many writings refer to the union between God and the Shechinah. In addition, the Shechinah is a protection shield of the Creator for all those who connect to the Tree of Life.

Teshuvah **(Repentance)** – Meaning literally "to return," *Teshuvah* is the process of going back to an earlier phase where things were connected to the source. When we "short circuit" (i.e. make a wrong choice) and conduct ourselves with selfishness, we disconnect from the Light of the Creator and attract chaos. *Teshuvah* is designed to reverse our negative consciousness through positive transformation, thus allowing us to reconnect with the Light of the Creator. When we take responsibility and own up to our past mistakes, we preemptively remove whatever chaos and pain we might face in the future as a result of our negativity.

This World – The physical world that we live in, where we are subject to the laws of cause and effect, and bound by the limitations of time, space, and motion. Also called the 1 Percent Reality and the Illusionary World. See also: World to Come

Torah – There is both the Written Torah and the Oral Torah. The Written Torah is comprised of the five books of Moses. The Oral Torah is the interpretation of the Written Torah, which the Sages received orally from Moses to Joshua to the Elders, and every generation from teacher to student, until the compilation of the Mishna and the Talmud. The Zohar is part of the Oral Torah, and deals with the soul (secrets) of the Torah and the metaphysical laws; whereas the Mishnah and Talmud deal with the body of the Torah and the corporeal laws.

Tractate – The Talmud and Mishnah are each split into six sections, each of which is further divided into subsections called *Masechet* (Tractates). Each subsection is given a name to describe the topic of discussion.

Tzadik (**Righteous Soul**) – A person who is completely devoted to working on transforming his or her negative traits and to sharing unconditionally with others. The Midrash also tells us that this is a person whose positive actions outweigh his or her negative actions. The terms "righteous" and "wicked" can also relate to the inner righteous and wicked parts of ourselves.

Tzelem (Image, shadow) – The clothing of the Mochin as they go to the Lower Partzuf. This clothing is created by the Returning Light of the Lower Partzuf. The *Tzelem* is divided into three main aspects. The first and highest is called Mem (מ) of the *Tzelem*. The second is called Lamed (ל) of the *Tzelem*. And the third and the lowest is called Tzadik (צ) of the *Tzelem*.

Tzimtzum – The ability to restrain the Desire to Receive. The original restriction. In the process of spiritual Creation, we have two Tzimtzums. The First Tzimtzum was in the Endless World in order to give the Vessel the opportunity to remove Bread of Shame. The Second Tzimtzum came to complete and to correct the shattered Vessel.

Upper Three – the head of a Partzuf, represented by Chochmah, Binah. and Da'at. The head represents cause and potential, which is more powerful than the Lower Six or body, but the body is what manifests. Similarly, the head or Upper Three represents control, as the body is controlled by the head. A Partzuf or Sefira without the Upper Three is considered incomplete. The Upper Three can also refer to the Mochin. See also: Mochin, Lower Seven

Vav Ketzavot – Literally means "Six Edges" and represents the body of a spiritual structure, comprised of the Lower Six Sefirot: Chesed, Gevurah, Tiferet, Netzach, Hod, and Yesod. The head of a spiritual structure is called *Gimel Rishonot* (Upper Three Sefirot), which are: Chochmah, Binah, and Da'at.

Vowels – In Hebrew and Aramaic, the vowels of words are marked with dots and lines instead of letters. In the Torah scroll there are only letters; but when one reads from the Torah scroll he must learn the vowels and the cantillation marks to consider it a valid Torah reading. See also: cantillation marks

Workings of Creation (*Ma'aseh Beresheet*) – A concept referring both to the creation of the world in six days, as described in the Book of Genesis, and to the Study of the Ten Luminous Emanations. The greatest kabbalists were able to tap into *Ma'aseh Beresheet* and could perform miracles for others in need, miracles that defied the laws of nature that were established in the moment of Creation. *Ma'aseh Beresheet* is taught to one student at a time in one-on-one study, and only few select students in each generation have the merit of achieving this level.

Workings of the Chariot (*Ma'aseh Merkavah*) – The study of the *Merkavah* (Chariot or Assembling) is a deep, secret kabbalistic study that refers to the structure and hierarchy of the Upper Worlds. Being a study above and beyond logic, *Ma'aseh Merkavah* is a level of consciousness that should be studied by a qualified kabbalist on his own.

World to Come – A realm where only happiness, fulfillment, love, and joy exist—the 99 Percent Realm of the Light of the Creator. The kabbalists explain that the World to Come exists in each and every moment of our lives. Every action of ours creates an effect that comes back to us either for good and for bad, and through the way we live our lives, we can create worlds according to our design. The World to Come is commonly referred to as "the reality of life after life." See also: This World

Worlds – A term used in the Study of the Ten Luminous Emanations to refer to the Five Spiritual Worlds. There are five channels that bring the Light down to our mundane reality. When these channels are filled with Light, we call them Worlds. Each World represents a different level of consciousness that is related to a level of veil that covers the Light. The word *olam* in Hebrew means "disappearance," referring to the fact that only when the Light is concealed can a reality be revealed. The Five Spiritual Worlds, from highest to lowest, are: Primordial Man (Adam Kadmon), Emanation (Atzilut), Creation (Briyah), Formation (Yetzirah), and Action (Asiyah).

Yaakov - The outer Partzuf of Zeir Anpin corresponding to the Six Edges of Zeir Anpin.

Yisrael – The inner Partzuf of Zeir Anpin corresponding to the Mochin of Zeir Anpin.

Zivug (Unification) – The Nature of the Supernal Light is to emanate illumination to the Lower Worlds for all eternity. Because of the Masach, the Vessel cannot connect. Therefore, when the Vessel is ready (by Returning Light or by elevating Mayin Nukvin) to connect with the Light it is called *Zivug*. *Zivug* literally means "unification," which represents the unification of Light and Vessel, and between Zeir Anpin and Nukva.

Appendix C

Hebrew Letters

Letter	Name	Numerical Value
א	Alef	1
ב	Bet	2
ג	Gimel	3
ד	Dalet	4
ה	Hei	5
ו	Vav	6
ז	Zayin	7
ח	Chet	8
ט	Tet	9
י	Yud	10
כ	Kaf	20
ל	Lamed	30
מ	Mem	40
נ	Nun	50
ס	Samech	60
ע	Ayin	70
פ	Pei	80
צ	Tzadi	90
ק	Kof	100
ר	Resh	200
ש	Shin	300
ת	Tav	400

Five Final Letters

When these five letters appear at the end of a word they change shape:

Letter	Final Letter	Name	Numerical Value
מ	ם	Mem	40
נ	ן	Nun	50
צ	ץ	Tzadi	90
פ	ף	Pei	80
כ	ך	Kaf	20

The Hebrew Vowels, and the Sefira They Represent

We will use the letter Alef and a demonstration of
how the vowels appear on any letter

Letter	Name	Numerical Value
אָ	Kamatz	Keter
אַ	Patach	Chochmah
אֵ	Tzere	Binah
אֶ	Segol	Chesed
אְ	Shva	Gevurah
אֹ אוֹ	Cholam	Tiferet
אִ	Chirik	Netzach
אֻ	Shuruk	Hod
אוּ	Shuruk Vav	Yesod